KONI
BUS TRUCK & TRAILER
YOU'LL GO THE DISTANCE

More safety and comfort?
Rely on KONI Bus dampers

KONI is the leading manufacturer of high quality shock absorbers for buses and coaches. When it comes to safety, road holding and comfort KONI dampers are the reliable solution.

ROADLINK INTERNATIONAL®

Roadlink International Ltd is the exclusive UK and Ireland concessionaire for KONI truck, trailer and bus shock absorbers.

Strawberry Lane, Willenhall, West Midlands, WV13 3RL
Sales Tel: +44 (0)1902 636206   Sales Fax: +44 (0)1902 631515
e-mail: sales@roadlink-international.co.uk
Web Site: www.roadlink-international.co.uk

Take our 3 issue trial today*, and you will receive your first issue for FREE!

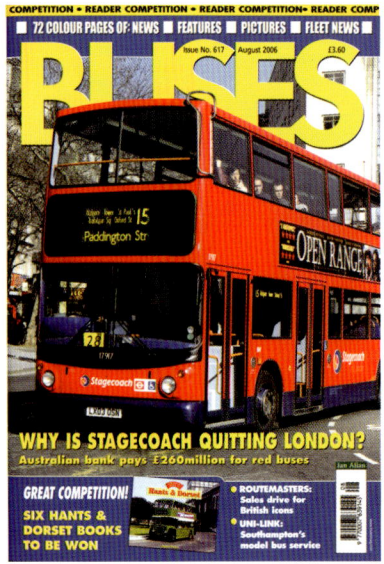

The UK's biggest selling PSV magazine

Delivering prompt and informed coverage every month, **BUSES** magazine has provided an essential overview of the UK's PSV industry for over fifty-five years.

Supported by quality editorial features and the latest news, **BUSES** magazine is essential reading for decision-makers within the bus industry.

The magazine is notable for its most unique feature, 'Fleet News', now an 18-page section detailing the latest additions to and departures from major and less major bus and coach fleets in the UK and Ireland.

Every month **BUSES** editorial features cover key areas of interest, including vehicle operation, technical developments, ticketing and publicity.

Subscribe today to receive **BUSES** on your desk every month, and keep abreast of the latest news and developments in the bus industry.

Great subscriber benefits!

A subscription to **BUSES** comes with **FREE MEMBERSHIP** to the Ian Allan Publishing Subs Club.

As a member of the **Ian Allan Publishing Subs Club**, you will receive a personalised Subscription Loyalty Card, plus a quarterly newsletter with great subscriber benefits, discounts, offers and competitions!

BUSES PRIORITY ORDER FORM   (Photocopies acceptable)

I would like to subscribe to *Buses*:   1 - Debit / Credit card   LRB07

☐ 3 issues trial subscription   **£7.20**   Please debit my:
☐ 1 year full UK subscription   **£43.20**   ☐ Mastercard   ☐ Visa   ☐ Switch / Maestro

Mr/Mrs/Miss/Ms: _____
Forename: _____   Exp date:_____ Start date: _____
Surname: _____   Issue no: ____ Date:_____
Address: _____   Cardholders signature:_____

2 - Cheque

I enclose a cheque to the value of _____
(please make cheque payable to Ian Allan Publishing Ltd Eurocheques are not accepted)

Post Code: _____   3 - Invoice
Tel No.: _____
Email: _____   ☐ Please invoice me

Return to: Subscriptions Dept, Ian Allan Publishing Ltd, Riverdene Business Park, Molesey Road, Hersham, Surrey, KT12 4RG

* Offer valid until 31st January 2007.

THE LITTLE RED BOOK 2007

THE PASSENGER TRANSPORT DIRECTORY FOR THE BRITISH ISLES

Editor: Tony Pattison

Riverdene Business Park, Molesey Road, Hersham, Surrey KT12 4RG
Tel: 01932 266600 Fax: 01932 266601

PSV GLASS - WE'VE GOT IT COVERED!

It would be nice to think that there really was one place to go for all your public service vehicle glass solutions. There is - PSV Glass can help you with all aspects of replacement glazing:

IMMEDIATE PARTS IDENTIFICATION > FULL STOCK RANGE > NATIONWIDE DELIVERY SERVICE

ON-SITE TECHNICAL SUPPORT > CUSTOMISED GLASS STORAGE SYSTEMS

MANAGED IMPREST STOCK > GLASS INSTALLATION TRAINING > GLASS ASSOCIATED PRODUCTS

GLASS FILMING PROTECTION MANAGEMENT

Just call PSV Glass on 01494 533131 or visit www.psvglass.co.uk

contents

List of Abbreviations	**4**
Index to Advertisers	**4**
Foreword	**6**
Section 1: *Trade Directory*	**7**
Section 2: *Tendering & Regulatory Authorities*	**63**
Traffic Commissioners,	**65**
Department for Transport	**68**
Section 3: *Organisations and Societies*	**71**
Section 4: *British Isles Operators*	**84**
Section 5: *Index (Trade)*	**234**
Index (British Isles Operators)	**240**

List of Abbreviations

Acct = Accountant
Admin = Administrative
Asst = Assistant
Ch = Chief
Chmn = Chairman
Co = Company
Comm Man = Commercial Manager
Cont = Controller
Dep = Deputy
Dir = Director
Eng = Engineer
Exec = Executive
Fin = Financial
Gen Man = General Manager
Insp = Inspector
Jnt = Joint
Man = Manager
Man Dir = Managing Director
Mktg = Marketing
Off = Officer
Op = Operating
Ops = Operations
Plan = Planning
Pres = President
Prin = Principal
Prop = Proprietor(s)
Ptnrs = Partner(s)
Reg Off = Registered Office
sd = single-deck bus
Sec = Secretary
Supt = Superintendent
Svce = service
Traf Man = Traffic Manager
Traf Supt = Traffic Superintendent
Tran Man = Transport Manager

Index to Advertisers

A's Models of Bolton	37
Airconco	18
Camira	48
Chapman Driver Seating	42
Cobus	20
Crewe Engines	29
Cummins-Allison Ltd	24
Grasshopper Inn	136
H L Smith	47
Ian Allan Publishing	iv, 62, 70
Midland Counties Publications	16
Mirror Image Models - *see* A's Models of Bolton	
Partline	Outside back cover
Prestolite	27
PSV Glass	Front cover, 2
PSV Products	19
Roadlink International Ltd	Front endpaper
Scan Coin	23
Specialist Training	60
Transport Benevolent Fund	Bookmark
Trimplex Safety Tread Ltd	33
Unitec	5
VIP Group	Front endpaper
ZF Great Britain	46
Walsh's Engineering	30

LITTLE RED BOOK

For information regarding a free listing contact:
The Editor, Little Red Book,
c/o Ian Allan Publishing Ltd, Riverdene Business Park, Hersham, Surrey KT12 4RG

For information regarding advertising contact: David Lane, Little Red Book Advertising, Foundry Road, Stamford, Lincolnshire PE9 2PP
Tel: 01780 484632   Fax: 01780 763388.

First published 2006

ISBN (10) 0 7110 3210 6
ISBN (13) 978 0 7110 3210 1

All rights reserved. No part of this book may be reproduced or transmitted in any form or by any means, electronic or mechanical, including photocopying, recording or by any information storage and retrieval system, without permission from the Publisher in writing.

© Ian Allan Publishing Ltd 2006

Published by Ian Allan Publishing; an imprint of Ian Allan Publishing Ltd, Riverdene Business Park, Hersham, Surrey KT12 4RG; and printed by Ian Allan Printing Ltd, Riverdene Business Park, Hersham, Surrey KT12 4RG.

Code: 0609/A1

Visit the Ian Allan Publishing web site:
www.ianallanpublishing.com

Your Complete Aftersales Service...

...dedicated to all makes of bus and coach

- London Service Centre
- Rotherham Service Centre
- Cumbernauld Service Centre
- All Makes Parts Supply - Nationwide
- All Makes Accident Damage & Mechanical Repairs
- Mobile Technicians
- Technical Services & Training
- Speedline dedicated Warranty Response

At Unitec our priority is getting and keeping your vehicles on the road... whatever make, whatever model we're here to help you.

Whether it's servicing, repairs, parts or training, call us today... ...we are here to help.

Service

London	01708 892440	london.service@optare.com
Rotherham	01709 535101	rotherham.service@optare.com
Scotland	01236 726738	scotland.service@optare.com

Parts

Call	01709 792 000
Fax	01709 792 009
email	parts@optare.com

UniTec

Unitec is a division of the Optare Group

Foreword

New for *LRB 2007* is a sub-section in the Vehicle Suppliers and Dealers section called Bus Rapid Transit vehicles. This section was mainly set up to feature the advanced Wright-bodied StreetCar, and reflects the potential importance of this revolutionary vehicle in the UK and world-wide rapid transit scene.

We have also re-named the Trade Directory from A-Z Listing of Bus, Coach & Tram Suppliers to A-Z Listing of Bus, Coach & Rapid Transit Suppliers and the Tramway & Light Transit Equipment sub-section in the Trade Directory to Rapid Transit/Priority Equipment.

Also new for the 2007 edition is the addition of two sections in the A-Z Manufacturers and Suppliers section - Cleaning Services, Lifting Equipment and Vehicle Certification.

More than 70 entries have been added to the address list in 2006.

We are very grateful to all who returned their entries - we know it is not easy to find the time to do chores like this. This year we were able to update many more entries than last year through replies received and further research carried out - thank you to all who replied and helped with the research.

If there is no change to your entry there is no need to re-write it all - just say something like "as for last year" but please say who you are. We have had forms returned complete but with no indication as to who they are from.

For the next edition we hope to include a category for operators offering wedding transport. We also hope to expand the coach parking listings in the A-Z section.

There will be the continuing challenge of sorting out the problem of entries for which there has been no reply for a number of years and for which it has been impracticable to gain information from other sources. We have increased the input from other experts in the bus industry so that more accuracy can be attained. Some pruning has been carried out in this edition and will be taken forward for the next.

Tony Pattison, Editor
June 2006

Acknowledgements

I would like to thank Ian Barlex and Chris Bushell for their major help in updating and correcting many entries throughout the whole book.

I am very grateful to Alan Butcher for all his help and advice with layout, production and support for both the entries and the mailing list.

Thanks, too, must go to our many advertisers who support the Little Red Book. Please use them and say you saw the advert in the LRB.

I would also like to thank Mary Webb and Colin Oggelsby for their substantial input to the current edition and Ann Pattison for compiling the index.

How *LRB* entries are compiled

As usual, every operator, manufacturer, supplier and other organisation featured in *LRB 2006* received an invitation to correct their entry for this edition free of charge.

Not all operators responded, which means that some existing unchanged entries are repeated. This is done reluctantly, and we are aware that there must be some entries for companies that are no longer in business; unless we are told of these, perhaps by neighbouring operators, it is impossible to follow up every non-response, although we do try to correct as much information as possible from whatever sources we can obtain. We have used an asterisk to signify those companies that have responded this time.

By the same token, new entrants to the bus and coach market should not wait for *LRB* to make contact. If you are in the bus or coach business, and would like to appear (free of charge) in the next *LRB*, please write to the Editor of *LRB* at Ian Allan Publishing Ltd, Riverdene Business Park, Molesey Road, Hersham, Surrey KT12 4RG, requesting to receive a form for the next edition.

LRB is used by a substantial number of bus and coach operators, as well as by national and local government, trade organisations, tendering authorities, group travel organisers, hotels and leisure attractions.

section 1
Trade Directory

Vehicle suppliers and dealers	**8**
A-Z listing of suppliers and manufacturers	**17**
Bus & Coach industry service providers	**50**

VEHICLE SUPPLIERS & DEALERS

Full-size bus and coach chassis and integrals

ALEXANDER DENNIS LTD
91 Glasgow Road, Falkirk FK1 4JB
Tel: 01324 621672
Web site: www.alexander-dennis.com
Range: rear-engined low-floor single-deck bus, chassis for rear-engined low-floor midibus, rear-engined low-floor single-deck bus, mid-engined coach, rear-engined coach, rear-engined low-floor double-deck bus, two- or three-axle, low-floor schoolbus.

AUTOSAN UK
UK Supplier: **Autoholdings**
Bedworth Road, Coventry CV6 6BP
Tel: 024 7636 0011
Web site: www.autosanuk.com
Range: High-floor school bus, single-deck bus, coach

AYATS
UK Supplier: **AYATS (GB) LTD**
Meadow Drive, Earith, Cambridge PE28 3SA
Tel: 01487 843333
Fax: 01487 843285
E-mail: david@sunfunholidays.co.uk
Web site: www.carroceriasayats.es
   Ireland supplier: **BARTONS TRANSPORT**
   Straffan Road, Maynooth, Co Kildare
   Tel: 00 353 1 628 6026
   Fax: 00 353 1 628 6722
   E-mail: info@bartons-transport.ie
Models: Rear-engined integral coach range - up to 15m

BMC UK LTD
UK Supplier: **Autoholdings**
Bedworth Road, Coventry CV6 6BP
Tel: 024 7636 3003
Website: www.bmcukltd.com
Models: integral front-engined schoolbus, integral front-engined midicoach, integral rear-engined 11m low-floor single-deck bus

IRISBUS (UK) LTD
Iveco House, Station Road, Watford WD17 1SR
Tel: 01923 259660
Fax: 01923 259623
E-mail: info@irisbus.co.uk
Web site: www.irisbus.co.uk
   UK Supplier: **UK COACH & BUS**
   Carlton House, Euroway Estate, Hellaby, Rotherham S66 8QL
   Tel: 01709 705570
   Fax: 01709 705569
   Web site: www.uk-cb.com
Models: midibus, low-floor midibus, minibuses, guided bus system, low-floor rear-engined single-deck bus, rear-engined single-deck coach.

KING LONG PLC
UK Supplier: **Autoholdings**
Bedworth Road, Coventry CV6 6BP
Tel: 024 7636 3004
Models: single-deck coach

MAN
UK Supplier: **Neoman Bus UK**
Frankland Road, Blagrove, Swindon SN5 8YU
Web site: www.man.co.uk
UK Dealer: **Mentor Coach & Bus Ltd**
Carlton House, Euroway Industrial Estate, Hellaby, Rotherham S66 8QL
Tel: 01709 700600
Web site: www.mentorplc.com
   Ireland supplier: **BRIAN NOONE**
   Straffan Road, Maynooth, Co Kildare
   Tel: 00 353 1 628 6311
   Fax: 00 353 1 628 5404
   Web site: www.briannooneltd.ie
Models: single-deck low-floor bus, rear-engined coach

MERCEDES-BENZ
UK Supplier: **EvoBus (UK) Ltd**, Cross Point Business Park, Ashcroft Way, Coventry CV2 2TU
Tel: 024 7662 6000
Website: www.evobus.co.uk
Models: rear-engine coach, rear-engine integral low-floor single-deck bus, rear-engine integral low-floor single-deck articulated bus

NEOPLAN
UK Supplier: **Neoman UK**
UK Dealer: **Mentor Coach & Bus Ltd**
Carlton House, Euroway Industrial Estate, Hellaby, Rotherham S66 8QL
Tel: 01709 705570
Fax: 01709 705569
E-mail: sales@mentorplc.com
Web site: www.mentorplc.com
Models: single-deck and double-deck rear-engine integral coaches

*OPTARE GROUP LTD
Manston Lane, Leeds LS15 8SU
Tel: 0113 264 5182
Fax: 0113 260 6635
E-mail: info@optare.com
Web site: www.optare.com
Models: low-floor minibus, rear-engined integral low-floor single-deck midibus, rear-engined integral low-floor single-deck bus
   UK supplier: ***OPTARE COACH SALES**
   Denby Way, Hellaby Industrial Estate, Hellaby, Rotherham S66 8HR
   Tel: 01709 535120
   Fax: 01709 535102
   E-mail: coachsales@optare.com
   Web site: www.optare.com

*PLAXTON
Plaxton Park, Cayton Low Road, Eastfield, Scarborough YO11 3BY
Tel: 01723 581500
Fax: 01723 5813238
E-mail: sales@plaxtonlimited.co.uk
Web site: www.plaxtonlimited.co.uk
Range: coaches, buses, midicoach and midibus bodies

SCANIA
Scania Bus & Coach UK Ltd, Claylands Avenue, Worksop S81 7DJ
Tel: 01909 500822
Web site: www.scaniabusand coach.com
Range: rear-engined low-floor single-deck and double-deck bus chassis, integral low-floor single-deck bus, integral low-floor double-deck bus, rear-engined coach.

SETRA
UK Supplier: **EvoBus (UK) Ltd** Cross Point Business Park, Ashcroft Way, Coventry CV2 2TU
Tel: 024 7662 6000
Fax: 024 7662 6020
Website: www.evobus.com, www.setra.de
Models: rear-engined integral coaches

VAN HOOL
Bernard Van Hoolstraat 58, B-2500 Lier-Koningshooikt, Belgium
Tel: 00 32 3 420 20 20
Fax: 00 32 3 482 33 68
Website: www.vanhool.be

Models: integral coaches

VDL BOVA
Web site: www.vdlbova.nl
UK Suppliers: *MOSELEY (PCV) LTD
Elmsall Way, Dale Lane, South Elmsall, Pontefract WF9 2XS
Tel: 01977 609000
Fax: 01977 609900
Web site: www.moseleycoachsales.co.uk
MOSELEY IN THE SOUTH LTD
Summerfield Avenue, Chelston Business Park, Wellington TA21 9JF
Tel: 01823 653000
Fax: 01823 663502
E-mail: enquiries@moseleysouth.co.uk
Models: Lexio, Magiq, Futura single-deck luxury coach; *Synergy* double-deck coach

VDL BUS INTERNATIONAL
UK Supplier: **ARRIVA BUS AND COACH LTD**
Lodge Garage, Whitehall Road West, Gomersal BD19 4BJ
Tel: 01274 681144
Fax: 01274 651198
Web site: www.arriva.co.uk, www.vdlbus.nl
E-mail: busandcoachsales@arriva.co.uk
Models: rear-engined low-floor single-deck bus, rear-engined low-floor double-deck bus, rear-engined coach, rear-engined three-axle single- or double-deck coach.

VOLVO BUS LTD
Wedgnock Lane, Warwick CV34 5YA
Tel: 01926 401777
Fax: 01926 407407
Website: www.volvobuses.volvo.co.uk, www.volvo.com
Models: rear-engined low-floor single-deck bus, rear-engined low-floor articulated single-deck bus, mid-engined coach, rear-engined integral coach, rear-engined low-floor double-deck bus.

Bus Rapid Transit Vehicles

IRISBUS (UK) LTD
Iveco House, Station Road, Watford WD17 1SR
Tel: 01923 259660
Fax: 01923 259623
E-mail: info@irisbus.co.uk
Web site: www.irisbus.co.uk
Models: guided bus system

MINITRAM SYSTEMS LTD
12 Waterloo Park Estate, Bidford on Avon B50 4JH
Tel: 01789 490707
Fax: 01789 490592
E-mail: enquiries@tdi.uk.com
Website: www.minitram.com
Models: Rubber tyre-guided/unguided/rail 7.8m vehicle

VOLVO BUS LTD
Wedgnock Lane, Warwick CV34 5YA
Tel: 01926 401777
Fax: 01926 407407
Website: www.volvobuses.volvo.co.uk, www.volvo.com
Models: rear-engined low-floor single-deck bus, rear-engined low-floor articulated single-deck bus, rear-engined low-floor double-deck bus *(chassis can be equipped with guidewheels for operation on guideways).*

*WRIGHTBUS LTD
Galgorm, Ballymena, Northern Ireland BT42 1PY
Tel: 028 2564 1212
Fax: 028 2564 9703
E-mail: info@wright-bus.com
Web site: www.wright-bus.com
Models: StreetCar rapid transit vehicle *(further models - see bodybuilders section).*

Light Rail Vehicles

ALSTOM TRANSPORT
Worldwide headquarters: 48 rue Albert Dhalenne, F-93482 Saint-Ouen Cedex, France
Tel: 00 33 1 41 66 90 00
Fax: 00 33 1 41 66 96 66
Web site: www.transport.alstom.com
Models: rail vehicles including light rail vehicles, traction equipment, infrastructure and maintenance services.

BOMBARDIER TRANSPORTATION
Management Office: 1101 Parent Street, Saint-Bruno, Quebec J3V 6E6, Canada
Tel: 00 1 450 441 20 20
Fax: 00 1 450 441 15 15
Web site: www.transportation.bombardier.com
BOMBARDIER TRANSPORTATION METROS
Litchurch Lane, Derby DE24 8AD
Tel: 01332 344666
Fax: 01332 266271
Models: light rail vehicles, trams, guided or unguided bi-mode rubber tyred electric vehicle.

MINITRAM SYSTEMS LTD
12 Waterloo Park Estate, Bidford on Avon B50 4JH
Tel: 01789 490707
Fax: 01789 490592
E-mail: enquiries@tdi.uk.com
Website: www.minitram.com
Models: Rubber tyre-guided/unguided/rail 7.8m vehicle

*PARRY PEOPLE MOVERS LTD
Overend Road, Cradley Heath, Dudley B64 7DD
Tel: 01384 569553
Fax: 01384 637753
E-mail: jpmparry@aol.com
Website: www.parrypeoplemovers.com, www.parrytech.com
Models: Ultra light rail vehicles and trams

TRAM POWER LTD
Unit 4, Carraway Road, Gillmoss Industrial Estate, Liverpool L11 0EE
Tel: 0151 547 1425
Fax: 0151 546 6066
Website: www.trampower.co.uk/CityClass.html
Models: Articulated lightweight low-cost tram

Bodybuilders (large vehicles)

ALEXANDER DENNIS
91 Glasgow Road, Falkirk FK1 4JB
Web site: www.alexander-dennis.com
Tel: 01324 621672
Range: double-deck low-floor bus, single-deck low-floor bus, single-deck low-floor midibus, low-floor schoolbus.

SALVADOR CAETANO (UK) LTD
Mill Lane, Heather, Coalville LE67 2QA
Web site: www.caetano.co.uk
Tel: 01530 263333
Fax: 01530 263379
E-mail: enquiries@caetano.co.uk

SC COACHBUILDERS LTD
Hambledon Road, Waterlooville PO7 7UA
Tel: 023 9225 8211
Fax: 023 9225 5611
E-mail: sccaetano.co.uk
Web site: www.caetano.co.uk
Models: single-deck coach, single-deck low-floor midibus.

EAST LANCASHIRE COACHBUILDERS LTD
Lower Philips Road, Whitebirk Industrial Estate, Blackburn BB1 5UD
Tel: 01254 504150
Fax: 01254 504197
E-mail: john.horn@elcb.co.uk
Web site: www.elcb.co.uk
Models: double-deck low-floor bus, single-deck low floor bus, single-deck low-floor midibus

ESKER BUS & COACH SALES LTD
Comagh Business Park, Kilbeggan, Co Westmeath, Ireland
Tel: 00 353 506 33070
Fax: 00 353 506 33070
E-mail: info@eskerbusandcoach.com
Web site: www.eskerbusandcoach.com
Models: single-deck coach, single-deck low-floor midibus.

IRIZAR
UK spares supplier: *TRAMONTANA
Chapelknowe Road, Carfin, Motherwell ML1 5LE
Tel: 01698 861790
Fax: 01698 860778
E-mail: wdt90@tiscali.co.uk
Web site: tramontanacoach.co.uk

JONCKHEERE
Importer: **Volvo Coach Sales (Loughborough) Ltd**, Brisco Avenue, Loughborough LE11 5HP
Tel: 01509 217777
Fax: 01509 260978
Models: single-deck coach
   UK service: *TRAMONTANA
   Chapelknowe Road, Carfin, Motherwell ML1 5LE
   Tel: 01698 861790
   Fax: 01698 860778
   E-mail: wdt90@tiscali.co.uk
   Web site: tramontanacoach.co.uk

*LEICESTER CARRIAGE BUILDERS
Marlow Road, Leicester LE3 2BQ
Tel: 0116 282 4270
Fax: 0116 263 0554
E-mail: rick.johnson@midlandsco-op.com
Web site: www.leicestercarriagebuilders.co.uk

*MCV BUS AND COACH LTD
Sterling Place, Elean Business Park, Sutton, Ely CB6 2QE
Tel: 01353 773000
Fax: 01353 773001

*MOSELEY (PCV) LTD
Elmsall Way, Dale Lane, South Elmsall, Pontefract WF9 2XS
Tel: 01977 609000
Fax: 01977 609900
Web site: www.moseleycoachsales.co.uk

NEOPLAN
UK Supplier: **MENTOR**
Mentor Coach & Bus Ltd, Carlton House, Euroway Industrial Estate, Hellaby, Rotherham S66 8QL
Tel: 01709 700600
Fax: 01709 700007
E-mail: sales@mentorplc.com
Web site: www.mentorplc.com
Models: single-deck coach, also integral coach.

NOGE
UK Supplier: **MENTOR**
Mentor Coach & Bus Ltd, Carlton House, Euroway Industrial Estate, Hellaby, Rotherham S66 8QL
Tel: 01709 700600
Fax: 01709 700007
E-mail: sales@mentorplc.com
Web site: www.mentorplc.com
   Ireland supplier: **BRIAN NOONE**
   Straffan Road, Maynooth, Co Kildare
   Tel: 00 353 1 628 6311
   Fax: 00 353 1 628 5404
Models: two-axle and three-axle integral coach bodies.

OPTARE LTD
Manston Lane, Leeds LS15 8SU
Tel: 0113 264 5182
Fax: 0113 260 6635
E-mail: info@optare.com
Web site: www.optare.com
Models: double-deck and single-deck buses, also integral
   UK supplier: **OPTARE COACH SALES**
   Denby Way, Hellaby Industrial Estate, Hellaby, Rotherham S66 8HR
   Tel: 01709 535120
   Fax: 01709 535102
   E-mail: coachsales@optare.com
   Web site: www.optare.com

*PLAXTON
Plaxton Park, Cayton Low Road, Eastfield, Scarborough YO11 3BY
Tel: 01723 581500
Fax: 01723 5813238
E-mail: sales@plaxtonlimited.co.uk
Web site: www.plaxtonlimited.co.uk
Range: coaches, buses, midicoach and midibus bodies

VAN HOOL
Bernard Van Hoolstraat 58, B-2500 Lier-Koningshooikt, Belgium
Tel: 00 32 3 420 20 20
Fax: 00 32 3 482 33 60
E-mail: info@vanhool.be
Web site: www.vanhool.be
Models: coach bodies

*WRIGHTBUS LTD
Galgorm, Ballymena, Northern Ireland BT42 1PY
Tel: 028 2564 1212
Fax: 028 2564 9703
E-mail: info@wright-bus.com
Web site: www.wright-bus.com
Models: double-deck low-floor bus body, single-deck low-floor articulated bus body, FTR advanced bus rapid transit vehicle, single-deck low-floor bus, single-deck low-entry coach, single-deck low-floor midibus.

Chassis and integral vehicles (small vehicles - under 9m)

ALEXANDER DENNIS
Dennis Way, Guildford GU1 1AF
Tel: 01483 571271
Range: rear-engined low-floor midibus

FORD MOTOR COMPANY
Ford Motor Co Ltd, Eagle Way, Brentwood CM13 3BW
Tel: 0845 7111 888
Web site: www.fordvans.co.uk/peoplemovers
Models: Transit, complete minibus or chassis-cowl.

IRISBUS (UK) LTD
Iveco House, Station Road, Watford WD17 1SR
Tel: 01923 259660
Fax: 01923 259623
E-mail: info@irisbus.co.uk
Web site: www.irisbus.co.uk

JOHN BRADSHAW LTD
New Lane, Stibbington, Peterborough PE8 6LW
Tel: 01780 781801
Web site: www.john-bradshaw.co.uk
Models: Electric minibus/taxi

KVC MANUFACTURING LTD
Comagh Business Park, Kilbeggan, Co Westmeath, Ireland
Tel: 00 353 506 32699
Fax: 00 353 506 32691
E-mail: info@kvc.ie
Web site: www.kvc.ie

LDV LTD
Bromford House, Drews Lane, Birmingham B8 2QG
Tel: 0121 322 2000
Fax: 0121 327 4487
Web site: www.ldv.co.uk
Models: Complete minibus or chassis-cowl

LEYLAND PRODUCT DEVELOPMENTS LTD
Aston Way, Leyland, Preston PR26 7TZ
Tel: 01772 435834
Web site: www.lpdl.co.uk
Models: CNG, LPG and electric low-floor minibus conversions

MERCEDES-BENZ
UK Supplier: **EvoBus (UK) Ltd**, Ashcroft Way, Cross Point Business Park, Ashcroft Way, Coventry CV2 2TU
Tel: 024 7662 6000
Fax: 024 7662 6034
Web site: www.evobus.com
Models: Complete low-floor minibus or chassis cowl

MINITRAM SYSTEMS LTD
12 Waterloo Park Estate, Bidford on Avon B50 4JH
Tel: 01789 490707
Fax: 01789 490592
E-mail: enquiries@tdi.uk.com
Web site: www.minitram.com
Models: Rubber tyre-guided/unguided/rail 7.8m vehicle

*NU-TRACK LTD
Steeple Industrial Estate, Antrim BT41 1AB.
Tel: 028 94 469 550
Fax: 028 94 465 430
E-mail: enquiries@nu-track.co.uk

OPTARE LTD
Manston Lane, Leeds LS15 8SU
Tel: 0113 264 5182
Fax: 0113 260 6635
Web site: www.optare.com
Models: front-engined integral low-floor minibus, rear-engined integral low-floor midibus.
  UK supplier: **OPTARE COACH SALES**
  Denby Way, Hellaby Industrial Estate, Hellaby, Rotherham S66 8HR
  Tel: 01709 535120
  Fax: 01709 535102
  E-mail: coachsales@optare.com
  Web site: www.optare.com

PARRY PEOPLE MOVERS LTD
Overend Road, Cradley Heath, Dudley B64 7DD
Tel: 01384 569553
Fax: 01384 637753
E-mail: jpmparry@aol.com
Website: www.parrypeoplemovers.com
Models: Small light rail vehicles and trams

PIAGGIO LTD
J D Thompson Motors Ltd, 260-264 Hatfield Road, St Albans AL1 4UN
Tel: Sales: 01727 850808 Service: 01727 834605
Fax: 01727 847974
Web site: www.piaggio-center.co.uk/porter.php
Models: 6-seat minibus

RENAULT UK LTD
Rivers Office Park, Denham Way, Maple Cross, Rickmansworth WD3 9YS
Tel: 01923 855500
Web site: www.renault.co.uk
Models: Complete minibus or chassis-cowl; electric vehicle.

TOYOTA (GB) PLC
Great Burgh, Burgh Heath, Epsom KT18 5UX
Tel: 01737 363633
Mobile: 07785 238798
E-mail: steve.prime@tgb.toyota.co.uk
Web site: www.toyota.com
  UK suppliers:
  A&D Coach Sales
  Tel: 01884 860767
  *Holloway Commercials
  Tel: 01902 636661
  Salvador Caetano
  Tel: 01530 26333
Models: Optimo midicoach, chassis cowl

VAUXHALL MOTORS LTD
Luton LU1 3YT
Tel: 020 7439 0303
Vauxhall Mobility: 0800 731 5267
Web site: www.vauxhall.co.uk
Models: Complete minibus or chassis-cowl.

VOLKSWAGEN COMMERCIAL VEHICLES
Yeomans Drive, Blakelands, Milton Keynes MK14 5AN
Web site: www.volkswagen-vans.co.uk
Models: Complete minibus or chassis-cowl.

Bodybuilders (small vehicles) Minibus conversions

ADVANCED VEHICLE BUILDERS
Upper Mantle Close, Clay Cross S45 9NU
Tel: 01246 250022
Fax: 01246 250016
E-mail: info@minibus.co.uk

BLUEBIRD VEHICLES LTD
Unit 7, Plaxton Park, Cayton Low Road, Eastfield, Scarborough YO11 3BY
Tel: 01723 860800
Web site: www.bluebirdvehicles.com

BURNT TREE VEHICLE SOLUTIONS
Burnt Tree House, Knights Way, Battlefield Enterprise Park, Harlescott Lane, Shrewsbury SY1 3JE
Tel: 01743 457650
Web site: www.burnt-tree.co.uk

CHASSIS DEVELOPMENTS
Grovebury Road, Leighton Buzzard LU7 8SL
Tel: 01525 374151
Web site: www.chassisdevelopments.co.uk

*CONCEPT COACHCRAFT
Far Cromwell Road, Bredbury, Stockport SK6 2SE
Tel: 0161 406 9322
Fax: 0161 406 9588
E-mail: sales@conceptcoachcraft.com
Web site: www.conceptcoachcraft.com

COURTSIDE CONVERSIONS LTD
1 Woodward Road, Howden Industrial Estate, Tiverton EX16 5HS
Tel: 01884 256048
Fax: 01884 256087
E-mail: courtsidesales@aol.com

CROWN COACHBUILDERS LTD
32 Flemington Industrial Park, Flemington, Motherwell ML1 1SN
Tel: 01698 276087
Fax: 01698 276144
E-mail: davidgreer@hotmail.com
Web site: www.crowncoachbuilders.co.uk

CVI (COMMERCIAL VEHICLE INNOVATION)
Moorfoot View, Bilston, Edinburgh EH25 9SL
Tel: 0131 473 9300
Web site: www.c-v-i.co.uk

DRIVELINE
Canal Gate Park, Nottingham Road, Spondon, Derby DE21 7SN
Tel: 01332 544111
Fax: 01332 544222

ESKER BUS & COACH SALES LTD
Comagh Business Park, Kilbeggan, Co Westmeath, Ireland
Tel: 00 353 506 33070
Fax: 00 353 506 33070
E-mail: info@eskerbusandcoach.com
Web site: www.eskerbusandcoach.com

Trade Directory

Trade Directory

*ESKER BUS & COACH (UK) LTD
Unit 3, Haigh Moor Drive, Brooklands Park, Church Lane, Dinnington, Sheffield S25 2JY
Tel: 01909 552244
Fax: 01909 569242
E-mail: info@eskerbusandcoach.co.uk
Web site: www.eskerbusandcoach.co.uk

EURO COACH BUILDERS LTD
Deerybeg Industrial Estate, Gweedore, Co Donegal, Ireland
Tel: 00 353 75 31528
Fax: 00 353 75 31930
Web site: www.eurocoachbuilders.ie

*EXCEL CONVERSIONS LTD
Excel House, Durham Lane, Armthorpe, Doncaster DN3 3FE
Tel: 01302 835388
Fax: 01302 835389
E-mail: admin@excelconversions.co.uk
Web site: www.excelconversions.co.uk

FRANK GUY LTD
Bridge Street, Clay Cross S45 9NG.
Tel: 01246 851222
Fax: 01246 250277
E-mail: sales@ frank-guy.co.uk
Web site: www.frank-guy.co.uk

GM COACHWORK LTD
Trusham, Newton Abbot TQ13 0NX
Tel: 01626 853050
Fax: 01626 853083
Web site: www.gmcoachwork.co.uk

INDCAR SA
Poligono Industrial Torres Pujals, E-17401 Arbucies (Girona), Spain
Web site: www.indar.com

JDC - JOHN DENNIS COACHBUILDERS
25 Westfield Road, Guildford GU1 1RR
Tel: 01483 501457
Web site: www.jdcbus.co.uk

JUBILEE AUTOMOTIVE GROUP
Woden Road South, Wednesbury WS10 0NQ
Tel: 0121 502 2252
Fax: 0121 502 2258
E-mail: sales@jubileeauto.co.uk

*LEICESTER CARRIAGE BUILDERS
Marlow Road, Leicester LE3 2BQ
Tel: 0116 282 4270
Fax: 0116 263 0554
E-mail: rick. johnson@midlandsco-op.com
Web site: www.leicestercarriagebuilders.co.uk

*MCV BUS AND COACH LTD
Sterling Place, Elean Business Park, Sutton, Ely CB6 2QE
Tel: 01353 773000
Fax: 01353 773001

*MELLOR COACHCRAFT
Miall Street, Rochdale OL11 1HY
Tel: 01706 860610
Fax: 01706 860042
E-mail: mcsales@woodhall-nicholson.co.uk
Web site: www.woodhall-nicholson.co.uk

*MINIBUS OPTIONS LTD
Bingswood Industrial Estate, Whaley Bridge, High Peak SK23 7LY
Tel: 01663 735355
Fax: 01663 735352
E-mail: info@minibusoptions.co.uk
Web site: www.minibusoptions.co.uk

*NU-TRACK LTD
Steeple Industrial Estate, Antrim BT41 1AB.
Tel: 028 9446 9550
Fax: 028 9446 5430
E-mail: enquiries@nu-track.co.uk

OLYMPUS COACHCRAFT LTD
7 Temperance Street, Manchester M12 6DX
Tel/Fax: 0161 273 4259
E-mail: geoffolympus@aol.com
Web site: www.olympuscoaches.co.uk

OPTARE LTD
Manston Lane, Leeds, LS15 8SU
Tel: 0113 264 5182
Fax: 0113 260 6635
Web site: www.optare.com

PLAXTON LIMITED
Plaxton Park, Cayton Low Road, Eastfield, Scarborough YO11 3BY
Tel: 01723 581500
Fax: 01723 5813238
Web site: www.plaxtonlimited.co.uk
Range: coaches; midicoach and midibus bodies.

PVS MANUFACTURING LTD
8 Ardboe Business Park, Kilmascally Road, Ardboe, Dungannon BT71 5BP
Tel: 028 8673 6969
Fax: 028 8673 7178
E-mail: mail@pvsltd.com
Web site: www.conversionspecialists.com

STANFORD COACH WORKS
Mobility House, Stanhope Industrial Park, Wharf Road, Stanford-le-Hope SS17 0EH
Tel: 01375 676088
Fax: 01375 677999
E-mail: sales@stanfordcoachworks.co.uk
Web site: www.stanfordcoachworks.co.uk
Range: mini- and midibuses, mini- and midicoaches

JOHN STEWART & CO (WISHAW) LTD
Smith Avenue, Garrion Business Park, Wishaw ML2 0RY
Tel: 01698 373483
Fax: 01698 357185

TAWE COACHBUILDERS LTD
Tawe House, Alloy Industrial Estate, Pontardawe SA8 4EN
Tel: 01792 832040
Fax: 01792 832041
Web site: www.tawecoachbuildersltd.co.uk

TVAC (THE VEHICLE APPLICATION CENTRE)
Centurion Way, Leyland PR26 6TZ
Tel: 01772 457116
Web site: www.tvac.com
Range: low-floor mini- and midibuses, mini- and midicoaches

UVMODULAR
Locksley Road, Armytage Road Industrial Estate, Brighouse HD6 1QF
Tel: 01484 400200
Fax: 01484 401125
E-mail: sales@uvmodular.co.uk

WILKER GROUP
Frederick Street, Clara, Co Offaly, Ireland
Tel: 00 353 506 31010
E-mail: info@wilkergroup.com
UK subsidiary
Sandy lane, Ettiley Heath, Sandbach CW11 3NG
Tel: 01270 705999
E-mail: info.uk@wilkergroup.com
Range: low-floor mini- and midibuses, mini- and midicoaches

Dealers

AD COACH SALES
Newbridge Coach Depot, Witheridge EX16 8PY
Tel: 01884 860767
E-mail: ggoodwin@adcoachsales.co.uk
Web site: www.adcoachsales.co.uk

Trade Directory

AJP COMMERCIALS
305-317 Wednesbury Road, Walsall WS2 9QJ
Tel: 01922 639652
Fax: 01922 611700

ALLIED VEHICLES LTD
230 Balmore Road, Glasgow G22 6LJ
Tel: 0800 916 3046
Web site: www.alliedvechicles.co.uk/bus
E-mail: info@alliedvechicles.co.uk

ARRIVA BUS AND COACH LTD
Lodge Garage, Whitehall Road West, Gomersal BD19 4BJ
Tel: 01274 681144
Web site: www.arriva.co.uk
E-mail: busandcoachsales@arriva.co.uk

AVONDALE INTERNATIONAL LTD
451 Clifton Drive North, Lytham St Annes FY8 2PS
Tel: 01253 727211
Fax: 01253 714210

B.A.S.E. LTD
Crosse Hall Street, Chorley PR6 0QQ
Tel: 01254 685599
Web site: www.basecoachsales.co.uk

BLYTHSWOOD MOTORS LTD
1175 Argyle Street, Glasgow G3 8TQ
Tel: 0141 221 3165
Fax: 0141 221 3172
E-mail: blythswoodmotors@aol.com
Web site: www.blythswoodmotors.co.uk

BN - BRIAN NOONE
Straffan Road, Maynooth, Co Kildare, Ireland
Tel: 00 353 1 628 6311
Web site: www.briannooneltd.ie

*BOB VALE COACH SALES
Kingshill House, Spurlands End Road, Great Kingshill, High Wycombe HP15 6PE
Tel: 01494 716996
Fax: 01494 716331
E-mail: bobvalecoachsale@btconnect.com
Web site: www.bobvalecoachsale.com

BRIAN NOONE
Straffan Road, Maynooth, Co Kildare, Ireland
Tel: 00 353 1 628 6311
Fax: 00 353 1 628 5404

*BRISTOL BUS & COACH SALES
6/7 Freestone Road, St Philips, Bristol BS2 0QN
Tel: 0117 971 0251
Fax: 0117 972 3121
E-mail: andrew.munden@bristolbusandcoach.co.uk
Web site: www.bristolbusandcoach.co.uk

*BRITISH BUS SALES
c/o Mike Nash, PO Box 534, Dorking RH5 5XB
Tel: 07836 656692
E-mail: nashionalbus1@btconnect.com
Web site: www.britishbussales.co.uk

SALVADOR CAETANO (UK) LTD
Mill Lane, Heather, Coalville LE67 2QA
Tel: 01530 263333
Fax: 01530 263379
E-mail: enquiries@caetano.co.uk
Web site: www.caetano.co.uk
Models: single-deck coach, single-deck low-floor midibus.

DAWSONRENTALS BUS AND COACH LTD
Delaware Drive, Tongwell, Milton Keynes MK15 8JH
Tel: 01908 218111
Fax: 01908 610156
E-mail: info@dawsongroup.co.uk
Web site: www.dawsongroup.co.uk

EAST LANCASHIRE COACHBUILDERS LTD
Lower Philips Road, Whitebirk Industrial Estate, Blackburn BB1 5UD
Tel: 01254 504150
Fax: 01254 504197
E-mail: john.horn@elcb.co.uk
Web site: www.elcb.co.uk

ENSIGN BUS CO LTD
Juliette Close, Purfleet Industrial Estate, Purfleet RM15 4YF
Tel: 01708 865656
Fax: 01708 864340
E-mail: sales@ensignbus.com
Web site: www.ensignbus.com

ERRINGTONS OF EVINGTON LTD
Glenrise Garage, London Road (A6), Oadby LE2 4RG
Tel: 0116 259 2131
Fax: 0116 259 2313

EVOBUS (UK) LTD
Ashcroft Way, Cross Point Business Park, Ashcroft Way, Coventry CV2 2TU
Tel: 024 7662 6000
Fax: 024 7662 6020
Web site: www.evobus.com

DAVID FISHWICK VEHICLE SALES
North Valley, Colne BB8 0RF
Tel: 01282 615138/867772

FLEET AUCTION GROUP
Brindley Road, Stephenson Industrial park, Coalville LE67 3HG
Tel: 01530 833535
E-mail: fleet.master@btinternet.com
Web site: www.fleetauctiongroup.com

FLEETMASTER BUS & COACH LTD
Regent House, Silverwood, Snow Hill, Copthorne RH10 3ED
Tel: 01342 859058
Fax: 01342 859059
E-mail: fleet.master@btinternet.com
Web site: www.fleetmaster.co.uk

FURROWS COMMERCIAL VEHICLES
Kemberton Road, Halesfield, Telford TF7 4QS
Tel: 01952 684433

GM COACHWORK LTD
Teign Valley, Trusham, Newton Abbot TQ13 0NX
Tel: 01626 853050
Fax: 01626 853083
Web site: www.gmcoachwork.co.uk
E-mail: david.vadght@gmcoachwork.co.uk

THOMAS HARDIE - WIGAN
Lockett Road, Ashton-in-Makerfield WN4 8DE
Tel: 01942 505124
Fax: 01942 505119

IAN GORDON COMMERCIALS
Schawkark Garage, Stair KA5 5JA
Tel: 01292 591764

*HOLLOWAY COMMERCIALS
60 Walsall Road, Willenhall WV13 2EF
Tel: 01902 636661
Fax: 01902 609652
E-mail: sales@hollowaycommercials.co.uk
Web site: www.hollowaycommercials.co.uk

B & D HOLT LTD
Cuthbert Street, Bolton BL3 3SD
Tel: 01204 650999
Fax: 01204 665300
E-mail: bevholt@bdholt.co.uk
Web site: www.bdholt.co.uk

IRISH COMMERCIALS (SALES)
Naas, Co Kildare, Ireland

LVD
Leinster Vehicle Distributors Ltd, Urlingford, Co Kilkenny, Ireland
Tel: 00 353 56 31189/88 3 1899
Web site: www.lvd.ie

LONDON BUS EXPORT
PO Box 12, Chepstow NP6 7NQ
Tel: 01291 689741
Fax: 01291 681361
E-mail: lonbusco@globalnet.co.uk
Web site: www.london.bus.co.uk

LOUGHSHORE AUTOS LTD
26 Killycanavan Road, Ardboe, Dungannon BT71 5BP
Tel: 028 8673 7325
Fax: 028 8673 5882
E-mail: michael@loughshoreautosltd.com
Web site: www.loughshoreautosltd.com

MAJORLINE ENGINEERING LTD
Baybridge Industrial Units, Baybridge Lane, Owslebury, Winchester SO21 1JN
Tel: 01962 777077
Fax: 01962 777661, 777667
E-mail: majorline@compuserve.com

MASS SPECIAL ENGINEERING LTD
Anston, Sheffield S25 4SD
Tel: 01909 550480
Fax: 01909 550486

MENTOR COACH & BUS LTD
Carlton House, Euroway Industrial Estate, Hellaby, Rotherham S66 8QL
Tel: 01709 700600
Fax: 01709 700007
E-mail: sales@mentorplc.com
Web site: www.mentorplc.com

MID WEST CHELTENHAM LTD
The Coach Centre, Golden Valley, Staverton, Cheltenham GL51 0TE
Tel: 01452 859111
Fax: 01452 859222
Web site: www.bussales.co.uk

MISTRAL GROUP (UK) PLC
PO Box 130, Knutsford WA16 6AG
Tel: 0870 241 5786
Fax: 0870 241 5784
E-mail: sales@mistral-group.com
Web site: www.mistral-group.com

*MOSELEY (PCV) LTD
Elmsall Way, Dale Lane, South Elmsall, Pontefract WF9 2XS
Tel: 01977 609000
Fax: 01977 609900
Web site: www.moseleycoachsales.co.uk

MOSELEY IN THE SOUTH LTD
Summerfield Avenue, Chelston Business Park, Wellington TA21 9JF
Tel: 01823 653000
Fax: 01823 663502
E-mail: enquiries@moseleysouth.co.uk

MOSELEY DISTRIBUTORS
Rydenmains, Condoratt Road, Glenmavis, Airdrie ML6 0PP
Tel: 01236 750501
E-mail: enquiries@moseleydistributors.co.uk

MIKE NASH
See British Bus Sales (above)

*NEXT BUS LTD
Vincients Road, Bumpers Farm Industrial Estate, Chippenham SN14 6QA
Tel: 01249 462462
Fax: 01249 448844
E-mail: sales@next-bus.co.uk
Web site: www.next-bus.co.uk

W. NORTHS (PV) LTD
Moor Lane Trading Estate, Sherburn in Elmet LS25 6ET
Tel: 01977 682415
Fax: 01977 681119

OPTARE COACH SALES
Denby Way, Hellaby Industrial Estate, Hellaby, Rotherham S66 8HR
Tel: 01709 535120
Fax: 01709 535102
E-mail: coachsales@optare.com
Web site: www.optare.com

OWENS OF OSWESTRY BMC
Unit 3, Foxen Monor Industrial Park, Four Crosses, Llanymynech SY22 6ST
Tel: 01691 652126
Fax: 01691 831142
E-mail: sales@owens-bmc.co.uk
Web site: www.owens-bmc.co.uk

H W PICKRELL
Gardiners Lane North, Crays Hill, Billericay CM11 2XE
Tel: 01268 521033
Fax: 01268 284951
Web site: www.hwpickrell.co.uk

*PLAXTON COACH SALES CENTRE
Ryton Road, Anston, Sheffield S25 4DL
Tel: 01909 551155
Fax: 01909 567994
E-mail: coaches@plaxtonlimited.co.uk
Web site: www.plaxtonlimited.co.uk

SCANIA BUS & COACH UK LTD
Claylands Avenue, Worksop S81 7DJ
Tel: 01909 500822
Web site: www.scaniabusandcoach.com

SOMERBUS
Paulton, Bristol BS39 7YR
Tel/Fax: 01761 415456
Web site: www.somerbus.co.uk
E-mail: somerbus@tinyworld.co.uk

*SOUTHDOWN PSV LTD
Silverwood, Snow Hill, Copthorne RH10 3EN
Tel: 01342 715222
Fax: 01342 719619
E-mail: bussales@southdownpsv.co.uk
Web site: www.southdownpsv.co.uk

*STAFFORD BUS CENTRE
Moorfields Industrial Estate, Cotes Heath ST21 6QY
Tel: 01782 791774
Fax: 01782 791721
E-mail: martin@staffordbuscentre.com
Web site: www.staffordbuscentre.com

STEPHENSONS OF ESSEX
Riverside Industrial Estate, South Street, Rochford SS4 1BS
Tel: 01702 541511

STOKE TRUCK & BUS CENTRE
Bute Street, Fenton, Stoke-on-Trent ST4 3PS
Tel: 01782 598310
Fax: 01782 598674
Web site: www.bmcstoke.co.uk

TAYLOR COACH SALES
102 Beck Road, Isleham, Ely CB7 5QP
Tel (mobile): 07850 241848
Tel: 01638 780010

TOYOTA (GB) PLC
Great Burgh, Burgh Heath, Epsom KT18 5UX
Tel: 01737 363633
Fax: 01737 367713
E-mail: steve.prime@tgb.toyota.co.uk
Web site: www.toyota.com
   UK suppliers:
   A&D Coach Sales
   Tel: 01884 860767

*Holloway Commercials
Tel: 01902 636661
Salvador Caetano
Tel: 01530 263333

*TRAMONTANA
Chapelknowe Road, Carfin, Motherwell ML1 5LE
Tel: 01698 861790
Fax: 01698 860778
E-mail: wdt90@tiscali.co.uk
Web site: tramontanacoach.co.uk

UK COACH & BUS
Carlton House, Euroway Estate, Hellaby, Rotherham S66 8QL
Tel: 01709 705570
Fax: 01709 705569
Web site: www.uk-cb.com

*USED COACH SALES
PO Box 166, Warrington WA4 5FG
Tel: 0870 062 0616
Fax: 0870 062 4499
Web site: www.usedcoachsales.co.uk

VENTURA BUS + COACH SALES
Unit 39, Hobbs Industrial Estate, Newchapel, Lingfield RH7 6HN
Tel: 01342 835206
Fax: 01342 835813
E-mail:info@venturasales.co.uk

VOLVO TRUCK & BUS LTD
Wedgnock Lane, Warwick CV34 5YA
Tel: 01926 401777
Fax: 01926 407407
Web site: www.volvobuses.com, www.volvo.com

VOLVO COACH CENTRE
Brisco Avenue, off Belton Road West, Loughborough LE11 5HP
Tel: 01509 634261
Fax: 01509 239362
Web site: www.volvo.com, www.volvobuses.volvo.co.uk

WACTON COACH SALES & SERVICES
Linton Trading Estate, Bromyard HR7 4QL
Tel: 01885 482782
Fax: 01885 482127

*WEALDEN PSV LTD
The Bus Garage, 64 Whetsted Road, Five Oak Green, Tonbridge TN12 6RT
Tel: 01892 833830
Fax: 01892 836977
E-mail: sales@wealdenpsv.co.uk
Web site: www.wealdenpsv.co.uk

ALAN WHITE COACH SALES
135 Nutwell Lane, Doncaster DN3 3JR
Tel: 01302 833203
Fax: 01302 831756
E-mail: sales@alanwhitecoachsales.com
Web site: www.alanwhitecoachsales.com

TREVOR WIGLEY & SONS BUS LTD
Baulder Bridge Road, Carlton, Barnsley S71 3HJ
Tel: 01226 713636/716479
E-mail: wigleys@btconnect.com
Web site: www.twigley.com

*YORKSHIRE BUS & COACH SALES
254A West Ella Road, West Ella, Hull HU10 7SF
Tel: 01482 653302
Fax: 01482 653302

Do you want to keep your
LITTLE RED BOOK
up-to-date?
Buses **magazine is now carrying**
updates every month.
See opposite title page
for Subscription details

Interested in Transport subjects?

Like a good read?
FREE?
send for our illustrated catalogue

Call 01455 254 470 or write to:

Midland Counties Publications
4 Watling Drive, Hinckley,
Leicestershire LE10 3EY

E-mail midlandbooks@compuserve.com
www.midlandcountiessuperstore.com

A-Z Listing of Bus, Coach & Tram Suppliers

Trade Directory

LIST OF CATEGORIES

Air Conditioning/Ventilation
Audio/Video Systems
Badges - Drivers/Conductors
Batteries
Bicycle Carriers
Body/Electrical Repairs & Refurbishing
Brakes & Brake Linings
Bus Stops/Shelters - see Shelters/Street Furniture
Cash Handling Equipment
Chassis Lubricating Systems
Clutches
Cooling Systems
Destination Indicator Equipment
Door Operating Gear
Drinks Dispensing Equipment
Driving Axles and Gears
Electrical Equipment
Electronic Control
Emission Control Devices
Engineering
Engines
Engine Oil Drain Valves
Exhaust Systems
Fans & Drive Belts
Fare Boxes
Fire Extinguishers
First Aid Equipment
Floor Covering
Fuel, Fuel Management & Lubricants
Garage Equipment
Gearboxes
Hand Driers (Coach Mounted)
Handrails
Headrest Covers/Curtains
Heating & Ventilation Systems
Hub Odometers
In-Coach Catering Equipment
Information Displays - see Passenger Information Systems
Labels, Nameplates & Decals
Lifting Equipment
Lifts/Ramps (Passenger)
Lighting/Lighting Systems
Model Buses
Oil Management Systems
Painting/Signwriting
Parts Suppliers
Passenger Information Systems
Pneumatic Valves/Cylinders
Rapid Transit/Priority Equipment
Repairs/refurbishment - see Body/Electrical Repairs
Retarders & Speed Control Systems
Reversing Safety Systems
Roller Blinds - Passenger/Driver
Roof Lining Fabrics
Seat Belts
Seats, Seat Cushions & Seat Frames
Shelters/Street Furniture
Shock Absorbers/Suspension
Steering
Surveillance Systems
Tachograph Calibrators
Tachograph Chart Analysis Service
Tachographs
Tickets, Ticket machines and Ticket Systems
Timetable Display Frames
Toilet Equipment
Transmission Overhaul
Tree Guards
Tyres
Uniforms
Upholstery
Vacuum Systems
Vehicle Washing and Washers
Wheeltrims & Covers
Windows & Windscreens

INDUSTRY SERVICE PROVIDERS

Accident Investigation
Accountancy & Audit
Advertising Contractors
Advisory Services
Artwork
Auctioneers & Valuators
Breakdown & Recovery Services
Cleaning Services
Coach Driver Agency
Coach Hire Broker
Coach Interchange & Parking Facilities
Computer Systems/Software
Consultants
Driver Supply
Driver Training
Exhibition Organisers
Ferry Operators
Finance & Leasing
Graphic Design
Hotels & Refreshment Facilities
Insurance
Legal & Operations Advisors
Life Insurance & Pensions
Livery Design
Maps for the Bus industry
Marketing Services
Mechanical Investigation
On-Bus Advertising
Printing
Promotional Material
Publications - Magazines & Books
Quality Management Systems
Refreshment Facilities
Timetable Production
Tour Wholesalers
Training & Marketing Services
Vehicle Certification

Coach & Bus Air Conditioning

Approved Service Centre

We are also experienced in other manufacturers systems.

- Servicing
- Repairs
- Parts

Tel: **0845 402 401 4**   www.airconco.ltd.uk
Unit 10, Middleton Trade Park, Oldham Rd, Middleton, Manchester, M24 1QZ

Air Conditioning/Ventilation

*AIRCONCO
Unit 10, Middleton Trade Park, Oldham Road, Middleton, Manchester M24 1QZ
Tel: 0845 402 4014
Fax: 0845 402 4041
E-mail: mail@airconco.uk
Web site: www.airconco.ltd.uk

AMA LTD
Unit 17, Springmill Industrial Estate, Avening Road, Nailsworth GL6 0BH
Tel: 01453 832884
Fax: 01453 832040
E-mail: ama@ftech.co.uk

BROXWOOD VEHICLE SPECIALISTS
Unit 2 Parkside Garage, Old Stafford Road, Wolverhampton WV10 7PH
Tel: 01902 798770
Fax: 01902 798564
E-mail: saks@broxwood.net
Web site: www.broxwood.net

CARRIER SUTRAK
Unit 6, I O Centre, Barn Way, Lodge Farm Industrial Estate, Northampton NN5 7UW
Tel: 01604 581468
Fax: 01604 758132
E-mail: kim.neale@carrier.utc.com

*CLAYTON HEATERS LTD
Hunter Terrace, Fletchworth Gate, Burnsall Road, Coventry CV5 6SP
Tel: 02476 691916
Fax: 02476 691969
E-mail: admin@claytoncc.co.uk
Web site: www.claytoncc.co.uk

COLDCARE
Unit 10, Langley Wharf, Railway Terrace, Kings Langley WD4 8JE
Tel: 01923 261177
Fax: 01923 264058
E-mail: sales@coldcare-refrigeration.co.uk
Web site: www.coldcare-refrigeration.co.uk

CONSERVE (UK) LTD
Suite 7, Logistics House, Kingsthorpe Road, Northampton NN2 6LJ
Tel: 01604 710055
Fax: 01604 710065
E-mail: information@conserveuk.co.uk
Web site: www.conserveuk.co.uk

CREST COACH CONVERSIONS
Unit 5, Holmeroyd Road, Bentley Moor Lane, Carcroft, Doncaster DN6 7BH
Tel: 01302 723723
Fax: 01302 724724

*EBERSPACHER (UK) LTD
Headlands Business Park, Salisbury Road, Ringwood BH24 3PB
Tel: 01425 480151
Fax: 01425 480152
E-mail: enquiries@eberspacher.com
Web site: www.eberspacher.com

HISPACOLD
See: Clayton Heaters above
Web Site: www.hispacold.es

JAYCAS MINIBUS SALES
11 John Street, Bamber Bridge, Preston PR5 6TJ
Tel/Fax: 01772 321491
E-mail: john@minibusjaycas.co.uk

*THE LAWTON MOTOR BODY BUILDING CO LTD
Knutsford Road, Church Lawton, Stoke-on-Trent ST7 3DN
Tel: 01270 882056
Fax: 01270 883014
E-mail: info@lawtonmotorbody.co.uk
Web site: www.lawtonmotorbody.co.uk

M A C LTD
Unit 8, Oldends Lane Industrial Estate, Oldends Lane, Stonehouse GL10 3RQ
Tel: 01453 828781
Fax: 01453 828167
E-mail: sales@macai.uk.com
Web site: www.macair.uk.com

*NEALINE WINDSCREEN WIPER PRODUCTS
Unit 1, The Sidings Industrial Estate, Birdingbury Road, Marton CV23 9RX
Tel: 01926 633256
Fax: 01926 632600

*PACET MANUFACTURING LTD
Wyebridge House, Cores End Road, Bourne End SL8 5HH
Tel: 01628 526754
Fax: 01628 810080
E-mail: sales@pacet.co.uk
Web site: www.pacet.co.uk

*PLAXTON COACH SALES CENTRE
Ryton Road, Anston, Sheffield S25 4DC
Tel: 01909 551155
Fax: 01909 567994
E-mail: coaches@plaxtonlimited.co.uk
Web site: www.plaxtonlimited.co.uk

SCANIA
Scania Bus & Coach (UK) Ltd, Claylands Avenue, Worksop S81 7DJ.
Tel: 01909 500822.
Fax: 01909 500165

SUTRAK
See Carrier Sütrak, above.

*UNITEC
Parts Division, Denby Way, Hellaby, Rotherham S66 8HR
Tel: 01709 792000
Fax: 01709 792009
E-mail: parts@optare.com

*UNITEC LONDON
Unit 5, Gateway 25, Weston Avenue, West Thurrock RM20 3ZD
Tel: 01708 892440
Fax: 01708 862125
E-mail: london.service@optare.com

*UNITEC ROTHERHAM
Denby Way, Hellaby, Rotherham S66 8HR
Tel: 01709 535101
Fax: 01709 535103
E-mail: rotherham.service@optare.com

*UNITEC SCOTLAND
Unit 7, Cumbernauld Business Park, Ward Park Road, Cumbernauld G67 3JZ
Tel: 01236 726738
Fax: 01236 795651
E-mail: scotland.service@optare.com

UWE VERKEN AB (UK branch)
Meadow Works, Walton Summit Industrial Estate, Bamber Bridge, Preston PR5 8AL
Tel: 0700 289 3893
Fax: 0700 289 3329
E-mail: uwe.uk@btinternet.com

WEBASTO PRODUCT UK LTD
Webasto House, White Rose Way, Doncaster Carr DN4 5JH
Tel: 01302 322232
Fax: 01302 322231
E-mail: info@webastouk.com
Web site: www.webasto.co.uk

Audio/Video Systems

AFTERMARKET COACH SUPPLIES (UK) LTD
Unit A, Shipmans Yard, Station Road, Rushton NN14 1RL
Tel: 01536 711310
Fax: 01536 710033
Web site: www.acsuk.freeuk.com

AUTOSOUND LTD
4 Lister Street, Dudley Hill, Bradford BD4 9PQ
Tel: 01274 688990
Fax: 01274 651318
Web site: www.autosound.co.uk
E-mail: sales@autosound.co.uk

Trade Directory

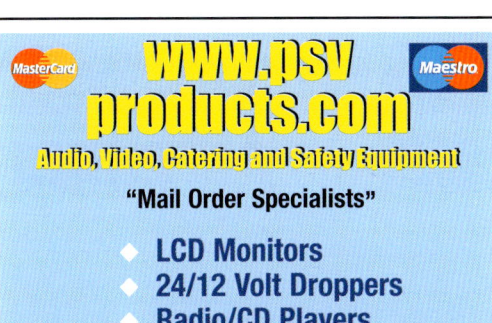

*AVT SYSTEMS LTD
Unit 3, Tything Road, Arden Forest Trading Estate, Alcester B49 6ES
Tel: 01789 400357
Fax: 01789 400359
E-mail: enquiries@avtsystems.co.uk
Web site: www.avtsystems.co.uk

BROXWOOD VEHICLE SPECIALISTS
Unit 2 Parkside Garage, Old Stafford Road, Wolverhampton WV10 7PH
Tel: 01902 798770
Fax: 01902 798564
E-mail: saks@broxwood.net
Web site: www.broxwood.net

CYBERLYNE COMMUNICATIONS LTD
Unit 5, Hatfield Way, South Church Industrial Estate, Bishop Auckland DL14 6XB
Tel: 01388 773761
Fax: 01388 773778
E-mail: david@cyberlynecommunications.co.uk
Web site: www.cyberlynecommunications.co.uk

EXPRESS COACH REPAIRS LTD
Outgang Lane, Pickering YO18 7EL
Tel: 01751 475215.

FCAV & CO
Brooklyn House, Coleford Road, Bream GL15 6EU
Tel: 01594 564552
Fax: 01594 564556
E-mail: sales@coachaudiovisual.co.uk
Web site: www.coachaudiovisual.co.uk

INOVAS LTD
1 Glenbervie Business Park, Larbert, Falkirk FK5 4RB
Tel: 01324 682268
Fax: 01324 682269
Web site: www.inovas.co.uk
E-mail: info@inovas.co.uk

JAYCAS MINIBUS SALES
11 John Street, Bamber Bridge, Preston PR5 6TJ
Tel/Fax: 01772 321491
E-mail: john@minibusjaycas.co.uk

*THE LAWTON MOTOR BODY BUILDING CO LTD
Knutsford Road, Church Lawton, Stoke-on-Trent ST7 3DN
Tel: 01270 882056
Fax: 01270 883014
E-mail: info@lawtonmotorbody.co.uk
Web site: www.lawtonmotorbody.co.uk

MENTOR
Mentor Coach & Bus Ltd, Carlton House, Euroway Industrial Estate, Hellaby, Rotherham S66 8QL
Tel: 01709 700600
Fax: 01709 700007
E-mail: sales@mentorplc.com
Web site: www.mentorplc.com

*PSV PRODUCTS
PO Box 166, Warrington WA4 5FG
Tel: 0870 062 4488
Fax: 0870 062 4499
E-mail: mike@psvproducts.com
Web site: www.psvproducts.com

*UNITEC
Parts Division, Denby Way, Hellaby, Rotherham S66 8HR
Tel: 01709 792000
Fax: 01709 792009
E-mail: parts@optare.com

Badges - Drivers/Conductors

ABBOT BROWN
Barnfleet Works, Fleet Street, Beaminster DT8 3EJ
Tel: 01308 862404
Fax: 01308 863402
E-mail: sales@abbotbrown.co.uk

*FIRST CHOICE NAMEPLATES, LABELS & SIGNS
Lynden 2c, Russell Avenue, Balderton, Newark NG24 3BT
Tel: 01636 678035
Fax: 01636 707066
E-mail: firstchoice@handbag.com

MARK TERRILL PSV BADGES
5 De Grey Close, Lewes BN7 2JR
Tel: 01273 474816
Fax: 01273 474816
Mobile: 07770 666159

TRANSPORTATION MANAGEMENT SOLUTIONS
PO Box 15174, Glasgow G3 6WB
Tel: 0141 332 4733
Fax: 0141 354 0076
E-mail: tramsol@aol.com

Batteries

BETA RESEARCH & DEVELOPMENT/ZEBRA BATTERIES
50 Goodsmoor Road, Sinfin, Derby DE24 9GN
Tel: 01332 770500
Web site: www.betard.co.uk

*BRITISH BUS SALES
c/o Mike Nash, PO Box 534, Dorking RH5 5XB
Tel: 07836 656692
E-mail: nashionalbus1@btconnect.com
Web site: www.britishbussales.co.uk

*CUMMINS UK
Rutherford Drive, Park Farm South, Wellingborough NN8 6AN
Tel: 01933 334200
Fax: 01933 334198
E-mail: cduksales@cummins.com
Web site: www.cummins-uk.com

ENECO LTD
Unit 6, Spring Copse Business Park, Slinfold RH13 0SZ
Tel: 01403 790114
Web site: www.eneco.co.uk

THOMAS HARDIE – WIGAN
Lockett Road, Ashton-in-Makerfield WN4 8DE.
Tel: 01942 505124
Fax: 01942 505119

LEXCEL POWER SYSTEMS PLC
35 Manor Road, Henley on Thames
RG9 1LU.
Tel: 01491 874414
E-mail: sales@lexcelpower.com
Web site: www.lexcelpower.com

MASS SPECIAL ENGINEERING LTD
Anston, Sheffield S25 4SD
Tel: 01909 550480
Fax: 01909 550486

MENTOR COACH & BUS LTD
Carlton House, Euroway Industrial Estate,
Hellaby, Rotherham S66 8QL
Tel: 01709 700600
Fax: 01709 700007
E-mail: sales@mentorplc.com
Web site: www.mentorplc.com

MULTIPART PSV
Pilling Lane, Chorley PR7 3EL.
Tel: 01257 225577
Fax: 01257 225575
E-mail: info@multipart.com
Web site: www.multipart.com

*PLAXTON COACH SALES CENTRE
Ryton Road, Anston, Sheffield S25 4DC
Tel: 01909 551155
Fax: 01909 567994
E-mail: coaches@plaxtonlimited.co.uk
Web site: www.plaxtonlimited.co.uk

POWER BATTERIES (GB) LTD
Units 5-8, Canal View Business Park,
Wheelhouse Road, Rugeley WS15 1UY
Tel: 01889 571100
Web site: www.bannerbatteriescom

*UNITEC
Parts Division, Denby Way, Hellaby,
Rotherham S66 8HR
Tel: 01709 792000
Fax: 01709 792009
E-mail: parts@optare.com

*UNITEC LONDON
Unit 5, Gateway 25, Weston Avenue,
West Thurrock RM20 3ZD
Tel: 01708 892440
Fax: 01708 862125
E-mail: london.service@optare.com

*UNITEC ROTHERHAM
Denby Way, Hellaby, Rotherham
S66 8HR
Tel: 01709 535101
Fax: 01709 535103
E-mail: rotherham.service@optare.com

*UNITEC SCOTLAND
Unit 7, Cumbernauld Business Park,
Ward Park Road, Cumbernauld G67 3JZ
Tel: 01236 726738
Fax: 01236 795651
E-mail: scotland.service@optare.com

VARTA AUTOMOTIVE BATTERIES LTD
Broadwater Park, North Orbital Road,
Denham UB9 5AG
Tel: 01895 838999
Fax: 01895 838981
Web site: www.varta.co.uk

Body/Electrical Repairs & Refurbishing

AD COACH SALES
Newbridge Coach Depot, Witheridge EX16 8PY
Tel: 01884 860787
Fax: 01884 860711
E-mail: ggoodwin@adcoachsales.co.uk
Web site: www.adcoachsales.co.uk

AVS STEPS LTD
Alders Farmhouse, Alders Lane, Whixall
SY13 2BR
Tel: 01948 880010
Fax: 01948 880020
Web site: www.avssteps.co.uk

BLACKPOOL COACH SERVICES
Moss Hey Garage, Chapel Road, Blackpool
FY4 5HU.
Tel/Fax: 01253 698686

BRISTOL BUS & COACH SALES
6/7 Freestone Road, St Philips, Bristol
BS2 0QN
Tel: 0117 971 0251
Fax: 0117 972 3121
E-mail: andrew.munden@bristolbusandcoach.com
Web site: www.bristolbusandcoach.co.uk

BROXWOOD VEHICLE SPECIALISTS
Unit 2 Parkside Garage, Old Stafford Road,
Wolverhampton WV10 7PH
Tel: 01902 798770
Fax: 01902 798564
E-mail: saks@broxwood.net
Web site: www.broxwood.net

BULWARK BUS & COACH ENGINEERING LTD
Gate 3, Bulwark Industrial Estate, Chepstow
NP16 5QZ
Tel: 01291 622326
Fax: 01291 622726.

CARLYLE BUS & COACH LTD
Great Bridge Street, Swan Village, West
Bromwich B70 0X4
Tel: 0121 524 1200
Fax: 0121 524 1201
E-mail: admin@carlyleplc.co.uk

*COBUS UK
Carnaby Industrial Estate, Bridlington
YO15 3QY
Tel: 01262 603 829
Fax: 01262 606 738
E-mail: cobus@btconnect.com

CREST COACH CONVERSIONS
Unit 5, Holmeroyd Road, Bentley Moor
Lane, Carcroft, Doncaster DN6 7BH
Tel: 01302 723723
Fax: 01302 724724

CROWN COACHBUILDERS LTD
32 Flemington Industrial Park, Flemington,
Motherwell ML1 1SN
Tel: 01698 276087
Fax: 01698 276144
E-mail: davidgreer@hotmail.com
Web site: www.crowncoachbuilders.co.uk

DRURY & DRURY
Unit 6, Cobbs Wood Industrial Estate,
Brunswick Road, Ashford TN23 1EH
Tel: 01303 610555.
Fax: 01303 610666.
E-mail: martinstrange@channelcommercials.co.uk

EAST LANCASHIRE COACHBUILDERS LTD (ELC)
Lower Philips Road, Whitebirk Industrial
Estate, Blackburn BB1 5UD
Tel: 01254 504150
Fax: 01254 504197
E-mail: john.horn@elcb.co.uk
Web site: www.elcb.co.uk

*EASTGATE COACH TRIMMERS
3 Thornton Road Industrial Estate, Pickering
YO18 7HZ
Tel/Fax: 01751 472229
E-mail: info@eastgate-coachtrimmers.co.uk

EXPRESS COACH REPAIRS LTD
Outgang Lane, Pickering YO18 7EL.
Tel: 01751 475215.

GHE
Unit 30, Fort Industrial Park, Fort Parkway,
Castle Bromwich B35 7AR.
Tel: 0121 747 4400.
Fax: 0121 747 4977.

HANTS & DORSET TRIM LTD
Canada Road, West Wellow SO51 6DE.
Tel: 023 8033 4335

THOMAS HARDIE – WIGAN
Lockett Road, Ashton-in-Makerfield, Wigan
WN4 8DE.
Tel: 01942 505124.
Fax: 01942 505119

Trade Directory

*HATTS COACHWORKS & SERVICES
Foxham, Chippenham SN15 4NB
Tel: 01249 740444
Fax: 01249 740447
E-mail: adrian@hattstravel.co.uk
Web site: www.hattstravel.co.uk

INVERTEC LTD
Whelford Road, Fairford GL7 4DT
Tel: 01285 713550
Fax: 01285 713548
Mobile: 07802 793828
E-mail: ian@invertec.co.uk
Web site: www.invertec.co.uk

KENT COACHWORKS
Lower Road, Northfleet DA11 9BB.
Tel: 01474 330320.
Fax: 01474 330321
Web site: www.londoncoaches.com.

*THE LAWTON MOTOR BODY BUILDING CO LTD
Knutsford Road, Church Lawton, Stoke-on-Trent ST7 3DN
Tel: 01270 882056
Fax: 01270 883014
E-mail: info@lawtonmotorbody.co.uk
Web site: www.lawtonmotorbody.co.uk

LEICESTER CARRIAGE BUILDERS
Marlow Road, Leicester LE3 2BQ
Tel: 0116 282 4270
Fax: 0116 263 0554
E-mail: rick. johnson@midlandsco-op.com
Web site:
www.leicestercarriagebuilders.co.uk

MARTYN INDUSTRIALS LTD
5 Brunel Way, Durranhill Industrial Esate, Carlisle CA1 3NQ
Tel: 01228 544000
Fax: 01228 544001
E-mail: enquiries@martyn-industrials.co.uk
Web site: www.martyn-industrials.com

MASS SPECIAL ENGINEERING LTD
Anston, Sheffield S25 4SD.
Tel: 01909 550480.
Fax: 01909 550486.

MCV BUS & COACH LTD
Sterling Place, Elean Business Park, Sutton CB6 2QE
Tel: 01353 773000
Fax: 01353 773001
E-mail: vernon.edwards@mcv-uk.com

*MELLOR COACHCRAFT
Miall Street, Rochdale OL11 1HY
Tel: 01706 860610
Fax: 01706 860042
E-mail: mcsales@woodhall-nicholson.co.uk
Web site: www.woodhall-nicholson.co.uk

MENTOR
Mentor Coach & Bus Ltd, Carlton House, Euroway Industrial Estate, Hellaby, Rotherham S66 8QL
Tel: 01709 700600
Fax: 01709 700007
E-mail: sales@mentorplc.com
Web site: www.mentorplc.com

MOSELEY (PCV) LTD
Elmsall Way, Dale Lane, South Elmsall WF9 2XS
Tel: 01977 609000
Fax: 01977 609900

MULTIPART PSV
Pilling Lane, Chorley PR7 3EL
Tel: 01257 225577
Fax: 01257 225575
E-mail: info@multipart.com
Web site: www.multipart.com

*NEXT BUS LTD
Vincients Road, Bumpers Farm Industrial Estate, Chippenham SN14 6QA
Tel: 01249 462462
Fax: 01249 448844
E-mail: sales@next-bus.co.uk
Web site: www.next-bus.co.uk

*NORBURY BLINDS LTD
41-45 Hanley Street, Newtown, Birmingham B19 3SP
Tel: 0121 359 4311
Fax: 0121 359 6388
E-mail: info@norbury-blinds.com
Web site: www.norbury-blinds.com

OLYMPUS COACHCRAFT LTD
7 Temperance Street, Manchester M12 6HR
Tel/Fax: 0161 273 4259
E-mail: geoffolympus@aol.com
Web site: www.olympuscoaches.co.uk

*PLAXTON
Plaxton Park, Cayton Low Road, Eastfield, Scarborough YO11 3BY
Tel: 01723 581500
Fax: 01723 5813238
E-mail: sales@plaxtonlimited.co.uk
Web site: www.plaxtonlimited.co.uk

*PLAXTON COACH SALES CENTRE
Ryton Road, Anston, Sheffield S25 4DC
Tel: 01909 551155
Fax: 01909 567994
E-mail: coaches@plaxtonlimited.co.uk
Web site: www.plaxtonlimited.co.uk

*RH BODYWORKS
A140 Ipswich Road, Brome Eye IP23 8AW
Tel: 01379 870666
Fax: 01379 871140
E-mail: mike.ball@rhbodywork.co.uk
Web site: www.rhbodyworks.co.uk

*TRAMONTANA
Chapelknowe Road, Carfin, Motherwell ML1 5LE
Tel: 01698 861790
Fax: 01698 860778
E-mail: wdt90@tiscali.co.uk
Web site: tramontanacoach.co.uk

*TRUCKALIGN CO LTD
VIP Trading Estate, Anchor & Hope Lane, London SE7 7RY
Tel: 020 8858 3781
Fax: 020 8858 3781

*UNITEC
Parts Division, Denby Way, Hellaby, Rotherham S66 8HR
Tel: 01709 792000
Fax: 01709 792009
E-mail: parts@optare.com

*UNITEC LONDON
Unit 5, Gateway 25, Weston Avenue, West Thurrock RM20 3ZD
Tel: 01708 892440
Fax: 01708 862125
E-mail: london.service@optare.com

*UNITEC ROTHERHAM
Denby Way, Hellaby, Rotherham S66 8HR
Tel: 01709 535101
Fax: 01709 535103
E-mail: rotherham.service@optare.com

*UNITEC SCOTLAND
Unit 7, Cumbernauld Business Park, Ward Park Road, Cumbernauld G67 3JZ
Tel: 01236 726738
Fax: 01236 795651
E-mail: scotland.service@optare.com

VOLVO COACH CENTRE
Brisco Avenue, off Belton Road West, Loughborough LE11 5HP
Tel: 01509 217777
Fax: 01509 260978

*WRIGHTBUS LTD
Galgorm, Ballymena BT42 1PY
Tel: 028 2564 1212
Fax: 028 2564 9703
E-mail: info@wright-bus.com
Web site: www.wright-bus.com

Bicycle Carriers

JES BUSCYCLE
27-33 High Street, Totton SO40 9HL
Tel: 023 8066 3535

Brakes and Brake Linings

ARVIN MERITOR
Unit 21, Suttons Park Avenue, Reading RG6 1LA.
Tel: 0118 935 9126
Fax: 0118 935 9138
E-mail: james.randall@arvinmeritor.com
Web site: www.arvinmeritor.com

AUTOMOTIVE PRODUCTS GROUP LTD – AP BORG & BECK / AP LOCKHEED
Tachbrook Road, Leamington Spa CV31 3ER.
Tel: 01926 470000.
Fax: 01926 472000.

BBA FRICTION LTD
PO Box 18, Hunsworth Lane BD19 3UJ.
Tel: 01274 854000.
Fax: 01274 854001.

BROXWOOD VEHICLE SPECIALISTS
Unit 2 Parkside Garage, Old Stafford Road, Wolverhampton WV10 7PH
Tel: 01902 798770
Fax: 01902 798564
E-mail: saks@broxwood.net
Web site: www.broxwood.net

*DIRECT PARTS LTD
Unit 1, Churnet Court, Churnetside Business Park, Harrison Way, Cheddleton ST13 7EF
Tel: 01538 361777
Fax: 01538 369100
E-mail: sales@direct-group.co.uk
Web site: www.direct-group.co.uk

*ERENTEK LTD
Malt Kiln Lane, Waddington, Lincoln
LN5 9RT
Tel: 01522 720065
Fax: 01522 729155
E-mail: sale@erentek.co.uk
Web site: www.erentek.co.uk

*HART BROTHERS (ENGINEERING) LTD
Soho Works, Soho Street, Oldham OL4 2AD
Tel: 0161 737 6791

*IMEXPART LTD
Links 31, Willowbridge Way, Whitwood,
Castleford WF10 5NP
Tel: 01977 553936
Fax: 01977 604684
E-mail: parts@imexpart.com
Web site: www.imexpart.com

*IMPERIAL ENGINEERING
Delamare Road, Cheshunt EN8 9UD
Tel: 01992 6342555
Fax: 01992 630506
E-mail: sales@imperialengineering.co.uk
Web site: www.imperialengineering.co.uk

KELLETT (UK) LTD
8 Stevenson Way, Sheffield S9 3WZ.
Tel: 0114 261 1122.
Fax: 0114 261 1199.
E-mail: sales@kellett.co.uk

KNORR-BREMSE SYSTEMS FOR COMMERCIAL VEHICLES LTD
Douglas Road, Kingswood, Bristol BS15 8NL.
Tel: 0117 984 6100.
Fax: 0117 984 6101.
Web site: www.knorr-bremse.com

*MCE LTD (WABCO AGENTS)
Firbank Way, Leighton Buzzard LU7 4YP
Tel: 01525 375301
Fax: 01525 850967
Web site: www.mce-ltd.com

MAJORLINE ENGINEERING LTD
Baybridge Industrial Units, Baybridge Lane,
Owslebury, Winchester SO21 1JN.
Tel: 01962 777077.
Fax: 01962 777661, 777667
E-mail: majorline@compuserve.com

MULTIPART PSV
Pilling Lane, Chorley PR7 3EL.
Tel: 01257 225577.
Fax: 01257 225575.
E-mail: info@multipart.com
Web site: www.multipart.com

*PARTLINE LTD
Dockfield Road, Shipley BD17 7AZ
Tel: 01274 531531
Fax: 01274 531088
E-mail: sales@partline.co.uk
Web site: www.partline.co.uk

*ROADLINK INTERNATIONAL LTD
Strawberry Lane, Willenhall WV13 3RL
Tel: 01902 636210
Fax: 01902 606604
E-mail: sales@roadlink-international.co.uk
Web site: www.roadlink-international.co.uk

*SERGEANT (P&P) LTD
PO Box 11, New Hall Lane, Hoylake
CH47 4DH
Tel: 0151 632 5903
Fax: 0151 632 5908
E-mail: enq@sergeant.co.uk
Web site: www.sergeant.co.uk

*UNITEC
Parts Division, Denby Way, Hellaby,
Rotherham S66 8HR
Tel: 01709 792000
Fax: 01709 792009
E-mail: parts@optare.com

*UNITEC LONDON
Unit 5, Gateway 25, Weston Avenue,
West Thurrock RM20 3ZD
Tel: 01708 892440
Fax: 01708 862125
E-mail: london.service@optare.com

*UNITEC ROTHERHAM
Denby Way, Hellaby, Rotherham
S66 8HR
Tel: 01709 535101
Fax: 01709 535103
E-mail: rotherham.service@optare.com

*UNITEC SCOTLAND
Unit 7, Cumbernauld Business Park,
Ward Park Road, Cumbernauld G67 3JZ
Tel: 01236 726738
Fax: 01236 795651
E-mail: scotland.service@optare.com

WABCO AUTOMOTIVE UK
Texas Street, Leeds LS27 0HQ
Tel: 0113 251 2510
Fax: 0113 251 2844

Cash Handling Equipment

CASH PROCESSING SOLUTIONS LTD
Unit 26-27, Portland Court, Kingsway, Luton
LU4 8HA
Tel: 01582 402318
Fax: 01582 402318
E-mail: info@cashprocessing.co.uk
Web site: www.cashprocessing.co.uk

*CUMMINS-ALLISON LTD
William H Klotz House, Colonnade
Point, Central Boulevard, Progolis Park,
Coventry CV6 4BU
Tel: 024 7633 9810
Fax: 024 7633 9811
E-mail: sales@cummins-allison.co.uk
Web site: www.cumminsallison.co.uk

*ETM SOFTWARE SERVICES
9 Dorset Avenue, Ferndown BH22 8HJ
Tel: 01202 246710
E-mail: info@etmss.com
Web site: www.etmss.com

JOHN GROVES TICKET SYSTEMS
Unit 5, Rennie Business Units, Factory
Place, Saltcoats KA21 5LZ
Tel: 01294 471133
Fax: 01294 471166
Web site: www.cambist.se

*MARK TERRILL TICKET MACHINERY
5 De Grey Close, Lewes BN7 2JR.
Tel: 01273 474816
Fax: 01273 474816
E-mail: mark.terrill@ukonline.co.uk

*SCAN COIN LTD
110 Broadway, Salford Quays M50 2UW
Tel: 0161 873 0500
Fax: 0161 873 0501
E-mail: sales@scancoin.co.uk
Web site: www.scancoin.co.uk

*TRANSPORT TICKET SERVICES LTD
Yew Tree Cottage, Newcastle, Monmouth
NP25 5NT
Tel/Fax: 01600 750650
E-mail: tts@waitrose.com, ticket-machine@waitrose.com

Chassis Lubricating Systems

MULTIPART PSV
Pilling Lane, Chorley PR7 3EL
Tel: 01257 225577
Fax: 01257 225575
E-mail: info@multipart.com
Web site: www.multipart.com

Clutches

*ASHLEY BANKS LTD
5 King Street Estate, Langtoft, Peterborough
PE6 9NF
Tel: 01778 560651
Fax: 01778 560721
E-mail: user@ashleybanks.fsnet.co.uk

AUTOMOTIVE PRODUCTS GROUP LTD – AP BORG & BECK / AP LOCKHEED
Tachbrook Road, Leamington Spa
CV31 3ER.
Tel: 01926 470000.
Fax: 01926 472000.

BBA FRICTION LTD
PO Box 18, Hunsworth Lane, Cleckheaton
BD19 3UJ.
Tel: 01274 854000.
Fax: 01274 854001.

BORG & BECK
See Automotive Products, above.

BROXWOOD VEHICLE SPECIALISTS
Unit 2 Parkside Garage, Old Stafford Road,
Wolverhampton WV10 7PH
Tel: 01902 798770
Fax: 01902 798564
E-mail: saks@broxwood.net
Web site: www.broxwood.net

BUSS BIZZ
Goughs Transport Depot, Morestead,
Winchester SO21 1JD.
Tel: 01962 715555/66.
Fax: 01962 714868.

COACH-AID
Unit 2, Brindley Close, Tollgate Industrial
Estate, Stafford ST16 3SU
Tel: 01785 222666
E-mail: workshop@coach-aid.com
Web site: www.coach-aid.com

EATON LTD
Truck Components Marketing, PO Box 11,
Worsley Road North,
Worsley M28 5GJ.
Tel: 01204 797219.
Fax: 01204 797204.

⦿ SCAN COIN

AUTOMATED CASH DEPOSITING SYSTEM

Fast and accurate processing of bank notes, coins and transport tokens plus dropsafe for depositing of non-cash items.

Safe, secure and easy to use.

Network capability

Fast coin deposit

High capacity printer

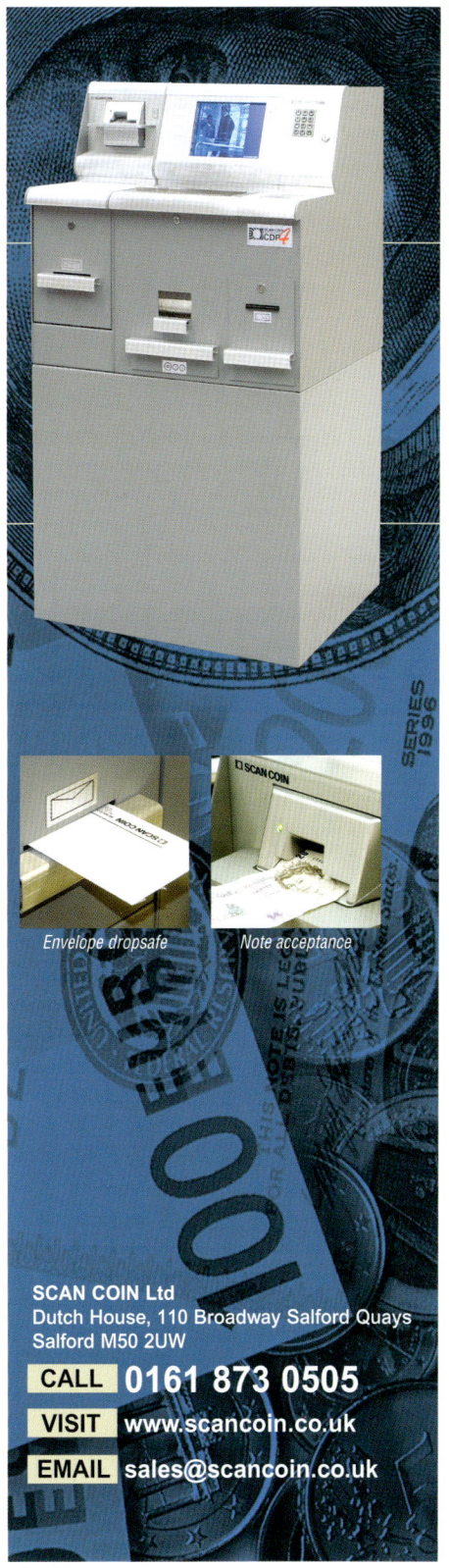

Envelope dropsafe

Note acceptance

- Easy to install, through-the-wall or free-standing
- Front or rear access for changing vaults and for servicing
- Fully customisable user interface
- All totals displayed on-screen
- Multiple coin acceptance and value counting
- Bank notes accepted in any direction
- Vehicle defect reporting
- Exchange rates can be programmed into the system
- Wide range of additional software available

SCAN COIN Ltd
Dutch House, 110 Broadway Salford Quays
Salford M50 2UW

CALL 0161 873 0505
VISIT www.scancoin.co.uk
EMAIL sales@scancoin.co.uk

Trade Directory

transport counts on it

The Jetsort range of coin counter/sorters are Euro ready

High speed, high volume coin processing

Counts & sorts up to 9 denominations at 6000 mixed coins a minute

Optional dual bag and coin discrimination
Integrates with industry standard software

We also provide a range of note counters and mixed note scanners

CUMMINS COUNTS EURO

CUMMINS
CUMMINS-ALLISON LTD.

0800 0186484
www.cumminsallison.co.uk

***IMEXPART LTD**
Links 31, Willowbridge Way, Whitwood, Castleford WF10 5NP
Tel: 01977 553936
Fax: 01977 604684
E-mail: parts@imexpart.com
Web site: www.imexpart.com

KELLETT (UK) LTD
8 Stevenson Way, Sheffield S9 3WZ.
Tel: 0114 261 1122.
Fax: 0114 261 1199.
E-mail: sales@kellett.co.uk

MAJORLINE ENGINEERING LTD
Baybridge Industrial Units, Baybridge Lane, Owslebury, Winchester SO21 1JN.
Tel: 01962 777077.
Fax: 01962 777661, 777667
E-mail: majorline@compuserve.com

MENTOR
Mentor Coach & Bus Ltd, Carlton House, Euroway Industrial Estate, Hellaby, Rotherham S66 8QL
Tel: 01709 700600
Fax: 01709 700007
E-mail: sales@mentorplc.com
Web site: www.mentorplc.com

MULTIPART PSV
Pilling Lane, Chorley PR7 3EL.
Tel: 01257 225577.
Fax: 01257 225575.
E-mail: info@multipart.com
Web site: www.multipart.com

***PARTLINE LTD**
Dockfield Road, Shipley BD17 7AZ
Tel: 01274 531531
Fax: 01274 531088
E-mail: sales@partline.co.uk
Web site: www.partline.co.uk

***SERGEANT (P&P) LTD**
PO Box 11, New Hall Lane, Hoylake CH47 4DH
Tel: 0151 632 5903
Fax: 0151 632 5908
E-mail: enq@sergeant.co.uk
Web site: www.sergeant.co.uk

***SHAWSON SUPPLY LTD**
12 Station Road, Saintfield BT24 7DU
Tel: 028 9751 0994
Fax: 028 9751 0816
E-mail: shawsondiesel@btopenworld.com
Web site: www.shawsonsupply.com

***UNITEC**
Parts Division, Denby Way, Hellaby, Rotherham S66 8HR
Tel: 01709 792000
Fax: 01709 792009
E-mail: parts@optare.com

***UNITEC LONDON**
Unit 5, Gateway 25, Weston Avenue, West Thurrock RM20 3ZD
Tel: 01708 892440
Fax: 01708 862125
E-mail: london.service@optare.com

***UNITEC ROTHERHAM**
Denby Way, Hellaby, Rotherham S66 8HR
Tel: 01709 535101
Fax: 01709 535103
E-mail: rotherham.service@optare.com

***UNITEC SCOTLAND**
Unit 7, Cumbernauld Business Park, Ward Park Road, Cumbernauld G67 3JZ
Tel: 01236 726738
Fax: 01236 795651
E-mail: scotland.service@optare.com

Cooling Systems

BROXWOOD VEHICLE SPECIALISTS
Unit 2 Parkside Garage, Old Stafford Road, Wolverhampton WV10 7PH
Tel: 01902 798770
Fax: 01902 798564
E-mail: saks@broxwood.net
Web site: www.broxwood.net

*DIRECT PARTS LTD
Unit 1, Churnet Court, Churnetside Business Park, Harrison Way, Cheddleton ST13 7EF
Tel: 01538 361777
Fax: 01538 369100
E-mail: sales@direct-group.co.uk
Web site: www.direct-group.co.uk

*IMEXPART LTD
Links 31, Willowbridge Way, Whitwood, Castleford WF10 5NP
Tel: 01977 553936
Fax: 01977 604684
E-mail: parts@imexpart.com
Web site: www.imexpart.com

*THE LAWTON MOTOR BODY BUILDING CO LTD
Knutsford Road, Church Lawton, Stoke-on-Trent ST7 3DN
Tel: 01270 882056
Fax: 01270 883014
E-mail: info@lawtonmotorbody.co.uk
Web site: www.lawtonmotorbody.co.uk

MAJORLINE ENGINEERING LTD
Baybridge Industrial Units, Baybridge Lane, Owslebury, Winchester SO21 1JN
Tel: 01962 777077.
Fax: 01962 777661, 777667
E-mail: majorline@compuserve.com

MULTIPART PSV
Pilling Lane, Chorley PR7 3EL.
Tel: 01257 225577
Fax: 01257 225575
E-mail: info@multipart.com
Web site: www.multipart.com

*PARTLINE LTD
Dockfield Road, Shipley BD17 7AZ
Tel: 01274 531531
Fax: 01274 531088
E-mail: sales@partline.co.uk
Web site: www.partline.co.uk

SILFLEX LTD
Coed Cae Lane Industrial Estate, Pontyclun CF72 9HJ
Tel: 01443 238464
Fax: 01443 237781
E-mail: silflex@silflex.com
Web site: www.silflex.com

*UNITEC LONDON
Unit 5, Gateway 25, Weston Avenue, West Thurrock RM20 3ZD
Tel: 01708 892440
Fax: 01708 862125
E-mail: london.service@optare.com

*UNITEC ROTHERHAM
Denby Way, Hellaby, Rotherham S66 8HR
Tel: 01709 535101
Fax: 01709 535103
E-mail: rotherham.service@optare.com

*UNITEC SCOTLAND
Unit 7, Cumbernauld Business Park, Ward Park Road, Cumbernauld G67 3JZ
Tel: 01236 726738
Fax: 01236 795651
E-mail: scotland.service@optare.com

Destination Indicator Equipment

BRIGHT-TECH DEVELOPMENTS LTD
Fleets Point House, Willis Way, Poole BH15 3SS
Tel: 01202 679627
E-mail: sales@bright-tech.co.uk
Web site: www.bright-tech.co.uk

HANOVER DISPLAYS LTD
Unit 24, Cliffe Industrial Estate, Lewes BN8 6JL
Tel: 01273 477528
Fax: 01273 407766
E-mail: nrobertson@hanoverdisplays.com
Web site: www.hanoverdisplays.com

INDICATORS INTERNATIONAL LTD
41 Aughrim Road, Magherafelt BT45 6JX.
Tel: 028 7963 2591.
Fax: 028 7963 3927.
E-mail: sales@indicators-int.com
Web site: www.indicators-int.com

INVERTEC LTD
Whelford Road, Fairford GL7 4DT
Tel: 01285 713550
Fax: 01285 713548
Mobile: 07802 793828
E-mail: ian@invertec.co.uk
Web site: www.invertec.co.uk

*McKENNA BROTHERS LTD
McKenna House, Jubilee Road, Middleton, Manchester M24 2LX
Tel: 0161 655 3244
Fax: 0161 655 3059
E-mail: info@mckennabrothers.co.uk
Web site: www.mckennabrothers.co.uk

MULTIPART PSV
Pilling Lane, Chorley PR7 3EL.
Tel: 01257 225577.
Fax: 01257 225575.
E-mail: info@multipart.com
Web site: www.multipart.com

*NORBURY BLINDS LTD
41-45 Hanley Street, Newtown, Birmingham B19 3SP
Tel: 0121 359 4311
Fax: 0121 359 6388
E-mail: info@norbury-blinds.com
Web site: www.norbury-blinds.com

PERCY LANE PRODUCTS LTD
Lichfield Road, Tamworth B79 7TL
Tel: 01827 63821
Fax: 01827 310159
E-mail: sales@percy-lane.co.uk
Web site: www.percy-lane.co.uk

*PLAXTON COACH SALES CENTRE
Ryton Road, Anston, Sheffield S25 4DL
Tel: 01909 551155
Fax: 01909 567994
E-mail: coaches@plaxtonlimited.co.uk
Web site: www.plaxtonlimited.co.uk

*TOP GEARS DESTINATIONS
46 Fulwood Hall Lane, Fulwood, Preston PR2 8DD
Tel/Fax: 01772 700536
E-mail: steve@pitlane-2000.com
Web site: www.pitlane-2000.com

WEBASTO PRODUCT UK LTD
Webasto House, White Rose Way, Doncaster Carr DN4 5JH
Tel: 01302 322232
Fax: 01302 322231
E-mail: info@webastouk.com
Web site: www.webasto.co.uk

Door Operating Gear

AIR DOOR SERVICES
The Pavilions, Holly Lane Industrial Estate, Atherstone CV9 2QZ
Tel: 01827 11660
Fax: 01827 713577
E-mail: airdoorservices@aol.com

CARLYLE BUS & COACH LTD
Great Bridge Street, Swan Village, West Bromwich B70 0X4
Tel: 0121 524 1200
Fax: 0121 524 1201
E-mail: admin@carlyleplc.co.uk

DEANS POWERED DOORS
PO Box 8, Borwick Drive, Grovehill, Beverley HU17 0HQ
Tel: 01482 868111
Fax: 01482 881890
E-mail: info@deans-doors.com

*ERENTEK LTD
Malt Kiln Lane, Waddington, Lincoln LN5 9RT
Tel: 01522 720065
Fax: 01522 729155
E-mail: sale@erentek.co.uk
Web site: www.erentek.co.uk

KELLETT (UK) LTD
8 Stevenson Way, Sheffield S9 3WZ.
Tel: 0114 261 1122.
Fax: 0114 261 1199.
E-mail: sales@kellett.co.uk

KNORR-BREMSE SYSTEMS FOR COMMERCIAL VEHICLES LTD
Douglas Road, Kingswood, Bristol BS15 8NL.
Tel: 0117 984 6100.
Fax: 0117 984 6101.
Web site: www.knorr-bremse.com

*THE LAWTON MOTOR BODY BUILDING CO LTD
Knutsford Road, Church Lawton, Stoke-on-Trent ST7 3DN
Tel: 01270 882056
Fax: 01270 883014
E-mail: info@lawtonmotorbody.co.uk
Web site: www.lawtonmotorbody.co.uk

MULTIPART PSV
Pilling Lane, Chorley PR7 3EL.
Tel: 01257 225577.
Fax: 01257 225575.
E-mail: info@multipart.com
Web site: www.multipart.com

MET UK LIMITED
PO Box 205, Southam CV47 0ZL
Tel: 01926 813938
Fax: 01926 814898
E-mail: met.uk@btinternet.com

*NEXT BUS LTD
Vincients Road, Bumpers Farm Industrial Estate, Chippenham SN14 6QA
Tel: 01249 462462
Fax: 01249 448844
E-mail: sales@next-bus.co.uk
Web site: www.next-bus.co.uk

PETERS DOOR SYSTEMS LTD
Bradbury Drive, Springwood Industrial Estate, Braintree CM7 2ET
Tel: 01376 555277
Fax: 01376 555292
E-mail: petersdoors@petersdoors.co.uk

*PLAXTON
Plaxton Park, Cayton Low Road, Eastfield, Scarborough YO11 3BY
Tel: 01723 581500
Fax: 01723 5813238
E-mail: sales@plaxtonlimited.co.uk
Web site: www.plaxtonlimited.co.uk

*PLAXTON COACH SALES CENTRE
Ryton Road, Anston, Sheffield S25 4DL
Tel: 01909 551155
Fax: 01909 567994
E-mail: coaches@plaxtonlimited.co.uk
Web site: www.plaxtonlimited.co.uk

*PNEUMAX LTD
Unit 8, Venture Industrial Park, Fareham Road, Gosport PO13 0BA
Tel: 01329 823999
Fax: 01329 822345
E-mail: sales@pneumax.co.uk
Web site: www.pneumax.co.uk

*UNITEC
Parts Division, Denby Way, Hellaby, Rotherham S66 8HR
Tel: 01709 792000
Fax: 01709 792009
E-mail: parts@optare.com

*UNITEC LONDON
Unit 5, Gateway 25, Weston Avenue, West Thurrock RM20 3ZD
Tel: 01708 892440
Fax: 01708 862125
E-mail: london.service@optare.com

*UNITEC ROTHERHAM
Denby Way, Hellaby, Rotherham S66 8HR
Tel: 01709 535101
Fax: 01709 535103
E-mail: rotherham.service@optare.com

*UNITEC SCOTLAND
Unit 7, Cumbernauld Business Park, Ward Park Road, Cumbernauld G67 3JZ
Tel: 01236 726738
Fax: 01236 795651
E-mail: scotland.service@optare.com

VAPOR-STONE UK LTD
2nd Avenue, Centrum 100, Burton-on-Trent DE14 3WF
Tel: 01283 743300
Fax: 01283 743333
Web site: www.wabtec.com

WABCO AUTOMOTIVE UK LTD
Texas Street, Morley LS27 0HQ.
Tel: 0113 251 2510
Fax: 0113 251 2844

Drinks Dispensing Equipment

BRADTECH LTD
Unit 3, Ladford Covert, Seighford, Stafford ST18 9QD
Tel: 01785 282800
E-mail: sales@bradtech.ltd.uk
Web site: www.bradtech.ltd.uk

DRINKMASTER LTD
Plymouth Road, Liskeard PL14 3PG
Tel: 01579 342082
Fax: 01579 342591
E-mail: info@drinkmaster.co.uk
Web site: www.drinkmaster.co.uk

*PLAXTON
Plaxton Park, Cayton Low Road, Eastfield, Scarborough YO11 3BY
Tel: 01723 581500
Fax: 01723 5813238
E-mail: sales@plaxtonlimited.co.uk
Web site: www.plaxtonlimited.co.uk

*PSV PRODUCTS
PO Box 166, Warrington WA4 5FG
Tel: 0870 062 4488
Fax: 0870 062 4499
E-mail: mike@psvproducts.com
Web site: www.psvproducts.com

SHADES TECHNICS
Marshgate Drive, Hertford SG13 7AJ
Tel: 01992 501683
Fax: 01992 501669
E-mail: sales@shades-technics.com
Web site: www.shades-technics.com

Driving Axles & Gears

ALBION AUTOMOTIVE LTD
South Street, Scotstoun, Glasgow G14 0DT.
Tel: 0141 434 2400.
Fax: 0141 959 6362
E-mail: sales@albion_auto.co.uk
Web site: www.albion_auto.co.uk

ARVIN MERITOR
Unit 21, Suttons Park Avenue, Reading RG6 1LA.
Tel: 0118 935 9126
Fax: 0118 935 9138
E-mail: james.randall@arvinmeritor.com
Web site: www.arvinmeritor.com

BUSS BIZZ
Goughs Transport Depot, Morestead, Winchester SO21 1JD.
Tel: 01962 715555/66.
Fax: 01962 714868.

*CRESCENT FACILITIES LTD
72 Willow Crescent, Chapeltown, Sheffield S35 1QS
Tel/fax: 0114 2451050
E-mail: cfl.chris@btinternet.com
Web site: www.cflparts.com

EATON LTD
Truck Components Marketing, PO Box 11, Worsley Road North, Worsley M28 5GJ
Tel: 01204 797219.
Fax: 01204 797204.

*HART BROTHERS (ENGINEERING) LTD
Soho Works, Soho Street, Oldham OL4 2AD
Tel: 0161 737 6791

*HL SMITH TRANSMISSIONS LTD
Enterprise Business Park, Cross Road, Albrighton, Wolverhampton WV7 3BJ
Tel: 01902 373011
Fax: 01902 373608

*IMPERIAL ENGINEERING
Delamare Road, Cheshunt EN8 9UD
Tel: 01992 6342555
Fax: 01992 630506
E-mail: sales@imperialengineering.co.uk
Web site: www.imperialengineering.co.uk

LH GROUP (SERVICES) LTD
Graycar Business Park, Barton Turns, Barton Under Needwood DE13 8EN.
Tel: 01283 713615.
Fax: 01283 713551.
E-mail: l/h/llords@classic.msn.com

MAJORLINE ENGINEERING LTD
Baybridge Industrial Units, Baybridge Lane, Owslebury, Winchester SO21 1JN.
Tel: 01962 777077.
Fax: 01962 777661, 777667
E-mail: majorline@compuserve.com

MULTIPART PSV
Pilling Lane, Chorley PR7 3EL.
Tel: 01257 225577.
Fax: 01257 225575.
E-mail: info@multipart.com
Web site: www.multipart.com

*NEXT BUS LTD
Vincients Road, Bumpers Farm Industrial Estate, Chippenham SN14 6QA
Tel: 01249 462462
Fax: 01249 448844
E-mail: sales@next-bus.co.uk
Web site: www.next-bus.co.uk

*UNITEC
Parts Division, Denby Way, Hellaby, Rotherham S66 8HR
Tel: 01709 792000
Fax: 01709 792009
E-mail: parts@optare.com

*ZF POWERTRAIN
Stringes Close, Willenhall WV13 1LE
Tel: 01902 366000
Fax: 01902 366504
E-mail: sales@powertrain.org.uk
Web site: www.powertrain.org.uk

Electrical Equipment

AFTERMARKET COACH SUPPLIES (UK) LTD
Unit A, Shipmans Yard, Station Road, Rushton NN14 1RL
Tel: 01536 711310
Fax: 01536 710033
Web site: www.acsuk.freeuk.com

BRITAX PMG LTD
Bressingby Industrial Estate, Bridlington YO16 4SJ
Tel: 01262 670161
Fax: 01262 605666
E-mail: info@britax-pmg.com
Web site: www.britax-pmg.com

CARLYLE BUS & COACH LTD
Great Bridge Street, Swan Village, West Bromwich B70 0X4
Tel: 0121 524 1200
Fax: 0121 524 1201
E-mail: admin@carlyleplc.co.uk

*CRESCENT FACILITIES LTD
72 Willow Crescent, Chapeltown, Sheffield S35 1QS
Tel/fax: 0114 2451050
E-mail: cfl.chris@btinternet.com
Web site: www.cflparts.com

Trade Directory

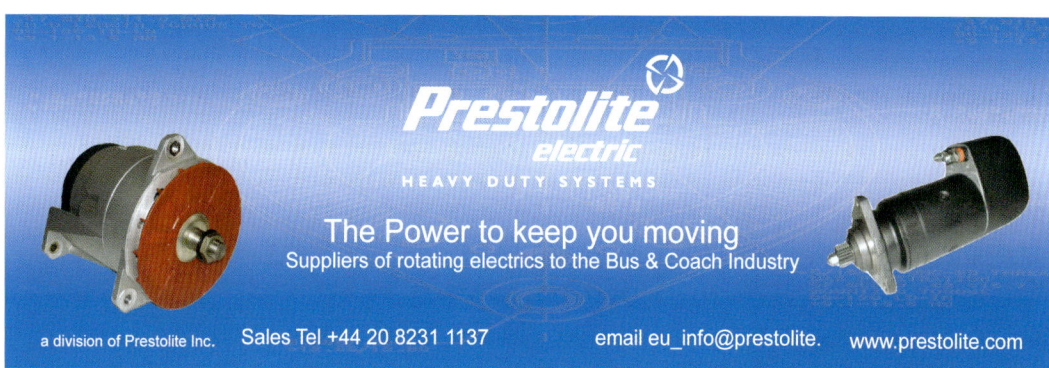

Prestolite electric
HEAVY DUTY SYSTEMS
The Power to keep you moving
Suppliers of rotating electrics to the Bus & Coach Industry
a division of Prestolite Inc.   Sales Tel +44 20 8231 1137   email eu_info@prestolite.com   www.prestolite.com

*DIRECT PARTS LTD
Unit 1, Churnet Court, Churnetside Business Park, Harrison Way, Cheddleton ST13 7EF
Tel: 01538 361777
Fax: 01538 369100
E-mail: sales@direct-group.co.uk
Web site: www.direct-group.co.uk

*ETM SOFTWARE SERVICES
9 Dorset Avenue, Ferndown BH22 8HJ
Tel: 01202 246710
E-mail: info@etmss.com
Web site: www.etmss.com

*IMEXPART LTD
Links 31, Willowbridge Way, Whitwood, Castleford WF10 5NP
Tel: 01977 553936
Fax: 01977 604684
E-mail: parts@imexpart.com
Web site: www.imexpart.com

INTELLITEC LTD
VIP Trading Estate, Anchor & Hope Lane, London SE7 7RY
Tel/Fax: 020 8858 3781

INVERTEC LTD
Whelford Road, Fairford GL7 4DT
Tel: 01285 713550
Fax: 01285 713548
Mobile: 07802 793828
E-mail: ian@invertec.co.uk
Web site: www.invertec.co.uk

LEXCEL POWER SYSTEMS PLC
35 Manor Road, Henley on Thames RG9 1LU.
Tel: 01491 874414.
E-mail: sales@lexcelpower.com
Web site: lexcelpower.com

MAJORLINE ENGINEERING LTD
Baybridge Industrial Units, Baybridge Lane, Owslebury, Winchester SO21 1JN.
Tel: 01962 777077.
Fax: 01962 777661, 777667
E-mail: majorline@compuserve.com

MULTIPART PSV
Pilling Lane, Chorley PR7 3EL.
Tel: 01257 225577
Fax: 01257 225575
E-mail: info@multipart.com
Web site: www.multipart.com

*NEALINE WINDSCREEN WIPER PRODUCTS
Unit 1, The Sidings Industrial Estate, Birdingbury Road, Marton CV23 9RX
Tel: 01926 633256
Fax: 01926 632600

*NEXT BUS LTD
Vincients Road, Bumpers Farm Industrial Estate, Chippenham SN14 6QA
Tel: 01249 462462
Fax: 01249 448844
E-mail: sales@next-bus.co.uk
Web site: www.next-bus.co.uk

PACEL ELECTRONICS
Fleets Point House, Willis Way, Poole BH15 3SS
Tel: 01202 676616
Fax: 01202 681357
E-mail: sales@pacel.co.uk
Web site: www.pacel.co.uk

*PARTLINE LTD
Dockfield Road, Shipley BD17 7AZ
Tel: 01274 531531
Fax: 01274 531088
E-mail: sales@partline.co.uk
Web site: www.partline.co.uk

*PLAXTON
Plaxton Park, Cayton Low Road, Eastfield, Scarborough YO11 3BY
Tel: 01723 581500
Fax: 01723 5813238
E-mail: sales@plaxtonlimited.co.uk
Web site: www.plaxtonlimited.co.uk

*PLAXTON COACH SALES CENTRE
Ryton Road, Anston, Sheffield S25 4DL
Tel: 01909 551155
Fax: 01909 567994
E-mail: coaches@plaxtonlimited.co.uk
Web site: www.plaxtonlimited.co.uk

*PNEUMAX LTD
Unit 8, Venture Industrial Park, Fareham Road, Gosport PO13 0BA
Tel: 01329 823999
Fax: 01329 822345
E-mail: sales@pneumax.co.uk
Web site: www.pneumax.co.uk

*PRESTOLITE ELECTRIC
Unit 48, The Metropolitan Park, 12-16 Bristol Road, Greenford UB6 8UP
Tel: 020 8231 1137
E-mail: eu_info@prestolite.com
Web site: www.prestolite.com

*UNITEC
Parts Division, Denby Way, Hellaby, Rotherham S66 8HR
Tel: 01709 792000
Fax: 01709 792009
E-mail: parts@optare.com

Electronic Control

ACTIA UK LTD
Unit 81, Mochdre Industrial Estate, Newtown SY16 4LE
Tel: 01686 621067
Fax: 01686 621068
E-mail: mail@actia.co.uk
Web site: www.actia.co.uk

*AVT SYSTEMS LTD
Unit 3, Tything Road, Arden Forest Trading Estate, Alcester B49 6ES
Tel: 01789 400357
Fax: 01789 400359
E-mail: enquiries@avtsystems.co.uk
Web site: www.avtsystems.co.uk

*BRITISH BUS SALES
c/o Mike Nash, PO Box 534, Dorking RH5 5XB
Tel: 07836 656692
E-mail: nashionalbus1@btconnect.com
Web site: www.britishbussales.co.uk

INTELLITEC LTD
VIP Trading Estate, Anchor & Hope Lane, London SE7 7RY
Tel/Fax: 020 8858 3781

KNORR-BREMSE SYSTEMS FOR COMMERCIAL VEHICLES LTD
Douglas Road, Kingswood, Bristol BS15 8NL.
Tel: 0117 984 6100.
Fax: 0117 984 6101.
Web site: www.knorr-bremse.com

*NORBURY BLINDS LTD
41-45 Hanley Street, Newtown, Birmingham B19 3SP
Tel: 0121 359 4311
Fax: 0121 359 6388
E-mail: info@norbury-blinds.com
Web site: www.norbury-blinds.com

*UNITEC
Parts Division, Denby Way, Hellaby, Rotherham S66 8HR
Tel: 01709 792000
Fax: 01709 792009
E-mail: parts@optare.com

VDO KIENZLE UK LTD
36 Gravelly Industrial Park, Birmingham B24 8TA.
Tel: 0121 326 1234.
Fax: 0121 326 1299.

WABCO AUTOMOTIVE UK
Texas Street, Morley LS27 0HQ.
Tel: 0113 251 2510.
Fax: 0113 251 2844.

Emission Control Devices

*CUMMINS UK
Rutherford Drive, Park Farm South, Wellingborough NN8 6AN
Tel: 01933 334200
Fax: 01933 334198
E-mail: cduksales@cummins.com
Web site: www.cummins-uk.com

*DINEX EXHAUSTS LTD
14 Chesford Garage, Woolston, Warrington WA1 4RE
Tel: 01925 849849
Fax: 01925 849850
E-mail: enquiries@dinex.co.uk
Web site: www.dinex.dk

MULTIPART PSV
Pilling Lane, Chorley PR7 3EL.
Tel: 01257 225577.
Fax: 01257 225575.
E-mail: info@multipart.com
Web site: www.multipart.com

*PLAXTON
Plaxton Park, Cayton Low Road, Eastfield, Scarborough YO11 3BY
Tel: 01723 581500
Fax: 01723 5813238
E-mail: sales@plaxtonlimited.co.uk
Web site: www.plaxtonlimited.co.uk

*UNITEC
Parts Division, Denby Way, Hellaby, Rotherham S66 8HR
Tel: 01709 792000
Fax: 01709 792009
E-mail: parts@optare.com

Engineering

ARRIVA BUS AND COACH LTD
Lodge Garage, Whitehall Road West, Gomersal BD19 4BJ.
Tel: 01274 681144
Fax: 01274 651198
Web site: www.arriva.co.uk
E-mail: busandcoachsales@arriva.co.uk

*BRITISH BUS SALES
c/o Mike Nash, PO Box 534, Dorking RH5 5XB
Tel: 07836 656692
E-mail: nashionalbus1@btconnect.com
Web site: www.britishbussales.co.uk

BROXWOOD VEHICLE SPECIALISTS
Unit 2 Parkside Garage, Old Stafford Road, Wolverhampton WV10 7PH
Tel: 01902 798770
Fax: 01902 798564
E-mail: saks@broxwood.net
Web site: www.broxwood.net

BUSS BIZZ
Goughs Transport Depot, Morestead, Winchester SO21 1JD.
Tel: 01962 715555/66.
Fax: 01962 714868.

*CUMMINS UK
Rutherford Drive, Park Farm South, Wellingborough NN8 6AN
Tel: 01933 334200
Fax: 01933 334198
E-mail: cduksales@cummins.com
Web site: www.cummins-uk.com

*DIRECT PARTS LTD
Unit 1, Churnet Court, Churnetside Business Park, Harrison Way, Cheddleton ST13 7EF
Tel: 01538 361777
Fax: 01538 369100
E-mail: sales@direct-group.co.uk
Web site: www.direct-group.co.uk

*ERENTEK LTD
Malt Kiln Lane, Waddington, Lincoln LN5 9RT
Tel: 01522 720065
Fax: 01522 729155
E-mail: sale@erentek.co.uk
Web site: www.erentek.co.uk

FTA VEHICLE INSPECTION SERVICE
Hermes House, St John's Road, Tunbridge Wells TN4 9UZ.
Tel: 01892 526171
Fax: 01892 534989
E-mail: enquiries@fta.co.uk
Web site: www.fta.co.uk

THOMAS HARDIE – WIGAN
Lockett Road, Ashton-in-Makerfield, Wigan WN4 8DE.
Tel: 01942 505124.
Fax: 01942 505119.

*HART BROTHERS (ENGINEERING) LTD
Soho Works, Soho Street, Oldham OL4 2AD
Tel: 0161 737 6791

HILTECH DEVELOPMENTS LTD
22 Larbre Crescent, Whickham, Newcastle upon Tyne NE16 5YG.
Tel: 0191 488 6258.
Fax: 0191 488 9158.
E-mail: info@hiltechdevelopments.com
Web site: www.hiltechdevelopments.com

*IMEXPART LTD
Links 31, Willowbridge Way, Whitwood, Castleford WF10 5NP
Tel: 01977 553936
Fax: 01977 604684
E-mail: parts@imexpart.com
Web site: www.imexpart.com

*IMPERIAL ENGINEERING
Delamare Road, Cheshunt EN8 9UD
Tel: 01992 6342555
Fax: 01992 630506
E-mail: sales@imperialengineering.co.uk
Web site: www.imperialengineering.co.uk

JBF SERVICES LTD
Southedge Works, Hipperholme, Halifax HX3 8EF
Tel: 01422 202840
Fax: 01422 206070
E-mail: jbfservices@aol.com

MENTOR
Mentor Coach & Bus Ltd, Carlton House, Euroway Industrial Estate, Hellaby, Rotherham S66 8QL
Tel: 01709 700600
Fax: 01709 700007
E-mail: sales@mentorplc.com
Web site: www.mentorplc.com

MAJORLINE ENGINEERING LTD
Baybridge Industrial Units, Baybridge Lane, Owslebury, Winchester SO21 1JN.
Tel: 01962 777077.
Fax: 01962 777661, 777667
E-mail: majorline@compuserve.com

*MCE LTD
Firbank Way, Leighton Buzzard LU7 4YP
Tel: 01525 375301
Fax: 01525 850967
Web site: www.mce-ltd.com

MASS SPECIAL ENGINEERING LTD
Anston, Sheffield S25 4SD
Tel: 01909 550480.
Fax: 01909 550486.

*NEXT BUS LTD
Vincients Road, Bumpers Farm Industrial Estate, Chippenham SN14 6QA
Tel: 01249 462462
Fax: 01249 448844
E-mail: sales@next-bus.co.uk
Web site: www.next-bus.co.uk

*PLAXTON
Plaxton Park, Cayton Low Road, Eastfield, Scarborough YO11 3BY
Tel: 01723 581500
Fax: 01723 5813238
E-mail: sales@plaxtonlimited.co.uk
Web site: www.plaxtonlimited.co.uk

*PNEUMAX LTD
Unit 8, Venture Industrial Park, Fareham Road, Gosport PO13 0BA
Tel: 01329 823999
Fax: 01329 822345
E-mail: sales@pneumax.co.uk
Web site: www.pneumax.co.uk

QUEENSBRIDGE (PSV) LTD
Longlands Industrial Estate, Milner Way, Ossett WF5 9JE
Tel: 01924 281871
Fax: 01924 281807
E-mail: craig@queensbridgeltd.co.uk
Web site: www.queensbridgeltd.co.uk

Trade Directory

Mercedes engines

Highest quality, Lowest price.
Direct from the Uk's No.1 for 25 years.

also..   IVECO VOLVO DAF

Join the UK's major bus & coach groups and choose Crewe Engines for Mercedes-Benz engines. From fast delivery of an exchange engine to collection of your vehicle and fitting of the engine, we have the expertise and resources to provide great service at very competitive prices.

ENGINES
- UK's No.1 for remanufactured Mercedes engines
- Also MAN, Cummins, Iveco, Volvo, DAF, etc
- Petrol & diesel, 1950's to present day, 4 cyl to V12
- Fast, friendly & efficient - excellent reputation

ENGINE PARTS
- Full range of highest quality original equipment parts
- Pistons, crankshaft bearings, gasket sets, etc
- Cylinder heads, camshafts, crankshafts, etc

Call now for a quote or free info-pack
☎ **01270 526333**

www.creweengines.co.uk
e-mail: sales@creweengines.co.uk

Crewe Engines Ltd

TRANSPORT DESIGN INTERNATIONAL
12 Waterloo Road Estate, Bidford on Avon
B50 4JH
Tel: 01789 490370
Fax: 01789 490592
E-mail:enquiries@tdi.uk.com
Web site: www.tdi.uk.com

*UNITEC
Parts Division, Denby Way, Hellaby,
Rotherham S66 8HR
Tel: 01709 792000
Fax: 01709 792009
E-mail: parts@optare.com

*UNITEC LONDON
Unit 5, Gateway 25, Weston Avenue,
West Thurrock RM20 3ZD
Tel: 01708 892440
Fax: 01708 862125
E-mail: london.service@optare.com

*UNITEC ROTHERHAM
Denby Way, Hellaby, Rotherham
S66 8HR
Tel: 01709 535101
Fax: 01709 535103
E-mail: rotherham.service@optare.com

*UNITEC SCOTLAND
Unit 7, Cumbernauld Business Park,
Ward Park Road, Cumbernauld G67 3JZ
Tel: 01236 726738
Fax: 01236 795651
E-mail: scotland.service@optare.com

Engines

BUSS BIZZ
Goughs Transport Depot, Morestead,
Winchester SO21 1JD.
Tel: 01962 715555/66.
Fax: 01962 714868.

*CRAIG TILSEY & SON LTD
Unit 7, Moorfield Industrial Estate, Cotes
Heath, Stoke-on-Trent ST21 6QY
Tel: 01782 791524
Fax: 01782 791316
E-mail:
maureen@eyremaureen.wanadoo.co.uk

*CREWE ENGINES
Warmingham Road, Crewe CW1 4PQ
Tel: 01270 526333
Fax: 01270 526433
E-mail: sales@creweengines.co.uk
Web site: www.creweengines.co.uk

*CUMMINS UK
Rutherford Drive, Park Farm South,
Wellingborough NN8 6AN
Tel: 01933 334200
Fax: 01933 334198
E-mail: cduksales@cummins.com
Web site: www.cummins-uk.com

DAF COMPONENTS LTD
Eastern Bypass, Thame OX9 3FB
Tel: 01844 261111
Fax: 01844 217111
Web site: www.daftrucks.com.

DAYCO – TRANSPORT & TRADE DISTRIBUTION LTD
Davis House, Lodge Causeway Trading
Estate, Fishponds, Bristol BS16 3JB.
Tel: 0117 965 9999.
Fax: 0117 965 4724.

DIESEL POWER ENGINEERING
Goughs Transport Depot, Morestead,
Winchester SO21 1JD.
Tel/Fax: 01962 711314

IVECO
Iveco Ford Truck Ltd, Iveco Ford House,
Station Road, Watford WD1 1SR.
Tel: 01923 246400.
Fax: 01923 240574.

LH GROUP (SERVICES) LTD
Graycar Business Park, Barton Turns,
Barton Under Needwood DE13 8EN.
Tel: 01283 713615.
Fax: 01283 713551.
E-mail: l/h/llords@classic.msn.com

MAJORLINE ENGINEERING LTD
Baybridge Industrial Units, Baybridge Lane,
Owslebury, Winchester SO21 1JN.
Tel: 01962 777077.
Fax: 01962 777661, 777667
E-mail: majorline@compuserve.com

MAN TRUCK & BUS UK LTD
Frankland Road, Blagrove, Swindon
SN5 8YU.
Tel: 01793 448000.
Fax: 01793 448262.

Trade Directory

MULTIPART PSV
Pilling Lane, Chorley PR7 3EL.
Tel: 01257 225577.
Fax: 01257 225575.
E-mail: info@multipart.com
Web site: www.multipart.com

*NEXT BUS LTD
Vincients Road, Bumpers Farm Industrial Estate, Chippenham SN14 6QA
Tel: 01249 462462
Fax: 01249 448844
E-mail: sales@next-bus.co.uk
Web site: www.next-bus.co.uk

PERKINS GROUP LTD
Peterborough PE1 5NA.
Tel: 01733 567474.
Fax: 01733 582240.
Web site: www.perkins.com

QUEENSBRIDGE (PSV) LTD
Longlands Industrial Estate, Milner Way, Ossett WF5 9JE
Tel: 01924 281871
Fax: 01924 281807
E-mail: craig@queensbridgeltd.co.uk
Web site: www.queensbridgeltd.co.uk

*SHAWSON SUPPLY LTD
12 Station Road, Saintfield BT24 7DU
Tel: 028 9751 0994
Fax: 028 9751 0816
E-mail: shawsondiesel@btopenworld.com
Web site: www.shawsonsupply.com

*UNITEC
Parts Division, Denby Way, Hellaby, Rotherham S66 8HR
Tel: 01709 792000
Fax: 01709 792009
E-mail: parts@optare.com

*UNITEC LONDON
Unit 5, Gateway 25, Weston Avenue, West Thurrock RM20 3ZD
Tel: 01708 892440
Fax: 01708 862125
E-mail: london.service@optare.com

*UNITEC ROTHERHAM
Denby Way, Hellaby, Rotherham S66 8HR
Tel: 01709 535101
Fax: 01709 535103
E-mail: rotherham.service@optare.com

*UNITEC SCOTLAND
Unit 7, Cumbernauld Business Park, Ward Park Road, Cumbernauld G67 3JZ
Tel: 01236 726738
Fax: 01236 795651
E-mail: scotland.service@optare.com

*WALSH'S ENGINEERING
Barton Moss Road, Eccles, Manchester M30 7RL
Tel: 0161 787 7017
Fax: 0161 787 7038
E-mail: walshs@gardnerdiesel.co.uk
Website: www.gardnerdiesel.co.uk

WEALDSTONE ENGINEERING
Sanders Lodge Industrial Estate, Rushden NN10 6AZ.
Tel: 01933 316622.
Fax: 01933 358742.
Web site: www.wealdstone.co.uk

Engine Oil Drain Valves

*FUMOTO ENGINEERING OF EUROPE
Normandy House, 35 Glategny Esplanade, St Peter Port, Guernsey GY1 2BP
Tel: 01481 716987
Fax: 01481 700374
E-mail: info@fumoto-valve.com

MARTYN INDUSTRIALS LTD
5 Brunel Way, Durranhill Industrial Esate, Carlisle CA1 3NQ
Tel: 01228 544000
Fax: 01228 544001
E-mail: enquiries@martyn-industrials.co.uk
Web site: www.martyn-industrials.com

MULTIPART PSV
Pilling Lane, Chorley PR7 3EL.
Tel: 01257 225577.
Fax: 01257 225575.
E-mail: info@multipart.com
Web site: www.multipart.com

*PARTLINE LTD
Dockfield Road, Shipley BD17 7AZ
Tel: 01274 531531
Fax: 01274 531088
E-mail: sales@partline.co.uk
Web site: www.partline.co.uk

WALSH'S ENGINEERING LTD

COMMERCIAL DIESEL ENGINE SPECIALISTS
Barton Moss Road. Eccles. Manchester. M30 7RL

SUPPLIERS OF ALL TYPES OF RECONDITIONED ENGINE UNITS, PARTS AND SERVICE TO THE TRANSPORT INDUSTRY

FOR DETAILS CONTACT

CHARLIE HUGHES
OR
STEVE BRADLEY

TEL:- 0161 787 7017 FAX:- 0161 787 7038
E-MAIL:-walshs@gardnerdiesel.co.uk

Trade Directory

WALLMINSTER LTD
Unit 22, Chelsea Wharf, 15 Lots Road, London SW10 0QJ
Tel: 020 7352 2727
Fax: 020 7352 3990
E-mail: info@tankcontainers.co.uk

Exhaust Systems

ARVIN MERITOR
Unit 21, Suttons Park Avenue, Reading RG6 1LA.
Tel: 0118 935 9126
Fax: 0118 935 9138
E-mail: james.randall@arvinmeritor.com
Web site: www.arvinmeritor.com

*ASHLEY BANKS LTD
5 King Street Estate, Langtoft, Peterborough PE6 9NF
Tel: 01778 560651
Fax: 01778 560721
E-mail: user@ashleybanks.fsnet.co.uk

BROXWOOD VEHICLE SPECIALISTS
Unit 2 Parkside Garage, Old Stafford Road, Wolverhampton WV10 7PH
Tel: 01902 798770
Fax: 01902 798564
E-mail: saks@broxwood.net
Web site: www.broxwood.net

BUSS BIZZ
Goughs Transport Depot, Morestead, Winchester SO21 1JD.
Tel: 01962 715555/66.
Fax: 01962 714868.

CARLYLE BUS & COACH LTD
Great Bridge Street, Swan Village, West Bromwich B70 0X4
Tel: 0121 524 1200
Fax: 0121 524 1201
E-mail: admin@carlyleplc.co.uk

*CRESCENT FACILITIES LTD
72 Willow Crescent, Chapeltown, Sheffield S35 1QS
Tel/fax: 0114 2451050
E-mail: cfl.chris@btinternet.com
Web site: www.cflparts.com

*EMINOX LTD
North Warren Road, Gainsborough DN21 2TU
Tel: 01427 810088
Fax: 01427 810061
E-mail: marketing@eminox.com
Web site: www.eminox.com

*IMEXPART LTD
Links 31, Willowbridge Way, Whitwood, Castleford WF10 5NP
Tel: 01977 553936
Fax: 01977 604684
E-mail: parts@imexpart.com
Web site: www.imexpart.com

MAJORLINE ENGINEERING LTD
Baybridge Industrial Units, Baybridge Lane, Owslebury, Winchester SO21 1JN.
Tel: 01962 777077.
Fax: 01962 777661, 777667
E-mail: majorline@compuserve.com

*PARTLINE LTD
Dockfield Road, Shipley BD17 7AZ
Tel: 01274 531531
Fax: 01274 531088
E-mail: sales@partline.co.uk
Web site: www.partline.co.uk

*UNITEC
Parts Division, Denby Way, Hellaby, Rotherham S66 8HR
Tel: 01709 792000
Fax: 01709 792009
E-mail: parts@optare.com

*UNITEC LONDON
Unit 5, Gateway 25, Weston Avenue, West Thurrock RM20 3ZD
Tel: 01708 892440
Fax: 01708 862125
E-mail: london.service@optare.com

*UNITEC ROTHERHAM
Denby Way, Hellaby, Rotherham S66 8HR
Tel: 01709 535101
Fax: 01709 535103
E-mail: rotherham.service@optare.com

*UNITEC SCOTLAND
Unit 7, Cumbernauld Business Park, Ward Park Road, Cumbernauld G67 3JZ
Tel: 01236 726738
Fax: 01236 795651
E-mail: scotland.service@optare.com

Fans & Drive Belts

BROXWOOD VEHICLE SPECIALISTS
Unit 2 Parkside Garage, Old Stafford Road, Wolverhampton WV10 7PH
Tel: 01902 798770
Fax: 01902 798564
E-mail: saks@broxwood.net
Web site: www.broxwood.net

CARLYLE BUS & COACH LTD
Great Bridge Street, Swan Village, West Bromwich B70 0X4
Tel: 0121 524 1200
Fax: 0121 524 1201
E-mail: admin@carlyleplc.co.uk

*CRESCENT FACILITIES LTD
72 Willow Crescent, Chapeltown, Sheffield S35 1QS
Tel/fax: 0114 2451050
E-mail: cfl.chris@btinternet.com
Web site: www.cflparts.com

*CUMMINS UK
Rutherford Drive, Park Farm South, Wellingborough NN8 6AN
Tel: 01933 334200
Fax: 01933 334198
E-mail: cduksales@cummins.com
Web site: www.cummins-uk.com

*DIRECT PARTS LTD
Unit 1, Churnet Court, Churnetside Business Park, Harrison Way, Cheddleton ST13 7EF
Tel: 01538 361777
Fax: 01538 369100
E-mail: sales@direct-group.co.uk
Web site: www.direct-group.co.uk

*IMEXPART LTD
Links 31, Willowbridge Way, Whitwood, Castleford WF10 5NP
Tel: 01977 553936
Fax: 01977 604684
E-mail: parts@imexpart.com
Web site: www.imexpart.com

MAJORLINE ENGINEERING LTD
Baybridge Industrial Units, Baybridge Lane, Owslebury, Winchester SO21 1JN.
Tel: 01962 777077.
Fax: 01962 777661, 777667
E-mail: majorline@compuserve.com

MULTIPART PSV
Pilling Lane, Chorley PR7 3EL.
Tel: 01257 225577.
Fax: 01257 225575.
E-mail: info@multipart.com
Web site: www.multipart.com

*PARTLINE LTD
Dockfield Road, Shipley BD17 7AZ
Tel: 01274 531531
Fax: 01274 531088
E-mail: sales@partline.co.uk
Web site: www.partline.co.uk

PIONEER WESTON
Smithfold Lane, Worsley, Manchester M28 0GP.
Tel: 0161 703 2000
Fax: 0161 703 2025
E-mail: pioneer.weston@wyko.co.uk

QUEENSBRIDGE (PSV) LTD
Longlands Industrial Estate, Milner Way, Ossett WF5 9JE
Tel: 01924 281871
Fax: 01924 281807
E-mail: craig@queensbridgeltd.co.uk
Web site: www.queensbridgeltd.co.uk

*UNITEC
Parts Division, Denby Way, Hellaby, Rotherham S66 8HR
Tel: 01709 792000
Fax: 01709 792009
E-mail: parts@optare.com

Fare Boxes

CUBIC TRANSPORTATION SYSTEMS LTD
AFC House, Honeycrock Lane, Salfords RH1 5LA
Tel: 01737 782200
Fax: 01737 789759
Web site: www.cubic.com

*ETM SOFTWARE SERVICES
9 Dorset Avenue, Ferndown BH22 8HJ
Tel: 01202 246710
E-mail: info@etmss.com
Web site: www.etmss.com

JOHN GROVES TICKET SYSTEMS
Unit 5, Rennie Business Units, Factory Place, Saltcoats KA21 5LZ
Tel: 01294 471133
Fax: 01294 471166
Web site: www.cambist.se

*MARK TERRILL TICKET MACHINERY
5 De Grey Close, Lewes BN7 2JR.
Tel: 01273 474816
Fax: 01273 474816
E-mail: mark.terrill@ukonline.co.uk

Fire Extinguishers

*ASHLEY BANKS LTD
5 King Street Estate, Langtoft, Peterborough PE6 9NF
Tel: 01778 560651
Fax: 01778 560721
E-mail: user@ashleybanks.fsnet.co.uk

BROXWOOD VEHICLE SPECIALISTS
Unit 2 Parkside Garage, Old Stafford Road, Wolverhampton WV10 7PH
Tel: 01902 798770
Fax: 01902 798564
E-mail: saks@broxwood.net
Web site: www.broxwood.net

CARLYLE BUS & COACH LTD
Great Bridge Street, Swan Village, West Bromwich B70 0X4
Tel: 0121 524 1200
Fax: 0121 524 1201
E-mail: admin@carlyleplc.co.uk

FIREMASTER EXTINGUISHER LTD
Firex House, 174-176 Hither Green Lane, London SE13 6QB
Tel: 020 8852 8585
Fax: 020 8297 8020
E-mail: info@firemaster.co.uk
Web site: www.firemaster.co.uk

HAPPICH V & I COMPONENTS LTD
Unit 30/31, Fort Industrial Park, Fort Parkway, Castle Bromwich B35 7AR.
Tel: 0121 747 4400
Fax: 0121 747 4977
E-mail: sales@happich.co.uk
Web site: www.happich.co.uk

KELLETT (UK) LTD
8 Stevenson Way, Sheffield S9 3WZ.
Tel: 0114 261 1122.
Fax: 0114 261 1199.
E-mail: sales@kellett.co.uk

*THE LAWTON MOTOR BODY BUILDING CO LTD
Knutsford Road, Church Lawton, Stoke-on-Trent ST7 3DN
Tel: 01270 882056
Fax: 01270 883014
E-mail: info@lawtonmotorbody.co.uk
Web site: www.lawtonmotorbody.co.uk

MENTOR
Mentor Coach & Bus Ltd, Carlton House, Euroway Industrial Estate, Hellaby, Rotherham S66 8QL
Tel: 01709 700600
Fax: 01709 700007
E-mail: sales@mentorplc.com
Web site: www.mentorplc.com

MULTIPART PSV
Pilling Lane, Chorley PR7 3EL.
Tel: 01257 225577.
Fax: 01257 225575.
E-mail: info@multipart.com
Web site: www.multipart.com

*PARTLINE LTD
Dockfield Road, Shipley BD17 7AZ
Tel: 01274 531531
Fax: 01274 531088
E-mail: sales@partline.co.uk
Web site: www.partline.co.uk

PLAXTON
Plaxton Park, Cayton Low Road, Eastfield, Scarborough YO11 3BY
Tel: 01723 581500
Fax: 01723 5813238
E-mail: sales@plaxtonlimited.co.uk
Web site: www.plaxtonlimited.co.uk

*PLAXTON COACH SALES CENTRE
Ryton Road, Anston, Sheffield S25 4DL
Tel: 01909 551155
Fax: 01909 567994
E-mail: coaches@plaxtonlimited.co.uk
Web site: www.plaxtonlimited.co.uk

*PSV PRODUCTS
PO Box 166, Warrington WA4 5FG
Tel: 0870 062 4488
Fax: 0870 062 4499
E-mail: mike@psvproducts.com
Web site: www.psvproducts.com

SAFEGUARD
Kiln Lane, Swindon SN2 2NP
Tel: 01793 512999
Fax: 01793 511345

First Aid Equipment

*ASHLEY BANKS LTD
5 King Street Estate, Langtoft, Peterborough PE6 9NF
Tel: 01778 560651
Fax: 01778 560721
E-mail: user@ashleybanks.fsnet.co.uk

BROXWOOD VEHICLE SPECIALISTS
Unit 2 Parkside Garage, Old Stafford Road, Wolverhampton WV10 7PH
Tel: 01902 798770
Fax: 01902 798564
E-mail: saks@broxwood.net
Web site: www.broxwood.net

CARLYLE BUS & COACH LTD
Great Bridge Street, Swan Village, West Bromwich B70 0X4
Tel: 0121 524 1200
Fax: 0121 524 1201
E-mail: admin@carlyleplc.co.uk

FIREMASTER EXTINGUISHER LTD
Firex House, 174-176 Hither Green Lane, London SE13 6QB
Tel: 020 8852 8585
Fax: 020 8297 8020
E-mail: info@firemaster.co.uk
Web site: www.firemaster.co.uk

HAPPICH V & I COMPONENTS LTD
Unit 30/31, Fort Industrial Park, Fort Parkway, Castle Bromwich B35 7AR
Tel: 0121 747 4400
Fax: 0121 747 4977
E-mail: sales@happich.co.uk
Web site: www.happich.co.uk

*THE LAWTON MOTOR BODY BUILDING CO LTD
Knutsford Road, Church Lawton, Stoke-on-Trent ST7 3DN
Tel: 01270 882056
Fax: 01270 883014
E-mail: info@lawtonmotorbody.co.uk
Web site: www.lawtonmotorbody.co.uk

MULTIPART PSV
Pilling Lane, Chorley PR7 3EL.
Tel: 01257 225577.
Fax: 01257 225575.
E-mail: info@multipart.com
Web site: www.multipart.com

*PARTLINE LTD
Dockfield Road, Shipley BD17 7AZ
Tel: 01274 531531
Fax: 01274 531088
E-mail: sales@partline.co.uk
Web site: www.partline.co.uk

*PLAXTON
Plaxton Park, Cayton Low Road, Eastfield, Scarborough YO11 3BY
Tel: 01723 581500
Fax: 01723 5813238
E-mail: sales@plaxtonlimited.co.uk
Web site: www.plaxtonlimited.co.uk

*PLAXTON COACH SALES CENTRE
Ryton Road, Anston, Sheffield S25 4DL
Tel: 01909 551155
Fax: 01909 567994
E-mail: coaches@plaxtonlimited.co.uk
Web site: www.plaxtonlimited.co.uk

*PSV PRODUCTS
PO Box 166, Warrington WA4 5FG
Tel: 0870 062 4488
Fax: 0870 062 4499
E-mail: mike@psvproducts.com
Web site: www.psvproducts.com

SAFEGUARD
Kiln Lane, Swindon SN2 2NP
Tel: 01793 512999
Fax: 01793 511345

*TRAMONTANA
Chapelknowe Road, Carfin, Motherwell ML1 5LE
Tel: 01698 861790
Fax: 01698 860778
E-mail: wdt90@tiscali.co.uk
Web site: tramontanacoach.co.uk

Floor Coverings

*ALTRO
Works Road, Letchworth SG6 1NW
Tel: 01462 480480
Fax: 01462 480010
E-mail: lkni@altro.co.uk
Web site: www.altrotransfloor.com

AUTOMATE WHEEL COVERS LTD
California Mills, Oxford Road, Gomersal, Cleckheaton BD19 4HQ
Tel: 01274 862700
Fax: 01274 851989
E-mail: sales@wheelcovers.co.uk
Web site: www.euroliners.com

*AUTOMOTIVE TEXTILE INDUSTRIES
Unit 15 & 16, Priest Court, Springfield Business Park, Grantham NG31 7BG
Tel: 01476 593050
Fax: 01476 593607
E-mail: sales@autotex.com
Web site: www.autotex.com

BROXWOOD VEHICLE SPECIALISTS
Unit 2 Parkside Garage, Old Stafford Road, Wolverhampton WV10 7PH
Tel: 01902 798770
Fax: 01902 798564
E-mail: saks@broxwood.net
Web site: www.broxwood.net

Trade Directory

CARLYLE BUS & COACH LTD
Great Bridge Street, Swan Village, West Bromwich B70 0X4
Tel: 0121 524 1200
Fax: 0121 524 1201
E-mail: admin@carlyleplc.co.uk

COACH CARPETS
Unit 12, Hamilton Street, Blackburn BB2 4AJ.
Tel: 01254 53549.
Fax: 01254 261873.

FIRTH FURNISHINGS LTD
PO Box 22, Flush Mills, Heckmondwike WF16 0EP.
Tel: 01924 406141.
Fax: 01924 401128.

*THE LAWTON MOTOR BODY BUILDING CO LTD
Knutsford Road, Church Lawton, Stoke-on-Trent ST7 3DN
Tel: 01270 882056
Fax: 01270 883014
E-mail: info@lawtonmotorbody.co.uk
Web site: www.lawtonmotorbody.co.uk

MARTYN INDUSTRIALS LTD
5 Brunel Way, Durranhill Industrial Esate, Carlisle CA1 3NQ
Tel: 01228 544000
Fax: 01228 544001
E-mail: enquiries@martyn-industrials.co.uk
Web site: www.martyn-industrials.com

MULTIPART PSV
Pilling Lane, Chorley PR7 3EL.
Tel: 01257 225577.
Fax: 01257 225575.
E-mail: info@multipart.com
Web site: www.multipart.com

*TIFLEX LTD
Tiflex House, Liskeard PL14 4NB
Tel: 01579 320808
Fax: 01579 320802
E-mail: marketing@tiflex.co.uk
Web site: www.tiflex.co.uk

*TRIMPLEX SAFETY TREAD LTD
Trident Works, Mulberry Way, Belvedere DA17 6AN
Tel: 020 8311 2101
Fax: 020 8312 1400
E-mail: ead@btconnect.com
Web site: www.safetytread.co.uk

Fuel, Fuel Management & Lubricants

CENTAUR FUEL MANAGEMENT LTD
Clifton Technology Park, Wynne Avenue, Clifton M27 8FF
Tel: 0161 793 6323
Fax: 0161 794 8031

*CUMMINS UK
Rutherford Drive, Park Farm South, Wellingborough NN8 6AN
Tel: 01933 334200
Fax: 01933 334198
E-mail: cduksales@cummins.com
Web site: www.cummins-uk.com

INTERLUBE SYSTEMS LTD
St Modwen Road, Plymouth PL6 8LH
Tel: 01752 676000
Fax: 01752 676001
E-mail: info@interlubesystems.com
Web site: www.interlubesystems.com

JMW
Systems House, Pentland Industrial Estate, Loanhead EH20 9QH
Tel: 0131 440 3633
Fax: 0131 440 3637
E-mail: enquiries@jmw-group.co.uk
Web site: www.jmw-group.co.uk

MULTIPART PSV
Pilling Lane, Chorley PR7 3EL.
Tel: 01257 225577.
Fax: 01257 225575.
E-mail: info@multipart.com
Web site: www.multipart.com

VBI TRISCAN
Harwood Street, Blackburn BB1 3BD
Tel: 0870 445 2952
Fax: 01254 680 381
E-mail: info@vbilimited.com
Web site: www.vbilimited.com

Garage Equipment

*BUTTS OF BAWTRY GARAGE EQUIPMENT
Station Yard, Station Road, Bawtry, Doncaster DN10 6QD
Tel: 01302 710868
Fax: 01302 719481
E-mail: info@jhmbuttco.com
Web site www.jhmbuttco.com

TERENCE BARKER TANKS
Tel: 01376 330661
E-mail: terencebarkertanks.co.uk
Web site: www.terencebarkertanks.co.uk

*DIRECT PARTS LTD
Unit 1, Churnet Court, Churnetside Business Park, Harrison Way, Cheddleton ST13 7EF
Tel: 01538 361777
Fax: 01538 369100
E-mail: sales@direct-group.co.uk
Web site: www.direct-group.co.uk

GEMCO EQUUIPMENT LTD
153-156 Bridge Street, Northampton NN1 1QG
Tel: 01604 828600
Fax: 01604 633159
E-mail: sales@gemco.co.uk
Web site: www.gemco.co.uk

*MAJORLIFT HYDRAULIC EQUIPMENT LTD
Arnold's Field Industrial Estate, Wickwar, Wotton-under-Edge GL12 8JD
Tel: 01454 299299
Fax: 01454294003
Web site: www.majorlift.com
E-mail: info@majorlift.com

*SOMERS TOTALKARE LTD
15 Forge Trading Estate, Mucklow Hill, Halesowen B62 8TR
Tel: 0121 585 2700
Fax: 0121 585 2725
E-mail: sales@somerstotalkare.co.uk
Web site: www.somerstotalkare.co.uk

STERTIL UK LTD
Unit A, Brackmills Business Park, Caswell Road, Northampton NN4 7PW
Tel: 01604 677384
Fax: 01604 765181
E-mail: info@stertil.com
Web site: www.stertil.com

PHIL STOCKFORD GARAGE EQUIPMENT
7 Badger Way, North Cheshire Trading Estate, Prenton CH43 3HQ
Tel: 0151 609 1007
Fax: 0151 609 1008

VARLEY & GULLIVER LTD
Alfred Street, Sparkbrook, Birmingham B12 8JR.
Tel: 0121 773 2441.
Fax: 0121 766 6875.

V L TEST SYSTEMS LTD
3-4 Middle Slade, Buckingham Industrial Park, Buckingham MK18 1WA
Tel: 01280 822488
Fax: 01280 822489
E-mail: sales@vltestuk.com
Web site: www.vltest.com

Gearboxes

ALLISON TRANSMISSION
Allison House, 36 Duncan Close, Moulton Park, Northampton NN3 6WL

DAVID BROWN VEHICLE TRANSMISSIONS LTD
Park Gear Works, Lockwood, Huddersfield HD4 5DD.
Tel: 01484 422180
Fax: 01484 435292

BUSS BIZZ
Goughs Transport Depot, Morestead, Winchester SO21 1JD.
Tel: 01962 715555/66.
Fax: 01962 714868.

EATON LTD
Truck Components Marketing, PO Box 11, Worsley Road North, Worsley M28 5GJ
Tel: 01204 797219.
Fax: 01204 797204.

GARDNER PARTS LTD
Barton Hall, Hardy Street, Eccles M30 7WA.
Tel: 0161 278 9200
Fax: 0161 787 7549.

*HART BROTHERS (ENGINEERING) LTD
Soho Works, Soho Street, Oldham OL4 2AD
Tel: 0161 737 6791

*HL SMITH TRANSMISSIONS LTD
Enterprise Business Park, Cross Road, Albrighton, Wolverhampton WV7 3BJ
Tel: 01902 373011
Fax: 01902 373608

LH GROUP (SERVICES) LTD
Graycar Business Park, Barton Turns, Barton Under Needwood DE13 8EN.
Tel: 01283 713615.
Fax: 01283 713551.
E-mail: l/h/llords@classic.msn.com

MAJORLINE ENGINEERING LTD
Baybridge Industrial Units, Baybridge Lane, Owslebury, Winchester SO21 1JN.
Tel: 01962 777077
Fax: 01962 777661, 777667
E-mail: majorline@compuserve.com

MULTIPART PSV
Pilling Lane, Chorley PR7 3EL.
Tel: 01257 225577.
Fax: 01257 225575.
E-mail: info@multipart.com
Web site: www.multipart.com

*NEXT BUS LTD
Vincients Road, Bumpers Farm Industrial Estate, Chippenham SN14 6QA
Tel: 01249 462462
Fax: 01249 448844
E-mail: sales@next-bus.co.uk
Web site: www.next-bus.co.uk

QUEENSBRIDGE (PSV) LTD
Longlands Industrial Estate, Milner Way, Ossett WF5 9JE
Tel: 01924 281871
Fax: 01924 281807
E-mail: craig@queensbrigeltd.co.uk
Web site: www.queensbrigeltd.co.uk

*SHAWSON SUPPLY LTD
12 Station Road, Saintfield BT24 7DU
Tel: 028 9751 0994
Fax: 028 9751 0816
E-mail: shawsondiesel@btopenworld.com
Web site: www.shawsonsupply.com

*UNITEC
Parts Division, Denby Way, Hellaby, Rotherham S66 8HR
Tel: 01709 792000
Fax: 01709 792009
E-mail: parts@optare.com

*UNITEC LONDON
Unit 5, Gateway 25, Weston Avenue, West Thurrock RM20 3ZD
Tel: 01708 892440
Fax: 01708 862125
E-mail: london.service@optare.com

*UNITEC ROTHERHAM
Denby Way, Hellaby, Rotherham S66 8HR
Tel: 01709 535101
Fax: 01709 535103
E-mail: rotherham.service@optare.com

*UNITEC SCOTLAND
Unit 7, Cumbernauld Business Park, Ward Park Road, Cumbernauld G67 3JZ
Tel: 01236 726738
Fax: 01236 795651
E-mail: scotland.service@optare.com

VOITH TURBO LTD
Regent House, Rump Lane, Hayes UB3 3BP
Tel: 020 8561 2131
Fax: 020 8569 1726
E-mail: turbo.uk@voith.com
Web site: www.voith.com

*VOR TRANSMISSIONS LTD
Little London House, St Anne's Road, Willenhall WV13 1DT
Tel: 0800 018 4141
Fax: 01902 603868
E-mail: vor@globalnet.co.uk
Web site: www.vor.co.uk

TREVOR WIGLEY & SONS BUS LTD
Baulder Bridge Road, Carlton, Barnsley S71 3HJ
Tel: 01226 713636/716479
E-mail: wigleys@btconnect.com
Web site: www.twigley.com

*ZF POWERTRAIN
Stringes Close, Willenhall WV13 1LE
Tel: 01902 366000
Fax: 01902 366504
E-mail: sales@powertrain.org.uk
Web site: www.powertrain.org.uk

Hand Driers (in coaches)

BRADTECH LTD
Unit 3, Ladford Covert, Seighford, Stafford ST18 9QD
Tel: 01785 282800
Fax: 01785 282558
E-mail: sales@bradtech.ltd.uk

SHADES TECHNICS
Marshgate Drive, Hertford SG13 7AJ
Tel: 01992 501683
Fax: 01992 501669
E-mail: sales@shades-technics.com
Web site: www.shades-technics.com

Handrails

*ABACUS TUBULAR PRODUCTS LTD
Abacus House, Highlode Industrial Estate, Ramsey PE26 2RB
Tel: 01487 710700
Fax: 01487 710626
E-mail: info@abacus-tp.com
Web site: www.abacus-tp.com

CARLYLE BUS & COACH LTD
Great Bridge Street, Swan Village, West Bromwich B70 0X4
Tel: 0121 524 1200
Fax: 0121 524 1201
E-mail: admin@carlyleplc.co.uk

CROWN COACHBUILDERS LTD
32 Flemington Industrial Park, Flemington, Motherwell ML1 1SN.
Tel: 01698 276087.
Fax: 01698 276144.
E-mail: davidgreer@hotmail.com
Web site: www.crowncoachbuilders.co.uk

DEANS POWERED DOORS
PO Box 8, Borwick Drive, Grovehill, Beverley HU17 0HQ
Tel: 01482 868111
Fax: 01482 881890
E-mail: info@deans-doors.com

*GABRIEL & CO LTD
Abro Works, 10 Hay Hall Road, Tyseley, Birmingham B11 2AU
Tel: 0121 248 3333
Fax: 0121 248 3330
E-mail: contact@gabrielco.com
Web site: www.gabrielco.com

HAPPICH V & I COMPONENTS LTD
Unit 30/31, Fort Industrial Park, Fort Parkway, Castle Bromwich B35 7AR.
Tel: 0121 747 4400
Fax: 0121 747 4977
E-mail: sales@happich.co.uk
Web site: www.happich.co.uk

JBF SERVICES LTD
Southedge Works, Hipperholme, Halifax HX3 8EF
Tel: 01422 202840
Fax: 01422 206070
E-mail: jbfservices@aol.com

*THE LAWTON MOTOR BODY BUILDING CO LTD
Knutsford Road, Church Lawton, Stoke-on-Trent ST7 3DN
Tel: 01270 882056
Fax: 01270 883014
E-mail: info@lawtonmotorbody.co.uk
Web site: www.lawtonmotorbody.co.uk

*PLAXTON
Plaxton Park, Cayton Low Road, Eastfield, Scarborough YO11 3BY
Tel: 01723 581500
Fax: 01723 5813238
E-mail: sales@plaxtonlimited.co.uk
Web site: www.plaxtonlimited.co.uk

*PLAXTON COACH SALES CENTRE
Ryton Road, Anston, Sheffield S25 4DL
Tel: 01909 551155
Fax: 01909 567994
E-mail: coaches@plaxtonlimited.co.uk
Web site: www.plaxtonlimited.co.uk

Headrest Covers & Curtains

DUOFLEX LTD
Trimmingham House, 2 Shires Road, Buckingham Road Industrial Estate, Brackley NN13 7EZ
Tel: 01280 701366
Fax: 01280 704799
E-mail: sales@duoflex.co.uk
Web site: www.duoflex.co.uk

*THE LAWTON MOTOR BODY BUILDING CO LTD
Knutsford Road, Church Lawton, Stoke-on-Trent ST7 3DN
Tel: 01270 882056
Fax: 01270 883014
E-mail: info@lawtonmotorbody.co.uk
Web site: www.lawtonmotorbody.co.uk

ORVEC INTERNATIONAL LTD
Malmo Road, Hull HU7 0YF.
Tel: 01482 879146
Fax: 01482 878989.
E-mail: service@orvec.co.uk
Web site: www.orvec.co.uk

Heating & Systems

AMA LTD
Unit 17, Springmill Industrial Estate, Avening Road, Nailsworth GL6 0BH.
Tel: 01453 832884.
Fax: 01453 832040.
E-mail: ama@ftech.co.uk

CARLYLE BUS & COACH LTD
Great Bridge Street, Swan Village, West Bromwich B70 0X4
Tel: 0121 524 1200
Fax: 0121 524 1201
E-mail: admin@carlyleplc.co.uk

CARRIER SUTRAK
Unit 6, I O Centre, Barn Way, Lodge Farm Industrial Estate, Northampton NN5 7UW
Tel: 01604 581468
Fax: 01604 758132
E-mail: kim.neale@carrier.utc.com

*CLAYTON HEATERS LTD
Hunter Terrace, Fletchworth Gate, Burnsall Road, Coventry CV5 6SP
Tel: 02476 691916
Fax: 02476 691969
E-mail: admin@claytoncc.co.uk
Web site: www.claytoncc.co.uk

CONSERVE (UK) LTD
Suite 7, Logistics House, Kingsthorpe Road, Northampton NN2 6LJ
Tel: 01604 710055
Fax: 01604 710065
E-mail: information@conserveuk.co.uk
Web site: www.conserveuk.co.uk

*EBERSPACHER (UK) LTD
Headlands Business Park, Salisbury Road, Ringwood BH24 3PB
Tel: 01425 480151
Fax: 01425 480152
E-mail: enquiries@eberspacher.com
Web site: www.eberspacher.com

HAPPICH V & I COMPONENTS LTD
Unit 30/31, Fort Industrial Park, Fort Parkway, Castle Bromwich B35 7AR.
Tel: 0121 747 4400
Fax: 0121 747 4977
E-mail: sales@happich.co.uk
Web site: www.happich.co.uk

*KARIVE LIMITED
PO Box 205, Southam CV47 0ZL
Tel: 01926 813938
Fax: 01926 814898
E-mail: karive.ltd@btinternet.com
Web site: www.karive.co.uk

*THE LAWTON MOTOR BODY BUILDING CO LTD
Knutsford Road, Church Lawton, Stoke-on-Trent ST7 3DN
Tel: 01270 882056
Fax: 01270 883014
E-mail: info@lawtonmotorbody.co.uk
Web site: www.lawtonmotorbody.co.uk

*NEALINE WINDSCREEN WIPER PRODUCTS
Unit 1, The Sidings Industrial Estate, Birdingbury Road, Marton CV23 9RX
Tel: 01926 633256
Fax: 01926 632600

*PACET MANUFACTURING LTD
Wyebridge House, Cores End Road, Bourne End SL8 5HH
Tel: 01628 526754
Fax: 01628 810080
E-mail: sales@pacet.co.uk
Web site: www.pacet.co.uk

*PLAXTON COACH SALES CENTRE
Ryton Road, Anston, Sheffield S25 4DL
Tel: 01909 551155
Fax: 01909 567994
E-mail: coaches@plaxtonlimited.co.uk
Web site: www.plaxtonlimited.co.uk

*UNITEC
Parts Division, Denby Way, Hellaby, Rotherham S66 8HR
Tel: 01709 792000
Fax: 01709 792009
E-mail: parts@optare.com

UWE VERKEN AB (UK branch)
Meadow Works, Walton Summit Industrial Estate, Bamber Bridge, Preston, PR5 8AL.
Tel: 07002 893893.
Fax: 07002 893329.
E-mail: uwe.uk@btinternet.com

WEBASTO PRODUCT UK LTD
Webasto House, White Rose Way, Doncaster Carr DN4 5JH
Tel: 01302 322232
Fax: 01302 322231
E-mail: info@webastouk.com
Web site: www.webasto.co.uk

Hub Odometers

KELLETT (UK) LTD
8 Stevenson Way, Sheffield S9 3WZ.
Tel: 0114 261 1122
Fax: 0114 261 1199
E-mail: sales@kellett.co.uk

MULTIPART PSV
Pilling Lane, Chorley PR7 3EL.
Tel: 01257 225577.
Fax: 01257 225575.
E-mail: info@multipart.com
Web site: www.multipart.com

*PARTLINE LTD
Dockfield Road, Shipley BD17 7AZ
Tel: 01274 531531
Fax: 01274 531088
E-mail: sales@partline.co.uk
Web site: www.partline.co.uk

PIONEER WESTON
Smithfold Lane, Worsley, Manchester M28 0GP.
Tel: 0161 703 2000
Fax: 0161 703 2025
E-mail: pioneer.weston@wyko.co.uk

*ROADLINK INTERNATIONAL LTD
Strawberry Lane, Willenhall WV13 3RL
Tel: 01902 636210
Fax: 01902 606604
E-mail: sales@roadlink-international.co.uk
Web site: www.roadlink-international.co.uk

In-coach Entertainment

*AVT SYSTEMS LTD
Unit 3, Tything Road, Arden Forest Trading Estate, Alcester B49 6ES
Tel: 01789 400357
Fax: 01789 400359
E-mail: enquiries@avtsystems.co.uk
Web site: www.avtsystems.co.uk

BRADTECH LTD
Unit 3, Ladford Covert, Seighford, Stafford ST18 9QD
Tel: 01785 282800
Fax: 01785 282558
E-mail: sales@bradtech.ltd.uk

EXPRESS COACH REPAIRS LTD
Outgang Lane, Pickering YO18 7EL.
Tel: 01751 475215.

*PLAXTON COACH SALES CENTRE
Ryton Road, Anston, Sheffield S25 4DL
Tel: 01909 551155
Fax: 01909 567994
E-mail: coaches@plaxtonlimited.co.uk
Web site: www.plaxtonlimited.co.uk

*PSV PRODUCTS
PO Box 166, Warrington WA4 5FG
Tel: 0870 062 4488
Fax: 0870 062 4499
E-mail: mike@psvproducts.com
Web site: www.psvproducts.com

SHADES TECHNICS
Marshgate Drive, Hertford SG13 7AJ
Tel: 01992 501683
Fax: 01992 501669
E-mail: sales@shades-technics.com
Web site: www.shades-technics.com

Labels, Nameplates & Decals

*FIRST CHOICE NAMEPLATES, LABELS & SIGNS
Lynden 2c, Russell Avenue, Balderton, Newark NG24 3BT
Tel: 01636 678035
Fax: 01636 707066
E-mail: firstchoice@handbag.com

*THE LAWTON MOTOR BODY BUILDING CO LTD
Knutsford Road, Church Lawton, Stoke-on-Trent ST7 3DN
Tel: 01270 882056
Fax: 01270 883014
E-mail: info@lawtonmotorbody.co.uk
Web site: www.lawtonmotorbody.co.uk

*McKENNA BROTHERS LTD
McKenna House, Jubilee Road, Middleton, Manchester M24 2LX
Tel: 0161 655 3244
Fax: 0161 655 3059
E-mail: info@mckennabrothers.co.uk
Web site: www.mckennabrothers.co.uk

Lifting Equipment

*AUTOLIFT LTD
Forge House, Norwell Woodhouse, Newark NG23 6NG
Tel: 01636 636586
Fax: 01636 636101
E-mail: info@autolift.freeserve.co.uk

*PLAXTON
Plaxton Park, Cayton Low Road, Eastfield, Scarborough YO11 3BY
Tel: 01723 581500
Fax: 01723 5813238
E-mail: sales@plaxtonlimited.co.uk
Web site: www.plaxtonlimited.co.uk

Lifts/Ramps (Passenger)

*COMPAK RAMPS LTD
VIP Trading Estate, Anchor & Hope Lane, London SE7 7RY
Tel/Fax: 020 8858 3781

CROWN COACHBUILDERS LTD
32 Flemington Industrial Park, Flemington, Motherwell ML1 1SN.
Tel: 01698 276087
Fax: 01698 276144
E-mail: davidgreer@hotmail.com
Web site: www.crowncoachbuilders.co.uk

*HATTS COACHWORKS & SERVICES
Foxham, Chippenham SN15 4NB
Tel: 01249 740444
Fax: 01249 740447
E-mail: adrian@hattstravel.co.uk
Web site: www.hattstravel.co.uk

MARTYN INDUSTRIALS LTD
5 Brunel Way, Durranhill Industrial Estate, Carlisle CA1 3NQ
Tel: 01228 544000
Fax: 01228 544001
E-mail: enquiries@martyn-industrials.co.uk
Web site: www.martyn-industrials.com

PASSENGER LIFT SERVICES LTD
Unit 10, Crystal Drive, Sandwell Business Park, Smethwick B66 1QG.
Tel: 0121 552 0600.
Fax: 0121 552 0200.
Web site: www.pls-access.co.uk

PERCY LANE PRODUCTS LTD
Lichfield Road, Tamworth B79 7TL
Tel: 01827 63821
Fax: 01827 310159
E-mail: sales@percy-lane.co.uk
Web site: www.percy-lane.co.uk

*PNEUMAX LTD
Unit 8, Venture Industrial Park, Fareham Road, Gosport PO13 0BA
Tel: 01329 823999
Fax: 01329 822345
E-mail: sales@pneumax.co.uk
Web site: www.pneumax.co.uk

RATCLIFF TAIL LIFTS LTD
Bessemer Road, Welwyn Garden City AL7 1ET
Tel: 01707 325571
Fax: 01707 327752
Web site: www.ratcliff.co.uk

RICON UK LIMITED
Littlemoss Business Park, Littlemoss Road, Droylsden, Manchester M43 7EF
Tel: 0800 435677
Fax: 0161 301 6050
E-mail: info@riconuk.com
Web site: www.riconuk.com

*TRUCKALIGN CO LTD
VIP Trading Estate, Anchor & Hope Lane, London SE7 7RY
Tel: 020 8858 3781
Fax: 020 8858 3781

Lighting & Lighting Design

ATLAS LIGHTING COMPONENTS
3 King George Close, Eastern Avenue, West Romford RM7 7PP.
Tel: 01708 776375
Fax: 01708 776376

BRITAX PMG LTD
Bressingby Industrial Estate, Bridlington YO16 4SJ
Tel: 01262 670161
Fax: 01262 605666
E-mail: info@britax-pmg.com
Web site: www.britax-pmg.com

CARLYLE BUS & COACH LTD
Great Bridge Street, Swan Village, West Bromwich B70 0X4
Tel: 0121 524 1200
Fax: 0121 524 1201
E-mail: admin@carlyleplc.co.uk

CSM LIGHTING
Suite 1b, Cobb House, Oyster Lane, Byfleet KT14 7DU
Tel: 01932 349661
Fax: 01932 349991
Web site: www.csmauto.com

HAPPICH V & I COMPONENTS LTD
Unit 30/31, Fort Industrial Park, Fort Parkway, Castle Bromwich B35 7AR.
Tel: 0121 747 4400
Fax: 0121 747 4977
E-mail: sales@happich.co.uk
Web site: www.happich.co.uk

*IMEXPART LTD
Links 31, Willowbridge Way, Whitwood, Castleford WF10 5NP
Tel: 01977 553936
Fax: 01977 604684
E-mail: parts@imexpart.com
Web site: www.imexpart.com

INVERTEC LTD
Whelford Road, Fairford GL7 4DT
Tel: 01285 713550
Fax: 01285 713548
Mobile: 07802 793828
E-mail: ian@invertec.co.uk
Web site: www.invertec.co.uk

KELLETT (UK) LTD
8 Stevenson Way, Sheffield S9 3WZ.
Tel: 0114 261 1122.
Fax: 0114 261 1199.
E-mail: sales@kellett.co.uk

MULTIPART PSV
Pilling Lane, Chorley PR7 3EL.
Tel: 01257 225577.
Fax: 01257 225575.
E-mail: info@multipart.com
Web site: www.multipart.com

*PARTLINE LTD
Dockfield Road, Shipley BD17 7AZ
Tel: 01274 531531
Fax: 01274 531088
E-mail: sales@partline.co.uk
Web site: www.partline.co.uk

*UNITEC
Parts Division, Denby Way, Hellaby, Rotherham S66 8HR
Tel: 01709 792000
Fax: 01709 792009
E-mail: parts@optare.com

Model Buses

*MIRROR IMAGE MODELS
A's Models of Bolton, (Dept. LRB/MIM), PO Box 514, Bolton BL1 5YD
Tel: 01204 467 961.
Web site: www.mirror-image-models.org.uk

Oil Management Systems

*IMEXPART LTD
Links 31, Willowbridge Way, Whitwood, Castleford WF10 5NP
Tel: 01977 553936
Fax: 01977 604684
E-mail: parts@imexpart.com
Web site: www.imexpart.com

INTERLUBE SYSTEMS LTD
St Modwen Road, Plymouth PL6 8LH
Tel: 01752 676000
Fax: 01752 676001
E-mail: info@interlubesystems.com
Web site: www.interlubesystems.com

STERTIL UK LTD
Unit A, Brackmills Business Park, Caswell Road, Northampton NN4 7PW
Tel: 01604 677384
Fax: 01604 765181
E-mail: info@stertil.com
Web site: www.stertil.com

Painting & Signwriting

BLACKPOOL COACH SERVICES
Moss Hey Garage, Chapel Road, Blackpool FY4 5HU.
Tel/Fax: 01253 698686

BRITISH BUS SALES
c/o Mike Nash, PO Box 534, Dorking RH5 5XB
Tel: 07836 656692
E-mail: nashionalbus1@btconnect.com
Web site: www.britishbussales.co.uk

BROXWOOD VEHICLE SPECIALISTS
Unit 2 Parkside Garage, Old Stafford Road, Wolverhampton WV10 7PH
Tel: 01902 798770
Fax: 01902 798564
E-mail: saks@broxwood.net
Web site: www.broxwood.net

BULWARK BUS & COACH ENGINEERING LTD
Gate 3, Bulwark Industrial Estate, Chepstow NP16 5QZ
Tel: 01291 622326.
Fax: 01291 622726.

DRURY & DRURY
Unit 6, Cobbs Wood Industrial Estate, Brunswick Road, Ashford TN23 1EH.
Tel: 01303 610555.
Fax: 01303 610666.
E-mail: martinstrange@channelcommercials.co.uk

EXPRESS COACH REPAIRS LTD
Outgang Lane, Pickering YO18 7EL.
Tel: 01751 475215.

HANTS & DORSET TRIM LTD
Canada Road, West Wellow SO51 6DE.
Tel: 023 8033 4335

*HATTS COACHWORKS & SERVICES
Foxham, Chippenham SN15 4NB
Tel: 01249 740444
Fax: 01249 740447
E-mail: adrian@hattstravel.co.uk
Web site: www.hattstravel.co.uk

*THE LAWTON MOTOR BODY BUILDING CO LTD
Knutsford Road, Church Lawton, Stoke-on-Trent ST7 3DN
Tel: 01270 882056
Fax: 01270 883014
E-mail: info@lawtonmotorbody.co.uk
Web site: www.lawtonmotorbody.co.uk

*McKENNA BROTHERS LTD
McKenna House, Jubilee Road, Middleton, Manchester M24 2LX
Tel: 0161 655 3244
Fax: 0161 655 3059
E-mail: info@mckennabrothers.co.uk
Web site: www.mckennabrothers.co.uk

*NORBURY BLINDS LTD
41-45 Hanley Street, Newtown, Birmingham B19 3SP
Tel: 0121 359 4311
Fax: 0121 359 6388
E-mail: info@norbury-blinds.com
Web site: www.norbury-blinds.com

*PLAXTON
Plaxton Park, Cayton Low Road, Eastfield, Scarborough YO11 3BY
Tel: 01723 581500
Fax: 01723 5813238
E-mail: sales@plaxtonlimited.co.uk
Web site: www.plaxtonlimited.co.uk

*PLAXTON COACH SALES CENTRE
Ryton Road, Anston, Sheffield S25 4DL
Tel: 01909 551155
Fax: 01909 567994
E-mail: coaches@plaxtonlimited.co.uk
Web site: www.plaxtonlimited.co.uk

Mirror Image Models
Model bus kits made from resin 3 piece body shells with plastic glazing. White metal wheels plus etched brass parts
Kit M10 Bristol Lodekka FSF / Eastern Coach Works as built c1960 and operated by United and other Tilling Group companies, with different front panels.
£37 including P&P
Please make cheques and postal orders payable to MIRROR IMAGE MODELS
A's Models of Bolton, (Dept. LRB/MIM), PO Box 514, Bolton, BL1 5YD.
Please ring between 9:30am-8:00pm 6 Days.
Tel: 01204 467 961.
www.mirror-image-models.org.uk
These models are kits not toys. West Midlands buses made to order

*RH BODYWORKS
A140 Ipswich Road, Brome Eye IP23 8AW
Tel: 01379 870666
Fax: 01379 871140
E-mail: mike.ball@rhbodywork.co.uk
Web site: www.rhbodyworks.co.uk

*UNITEC LONDON
Unit 5, Gateway 25, Weston Avenue, West Thurrock RM20 3ZD
Tel: 01708 892440
Fax: 01708 862125
E-mail: london.service@optare.com

*UNITEC ROTHERHAM
Denby Way, Hellaby, Rotherham S66 8HR
Tel: 01709 535101
Fax: 01709 535103
E-mail: rotherham.service@optare.com

*UNITEC SCOTLAND
Unit 7, Cumbernauld Business Park, Ward Park Road, Cumbernauld G67 3JZ
Tel: 01236 726738
Fax: 01236 795651
E-mail: scotland.service@optare.com

VOLVO COACH CENTRE
Brisco Avenue, off Belton Road West, Loughborough LE11 5HP.
Tel: 01509 217777.
Fax: 01509 260978.

Parts Suppliers

AIR DOOR SERVICES
Unit D, The Pavillions, Holly Lane Industrial Estate, Atherstone CV9 2QZ.
Tel: 01827 711660.
Fax: 01827 713577.
Web site: www.airdoorservices.co.uk

ARRIVA BUS AND COACH LTD
Lodge Garage, Whitehall Road West, Gomersal BD19 4BJ.
Tel: 01274 681144
Fax: 01274 651198
Web site: www.arriva.co.uk
E-mail: busandcoachsales@arriva.co.uk

*ASHLEY BANKS LTD
5 King Street Estate, Langtoft, Peterborough PE6 9NF
Tel: 01778 560651
Fax: 01778 560721
E-mail: user@ashleybanks.fsnet.co.uk

M BARNWELL SERVICES LTD
Reginald Road, Smethwick B67 5AS
Tel: 0121 420 0700
Fax: 0121 420 3080
E-mail: sales@barnwell.co.uk

*BRITISH BUS SALES
c/o Mike Nash, PO Box 534, Dorking RH5 5XB
Tel: 07836 656692
E-mail: nashionalbus1@btconnect.com
Web site: www.britishbussales.co.uk

BRT BEARINGS LTD
Algores Way, Wisbech PE13 2TQ
Tel: 01945 464097
Fax: 01945 464523
Web site: www.brt-bearings.com
Email: brt.sales@brt-bearings.com

BROXWOOD VEHICLE SPECIALISTS
Unit 2 Parkside Garage, Old Stafford Road, Wolverhampton WV10 7PH
Tel: 01902 798770
Fax: 01902 798564
E-mail: saks@broxwood.net
Web site: www.broxwood.net

BUSS BIZZ
Goughs Transport Depot, Morestead, Winchester SO21 1JD.
Tel: 01962 715555/66.
Fax: 01962 714868.

CARLYLE BUS & COACH LTD
Great Bridge Street, Swan Village, West Bromwich B70 0X4
Tel: 0121 524 1200
Fax: 0121 524 1201
E-mail: admin@carlyleplc.co.uk

CONSERVE (UK) LTD
Suite 7, Logistics House, 1 Horsley Road, Kingsthorpe Road, Northampton NN2 6LJ
Tel: 01604 710055
Fax: 01604 710065
E-mail: information@conserveuk.co.uk
Web site: www.conserveuk.co.uk

*CRESCENT FACILITIES LTD
72 Willow Crescent, Chapeltown, Sheffield S35 1QS
Tel/fax: 0114 2451050
E-mail: cfl.chris@btinternet.com
Web site: www.cflparts.com

CREST COACH CONVERSIONS
Unit 5, Holmeroyd Road, Bentley Moor Lane, Carcroft, Doncaster DN6 7BH
Tel: 01302 723723
Fax: 01302 724724

*CREWE ENGINES
Warmingham Road, Crewe CW1 4PQ
Tel: 01270 526333
Fax: 01270 526433
E-mail: sales@creweengines.co.uk
Web site: www.creweengines.co.uk

*CUMMINS UK
Rutherford Drive, Park Farm South, Wellingborough NN8 6AN
Tel: 01933 334200
Fax: 01933 334198
E-mail: cduksales@cummins.com
Web site: www.cummins-uk.com

*DIRECT PARTS LTD
Unit 1, Churnet Court, Churnetside Business Park, Harrison Way, Cheddleton ST13 7EF
Tel: 01538 361777
Fax: 01538 369100
E-mail: sales@direct-group.co.uk
Web site: www.direct-group.co.uk

FLIGHTS COACH TRAVEL LTD
Beacon House, Long Acre, Birmingham B7 5JJ
Tel: 0121 322 2222.
Fax: 0121 322 2224.
E-mail: sales@motorcoach.co.uk

GARDNER PARTS LTD
Barton Hall, Hardy Street, Eccles, Manchester M30 7WA.
Tel: 0161 278 9200
Fax: 0161 787 7549.

HAPPICH V & I COMPONENTS LTD
Unit 30/31, Fort Industrial Park, Fort Parkway, Castle Bromwich B35 7AR.
Tel: 0121 747 4400
Fax: 0121 747 4977
E-mail: sales@happich.co.uk
Web site: www.happich.co.uk

THOMAS HARDIE – WIGAN
Lockett Road, Ashton-in-Makerfield WN4 8DE
Tel: 01942 505124.
Fax: 01942 505119.

*HART BROTHERS (ENGINEERING) LTD
Soho Works, Soho Street, Oldham OL4 2AD
Tel: 0161 737 6791

*IMEXPART LTD
Links 31, Willowbridge Way, Whitwood, Castleford WF10 5NP
Tel: 01977 553936
Fax: 01977 604684
E-mail: parts@imexpart.com
Web site: www.imexpart.com

*IMPERIAL ENGINEERING
Delamare Road, Cheshunt EN8 9UD
Tel: 01992 6342555
Fax: 01992 630506
E-mail: sales@imperialengineering.co.uk
Web site: www.imperialengineering.co.uk

*KARIVE LIMITED
PO Box 205, Southam CV47 0ZL
Tel: 01926 813938
Fax: 01926 814898
E-mail: karive.ltd@btinternet.com
Web site: www.karive.co.uk

KELLETT (UK) LTD
8 Stevenson Way, Sheffield S9 3WZ
Tel: 0114 261 1122.
Fax: 0114 261 1199.
E-mail: sales@kellett.co.uk

KNORR-BREMSE SYSTEMS FOR COMMERCIAL VEHICLES LTD
Douglas Road, Kingswood, Bristol BS15 8NL.
Tel: 0117 984 6100
Fax: 0117 984 6101.
Web site: www.knorr-bremse.com

*THE LAWTON MOTOR BODY BUILDING CO LTD
Knutsford Road, Church Lawton, Stoke-on-Trent ST7 3DN
Tel: 01270 882056
Fax: 01270 883014
E-mail: info@lawtonmotorbody.co.uk
Web site: www.lawtonmotorbody.co.uk

MAJORLINE ENGINEERING LTD
Baybridge Industrial Units, Baybridge Lane, Owslebury, Winchester SO21 1JN.
Tel: 01962 777077.
Fax: 01962 777661, 777667
E-mail: majorline@compuserve.com

MOCAP LIMITED
Hortonwood 35, Telford TF1 7YW
Tel: 01952 670247
Fax: 01952 670241
Web site: www.mocap.co.uk
E-mail: sales@mocap.co.uk

MULTIPART PSV
Pilling Lane, Chorley PR7 3EL.
Tel: 01257 225577.
Fax: 01257 225575.
E-mail: info@multipart.com
Web site: www.multipart.com

Trade Directory

*NEXT BUS LTD
Vincients Road, Bumpers Farm Industrial Estate, Chippenham SN14 6QA
Tel: 01249 462462
Fax: 01249 448844
E-mail: sales@next-bus.co.uk
Web site: www.next-bus.co.uk

*NORBURY BLINDS LTD
41-45 Hanley Street, Newtown, Birmingham B19 3SP
Tel: 0121 359 4311
Fax: 0121 359 6388
E-mail: info@norbury-blinds.com
Web site: www.norbury-blinds.com

*PARTLINE LTD
Dockfield Road, Shipley BD17 7AZ
Tel: 01274 531531
Fax: 01274 531088
E-mail: sales@partline.co.uk
Web site: www.partline.co.uk

PIONEER WESTON
Smithfold Lane, Worsley, Manchester M28 0GP.
Tel: 0161 703 2000.
Fax: 0161 703 2025
E-mail: pioneer.weston@wyko.co.uk

*PLAXTON
Plaxton Park, Cayton Low Road, Eastfield, Scarborough YO11 3BY
Tel: 01723 581500
Fax: 01723 5813238
E-mail: sales@plaxtonlimited.co.uk
Web site: www.plaxtonlimited.co.uk

*PLAXTON COACH SALES CENTRE
Ryton Road, Anston, Sheffield S25 4DL
Tel: 01909 551155
Fax: 01909 567994
E-mail: coaches@plaxtonlimited.co.uk
Web site: www.plaxtonlimited.co.uk

*PNEUMAX LTD
Unit 8, Venture Industrial Park, Fareham Road, Gosport PO13 0BA
Tel: 01329 823999
Fax: 01329 822345
E-mail: sales@pneumax.co.uk
Web site: www.pneumax.co.uk

QUEENSBRIDGE (PSV) LTD
Longlands Industrial Estate, Milner Way, Ossett WF5 9JE
Tel: 01924 281871
Fax: 01924 281807
E-mail: craig@queensbridgeltd.co.uk
Web site: www.queensbridgeltd.co.uk

*ROADLINK INTERNATIONAL LTD
Strawberry Lane, Willenhall WV13 3RL
Tel: 01902 636210
Fax: 01902 606604
E-mail: sales@roadlink-international.co.uk
Web site: www.roadlink-international.co.uk

*SHAWSON SUPPLY LTD
12 Station Road, Saintfield BT24 7DU
Tel: 028 9751 0994
Fax: 028 9751 0816
E-mail: shawsondiesel@btopenworld.com
Web site: www.shawsonsupply.com

*TRAMONTANA
Chapelknowe Road, Carfin, Motherwell ML1 5LE
Tel: 01698 861790
Fax: 01698 860778
E-mail: wdt90@tiscali.co.uk
Web site: tramontanacoach.co.uk

TREVOR WIGLEY & SON BUS LTD
Passenger Vehicle Dismantling/Spares Works: Boulder Bridge Lane, off Shaw Lane, Barnsley S71 3HJ
Correspondence: 148 Royston Road, Cudworth, Barnsley S72 8BN
Tel: 01226 723147
Fax: 01226 700199

*UNITEC
Parts Division, Denby Way, Hellaby, Rotherham S66 8HR
Tel: 01709 792000
Fax: 01709 792009
E-mail: parts@optare.com

VOLVO COACH CENTRE
Brisco Avenue, off Belton Road West, Loughborough LE11 5HP.
Tel: 01509 217777.
Fax: 01509 260978.

WABCO AUTOMOTIVE UK LTD
Texas Street, Morley LS27 0HQ.
Tel: 0113 251 2510.
Fax: 0113 251 2844.

WACTON COACH SALES & SERVICES
Linton Trading Estate, Bromyard HR7 4QL.
Tel: 01885 482782.
Fax: 01885 482127

*WALSH'S ENGINEERING
Barton Moss Road, Eccles, Manchester M30 7RL
Tel: 0161 787 7017
Fax: 0161 787 7038
E-mail: walshs@gardnerdiesel.co.uk
Website: www.gardnerdiesel.co.uk

*ZF POWERTRAIN
Stringes Close, Willenhall WV13 1LE
Tel: 01902 366000
Fax: 01902 366504
E-mail: sales@powertrain.org.uk
Web site: www.powertrain.org.uk

Passenger Information Systems

HANOVER DISPLAYS LTD
Unit 24, Cliffe Industrial Estate, Lewes BN8 6JL
Tel: 01273 477528
Fax: 01273 407766
E-mail: hanover@hanoverdisplays.com
Web site: www.hanoverdisplays.com

JOURNEY PLAN LTD
12 Abbey Park Place, Dunfermline KY12 7PD
Tel: 01383 731048
Web site: journeyplan.co.uk

*McKENNA BROTHERS LTD
McKenna House, Jubilee Road, Middleton, Manchester M24 2LX
Tel: 0161 655 3244
Fax: 0161 655 3059
E-mail: info@mckennabrothers.co.uk
Web site: www.mckennabrothers.co.uk

*NORBURY BLINDS LTD
41-45 Hanley Street, Newtown, Birmingham B19 3SP
Tel: 0121 359 4311
Fax: 0121 359 6388
E-mail: info@norbury-blinds.com
Web site: www.norbury-blinds.com

SSL SIMULATION SYSTEMS LTD
Unit 12, Market Industrial Estate, Yatton BS49 4RF
Tel: 01934 838803
Fax: 01934 876202
E-mail: ssl@simulation-systems.co.uk
Web site: www.simulation-systems.co.uk

*VULTRON INTERNATIONAL LTD
Unit 2, Stadium Way, Elland Road, Leeds LS11 0EW
Tel: 0113 387 7310
Fax: 0113 387 7317
E-mail: jmoorhouse@vultron.co.uk

*WRIGHTBUS LTD
Galgorm, Ballymena BT42 1PY
Tel: 028 2564 1212
Fax: 028 2564 9703
E-mail: info@wright-bus.com
Web site: www.wright-bus.com

Pneumatic Valves/Cylinders

*PNEUMAX LTD
Unit 8, Venture Industrial Park, Fareham Road, Gosport PO13 0BA
Tel: 01329 823999
Fax: 01329 822345
E-mail: sales@pneumax.co.uk
Web site: www.pneumax.co.uk

*UNITEC
Parts Division, Denby Way, Hellaby, Rotherham S66 8HR
Tel: 01709 792000
Fax: 01709 792009
E-mail: parts@optare.com

Rapid Transit/ Priority Equipment

ALSTOM TRANSPORT SA
48 rue Albert Dhalenne, F-93482 Saint-Ouen Cedex, France
Tel: 00 33 1 41 66 90 00
Fax: 00 33 1 41 66 96 66
Web site: www.transport.alstom.com

BALFOUR BEATTY RAIL PLANT LTD
PO Box 5065, Raynesway, Derby DE21 7QZ
Tel: 01332 661491
Fax: 01332 288222
Web site: www.bbrail.com

BRECKNELL WILLIS & CO LTD
PO Box 10, Chard TA20 2DE
Tel: 01460 64941
Fax: 01460 66122
Web site: www.brecknell-willis.co.uk

Trade Directory

BRISTOL ELECTRIC RAILBUS LTD
Heron House, Chiswick Mall, London W4 2PR
Tel: 020 8995 3000
Fax: 020 8994 6060
E-mail: james@skinner.demon.co.uk

JMW
Systems House, Pentland Industrial Estate, Loanhead EH20 9QH
Tel: 0131 440 3633
Fax: 0131 440 3637
E-mail: enquiries@jmw-group.co.uk
Web site: www.jmw-group.co.uk

***PRE METRO OPERATION LTD**
21 Woodglade Croft, Kings Norton, Birmingham B38 8TD
Tel: 0121 243 9906
Fax: 0121 243 9906
E-mail: premetro@aol.com
Web site: www.parrytech.com

SIEMENS TRAFFIC CONTROLS LTD
Sopers Lane, Poole BH17 7ER
Tel: 01202 782000
Web site: www.siemenstraffic.com

SUSTRACO LTD
Heron House, Chiswick Mall, London W4 2PR
Tel: 020 8995 3000
Fax: 020 8994 6060
Web site: www.ultralightrail.com

Repairs/Refurbishment
- see body repairs above

Retarders & Speed Control Systems

BUSS BIZZ
Goughs Transport Depot, Morestead, Winchester SO21 1JD.
Tel: 01962 715555/66.
Fax: 01962 714868.

CHASSIS DEVELOPMENTS LTD
Grovebury Road, Leighton Buzzard LU7 8SL.
Tel: 01525 374151.
Fax: 01525 370127
Web site: www.chassisdevelopments.co.uk

LH GROUP (SERVICES) LTD
Graycar Business Park, Barton Turns, Barton Under Needwood DE13 8EN.
Tel: 01283 713615.
Fax: 01283 713551.
E-mail: l/h/llords@classic.msn.com

MULTIPART PSV
Pilling Lane, Chorley PR7 3EL.
Tel: 01257 225577.
Fax: 01257 225575.
E-mail: info@multipart.com
Web site: www.multipart.com

*SERGEANT (P&P) LTD
PO Box 11, New Hall Lane, Hoylake CH47 4DH
Tel: 0151 632 5903
Fax: 0151 632 5908
E-mail: enq@sergeant.co.uk
Web site: www.sergeant.co.uk

TELMA RETARDER LTD
25 Clarke Road, Mount Farm, Milton Keynes MK1 1LG
Tel: 01908 642822
Fax: 01908 641348
E-mail: telma@telma.co.uk
Web site: www.telma.co.uk

VOITH TURBO LTD
Regent House, Rump Lane, Hayes UB3 3BP
Tel: 020 8561 2131
Fax: 020 8569 1726
E-mail:turbo.uk@voith.com
Web site: www.voith.com

WABCO AUTOMOTIVE UK LTD
Texas Street, Morley LS27 0HQ.
Tel: 0113 251 2510.
Fax: 0113 251 2844

Reversing Safety Systems

AUTOSOUND LTD
4 Lister Street, Dudley Hill, Bradford BD4 9PQ
Tel: 01274 688990
Fax: 01274 651318
Web site: www.autosound.co.uk
E-mail: sales@autosound.co.uk

*AVT SYSTEMS LTD
Unit 3, Tything Road, Arden Forest Trading Estate, Alcester B49 6ES
Tel: 01789 400357
Fax: 01789 400359
E-mail: enquiries@avtsystems.co.uk
Web site: www.avtsystems.co.uk

BRIGADE ELECTRONICS plc
Brigade House, The Mills, Station Road, South Darenth DA4 9BD
Tel: 0870 774 1500
Fax: 0870 774 1502
E-mail: sales@brigade-electronics.co.uk
Web site: www.brigade-electronics.co.uk, www.bbs-tek.com

BROXWOOD VEHICLE SPECIALISTS
Unit 2 Parkside Garage, Old Stafford Road, Wolverhampton WV10 7PH
Tel: 01902 798770
Fax: 01902 798564
E-mail: saks@broxwood.net
Web site: www.broxwood.net

CARLYLE BUS & COACH LTD
Great Bridge Street, Swan Village, West Bromwich B70 0X4
Tel: 0121 524 1200
Fax: 0121 524 1201
E-mail: admin@carlyleplc.co.uk

CLAN TOOLS & PLANT LTD
3 Greenhill Avenue, Giffnock, Glasgow G46 6QX.
Tel: 0141 638 8040.
Fax: 0141 638 8881.

CYBERLYNE COMMUNICATIONS LTD
Unit 5, Hatfield Way, South Church Industrial Esate, Bishop Auckland DL14 6XF
Tel: 01388 773761
Fax: 01388 773778
E-mail: david@cyberlynecommunications.co.uk
Web site: www.cyberlynecommunications.co.uk

KELLETT (UK) LTD
8 Stevenson Way, Sheffield S9 3WZ.
Tel: 0114 261 1122.
Fax: 0114 261 1199.
E-mail: sales@kellett.co.uk

*PARTLINE LTD
Dockfield Road, Shipley BD17 7AZ
Tel: 01274 531531
Fax: 01274 531088
E-mail: sales@partline.co.uk
Web site: www.partline.co.uk

*PLAXTON COACH SALES CENTRE
Ryton Road, Anston, Sheffield S25 4DL
Tel: 01909 551155
Fax: 01909 567994
E-mail: coaches@plaxtonlimited.co.uk
Web site: www.plaxtonlimited.co.uk

Roller Blinds - Passenger & Driver

CARLYLE BUS & COACH LTD
Great Bridge Street, Swan Village, West Bromwich B70 0X4
Tel: 0121 524 1200
Fax: 0121 524 1201
E-mail: admin@carlyleplc.co.uk

HAPPICH V & I COMPONENTS LTD
Unit 30/31, Fort Industrial Park, Fort Parkway, Castle Bromwich B35 7AR.
Tel: 0121 747 4400
Fax: 0121 747 4977
E-mail: sales@happich.co.uk
Web site: www.happich.co.uk

*NORBURY BLINDS LTD
41-45 Hanley Street, Newtown, Birmingham B19 3SP
Tel: 0121 359 4311
Fax: 0121 359 6388
E-mail: info@norbury-blinds.com
Web site: www.norbury-blinds.com

WIDNEY UK LTD
Plume Street, Aston, Birmingham B6 7SA
Tel: 0121 327 5500
Fax: 0121 328 2466
E-mail: richard@widney.co.uk

Roof-Lining Fabrics

AUTOMATE WHEEL COVERS LTD
California Mills, Oxford Road, Gomersal BD19 4HQ
Tel: 01274 862700
Fax: 01274 851989
E-mail: sales@wheelcovers.co.uk
Web site: www.euroliners.com

Trade Directory

*AUTOMOTIVE TEXTILE INDUSTRIES
Unit 15 & 16, Priest Court, Springfield
Business Park, Grantham NG31 7BG
Tel: 01476 593050
Fax: 01476 593607
E-mail: sales@autotex.com
Web site: www.autotex.com

HAPPICH V & I COMPONENTS LTD
Unit 30/31, Fort Industrial Park, Fort
Parkway, Castle Bromwich B35 7AR.
Tel: 0121 747 4400
Fax: 0121 747 4977
E-mail: sales@happich.co.uk
Web site: www.happich.co.uk

*THE LAWTON MOTOR BODY BUILDING CO LTD
Knutsford Road, Church Lawton, Stoke-on-Trent ST7 3DN
Tel: 01270 882056
Fax: 01270 883014
E-mail: info@lawtonmotorbody.co.uk
Web site: www.lawtonmotorbody.co.uk

Seat belts/restraint systems

*ABACUS TUBULAR PRODUCTS LTD
Abacus House, Highlode Industrial Estate,
Ramsey PE26 2RB
Tel: 01487 710700
Fax: 01487 710626
E-mail: info@abacus-tp.com
Web site: www.abacus-tp.com

CARLYLE BUS & COACH LTD
Great Bridge Street, Swan Village, West
Bromwich B70 0X4
Tel: 0121 524 1200
Fax: 0121 524 1201
E-mail: admin@carlyleplc.co.uk

ELITE SEATBELT SPECIALIST LTD
Unit 6, Adswood Road Industrial Estate,
Stockport SK3 8LF.
Tel: 0161 480 0617.
Fax: 0161 480 3099.
E-mail: elite.seatbelts@btinternet.com
Web site: www.seatbelts.co.uk
Mobile: 0467 486 700 (0161 976 1280 after hours).

*HATTS COACHWORKS & SERVICES
Foxham, Chippenham SN15 4NB
Tel: 01249 740444
Fax: 01249 740447
E-mail: adrian@hattstravel.co.uk
Web site: www.hattstravel.co.uk

*THE LAWTON MOTOR BODY BUILDING CO LTD
Knutsford Road, Church Lawton, Stoke-on-Trent ST7 3DN
Tel: 01270 882056
Fax: 01270 883014
E-mail: info@lawtonmotorbody.co.uk
Web site: www.lawtonmotorbody.co.uk

*MTB EQUIPMENT LTD
Sixth Avenue, Zone Two, Deeside Industrial
Park, Deeside CH5 2LB
Tel: 0870 870 1282
Fax: 01244 289 818
E-mail: info@mtb-equipment.com
Web site: www.mtb-equipment.com

MULTIPART PSV
Pilling Lane, Chorley PR7 3EL.
Tel: 01257 225577.
Fax: 01257 225575.
E-mail: info@multipart.com
Web site: www.multipart.com

*PARTLINE LTD
Dockfield Road, Shipley BD17 7AZ
Tel: 01274 531531
Fax: 01274 531088
E-mail: sales@partline.co.uk
Web site: www.partline.co.uk

*PLAXTON
Plaxton Park, Cayton Low Road, Eastfield,
Scarborough YO11 3BY
Tel: 01723 581500
Fax: 01723 5813238
E-mail: sales@plaxtonlimited.co.uk
Web site: www.plaxtonlimited.co.uk

*PLAXTON COACH SALES CENTRE
Ryton Road, Anston, Sheffield S25 4DL
Tel: 01909 551155
Fax: 01909 567994
E-mail: coaches@plaxtonlimited.co.uk
Web site: www.plaxtonlimited.co.uk

Q'STRAINT
73-76 John Wilson Business Park,
Whitstable CT5 3QU
Tel: 01227 773035
Fax: 01227 770035
E-mail: info@qstraint.co.uk
Web site: www.qstraint.com

SAFETEX LTD
Unit 16/17, Bookham Industrial Park,
Church Road, Bookham KT23 3EV
Tel: 01372 451272
Fax: 01372 451282
E-mail: sales@safetex.com
Web site: www@safetex.com

SECURON (AMERSHAM) LTD
Winchmore Hill, Amersham HP7 0NZ.
Tel: 01494 434455.
Fax: 01494 726499.
E-mail: securon@securon.co.uk
Web site: www.securon.co.uk

*TRAMONTANA
Chapelknowe Road, Carfin, Motherwell
ML1 5LE
Tel: 01698 861790
Fax: 01698 860778
E-mail: wdt90@tiscali.co.uk
Web site: tramontanacoach.co.uk

Seats/seat cushions & seat frames

*ABACUS TUBULAR PRODUCTS LTD
Abacus House, Highlode Industrial Estate,
Ramsey PE26 2RB
Tel: 01487 710700
Fax: 01487 710626
E-mail: info@abacus-tp.com
Web site: www.abacus-tp.com

ARDEE COACH TRIM LTD
Artnalivery, Ardee, Co Louth, Ireland
Tel: 00 353 41 685 3599
Web site: www.ardeecoachtrim.com

BERNSTEIN ENGINEERING LTD
Unit 1, Colne Way Court, Colne Way,
Watford WD24 7NE
Tel: 01923 239996
Fax: 01923 252633

CARLYLE BUS & COACH LTD
Great Bridge Street, Swan Village, West
Bromwich B70 0X4
Tel: 0121 524 1200
Fax: 0121 524 1201
E-mail: admin@carlyleplc.co.uk

CHAPMAN DRIVER SEATING
68 Burners Lane, Kiln Farm, Milton
Keynes MK11 3HD
Tel: 0845 838 2305
Fax: 0845 838 2909

COGENT PASSENGER SEATING LTD
Prydwen Road, Swansea West Industrial
Estate, Swansea SA5 4HN
Tel: 01792 585444
Fax: 01792 588191
Web site: www.cogent.demon.co.uk
E-mail: seats@cogent.demon.co.uk

DUOFLEX LTD
Trimmingham House, 2 Shires Road,
Buckingham Road Industrial Estate,
Brackley NN13 7EZ
Tel: 01280 701366
Fax: 01280 704799
E-mail: sales@duoflex.co.uk
Web site: www.duoflex.co.uk

HAPPICH V & I COMPONENTS LTD
Unit 30/31, Fort Industrial Park, Fort
Parkway, Castle Bromwich B35 7AR.
Tel: 0121 747 4400
Fax: 0121 747 4977
E-mail: sales@happich.co.uk
Web site: www.happich.co.uk

*INTERFACE FABRICS LTD
Hopton Mills, Mirfield WF1 8HE
Tel: 01924 490591
Web site: www.interfacefabrics.com

JBF SERVICES LTD
Southedge Works, Hipperholme, Halifax
HX3 8EF
Tel: 01422 202840
Fax: 01422 206070
E-mail: jbfservices@aol.com

KAB SEATING LTD
Round Spinney, Northampton NN3 8RS
Tel: 01604 790500
Fax: 01604 790155

LUNAR SEATING LTD
Unit 3, Packhorse Place, Watling Street,
Kensworth LU6 3QU
Tel: 01582 841535
Fax: 01582 841749
E-mail: sue@lunar-seating.co.uk

MAJORLINE ENGINEERING LTD
Baybridge Industrial Units, Baybridge Lane,
Owslebury, Winchester SO21 1JN.
Tel: 01962 777077.
Fax: 01962 777661, 777667
E-mail: majorline@compuserve.com

Trade Directory

CHAPMAN
DRIVER SEATING

www.chapmandriverseating.com

Contact Details
☎ 0845 838 2305
📠 0845 838 2909

---

*MTB EQUIPMENT LTD
Sixth Avenue, Zone Two, Deeside Industrial Park, Deeside CH5 2LB
Tel: 0870 870 1282
Fax: 01244 289 818
E-mail: info@mtb-equipment.com
Web site: www.mtb-equipment.com

METRONET (REW) LTD
130 Bollo Lane, London W3 8BZ.
Tel: 020 7918 6666.
Fax: 020 7918 6599.
E-mail: fraser@r-e-w.co.uk
Web site: www.r-e-w.co.uk

PHOENIX SEATING LTD
Unit 47, Bay 3, Second Avenue, Pensnett Estate, Kingswinford DY6 7UZ
Tel: 01384 296622

*PLAXTON COACH SALES CENTRE
Ryton Road, Anston, Sheffield S25 4DL
Tel: 01909 551155
Fax: 01909 567994
E-mail: coaches@plaxtonlimited.co.uk
Web site: www.plaxtonlimited.co.uk

RESCROFT LTD
20 Oxleasow Road, East Moons Moat, Redditch B98 0RE
Tel: 01527 521300
Fax: 01527 521301
Web site: www.rescroft.com
E-mail: enquiries@rescroft.com

SCANDUS UK
Unit 21, Gainsborough Trading Estate, Rufford Road, Stourbridge DY9 7ND
Tel: 01384 443409
Fax: 01384 443 932
Web site: www.scandusuk.co.uk

TUBE PRODUCTS LTD
PO Box 13, Oldbury, Warley B69 4PF.
Tel: 0121 552 1511.
Fax: 0121 544 6026.

WOODBRIDGE FOAM UK LTD
Caxton Road, Elms Industrial Estate, Bedford MK41 0EJ.
Tel: 01234 211333.
Fax: 01234 272047

Shelters/Street Furniture

BUS SHELTERS LTD
Dyffryn Business Park, Llantwit Major Road, Llandow CF71 7PY
Tel: 01446 795444
Fax: 01446 793344
E-mail: bus@shelters.demon.co.uk

CARMANAH UK
68 Basepoint Business Centre, Metcalf Way, Crawley RH11 7XX
Tel: 0870 345 9548 0208 323 8028
E-mail: info@carmanah.co.uk
Web site: www.carmanah.co.uk

*FIRST CHOICE NAMEPLATES, LABELS & SIGNS
Lynden 2c, Russell Avenue, Balderton, Newark NG24 3BT
Tel: 01636 678035
Fax: 01636 707066
E-mail: firstchoice@handbag.com

*GABRIEL & COMPANY LTD
Abro Works, 10 Hay Hall Road, Tyseley, Birmingham B11 2AU
Tel: 0121 248 3333
Fax: 0121 248 3330
E-mail: contact@gabrielco.com
Web site: www.gabrielco.com

MACEMAIN + AMSTAD
Boyle Road, Willowbrook Industrial Estate, Corby NN17 5XU
Tel: 01536 401331
Fax: 01536 401298
E-mail: enquiries@macemainamstad.com
Web site: www.macemainamstad.com

*PSV GLASS
Central Distribution Centre
Hillbottom Road, High Wycombe HP12 4HJ
Tel: 01494 533131
Fax: 01494 462675
Northern Distribution Centre
Stakehill Distribution Park, Middleton, Greater Manchester M24 2FL
Scottish Distribution Centre
Bessemer Drive, Kelvin Industrial Estate, East Kilbride G75 0QX
E-mail: sales@psvglass.co.uk
Web site: www.psvglass.co.uk

QUEENSBURY SHELTERS
Queensbury House, Fitzherbert Road, Farlington, Portsmouth PO6 1SE
Tel: 023 9221 0052
Fax: 023 9221 0059
Web site: www.queensbury.org

TRUEFORM ENGINEERING LTD
Unit 4, Pasadena Trading Estate, Pasadena Close, Hayes UB3 3NQ
Tel: 020 8561 4959
Fax: 020 8848 1397
E-mail: sales@trueform.co.uk
Web site: www..trueform.co.uk

WHITELEY ELECTRONICS
Victoria Street, Mansfield NG18 5RW
Tel: 01623 415600
E-mail: sales@whiteleyelectronics.com
Web site: www.whiteleyelectronics.com

Shock Absorbers/Suspension

*ASHLEY BANKS LTD
5 King Street Estate, Langtoft, Peterborough PE6 9NF
Tel: 01778 560651
Fax: 01778 560721
E-mail: user@ashleybanks.fsnet.co.uk

BROXWOOD VEHICLE SPECIALISTS
Unit 2 Parkside Garage, Old Stafford Road, Wolverhampton WV10 7PH
Tel: 01902 798770
Fax: 01902 798564
E-mail: saks@broxwood.net
Web site: www.broxwood.net

*CRESCENT FACILITIES LTD
72 Willow Crescent, Chapeltown, Sheffield S35 1QS
Tel/fax: 0114 2451050
E-mail: cfl.chris@btinternet.com
Web site: www.cflparts.com

Trade Directory

*DIRECT PARTS LTD
Unit 1, Churnet Court, Churnetside Business Park, Harrison Way, Cheddleton ST13 7EF
Tel: 01538 361777
Fax: 01538 369100
E-mail: sales@direct-group.co.uk
Web site: www.direct-group.co.uk

*ERENTEK LTD
Malt Kiln Lane, Waddington, Lincoln LN5 9RT
Tel: 01522 720065
Fax: 01522 729155
E-mail: sale@erentek.co.uk
Web site: www.erentek.co.uk

*HART BROTHERS (ENGINEERING) LTD
Soho Works, Soho Street, Oldham OL4 2AD
Tel: 0161 737 6791

*IMEXPART LTD
Links 31, Willowbridge Way, Whitwood, Castleford WF10 5NP
Tel: 01977 553936
Fax: 01977 604684
E-mail: parts@imexpart.com
Web site: www.imexpart.com

KELLETT (UK) LTD
8 Stevenson Way, Sheffield S9 3WZ.
Tel: 0114 261 1122.
Fax: 0114 261 1199.
E-mail: sales@kellett.co.uk

MAJORLINE ENGINEERING LTD
Baybridge Industrial Units, Baybridge Lane, Owsleybury, Winchester SO21 1JN.
Tel: 01962 777077.
Fax: 01962 777661, 777667
E-mail: majorline@compuserve.com

MULTIPART PSV
Pilling Lane, Chorley PR7 3EL.
Tel: 01257 225577.
Fax: 01257 225575.
E-mail: info@multipart.com
Web site: www.multipart.com

*NEXT BUS LTD
Vincients Road, Bumpers Farm Industrial Estate, Chippenham SN14 6QA
Tel: 01249 462462
Fax: 01249 448844
E-mail: sales@next-bus.co.uk
Web site: www.next-bus.co.uk

*PARTLINE LTD
Dockfield Road, Shipley BD17 7AZ
Tel: 01274 531531
Fax: 01274 531088
E-mail: sales@partline.co.uk
Web site: www.partline.co.uk

*POLYBUSH
Clywedog Road South, Wrexham Industrial Estate, Wrexham LL13 9XS
Tel: 01978 664316
Fax: 01978 661190
E-mail: sales@polybush.co.uk
Web site: www.polybush.co.uk

*ROADLINK INTERNATIONAL LTD
Strawberry Lane, Willenhall WV13 3RL
Tel: 01902 636210
Fax: 01902 606604
E-mail: sales@roadlink-international.co.uk
Web site: www.roadlink-international.co.uk

*SHAWSON SUPPLY LTD
12 Station Road, Saintfield BT24 7DU
Tel: 028 9751 0994
Fax: 028 9751 0816
E-mail: shawsondiesel@btopenworld.com
Web site: www.shawsonsupply.com

*UNITEC
Parts Division, Denby Way, Hellaby, Rotherham S66 8HR
Tel: 01709 792000
Fax: 01709 792009
E-mail: parts@optare.com

Steering

BROXWOOD VEHICLE SPECIALISTS
Unit 2 Parkside Garage, Old Stafford Road, Wolverhampton WV10 7PH
Tel: 01902 798770
Fax: 01902 798564
E-mail: saks@broxwood.net
Web site: www.broxwood.net

*CRESCENT FACILITIES LTD
72 Willow Crescent, Chapeltown, Sheffield S35 1QS
Tel/fax: 0114 2451050
E-mail: cfl.chris@btinternet.com
Web site: www.cflparts.com

*DIRECT PARTS LTD
Unit 1, Churnet Court, Churnetside Business Park, Harrison Way, Cheddleton ST13 7EF
Tel: 01538 361777
Fax: 01538 369100
E-mail: sales@direct-group.co.uk
Web site: www.direct-group.co.uk

*HL SMITH TRANSMISSIONS LTD
Enterprise Business Park, Cross Road, Albrighton, Wolverhampton WV7 3BJ
Tel: 01902 373011
Fax: 01902 373608

*IMEXPART LTD
Links 31, Willowbridge Way, Whitwood, Castleford WF10 5NP
Tel: 01977 553936
Fax: 01977 604684
E-mail: parts@imexpart.com
Web site: www.imexpart.com

*IMPERIAL ENGINEERING
Delamare Road, Cheshunt EN8 9UD
Tel: 01992 6342555
Fax: 01992 630506
E-mail: sales@imperialengineering.co.uk
Web site: www.imperialengineering.co.uk

MAJORLINE ENGINEERING LTD
Baybridge Industrial Units, Baybridge Lane, Owsleybury, Winchester SO21 1JN.
Tel: 01962 777077.
Fax: 01962 777661, 777667
E-mail: majorline@compuserve.com

MULTIPART PSV
Pilling Lane, Chorley PR7 3EL.
Tel: 01257 225577.
Fax: 01257 225575.
E-mail: info@multipart.com
Web site: www.multipart.com

*NEXT BUS LTD
Vincients Road, Bumpers Farm Industrial Estate, Chippenham SN14 6QA
Tel: 01249 462462
Fax: 01249 448844
E-mail: sales@next-bus.co.uk
Web site: www.next-bus.co.uk

*PARTLINE LTD
Dockfield Road, Shipley BD17 7AZ
Tel: 01274 531531
Fax: 01274 531088
E-mail: sales@partline.co.uk
Web site: www.partline.co.uk

*PSS - STEERING & HYDRAULICS DIVISION
Folgate Road, North Walsham NR28 0AJ
Tel: 01692 406017
Fax: 01692 406957
E-mail: sales@pss.co.uk
Web site: www.pss.co.uk

*ROADLINK INTERNATIONAL LTD
Strawberry Lane, Willenhall WV13 3RL
Tel: 01902 636210
Fax: 01902 606604
E-mail: sales@roadlink-international.co.uk
Web site: www.roadlink-international.co.uk

*SHAWSON SUPPLY LTD
12 Station Road, Saintfield BT24 7DU
Tel: 028 9751 0994
Fax: 028 9751 0816
E-mail: shawsondiesel@btopenworld.com
Web site: www.shawsonsupply.com

*UNITEC
Parts Division, Denby Way, Hellaby, Rotherham S66 8HR
Tel: 01709 792000
Fax: 01709 792009
E-mail: parts@optare.com

*UNITEC LONDON
Unit 5, Gateway 25, Weston Avenue, West Thurrock RM20 3ZD
Tel: 01708 892440
Fax: 01708 862125
E-mail: london.service@optare.com

*UNITEC ROTHERHAM
Denby Way, Hellaby, Rotherham S66 8HR
Tel: 01709 535101
Fax: 01709 535103
E-mail: rotherham.service@optare.com

*UNITEC SCOTLAND
Unit 7, Cumbernauld Business Park, Ward Park Road, Cumbernauld G67 3JZ
Tel: 01236 726738
Fax: 01236 795651
E-mail: scotland.service@optare.com

*ZF POWERTRAIN
Stringes Close, Willenhall WV13 1LE
Tel: 01902 366000
Fax: 01902 366504
E-mail: sales@powertrain.org.uk
Web site: www.powertrain.org.uk

Surveillance Systems

AFTERMARKET COACH SUPPLIES (UK) LTD
Unit A, Shipmans Yard, Station Road, Rushton NN14 1RL
Tel: 01536 711310
Fax: 01536 710033
Web site: www.acsuk.freeuk.com

Trade Directory

AUTOSOUND LTD
4 Lister Street, Dudley Hill, Bradford
BD4 9PQ
Tel: 01274 688990
Fax: 01274 651318
Web site: www.autosound.co.uk
E-mail: sales@autosound.co.uk

*AVT SYSTEMS LTD
Unit 3, Tything Road, Arden Forest Trading Estate, Alcester B49 6ES
Tel: 01789 400357
Fax: 01789 400359
E-mail: enquiries@avtsystems.co.uk
Web site: www.avtsystems.co.uk

CLAN TOOLS & PLANT LTD
3 Greenhill Avenue, Giffnock, Glasgow G46 6QX.
Tel: 0141 638 8040.
Fax: 0141 638 8881.

CYBERLYNE COMMUNICATIONS LTD
Unit 5, Hatfield Way, South Church Industrial Esate, Bishop Auckland DL14 6XF
Tel: 01388 773761
Fax: 01388 773778
E-mail: david@cyberlynecommunications.co.uk
Web site: www.cyberlynecommunications.co.uk

KELLETT (UK) LTD
8 Stevenson Way, Sheffield S9 3WZ.
Tel: 0114 261 1122.
Fax: 0114 261 1199.
E-mail: sales@kellett.co.uk

KNORR-BREMSE SYSTEMS FOR COMMERCIAL VEHICLES LTD
Douglas Road, Kingswood, Bristol BS15 8NL.
Tel: 0117 984 6100.
Fax: 0117 984 6101.
Web site: www.knorr-bremse.com

LOOK CCTV LTD
Look House, Aldon Road, Poulton-le-Fylde FY6 8JL
Tel: 01253 891222
Fax: 01253 891221
Web site: www.look-cctv.co.uk
E-mail: enquiries@look-cctv.co.uk

MAJORLINE ENGINEERING LTD
Baybridge Industrial Units, Baybridge Lane, Owslebury, Winchester SO21 1JN.
Tel: 01962 777077.
Fax: 01962 777661, 777667
E-mail: majorline@compuserve.com

MULTIPART PSV
Pilling Lane, Chorley PR7 3EL.
Tel: 01257 225577.
Fax: 01257 225575.
E-mail: info@multipart.com
Web site: www.multipart.com

*PSV PRODUCTS
PO Box 166, Warrington WA4 5FG
Tel: 0870 062 4488
Fax: 0870 062 4499
E-mail: mike@psvproducts.com
Web site: www.psvproducts.com

*VERIFEYE (UK) LTD
Unit 1, Branksome Business Centre, Cortry Close, Poole BH12 4BQ
Tel: 02380 284727
E-mail: sales@verifeye.co.uk
Web site: www.verifeye.com

WABCO AUTOMOTIVE UK LTD
Texas Street, Morley LS27 0HQ.
Tel: 0113 251 2510
Fax: 0113 251 2844

WEBASTO PRODUCT UK LTD
Webasto House, White Rose Way, Doncaster Carr DN4 5JH
Tel: 01302 322232
Fax: 01302 322231
E-mail: info@webastouk.com
Web site: www.webasto.co.uk

Tachographs

CHASSIS DEVELOPMENTS LTD
Grovebury Road, Leighton Buzzard LU7 8SL.
Tel: 01525 374151.
Fax: 01525 370127.

ERF MEDWAY LTD
Sir Thomas Longley Road, Medway City Estate, Rochester ME2 4QW.
Tel: 01634 711144.
Fax: 01634 711188.

THOMAS HARDIE – WIGAN
Lockett Road, Ashton-in-Makerfield WN4 8DE.
Tel: 01942 505124.
Fax: 01942 505119.

MAJORLINE ENGINEERING LTD
Baybridge Industrial Units, Baybridge Lane, Owslebury, Winchester SO21 1JN.
Tel: 01962 777077.
Fax: 01962 777661, 777667
E-mail: majorline@compuserve.com

MULTIPART PSV
Pilling Lane, Chorley PR7 3EL.
Tel: 01257 225577
Fax: 01257 225575.
E-mail: info@multipart.com
Web site: www.multipart.com

*PARTLINE LTD
Dockfield Road, Shipley BD17 7AZ
Tel: 01274 531531
Fax: 01274 531088
E-mail: sales@partline.co.uk
Web site: www.partline.co.uk

*PLAXTON
Plaxton Park, Cayton Low Road, Eastfield, Scarborough YO11 3BY
Tel: 01723 581500
Fax: 01723 5813238
E-mail: sales@plaxtonlimited.co.uk
Web site: www.plaxtonlimited.co.uk

*PLAXTON COACH SALES CENTRE
Ryton Road, Anston, Sheffield S25 4DL
Tel: 01909 551155
Fax: 01909 567994
E-mail: coaches@plaxtonlimited.co.uk
Web site: www.plaxtonlimited.co.uk

SIEMENS VDO TRADING LTD
36 Gravelly Industrial Park, Birmingham B24 8TA
Tel: 0121 326 1234
Fax: 0121 326 1299
Web site: www.siemens-datatrack.com

*UNITEC LONDON
Unit 5, Gateway 25, Weston Avenue, West Thurrock RM20 3ZD
Tel: 01708 892440
Fax: 01708 862125
E-mail: london.service@optare.com

*UNITEC ROTHERHAM
Denby Way, Hellaby, Rotherham S66 8HR
Tel: 01709 535101
Fax: 01709 535103
E-mail: rotherham.service@optare.com

*UNITEC SCOTLAND
Unit 7, Cumbernauld Business Park, Ward Park Road, Cumbernauld G67 3JZ
Tel: 01236 726738
Fax: 01236 795651
E-mail: scotland.service@optare.com

*WARD INTERNATIONAL CONSULTING LTD
Funtley Court, 19 Funtley Hill, Fareham PO16 7UY
Tel: 01329 280280
Fax: 01329 221010
E-mail: info@wardint.co.uk
Web site: www.wardint.com

Tachograph Calibrators

MAJORLINE ENGINEERING LTD
Baybridge Industrial Units, Baybridge Lane, Owslebury, Winchester SO21 1JN.
Tel: 01962 777077.
Fax: 01962 777661, 777667
E-mail: majorline@compuserve.com

*MCE LTD
Firbank Way, Leighton Buzzard LU7 4YP
Tel: 01525 375301
Fax: 01525 850967
Web site: www.mce-ltd.com

*PLAXTON
Plaxton Park, Cayton Low Road, Eastfield, Scarborough YO11 3BY
Tel: 01723 581500
Fax: 01723 5813238
E-mail: sales@plaxtonlimited.co.uk
Web site: www.plaxtonlimited.co.uk

*PLAXTON COACH SALES CENTRE
Ryton Road, Anston, Sheffield S25 4DL
Tel: 01909 551155
Fax: 01909 567994
E-mail: coaches@plaxtonlimited.co.uk
Web site: www.plaxtonlimited.co.uk

SIEMENS VDO TRADING LTD
36 Gravelly Industrial Park, Birmingham B24 8TA
Tel: 0121 326 1234
Fax: 0121 326 1299
Web site: www.siemens-datatrack.com

*UNITEC LONDON
Unit 5, Gateway 25, Weston Avenue, West Thurrock RM20 3ZD
Tel: 01708 892440
Fax: 01708 862125
E-mail: london.service@optare.com

*UNITEC ROTHERHAM
Denby Way, Hellaby, Rotherham S66 8HR
Tel: 01709 535101
Fax: 01709 535103
E-mail: rotherham.service@optare.com

*UNITEC SCOTLAND
Unit 7, Cumbernauld Business Park, Ward Park Road, Cumbernauld G67 3JZ
Tel: 01236 726738
Fax: 01236 795651
E-mail: scotland.service@optare.com

VISECT LTD (TACH:TRAK)
PO Box 1478, Pill BS20 0DZ
Tel: 01275 372274
Fax: 01275 375091

Tachograph Chart Analysis Service

*IBPTS
43 Cage Lane, Felixstowe IP11 9BJ
Tel: 01394 672344
Fax: 01394 672344
E-mail: info@ibpts.com
Web site: www.ibpts.com

CHASSIS DEVELOPMENTS LTD
Grovebury Road, Leighton Buzzard LU7 8SL.
Tel: 01525 374151.
Fax: 01525 370127.

SIEMENS VDO TRADING LTD
36 Gravelly Industrial Park, Birmingham B24 8TA
Tel: 0121 326 1234
Fax: 0121 326 1299
Web site: www.siemens-datatrack.com

TACHOGRAPH BUREAUX LTD
Lodge Farm, Kineton CV35 0JH
Tel/Fax: 01926 641224
E-mail: peter.day@tachograph-bureaux.co.uk
Web site: www.tachograph-bureaux.co.uk

Tickets, Ticket Machines and Ticket Systems

ACT - APPLIED CARD TECHNOLOGIES
Langley Gate, Kington Langley, Chippenham SN15 5SE
Tel: 01249 751 200
Fax: 01249 751 201
Email: info@card.co.uk
Web site: www.card.co.uk

ALMEX INFORMATION SYSTEMS
Metric House, Love Lane, Cirencester GL7 1YG
Tel: 01285 651441
Fax: 01285 650633
E-mail: info@almex.co.uk
Web site: www.almex.co.uk

ATOS ORIGIN
4 Triton Square, Regents Place, London NW1 3HG
Tel: 020 7830 4444
Fax: 020 7830 4445
Web site: www.atosorigin.co.uk

BEMROSEBOOTH LTD
Stockholm Road, Sutton Fields Industrial Estate, Hull HU7 0XY
Tel: 01482 826343
Fax: 01482 371386
E-mail: lprecious@bemrosebooth.com
Web site: www.bemrosebooth.com

*BRITANNIA ROLL/TICKETMEDIA
Maple Works, Old Shoreham Road, Hove BN3 7ED
Tel: 01273 726325
Fax: 01273 324936
E-mail: edmund.jackson@ticketmedia.com
Web site: www.ticketmedia.com

CANN PRINT
Block C, Unit 2, Crookedholm Commercial Centre, Mainroad, Crookedholm, Kilmarnock KA3 6JT
Tel/Fax: 01563 572440

CUBIC TRANSPORTATION SYSTEMS LTD
AFC House, Honeycrock Lane, Salfords, Redhill RH1 5LA
Tel: 01737 782200
Fax: 01737 789759
Web site: www.cubic.com

DE LA RUE
De La Rue House, Jays Close, Viables, Basingstoke RG22 4BS
Tel: 01256 605000
Fax: 01256 605004
Web site: www.delarue.com

*KEITH EDMONDSON
The Garden House, Tittensor, Stoke-on-Trent ST12 9HQ
Tel: 01782 372305
Fax: 01782 351136
E-mail: kedmo.ticket@zoom.co.uk
Web site: www.ticketrolls.co.uk

*ETM SOFTWARE SERVICES
9 Dorset Avenue, Ferndown BH22 8HJ
Tel: 01202 246710
E-mail: info@etmss.com
Web site: www.etmss.com

JOHN GROVES TICKET SYSTEMS
Unit 5, Rennie Business Units, Factory Place, Saltcoats KA21 5LZ
Tel: 01294 471133
Fax: 01294 471166
Web site: www.cambist.se

INIT
Broadway Business Centre, 32a Stoney Street, The Lace Market, Nottingham NG1 1LL
Tel: 0115 988 6916
Web site: www.init-ka.de

*MARK TERRILL TICKET MACHINERY
5 De Grey Close, Lewes BN7 2JR.
Tel: 01273 474816
Fax: 01273 474816
E-mail: mark.terrill@ukonline.co.uk

PAYPOINT PLC
1 The Boulevard, Shire Park, Welwyn Garden City AL7 1EL
Tel: 01707 60300
Email: grahambloye@paypoint.co.uk
Web site: www.paypoint.co.uk

*SCAN COIN LTD
110 Broadway, Salford Quays M50 2UW
Tel: 0161 873 0500
Fax: 0161 873 0501
E-mail: sales@scancoin.co.uk
Web site: www.scancoin.co.uk

SCHADES LTD
Brittain Drive, Codnor Gate Business Park, Ripley DE5 3RZ
Tel: 01773 748721
Fax: 01773 745601
Web site: www.schades.com
E-mail: sales@schades.co.uk

STUART MANUFACTURING CO LTD
Craft House, 135 Hayes Lane, Kenley CR8 5JR
Tel: 020 8668 8107
Fax: 020 8668 8277
E-mail: sales@smco.co.uk
Web site: www.smco.co.uk

THE THOMAS AUTOMATICS CO LTD
Bishop Meadow Road, Loughborough LE11 5RE
Tel: 01509 267611
Fax: 01509 266836
E-mail: sales@thomasa.co.uk
Web site: www.thomasa.co.uk

*TRANSPORT TICKET SERVICES LTD
Yew Tree Cottage, Newcastle, Monmouth NP25 5NT
Tel/Fax: 01600 750650
E-mail: tts@waitrose.com, ticket-machine@waitrose.com

*WAYFARER TRANSIT SYSTEMS LTD
10 Willis Way, Fleets Industrial Estate, Poole BH15 3SS
Tel: 01202 339339
Fax: 01202 339369
E-mail: sales@wayfarer.co.uk
Web site: www.wayfarer.co.uk

*WRIGHTBUS LTD
Galgorm, Ballymena BT42 1PY
Tel: 028 2564 1212
Fax: 028 2564 9703
E-mail: info@wright-bus.com
Web site: www.wright-bus.com

Timetable Display Frames

*M BISSELL DISPLAY LTD
Spring Road, Walsall WS4 1QQ
Tel: 01922 692300
Fax: 01922 693830
E-mail: sales@bisselldisplay.com
Web site: www.bisselldisplay.com

BROADWATER MOULDINGS LTD
Horham, Eye IP21 5JL.
Tel: 01379 384145.
Fax: 01379 384150

*FIRST CHOICE NAMEPLATES, LABELS & SIGNS
Lynden 2c, Russell Avenue, Balderton, Newark NG24 3BT
Tel: 01636 678035
Fax: 01636 707066
E-mail: firstchoice@handbag.com

ZF Aftermarket Support
Your first and last call for ZF parts and service

Adtec Aerauto
Ireland
00 353 (0)46 9055126

Ecodrive
Scotland
0141 774 0808

Ecodrive
Northern England
North Wales
01204 701 812

Powertrain
Central and Southern England
South Wales
01902 366 000

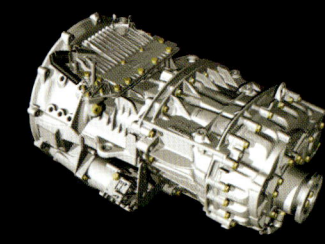

 For ZF Service Solutions call:
0870 607 1231

Toilet Equipment

BRADTECH LTD
Unit 3, Ladford Covert, Seighford, Stafford ST18 9QD
Tel: 01785 282800
E-mail: sales@bradtech.ltd.uk
Web site: www.bradtech.ltd.uk

CARLYLE BUS & COACH LTD
Great Bridge Street, Swan Village, West Bromwich B70 0X4
Tel: 0121 524 1200
Fax: 0121 524 1201
E-mail: admin@carlyleplc.co.uk

ELSAN LTD
Bellbrook Park, Uckfield TN22 1QF
Tel: 01825 748200
Fax: 01825 761212
E-mail: sales@elsan.co.uk
Web site: www.elsan.co.uk

EXPRESS COACH REPAIRS LTD
Outgang Lane, Pickering YO18 7EL.
Tel: 01751 475215.

*THE LAWTON MOTOR BODY BUILDING CO LTD
Knutsford Road, Church Lawton, Stoke-on-Trent ST7 3DN
Tel: 01270 882056
Fax: 01270 883014
E-mail: info@lawtonmotorbody.co.uk
Web site: www.lawtonmotorbody.co.uk

*PSV PRODUCTS
PO Box 166, Warrington WA4 5FG
Tel: 0870 062 4488
Fax: 0870 062 4499
E-mail: mike@psvproducts.com
Web site: www.psvproducts.com

SHADES TECHNICS
Marshgate Drive, Hertford SG13 7AJ
Tel: 01992 501683
Fax: 01992 501669
E-mail: sales@shades-technics.com
Web site: www.shades-technics.com

METRONET (REW) LTD
130 Bollo Lane, London W3 8BZ.
Tel: 020 7918 6666.
Fax: 020 7918 6599.
E-mail: fraser@r-e-w.co.uk
Web site: www.r-e-w.co.uk

MULTIPART PSV
Pilling Lane, Chorley PR7 3EL.
Tel: 01257 225577.
Fax: 01257 225575.
E-mail: info@multipart.com
Web site: www.multipart.com

*SHAWSON SUPPLY LTD
12 Station Road, Saintfield BT24 7DU
Tel: 028 9751 0994
Fax: 028 9751 0816
E-mail: shawsondiesel@btopenworld.com
Web site: www.shawsonsupply.com

*UNITEC
Parts Division, Denby Way, Hellaby, Rotherham S66 8HR
Tel: 01709 792000
Fax: 01709 792009
E-mail: parts@optare.com

*UNITEC LONDON
Unit 5, Gateway 25, Weston Avenue, West Thurrock RM20 3ZD
Tel: 01708 892440
Fax: 01708 862125
E-mail: london.service@optare.com

*UNITEC ROTHERHAM
Denby Way, Hellaby, Rotherham S66 8HR
Tel: 01709 535101
Fax: 01709 535103
E-mail: rotherham.service@optare.com

*UNITEC SCOTLAND
Unit 7, Cumbernauld Business Park, Ward Park Road, Cumbernauld G67 3JZ
Tel: 01236 726738
Fax: 01236 795651
E-mail: scotland.service@optare.com

VOITH TURBO LTD
Regent House, Rump Lane, Hayes UB3 3BP
Tel: 020 8561 2131
Fax: 020 8569 1726
E-mail:turbo.uk@voith.com
Web site: www.voith.com

*VOR TRANSMISSIONS LTD
Little London House, St Anne's Road, Willenhall WV13 1DT
Tel: 0800 018 4141
Fax: 01902 603868
E-mail: vor@globalnet.co.uk
Web site: www.vor.co.uk

*ZF POWERTRAIN
Stringes Close, Willenhall WV13 1LE
Tel: 01902 366000
Fax: 01902 366504
E-mail: sales@powertrain.org.uk
Web site: www.powertrain.org.uk

Transmission Overhaul

BUSS BIZZ
Goughs Transport Depot, Morestead, Winchester SO21 1JD.
Tel: 01962 715555/66.
Fax: 01962 714868.

GARDNER PARTS LTD
Barton Hall, Hardy Street, Eccles, Manchester M30 7WA.
Tel: 0161 278 9200
Fax: 0161 787 7549.

*HL SMITH TRANSMISSIONS LTD
Enterprise Business Park, Cross Road, Albrighton, Wolverhampton WV7 3BJ
Tel: 01902 373011
Fax: 01902 373608

LH GROUP (SERVICES) LTD
Graycar Business Park, Barton Turns, Barton Under Needwood DE13 8EN.
Tel: 01283 713615.
Fax: 01283 713551.
E-mail: l/h/llords@classic.msn.com

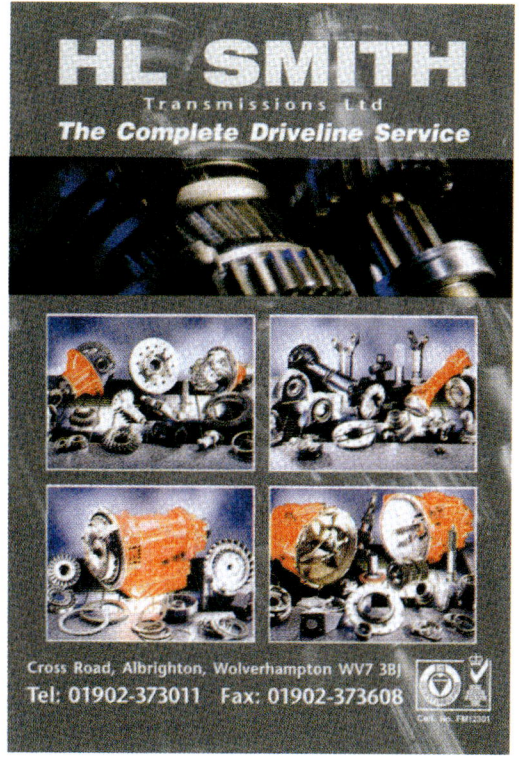

Trade Directory

Interface Fabrics, the company behind the Furtex brand, has changed. We're now Camira, providing an unrivalled one-stop-shop in fabrics for the mass passenger transportation market.

- traditional wool moquettes through to flat wovens
- seating upholstery, wall & ceiling trims, anti-macassars and curtaining
- available on an ex-stock basis
- custom made service available
- recognised for environmental best practice including green electricity, energy management and recycling initiatives

camira

www.camirafabrics.com

Tree Guards

*GABRIEL & CO LTD
Abro Works, 10 Hay Hall Road, Tyseley, Birmingham B11 2AU
Tel: 0121 248 3333
Fax: 0121 248 3330
E-mail: contact@gabrielco.com
Web site: www.gabrielco.com

Tyres

DUNLOP TYRES LTD
TyreFort, 88-98 Wingfoot Way, Birmingham B24 9HY
Tel: 0121 306 6000
Web site: www.dunloptyres.co.uk

SNOWCHAINS EUROPRODUCTS
Borough Green TN15 8DG
Tel: 01732 884408
Web site: www.snowchains.co.uk

*UNITEC LONDON
Unit 5, Gateway 25, Weston Avenue, West Thurrock RM20 3ZD
Tel: 01708 892440
Fax: 01708 862125
E-mail: london.service@optare.com

*UNITEC ROTHERHAM
Denby Way, Hellaby, Rotherham S66 8HR
Tel: 01709 535101
Fax: 01709 535103
E-mail: rotherham.service@optare.com

*UNITEC SCOTLAND
Unit 7, Cumbernauld Business Park, Ward Park Road, Cumbernauld G67 3JZ
Tel: 01236 726738
Fax: 01236 795651
E-mail: scotland.service@optare.com

Uniforms

ALLEN & DOUGLAS CORPORATE CLOTHING LTD
Compton Park, Wildmere Road, Banbury OX16 3EZ
Tel: 01295 228456
Fax: 01295 278972
E-mail: telesales@aandd.co.uk
Web site: www.aandd.co.uk

LEISUREWEAR DIRECT LTD
Harpur Hill Industrial Estate, Harpur Hill, Buxton SK17 9JL
Tel: 01298 74737
Fax: 01298 71674
E-mail: jane@leisureweardirect.com
Web site: www.leisureweardirect.com

IMAGE FIRST CORPORATE CLOTHING LTD
11 Hudswell Road, Leeds LS10 1AG
Tel: 0113 243 3855
Fax: 0113 242 1040
E-Mail: rob@image-first.co.uk
Web site: www.image-first.co.uk

R&J HANDLEY UNIFORM
27-29 Barkston House, Croydon Street, Leeds LS11 9RT.
Tel: 0113 245 7008
Fax: 0113 245 7009
E-mail: tor@tordesigns.com

*RAINBOW CORPORATEWEAR
Gosforth Road, Derby DE24 8HU
Tel: 01332 342616
Fax: 01332 362328
www.rainbow-corporatewear.co.uk

TALISMAN
26 North Road, Yate BS37 7DA
Tel: 01454 335155
Fax: 01454 335133
E-mail: sales@talisman.ms.com
Web site: www.talisman.ms.com

Upholstery

ABACUS TUBULAR PRODUCTS LTD
Abacus House, Highlode Industrial Estate, Ramsey PE26 2RB
Tel: 01487 710700
Fax: 01487 710626
E-mail: info@abacus-tp.com
Web site: www.abacus-tp.com

*AUTOMOTIVE TEXTILE INDUSTRIES
Unit 15 & 16, Priest Court, Springfield Business Park, Grantham NG31 7BG
Tel: 01476 593050
Fax: 01476 593607
E-mail: sales@autotex.com
Web site: www.autotex.com

*BLACKPOOL TRIM SHOPS LTD
Brun Grove, Blackpool FY1 6PG
Tel: 01253 766762
Fax: 01253 798443
E-mail: sales@blackpooltrimshops.co.uk
Web site: www.blackpooltrimshops.co.uk

BRIDGE OF WEIR LEATHER CO LTD
Clydesdale Works, Bridge of Weir PA11 3LF.
Tel: 01505 612132.
Fax: 01505 614964.

DUOFLEX LTD
Trimmingham House, 2 Shires Road, Buckingham Road Industrial Estate, Brackley NN13 7EZ
Tel: 01280 701366
Fax: 01280 704799
E-mail: sales@duoflex.co.uk
Web site: www.duoflex.co.uk

EXPRESS COACH REPAIRS LTD
Outgang Lane, Pickering YO18 7EL.
Tel: 01751 475215.

FIRTH FURNISHINGS LTD
PO Box 22, Flush Mills, Heckmondwike WF16 0EP.
Tel: 01924 406141.
Fax: 01924 401128.

*INTERFACE FABRICS LTD
Hopton Mills, Mirfield WF1 8HE
Tel: 01924 490591
Web site: www.interfacefabrics.com

JOHN HOLDSWORTH & CO LTD
Shaw Lodge Mills, Halifax HX3 9ET
Tel: 01422 433000
Fax: 01422 433300
E-mail: info@holdsworth.co.uk
Web site: www.holdsworth.co.uk

*THE LAWTON MOTOR BODY BUILDING CO LTD
Knutsford Road, Church Lawton, Stoke-on-Trent ST7 3DN
Tel: 01270 882056
Fax: 01270 883014
E-mail: info@lawtonmotorbody.co.uk
Web site: www.lawtonmotorbody.co.uk

MARTYN INDUSTRIALS LTD
5 Brunel Way, Durranhill Industrial Esate, Carlisle CA1 3NQ
Tel: 01228 544000
Fax: 01228 544001
E-mail: enquiries@martyn-industrials.co.uk
Web site: www.martyn-industrials.com

METRONET (REW) LTD
130 Bollo Lane, London W3 8BZ.
Tel: 020 7918 6666.
Fax: 020 7918 6599.
E-mail: fraser@r-e-w.co.uk
Web site: www.r-e-w.co.uk

WIDNEY UK LTD
Plume Street, Aston, Birmingham B6 7SA.
Tel: 0121 327 5500.
Fax: 0121 328 2466.
E-mail: richard@widney.co.uk

Vacuum Systems

*SMART CENTRAL COACH SYSTEMS
1 Eastholme Court, Belmont, Hereford HR2 7UH
Tel: 01432 276380
Fax: 01432 351800
Web site: www.smartcoachsystems.co.uk
E-mail: info@smartcoachsystems.co.uk

Vehicle Washing & Washers

CRYSTALKLEEN LTD
8 Fifth Avenue, Hayes UB3 2ER
Tel: 020 8581 0599
Email: crystalkleen@blueyonder.co.uk

*ATLANTIS INTERNATIONAL LTD
18 Weldon Road, Loughborough LE11 5RA
Tel: 01509 233770
Fax: 01509 210542
E-mail: peterspencer@atlantisint.co.uk
Web site: www.atlantisint.co.uk

MONOWASH (BRUSH REPLACEMENT SERVICE)
8 Contessa Close, Farnborough BR6 7ER.
Tel: 01689 860061.
Fax: 01689 861469

NATIONWIDE CLEANING & SUPPORT SERVICES LTD
Airport House, Purley Way, Croydon CR0 0XZ
Tel: 020 8288 3580
Web site: www.nationwidefm.com

SMITH BROS & WEBB
Britannia House, Arden Forest Industrial Estate, Alcester B49 6EX
Tel: 01789 400096
Fax: 01789 400231
E-mail: jbp@vehicle-washing-systems.co.uk
Web site: www.vehicle-washing-systems.co.uk

*SOMERS TOTALKARE LTD
15 Forge Trading Estate, Mucklow Hill, Halesowen B62 8TR
Tel: 0121 585 2700
Fax: 0121 585 2725
E-mail: sales@somerstotalkare.co.uk
Web site: www.somerstotalkare.co.uk

*WINDOW CLEAN SERVICES
309 Cow Gate, Edinburgh EH1 1NA
Tel: 0131 556 5720.
Fax: 0131 558 7377

Wheeltrims & Covers

AUTOMATE WHEEL COVERS LTD
California Mills, Oxford Road, Gomersal BD19 4HQ
Tel: 01274 862700
Fax: 01274 851989
E-mail: sales@wheelcovers.co.uk
Web site: www.euroliners.com

HATCHER COMPONENTS LTD
Broadwater Road, Framlingham IP13 9LL.
Tel: 01728 723675.
Fax: 01728 724475.

J. HIPWELL & SON
427 Warwick Road, Greet, Birmingham B20 1JE.
Tel: 0121 706 7175.
Fax: 0121 706 0502

*THE LAWTON MOTOR BODY BUILDING CO LTD
Knutsford Road, Church Lawton, Stoke-on-Trent ST7 3DN
Tel: 01270 882056
Fax: 01270 883014
E-mail: info@lawtonmotorbody.co.uk
Web site: www.lawtonmotorbody.co.uk

*UNITEC
Parts Division, Denby Way, Hellaby, Rotherham S66 8HR
Tel: 01709 792000
Fax: 01709 792009
E-mail: parts@optare.com

Windows and Windscreens

AUTOGLASS COACH & BUS SERVICES
PO Box 343, Goldington Road, Bedford MK40 3BX.
Tel: 01234 279572.
Fax: 01234 279460.
Central control: Tel: 0800 222777.
Tel: 01234 279559

BRITAX PMG LTD
Bressingby Industrial Estate, Bridlington YO16 4SJ
Tel: 01262 670161
Fax: 01262 605666
E-mail: info@britax-pmg.com
Web site: www.britax-pmg.com

CARLYLE BUS & COACH LTD
Great Bridge Street, Swan Village, West Bromwich B70 0X4
Tel: 0121 524 1200
Fax: 0121 524 1201
E-mail: admin@carlyleplc.co.uk

EXPRESS COACH REPAIRS LTD
Outgang Lane, Pickering YO18 7EL
Tel: 01751 475215.

B HEPWORTH & CO LTD
Hepworth House, Brook Street, Redditch B98 8NF
Tel: 01527 61243
Fax: 01527 66836
Web site: www.b-hepworth.com
E-mail: bhepworth@b-hepworth.com

INDUSTRIAL & COMMERCIAL WINDOW CO LTD
Unit 2, Caldervale Industrial Estate, Horbury Junction, Wakefield WF4 5ER.
Tel: 01924 260106.
Fax: 01924 260152.

*J W GLASS LTD
Units 6 & 7, Scropton Road, Hatton DE65 5DT
Tel: 01283 520202
Fax: 01283 520022
E-mail: info@jwglass.co.uk
Web site: www.jwglass.co.uk

*THE LAWTON MOTOR BODY BUILDING CO LTD
Knutsford Road, Church Lawton, Stoke-on-Trent ST7 3DN
Tel: 01270 882056
Fax: 01270 883014
E-mail: info@lawtonmotorbody.co.uk
Web site: www.lawtonmotorbody.co.uk

MULTIPART PSV
Pilling Lane, Chorley PR7 3EL.
Tel: 01257 225577.
Fax: 01257 225575.
E-mail: info@multipart.com
Web site: www.multipart.com

*NEALINE WINDSCREEN WIPER PRODUCTS
Unit 1, The Sidings Industrial Estate, Birdingbury Road, Marton CV23 9RX
Tel: 01926 633256
Fax: 01926 632600

*PARTLINE LTD
Dockfield Road, Shipley BD17 7AZ
Tel: 01274 531531
Fax: 01274 531088
E-mail: sales@partline.co.uk
Web site: www.partline.co.uk

PERCY LANE PRODUCTS LTD
Lichfield Road, Tamworth B79 7TL
Tel: 01827 63821
Fax: 01827 310159
E-mail: sales@percy-lane.co.uk
Web site: www.percy-lane.co.uk

*PLAXTON COACH SALES CENTRE
Ryton Road, Anston, Sheffield S25 4DL
Tel: 01909 551155
Fax: 01909 567994
E-mail: coaches@plaxtonlimited.co.uk
Web site: www.plaxtonlimited.co.uk

*PSV GLASS
Central Distribution Centre
Hillbottom Road, High Wycombe HP12 4HJ
Tel: 01494 533131
Fax: 01494 462675
Northern Distribution Centre
Stakehill Distribution Park, Middleton, Greater Manchester M24 2FL
Scottish Distribution Centre
Bessemer Drive, Kelvin Industrial Estate, East Kilbride G75 0QX
E-mail: sales@psvglass.co.uk
Web site: www.psvglass.co.uk

*UNITEC
Parts Division, Denby Way, Hellaby, Rotherham S66 8HR
Tel: 01709 792000
Fax: 01709 792009
E-mail: parts@optare.com

*UNITEC LONDON
Unit 5, Gateway 25, Weston Avenue, West Thurrock RM20 3ZD
Tel: 01708 892440
Fax: 01708 862125
E-mail: london.service@optare.com

*UNITEC ROTHERHAM
Denby Way, Hellaby, Rotherham S66 8HR
Tel: 01709 535101
Fax: 01709 535103
E-mail: rotherham.service@optare.com

*UNITEC SCOTLAND
Unit 7, Cumbernauld Business Park, Ward Park Road, Cumbernauld G67 3JZ
Tel: 01236 726738
Fax: 01236 795651
E-mail: scotland.service@optare.com

VOLVO COACH CENTRE
Brisco Avenue, off Belton Road West, Loughborough LE11 5HP.
Tel: 01509 217777.
Fax: 01509 260978.

WIDNEY UK LTD
Plume Street, Aston, Birmingham B6 7SA.
Tel: 0121 327 5500.
Fax: 0121 328 2466.
E-mail: richard@widney.co.uk

INDUSTRY SERVICE PROVIDERS

Accident Investigation

KERNOW ASSOCIATES
18 Tresawla Court, Tolvaddon, Camborne TR14 0HF.
Tel/Fax: 01209 711870.
E-mail: 106472.3264@compuserve.com

Accountancy & Audit

BARRONS CHARTERED ACCOUNTANTS
Monometer House, Rectory Grove, Leigh on Sea SS9 2HN
Tel: 01702 481910
Fax: 01702 481911
E-mail: mail@barrons-bds.com
Web site: www.barrons-bds.com

Advertising Contractors

DECKER MEDIA LTD
Decker House, Lowater Street, Carlton, Nottingham NG4 1JJ
Tel: 0115 940 2406.
Fax: 0115 940 2407.
E-mail: sales@deckermedia.co.uk,
Web site: www.deckermedia.co.uk

Advisory Services

*ADGROUP LTD
Ad House, East Parade, Harrogate HG1 5LT
Tel: 01423 526253
Fax: 01423 502522
E-mail: info@adbus.info
Web site: www.adbus.info

AD COACH SALES
Newbridge Coach Depot, Witheridge EX16 8PY
Tel: 01884 860787
Fax: 01884 860711
E-mail: ggoodwin@adcoachsales.co.uk
Web site: www.adcoachsales.co.uk

ADG TRANSPORT CONSULTANCY
Oak Cottage, Royal Oak, Machen CF83 8SN
Tel: 01633 441491
Fax: 01633 440591
E-mail: a.dgettins@btinternet.com

AKM TECHSERVICES
Unit F2, Scope House, Weston Road, Crewe CW1 6DD
Tel: 01270 250829
E-mail: akmtec@aol.com

ANDY IZATT
10 Briton Court, St Thomas's Road, Spalding PE11 2TS
Tel: 01775 712542
E-mail: andy.izatt@btinternet.com
Web site: andy.izatt.btinternet.co.uk

*AUSTIN ANALYTICS
Crown House, 183 High Street, Bottisham, Cambridge CB5 9BB
Tel: 01223 813151
Fax: 07005 946854
E-mail: john@j-austin.co.uk
Web site: www.analytics.co.uk

*BORLAND, WINDER-DIXON LLP
3 Axe View, Axe Road, Drimpton, Beaminster DT8 3RJ
Tel: 01460 72769
Fax: 01460 72769
E-mail: chris.borland@tiscali.co.uk

CAPOCO DESIGN
Stone Cross House, Chickgrove, Salisbury SP3 6NA
Tel: 01722 716722
Fax: 01722 716226

*COLIN BUCHANAN
Newcombe House, 45 Notting Hill Gate, London W11 3PB
Tel: 020 7309 7000
Fax: 020 7309 0906
E-mail: london@cbuchanan.co.uk
Web site: www.cbuchanan.co.uk

*COACH DIRECT
The Coach House, 22 South Street, Rochford SS4 1BQ
Tel: 0870 550 2069
Fax: 0870 070 2069
E-mail: info@coachdirect.co.uk
Web site: www.coachdirect.co.uk

*CREATIVE MANAGEMENT DEVELOPMENT LTD
52 Okebourne Park, Liden, Swindon SN3 6AJ
Tel: 07771 732185
Fax: 01793 491786
E-mail: jowencmd@aol.com
Web site: www.cmd-training.co.uk

*ELLIS TRANSPORT SERVICES
61 Bodycoats Road, Chandlers Ford SO53 2HA
Tel: 023 8027 0447
Fax: 023 8027 6736
E-mail: info@ellistransportservices.co.uk

ETM SOFTWARE SERVICES
9 Dorset Avenue, Ferndown BH22 8HJ
Tel: 01202 246710
Fax: 01202 687537
E-mail: info@etmss.com
Web site: www.etmss.com

Trade Directory

FCAV & CO
Brooklyn House, Coleford Road, Bream
GL15 6EU
Tel: 01594 564552
Fax: 01594 564556
E-mail: info@fcav.co.uk
Web site: www.fcav.co.uk

*GOSKILLS
Concorde House, Trinity Park, Solihull
B37 7UQ
Tel: 0121 635 5520
Fax: 0121 635 5521
E-mail: info@goskills.org
Web site: www.goskills.org

*MINIMISE YOUR RISK
11 Chatsworth Park, Telscombe Cliffs
BN10 7DZ
Tel: 01273 580189
Fax: 01273 580189
E-mail: minimise@btconnect.com
Web site: www.minimiseyourrisk.co.uk

MVA
MVA House, Victoria Way, Woking
GU21 1DD
Tel: 01483 755207
Web site: www.mva-group.com

*PROFESSIONAL TRANSPORT SERVICES
12 Silverdale, Stanford-le-Hope SS17 8BG
Tel: 01375 675262
Web site: www.proftranserv.co.uk
E-mail: enquiries@proftranserv.com

*STEPHEN C MORRIS
PO Box 119, Shepperton TW17 8UX
Tel: 01932 232574
E-mail: buswriter@btinternet.com

*SALTIRE COMMUNICATIONS
39 Lilyhill Terrace, Edinburgh EH8 7DR
Tel: 0131 652 0205
E-mail: gavin-booth@btconnect.com

TRANSPORTATION MANAGEMENT SOLUTIONS
PO Box 15174, Glasgow G3 6WB.
Tel: 0141 332 4733.
Fax: 0141 354 0076.
E-mail: tramsol@aol.com

*WARD INTERNATIONAL CONSULTING LTD
Funtley Court, 19 Funtley Hill, Fareham
PO16 7UY
Tel: 01329 280280
Fax: 01329 221010
E-mail: info@wardint.co.uk
Web site: www.wardint.com

Artwork

*ADGROUP LTD
Ad House, East Parade, Harrogate HG1 5LT
Tel: 01423 526253
Fax: 01423 502522
E-mail: info@adbus.info
Web site: www.adbus.info

BEST IMPRESSIONS
15 Starfield Road, London W12 9SN
Tel: 020 8740 6443
Fax: 020 8740 9134
E-mail: talk2us@best-impressions.co.uk
Web site: www.best-impressions.co.uk

BRITANNIA ROLL/TICKETMEDIA
Maple Works, Old Shoreham Road, Hove
BN3 7ED
Tel: 01273 726325
Fax: 01273 324936
E-mail: edmund.jackson@ticketmedia.com
Web site: www.ticketmedia.com

FIGUREHEAD DATA SYSTEMS
Felindre, Swansea SA5 7PP
Tel: 01792 883155
Fax: 01792 884934
E-mail: BusTimes@aol.com
Web site: www.bustimes.com

FWT
Whittington House, 764-768 Holloway Road,
London N19 3JQ
Tel: 020 7281 2161
Fax: 020 7281 4117
E-mail: sales@fwt.co.uk
Web site: www.fwt.co.uk

TONY GREAVES GRAPHICS
19 Perth Mount, Horsforth, Leeds LS18 5SH
Tel/Fax: 0113 258 4795
E-mail: tony@greavesgraphics.fsnet.co.uk

*HATTS COACHWORKS & SERVICES
Foxham, Chippenham SN15 4NB
Tel: 01249 740444
Fax: 01249 740447
E-mail: adrian@hattstravel.co.uk
Web site: www.hattstravel.co.uk

MCV BUS & COACH LTD
Sterling Place, Elean Business Park, Sutton
CB6 2QE
Tel: 01353 773000
Fax: 01353 773001
E-mail: vernon.edwards@mcv-uk.com

NEERMAN & PARTNERS
c/o 22 Larbre Crescent, Whickham,
Newcastle-upon-Tyne NE16 5YG
Tel: 0191 488 6258
Web site: www.neerman.net
E-mail: executive@neerman.net

*PLUM CREATIONS
Plum Publishing Ltd, Suite 1, Cornerstone
House, Stafford Park 13, Telford TF3 3AZ
Tel: 01952 204920
Fax: 01952 204929
E-mail: steve.rooney@busandcoach.com
Web site: www.busandcoach.com

*TIME TRAVEL UK
247 Bradford Road, Stanningley, Pudsey
LS28 6QB
Tel: 0113 255 1188
E-mail: nick.baldwin@tinyworld.co.uk

Breakdown & Recovery Services

NB - Operator lists also indicate bus and coach operators able to provide breakdown and recovery services.

AD COACH SALES
Newbridge Coach Depot, Witheridge
EX16 8PY
Tel: 01884 860787
Fax: 01884 860711
E-mail: ggoodwin@adcoachsales.co.uk
Web site: www.adcoachsales.co.uk

*BRITISH BUS SALES
c/o Mike Nash, PO Box 534, Dorking
RH5 5XB
Tel: 07836 656692
E-mail: nashionalbus1@btconnect.com
Web site: www.britishbussales.co.uk

*BUZZLINES LTD
Unit G1, Lympne Industrial Park, Hythe
CT21 4LR
Tel: 01303 261870
Fax: 01303 230093
Web site: www.buzzlines.co.uk

COACH-AID
Unit 2, Brindley Close, Tollgate Industrial
Estate, Stafford ST16 3SU
Tel: 01785 222666
E-mail: workshop@coach-aid.com
Web site: www.coach-aid.com

DRURY & DRURY
Unit 6, Cobbs Wood Industrial Estate,
Brunswick Road, Ashford TN23 1EH.
Tel: 01303 610555.
Fax: 01303 610666.
E-mail: martinstrange@channelcommercials.co.uk

*HATTS COACHWORKS & SERVICES
Foxham, Chippenham SN15 4NB
Tel: 01249 740444
Fax: 01249 740447
E-mail: adrian@hattstravel.co.uk
Web site: www.hattstravel.co.uk

LANTERN RECOVERY SPECIALISTS PLC
Lantern House, 39/41 High Street, Potters
Bar EN6 5AJ
Tel: 0870 6090333
Fax: 01707 640450
Web site: www.lrs.uk.com
E-mail: bob@lrs.uk.com

THOMAS HARDIE – WIGAN
Lockett Road, Ashton-in-Makerfield
WN4 8DE.
Tel: 01942 505124
Fax: 01942 505119

MASS SPECIAL ENGINEERING LTD
Anston, Sheffield S25 4SD.
Tel: 01909 550480.
Fax: 01909 550486.

*TRUCKALIGN CO LTD
VIP Trading Estate, Anchor & Hope Lane,
London SE7 7RY
Tel: 020 8858 3781
Fax: 020 8858 3781

*UNITEC LONDON
Unit 5, Gateway 25, Weston Avenue,
West Thurrock RM20 3ZD
Tel: 01708 892440
Fax: 01708 862125
E-mail: london.service@optare.com

*UNITEC ROTHERHAM
Denby Way, Hellaby, Rotherham
S66 8HR
Tel: 01709 535101
Fax: 01709 535103
E-mail: rotherham.service@optare.com

*UNITEC SCOTLAND
Unit 7, Cumbernauld Business Park,
Ward Park Road, Cumbernauld G67 3JZ
Tel: 01236 726738
Fax: 01236 795651
E-mail: scotland.service@optare.com

Trade Directory

Coach Driver Agencies

DRIVER HIRE CANTERBURY
East Suite, Parsonage Office, Nackington, Canterbury CT4 7AD
Tel: 01227 479529
Fax: 01227 479531
E-mail: canterbury@driver-hire.co.uk

FRASER EAGLE MANAGEMENT SERVICES
Technology Management Centre, St James Square, Accrington BB5 0RE
Tel: 01254 357777
Fax: 01254 879461
E-mail: info@frasereagle.com
Web site: www.frasereagle.com

*IBPTS
43 Cage Lane, Felixstowe IP11 9BJ
Tel: 01394 672344
Fax: 01394 672344
E-mail: info@ibpts.com
Web site: www.ibpts.com

THE PENINSULA GROUP
Trematon Drive, St Peter's Way, Ivybridge PL21 0HT
Tel (office hrs): 01752 896471
Mobile/Direct: 07909 695438
Owner: Mike Yedermann **Touring Man**: Brian Madge
Associated companies: Peninsula Cars & Eastward Coaches (see operators section - Devon)

Cleaning services

*TARA SUPPORT SERVICES LTD
32 Derby Road, Enfield EN3 4AW
Tel: 0845 450 0607
Fax: 0845 450 0608
E-mail: info@tarasupport.co.uk
Web site: www.tarasupport.co.uk

Coach Hire Brokers

AVENTA
66B Victoria Road, Horley RH6 7PZ.
Tel: 01293 825001.
Fax: 01293 825002.
E-mail: info@aventa.co.uk
Web site: www.aventa.co.uk

*COACH DIRECT
The Coach House, 22 South Street, Rochford SS4 1BQ
Tel: 0870 550 2069
Fax: 0870 070 2069
E-mail: info@coachdirect.co.uk
Web site: www.coachdirect.co.uk

*COACHFINDER LTD
Woodbank House, 24 Matley Close, Newton, Hyde SK14 4UE
Tel: 0161 368 7877
Web site: www.coachfinder.uk.com

FRASER EAGLE MANAGEMENT SERVICES
Technology Management Centre, St James Square, Accrington BB5 0RE
Tel: 01254 357777
Fax: 01254 879461
E-mail: info@frasereagle.com
Web site: www.frasereagle.com

HAYWARD TRAVEL (CARDIFF)
2 Murch Crescent, Dinas Powys CF64 4RF
Tel: 029 2051 5551
Fax: 029 2051 5113
E-mail: haytvl@aol.com

*IBPTS
43 Cage Lane, Felixstowe IP11 9BJ
Tel: 01394 672344
Fax: 01394 672344
E-mail: info@ibpts.com
Web site: www.ibpts.com

*NEXT BUS LTD
Vincients Road, Bumpers Farm Industrial Estate, Chippenham SN14 6QA
Tel: 01249 462462
Fax: 01249 448844
E-mail: sales@next-bus.co.uk
Web site: www.next-bus.co.uk

Coach Interchange & Parking Facilities

T & E DOCHERTY
40 Bank Street, Irvine KA12 0LP
Tel: 01294 278440
Web site: www.coach-hires.co.uk

SAMMYS GARAGE
Victoria Coach Station, Arrivals Hall, 3 Eccleston Place, London SW1W 9NF
Tel: 020 7793 7533/7730/8867

*TOP LINE TRAVEL OF YORK LTD
23 Hospital Fields Road, Fulford Industrial Estate, York YO10 4EW
Tel: 01904 655585
Web site: www.toplinetravelofyork.co.uk

VICTORIA COACH STATION LTD
164 Buckingham Palace Road, London SW1W 9TP
Tel: 020 7824 0000
Fax: 020 7824 0008
Web site: www.tfl.co.uk

Computer Systems/Software

ACIS
ACIS House, Knaves Beech Business Centre, Loudwater HP10 9QR
Tel: 01628 524900
Fax: 01628 523222
E-mail: enquiries@acis.uk.com
Web site: www.acis.uk.com

AKM TECHSERVICES
Unit F2, Scope House, Weston Road, Crewe CW1 6DD
Tel: 01270 250829
E-mail: akmtec@aol.com

AUTOPRO SOFTWARE
1 Kingsmeadow, Norton Cross, Runcorn WA7 6PB
Tel: 01928 715962
Fax: 01928 714538
E-mail: sales@autoprouk.com
Web site: www.autoprosoftware.com

CYBERLYNE COMMUNICATIONS LTD
Unit 5, Hatfield Way, South Church Industrial Esate, Bishop Auckland DL14 6XF
Tel: 01388 773761
Fax: 01388 773778
E-mail: david@cyberlynecommunications.co.uk
Web site: www.cyberlynecommunications.co.uk

DISTINCTIVE SYSTEMS LTD
Amy Johnson Way, York YO30 4XT
Tel: 01904 692269
Fax: 01904 690810
E-mail: sales@distinctive-systems.com
Web site: www.distinctive-systems.com

ETM SOFTWARE SERVICES
9 Dorset Avenue, Ferndown BH22 8HJ
Tel: 01202 246710
Fax: 01202 687537
E-mail: info@etmss.com
Web site: www.etmss.com

FIGUREHEAD DATA SYSTEMS
Felindre, Swansea SA5 7PP
Tel: 01792 883155
Fax: 01792 884934
E-mail: BusTimes@aol.com
Web site: www.bustimes.com

*GRAMPIAN SOFTWARE
40 Carden Place, Aberdeen AB10 1UP
Tel: 01224 627600
Fax: 01224 627637
E-mail: info@grampian-software.co.uk
Web site: www.grampian-software.co.uk

JOHN GROVES TICKET SYSTEMS
Unit 5, Rennie Business Units, Factory Place, Saltcoats KA21 5LZ
Tel: 01294 471133
Fax: 01294 471166
Web site: www.cambist.se

INOVAS LTD
1 Glenbervie Business Park, Larbert, Falkirk FK5 4RB
Tel: 01324 682268
Fax: 01324 682269
Web site: www.inovas.co.uk
E-mail: info@inovas.co.uk

ROEVILLE COMPUTER SYSTEMS
Hay Green, Fishlake, Doncaster DN7 5JY
Tel: 01302 841333
Fax: 01302 843966
E-mail: sales@roeville.com
Web site: www.roeville.com

TACHOGRAPH BUREAUX LTD
Lodge Farm, Kineton CV35 0JH
Tel/Fax: 01926 641224
E-mail: peter.day@tachograph-bureaux.co.uk
Web site: www.tachograph-bureaux.co.uk

TAGTRONICS LTD
Suite 410, Daisyfield Business Centre, Appleby Street, Blackburn BB1 3BL
Tel: 01254 297732
Fax: 01254 698484
E-mail: info@tagtronics.co.uk
Web site: www.tagtronics.co.uk

Trade Directory

TRANMAN SOLUTIONS
Thornbury Office Park, Midland Way, Thornbury BS35 2BS.
Tel: 01454 874000.
Fax: 01454 874001.
E-mail: enquire@tranman.co.uk

*TRAVEL INFORMATION SYSTEMS
Grand Union House, 20 Kentish Town Road, London NW1 9NX
Tel: 020 7428 1288
Fax: 020 7267 2745
E-mail: enquiries@travelinfosystems.com
Web site: www.travelinfosystems.com

Consultants

ADG TRANSPORT CONSULTANCY
Oak Cottage, Royal Oak, Machen CF83 8SN
Tel: 01633 441491
Fax: 01633 440591
E-mail: a.dgettins@btinternet.com

AKM TECHSERVICES
Unit F2, Scope House, Weston Road, Crewe CW1 6DD
Tel: 01270 250829
E-mail: akmtec@aol.com

ATKINS
Television House, Mount Street, Manchester M2 5NT.
Tel: 0161 839 3113
Fax: 0161 839 3137
E-mail: peter.kelly@atkinsglobal.com
Web site: www.atkinsglobal.com

*AUSTIN ANALYTICS
Crown House, 183 High Street, Bottisham, Cambridge CB5 9BB
Tel: 01223 813151
Fax: 07005 946854
E-mail: john@j-austin.co.uk
Web site: www.analytics.co.uk

AUTOPRO SOFTWARE
1 Kingsmeadow, Norton Cross, Runcorn WA7 6PB
Tel: 01928 715962
Fax: 01928 714538
E-mail: sales@autoprouk.com
Web site: www.autoprosoftware.com

AVENTA
66B Victoria Road, Horley RH6 7DZ.
Tel: 01293 825001.
Fax: 01293 825002.
E-mail: info@aventa.co.uk
Web site: www.aventa.co.uk

BESTCHART LTD
6A Mims Yard, Down Road, Horndean, Waterlooville PO8 0YP
Tel: 023 9259 7707
Fax: 023 9259 1700
E-mail: info@bestchart.co.uk
Web site: www.bestchart.co.uk

*CAREYBROOK LTD
PO Box 205, Southam CV47 0ZL
Tel: 01926 813619
Fax: 01926 814898
E-mail: cb.ltd@btinternet.com
Web site: www.careybrook.com

COACH DIRECT
The Coach House, 22 South Street, Rochford SS4 1BQ
Tel: 0870 550 2069
Fax: 0870 070 2069
E-mail: info@coachdirect.co.uk
Web site: www.coachdirect.co.uk

*COLIN BUCHANAN
Newcombe House, 45 Notting Hill Gate, London W11 3PB
Tel: 020 7309 7000
Fax: 020 7309 0906
E-mail: london@cbuchanan.co.uk
Web site: www.cbuchanan.co.uk

*CREATIVE MANAGEMENT DEVELOPMENT LTD
52 Okebourne Park, Liden, Swindon SN3 6AJ
Tel: 07771 732185
Fax: 01793 491786
E-mail: jowencmd@aol.com
Web site: www.cmd-training.co.uk

CRONER CCH GROUP LTD
145 London Road, Kingston upon Thames KT2 6SR.
Tel: 020 8247 1261.
Fax: 020 8547 2638.
E-mail: info@croner.cch.co.uk

DCA DESIGN INTERNATIONAL
19 Church Street, Warwick CV34 4AB
Tel: 01926 499461
Fax: 01926 401134
Web site: www.dca-design.com/transport

*ELLIS TRANSPORT SERVICES
61 Bodycoats Road, Chandlers Ford SO53 2HA
Tel: 023 8027 0447
Fax: 023 8027 6736
E-mail: info@ellistransportservices.co.uk

ETM SOFTWARE SERVICES
9 Dorset Avenue, Ferndown BH22 8HJ
Tel: 01202 246710
Fax: 01202 687537
E-mail: info@etmss.com
Web site: www.etmss.com

FABER MAUNSELL
Imperial House, 31 Temple Street, Birmingham B2 5DB
Tel: 0870 905 0906
Web site: www.fabermaunsell.com

*R W FAULKS FCIT
Penthouse J, Ross Court, Putney Hill, London SW15 3NY
Tel: 020 8785 1584

FINANCIAL INSPECTION SERVICES LTD
PO Box 1075, Beaminster DT8 3YA.
Tel: 01460 74337.
Fax: 01460 72154.
E-mail: fininspect@aol.com

*LEONARD GREEN ASSOCIATES
2 Short Clough Close, Reedsholme, Rawtenstall BB4 8PT
Tel: 01706 218539
Fax: 01706 601485

HILTECH DEVELOPMENTS LTD
22 Larbre Crescent, Whickham, Newcastle upon Tyne NE16 5YG.
Tel: 0191 488 6258.
Fax: 0191 488 9158.
E-mail: info@hiltechdevelopments.com
Web site: www.hiltechdevelopments.com

*IBPTS
43 Cage Lane, Felixstowe IP11 9BJ
Tel: 01394 672344
Fax: 01394 672344
E-mail: info@ibpts.com
Web site: www.ibpts.com

JACOBS BABTIE GROUP LTD
School Green, Shinfield, Reading RG2 9HL.
Tel: 0118 988 1555.
Fax: 0118 988 1653.

KERNOW ASSOCIATES
18 Tresawla Court, Tolvaddon, Camborne TR14 0HF.
Tel/Fax: 01209 711870.
E-mail: 106472.3264@compuserve.com

*THOMAS KNOWLES - TRANSPORT CONSULTANT
41 Redhills, Eccleshall ST21 6JW
Tel: 01785 859414
Fax: 01785 859414
E-mail: twwknowles@hotmail.com

MASS SPECIAL ENGINEERING LTD
Anston, Sheffield S25 4SD.
Tel: 01909 550480.
Fax: 01909 550486.

MAUN INTERNATIONAL
New Cross House, 8-10 Mansfield Road, Sutton in Ashfield NG17 4GR.
Tel: 01623 555621.
Fax: 01623 555671.

*MINIMISE YOUR RISK
11 Chatsworth Park, Telscombe Cliffs BN10 7DZ
Tel: 01273 580189
Fax: 01273 580189
E-mail: minimise@btconnect.com
Web site: www.minimiseyourrisk.co.uk

MOTT MACDONALD
St Anne House, Wellesley House, Croydon CR9 2UL
Tel: 020 8774 2000
Fax: 020 8681 5706
E-mail: marketing@mottmac.com
Web site: www.mottmac.com

NEERMAN & PARTNERS
c/o 22 Larbre Crescent, Whickham, Newcastle-upon-Tyne NE16 5YG
Tel: 0191 488 6258
Web site: www.neerman.net
E-mail: executive@neerman.net

*PJ ASSOCIATES
27 Park End Street, Oxford OX1 1HU
Tel: 01865 724320
E-mail: mail@pj-associates.co.uk
Web site: www.pj-associates.co.uk

*PRE METRO OPERATION LTD
21 Woodglade Croft, Kings Norton, Birmingham B38 8TD
Tel: 0121 243 9906
Fax: 0121 243 9906
E-mail: premetro@aol.com

*PROFESSIONAL TRANSPORT SERVICES
12 Silverdale, Stanford-le-Hope, Essex SS17 8BG
Tel: 01375 675262
Web site: www.proftranserv.co.uk
E-mail: enquiries@proftranserv.co.uk

Trade Directory

*ROBERTSON TRANSPORT CONSULTING LTD
Field House, Braceby, Sleaford NG34 0SZ
Tel: 01529 497354
E-mail: robertson@rtclincs.co.uk

*SALTIRE COMMUNICATIONS
39 Lilyhill Terrace, Edinburgh EH8 7DR
Tel: 0131 652 0205
E-mail: gavin-booth@btconnect.com

*SPECIALIST
Tel: 0800 3283297
E-mail:
enquiries@specialisttraining.co.uk
Web site: www.specialisttraining.co.uk

TACHOGRAPH BUREAUX LTD
Lodge Farm, Kineton CV35 0JH
Tel/Fax: 01926 641224
E-mail: sales@tachograph-bureaux.co.uk

*TAS PARTNERSHIP LTD
Guildhall House, Guildhall Street, Preston PR1 3NU
Tel: 01772 204988
Fax: 01722 562070
E-mail: info@tas-part.co.uk
Web site: www.tas-part.co.uk

TRANSPORTATION MANAGEMENT SOLUTIONS
PO Box 15174, Glasgow G3 6WB.
Tel: 0141 332 4733.
Fax: 0141 354 0076.
E-mail: tramsol@aol.com

TRANSPORT DESIGN INTERNATIONAL
12 Waterloo Road Estate, Bidford on Avon B50 4JH
Tel: 01789 490370
Fax: 01789 490592
E-mail:enquiries@tdi.uk.com
Web site: www.tdi.uk.com

*VCA
No1, The Estate Office Centre, Eastgate Road, Bristol BS5 6XX
Tel: 0117 952 4126
Fax: 0117 952 4104
E-mail: paul.cooke@vca.gov.uk
Web site: www.vca.gov.uk

*WARD INTERNATIONAL CONSULTING LTD
Funtley Court, 19 Funtley Hill, Fareham PO16 7UY
Tel: 01329 280280
Fax: 01329 221010
E-mail: info@wardint.co.uk
Web site: www.wardint.com

Driver Supply

WEBB'S
St Peters Farm, Middle Drove, Peterborough PE14 8JJ
Tel: 01945 430123
E-mail: webb-s-cant@fsbdial.co.uk

Driver Training

ADG TRANSPORT CONSULTANCY
Oak Cottage, Royal Oak, Machen CF83 8SN
Tel: 01633 441491
Fax: 01633 440591
E-mail: a.dgettins@btinternet.com

*BUZZLINES LTD
Unit G1, Lympne Industrial Park, Hythe CT21 4LR
Tel: 01303 261870
Fax: 01303 230093
Web site: www.buzzlines.co.uk

*COACH DIRECT
The Coach House, 22 South Street, Rochford SS4 1BQ
Tel: 0870 550 2069
Fax: 0870 070 2069
E-mail: info@coachdirect.co.uk
Web site: www.coachdirect.co.uk

*CREATIVE MANAGEMENT DEVELOPMENT LTD
52 Okebourne Park, Liden, Swindon SN3 6AJ
Tel: 07771 732185
Fax: 01793 491786
E-mail: jowencmd@aol.com
Web site: www.cmd-training.co.uk

*D.A.T.S.
Dave's Accident & Training Services
9 Cheshire Close, Yate, Bristol BS37 5TQ
Tel: 07747 686789
E-mail: davepboulter@blueyonder.co.uk
Web site: www.datservices.org

*HATTS COACHWORKS & SERVICES
Foxham, Chippenham SN15 4NB
Tel: 01249 740444
Fax: 01249 740447
E-mail: adrian@hattstravel.co.uk
Web site: www.hattstravel.co.uk

INOVAS LTD
1 Glenbervie Business Park, Larbert, Falkirk FK5 4RB
Tel: 01324 682268
Fax: 01324 682269
Web site: www.inovas.co.uk
E-mail: info@inovas.co.uk

*MINIMISE YOUR RISK
11 Chatsworth Park, Telscombe Cliffs BN10 7DZ
Tel: 01273 580189
Fax: 01273 580189
E-mail: minimise@btconnect.com
Web site: www.minimiseyourrisk.co.uk

OMNIBUS TRAINING LTD
8 Lombard Road, London SW19 3TZ
Tel: 020 8543 4499
Fax: 020 8543 0011
E-mail: enquiries@omnibusltd.com

*PROFESSIONAL TRANSPORT SERVICES
12 Silverdale, Stanford-le-Hope SS17 8BG
Tel: 01375 675262
Web site: www.proftranserv.co.uk
E-mail: enquiries@proftranserv.com

SKILLPLACE TRAINING
Acacia Avenue, Sandfields Estate, Port Talbot SA12 7DW.
Tel: 01639 899849

*SPECIALIST
Tel: 0800 3283297
E-mail:
enquiries@specialisttraining.co.uk
Web site: www.specialisttraining.co.uk

VOSA
Vehicle & Operator Services Agency, Commercial Projects Unit, Berkeley House, Croydon Street, Bristol BS5 0DA
Tel: 0117 954 3359
Fax: 0117 954 3496
E-mail: commercial.training@vosa.gov.uk

Exhibition Organisers

COACH & BUS
PO Box 1359, Leamington Spa CV32 5GT.
Tel: 020 7240 5800.
Fax: 020 7240 5805.
E-mail: info@expom.co.uk
Web site: www.cpt-uk.org

COACH DISPLAYS LTD (**UK Coach Rally**)
21 The Poynings, Richings Park, Iver SL0 9DS
Tel: 01753 631170
Fax: 01753 655980
E-mail: info@coachdisplays.co.uk
Web site: www.coachdisplays.co.uk

EXPOMANAGEMENT LTD
Linden House, 21 Dormer Place, Leamington Spa CV32 5AA.
Tel: 01926 888123.
Fax: 01926 888004.
E-mail: info@expom.co.uk
Web site: www.expocoach.com

MCI EXHIBITIONS LTD
Starley House, Eaton Road, Coventry CV1 2FH.
Tel: 0870 330 7834.
Fax: 0870 076 3292
E-mail: john@motorcycleshow.co.uk
Web site: www.motorcycleshow.co.uk

Ferry Operators

BRITTANY FERRIES LTD
Group Travel, The Brittany Centre, Wharf Road, Portsmouth PO2 8RU
Tel: 0870 901 2100
Fax: 0870 901 3100
E-mail: grouptravel@brittany-ferries.com
Web site: www.brittany-ferries.com

CALEDONIAN MACBRAYNE LTD
Head Office, The Ferry Terminal, Gourock PA19 1QP
Tel: 01475 650100
Web site: www.calmac.co.uk

CONDOR FERRIES LTD
Condor House, New Harbour Road South, Hamworthy, Poole BH15 4AJ
Tel: 01305 776883
Web site: www.condorferries.co.uk

DFDS SEAWAYS
Scandinavia House, Refinery Road, Parkeston CO12 4QG
Tel: 08708 488 222
Web site: www.dfdsseaways.com

EUROTUNNEL
PO Box 2000, Folkestone CT18 8XY
Tel: 08702 430401
Fax: 01303 288909
Web site: www.eurotunnel.com

*FJORD LINE
Norway House, Royal Quays, North Shields NE29 6EG
Tel: 0191 296 1313
Fax: 0191 296 1540
E-mail: fjordline.uk@fjordline.com
Web site: www.fjordline.com

IRISH FERRIES LTD
Groups Department, Salt Island, Holyhead LL65 1DR
Tel: 0151 236 6921
Web site: www.irishferries.ie
www.irishferries.com

ISLE OF MAN STEAM PACKET COMPANY
Imperial Buildings, Douglas IM1 2BY
Tel: 01624 661661
Tel: 01624 645618
E-mail: resesteam-packet.com
Web site: www.steam-packet.com

NORFOLKLINE
Norfolk House, Eastern Dock, Dover CT16 1JA
Tel: 0870 870 1020
Web site: www.norfolkline.com

*P&O FERRIES
Channel House, Channel View Road, Dover CT17 9TJ
Tel: 08705 980444
Fax: 08707 625325
E-mail: groups@poferries.com
Web site: www.poferries.com

RED FUNNEL
Red Funnel Travel Centre, 12 Bugle Street, Southampton SO14 2JY
Tel: 0870 444 8898
E-mail: post@redfunnel.co.uk
Web site: www.redfunnel.co.uk

*SEAFRANCE
Whitfield Court, Honeywood Close, Whitfield CT16 3PX
Tel: 08705 301 301
Fax: 08700 644 775
E-mail: groups@seafrance.fr
Web site: www.seafrance.com

STENA LINE
Station Approach, Holyhead LL65 1DQ
Tel: 08705 204 402
Web site: www.stenaline.co.uk

SUPERFAST FERRIES
The Terminal Building, Port of Rosyth KY11 2XP
Tel: 0870 234 221
Web site: www.superfast.com

SWANSEA CORK FERRIES LTD
Harbour Office, Kings Dock, Swansea SA1 1SF
Tel: 01792 456116
Fax: 01792 644356
E-mail: scferries@aol.com
Web site: www.swanseacork.ie

*WIGHTLINK ISLE OF WIGHT FERRIES
70 Broad Street, Portsmouth PO1 2LB
Tel: 0870 582 7744
Fax: 023 9285 5257
E-mail: sales@wightlink.co.uk
Web site: www.wightlink.co.uk

Finance/Leasing

AD COACH SALES
Newbridge Coach Depot, Witheridge EX16 8PY
Tel: 01884 860787
Fax: 01884 860711
E-mail: ggoodwin@adcoachsales.co.uk
Web site: www.adcoachsales.co.uk

ARRIVA BUS AND COACH LTD
Lodge Garage, Whitehall Road West, Gomersal BD19 4BJ.
Tel: 01274 681144.
Fax: 01274 651198.
Web site: www.arriva.co.uk
E-mail: busandcoachsales@arriva.co.uk

DAWSONRENTALS BUS AND COACH LTD
Delaware Drive, Tongwell, Milton Keynes MK15 8JH
Tel: 01908 218111
Fax: 01908 610156
E-mail: info@dawsongroup.co.uk
Web site: www.dawsongroup.co.uk

HANSAR FINANCE LTD
Bridgeway House, Mellor Road, Cheadle Hulme SK8 5AU
Tel: 0161 488 4000
Fax: 0161 488 4567
Web site: www.hansar.co.uk

*LHE FINANCE LTD
21 Headlands Business Park, Salisbury Road, Ringwood BH24 3PB
Tel: 01425 474070
Fax: 01425 474090
E-mail: bhymers@lhefinance.co.uk
Web site: www.lhefinance.co.uk

MCV BUS & COACH LTD
Sterling Place, Elean Business Park, Sutton CB6 2QE
Tel: 01353 773000
Fax: 01353 773001
E-mail: vernon.edwards@mcv-uk.com

NORTON FOLGATE FG PLC
50A St Andrew Street, Hertford SG14 1JA.
Tel: 01992 537735
Fax: 01992 537733

MISTRAL GROUP (UK) PLC
PO Box 130, Knutsford WA16 6AG
Tel: 0870 2415786
Fax: 0870 241 5784
E-mail: sales@mistral-group.com
Web site: www.mistral-group.com

ROADLEASE
Crossroads, Anston, Sheffield S25 7ES.
Tel: 01909 551177.
Fax: 01909 567994.
E-mail: roadlease@kirkbycoachandbus.com
Web site: www.roadlease.com

VOLVO FINANCIAL SERVICES
Wedgnock Lane, Warwick CV34 5YA
Tel: 01926 498888
Fax: 01926 410278

Graphic Design

*ADGROUP LTD
Ad House, East Parade, Harrogate HG1 5LT
Tel: 01423 526253
Fax: 01423 502522
E-mail: info@adbus.info
Web site: www.adbus.info

BEST IMPRESSIONS
15 Starfield Road, London W12 9SN
Tel: 020 8740 6443
Fax: 020 8740 9134
E-mail: talk2us@best-impressions.co.uk
Web site: www.best-impressions.co.uk

FWT
Whittington House, 764-768 Holloway Road, London N19 3JQ
Tel: 020 7281 2161
Fax: 020 7281 4117
E-mail: sales@fwt.co.uk
Web site: www.fwt.co.uk

*HATTS COACHWORKS & SERVICES
Foxham, Chippenham SN15 4NB
Tel: 01249 740444
Fax: 01249 740447
E-mail: adrian@hattstravel.co.uk
Web site: www.hattstravel.co.uk

IMAGE & PRINT GROUP
Unit 9, Oakbank Industrial Estate, Garscube Road, Glasgow G20 7LU
Tel: 0141 353 1900
Fax: 0141 353 8611

*McKENNA BROTHERS LTD
McKenna House, Jubilee Road, Middleton, Manchester M24 2LX
Tel: 0161 655 3244
Fax: 0161 655 3059
E-mail: info@mckennabrothers.co.uk
Web site: www.mckennabrothers.co.uk

*NORBURY BLINDS LTD
41-45 Hanley Street, Newtown, Birmingham B19 3SP
Tel: 0121 359 4311
Fax: 0121 359 6388
E-mail: info@norbury-blinds.com
Web site: www.norbury-blinds.com

*PLUM CREATIONS
Plum Publishing Ltd, Suite 1, Cornerstone House, Stafford Park 13, Telford TF3 3AZ
Tel: 01952 204920
Fax: 01952 204929
E-mail: steve.rooney@busandcoach.com
Web site: www.busandcoach.com

*RH BODYWORKS
A140 Ipswich Road, Brome Eye IP23 8AW
Tel: 01379 870666
Fax: 01379 871140
E-mail: mike.ball@rhbodywork.co.uk
Web site: www.rhbodyworks.co.uk

*TIME TRAVEL UK
247 Bradford Road, Stanningley, Pudsey LS28 6QB
Tel: 0113 255 1188
E-mail: nick.baldwin@tinyworld.co.uk

Trade Directory

Hotels

CALOTELS HOTELS
88 Jordan Avenue, Stretton, Burton-on-Trent DE13 0JD
Tel: 01283 542455
Fax: 01283 542455

CIE TOURS INTERNATIONAL
Loveitts Farm, Brinklow CV23 0LG
Tel: 01788 833388
Fax: 01788 833710
E-mail: anne@ciegroups.freeserve.co.uk
Web site: www.cietours.co.uk

*GRASSHOPPER INN
Moorhouse, Westerham TN16 2EU
Tel: 01959 563136
E-mail: info@grasshopperinn.co.uk
Web site: www.grasshopperinn.co.uk

*GREATDAYS TRAVEL GROUP
2 Stamford Park Road, Altrincham WA15 9EN
Tel: 0161 928 9966
Fax: 0161 928 1332
E-mail: sales@greatdays.co.uk
Web site: www.greatdays.co.uk

GREATDAYS TRAVEL GROUP, LONDON
10 Thurloe Place, London SW7 2RZ
Tel: 020 7581 5606
Fax: 020 7225 0068
E-mail: sales@london.greatdays.co.uk
Web site: www.greatdays.co.uk

STAGE HOTEL – LEICESTER
299 Leicester Road, (A5199) Wigston Fields, Leicester LE18 1JW
Tel: 0116 288 6161
Fax: 0116 281 1874

*TRAVELPATH 3000
PO Box 32, Grantham NG31 7JA
Tel: 01476 570187
Fax: 01476 572718
E-mail: jon@travelpath-uk.com
Web site: www.travelpath3000.com

Insurance

*BELMONT INTERNATIONAL LTD
Becket House, Vestry Road, Otford, Sevenoaks TN14 5EL
Tel: 01732 744700
Fax: 01732 744726
ite: www.belmontint.com
E-mail: sales@belmontint.com

R. L. DAVISON & CO LTD
Bury House, 31 Bury Street, London EC3A 5AH.
Tel: 020 7816 9876.
Fax: 020 7816 9880.

P J HAYMAN & CO LTD
Stansted House, Rowlands Castle PO9 6BR
Tel: 0845 6020 020
Web site: www.pjhayman.com

OMNI WHITTINGTONS
Arthur Castle House, 33 Creechurch Lane, London EC3A 5EB
Tel: 020 7709 9991
Fax: 020 7456 1225.

*RIGTON INSURANCE SERVICES LTD
Alexander House, Orchard Way, Oxford Road, Guiseley LS20 9AT
Tel: 01943 879539
Fax: 01943 875529
E-mail: enquiries@rigtoninsurance.co.uk
Web site: www.rigtoninsurance.co.uk

*TOWERGATE CHAPMAN STEVENS
Towergate House, 22 Wintersells Road, Wintersells Business Park, Byfleet KT14 7LF
Tel: 01932 334140
Fax: 01932 351238
E-mail: tcs@towergate.co.uk
Web site: www.towergatechapmanstevens.co.uk

VOLVO INSURANCE SERVICES
Wedgnock Lane, Warwick CV34 5YA
Tel: 01926 401777.
Fax: 01926 407407.
Web site: www.volvobuses.volvo.co.uk
www.volvo.com

*WILLIS LTD
10 Trinity Square, London EC3P 3AX
Tel: 020 7488 8111
Fax: 020 7975 2884
E-mail: warren.dann@willis.com
Web site: www.willis.com

WILSURE INSURANCE BROKERS
9 Crusader Business Park, Stephenson Road West, Clacton on Sea CO15 4TN.
Tel: 01255 420564.
Fax: 01255 222764.
E-mail: info@wilsure.co.uk
Web site: www.wilsure.co.uk

WRIGHTSURE GROUP
799 London Road, West Thurrock RM20 3LH.
Tel: 01708 865553.
Fax: 01708 865100.
E-mail: info@wrightsure.com
Web site: www.wrightsure.com

Legal & Operations Advisers

*BORLAND, WINDER-DIXON LLP
3 Axe View, Axe Road, Drimpton, Beaminster DT8 3RJ
Tel: 01460 72769
Fax: 01460 72769
E-mail: chris.borland@tiscali.co.uk

*COACH DIRECT
The Coach House, 22 South Street, Rochford SS4 1BQ
Tel: 0870 550 2069
Fax: 0870 070 2069
E-mail: info@coachdirect.co.uk
Web site: www.coachdirect.co.uk

*ELLIS TRANSPORT SERVICES
61 Bodycoats Road, Chandlers Ford SO53 2HA
Tel: 023 8027 0447
Fax: 023 8027 6736
E-mail: info@ellistransportservices.co.uk

FREIGHT TRANSPORT ASSOCIATION
Hermes House, St John's Road, Tunbridge Wells TN4 9UZ.
Tel: 01892 526171
Fax: 01892 534989
E-mail: enquiries@fta.co.uk
Web site: www.fta.co.uk

KERNOW ASSOCIATES
18 Tresawla Court, Tolvaddon, Camborne TR14 0HF.
Tel/Fax: 01209 711870.
E-mail: 106472.3264@compuserve.com

*PROFESSIONAL TRANSPORT SERVICES
12 Silverdale, Stanford-le-Hope, Essex SS17 8BG
Tel: 01375 675262
Web site: www.proftranserv.co.uk
E-mail: enquiries@proftranserv.com

*WARD INTERNATIONAL CONSULTING LTD
Funtley Court, 19 Funtley Hill, Fareham PO16 7UY
Tel: 01329 280280
Fax: 01329 221010
E-mail: info@wardint.co.uk
Web site: www.wardint.com

WEDLAKE SAINT
14 John Street, London WC1N 2EB.
Tel: 020 7405 9446.
Fax: 020 7242 9877.

Life Insurance & Pensions

*RIGTON INSURANCE SERVICES LTD
Alexander House, Orchard Way, Oxford Road, Guiseley LS20 9AT
Tel: 01943 879539
Fax: 01943 875529
E-mail: enquiries@rigtoninsurance.co.uk
Web site: www.rigtoninsurance.co.uk

WILSURE INSURANCE BROKERS
9 Crusader Business Park, Stephenson Road West, Clacton on Sea CO15 4TN.
Tel: 01255 420564.
Fax: 01255 222764.
E-mail: info@wilsure.co.uk
Web site: www.wilsure.co.uk

Livery Design

*ADGROUP LTD
Ad House, East Parade, Harrogate HG1 5LT
Tel: 01423 526253
Fax: 01423 502522
E-mail: info@adbus.info
Web site: www.adbus.info

BEST IMPRESSIONS
15 Starfield Road, London W12 9SN
Tel: 020 8740 6443
Fax: 020 8740 9134
E-mail: talk2us@best-impressions.co.uk
Web site: www.best-impressions.co.uk

BROXWOOD VEHICLE SPECIALISTS
Unit 2 Parkside Garage, Old Stafford Road,
Wolverhampton WV10 7PH
Tel: 01902 798770
Fax: 01902 798564
E-mail: saks@broxwood.net
Web site: www.broxwood.net

DRURY & DRURY
Unit 6, Cobbs Wood Industrial Estate,
Brunswick Road, Ashford TN23 1EH.
Tel: 01303 610555.
Fax: 01303 610666.
E-mail:
martinstrange@channelcommercials.co.uk

TONY GREAVES GRAPHICS
19 Perth Mount, Horsforth, Leeds LS18 5SH
Tel/Fax: 0113 258 4795
E-mail: tony@greavesgraphics.fsnet.co.uk

*HATTS COACHWORKS & SERVICES
Foxham, Chippenham SN15 4NB
Tel: 01249 740444
Fax: 01249 740447
E-mail: adrian@hattstravel.co.uk
Web site: www.hattstravel.co.uk

*McKENNA BROTHERS LTD
McKenna House, Jubilee Road, Middleton,
Manchester M24 2LX
Tel: 0161 655 3244
Fax: 0161 655 3059
E-mail: info@mckennabrothers.co.uk
Web site: www.mckennabrothers.co.uk

NEERMAN & PARTNERS
c/o 22 Larbre Crescent, Whickham,
Newcastle-upon-Tyne NE16 5YG
Tel: 0191 488 6258
Web site: www.neerman.net
E-mail: executive@neerman.net

*NORBURY BLINDS LTD
41-45 Hanley Street, Newtown, Birmingham
B19 3SP
Tel: 0121 359 4311
Fax: 0121 359 6388
E-mail: info@norbury-blinds.com
Web site: www.norbury-blinds.com

*PLUM CREATIONS
Plum Publishing Ltd, Suite 1, Cornerstone
House, Stafford Park 13, Telford TF3 3AZ
Tel: 01952 204920
Fax: 01952 204929
E-mail: steve.rooney@busandcoach.com
Web site: www.busandcoach.com

*RH BODYWORKS
A140 Ipswich Road, Brome Eye IP23 8AW
Tel: 01379 870666
Fax: 01379 871140
E-mail: mike.ball@rhbodywork.co.uk
Web site: www.rhbodyworks.co.uk

*TIME TRAVEL UK
247 Bradford Road, Stanningley, Pudsey
LS28 6QB
Tel: 0113 255 1188
E-mail: nick.baldwin@tinyworld.co.uk

Maps for the Bus Industry

BEST IMPRESSIONS
15 Starfield Road, London W12 9SN
Tel: 020 8740 6443
Fax: 020 8740 9134
E-mail: talk2us@best-impressions.co.uk
Web site: www.best-impressions.co.uk

FIGUREHEAD DATA SYSTEMS
Felindre, Swansea SA5 7PP
Tel: 01792 883155
Fax: 01792 884934
E-mail: BusTimes@aol.com
Web site: www.bustimes.com

FWT
Whittington House, 764-768 Holloway Road,
London N19 3JQ
Tel: 020 7281 2161
Fax: 020 7281 4117
E-mail: sales@fwt.co.uk
Web site: www.fwt.co.uk

TONY GREAVES GRAPHICS
19 Perth Mount, Horsforth, Leeds LS18 5SH
Tel/Fax: 0113 258 4795
E-mail: tony@greavesgraphics.fsnet.co.uk

IMAGE & PRINT GROUP
Unit 9, Oakbank Industrial Estate, Garscube
Road, Glasgow G20 7LU.
Tel: 0141 353 1900.
Fax: 0141 353 8611.
E-mail: alan@imageandprint.co.uk
Web site: www.imageandprint.co.uk

PINDAR PLC
31 Edison Road, Aylesbury HP19 8TE
Tel: 01296 390100
Fax: 01296 381233
Web site: www.pindar.com

*TIME TRAVEL UK
247 Bradford Road, Stanningley, Pudsey
LS28 6QB
Tel: 0113 255 1188
E-mail: nick.baldwin@tinyworld.co.uk

Marketing Services

ADG TRANSPORT CONSULTANCY
Oak Cottage, Royal Oak, Machen
CF83 8SN
Tel: 01633 441491
Fax: 01633 440591
E-mail: a.dgettins@btinternet.com

AVENTA
66B Victoria Road, Horley RH6 7DZ.
Tel: 01293 825001.
Fax: 01293 825002.
E-mail: info@aventa.co.uk
Web site: www.aventa.co.uk

*COACH DIRECT
The Coach House, 22 South Street,
Rochford SS4 1BQ
Tel: 0870 550 2069
Fax: 0870 070 2069
E-mail: info@coachdirect.co.uk
Web site: www.coachdirect.co.uk

*CREATIVE MANAGEMENT DEVELOPMENT LTD
52 Okebourne Park, Liden, Swindon
SN3 6AJ
Tel: 07771 732185
Fax: 01793 491786
E-mail: jowencmd@aol.com
Web site: www.cmd-training.co.uk

KERNOW ASSOCIATES
18 Tresawla Court, Tolvaddon, Camborne
TR14 0HF.
Tel/Fax: 01209 711870.
E-mail: 106472.3264@compuserve.com

Mechanical Investigation

KERNOW ASSOCIATES
18 Tresawla Court, Tolvaddon, Camborne
TR14 0HF.
Tel/Fax: 01209 711870.
E-mail: 106472.3264@compuserve.com

*UNITEC LONDON
Unit 5, Gateway 25, Weston Avenue,
West Thurrock RM20 3ZD
Tel: 01708 892440
Fax: 01708 862125
E-mail: london.service@optare.com

*UNITEC ROTHERHAM
Denby Way, Hellaby, Rotherham
S66 8HR
Tel: 01709 535101
Fax: 01709 535103
E-mail: rotherham.service@optare.com

*UNITEC SCOTLAND
Unit 7, Cumbernauld Business Park,
Ward Park Road, Cumbernauld G67 3JZ
Tel: 01236 726738
Fax: 01236 795651
E-mail: scotland.service@optare.com

On-Bus Advertising

*ADGROUP LTD
Ad House, East Parade, Harrogate HG1 5LT
Tel: 01423 526253
Fax: 01423 502522
E-mail: info@adbus.info
Web site: www.adbus.info

BEST IMPRESSIONS
15 Starfield Road, London W12 9SN
Tel: 020 8740 6443
Fax: 020 8740 9134
E-mail: talk2us@best-impressions.co.uk
Web site: www.best-impressions.co.uk

BRITANNIA ROLL/TICKETMEDIA
Maple Works, Old Shoreham Road, Hove
BN3 7ED
Tel: 01273 726325
Fax: 01273 324936
E-mail: edmund.jackson@ticketmedia.com
Web site: www.ticketmedia.com

DECKER MEDIA LTD
Decker House, Lowater Street, Carlton,
Nottingham NG4 1JJ
Tel: 0115 940 2406
Fax: 0115 940 2407
E-mail: sales@deckermedia.co.uk
Web site: www.deckermedia.co.uk

Trade Directory

NORBURY BLINDS LTD
41-45 Hanley Street, Newtown, Birmingham B19 3SP
Tel: 0121 359 4311
Fax: 0121 359 6388
E-mail: info@norbury-blinds.com
Web site: www.norbury-blinds.com

***TIME TRAVEL UK**
247 Bradford Road, Stanningley, Pudsey LS28 6QB
Tel: 0113 255 1188
E-mail: nick.baldwin@tinyworld.co.uk

Printing/Publishing

***BRITISH BUS PUBLISHING LTD**
16 St Margarets Drive, Telford TF1 3PH
Tel: 01952 255669
Fax: 01952 222397
E-mail: bill@britishbuspublishing.co.uk
Web site: www.britishbuspublishing.co.uk

***IAN ALLAN PRINTING LTD**
Riverdene Business Park, Molesey Road, Hersham KT12 4RG.
Tel: 01932 266600
Fax: 01932 266601
E-mail: jonathan.bingham@ianallanprinting.co.uk
Web site: www.ianallanprinting.co.uk

BEMROSEBOOTH LTD
Stockholm Road, Sutton Fields Industrial Estate, Hull HU7 0XY
Tel: 01482 826343
Fax: 01482 371386
E-mail: lprecious@bemrosebooth.com
Web site: www.bemrosebooth.com

BEST IMPRESSIONS
15 Starfield Road, London W12 9SN
Tel: 020 8740 6443
Fax: 020 8740 9134
E-mail: talk2us@best-impressions.co.uk
Web site: www.best-impressions.co.uk

THE HENRY BOOTH GROUP
Stockholm Road, Sutton Fields Industrial Estate, Hull HU7 0XY
Tel: 01482 826343.
Fax: 01482 839767.
E-mail: mshanley@henrybooth.co.uk
Web site: www.henrybooth.co.uk

BRITANNIA ROLL/TICKETMEDIA
Maple Works, Old Shoreham Road, Hove BN3 7ED
Tel: 01273 726325
Fax: 01273 324936
E-mail: edmund.jackson@ticketmedia.com
Web site: www.ticketmedia.com

FIGUREHEAD DATA SYSTEMS
Felindre, Swansea SA5 7PP
Tel: 01792 883155
Fax: 01792 884934
E-mail: BusTimes@aol.com
Web site: www.bustimes.com

*FIRST CHOICE NAMEPLATES, LABELS & SIGNS
Lynden 2c, Russell Avenue, Balderton, Newark NG24 3BT
Tel: 01636 678035
Fax: 01636 707066
E-mail: firstchoice@handbag.com

FWT
Whittington House, 764-768 Holloway Road, London N19 3JQ
Tel: 020 7281 2161
Fax: 020 7281 4117
E-mail: sales@fwt.co.uk
Web site: www.fwt.co.uk

TONY GREAVES GRAPHICS
19 Perth Mount, Horsforth, Leeds LS18 5SH
Tel/Fax: 0113 258 4795
E-mail: tony@greavesgraphics.fsnet.co.uk

IMAGE & PRINT GROUP
Unit 9, Oakbank Industrial Estate, Garscube Road, Glasgow G20 7LU
Tel: 0141 353 1900
Fax: 0141 353 8611
E-mail: alan@imageandprint.co.uk
Web site: www.imageandprint.co.uk

MIDLAND COUNTIES PUBLICATIONS
4 Watling Drive, Hinckley LE10 3EY
E-mail:midlandbooks@compuserve.com

*NORBURY BLINDS LTD
41-45 Hanley Street, Newtown, Birmingham B19 3SP
Tel: 0121 359 4311
Fax: 0121 359 6388
E-mail: info@norbury-blinds.com
Web site: www.norbury-blinds.com

PINDAR PLC
31 Edison Road, Aylesbury HP19 8TE
Tel: 01296 390100
Fax: 01296 381233
Web site: www.pindar.com

*PLUM CREATIONS
Plum Publishing Ltd, Suite 1, Cornerstone House, Stafford Park 13, Telford TF3 3AZ
Tel: 01952 204920
Fax: 01952 204929
E-mail: steve.rooney@busandcoach.com
Web site: www.busandcoach.com

*TIME TRAVEL UK
247 Bradford Road, Stanningley, Pudsey LS28 6QB
Tel: 0113 255 1188
E-mail: nick.baldwin@tinyworld.co.uk

*TRANSPORT STATIONERY SERVICES
61 Bodycoats Road, Chandlers Ford SO53 2HA
Tel: 07041 471008
Fax: 07041 471009
E-mail: info@transportstationeryservices.co.uk

Promotional Material

BEST IMPRESSIONS
15 Starfield Road, London W12 9SN
Tel: 020 8740 6443
Fax: 020 8740 9134
E-mail: talk2us@best-impressions.co.uk
Web site: www.best-impressions.co.uk

BRITANNIA ROLL/TICKETMEDIA
Maple Works, Old Shoreham Road, Hove BN3 7ED
Tel: 01273 726325
Fax: 01273 324936
E-mail: edmund.jackson@ticketmedia.com
Web site: www.ticketmedia.com

FWT
Whittington House, 764-768 Holloway Road, London N19 3JQ
Tel: 020 7281 2161
Fax: 020 7281 4117
E-mail: sales@fwt.co.uk
Web site: www.fwt.co.uk

*MARKET ENGINEERING
23a Parsons Street, Banbury OX16 5LY
Tel: 01295 277050
Fax: 01295 297030
E-mail: contact@m-eng.com
Web site: www.marketengineering.com

PINDAR PLC
31 Edison Road, Aylesbury HP19 8TE
Tel: 01296 390100
Fax: 01296 381233
Web site: www.pindar.com

*PLUM CREATIONS
Plum Publishing Ltd, Suite 1, Cornerstone House, Stafford Park 13, Telford TF3 3AZ
Tel: 01952 204920
Fax: 01952 204929
E-mail: steve.rooney@busandcoach.com
Web site: www.busandcoach.com

*PROFESSIONAL TRANSPORT SERVICES
12 Silverdale, Stanford-le-Hope, Essex SS17 8BG
Tel: 01375 675262
Web site: www.proftranserv.co.uk
E-mail: enquiries@proftranserv.com

*STEPHEN C MORRIS
PO Box 119, Shepperton TW17 8UX
Tel: 01932 232574
E-mail: buswriter@btinternet.com

*TIME TRAVEL UK
247 Bradford Road, Stanningley, Pudsey LS28 6QB
Tel: 0113 255 1188
E-mail: nick.baldwin@tinyworld.co.uk

TONY GREAVES GRAPHICS
19 Perth Mount, Horsforth, Leeds LS18 5SH
Tel/Fax: 0113 258 4795
E-mail: tony@greavesgraphics.fsnet.co.uk

Publications - Magazines & Books

*BRITISH BUS PUBLISHING LTD
16 St Margarets Drive, Telford TF1 3PH
Tel: 01952 255669
Fax: 01952 222397
E-mail: bill@britishbuspublishing.co.uk
Web site: www.britishbuspublishing.co.uk

*BUSES
Ian Allan Publishing Ltd
Riverdene Business Park, Molsey Road, Hersham KT12 4RG.
Tel: 01932 266600
Fax: 01932 266601
Web site: www.busesmag.com

BUS & COACH BUYER
The Publishing Centre, 1 Woolram Wygate, Spalding PE11 1NU
Tel: 01775 711777
Fax: 01775 711777
E-mail: bcbsales@busandcoachbuyer.com

*BUS & COACH PROFESSIONAL
Plum Publishing Ltd, Suite 1, Cornerstone House, Stafford Park 13, Telford TF3 3AZ
Tel: 01952 204920
Fax: 01952 204929
E-mail: steve.rooney@busandcoach.com
Web site: www.busandcoach.com

BUS USER
Bus Users UK, PO Box 320, Portsmouth PO5 3SD
Tel: 023 9281 4493
Fax: 023 9285 3080
Web site: www.bususers.org

*COACH & BUS WEEK
3 The Office Village, Cygnet Park, Hampton, Peterborough PE7 8FD
Tel: 01733 293240
Fax: 0845 2802927
E-mail: jacqui.grobler@rouncymedia.co.uk
Web site: www.cbwnet.co.uk

CRONER CCH GROUP LTD
145 London Road, Kingston upon Thames KT2 6SR
Tel: 020 8247 1261
Fax: 020 8547 2638
E-mail: info@croner.cch.co.uk

JANES URBAN TRANSPORT SYSTEMS
163 Brighton Road, Coulsdon CR5 2YH
Tel: 020 8700 3700
Web site:
www.janes.com/www.juts.janes.com

*PLUM CREATIONS
Plum Publishing Ltd, Suite 1, Cornerstone House, Stafford Park 13, Telford TF3 3AZ
Tel: 01952 204920
Fax: 01952 204929
E-mail: steve.rooney@busandcoach.com
Web site: www.busandcoach.com

ROUTE ONE
Expo Publishing, Suite 4, Century House, Towermead Business Park, Fletton, Peterborough PE2 9DY
Tel: 0870 241 8745
Fax: 0870 241 8891m
E-mail: mike.morgan@route-one.net
Web site: www.route.one.net

*SALTIRE COMMUNICATIONS
39 Lilyhill Terrace, Edinburgh EH8 7DR
Tel: 0131 652 0205
E-mail: gavin-booth@btconnect.com

*STEPHEN C MORRIS
PO Box 119, Shepperton TW17 8UX
Tel: 01932 232574
E-mail: buswriter@btinternet.com

TRAMWAYS & URBAN TRANSIT/LRTA PUBLICATIONS
13A The Precinct, Broxbourne EN10 7HY
Web site: www.lrta.org

*TIME TRAVEL UK
247 Bradford Road, Stanningley, Pudsey LS28 6QB
Tel: 0113 255 1188
E-mail: nick.baldwin@tinyworld.co.uk

TRANSIT
Landor Publishing, 3rd Floor Quadrant House, 250 Kennington Lane, London SE11 5RD
Tel: 020 7820 0848
Fax: 020 7587 0497

Quality Management Systems

FTA VEHICLE INSPECTION SERVICE
Hermes House, St John's Road, Tunbridge Wells TN4 9UZ.
Tel: 01892 526171
Fax: 01892 534989
E-mail: enquiries@fta.co.uk
Web site: www.fta.co.uk

*MYSTERY TRAVELLERS
6A Mims Yard, Down Road, Waterlooville PO8 0YP
Tel: 023 9259 7707
Fax: 023 9259 1700
E-mail: info@bestchart.co.uk
Web site: www.mysterytravellers.com

*VCA
No1, The Estate Office Centre, Eastgate Road, Bristol BS5 6XX
Tel: 0117 952 4126
Fax: 0117 952 4104
E-mail: paul.cooke@vca.gov.uk
Web site: www.vca.gov.uk

VOSA COMMERCIAL PROJECTS UNIT
Berkeley House, Croydon Street, Bristol BS5 0DA
Tel: 0117 954 3359
Fax: 0117 954 3496
E-mail: commercial.training@vosa.gov.uk

Refreshment Facilities

In this section we include brief directions and facilities, where available
Entries listed in county order

KENT

> ### *GRASSHOPPER INN
> Moorhouse, Westerham TN16 2EU
> **Tel**: 01959 563136
> **E-mail**: info@grasshopperinn.co.uk
> **Web site**: www.grasshopperinn.co.uk
> *on A25 near Westerham, Kent, close to M25 (jct 5 and 6); coffee, drinks, lunch dinner; large car park with coach bays*

Timetable Production

BEMROSEBOOTH LTD
Stockholm Road, Sutton Fields Industrial Estate, Hull HU7 0XY
Tel: 01482 826343
Fax: 01482 371386
E-mail: lprecious@bemrosebooth.com
Web site: www.bemrosebooth.com

BEST IMPRESSIONS
15 Starfield Road, London W12 9SN
Tel: 020 8740 6443
Fax: 020 8740 9134
E-mail: talk2us@best-impressions.co.uk
Web site: www.best-impressions.co.uk

FIGUREHEAD DATA SYSTEMS
Felindre, Swansea SA5 7PP
Tel: 01792 883155
Fax: 01792 884934
E-mail: BusTimes@aol.com
Web site: www.bustimes.com

*FIRST CHOICE NAMEPLATES, LABELS & SIGNS
Lynden 2c, Russell Avenue, Balderton, Newark NG24 3BT
Tel: 01636 678035
Fax: 01636 707066
E-mail: firstchoice@handbag.com

FWT
Whittington House, 764-768 Holloway Road, London N19 3JQ
Tel: 020 7281 2161
Fax: 020 7281 4117
E-mail: sales@fwt.co.uk
Web site: www.fwt.co.uk

TONY GREAVES GRAPHICS
19 Perth Mount, Horsforth, Leeds LS18 5SH
Tel/Fax: 0113 258 4795
E-mail: tony@greavesgraphics.fsnet.co.uk

*IBPTS
43 Cage Lane, Felixstowe IP11 9BJ
Tel: 01394 672344
Fax: 01394 672344
E-mail: info@ibpts.com
Web site: www.ibpts.com

IMAGE & PRINT GROUP
Unit 9, Oakbank Industrial Estate, Garscube Road, Glasgow G20 7LU.
Tel: 0141 353 1900.
Fax: 0141 353 8611.
E-mail: alan@imageandprint.co.uk
Web site: www.imageandprint.co.uk

*NORBURY BLINDS LTD
41-45 Hanley Street, Newtown, Birmingham B19 3SP
Tel: 0121 359 4311
Fax: 0121 359 6388
E-mail: info@norbury-blinds.com
Web site: www.norbury-blinds.com

*PLUM CREATIONS
Plum Publishing Ltd, Suite 1, Cornerstone House, Stafford Park 13, Telford TF3 3AZ
Tel: 01952 204920
Fax: 01952 204929
E-mail: steve.rooney@busandcoach.com
Web site: www.busandcoach.co.uk

*TIME TRAVEL UK
247 Bradford Road, Stanningley, Pudsey LS28 6QB
Tel: 0113 255 1188
E-mail: nick.baldwin@tinyworld.co.uk

PINDAR PLC
31 Edison Road, Aylesbury HP19 8TE
Tel: 01296 390100
Fax: 01296 381233
Web site: www.pindar.com

SOUTHERN VECTIS PLC
Nelson Road, Newport PO30 1RD.
Tel: 01983 812983.
E-mail: pwhite@southernvectis.com
Web site: www.southernvectis.com

*TIME TRAVEL UK
247 Bradford Road, Stanningley, Pudsey LS28 6QB
Tel: 0113 255 1188
E-mail: nick.baldwin@tinyworld.co.uk

*TRAVEL INFORMATION SYSTEMS
Grand Union House, 20 Kentish Town Road, London NW1 9NX
Tel: 020 7428 1288
Fax: 020 7267 2745
E-mail: enquiries@travelinfosystems.com
Web site: www.travelinfosystems.com

Tour Wholesalers

ALBATROSS TRAVEL GROUP LTD
Albatross House, 14 New Hythe Lane,
Larkfield ME20 6AB
Tel: 01732 879191
Fax: 01732 522968
E-mail: sales@albatross-tours.com
Web site: www.albatross-tours.com

BOTEL LTD
Botel House, 50 Northern Road, Wickersley,
Rotherham S66 1EN
Tel: 01709 703535
Fax: 01709 703525
Web site: www.botel.co.uk

CI COACHLINES
Pools Lane, Highwood, Chelmsford
CM1 3QL
Tel: 01245 248669
Fax: 01245 603534
E-mail: cicoachlines@btinternet.com

CIE TOURS IINTERNATIONAL
Loveitts Farm, Brinklow CV23 0LG
Tel: 01788 833388
Fax: 01788 833710
E-mail: anne@ciegroups.freeserve.co.uk
Web site: www.cietours.co.uk

*FJORD LINE
Norway House, Royal Quays, North Shields
NE29 6EG
Tel: 0191 296 1313
Fax: 0191 296 1540
E-mail: fjordline.uk@fjordline.com
Web site: www.fjordline.com

GREATDAYS TRAVEL GROUP
Travel House, 2 Stamford Park Road,
Altrincham WA15 9EN
Tel: 0161 928 9966
Fax: 0161 928 1332
E-mail: sales@greatdays.co.uk
Web site: www.greatdays.co.uk
Sales Dir: Paul Beaumont

*INDEPENDENT COACH TRAVEL (WHOLESALING) LTD
South Quay Travel and Leisure Ltd, Studios 20/21, Colman's Wharf, 45 Morris Road, London E14 6PA
Tel: 020 7538 4627
Fax: 020 7538 8239
E-mail: aheaton@ictsqt.co.uk
Web site: www.ictsqt.co.uk

*TRAVELPATH 3000
PO Box 32, Grantham NG31 7JA
Tel: 01476 570187
Fax: 01476 572718
E-mail: jon@travelpath-uk.com
Web site: www.travelpath3000.com

THE Trainers For The Passenger Transport Industry

- CPC Passenger National and International courses
- Digital Tachograph & Drivers' Hours courses
- Health & Safety training and consultancy
- Fleet driver training and consultancy
- Consistently high examination pass results

Contact us **NOW** to find out more
0800 3283297

enquiries@specialisttraining.co.uk
www.specialisttraining.co.uk
STCS RB167

Training Services

*BUZZLINES LTD
Unit G1, Lympne Industrial Park, Hythe
CT21 4LR
Tel: 01303 261870
Fax: 01303 230093
Web site: www.buzzlines.co.uk

*COACH DIRECT
The Coach House, 22 South Street,
Rochford SS4 1BQ
Tel: 0870 550 2069
Fax: 0870 070 2069
E-mail: info@coachdirect.co.uk
Web site: www.coachdirect.co.uk

*GOSKILLS
Concorde House, Trinity Park, Solihull
B37 7UQ
Tel: 0121 635 5520
Fax: 0121 635 5521
E-mail: info@goskills.org
Web site: www.goskills.org

*IBPTS
43 Cage Lane, Felixstowe IP11 9BJ
Tel: 01394 672344
Fax: 01394 672344
E-mail: info@ibpts.com
Web site: www.ibpts.com

*MARKET ENGINEERING
23a Parsons Street, Banbury OX16 5LY
Tel: 01295 277050
Fax: 01295 297030
E-mail: contact@m-eng.com
Web site: www.marketengineering.com

*MINIMISE YOUR RISK
11 Chatsworth Park, Telscombe Cliffs
BN10 7DZ
Tel: 01273 580189
Fax: 01273 580189
E-mail: minimise@btconnect.com
Web site: www.minimiseyourrisk.co.uk

OMNIBUS TRAINING LTD
8 Lombard Road, London SW19 3TZ
Tel: 020 8543 4499
Fax: 020 8543 0011
E-mail: enquiries@omnibusltd.com

*PROFESSIONAL TRANSPORT SERVICES
12 Silverdale, Stanford-le-Hope SS17 8BG
Tel: 01375 675262
Web site: www.proftranserv.co.uk
E-mail: enquiries@proftranserv.com

*SPECIALIST TRAINING & CONSULTANCY SERVICES LTD
Head Office, 6 Venture Court, Metcalfe Drive, Altham Industrial Estate, Accrington, Lancs BB5 5TU
Tel: 0800 3283297
Fax: 01282 687091
E-mail: enquiries@specialisttraining.co.uk
Web site: www.specialisttraining.co.uk

Vehicle Certification

*VCA
No1, The Estate Office Centre, Eastgate
Road, Bristol BS5 6XX
Tel: 0117 952 4126
Fax: 0117 952 4104
E-mail: paul.cooke@vca.gov.uk
Web site: www.vca.gov.uk

REVISED/ADDITIONAL/LATE ENTRIES

A-Z Listing of Suppliers / Services

Bodybuilders (small vehicles) Minibus conversions

*BLUEBIRD VEHICLES LTD
Unit 7, Plaxton Park, Cayton Low Road, Eastfield, Scarborough YO11 3BY
Tel: 01723 860800
Fax: 01723 585235
E-mail: info@bluebirdvehicles.com
Web site: www.bluebirdvehicles.com

Body repairs/refurbishing

*COBUS UK
Carnaby Industrial Estate, Bridlington YO15 3QY
Tel: 01262 603 829
Fax: 01262 606 738
E-mail: cobus@btconnect.com

Floor Coverings

*TRIMPLEX SAFETY TREAD LTD
Trident Works, Mulberry Way, Belvedere DA17 6AN
Tel: 020 8311 2101
Fax: 020 8312 1400
E-mail: safetytread@btconnect.com
Web site: www.safetytread.co.uk

Model Buses

*MIRROR IMAGE MODELS
A's Models of Bolton, (Dept. LRB/MIM), PO Box 514, Bolton BL1 5YD
Tel: 01204 467 961.
Web site: www.mirror-image-models.org.uk

Driver Training

*D.A.T.S.
Dave's Accident & Training Services
9 Cheshire Close, Yate, Bristol BS37 5TQ
Tel: 07747 686789
E-mail: davepboulter@blueyonder.co.uk
Web site: www.datservices.org

Consultants

*SPECIALIST TRAINING & CONSULTANCY SERVICES LTD
6 Venture Court, Metcalfe Drive, Altham Industrial Estate, Accrington BB5 5TU
Tel: 0800 3283297
Fax: 01282 687091
E-mail: enquiries@specialisttraining.co.uk
Web site: www.specialisttraining.co.uk

Driver Training

*SPECIALIST TRAINING & CONSULTANCY SERVICES LTD
6 Venture Court, Metcalfe Drive, Altham Industrial Estate, Accrington BB5 5TU
Tel: 0800 3283297
Fax: 01282 687091
E-mail: enquiries@specialisttraining.co.uk
Web site: www.specialisttraining.co.uk

Lifts/Ramps (Passenger)

*C N UNWIN LTD
Unwin House, The Horseshoe, Coat Road, Martock, Somerset TA12 6EY
Tel: 01935 827740
Fax: 01935 827760

Training Services

*SPECIALIST TRAINING & CONSULTANCY SERVICES LTD
6 Venture Court, Metcalfe Drive, Altham Industrial Estate, Accrington BB5 5TU
Tel: 0800 3283297
Fax: 01282 687091
E-mail: enquiries@specialisttraining.co.uk
Web site: www.specialisttraining.co.uk

SPECIAL OFFER

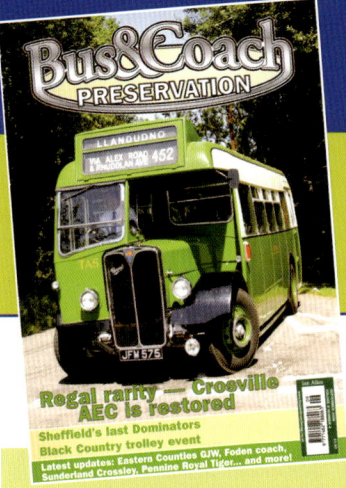

Subscribe today and receive
13 ISSUES for the PRICE OF 12*

BUS & COACH PRESERVATION offers a real insight into the preserved bus and coach world with the latest news and views of vehicle restoration, up-to-date events listings, comprehensive rally reports and superbly illustrated features in every single issue.

Great subscriber benefits!

A subscription to **BUS & COACH PRESERVATION** comes with **FREE MEMBERSHIP** to the **Ian Allan Publishing Subs Club**. As a member of the **Ian Allan Publishing Subs Club**, you will receive a personalised Subscription Loyalty Card, plus a quarterly newsletter with great subscriber benefits, discounts, offers and competitions!

SUBSCRIPTION PRICES
- 1 year UK £43.20
- 1 year Europe & ROI £49.20
- 1 year ROW economy airmail £51.00
- 1 year ROW 1st class airmail £60.00

Contact our subs hotline on: 01932 266622
to take advantage of this special offer and quote LRBBC
subs@ianallanpublishing.co.uk

*Offer valid until 31st January 2007.

NEW Edition

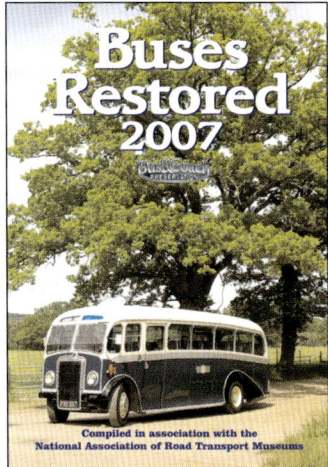

This is the invaluable annual guide to road transport museums throughout the British Isles, compiled by the National Association of Road Transport Museums. The new 2007 edition will be thoroughly updated and once again includes colour illustrations throughout

Softback | 235 x 172mm | 128pp

ISBN: 0 7110 3211 4

£13.99

Available from your local stockist, the Ian Allan Bookshops in Birmingham, Cardiff, London and Manchester or post free to UK addresses from our mail order department:

Ian Allan Publishing Mail Order Dept (BA) | 4 Watling Drive | Hinckley | Leics | LE10 3EY
Tel: 01455 254450 | Fax: 01455 233737
email: midlandbooks@compuserve.com | Visit our website: www.ianallansuperstore.com

section 2

Tendering & Regulatory Authorities

Tendering & Regulatory Authorities etc

PTAs	**64**
PTEs	**64**
Passenger Transport Regional Authorities	**65**
Transport Co-ordinating Officers	**65**
Traffic Commissioners	**68**
Department for Transport	**68**

Passenger Transport Authorities

Greater Manchester PTA:
PO Box 532, Town Hall, Manchester M60 2LA
 Tel: 0161 234 3335
 Fax: 0161 236 6459
 Chmn: Cllr J. R. Jones. **Vice-Chmn**: Cllr A Brett

Merseyside PTA:
24 Hatton Garden, Liverpool L3 2AN
 Tel: 0151 227 5181
 Fax: 0151 236 2457
 Chmn: Cllr Mark Dowd; **Vice-Chmn**: Cllr Hugh G. Lloyd;
 Clerk: Steve Maddox; **Gen Man Mersey Tunnels**: John Gillard.
Operates with Merseyside PTE (qv) as Merseytravel.

South Yorkshire PTA:
PO Box 37, Regent Street, Barnsley S70 2PQ.
 Tel: 01226 772848.
 Web site: www.southyorks.org.uk
 Chmn: Cllr J. M. Hoare; **Vice-Chmn**: Cllr M. Edgell;
 Clerk/Treasurer: W J Wilkinson.

Tyne & Wear PTA:
Civic Centre, Newcastle upon Tyne NE99 2BN.
 Tel: 0191 203 3209.
 Fax: 0191 203 3180.
 Chmn: Cllr T. D. Marshall; **Vice-Chairman & Monitoring Officer**: E. Holt; **Clerk**: K. G. Lavery; **Deputy Clerk & Treasurer**: D. Johnson; **Engineer**: J. Millar; **Legal advisor**: V. A. Dodds.

*West Midlands PTA:
Room 120, Centro House, 16 Summer Lane, Birmingham B19 3SD.
 Tel: 0121 214 7507
 Fax: 0121 233 1841
 Web site: www.wmpta.org.uk
 E-mail for Councillors: ptateam@centro.org.uk
 E-mail for Committee Team: ptateam@centro.org.uk
 Chair: Cllr G Clarke **Vice-Chair**: Cllr P Allen
 Clerk: Ms S Manzie **Deputy Clerk/Solicitor**: C Hinde **Treasurer**: Ms A Ridgewell
 Head of Communications: Conrad Jones

West Yorkshire PTA:
Wellington House, 40-50 Wellington Street, Leeds LS1 2DE.
 Tel: 0113 251 7272.
 Fax: 0113 251 7373.
 Chmn: Cllr J S King; **Vice-Chmn**: Cllr K Hussain
 Clerk to the Authority: K T Preston, OBE.

Passenger Transport Executives

*GMPTE

9 Portland Street, Manchester M60 1HX **Tel**: 0161 242 6000
Web site: www.gmpte.com
GMPTE is responsible to the Greater Manchester Passenger Transport Authority. The PTE is responsible for contracting socially necessary bus services and supporting the local rail service. It also owns the Metrolink light rail system on behalf of the Authority and is responsible for planning for the future of the Metrolink network.
GMPTE and the Authority are also committed to developing accessible transport, funding Ring and Ride, a fully accessible door to door transport service for people with mobility difficulties.
The PTE administers the concessionary fares scheme, which allows participants (pensioners, children and people with disabilities) either free or reduced rate travel. GMPTE owns and is responsible for the upkeep of bus stations and on-street infrastructure. It also provides information about public transport through telephone information lines, timetables, general publicity and Travelshops.

Director General: Chris Mulligan
 Deputy Director, General & Finance Director: Geoff Inskip
 Strategy Director: Keith Howcroft
 Projects Director: Michael Renshaw
 Organisational Development Director: Urvashi Bramwell
 Service Delivery Director: Denise Lennox

Merseyside Passenger Transport Authority and Executive (Merseytravel)

24 Hatton Garden, Liverpool L3 2AN **Tel**: 0151 227 5181
Fax: 0151 236 2457 **Web site**: www.merseytravel.gov.uk
Merseytravel ensures the availability of public transport in Merseyside, including financial support for the Merseyrail rail network and those bus services not provided for by the private sector.
 It also promotes public transport by providing bus stations and infrastructure, comprehensive travel tickets and free travel with minimum restrictions for the elderly and those with mobility difficulties.
 Merseytravel also owns and operates the Mersey ferries and Mersey tunnels.
Chair to PTA: Cllr M Dowd. **Vice-Chair to PTA**: Cllr H. Lloyd. **Chief Executive PTA & Director General PTE**: Neil Scales. **Clerk to PTA**: Steve Maddox. **Director of Resources**: John Wilkinson. **Director of Operations**: Brian Fisher. **Secretary, PTE**: Louise Outram. **Tunnels Manager**: John Gillard.

Nexus (Tyne & Wear PTE)

Nexus House, St James Boulevard, Newcastle upon Tyne NE1 4AX
Tel: 0191 203 3333 **Fax**: 0191 203 3180
Web site: www.nexus.org.uk
Metro: www.tyneandwearmetro.co.uk
Nexus operates within the policies of the Tyne & Wear Passenger Transport Authority. Nexus owns and operates both the Tyne & Wear Metro system and the Shields Ferry (between North Shields and South Shields). Nexus ensures that bus services not operated commercially are provided where there is evidence of social need; operates a demand-responsive transport system, U-call; and organises the provision of special transport for those who can only use ordinary public transport with difficulty if at all. Nexus adminsters the Concessionary Travel scheme and provides comprehensive travel information and sales outlets for countywide season tickets, as well as related administrative support for the scheme.
Rolling Stock: 90 light rail cars. **Ferries**: MFs 'Pride of the Tyne' and 'Shieldsman'

*South Yorkshire Passenger Transport Executive

PO Box 801, Exchange Street, Sheffield S2 5YT
Tel: 0114 276 7575 **Fax**: 0114 275 9908
Web site: www.sypte.co.uk
The Executive is responsible to the South Yorkshire Passenger Transport Authority.

*Centro (West Midlands Passenger Transport Executive)

16 Summer Lane, Birmingham B19 3SD **Tel**: 0121 200 2787
Fax: 0121 214 7010
Web site: www.centro.org.uk
The Executive is responsible to the West Midlands Passenger Transport Authority
Director General: vacant
Services Director: Robert Smith
Projects Director: Tom Magrath
Resources Director: Trevor Robinson
Member of Executive/Treasurer to PTA: Angie Rigwell
PTA Committee: Dan Essex, Marion Cheatham

West Yorkshire Passenger Transport Executive (Metro)

Wellington House, 40-50 Wellington Street, Leeds LS1 2DE
Tel: 0113 251 7272 **Fax**: 0113 251 7333
WYPTE activities are conducted under the corporate name Metro. Metro is financed and supported by the West Yorkshire Passenger Transport Authority.
Director General: Kieran Preston, OBE **Dir Corp Sers**: Sheena Pickersgill **Dir Pass Sers**: John Henkel **Dir Projects**: John Carr

Passenger Transport Regional Authorities

Strathclyde Partnership for Transport (SPT)

Consort House, 12 West George Street, Glasgow G2 1HN
Tel: 0141 332 6811 **Fax**: 0141 332 3076
Web site: www.spt.co.uk
Non Exec Dir: John Anderson

Transport *for* London

Windsor House, 42-50 Victoria Street, London SW1H 0TL
Tel: 020 7941 4500
Web Site: www.tfl.gov.uk
Transport *for* London (T*f*L) took over most of the functions of London Transport from July 2000. It is under the control of the Mayor of London and Greater London Authority. TfL assumed control of London Underground Ltd in 2003.

Commissioner for Transport: Peter Hendy, CBE
Managing Surface Transport: David Brown
Director of Operations: Mike Weston
Managing Director of Finance and Planning: Jay Walder
Director of Road Safety Unit: Chris Lines
Director of the Congestion Charge: Malcolm Murray-Clark
Director of Road Network Operations: Keith Ollier
Traffic Manager: Nick Morris
Managing Director for London Rail: Ian Brown
Head of London Trams: Phil Hewitt

T*f*L's subsidiary companies:

London Buses Ltd
172 Buckingham Palace Road, London SW1W 9TN.
Tel: 020 7222 5600.
Director of Performance: Clare Kavanagh

Victoria Coach Station Ltd
164 Buckingham Palace Road, London SW1W 9TP.
Tel: 020 7730 3466. **Fax**: 020 7730 2589

London River Services Ltd
55 Broadway, London SW1H 0BD. **Tel**: 020 7222 5600.

London Underground Ltd
55 Broadway, London SW1H 0BD. **Tel**: 020 7222 5600
Managing Director: Tim O'Toole

Transport Co-ordinating Officers

Under the Transport Act 1978 the non-Metropolitan Counties were given power to co-ordinate public transport facilities in their areas. From 1 April 1996 Welsh Counties and Scottish Regions were replaced by new single-tier authorities. At the same time certain English Counties were replaced by new single-tier authorities. The major role is now to secure socially necessary services which are not provided commercially. The names of most of the responsible officers are set out below.

ENGLAND

*****Bedfordshire County Council** - Chris Pettifer, Integrated Passenger Transport Manager, Integrated Passenger Transport Unit, Bedfordshire County Council, County Hall, Cauldwell Street, Bedford MK42 9AP
Tel: 01234 228881

Bracknell Forest Borough Council - R. Cook, Time Square, Bracknell RG12 1JD
Tel: 01344 424642.

Buckinghamshire - R. Slevin, County Passenger Transport Officer, County Hall, Aylesbury HP20 1YZ.
Tel: 01296 383751. **Fax**: 01296 383749.

Cambridgeshire - B. E. Jackson, Head of Passenger Transport, Department of Environment & Transport, Mailbox ET1015, Shire Hall, Castle Hill, Cambridge CB3 0AP.
Tel: 01223 717744. **Fax**: 01223 717789.

Cheshire - G. Goddard, County Transport Co-ordinator, Rivacre Business Centre, Mill Lane, Ellesmere Port CH66 3TL.
Tel: 01244 603218. **Fax**: 01244 603200.

*****Cornwall** - Stephen Nicholson, Principal Transport Officer, County Hall, Truro TR1 3AY
Tel: 01872 322003 (via call centre) **Fax**: 01872 323844
E-mail: snicholson@cornwall.gov.uk

*****Cumbria County Council** - The Courts, Carlisle CA3 8NA
Tel: 01228 606720 **Fax**: 01228 606755
E-mail: graham.whiteley@cumbriacc.gov.uk

Derbyshire - T. M. Hardy, Public Transport Manager, County Hall, Matlock DE4 3AG
Tel: 01629 580000. **Fax**: 01629 585740.

Devon - A. T. W. Davies, Head, Transport Co-ordination Service, Environment Directorate, County Hall, Exeter EX2 4QW
Tel: 01392 383244 **Fax**: 01392 382904
E-mail: tim.davies@devon.gov.uk

*****Dorset** - Barry Thirlwall, Passenger Transport Manager, County Hall, Dorchester DT1 1XJ
Tel: 01305 224537 **Fax**: 01305 225166
E-mail: b.thirlwall@dorsetcc.gov.uk
Web site: www.dorsetcc.gov.uk

Durham - Adrian J White, Business Manager Public Transport, Environment Dept, County Hall, Durham DH1 5UQ.
Tel: 0191 383 3435 **Fax**: 0191 383 4096.

*****East Riding of Yorkshire Council** - David Boden, Passenger Services Manager, Passenger Services Team, The Fleet Building, Grovehill Road, Beverley HU17 0JP
Tel: 01482 395521 **Fax**: 01482 395054
E-mail: david.boden@eastriding.gov.uk
Web site: www.eastriding.gov.uk

East Sussex - N Smith, Group Manager (Passenger Transport), Transport & Environment, East Sussex County Council, County Hall, St Anne's Crescent, Lewes BN7 1UE.
Tel: 01273 482326. **Fax**: 01273 474361.
E-mail: nick.smith@eastsussexcc.gov.uk

*****Essex** - J Pope, Group Manager, Passenger Transport, Highways & Transportation, County Hall, Chelmsford CM1 1QH
Tel: 01245 437506 **Fax**: 01245 496764
Web site: www.essexcc.gov.uk

Gloucestershire - Operations & Procurement Manager, Shire Hall, Bearland, Gloucester GL1 2TH
Tel: 01452 425968

*****Hampshire** - K Wilcox, Head of Passenger Transport, Hampshire County Council, Environment Department, The Castle, Winchester SO23 8UD.
Tel: 01962 846997 **Fax**: 01962 845855
E-mail: keith.wilcox@hants.gov.uk

Hartlepool Borough Council – Ian Jopling, Transport Team Leader, Department of Neighbourhood Services, Bryan Hanson House, Hanson Square, Hartlepool TS24 7BT
Tel: 01429 284140 **Fax**: 01429 860830
E-mail: ian.jopling@hartlepool.gov.uk
Web site: www.hartlepool.gov.uk

Hertfordshire County Council Passenger Transport Unit, PO Box 99, Hertford SG13 8TJ
Tel: 01992 556725
Web site: www.intalink.org.uk

Hull City Council
Web site: www.hullcc.gov

Isle of Wight Council - A A Morris, Transport Manager, Jubilee Stores, The Quay, Newport PO30 2EH
Tel: 01983 823710. **Fax**: 01983 823707.

Kent County Council - Julia Seaward, Head of Transport, Commercial Services, Kent County Council, Gibson Drive, Kings Hill, West Malling ME19 4QG
Tel: 01622 605091 **Fax**: 01622 605084
E-mail: passenger.transport@kent.gov.uk
Web site: www.kentpublictransport.info

Lancashire - Stuart Wrigley, Head of Transport Policy, PO Box 9, Guild House, Cross Street, Preston PR1 8RD
Tel: 01772 534660. **Fax**: 01772 533833

Leicestershire - Tony Kirk, Group Manager (Public Transport), Department of Highways, Transportation & Waste Management, County Hall, Glenfield, Leicester LE3 8RJ
Tel: 0116 265 6270 **Fax**: 0116 265 7181
E-mail: tkirk@leics.gov.uk
  Web site: www.leics.gov.uk

Lincolnshire - A R Cross, Head of Transport Services, 4th Floor, City Hall, Beaumont Fee, Lincoln LN1 1DN
Tel: 01522 553132 **Fax**: 01522 568735

*****Norfolk** - Tracey Jessop, Head of Passenger Transport, Department of Planning & Transportation, County Hall, Martineau Lane, Norwich NR1 2SG
Tel: 01603 224368 **Fax**: 01603 222144

Northamptonshire - Sustainable Transport Manager, Northamptonshire County Council, Riverside House, Riverside Way, Bedford Road, Northampton NN1 5NX
Tel: 01604 236711

Northumberland - John Hodgson, Network Development Officer, Integrated Transport Unit, Community and Environmental Services Directorate, Northumberland County Council, County Hall, Morpeth NE61 2EF
Tel: 01670 534837 **Fax**: 01670 533086
E-mail: jhodgson@northumberland.gov.uk

North Yorkshire - R Owens, Passenger Transport Officer, County Hall, Northallerton DL7 8AH
Tel: 01609 780780, Ext 2870 **Fax**: 01609 779838

*****Nottinghamshire County Council** - County Hall, West Bridgford, Nottingham NG2 7QP
Tel: 0115 982 3823 **E-mail**: enquiries@nottscc.gov.uk
Web site: www.nottinghamshire.gov.uk

Oxfordshire - R Helling, Public Transport Officer, Environmental Services, Speedwell House, Speedwell Street, Oxford OX1 1NE
Tel: 01865 815859 **Fax**: 01865 815085

Reading Borough Council – Mrs P Baxter, Civic Centre, Reading RG1 7TD
Tel: 0118 939 0813

Shropshire - K R Gallop, Principal Passenger Transport Officer, Environment Department, The Shirehall, Abbey Foregate, Shrewsbury SY2 6ND
Tel: 01743 253031 **Fax**: 01743 254382

Slough Borough Council - R Fraser, PO Box 570, Slough SL1 1FA

Somerset County Council - County Hall, The Crescent, Taunton TA20 1JS
Tel: 01823 356700 **Fax**: 01823 351356
E-mail: transport@somerset.gov.uk
Web site: www.somerset.gov.uk

Staffordshire - Charles Soutar, Head of Passenger Transport, Development Services Department, Riverway, Stafford ST16 3TJ
Tel: 01785 276735 **Fax**: 01785 276621

Suffolk - M Bradshaw, Public Transport Manager, Environment & Transport Department, Endeavour House, 8 Russell Road, Ipswich IP1 2BX
Tel: 01473 265050 **Fax**: 01473 216884
E-mail: mitchell.bradshaw@et.suffolkcc.gov.uk

*****Surrey County Council** - A Teer, Group Manager Passenger Transport, Room 306, County Hall, Penrhyn Road, Kingston-on-Thames KT1 2DY
Tel: 020 8541 9371 **Fax**: 020 8541 9389
E-mail: alan.teer@surreycc.gov.uk
Web site: surreycc.gov.uk/passenger_transport

*****Warwickshire** - K McGovern, Passenger Tranport Operations Manager, Warwickshire County Council, Environment & Economy Directorate, PO Box 43, Shire Hall, Warwick CV34 4SX
Tel: 01926 412930 **Fax**: 01926 418041
E-mail: passengertransport@warwickshire.gov.uk
Web site: www.warwickshire.gov.uk

West Berkshire Council - J Sherry, Market Street, Newbury
Tel: 01635 42400

*****West Sussex County Council** - Mark Miller, Group Manager, Transport Co-ordination, Highways and Transport, The Grange, Tower Street, Chichester PO19 1RH
Tel: 01243 777811 **Web site**: www.westsussex.gov.uk

*****Wiltshire** - I White, Passenger Transport Co-ordinator, Environmental Services Dept, County Hall, Trowbridge BA14 8JD
Tel: 01225 713322 **Fax**: 01225 713565

Royal Borough of Windsor & Maidenhead – E Mouser, Yorkstream House, St Ives Road, Maidenhead SL6 1RF
Tel: 01628 796732 **Fax**: 01628 796774

*****Wokingham** - Roland Clausen-Thue, Transport, Environment Service, Shute End, Wokingham RG40 1WL
Tel: 0118 974 6468 **Fax**: 0118 974 6486

*****Worcestershire County Council** - Passenger Transport Group, PO Box 82, Pershore Lane, Worcester WR4 0AA
Tel: 01905 768411 **Fax**: 01905 768438
Web site: www.worcestershire.gov.uk

WALES

*****Anglesey** - Isle of Anglesey County Council, Council Offices, Llangefni LL77 7TW
Tel: 01248 752300 **Fax**: 01248 724839
E-mail: dwrpl@anglesey.gov.uk **Web site**: www.anglesey.gov.uk

Blaenau Gwent - Blaenau Gwent County Borough Council, Municipal Offices, Civic Centre, Ebbw Vale NP3 6XB
Tel: 01495 350555. **Fax**: 01495 301255

*****Bridgend County Borough Council** - D H Beynon, Transport Co-ordinating Manager, Transport & Engineering, Morien House, Bennet Street, Bridgend CF31 3SH
Tel: 01656 643643. **Fax**: 01656 668126
Web site: www.bridgend.gov.uk

*****Caerphilly County Borough Council** - Huw Morgan, Principal Passenger Transport Officer, Directorate of the Environment, Council Offices, Pontllanfraith, Blackwood NP12 2YW.
Tel: 01495 235089 **Fax**: 01495 235045 **E-mail**: morgash@caerphilly.gov.uk **Web site**: www.caerphilly.gov.uk

Cardiff - Cardiff County Council, Traffic & Transportation Service, County Hall, Atlantic Wharf, Cardiff CF10 4UW

Cardiganshire - see Ceredigion

Carmarthenshire: Dir of Economic Development: Gerald Campbell Phillips. Carmarthenshire Council Council, County Hall, Carmarthen SA31 1JP.
Tel: 01267 234567. **Fax:** 01267 230848.

Ceredigion: Cyngor Sir Ceredigion, County Council, County Hall, Market Street, Aberaeron SA46 0AT.
Tel: 01545 572501 **Fax:** 01545 571089

Conwy - Conwy County Borough Council, Bodlondeb, Conwy LL32 8DU.
Tel: 01492 574000, 592114. **Fax:** 01492 592114.

Denbighshire - Denbighshire County Council, Council Offices, Wynnstay Road, Ruthin LL15 1AT.
Tel: 01824 706000 **Fax**: 01824 707446.
Public Transport: M G Rhodes, Passenger Transport Coordinator, Caledfryn, Smithfield Road, Denbigh LL16 3RJ.
Tel: 01824 706879. **Fax**: 01824 706970

Flintshire County Council - Directorate of Environment & Regeneration, County Hall, Mold CH7 6NG
Tel: 01352 704530 **Fax**: 01352 704540
Web site: www.flintshire.gov.uk

Gwynedd Council - M Cowban, Public Transport Officer, Council Offices, Shirehall 56, Caernarfon LL55 1SH.
Tel: 01286 679541 **Fax**: 01286 673324
E-mail: malcolmwaltercowban@gwynedd.gov.uk

Merthyr Tydfil - Martin Haworth, Senior Transport Officer, Merthyr Tydfil County Borough Council, Civic Centre, Castle Street, Merthyr Tydfil CF47 8AN
Tel: 01685 726288 **Fax**: 01685 387982
E-mail: martin.howarth@merthyr.gov.uk

Monmouthshire - Monmouthshire County Council, County Hall, Cwmbran NP44 2XH
Tel: 01633 644644 **Fax**: 01633 644701
E-mail: transport@monmouthshire.gov.uk
Web site: www.monmouthshire.gov.uk

Neath Port Talbot - Neath Port Talbot County Borough Council, Civic Centre, Port Talbot SA13 1PJ .
Tel: 01639 763333. **Fax**: 01639 763444.

Newport - Dir. of Development/Transport: Brian Adcock, Newport County Borough Council, Civic Centre, Newport NP9 4UR.
Tel: 01633 244491. **Fax**: 01633 244721

*****Pembrokeshire County Council** - M Hubert, Transport and Fleet Manager, County Hall, Haverfordwest SA61 1TP
Tel: 01437 764551 **Fax**: 01437 775008
E-mail: hubert.mathias@pembrokeshire.gov.uk

Powys - Transport Co-ordination Unit, County Hall, Llandrindod Wells LD1 5LG.
Tel: 01597 826260 **Fax**: 01597 826260.

Rhondda Cynon Taf - Rhondda Cynon Taf County Borough Council, The Pavilions, Cambrian Park, Clydach Vale CF40 2XX
Tel: 01443 424000. **Fax**: 01443 424027. Public Transport: D M Sherrard, Divisional Director (Transportation), Sardis House, Sardis Road, Pontypridd CF37 1DU
Tel: 01443 494700 **Fax**: 01443 494875

City & County of Swansea - Catherine Swain, Team Leader - Passenger Transport, Environment Department, County Hall, Oystermouth Road, Swansea SA1 3SN
Tel: 01792 636079 **Fax**: 01792 652712
E-mail: cath.swain@swansea.gov.uk
Web site: www.swansea.gov.uk

Torfaen - Torfaen County Borough Council, Civic Centre, Pontypool NP4 6YB.
Tel: 01495 762200. **Fax**: 01495 755513.

*****Vale of Glamorgan Council** - Transportation Unit, Dock Offices, Barry Docks, Barry CF63 4RT
Tel: 01446 704687 **Fax**: 01446 704891
E-mail: planning&transport@valeofglamorgan.gov.uk
Web site: www.valeofglamorgan.gov.uk

*****Wrexham** - Wrexham County Borough Council, Crown Buildings, Chester Street, Wrexham LL13 8BG
Tel: 01978 292000 **Fax**: 01978 292106

SCOTLAND

Aberdeen City - The Director, Environment & Infrastructure Services, Aberdeen City Council, St Nicholas House, Broad Street, Aberdeen AB10 1WL
Tel: 01224 523762. **Fax**: 01224 523764.
E-mail: rwaters@roads.aberdeen.net.uk.
Web site: www.aberdeencity.gov.uk

*****Aberdeenshire** - R McKenzie, Public Transport Manager, Aberdeenshire Council, Woodhill House, Westburn Road, Aberdeen AB16 5GB.
Tel: 01224 664585 **Fax**: 01224 662005
E-mail: richard.mckenzie@aberdeenshire.gov.uk
Web site: www.aberdeenshire.gov.uk

Angus Council - L Millar, Transport Manager, Angus Council, St James House, St James Road, Forfar DD8 2ZD
Tel: 01307 461774 **Fax**: 01307 473711
E-mail: millarle@angus.gov.uk
Web site: www.angus.gov.uk/transport

*****Argyll and Bute Council** - B D Blades, Public Transport Officer, Kilmory, Lochgilphead PA31 8RT
Tel: 01546 604360 **Fax**: 01546 604291
Web site: www.argyll-bute.gov.uk

Clackmannanshire - David Taylor, Public Transport Officer, Clackmannanshire Council, Lime Tree House, Alloa FK10 1EX.
Tel: 01259 452603 **Fax**: 01786 442739
E-mail: dtaylor@clacks.gov.uk **Web site**: www.clacksweb.org.uk

Dundee City - Mark Devine, Transport Officer, Dundee City Council, Planning & Transportation Department, Floor 16, Tayside House, Crichton Street, Dundee DD1 3RB.
Tel: 01382 433831. **Fax**: 01382 433313
E-mail: mark.devine@dundeecity.gov.uk.
Web site: www.dundeecity.gov.uk

*****Dumfries & Galloway** - D Kirkpatrick, Team leader (Passenger Transport), Dumfries & Galloway Council, Militia House, English Street, Dumfries DG1 2HR.
Tel: 01387 260133 **Fax**: 01387 260383

East Ayrshire - East Ayrshire Council, London Road, Kilmarnock KA3 7BU.

East Dunbartonshire - East Dunbartonshire Council, PO Box 4, Civic Way, Kirkintilloch G66 4TJ.

East Lothian - Transport Planning Manager, Department of Planning, East Lothian Council, 25 Court Street, Haddington EH41 3HA.

East Renfrewshire - East Renfrewshire Council, Eastwood Park, Rouken Glen Road, Giffnock G46 6UG.

City of Edinburgh Council - Max Thomson, Public Transport Manager, City Development, 1 Cockburn Street, Edinburgh EH1 1BJ
Tel: 0131 469 3631. **Fax**: 0131 469 3635.
E-mail: max.thomson@edinburgh.gov.uk

Falkirk - Stephen Bloomfield, Public Transport Co-ordinator, Development Services, Falkirk Council, Abbotsfold House, David's Loan, Falkirk FK2 7YZ.
Tel: 01324 504723. **Fax**: 01324 504914.

Fife - Trond Haugen, Transportation Manager - Transportation Services, Fife Council, Fife House, North Street, Glenrothes KY7 5LT.
Tel: 01592 413106. **Fax**: 01592 413061
E-mail: trond.haugen@fife.gov.uk

Highland - Transport Officer, Highland Council, Glenurquhart Road, Inverness IV3 5NX.
Tel: 01463 702612. **Fax**: 01463 702606.

Inverclyde - Inverclyde Council, Municipal Buildings, Greenock PA15 1LY.

Midlothian - Brian Sharkie, Public Transport Manager, Midlothian Council, Fairfield House, 8 Lothian Road, Dalkeith EH22 3ZN.
Tel: 0131 271 3520. **Fax**: 0131 271 3537.
E-mail: brian.sharkie@midlothian.gov.uk

Moray - Peter Findlay, Public Transport Manager, Moray Council, Council Office, Academy Street, Elgin IV30 1LL
Tel: 01343 562541. **Fax**: 01343 545628.
E-mail: peter.findlay@moray.gov.uk.

North Ayrshire - North Ayrshire Council, Cunningham House, Irvine KA12 8EE.

North Lanarkshire - North Lanarkshire Council, Po Box 14, Civic Centre, Motherwell ML1 1TW
Tel: 01224 664580. **Fax**: 01224 662005.

Orkney - Orkney Islands Council, Council Offices, School Place, Kirkwall KW15 1NY.

*****Perth & Kinross** - Andrew J Warrington, Public Transport Manager; The Environment Service, Pullar House, 35 Kinnoull Street, Perth PH1 5GD.
Tel: 01738 476530. **Fax**: 01738 476510.
E-mail: awarrington@pkc.gov.uk

Renfrewshire - Renfrewshire Council, North Building, Cotton Street, Paisley PA1 1WB.

Scottish Borders - B Young, Transport Policy Manager, Scottish Borders Council, Council Headquarters, Newtown St Boswells, Melrose TD6 0SA.
Tel: 01835 824000 **Fax**: 01835 823008

Shetland Islands - Ian Bruce, Service Manager - Transport Operations, Infrastructure Service Dept., Shetland Islands Council, Grantfield, Lerwick ZE1 0NT.
Tel: 01595 744872. **Fax**: 01595 744869.
E-mail: ian.bruce@sic.shetland.gov.uk

South Ayrshire - South Ayrshire Council, County Buildings, Wellington Square, Ayr KA7 1DR.

South Lanarkshire - South Lanarkshire Council, Council Offices, Almada Street, Hamilton ML3 0AA. *(No Public Transport responsibilities - see SPT)*

Stirling - Stirling Council, Council Headquarters, Viewforth, Stirling FK8 2ET.

West Dunbartonshire - West Dunbartonshire Council, Council Offices, Garshake Road, Dunbarton, G82 3PU. (No Public Transport responsibilities - see SPT)

Western Isles - Western Isles Council, Council Offices, Balivanich, Benbecula HS7 5LA.

*****West Lothian** - Roy Mitchell, Public Transport Manager, West Lothian Council, County Buildings, Linlithgow EH49 7EZ
Tel: 01506 775282. **Fax**: 01506 775265.
E-mail: roy.mitchell@westlothian.gov.uk .
Web site: www.westlothian.gov.uk

Traffic Commissioners

Web site: www.vosa.gov.uk

EASTERN TRAFFIC AREA
Terrington House, 13-15 Hills Road, Cambridge CB2 1NP
Tel: 01223 531060 **Fax**: 01223 309681
Traffic Commissioner: Geoffrey Simms
Deputy Traffic Commissioners: D. N. Stevens, R. C. Lockwood, M. J. Guy. **Area covered:** Leicestershire, Lincolnshire, Cambridgeshire, Norfolk, Suffolk, Essex, Bedfordshire, Northamptonshire, Hertfordshire, Buckinghamshire.

NORTH EASTERN TRAFFIC AREA
Hillcrest House, 386 Harehills Lane, Leeds LS9 6NF
Tel: 0870 606 0440 **Fax**: 0113 248 9607
Traffic Commissioner: Tom Macartney
Deputy Traffic Commissioners: M. Hinchcliffe, Ms L Perrett, P J Mulvenna
Area covered: Northumberland, Tyne & Wear, Co Durham, Yorkshire, Nottinghamshire
Web site: www.vosa.gov.uk

NORTH WESTERN TRAFFIC AREA
Hillcrest House, 386 Harehills Lane, Leeds LS9 6NF
Tel: 0870 606 0440 **Fax**: 0113 248 9607
Traffic Commissioner: Beverley Bell.
Deputy Traffic Commissioners: M Hinchcliffe, Ms L Perrett, P J Mulvenna
Area covered: Cumbria, Lancashire, Greater Manchester, Merseyside, Cheshire, Derbyshire.
Web site: www.vosa.gov.uk

*SCOTTISH TRAFFIC AREA
J Floor, 3 Lady Lawson Street, Edinburgh EH3 9SE
Tel: 0131 200 4955 **Fax**: 0131 229 0682
Traffic Commissioner: Miss Joan Aitken
Deputy Traffic Commissioner: R H McFarlane
Area covered: Scotland

*SOUTH EASTERN & METROPOLITAN TRAFFIC AREA
Ivy House, 3 Ivy Terrace, Eastbourne BN21 4QT.
Tel: 01323 452400. **Fax**: 01323 721057
Traffic Commissioner: Chris Heaps
Deputy Traffic Commissioners: M Kane, T Swan
Area covered: Greater London, Kent, Surrey, Sussex.

WELSH TRAFFIC AREA
38 George Road, Birmingham B15 1PL
Tel: 0121 609 6832 **Fax**: 0121 456 4241
Traffic Commissioner: David Dixon
Deputy Traffic Commissioners: A Jenkins, A L Maddrell, C R Seymour.
Area covered: Wales.

WEST MIDLAND TRAFFIC AREA
38 George Road, Birmingham B15 1PL
Tel: 0121 609 6832 **Fax**: 0121 456 4241
Traffic Commissioner: David Dixon.
Deputy Traffic Commissioners: A Jenkins, A L Maddrell, C R Seymour.
Area covered: Shropshire, Staffordshire, West Midlands, Warwickshire, Worcestershire, Herefordshire.

WESTERN TRAFFIC AREA
2 Rivergate, Bristol BS1 6EH
Tel: 0870 606 0440
Traffic Commissioner: Philip Brown.
Deputy Traffic Commissioners: Brig M. H. Turner, Mrs F. R. Burton, A. L. Maddrell.
Administrative Director: Tim Hughes.
Area covered: Cornwall, Devon, Somerset, Dorset, Hampshire, Wiltshire, Gloucestershire, Oxfordshire, Berkshire.

Office of Fair Trading

The Office of Fair Trading (OFT) plays a leading role in promoting and protecting consumer interests throughout the UK, while ensuring that businesses are fair and competitive. The tools to carry out this work are the powers granted to the OFT under consumer and competition legislation.
Address: Fleetbank House, 2-6 Salisbury Square, London EC4Y 8JX
Tel: 020 7211 8000 **Fax**: 020 7211 8800
Web site: www.oft.gov.uk
E-mail: enquiries@oft.gsi.gov.uk
Enquiries: 08457 22 44 99

Department for Transport

Eland House, Bressenden Place, London SW1E 5DU
Tel: 020 7944 3000
Web site: www.dft.gov.uk

Permanent Secretary: David Rowlands
Director of Communications: Charles Skinner
Director General, Railways: Dr Mike Mitchell

Executive Agencies: (includes:)
Driving Standards Agency (DSA)
Driver and Vehicle Licensing Agency (DVLA)
Highways Agency (HA)
Tel: 08457 50 40 30
Web Site: www.highways.gov.uk

*Vehicle Certification
*VCA
No1, The Estate Office Centre, Eastgate Road, Bristol BS5 6XX
Tel: 0117 952 4126
Fax: 0117 952 4104
E-mail: paul.cooke@vca.gov.uk
Web site: www.vca.gov.uk

Vehicle and Operator Services Agency (VOSA) (see also Driver Training A-Z Manufacturers section)
Web site: www.transportoffice.gov.uk

Advisory Non-Departmental Bodies: (includes:)

Commission for Integrated Transport
Chmn: Peter Hendy
Tel: 020 7944 8300
E-mail: cfit@dft.gsi.gov.uk

Disabled Persons Transport Advisory Committee
E-mail: dptac@dft.gsi.gov.uk

Executive Non-departmental Bodies: (includes:)
Health and Safety Commission
Health and Safety Executive

Tribunals
Traffic Areas

Public Corporations
Civil Aviation Authority
Transport for London

The Disabled Persons Transport Advisory Committee
Department for Transport
Great Minster House, 76 Marsham Street, London SW1P 4DR
Tel: 020 7944 8011
Minicom: 020 7944 3277
Fax: 020 7944 6998
E-mail: dptac@dft.gov.uk
Web site: www.dptac.gov.uk
Chair: Neil Betteridge
The Disabled Persons Transport Advisory Committee (DPTAC) is a statutory body established under Section 125 of the Transport Act 1985 to advise the Secretary of State for Transport on matters affecting the transport needs of disabled people. Membership is limited to a Chairman plus twenty members, at least half of whom must be disabled.

Mobility and Inclusion Unit
(address as above)
Tel: 020 7944 8021
Minicom: 020 7944 3277
Fax: 020 7944 6102
E-mail: miu@dft.gsi.gov.uk
Web site: www.dptac.gov.uk
Disability Rights Commission
Web site: www.drc-gb.org.uk

Rail Accident Investigation Branch
The Wharf, Stores Road, Derby DE21 4BA
Tel: 01332 253300
Fax: 01332 253301
E-mail: enquiries@raib.gov.uk
Web site: www.raib.gov.uk
RAIB is the independent railway accident investigation organisation for the UK and is listed in LRB because its remit covers street tramways.

Do you want to keep your
LITTLE RED BOOK
up-to-date?
Buses magazine is now carrying
updates every month.
See opposite title page
for Subscription details

section 3
Organisations and Societies

British Operators Organisations	*72*
Institutions	*72*
International Associations	*74*
Other Organisations	*74*
First Aid and Sports Associations	*76*
Trade Organisations	*76*
Societies	*77*
Passenger Transport Museums	*81*

British Operators' Organisations

*ALBUM - ASSOCIATION OF LOCAL BUS COMPANY MANAGERS

The Association represents the professional views of the Executive Directors of those bus companies owned by district council and major independent operators on matters specifically affecting locally-owned bus company management and operations.

Chairperson: M Robson, Ipswich Buses Ltd, 7 Constantine Road, Ipswich IP1 2DL **Tel**: 01473 232600
Secretary: S Burd, Blackpool Transport Services Ltd, Rigby Road, Blackpool FY1 5DD **Tel**: 01253 473041

*COACH OPERATORS FEDERATION

Oakwood, Radway, Sidmouth EX10 8TW
Tel: 07768 846138 **Fax**: 01395 513508
E-mail: john.reece@virgin.net
Web site: www.coachoperatorsfederation.co.uk
Secretary: Ted Reece

*THE COACH TOURISM COUNCIL

PO Box 750, Olney MK46 5WZ
Tel: 0870 850 2839
E-mail: admin@coachtourismcouncil.co.uk
Web site: www.coachtourismcouncil.co.uk
The CTC's mission is to promote tourism and travel by coach.

COMMUNITY TRANSPORT ASSOCIATION

Highbank, Halton Street, Hyde SK14 2NY
Tel: 0870 774 3586 **Fax**: 0870 774 3581
Advice Service Tel: 0845 130 6195
E-mail: CTAUK@CommunityTransport.com
Web site: www.CommunityTransport.com

The community transport sector is vast. There are over 100,000 minibuses serving over 10 million passengers every year being operated for use by voluntary and community groups, schools, colleges and Local Authorities, or to provide door-to-door transport for people who are unable to use other public transport. This door-to-door transport is not limited to minibuses though; there are very many voluntary car schemes throughout the UK where volunteers will use their own cars to provide transport for individuals. Overcoming social exclusion is at the heart of what community transport has always been about. The CTA is committed to helping its members achieve this objective in their area both in terms of the direct support it can offer such as training, developmental support etc. but also by lobbying on behalf of the movement with government and other important agencies.

*CONFEDERATION OF PASSENGER TRANSPORT UK

Imperial House, 15-19 Kingsway, London WC2B 6UN
Tel: 020 7240 3131 **Fax**: 020 7240 6565
E-mail: cpt@cpt-uk.org **Web site**: www.cpt-uk.org

The Confederation of Passenger Transport UK (CPT) is the trade association representing the UK's bus and coach operators and the light rail sector. CPT has wide responsibilities ranging from representation on government working parties (national, local, EU); establishing operating codes of practice; advising on legal, technical and mechanical standards; management of the Bonded Coach Holiday Scheme, a government recognised consumer travel protection scheme and Coachmarque, an industry quality standard; 24-hour Crisis Control service for members; organisation of industry events and the first point of contact for the media on transport and other related issues.

OFFICERS AND COUNCIL
President: Alan Scoles
Immediate Past President: Phil White CBE
Director General: B Nimick
Manager, Director General's Office: Miss L Tang
Finance Director: W Wright
Communications Director: S Posner
Public Affairs Officer: C Nice
Director of Membership: Peter Gomersall
Operations Director: S Salmon
Head of Coach Services & Deputy Director of Operations: A Edmondson
Technical Executive: C Copelin
Operations Executives: M James, J Burch
Fixed Track Executive: D Walmsley
Director, Government Relations, Northern Ireland: Karen Magill
The Ecos Centre, Broughshane Road, Ballymena, Co Antrim BT43 7QA
Tel: 0282 563 8938
Chair, CPT Northern Ireland: William Wright
Director of Government Relations, Scotland:
Mrs M Rodger, 29 Drumsheugh Gardens, Edinburgh EH3 7RN
Tel: 0131 272 2150 **Fax**: 0131 272 2152
Director of Government Relations, Wales:
J Pockett, 70 Hillside View, Craigwen, Pontypridd CF37 2LG
Tel: 01443 485814 **Fax**: 01443 485816

Regional Managers
East Midlands: Andrew Norman, 28 Coppice End Road, Allestree, Derby DE22 2TA **Tel**: 01332 242169
London & Home Counties: G Sutton, Imperial House, 15-19 Kingsway, London WC2B 6UN
Tel: 020 7240 3131. **Fax**: 020 7240 6565
Northern: David Holding, 6 The Dene, Chester Moor, Chester-le-Street DH2 3TB **Tel**: 0191 388 7694 **Fax**: 0191 388 7694
North Western: Leonard Green, 2 Short Clough Close, Reedsholme, Rawtenstall BB4 8PT **Tel**: 01706 218539 **Fax**: 01706 601485
Scotland: Gail Hume, 29 Drumsheugh Gardens, Edinburgh EH13 7RR **Tel**: 0131 272 2150 **Fax**: 0131 272 2152
Wales: E Marsh, Flat 102, The Aspect, 140 Queen Street, Cardiff CF10 2GP **Tel**: 029 2093 0069
West Midlands: G Sutton, Imperial House, 15-19 Kingsway, London WC2B 6UN. **Tel**: 020 7240 3131 **Fax**: 020 7240 6565
South West: R Anderson, Heather Cottage, Smokey Cross, Haytor, Newton Abbot TQ13 9QU
Tel: 01364 661365 **Fax**: 01752 777931
Yorkshire: G Peach, Green Acres, 332 Barnsley Road, Flockton WF4 4AT
Tel: 01924 840767 **Fax**: 01924 849685

PASSENGER TRANSPORT EXECUTIVE GROUP

Wellington House, 40-50 Wellington Street, Leeds LS1 2DE
Tel: 0113 251 7204 **Fax**: 0113 251 7333
Web site: www.pteg.net
Chair: Roy Wicks
PTEG brings together and promotes the interests of the six Passenger Transport Executives (PTEs) in England. Transport for London is an associate member.

Institutions

THE CHARTERED INSTITUTE OF LOGISTICS & TRANSPORT

Logistics & Transport Centre, Earlstrees Court, Earlstrees Road, Corby NN17 4AX
Tel: 01536 740100 **Fax:** 01536 740101
E-mail: enquiry@ciltuk.org.uk.
Web site: www.ciltuk.org.uk

The Chartered Institute of Logistics and Transport (UK) is the professional body for individuals and organisations involved in all disciplines, modes and aspects of logistics and transport.

The Institute's 22,000 members have privileged access to a range of benefits and services, which support them, professionally and personally, throughough their careers and help connect them with world-wide expertise.

For further information and to join please contact Membership Services, Tel: 01536 740104 or visit the CILT(UK) web site: www.ciltuk.org.uk

THE INSTITUTE OF THE MOTOR INDUSTRY

The Institute of the Motor Industry (IMI) is the major professional and awarding body for the motor industry. Established in 1920, the Institute performs the role of promoting and recognising professionalism in the motor industry and has some 25,000 members worldwide. Information is available on a wide variety of qualifications offered by the Institute including NVQs/SVQs, the 600 Series learning programmes and the Certificate of Management offered by the Awarding Body. There are six levels of membership, student, graduate, affiliate, associate, member and fellow.

OFFICERS AND VICE PRESIDENTS
Patron: HRH Prince Michael of Kent KCVO FIMI.
President: Rt Hon Lord Brabazon of Tara FIMI.
Honorary Treasurer: Martin Austin FIMI.
Vice Presidents: Sir T. Chinn CVO FIMI, Sir I Gibson CBE FIMI, T Gibson FIMI, P Johnson FIMI, J Hughes FIMI, M Marshall CBE FIMI, I McAllister CBE FIMI, J Neill CBE FIMI, Prof G Rhys OBE FIMI, Sir N Scheele FIMI, T Taylor FIMI, V Thomas CBE FIMI
Representative Vice Presidents:
The Presidents of:
Motor & Allied Trades Benevolent Fund: Mrs Sue Brownson OBE FIMI.
Retail Motor Industry Federation: John Bond-Smith FIMI.
Scottish Motor Trade Association: John Chessor FIMI.
Society of the Irish Motor Industry: Michael Forde.
Society of Motor Manufacturers & Traders: Nick Reilly FIMI.
Vehicle Builders & Repairers Association: Rt Hon Lord Strathcarron FIMI
Members of the Council of Management:
Chairman: Edward Ciack FIMI
Chief Executive Offierr: Sarah Sillars
Council of Management: M W Austin FIMI, G Braddock FIMI, C Brass MIMI, E Clark FIMI, S Collins MIMI, T Copley FIMI, S Collins MIMI, T Copley FIMI, I Creek FIMI, M Green FIMI, N Lindsay FIMI, J Livingstone FIMI, E Loft FIMI, F Maguire FIMI, K Muddimer FIMI, P Murphy FIMI, G Owen FIMI, J Simpkins FIMI, J Small FIMI, J Stone MIMI, M Trainer FIMI.
Company Secretary: Allan Tyrer.

OPERATING BOARD
Chief Executive: Peter Creasey FIMI
Company Secretary and Finance Director: Allan Tyrer
Director, Membership Services: Ian Philpott FIMI
Address: 'Fanshaws', Brickendon, Hertford SG13 8PQ.
Tel: 01992 511521. **Fax:** 01992 511548.
E-mail: imi@motor.org.uk **Website:** www.motor.org.uk

THE INSTITUTE OF TRANSPORT ADMINISTRATION

IOTA House, 7b St Leonards Road, Horsham RH13 6EH
Tel: 01403 242412 **Fax:** 01403 242413
E-mail: directors@iota.org.uk **Web site:** www.iota.org.uk
OFFICERS
President: D MacCuish
Trustees: Cllr G G Fiegel, J D Bailey, M Braid, I M Marshall
National Chairman: A Varney
National Chairman Elect: M Walker
National Vice Chairmen: T Dobson
National Treasurer: J Amos
Finance & General Purposes Chairman: J Amos
Membership/Training Chairman: A Whittington
External Affairs Chairman: G Fletcher
Director: J Miles

CHAIRMEN/HON SECRETARIES OF CENTRES
Bristol – Chairman: E J. Reece **Secretary:** Miss M Lane, 137 Hilston Avenue, Penn, Wolverhampton WV4 4SB
Cheshire, Mersey & North Wales – Chairman: F A Robertson **Secretary:** A Woolfall, 4 Mereworth Drive, Kingsmead, Northwich CW9 8W
Devon/Cornwall – Chairman: I A Smith **Secretary:** Ms J. M. Land, 44 Parkside Road, Westclyst, Pinhoe, Exeter EX1 3TN
East Anglia – Chairman: B Young. **Secretary:** A J Clay, RTT Training Services Ltd, Gippeswyk Hall, Gippeswyk Avenue, Ipswich IP2 9AF
Edinburgh – Chairman: K G Welch **Secretary:** C M McDaid, 46 Bervie Drive, Murieston, Livingston EH54 9HA
Essex – Chairman: A C Williams **Secretary:** B A Mason, 2 Regency Close, Runwell, Wickford SS11 7BN
Falkirk – Chairman: A Cormack **Secretary:** Mrs M Struthers, 48 Livingstone Drive, Laurieston-by-Falkirk FK2 9JW
Herts/Bucks & Beds – Chairman: A L Bell **Secretary:** M Mullet, 129 Littleworth Road, Downley, High Wycombe HP13 5UZ
Inverness – Chairman: G W Masson **Secretary:** Ms J C Morrison, 8 Mackenzie Road, Inverness IV2 3DF
Kent – Chairman: W Wilford **Secretary:** B W Freeman, 34 Hunters Way West, Chatham Kent ME5 7HL
Lancashire – Chairman: D Uttley **Secretary:** W A Jefferies, 34 Broadfield Drive, Penwortham, Preston PR1 9DU
Leeds – Chairman: J M Walker **Secretary:** D Russell, 4 Beechfield Drive, Harvest Meadows, Sharlston Common, Wakefield WF4 1EG
Leicester – Chairman: J D Bailey **Secretary:** Mrs A Coupland, 193 Bardon Road, Coalville, Leicester LE67 4BG
London Central – Chairman: A Varney **Secretary:** R A Ellis, Bridgeview, Hill Road, Borstal, Rochester ME1 3NN
Manchester – Chairman: H Haworth **Secretary:** J P Egan, 45 Sherway Drive, Timperley, Altrincham WA15 7NU
North East – Chairman: D Holland **Secretary:** T A Simpson, 11 Gleneagles Drive, Usworth, Washington NE37 1PL
Peterborough – Chairman: T Hill **Secretary:** C Brown, 18 Deeping St James Road, Northborough PE6 9BQ
Sheffield – Chairman: A Hawcroft **Secretary:** M Baines, 58 Hollins Spring Avenue, Dronfield S18 1RP
Southampton – Chairman: A Evans **Secretary:** R Brown, 25 Downscroft Gardens, Hedge End, Southampton SO30 4RR
South Wales – Chairman/Secretary: A. D. Gettins, Oak Cottage, Royal Oak, Machen CF83 8SN
Sussex – Chairman: I Greenlow **Secretary:** Julia Merton
Swindon – Chairman: D Brooks. **Secretary:** C Harling, 128 Beech Drive, Pinehurst, Swindon SN2 1JR

West Midlands – **Chairman/Secretary:** P Hastelow
Hamilton Cottage, 66 Duke Street, Cheltenham GL52 6BP

*THE INSTITUTION OF MECHANICAL ENGINEERS

1 Birdcage Walk, London SW1H 9JJ
Tel: 020 7222 7899. **Fax:** 020 7222 4557
Web site: www.imeche.org.uk
Founded in 1847
Chief Executive: Sir Michael Moore KBE LVO
President 2006/7: W A Osborn MBE, CEng, FIMechE
Engineering Director: Dr Colin Brown C Eng FIMechE
Incorporates as the Automobile Division the former Institution of Automobile Engineers and as the Railway Division the former Institution of Locomotive Engineers.

SOCIETY OF OPERATIONS ENGINEERS

22 Greencoat Place, London SW1P 1PR
Tel: 020 7630 1111 **Fax:** 020 7630 6677
E-mail: ian.chisholm@soe.org.uk **Web site:** www.soe.org.uk
The SOE is the umbrella professional body for those working in road transport and plant engineering. The Institute of Road Transport Engineers is a professional sector within the SOE.

TRL LTD (TRANSPORT RESEARCH LABORATORY)

Address: Old Wokingham Road, Crowthorne RG45 6AU.
Tel: 01344 770007 **Fax:** 01344 770880
E-mail: enquiries@trl.co.uk
Web site: www.trl.co.uk

International Associations

*INTERNATIONAL ROAD TRANSPORT UNION (IRU)

Founded in 1948 in Geneva, the IRU is an international association of national road transport federations which has consultative status in the United Nations. One of its two Transport Councils is concerned with road passenger transport.
General Secretariat: IRU, Centre International, 3 Rue de Varembe, B.P.44, 1211 Geneva 20, Switzerland
Tel: 00 41 22 918 2700 **Fax:** 00 41 22 918 2741
E-mail: info@iru.org **Web site:** www.iru.org

UITP, THE INTERNATIONAL ASSOCIATION OF PUBLIC TRANSPORT

President: Roberto Cavalieri (Italy)
Secretary General: Hans Rat
Offices: Rue Sainte Marie 6, B-1080 Bruxelles
Tel: 00 32 2 673 6100 **Fax:** 00 32 2 660 1072
Web site: www.uitp.com **E-mail:** administration@uitp.com

WORLD ROAD ASSOCIATION (PIARC)

Hon Sec/Hon Treas: Room 914, Sunley Tower, Piccadilly Plaza, Manchester M1 4BE **Tel:** 0161 930 5579
E-mail: piarc.bnc@highways.gsi.gov.uk
Web site: www.piarc.org
The Association is an international body with headquarters in Paris, administered by an elected President and other office bearers. Members are recruited from governments, local authorities, technical and industrial groups and private individuals whose interests are centred on roads and road traffic. The association is maintained by subscriptions from its members. International congresses are held every four years.
OFFICE BEARERS
President: O Michaud (Switzerland)
International Vice-Presidents: P Anguitas Salas (Chile),
C Jordan (Australia), K Ghellab (Morocco)
Secretary General: J F Corte, PIARC, La Grande Arche, Paroi Nord, Niveau 8, 92055 La Defense Cedex, France
Tel: 00 33 1 47 96 81 21 **Fax:** 00 33 1 49 00 02 02
The British National Committee's role is to ensure adequate representation of British methods and experience on PIARC's international committees and Congresses, to disseminate the findings of those committees and generally look after British interests. The present officers of this committee are:
Patron: Minister for Transport.
UK President: Sir Richard Mottram KCB
UK Chairman: W J McCoubrey
Vice-Chairman: S Clarke
Hon Treasurer: C B Goodwillie
Hon Secretary/Hon Treasurer: M Neave

Other Organisations

ASSOCIATION OF TRANSPORT CO-ORDINATING OFFICERS (ATCO)

Web site: www.atco.org.uk
Chairman: John Hodgkins
Chairman, Bus Sub-Committee: David Neilson

The Association of Transport Coordinating Officers was formed in 1974 to bring together local authority officers whose work involved what were then new county council responsibilities for passenger transport.

ATCO members include senior staff directly concerned with strategic policy development and implementation for securing of passenger transport services for a wide range of public authorities. These include shire counties and unitary councils in England, Wales and Scotland, Passenger Transport Executives, TfL, the Isle of Man, the States of Jersey and Northern Ireland.

Through exchanging information and views the Association helps formulate policies and standards and promotes transport initiatives aimed at achieving better passenger transport services for all.

Members give advice to the Local Government Association and the Convention of Scottish Local Authorities. ATCO cooperates with the Community Transport Association and Passenger Transport Executive Group.

BUS USERS UK

PO Box 320, Portsmouth PO5 3SD
Tel: 023 9281 4493 **Fax:** 023 9286 3080
E-mail: caroline@bususers.org **Web site:** www.bususers.org
Bus Users UK was formed in 1985 to bring together national and local organisations with an interest in bus services and concerned individual bus users to seek to give an effective voice to the consumer. It is actively involved in developing constructive dialogue between the users and providers of bus services. It publishes a quarterly newsletter – *Bus User*.
Chairman: Dr Caroline Cahm.
Vice Chairman: Gavin Booth
Secretary: Mrs Deirdre Parkinson
Treasurer: Stephen Le Bras
Areas Officer: Joe Lynch

Officer in Wales: Leo Markham, Bus Users UK Wales, 4 Wimmerfield Crescent, Swansea SA2 7BU
E-mail: leo@bususers.org
Bus User Editor: Stephen Morris, PO Box 119, Shepperton TW17 8UX **Tel:** 01932 232574 **Fax:** 01932 246394
E-mail: editor@bususers.org
Assistant Area Officer: Phil Tonks

BUSK

18 Windsor Road, Newport NP19 8NS
Tel: 01633 274944
E-mail: busk.beltupschoolkids@btopenworld.com
Formerly known for its Belt Up School Kids campaign, BUSK is now known through the European Union as an authority on vehicular safety for children and young people.

COACH DRIVERS CLUB

Unit 3, Jephson Court, Tancred Close, Queensway, Leamington Spa, Warwickshire CV31 3RZ
Tel: 01926 455266 **Fax:** 01926 888004
E-mail: barbara@expom.co.uk
Web site: www.coachdriversclub.com
Membership club for coach drivers, coaching and tourism. Offers accident cover, magazine, yearbook, members' website, legal advice.

GO SKILLS

Concorde House, Trinity Park, Solihull B37 7UQ
Tel: 0121 635 5520 **Fax:** 0121 635 5521
Web site: goskills.org
GoSkills is the Sector Skills Council for passenger transport.

*LIGHT RAIL TRANSIT ASSOCIATION

c/o Haslams, 133 Lichfield Street, Walsall WS1 1SL
Tel/Fax: 01487 834000
Web site: www.lrta.org
E.mail: development@lrta.org
Founded in 1937 to advocate and encourage interest in light rail and modern tramways. Monthly magazine is Tramways & Urban Transit. Membership enquiries to:
Membership Secretary: Roger Morris,
E-mail: membership@lrta.org
President: Michael Parker
Chairman: David F Russell
Deputy Chairman: Geoff Lusher

LOCAL GOVERNMENT ASSOCIATION

Local Government House, Smith Square, London SW1P 3HZ
Tel: 020 7664 3000 **Fax:** 020 7664 3030
Web Site: www.lga.gov.uk
The Local Government was formed by the merger of the Association of County Councils, the Association of District Councils and the Association of Metropolitan Authorities in 1997. The LGA has just under 500 members, including all 238 shire district councils; 36 metropolitan district councils; 34 county councils; 46 new unitary authorities; 33 London authorities; and 22 Welsh authorities. In addition, the LGA represents police authorities, fire authorities and passenger transport authorities. The LGA provides the national voice for local communities in England and Wales; its members represent over 50 million people, employ more than 2 million staff and spend over £65 billion on local services.

Amongst the LGA's policy priorities is integrated transport; local authorities lead the way in encouraging the use of public transport and thereby reducing congestion, ill-health and environmental damage through a programme of partnerships between local authorities and other agencies.

President: Lord Ouseley
Chair: Sir Andy Bruce-Lockhart OBE (Conservative, Kent CC)
Vice-Chairs: Sir Jeremy Beecham (Labour, Newcastle), Peter Chalke (Conservative, Wiltshire)
Deputy Chairs:
 Ian Swithenbank CBE (Labour, Northumberland)
 Chris Clarke OBE (Liberal Democrat, Somerset)
 Chloe Lambert (Independent, Aylesbury Vale)
 Margaret Eaton OBE (Conservative, Bradford)
Chief Executive: Sir Brian Briscoe
Director of Economic & Environmental Policy: Sarah Wood
Director of Communications & Public Affairs: Oona Muirhead
Programme Manager, Planning: Lee Searles

*LONDON TRAVELWATCH

6 Middle Street, London EC1A 7JA
Tel: 020 7505 9000 **Fax:** 020 7505 9003
Web site: www.londontravelwatch.org.uk
E-mail: info@londontravelwatch.org.uk
Formerly the London Transport Users Committee, London TravelWatch is the independent statutory body set up to represent the interests of the users of all transport for which the Greater London Authority and Transport for London is responsible for operating, providing, procuring and licensing. London TravelWatch is also the Rail Passengers Committee for London.
Chairperson: Brian Cooke, FInstTT
Chief Executive: Rufus Barnes

*ROAD .OPERATORS' SAFETY COUNCIL (ROSCO)

Cowley House, Watlington Road, Oxford OX4 6GA
Tel: 01865 775552 **Fax:** 01865 775552
E-mail: rosco-oxford@supanet.com
Web site: www.rosco.org.uk
Chairman: Peter Shipp
Secretary: Tony Beetham

THE ROYAL SOCIETY FOR THE PREVENTION OF ACCIDENTS

Edgbaston Park, 353 Bristol Road, Birmingham B5 7ST
Tel: 0121 248 2000. **Fax:** 0121 248 2001.
RoSPA promotes safety at work and in the home, at leisure and in schools, on (or near water) and on the roads, through providing information, publicity, training and consultancy.

The Society works with central and local government, the caring services, the police and public and private sector organisations large and small. Some work is funded by grant and sponsorship, but most relies on the support of the Society's membership.

The Society also produces and supplies a comprehensive selection of publications ranging from reference books to low-cost booklets for mass distribution.
Training Offered: Training courses cover practical skills and management training through to professional qualifications in Health and Safety.
Chief Executive: John Hooper
Head of Road Safety: Kevin Clinton
Director of Public Safety: J L Howard

*STATUS

c/o Michael Hughes, Manchester Metropolitan University, Chester Street, Manchester M1 5GD
Tel: 0161 247 6242
Fax: 0161 247 6779
Web site: www.status.org.uk
E-mail: m.p.hughes@mmu.ac.uk

STATUS provides members, from all areas of the specialist road transport industry, with engineering development and test services, technical legislative consultancy and a range of general technical information.

It is involved on behalf of its members in contributing to consultation documents, influencing transport related legislation and lobbying government departments and agencies.

The organisation can call on a diverse range of personnel to help deal with more difficult problems. A primary benefit is the availability of telephone consultancy on technical or legislative matters.

STATUS plays a prominent role in representing its members' interests on legislative matters and lobbies government agencies on behalf of members.

A monthly newsletter is published, featuring industry related stories.

TRANSPORT 2000

Transport 2000, 1st Floor, The Impact Centre, 12-18 Hoxton Street, London N1 6NG
Tel: 020 7613 0743 **Fax**: 020 7613 5280.
Web site: www.transport2000.org.uk
E-mail: info@transport2000.org.uk

Transport 2000 is a campaign and research group that seeks greener, cleaner transport patterns through greater use of public transport, walking and cycling.
President: Michael Palin
Executive Director: Stephen Joseph

*TRANSPORT BENEVOLENT FUND

87A Leonard Street, London EC2A 4QS
Tel: 0870 0000 172/173 Fax: 0870 831 2882
Web site: www.tbf.org.uk
E-mail: help@tbf.co.uk

TBF is a Registered Charity (No 1058032) and was founded in 1923. Membership is open to most staff engaged in the public transport industry. Members pay £1 a week and in return are granted, at the discretion of the Trustees, cash help, convalescence, recuperation, a wide range of complementary medical treatments, legal advice, and medical equipment in times of need. Membership covers the employee and their partner and dependent children. Subject to age and length of membership, free membership may be awarded on leaving the industry. There are payroll deduction facilities in many companies.
Director: Chris Godbold
Senior Trustee: Ray Jordan (President)
Patrons: Sir Wilfrid Newton, CBE (Past Chairman, London Transport), Brian Souter (Stagecoach Group), Lew Adams OBE (BT Police Authority), Moir Lockhead (FirstGroup), Peter Hendy and Dave Wetzel (Transport for London), Phil White (National Express), Robert Crow (RMT), Chris Moyes (Go-Ahead Group), Graham Stevenson (T&GWU), Gerry Doherty (TSSA), Keith Norman (ASLEF), David Martin (Arriva).

First Aid & Sports Accociations

*COACH & BUS FIRST AID ASSOCIATION

President: J. Mackie, Commercial Director, First Aberdeen; 395 King Street, Aberdeen AB24 5RD
Hon Secretary: D A Crew, 11 Chertsey Road, Windlesham GU20 6EN.
Tel: 01276 451977 (**Mobile**) 07721 457735
E-mail: david.crew1@BTinternet.com

Membership of the Association is open to all companies in the passenger transport industry for a nominal annual subscription. The Association is purely a non profit making voluntary body administered by an executive committee comprising the elected president, secretary and treasurer plus other members who meet four times per year.

CABFAA is supported by the Confederation of Passenger Transport. As no other representative body exists for the bus and coach industry to exchange views and be kept up to date on First Aid matters and legislation, it is hoped that all companies both large and small will give support to the Association.

*NATIONAL PASSENGER TRANSPORT SPORTS ASSOCIATION

President: Ian Davies
Secretary: V Hills, 2 St Aidans Avenue, Grangetown, Sunderland SR2 9SF
Tel: 0191 567 2504 **Fax**: 0191 203 3177
E-mail: nptsasec@btinternet.com

The association organises inter-company sporting activities for the bus, coach, light rail and heavy rail industries. Currently 16 different sports are covered, each with competitions through the year, with trophies provided often by bus sponsors. A regular magazine is published. Corporate membership is provided to large transport undertakings. Furher information is available from the Secretary, address above.

Trade Organisations and Associations

BEAMA LTD

Offices: Westminster Tower, 3 Albert Embankment, London SE1 7SL. **Tel:** 020 7793 3000. **Fax:** 020 7793 3003.
The British Electrotechnical & Allied Manufacturers' Association.
Founded 1902. Incorporated 1905.
Objects: By co-operative action to promote the interests of the industrial, electrical and electronic manufacturing industries of Great Britain.
Director-General: A. A. Bullen

FEDERATION OF ENGINE REMANUFACTURERS

Director: Brian Ludford
Address: 49 New Stone Avenue, Wembury, Plymouth PL9 0JT
Tel: 01752 863681 **Web Site**: www.fer.co.uk

FREIGHT TRANSPORT ASSOCIATION VEHICLE INSPECTION SERVICE

Address: Hermes House, St John's Road, Tunbridge Wells TN4 9UZ.
Tel: 01892 526171. **Web Site:** www.fta.co.uk.
The Freight Transport Association represents the interests of over 11,000 companies throughout the UK. FTA carries out over 100,000 vehicle inspections each year including many PSVs. The FTA Vehicle Inspection Service supports operators in maintaining their vehicles in a road-worthy condition - both mechanically and legally.
Further details from Alan Osborne, Head of Vehicle Inspection Services, FTA, Tunbridge Wells (01892 526171).
Publications: *Freight* (monthly journal), FTA Yearbook.
Chief Executive: Richard Turner.

*LOW CARBON VEHICLE PARTNERSHIP

17 Queen Anne's Gate, London SW1H 9BU
Tel: 020 7222 8000
E-mail: secretariat@lowcvp.org.uk
Web site: www.lowcvp.org.uk
The LowCVP is an action and advisory group providing a forum through which partners can work together towards shared goals and take the lead in the transition to a low-carbon future for road transport in the UK.
Bus Working Group Chmn: Rayner Mayer

MOTOR INDUSTRY RESEARCH ASSOCIATION (MIRA)

Registered Office: MIRA Ltd, Watling Street, Nuneaton CV10 0TU
Tel: 024 7635 5000. **Fax**: 024 7635 5355.
MIRA an independent product engineering and technology centre and offers skills in innovation, problem-solving and consultancy.
Chairman: C. Ennos.
Executive Directors:
Managing Director: J. R. Wood.
Director of Finance & Company Secretary: C. H. Phillipson.
Director of Engineering: G. Townsend.
Director of Research & Business Development:
  Dr V. Considine

*SOCIETY OF MOTOR MANUFACTURERS & TRADERS (SMMT)

Forbes House, Halkin Street, London SW1X 7DS.
Tel: 020 7235 7000
Web site: www.smmt.co.uk
E-mail: buscoachweb@smmt.co.uk

*THE VEHICLE BUILDERS & REPAIRERS ASSOCIATION LTD

Offices: Belmont House, Gildersome, Leeds LS27 7TW.
Tel: 0113 253 8333 **Fax**: 0113 238 0496
E-mail: vbra@vbra.co.uk **Web site**: www.vbra.co.uk
President: The Rt Hon Lord Strathcarron.
Director General: M Tagg
Journal Editor: Judi Barton

Societies

*THE ASSOCIATION OF FRIENDS OF THE BRITISH COMMERCIAL VEHICLE MUSEUM TRUST

The Association was formed when The British Commercial Vehicle Museum was opened in 1983. Its aims are to support the full-time staff in matters of publicity, fund raising, maintenance and documentation of exhibits, work in the archives, organising rallies, etc. Facilities for members include a newsletter, free admission to the museum to undertake museum work and socialise with colleagues. New members are always welcome and special rates exist for families, students and senior citizens.
Hon Chairman: H Hatcher
Hon Secretary: A Pritchard
Hon Treasurer: A Pritchard
Members of the Committee: E Simister, D Lewis, J Gardner
Museum Manager: A Buchan
Address: The British Commercial Vehicle Museum,
  King Street, Leyland, Preston PR25 2LE **Tel**: 01772 451011

*ASTON MANOR ROAD TRANSPORT MUSEUM

Contact address: The Old Tram Depot, 208-216 Witton Lane, Aston, Birmingham B6 6QE
Phone: 0121 322 2298
Web site: www.amrtm.org.uk
Company limited by guarantee. Registered as a charity.
The museum is uniquely housed in a former depot of Birmingham's first-generation tramways. The display of commercial and passenger vehicles reflects the history of construction and operation in the West Midlands, and there are numerous displays of transport artefacts, tickets, notices and photographs. Joining as a Friend of the Museum gives entitlement to free entry and a quarterly newsletter. The museum is open on Saturdays, Sundays and Bank Holidays throughout the year, with a range of special events featuring a free heritage bus service to and from the city centre.
Further information from:
Chairman: Geoff Lusher, 86 Heritage Court, Warstone Lane, Jewellery Quarter, Birmingham B18 6HU

BRITISH BUS PRESERVATION GROUP

25 Oldfield Road, Bexleyheath DA7 4DX
Membership enquiries: 51 Market Close, Shirebrook, Mansfield NG20 8AE
Tel: 07940 771439
Web site: www.bbpg.co.uk
E-mail: enquiries@bbpg.co.uk, john-witt@eurobell.co.uk
The BBPG was formed in 1990 and has been responsible for securing the future of more than 250 historic buses and coaches, many of which were saved at extremely short notice from being broken up. The society has more than 600 members, both individuals and preservation groups.The BBPG caters for all bus enthusiasts, whether or not they own a bus.
Chairman: Glyn Matthews.
General Secretary: Mike Lloyd.
Membership Secretary: Harry Glover

*BRITISH TROLLEYBUS SOCIETY

Formed as the Reading Transport Society in 1961, the title was changed to the present one in 1971, having acquired a number of trolleybuses for preservation from all over Britain. In 1969 it

founded the Trolleybus Museum at Sandtoft, near Doncaster, where its vehicles are housed and regularly operate on mains power from the overhead wiring. West Yorkshire Transport Circle merged into the Society in January 1991. Currently membership stands at about 320. Members receive a monthly journal *Trolleybus* containing news and articles from home and abroad. Additionally members can subscribe to *Bus Fare* and *Wheels*, monthly magazines for motorbus operation in the Thames Valley and West Yorkshire areas respectively. Monthly meetings are also held in Reading, London. and Bradford.
Chairman: G P Bilbe, 12 Belle Avenue, Reading RG6 7BL
Secretary: A. J. Barton, 2 Josephine Court, Southcote Road, Reading RG30 2DG.
Treasurer: R. V. Fawcett, 57 Sutcliffe Avenue, Earley RG6 7JN

*BUSES WORLDWIDE (BWW)

Web site: www.busesworldwide.org
Established in 1982 to associate those particularly interested in bus operation in countries other than their own. Meetings are held, a bi-monthly magazine is published and visits abroad are organised.
Chairman: R Stedall
Membership Secretary: S. Guess, 37 Oyster Lane, Byfleet KT14 7HS
News Editor: N. R. Bartlett, 1 Hopping Jacks Lane, Danbury, Chelmsford CM3 4PN.
Features Editor: D. Corke, 8 Priestland Gardens, Berkhamsted HP4 2GT.

*CLASSIC BUS HERITAGE TRUST (INCORPORATING THE ROUTEMASTER HERITAGE TRUST)

The Classic Bus Heritage Trust aims to advance preservation of buses and coaches by fostering the interests of the general public. It is a Registered Charity.
Treasurer & Hon Sec: W. Ackroyd, 1 Hawthorn Road, Send, Surrey GU23 6LH.

*ESSEX BUS ENTHUSIASTS' GROUP

Web site: www.essexbus.org.uk
This group was formed in 1962, under its previous title, Eastern National Enthusiasts' Group. The present title was adopted in 1987 to reflect more fully the activities of the group. A monthly magazine is circulated to all members giving information on all aspects of First Essex Buses, Thamesway, Colchester and Southend and all other operators in Essex. Meetings are arranged on a regular basis whilst tours are also organised. A range of publications and photographs is also available. Membership is open to all over the age of 12.
Membership Secretary: Derek Stebbing, Conifers, Thorpe Road, Weeley, Clacton-on-Sea CO16 9JJ
E-mail: derekstebbing@hotmail.com.

*HISTORIC COMMERCIAL VEHICLE SOCIETY

The Society was founded in 1958 and four years later absorbed the Vintage Passenger Vehicle Society and the London Vintage Taxi Club. Its membership of over 4,000 owns more than 6,000 preserved vehicles. Activities include the organisation of rallies, among them the well known London to Brighton and Trans-Pennine runs. The club caters for all commercial vehicles over 20 years old.
OFFICERS
President: Lord Montagu of Beaulieu
Senior Exec Officer and Vice-President: M. Banfield, Iden Grange, Cranbrook Road, Staplehurst TN12 0ET
Tel: 01580 892929. **Fax:** 01580 893227.
E-mail: hcvs@btinternet.com **Web site**: www.hcvs.co.uk

LEYLAND NATIONAL GROUP

Website: www.leylandnationalgroup.org
E-mail: enquiries@leylandnationalgroup.org
Address: 27 Dukeshill Road, Bracknell RG42 2DU
Tel: 01344 640095
The Leyland National Group was formed in 1997. Since then its growth has been rapid and it now has members not just throughout Britain but abroad as well. Although the group does not own vehicles itself, some of its members are bus owners. There are more than 100 Leyland Nationals from a variety of operators, preserved by group members. However, one does not need to own a bus to join the group, as membership is open to anyone with an interest in Leyland Nationals. Members receive a bi-monthly newsletter as well as other benefits. Please contact the Membership Secretary for more information about the group, the benefits of membership and to receive a membership application form.
Chairman: Alan Fairbrother
Address: 8 Lansdowne Road, Alton GU34 2HB
Tel: 01420 87482
E-mail: chairman@leylandnationalgroup.org
Secretary: Eddie Knorn
E-mail: secretary@leylandnationalgroup.org
Treasurer: Mike Bellinger
Publicity Officer: Paul Barrett
Membership Sec: Tim Wild
Address: 27 Dukeshill Road, Bracknell RG42 2DU
Tel: 01344 640095
E-mail: membership@leylandnationalgroup.org
Newsletter Editor: Anthony Poulton

LINCOLNSHIRE VINTAGE VEHICLE SOCIETY

Road Transport Museum, Whisby Road, North Hykeham LN6 5TR Tel: 01522 500566/689497
The LVVS was founded in 1959 by local businessmen with the aim of forming a road transport museum. Charitable status was obtained some time ago, and with a capital grant from its local district council, it has now completed the first stage of its new museum project. Over 60 vehicles dating from the 1920s to the 1980s can be seen in the new exhibition hall with many more in the workshop. Opening times November–April Sundays 13.00-16.00. May–October Mon-Fri 12.00-16.00, Sun 10.00-16.00.
Chairman: S Milner
Hon Treasurer: J Child
Secretary: Mrs J Jefford

*LONDON OMNIBUS TRACTION SOCIETY (LOTS)

Unit N305, Westminster Business Square, 1-45 Durham Street London SE11 5JH
Web site: www.lots.org.uk
Formed in 1964, LOTS has some 2,600 members and is the largest bus enthusiast society in the British Isles.
An Illustrated monthly newsletter is sent to all members. This covers all the current operators in the former London Transport area and includes General and Industry News, Route Developments, and Vehicle News for the former London Transport area as well as publicity, subsequent disposal information and service vehicles. Monthly meetings are usually held in central London featuring guest speakers, slide and film presentations during the year as well as the annual free bus rides from central London using vehicles of London interest.
Regular LOTS publications include fleet allocations and route

working publications as well as the annual *London Bus and Tram Fleetbook*. A quarterly 64 page glossy magazine, the *London Bus Magazine (LBM)* has been produced for over 30 years.

Regular sales lists are produced and sent out to all members. An information service is also available to all members to answer those historical queries.

The Autumn Transport Spectacular (ATS) is held in London every year and is one of London's biggest transport sales.

*THE M & D AND EAST KENT BUS CLUB

42 St Albans Hill, Hemel Hempstead HP3 9NG
Web site: www.mdekbusclub.org.uk **E-mail**: ndk@mdekbusclub.fsnet.co.uk

This club was formed in 1952 with the object of bringing together all those interested in road passenger transport in an area covering Kent and East Sussex. Facilities for members include a monthly news booklet (illustrated), information service, tours, meetings, vehicle photograph sales and vehicle preservation. A series of publications is also produced, including illustrated fleet histories.

Hon Chairman: J. V. Spillett
Hon Sec: P J Evans
Hon Editor: N D King
Hon Treasurer: N D King
Membership Officer: J. A. Fairley
Photographic Officer: R. A. Lewis
Sales Officer: J. M. Poultney
Tours Officer: D. R. Cobb
Management Committee: N. D. King, R. A. Lewis, J. V. Spillett, P. J. Evans, J. M. Poultney. Area Organisers in Ashford, Dover, Folkestone, Hastings, North-East Kent, Maidstone and the Medway Towns.

*NATIONAL TROLLEYBUS ASSOCIATION

15 Cambrian Crescent, Oulton Broad NR32 3HW
Web site: www.trolleybus.co.uk/nta

Formed in 1963, and incorporated in 1968 as The Trolleybus Museum Co Ltd. The vehicles and ancillary equipment collected by the NTA since its inception are now owned by the company, which is limited by guarantee and is a registered charity. Members receive *Trolleybus Magazine*, a printed and illustrated bi-monthly journal documenting all aspects of trolleybus operation past and present throughout the world.

Chairman: R. D. Helliar-Symons
Secretary: J. H. Ward
Treasurer: I Martin
Membership Secretary: I Martin
Enquiries: TMCMembSec@hotmail.com

*THE OMNIBUS SOCIETY

Website: www.omnibussoc.org.

The Omnibus Society was founded in 1929. Today it is a nationwide organisation with a network of provincial branches, offering a comprehensive range of facilities for those interested in the bus and coach industry. The Society has accumulated a wealth of information on public road transport. Members have the opportunity to receive and exchange data on every aspect of the industry including route developments, operational/traffic matters and fleet changes. Each branch has a full programme of activities and publishes its own Branch Bulletin to give local news of route changes, etc. A scheme exists whereby members subscribe to receive bulletins from branches other than that of which they are a member. A programme of indoor meetings is customary during winter, including film shows, invited speakers and discussions. In the summer months visits to manufacturers and tours to operators are featured.

OFFICERS
President: Chris Moyes OBE
Vice-Presidents: F P Groves, A W Mills, G Wedlake, T. F. McLachlan, K. W. Swallow, R. G. Westgate.
Chairman: B. Le Jeune.
Secretary: A. J. Francis, 185 Southlands Road, Bromley BR2 9QZ.
Treasurer: H. L. Barker, 31 High Street, Tarporley CW6 0DP.
Editor, Society's Publications: D. Brendan Chandler
Members of the Council: I. D. Barlex, J. Hart, D. M. Persson, D. Roy, J Howie and nominations from each branch
Branch Officers:
Midland Branch: C R Warn, 11 The Meadows, Shawbury, Shrewsbury SY4 4HS
South Wales and West Branch: A J Armstrong, 16 Stanley Grove, Weston-super-Mare BS23 3EB
Northern Branch: Philip Battersby, 12 Crescent Lodge, Tile Crescent, Middlesbrough TS5 6SF.
North Western & Yorkshire Branch: P. Wilkinson, 10 Bradley Close, Timperley, Altrincham WA15 6SH
Scottish Branch: I. Allan, 10 Miller Avenue, Crossford, Dunfermline KY12 8PY
Essex & South Suffolk Group: J. L. Rugg, 86 Worthing Road, Laindon SS15 6JU
East Midland Group: A. Oxley, 4 Gordon Close, Attenborough, Nottingham NN4 9UF
Herts & Beds Group: R. C. Barton, 5 Viscount Court, Knights Field, Luton LU2 7LD
London Historical Research Group: D A Ruddom, 57 Bluebridge Road, Brookmans Park, Hatfield AL9 7UW
Provincial Historical Research Group: A E Jones, 8 Poplar Drive, Church Stretton S76 7BW

*THE PSV CIRCLE

15 Port Close, Lordswood, Chatham ME5 8DU

The Circle is an association of over 2000 members, interested in various ways in the vehicles used by the passenger transport industry on the roads of the United Kingdom and abroad. Membership is open to all over the age of 16, and in certain exceptional cases to those under this age. News Sheets, comprising nine regional sections, are published each month, together with numerous supplements and fleet histories which fully record information relating to operators, chassis builders and body constructors. There is no entrance fee. Annual subscriptions vary with the number of regional news sheets required, with a minimum for one area and graded additional payments according to members' requirements. Frequent meetings, mainly of a social nature, are held in London and several provincial towns.

HONORARY OFFICERS
Chairman: C. R. Costella
Secretary: J E Skilling
Treasurer: M D Bissex
Managing Editor: S Curl

The above with another eight members constitute the Committee of Management, and for convenience all mail other than editorial matters is handled at the above address.

*RIBBLE ENTHUSIASTS' CLUB

23 Richmond Road, Hindley Green, Wigan WN2 4ND
Tel: 01942 253497
E-mail: ribbleecsec@tiscali.co.uk
Web site: http://homepage.manx.net/JHL/REC/index.htm

Founded in 1954 by the late T. B. Collinge for the study of road transport past and present and in particular Ribble Motor Services and associated companies. Meetings are held and a monthly news sheet produced.

Life President: A E Chapman
Life Vice President: M. Shires

Vice President: N Barrett
Committee Chairman: D Bailey MBE
Secretary/Tours: M J Yates, 23 Richmond Road, Hindley Green, Wigan WN2 4ND
Treasurer/Editor: R A Harpum, 22 Woodside Road, Ferndown BH22 9LD
Records: S Blake, 23 Fairfield Road, North Shore, Blackpool FY1 2RA
Sales Dept: Mr & Mrs B Ashcroft, 11 Regent Road, Walton le Dale, Preston PR5 4QA
Sales Dept: Assistant: Mrs J Yates, 23 Richmond Road, Hindley Green, Wigan WN2 4ND
Archive: B Ashcroft, 11 Regent Road, Walton Le Dale, Preston PR5 4QA

*ROADS AND ROAD TRANSPORT HISTORY ASSOCIATION

Web site: www.rrtha.org.uk
Founded in 1992, the association promotes, encourages and co-ordinates the study of the history of roads and road transport, both passenger and freight. It aims to encourage those interested in a particular aspect of transport to understand their chosen subject in the context of developments in other areas and at other periods. It publishes a newsletter four times a year and holds an annual conference each autumn.
Membership is open to professional bodies/transport societies, museums and individuals.
President: Professor John Hibbs, OBE
Chairman: Garry Turvey, CBE
Hon. Secretary: Christopher Hogan, 124 Shenstone Avenue, Stourbridge DY8 3EJ **E-mail**: roadsandRTHA@aol.com

*ROUTEMASTER OPERATORS & OWNERS ASSOCIATION

23 Oakhurst Drive, Crewe, Cheshire CW2 6UE
Tel: 0870 720 2920 **E-mail**: grahamsteph1011@hotmail.co.uk
Web Site: www.routemaster.org.uk
The Routemaster Operators & Owners Association provides assistance, advice and news for operators, owners and enthusiasts of these vehicles. From the specification of a screw to a complete bus, the Association provides authoritative technical information. Bus rallies and events are organised and other selected events are supported each year. Members receive a quarterly news magazine and discounts on parts and accessories including a maintenance manual, owners handbook technical bulletins, suppliers handbook, badges and transfers, window sealing rubber and many other unique products. Large batches of Routemaster spares have been acquired from the London bus operators including mechanical units, electrical items and bodywork spares.
President: Colin Curtis OBE
Secretary: Graham Meadows
Chairman: Andrew Morgan, 45 Princess Diana Drive, St Albans, Herts AL4 0DZ **E-mail**: andrewmorgan1368@tiscali.co.uk

*THE SAMUEL LEDGARD SOCIETY

C/O 58 Kirklees Drive, Farsley, Pudsey LS28 5TE
Tel: 0113 236 3695 **Fax**: 0113 259 1425
E-mail: rennison@mailcc.co.uk
Web site: wwwsamuelledgardsociety.org.uk
The Samuel Ledgard Society was formed in 1998 at the Rose & Crown Inn, Otley, during the second annual reunion of the devotees of this well-known bus company. Reunions are held twice yearly at Armley during April and Otley on or about October 14. A Christmas dinner is also part of the established calendar of events. The quarterly journal of the Society, *The Chat*, is published in March, June, September and December each year. Founding officers were Barry Rennison, Tony Greaves, and Don Bate, all of whom have a wealth of knowledge about the Samuel Ledgard company. Membership is open to all with a subscription of £5 - contact any member of the Committee for details.
Hon President: Samuel Ledgard Mather AMIRTE (Retd)
COMMITTEE
Chairman: Barry Rennison, 58 Kirklees Drive, Farsley, Pudsey LS28 5TE
Vice-Chairman, Magazine Editor & Publicity Officer:
Tony Greaves, 19 Perth Mount, Horsforth LS18 5SH
Treasurer: Bryan Whitham, 4 Airsdale Drive, Horsforth LS18 4ER
Secretary & Membership: Margaret Rennison, 58 Kirklees Drive, Farsley, Pudsey LS28 5TE

*SCOTTISH TRAMWAY & TRANSPORT SOCIETY

PO Box 7342, Glasgow G51 4YQ
Founded in 1951 as the Scottish Tramway Museum Society, the Society claims to be 'Scotland's foremost tramway enthusiast organisation', publishing books and videos on tramways and other transport subjects and supporting the National Tramway Museum. Monthly meetings and newsletter.
Hon Chairman: B M Longworth
Gen Secretary: H. McAulay
E-mail: stts-glasgow@virgin.net
Hon Treasurer: A. Ramsay
Members of Committee: A Murray, N Bates, A Muir, B Quinn, F W B Mitchell, K Darroch

SHEFFIELD BUS MUSEUM TRUST LTD

Tinsley Tram Sheds, Sheffield Road, Tinsley, Sheffield S9 2FY
Tel: 0114 255 3010
The Sheffield Bus Museum Trust was formed in 1987 with the purpose of co-ordinating the bus preservation movement in Sheffield and to establish a permanent museum. This has been achieved at the former Sheffield Tramways Company's Tinsley Tram Depot. The majority of the Trust's collection is local and extremely varied, ranging from a 1926 Sheffield tramcar to a 1985 Dennis Domino. In recent years the Museum Trust has benefitted from Heritage Fund Lottery grants. The museum is an educational charity and promotes an ever-expanding schools visits programme. The museum is open every Saturday and Sunday afternoon with special theme days from April to December.
Chairman: M W Greenwood
Membership Secretary: Dr. John Willis, 2 Pwll-Y-Waen, Ty'n-Y-Groes, Conwy LL32 8TQ.

*SOUTHDOWN ENTHUSIASTS' CLUB

Web site: www.southdownenthusiastsclub.org.uk
This club was founded in 1954 to bring together people interested in the vehicles, routes and history of Southdown Motor Services Ltd and now includes Stagecoach South (Hastings & District, South Coast Buses, Southdown, Hampshire Bus, Hants & Surrey, East Kent), Brighton & Hove, Eastbourne Buses and First Hampshire and Dorset. There is a monthly news publication and winter meetings. Membership is open to persons aged 14 years and over and details may be had from the Hon Secretary.
Hon Chairman: J Allpress, 9 Phoenix Way, Southwick, Brighton BN42 4HQ
Hon Secretary: N Simes, 11 High Cross Fields, Crowborough TN6 2SN
Hon Treasurer: D E Still, 12 Westway Close, Mile Oak, Portslade BN42 2RT

Hon Sales Officer: D Chalkley, 6 Valebridge Drive, Burgess Hill RH15 0RW
Hon News Sheet Editor: P Gainsbury, Park Cottage, Guestling TN35 4LT
Hon Publications Officer: J Smith, 1 Sackville Way, Worthing BN14 8BJ
Committee Member: J Barley, 84 Kipling Avenue, Brighton BN2 6UE.
Hon Photographic Officer: C Churchill, 53 Monks Close, Lancing BN15 9DB

*SWINDON VINTAGE OMNIBUS SOCIETY

10 Fraser Close, Nythe, Swindon SN3 3RP
Tel: 01793 526001
Preserved Daimler Weymann double deck, ex Swindon corporation society vehicle. Also Bristol RESL ECW ex-Thamesdown Transport.
Chairman: M. Naughton
Secretary: D. Nicol
Treasurer: D. Mundy

*THE TRANSPORT MUSEUM, WYTHALL

Birmingham & Midland Motor Omnibus Trust

The Transport Museum, Chapel Lane, Wythall B47 6JX
Web site: www.bammot.org.uk
E-mail: enquiries@bammot.org.uk
The Trust dates back to 1973, taking its present title in 1977, when it became a registered educational charity to establish and develop a regional transport museum.

Three large halls, the most recent built with the assistance of the Heritage Lottery Fund and opening in 2007, house a broad collection of around 100 buses, coaches, fire engines and battery-electric vehicles from all parts of the Midlands and beyond. Birmingham and the Black Country especially are featured, and the museum has a unique collection of buses and coaches designed, built and operated by Midland Red, a company which pioneered many technical innovations over a 50 year manufacturing period.

A museum archive to record the development of the bus and coach industry in the Midlands is also being established, with collections of photographs, uniforms, tickets, ticket equipment and street furniture.

Members receive the bi-monthly museum journal *Omnibus* containing details of museum developments. The museum is open to the public every weekend between Easter and the end of October. Special event days are held on some Sundays and holiday Mondays when vehicles are on display and historic bus services operate, including a link with Birmingham city centre. Also buses for hire - see West Midlands in Operators section.

*TRAMWAY & LIGHT RAILWAY SOCIETY

Web site: www.tramways.freeserve.co.uk
Founded in 1938, the Tramway & Light Railway Society caters for those interested in all aspects of tramways. Members receive *Tramfare*, a bi-monthly illustrated magazine. There are regular meetings throughout the country. The Society promotes tramway modelling, drawings, castings, and technical details are available to modellers. There are also comprehensive library facilities. For fuller details of the Society and of membership please write to the Membership Secretary.
HONORARY OFFICERS
President: P J Davis.

Vice-Presidents: E R Oakley, G. B. Claydon, C.B
Chairman: J R Prentice, 216 Brentwood Road, Romford RM1 2RP.
Secretary: G R Tribe, 47 Soulbury Road, Linslade, Leighton Buzzard LU7 7RW.
Membership Secretary: H J Leach, 6 The Woodlands, Brightlingsea CO7 0RY.

THE TRANSPORT TICKET SOCIETY

An association of students and collectors of passenger tickets and fare collection methods. Founded in 1946 the TTS now has some 500 members worldwide. An illustrated monthly Journal, and regular distributions of tickets, keep members up to date with both historical and recent developments in ticketing in all modes of transport. The TTS welcomes offers of obsolete tickets for distribution to members. Full details of membership together with a sample Journal will be sent on request to the TTS publicity officer, or visit the TTS website: www.transport-ticket.com.
Publicity Officer: Martin Rickitt, Bromes House, Isle Abbots, Taunton TA3 6RW. **Tel:** 01460 281228 **E-mail**: mrickitt@hotmail.com
Chairman: John Tolson
Membership Secretary: David Randall
General Secretary: Patrick Geall
Treasurer: Graham Wootton.
Managing Editor: David Harman

*THE TRANSPORT TRUST

202 Lambeth Road, London SE1 7JW
Tel: 020 7928 6464. **Fax:** 020 7928 6565. **E-mail**: hq@thetransporttrust.org.uk **Web Site**: www.thetransporttrust.org.uk
The national charity for the preservation and restoration of Britain's transport heritage.

Road Passenger Transport Museums

This list is in addition to those shown in the main Society section above

*ABBEY PUMPING STATION

Contact address: Corporation Road, Leicester LE4 5PX
Phone: 0116 299 5111
Fax: 0116 299 5125
Web site: www.leicester.gov.uk/museums, www.leicestermuseums.ac.uk

*AMBERLEY WORKING MUSEUM

Contact address: Amberley, Arundel BN18 9LT
Phone: 01798 831370
Fax: 01798 831831
E-mail: office@amberleymuseum.co.uk
Web site: www.amberleymuseum.co.uk

*ASTON MANOR ROAD TRANSPORT MUSEUM

(*See Societies section*)

BLACK COUNTRY LIVING MUSEUM TRANSPORT GROUP

Contact address: Tipton Road, Dudley DY1 4SQ
Phone: 0121 557 9643
Web site: wwww.bclm.co.uk

BRISTOL ROAD TRANSPORT COLLECTION
Contact address: William Staniforth, 37 Corbett Road, Birmingham B47 5LP (SAE please)
E-mail: william.staniforth@virgin.net

BRITISH COMMERCIAL VEHICLE MUSEUM
Contact address: King Street, Leyland PR25 2LE
Phone: 01772 451011
Fax: 01772 451015

*CASTLE POINT TRANSPORT MUSEUM
Contact address: 105 Point Road, Canvey Island SS8 7TP
Phone: 01268 684272

*CAVAN & LEITRIM RAILWAY
Contact address: Narrow Gauge Station, Station Road, Dromod, Co Leitrim, Ireland
Phone/fax: 00353 71 9638599
Web site: www.irish-railway.com
E-mail: info@irish-railway.com

*COBHAM BUS MUSEUM - THE LONDON BUS PRESERVATION TRUST LTD
Contact address: Redhill Road, Cobham, Surrey, KT11 1EF
Phone/Fax: 01932 868665
Web site: www.lbpt.org.uk
E-mail: cobhambusmuseum@aol.com

COVENTRY TRANSPORT MUSEUM
Contact address: Millenium Place, Hales Street, Coventry CV1 1PN
Phone: 024 7683 2425
Fax: 024 7683, 2465
E-mail: enquiries@transport-museum.com

DOVER TRANSPORT MUSEUM
Contact address: Willingdon Road, Port Zone White Cliffs Business Park, Whitfield, Dover CT16 2HJ
Phone: 01304 822409

*EAST ANGLIA TRANSPORT MUSEUM
Contact address: Chapel Road, Carlton Colville, Lowestoft NR33 8BL
Phone: 01502 518459
Fax: 01502 584658
E-mail: enquiries@eatm.org.uk
Web site: www.eatm.org.uk

GRAMPIAN TRANSPORT MUSEUM
Contact address: Alford AB33 8AE
Phone: 01975 562292
Fax: 01975 562180
E-mail: info@g-t-m.freeserve.co.uk
Web site: www.gtm.org.uk

IPSWICH TRANSPORT MUSEUM
Contact address: Old Trolleybus Depot, Cobham Road, Ipswich IP3 9JD
Phone: 01473 715666
E-mail: www.ipswichtransportmuseum.co.uk.html

*ISLE OF WIGHT BUS MUSEUM
Contact address: Seaclose Quay, Newport PO30 2EF
Phone: 01983 533352

*KEIGHLEY BUS MUSEUM TRUST
Contact address: 47 Brantfell Drive, Burnley BB12 8AW
Phone: 01282 413179
E-Mail: shmdboard@aol.com
Web site: www.kbmt.org.uk

LONDON'S TRANSPORT MUSEUM
Contact address: 39 Wellington Street, London WC2E 7BB.
Phone: 020 7379 6344; recorded information 020 7565 7299
E-mail: resources@ltmuseum.co.uk
Web site: www.ltmuseum.co.uk

*MANCHESTER MUSEUM OF TRANSPORT
Contact address: Boyle Street, Cheetham, Manchester M8 8UW
Phone: 0161 205 2122
Fax: 0161 202 1110
E-mail: busmuseum@btconnect.com
Web site: www.gmts.co.uk or www.manchester.bus.museum

MIDLAND ROAD TRANSPORT GROUP — BUTTERLEY
Contact address: 21 Ash Grove, Mastin Moor, Chesterfield S43 3AW
Phone: Midland Road Transport Group — 01246 473619 Midland Railway 01773 747674, Visitor Information Line (01773) 570140.

MUSEUM OF TRANSPORT
Contact address: Kelvin Hall, 1 Bunhouse Road, Glasgow G3 8DP
Phone: 0141 287 2720 (school bookings on 0141 565 4112/3)
Fax: 0141 287 2692

NATIONAL MUSEUM OF SCIENCE AND INDUSTRY
Contact address: Exhibition Road, London SW7 2DD
Phone: 0207 942 4105 or 01793 814466
E-mail: s.evans@nmsi.ac.uk

NORTH OF ENGLAND OPEN AIR MUSEUM
Contact address: Beamish DH9 0RG
Phone: 0191 370 4000
Fax: 0191 370 4001
E-mail: museum@beamish.org.uk
Web site: www.beamishmuseum.co.uk

*THE NATIONAL TRAMWAY MUSEUM
Crich, Matlock DE4 5DP
Tel: 01773 854321 **Fax:** 01773 854320
The Society was founded in 1955 to establish and operate a working tramway museum. The Museum is at Crich Tramway Village, Crich, near Matlock, in Derbyshire, and owns over 70 English, Irish, Scottish, Welsh and overseas tramcars. Members receive a copy of the Society's quarterly journal and can participate in the running of the museum.
Patron: HRH The Duke of Gloucester GCVO
Vice-Presidents: G. S. Hearse, W. G. S. Hyde, G. B. Claydon, D. J. H. Senior, A W Bond
Chairman: C. Heaton

Vice-Chairman: R T Pennyfather
Hon Secretary: I. M. Dougill
Hon Treasurer: P R Moore
Operations Superintendent: K. B. Hulme

*NORTH WEST MUSEUM OF ROAD TRANSPORT

Contact address: The Old Bus Depot, 51 Hall Street, St Helens WA10 1DU
E-mail: general@hallstreetdepot.info
Web site: www.hallstreetdepot.info
Due to open late 2006

NOTTINGHAM TRANSPORT HERITAGE CENTRE

Contact address: Mere Way, Ruddington, Nottingham NG11 6NX
Phone: 0115 940 5705
E-mail: aecley@aol.com
Web site: http://www.nthc.co.uk

OXFORD BUS MUSEUM

Contact address: Station Yard, Long Hanborough, Witney OX29 8LA
Phone: 01993 883617 (Answerphone) or 01993 881662

*SCOTTISH VINTAGE BUS MUSEUM

Contact address: M90 Commerce Park, Lathalmond, Dumfermline, Fife KY12 OSJ
Phone: 01383 623380
Website: www.busweb.co.uk/svbm

TAMESIDE TRANSPORT COLLECTION

Contact address: Roaches Industrial Estate, Manchester Road, Mossley, Greater Manchester

*THE TRANSPORT MUSEUM, WYTHALL

BIRMINGHAM & MIDLAND MOTOR OMNIBUS TRUST

(*See Societies section*)

TRANSPORT MUSEUM SOCIETY OF IRELAND

Contact address: Howth Castle Demesne, Howth, Dublin 13, Ireland
Phone: 00 353 1 832 0427

*TROLLEYBUS MUSEUM AT SANDTOFT

Contact address: Belton Road, Sandtoft, Doncaster DN8 5SX
Phone: 01724 711391
E-mail: enquiries@sandtoft.org.uk
Web site: www.sandtoft.org.uk

ULSTER FOLK & TRANSPORT MUSEUM

Contact address: Cultra, Holywood BT18 OEU
Phone: 028 9042 8428

WIRRAL TRANSPORT MUSEUM

Contact address: Pacific Road, Birkenhead L41 5HN
Phone: 0151 666 2756

Do you want to keep your
LITTLE RED BOOK
up-to-date?
Buses magazine is now carrying updates every month.
See opposite title page for Subscription details

section 4

British Isles Operators

Major Groups	85

English Operators
Bedfordshire	86
Berkshire (West Berkshire, Bracknell Forest, Reading, Slough, Windsor & Maidenhead, Wokingham)	87
Bristol	89
Buckinghamshire, Milton Keynes	90
Cambridgeshire and Peterborough City	92
Cheshire, Halton and Stockport	94
Cornwall	97
Cumbria	99
Derbyshire	101
Devon	104
Dorset, Bournemouth, Poole	108
Durham	110
East Sussex, Brighton & Hove	113
East Riding of Yorkshire, Kingston upon Hull	114
Essex	116
Gloucestershire	120
Greater Manchester, Bolton, Bury, Oldham, Rochdale, Salford, Tameside, Wigan	122
Hampshire	125
Herefordshire	128
Hertfordshire	129
Isle of Wight	132
Kent	133
Lancashire, Blackburn with Darwen, Blackpool, Wigan	137
Leicestershire, City of Leicester, Rutland	141
Lincolnshire	143
London	145
Merseyside area (St Helens, Knowsley, Liverpool, Sefton, Wirral)	151
Middlesex	152
Norfolk	154
North Lincolnshire, North East Lincolnshire	156
North Yorkshire, York	157
Northamptonshire	161
Northumberland	162
Nottinghamshire, Nottingham	163
Oxfordshire	166
Shropshire	167
Somerset, Bath & North East Somerset/North Somerset	169
South Yorkshire	172
Staffordshire	175
Suffolk	177
Surrey	179
Tyne & Wear	182
Warwickshire	183
West Midlands	184
West Sussex	188
West Yorkshire, Bradford, Calderdale, Kirklees, Leeds, Wakefield	190
Wiltshire	193
Worcestershire	196

Scottish Operators
Aberdeen, City of	198
Aberdeenshire	198
Angus	199
Argyll & Bute	199
Borders	200
Clackmannanshire	200
Dumfries & Galloway	201
Dundee, City of	201
East Ayrshire	202
East Lothian	202
East Renfrewshire	202
Edinburgh, City of	202
Falkirk	203
Fife	203
Glasgow, City of	204
Highland	204
Inverclyde	205
Midlothian	205
Moray	206
North Ayrshire	206
North Lanarkshire	207
Orkney	208
Perth & Kinross	208
Renfrewshire	209
Shetland	209
South Ayrshire	209
South Lanarkshire	210
Stirling	210
West Dunbartonshire	211
West Lothian	211
Western Isles	211

Isle of Man Operators
Isle of Man	212

Welsh Operators
Anglesey	213
Blaenau Gwent	213
Bridgend	213
Caerphilly	214
Cardiff	214
Carmarthenshire	215
Ceredigion	216
Conwy	216
Denbighshire	217
Flintshire	217
Gwynedd	217
Merthyr Tydfil	218
Monmouthshire	218
Neath & Port Talbot	219
Newport	219
Pembrokeshire	219
Powys	220
Rhondda, Cynon, Taff	221
Swansea	221
Torfaen	222
Vale of Glamorgan	222
Wrexham	222

Channel Islands Operators
Alderney	224
Guernsey	224
Jersey	224

Isles of Scilly Operators
Isle of Scilly	224

Northern Ireland Operators
Northern Ireland	225

Republic of Ireland Operators
Republic of Ireland	226

Unitary authorities are included within the postal boundaries.

MAJOR GROUPS

ARRIVA PLC
ADMIRAL WAY, DOXFORD INTERNATIONAL BUSINESS PARK, SUNDERLAND SR3 3XP
Tel: 0191 520 4000
E-mail: enquiries@arriva.co.uk
Website: www.arrivabus.co.uk
Chairman (Non Exec): Sir Richard Broadbent **Chief Executive**: David Martin **Group Man Dir (Finance)**: Steve Lonsdale **Non Exec Dirs**: Michael Allan, Veronica Palmer OBE, Simon Batey **Group Dev Dir**: Dom McKenna **Group Man Dir (Ops)/Dep Ch Exec**: David Martin **Group Man Dir (Corporate Affairs)**: Steve Clayton **Communications Dir**: Simon Craven **Dir, Business Support**: Bob Scowen
DEALERSHIP
ARRIVA BUS & COACH, LODGE GARAGE, WHITEHALL ROAD WEST, GOMERSAL, CLECKHEATON BD19 4BJ

ARRIVA PASSENGER SERVICES
5 DOMINUS WAY, LEICESTER LE3 2RP
Tel: 0116 240 5500
Fax: 0116 240 5501
Man Dir UK Regional Bus: Mike Cooper **Eng Dir**: Mark Bowd

BLAZEFIELD GROUP
PROSPECT PARK, BROUGHTON WAY, STARBECK, HARROGATE HG2 7NY
Tel: 01423 884020
Web site: www.blazefieldholdings.com
Chmn: C Beaumont **Dirs**: Giles Fearnley, Stuart Wilde
Subsidiary companies: Burnley & Pendle, Harrogate & District Travel Ltd, Keighley & District Travel Ltd, Lancashire United, Yorkshire Coastliner Ltd.
Blazefield Holdings is part of Transdev Group

FIRST
395 KING STREET, ABERDEEN AB24 5RP
Tel: 01224 650100
Fax: 01224 650140
Website: www.firstgroup.com
Chmn: Martin Gilbert **DepChmn/Ch Exec**: Moir Lockhead **Fin Dir**: Dean Finch **Dir, UK Bus**: Nicola Shaw **Ops Dir**: David Kaye **Comm Dir**: Leon Daniels **Senior Independent Non-Exec Dir**: David Dunn **Non Exec Dir**: Jim Forbes **Dir International Development**: David Leeder **UK Rail**: Andrew Haines **Dep UK Bus Dir**: David Kaye
Non-exec Dirs: David Begg, John Sievwright **Non-Exec Employee Dir**: Martyn Williams

*THE GO-AHEAD GROUP PLC

3RD FLOOR, 41-51 GREY STREET, NEWCASTLE UPON TYNE NE1 6EE
Tel: 0191 232 3123
Fax: 0191 221 0315
E-mail: admin@go-ahead.com
Website: www.go-ahead.com
Ch Exec: Chris Moyes **Fin Dir/Co Sec**: Ian Butcher **Dir**: Keith Ludeman **Non-Exec Chmn**: Sir Patrick Brown **Non-Exec Dirs**: Christopher Collins, Rupert Pennant-Rea
Fleet: 3371 - 1157 double-deck bus, 542 single-deck bus, 532 coach, 94 articulated bus, 1046 minibus/midibus.
Ops incl: local bus services, excursions & tours, express
Livery: local fleet identity
Ticket System: various
Subsidiary companies:
BUS: Birmingham Coach Company, Brighton & Hove Bus & Coach Company, Go North East, London General, London Central, Metrobus, Oxford Bus Company, Solent Blue Line, Southern Vectis, Wilts & Dorset
RAIL: Southern Railway, South Eastern
PARKING: Meteor
AVIATION SUPPORT SERVICES: Aviance, Plane Handling

NATIONAL EXPRESS GROUP PLC
75 DAVIES STREET, LONDON W1K 5HT
Tel: 020 7529 2000
Fax: 020 7529 2100
E-mail: info@natex.co.uk
Website: www.nationalexpress.com
Ch Ex: R Bowker **Ch Ex (National Express Corporation, USA)**: Keith Stock **Man Dir (AirLinks)**: Bill Cahill **Finance Director**: Adam Walker **Ch Ops Officer**: Ray O'Toole **Co Sec**: Tony McDonald **Group Customer Service Dir**: David Bird **Project Dir**: Alex Perry **Eurolines Vice President**: John Gilbert **Dir UK Bus Div**: Denis Wormwell **Ch Exec National Express Coaches**: Paul Bunting
Subsidiary companies
Bus and coach: National Express (nationwide express coach network using coaches hired in from local operators under contract). National Express owns Travel West Midlands, Travel Dundee and Travel London, Alsa (Spain). Eurolines UK
Rail: Central Trains, Midland Mainline, Silverlink, Gatwick Express, C2C, Maintrain, Travel Midland Metro
Overseas: National Express Corporation (USA) - Bauman, Crabtree-Harmaan, Durham Transportation, Robinson Bus, SSL, ATC, Forsythe & Associates, Intelitran, Multisystems, Stewart International; shareholding in Westbus.

STAGECOACH GROUP
10 DUNKELD ROAD, PERTH PH1 5TW
Tel: 01738 442111
Fax: 01738 643648
Web site: www.stagecoachgroup.com, www.megabus.com
Ch Exec: Brian Souter **Ch Exec (Rail)**: Ian Dobbs **Fin Dir**: Martin Griffiths **Man Dir (UK bus)**: Les Warneford **Exec Dir (Rail)**: Graham Eccles **Non-Exec Chmn**: Robert Spiers **Reg Dir NW**: Tom Wileman **Man Dir Scotland**: Robert Andrew **Non-Exec Dirs**: Ann Gloag, Ewan Brown, Iain Duffin, Janet Morgan, Russell Walls
Fleet: 2589 double-deck bus, 1408 single-deck bus, 334 coach, 27 double-deck coach, 35 articulated bus, 1536 midibus, 855 minibus.
Livery: Stagecoach
Ticket system: ERG/Wayfarer
Overseas Division: Coach USA
Rail Division: South West Trains, Island Line, joint venture Virgin Rail Group, Sheffield Supertram (Sheffield).

TRANSDEV PLC
GARRICK HOUSE, STAMFORD BROOK GARAGE, 74 CHISWICK HIGH ROAD, LONDON W4 1SY
Tel: 020 8400 6052
Fax: 020 8400 6053
E-mail: information@transdevplc.co.uk
Web site: www.transdevplc.co.uk
Ch Exec: Francois Xavier Perin **Ch Op Officer**: C Beaumont
Subsidiary companies: Blazefield Holdings, Bournemouth Transport, shareholder partner with Nottingham council with Nottingham City Transport, Nottingham Express Transit (joint with NCT), London United, London Sovereign.

WELLGLADE LTD
MANSFIELD ROAD, HEANOR, DERBY DE75 7BG.
Tel: 01773 536309
Fax: 01773 536310
Subsidiary companies: Trent-Barton Ltd, Kinchbus Ltd, Nottinghamshire & Derbyshire Traction Co Ltd.

BEDFORDSHIRE

AtoB TRAVEL (LUTON) LTD

UNIT 54, BILTON WAY, LUTON
LU1 1UU
Tel: 01582 733333
Fax: 01582 733331
Web site: www.atobexec.com
Fleet: 50 - coach, minicoach, midicoach
Chassis: incl. Ford. Mercedes.
Bodies: incl. Ford. Mercedes.
Ops incl: school contracts, private hire
Livery: Silver

ARRIVA THE SHIRES & ESSEX LTD

487 DUNSTABLE ROAD, LUTON
LU4 8DS
Tel: 01582 587000/08701 201088
Web site: www.arrivabus.co.uk
Fleetname: Arriva the Shires & Essex.
Man Dir: Paul Woolmore
Fleet: 550 - double-deck bus, single-deck bus, coach, minibus.
Chassis: incl. 4 Optare
Bodies: incl. 4 Optare
Ops incl: local bus services, school contracts, excursions & tours, private hire, express.
Livery: Aquamarine and Cream.
Ticket System: Wayfarer 3, Prestige.

*BARFORDIAN COACHES LTD

500 GOLDINGTON ROAD, BEDFORD
MK41 0DX
Tel: 01234 355440
Fax: 01234 355310
E-mail: info@barfordiancoaches.co.uk
Web site: www.barfordiancoaches.co.uk
Man Dir: P Bullard **Dir**: K Bullard **Ops Man**: K Hargreaves
Fleet: 24 - 5 double-deck bus, 1 single-deck bus, 12 coach, 2 double-deck coach, 1 midicoach, 1 minibus, 2 minibus.
Chassis: 1 Bedford. 11 Bova. 4 Leyland. 1 MCW. 3 Mercedes. 2 Neoplan. 1 Toyota. 1 Volvo.
Bodies: 2 Alexander. 11 Bova. 1 Caetano. 1 Duple. 2 ECW. 1 Jonckheere. 1 MCW. 1 Mellor. 2 Neoplan. 1 Plaxton. 1 other.
Ops incl: local bus services, school contracts, excursions & tours, private hire, continental tours.
Livery: Orange/Yellow/White
Ticket System: Almex

*CLASSIC COACHES

47 WELLINGTON STREET, LUTON
LU1 2QH
Tel: 01582 457008
Owner: R J Lush
Fleet: 7 - 5 coaches, 2 minibus.
Chassis: 2 DAF. 2 LDV. 2 Scania. 1 Volvo.
Bodies: 1 Berkhof. 1 Caetano. 2 LDV. 1 Plaxton. 2 Van Hool.
Ops incl: private hire, school contracts, excursions & tours, continental tours.
Livery: White

CEDAR COACHES

ARKWRIGHT ROAD, BEDFORD
MK42 0LE.
Tel: 01234 354054
Fax: 01234 219210
E-mail: nikki@cedarcoaches.co.uk
Web site: www.cedarcoaches.co.uk
Man Dir: Eric Reid **Co Sec**: Nichola Graham
Dirs: Donna Reid, Kevin Reid
Fleet: 30 - 17 double-deck bus, 4 single-deck bus, 6 coach, 1 double-deck coach, 2 minicoach.
Chassis: Ayats. Bova. Irisbus. Iveco. Leyland. Scania. Volvo.
Bodies: Ayats. Beulas. Bova
Ops incl: local bus services, school contracts, excursions & tours, private hire.
Livery: Red/Yellow

*CENTREBUS LTD

14 SEDGWICK ROAD, LUTON
LU4 9DT
Tel: 08707 444746
Web site: www.centrebus.co.uk
Man Dir: Peter Harvey **Ops Di**: Neil Harris
Fleet: 60 single-deck bus
Ops incl: local bus services
Livery: Blue/Orange
Ticket system: Wayfarer 3

CHILTERN TRAVEL

THE COACH HOUSE, BARFORD
ROAD, BLUNHAM MK44 3NA
Tel: 01234 295490
Fax: 01234 295490
E-mail: chilterntravel.coaches@virgin.net
Prop: Trevor Boorman
Fleet: 8 - 6 coach, 2 double-deck coach.
Chassis: 1 Bova. 2 DAF. 3 Mercedes-Benz. 2 Volvo.
Bodies: 1 Bova. 1 Jonckheere. 3 Mercedes-Benz. 3 Van Hool.
Ops incl: private hire, continental tours, school contracts, excursions & tours. **Livery**: White.

*CORPORATE COACHING

EAGLE HOUSE, EAGLE CENTRE
WAY, LUTON LU4 9US
Tel: 01525 715872
Fax: 01525 713020
E-mail: sales@corp-coach.co.uk
Web site: www.corp-coach.co.uk
Man Dir: Doreen Collins **Ops Dir**: Peter Collins
Fleet: 8 - 4 midicoach, 4 minicoach.
Chassis: 8 Mercedes-Benz.
Ops incl: private hire, express.
Livery: Blue/Silver

DUNN-LINE GROUP
See Nottinghamshire

*EXPRESSLINES LTD

UNIT 15, FENLAKE INDUSTRIAL
ESTATE, FENLAKE ROAD,
BEDFORD MK42 0HB
Tel: 01234 268704
Web site: www.expresslinesltd.co.uk
Fleet: 16 - 1 single-deck bus, 5 midicoach, 10 minicoach.
Chassis: 10 Ford Transit. 1 Leyland. 4 Mercedes-Benz. 1 Optare.
Bodies: 5 Optare. 1 Wadham Stringer.
Ops incl: local bus services, school contracts, private hire.
Livery: Red/White/Silver
Ticket System: Almex Microfare

FLIGHTS HALLMARK
See West Midlands

GRANT PALMER PASSENGER SERVICES

UNIT 2, LAWRENCE WAY,
DUNSTABLE LU6 1BD
Tel: 01582 600844
Ops incl: local bus services

*HERBERTS TRAVEL

UNIT 5, OLD ROWNEY FARM,
SHEFFORD SG17 5QH
Tel: 0845 0090 369
Fax: 01234 381117
Ops Dir: D S Dougall **Man Dir**: D M Dougall
Fleet Eng: S Myers
E-mail: booking@herberts-travel.co.uk
Web site: www.herberts-travel.co.uk
Fleet: 21 - 6 double-deck bus, 5 midibus, 4 midicoach, 1 minibus, 5 minicoach.
Chassis: 5 Ford Transit. 5 Leyland. 3 MCW. 4 Mercedes. 2 Optare. 1 Toyota. 1 Volvo.
Bodies: 4 Alexander. 1 Caetano. 2 ECW. 1 Leyland. 1 MCW. 4 Optare. 1 Plaxton. 6 other.
Ops incl: private hire, school contracts, local bus services.
Livery: White.
Ticket system: Wayfarer

*MARSHALLS COACHES LTD

FIRBANK WAY, LEIGHTON BUZZARD
LU7 4YP
Tel: 01525 376077
Fax: 01525 850967
Recovery: 01525 375301
E-mail: info@marshalls-coaches.co.uk
Web site: www.marshalls-coaches.co.uk
Props: G Marshall, Mrs S Marshall **Ops Man**: Ian White **Fleet Eng**: R Winters
Fleet: 21 - 19 coach, 1 double-deck coach, 1 midicoach.
Chassis: 4 Dennis. 2 Iveco. 1 Mercedes. 1 Neoplan. 1 Scania. 12 Volvo.
Bodies: 2 Beulas. 1 Caetano. 1 Ikarus. 5 Jonckheere. 1 Mercedes. 1 Neoplan. 10 Plaxton.
Ops incl: private hire, school contracts, local bus services.
Livery: Blue/Multicoloured.

NEWBOURNE COACHES
See London

RED KITE COMMERCIAL SERVICES

UNIT 2, LEYS YARD, DUNSTABLE ROAD, TILSWORTH, LEIGHTON BUZZARD LU7 9PU
Tel: 01525 211441.
Props: D. Hoar, R. H. Savage
Fleet: 18 - 15 double-deck bus, 3 coach.
Ops incl: local bus services, school contracts, excursions and tours, private hire, school contracts.
Livery: Red/Blue

SAFFORDS COACHES LTD

THE DRIFT, LITTLE GRANSDEN, SANDY SG19 3DW
Tel: 01767 677395
Fax: 01767 677742
Dirs: M. C. Safford, S. I. Gillett.
Fleet: 14 - 1 single-deck bus, 10 coach, 3 midicoach.
Chassis: 2 Mercedes, 12 Volvo.
Bodies: 1 Caetano, 1 Jonckheere, 12 Plaxton.
Ops incl: local bus services, school contracts, excursions & tours, private hire, continental tours.

Livery: White/Blue/Yellow.
Ticket System: Almex.

SHOREYS TRAVEL

119 CLOPHILL ROAD, MAULDEN MK45 2AE.
Tel: 01525 860694
Fax: 01525 861850.
E-mail: shoreystravel@talk21.com
Prop: E C J Shorey **Ptnrs**: D Shorey, G Shorey **Ch Eng**: D Bunker
Fleet: 8 - 7 double deck bus, 1 coach.
Chassis: ! Iveco. 1 Leyland. 6 MCW.
Bodies: 1 Beulas. 6 MCW. 1 Leyland.
Ops incl: school contracts, private hire.
Livery: White/Green
Ticket System: Wayfarer.

*TATES COACHES
See Hertfordshire

THREE STAR COACH HIRE

6 HIGH TOWN ROAD, LUTON LU2 0DD
Tel: 01582 722626
Fax: 01582 484034

E-mail: sales@bookthisbus.com
Ops Man: Kevin Green
Fleet: 14 - 5 coach, 3 midicoach, 4 minibus, 2 minicoach.
Chassis: 2 Dennis. 1 MAN. 2 Volvo.
Bodies: incl: 9 Mercedes.
Ops incl: local bus services, school contracts, private hire.
Livery: Blue

*VILLAGER MINIBUS (SHARNBROOK) LTD

SHARNBROOK UPPER SCHOOL, ODELL ROAD, SHARNBROOK MK44 1JL
Tel: 01234 781920
Fleet: 1 minibus
Chassis: 1 Ford
Ops incl: local bus services, private hire
Ticket system: printed book

BERKSHIRE
(WEST BERKSHIRE, BRACKNELL FOREST, READING, SLOUGH, WINDSOR & MAIDENHEAD, WOKINGHAM)

1ST CHOICE SCORPIO TRAVEL

67 WEST END COURT, WEST END LANE, STOKE POGES SL2 4NB
Tel: 01753 648435
Fax: 01753 644878
E-mail: admin@scorpiotravel.net
Web site: www.scorpiotravel.net
Ptnrs: Don Hughes, Gill Hughes.
Fleet: 1 coach
Chassis: Iveco
Body: Beulas
Ops incl: excursions & tours, private hire, continental tours.
Livery: Silver/Cerise/Teal

ALDERMASTON COACHES

ALDERMASTON RG7 5PP
Tel: 0118 971 3257
Fax: 0118 971 2722
Ptnrs: D. Arlott, T. Arlott, P. Arlott
Fleet: includes 1 midicoach, 1 minicoach.
Chassis: includes 4 Leyland.
Ops incl: private hire, school contracts.
Livery: White

BURGHFIELD MINI COACHES LTD

BURGHFIELD FARM, MILL ROAD, BURGHFIELD BRIDGE RG30 3SS
Tel/Fax: 0118 959 0719
E-mail: burghfield.coaches@virgin.net
Dir: Susan McCoud
Fleet: 38 - 30 minibus, 8 minicoach.
Chassis: Citroen. Dennis. Leyland. Mercedes-Benz. Optare. Renault.
Ops incl: local bus services, school contracts, private hire.

COURTNEY COACHES

TERRANOVA HOUSE, KILN LANE, BRACKNELL RG12 1NA
Tel: 01344 412302
Fax: 01344 868980/422278
E-mail: enquiries@courtneycoaches.com
Web site: www.courtneycoaches.com
Prop: Bill Courtney-Smith
Fleet: 37 - 5 double-deck bus, 11 coach, 3 double-deck, 4 single-deck bus, 14 minibus.
Chassis: 1 Ayats. 1 Iveco. 7 Leyland. 1 Marshall. 14 Mercedes. 1 Neoplan. 3 Optare. 2 Scania. 7 Volvo.
Ops incl: local bus services.
Livery: Orange/White.

FIRST IN BERKSHIRE

COLDBOROUGH HOUSE, MARKET STREET, BRACKNELL RG12 1JA
Tel: 01344 868688
Fax: 01344 868332
Web site: www.firstgroup.com
Man Dir: Tony Wilson **Comm Dir**: Andrew Taylor
Fleet: 115 - 6 double-deck bus, 68 single-deck bus, 24 midibus, 17 coach.
Chassis: 6 Bluebird. 55 Dennis. 8 Mercedes. 33 Scania. 13 Volvo.
Bodies: 19 Alexander. 8 Berkhof. 6 Bluebird. 1 Irizar. 8 Mercedes. 10 Northern Counties. 43 Plaxton. 20 Wright.
Ops incl: local bus services, school contracts, express.
Livery: FirstGroup/Green Line
Ticket System: Wayfarer

*HAYWARDS COACHES

169 NEW GREENHAM PARK, THATCHAM RG19 6HN
Tel: 01185 474561
Fax: 01635 821128
Dir: Simon Weaver
Fleet: 24 - 18 coach, 6 double-deck coach.
Chassis: 8 Bova. 7 Scania. 9 Volvo.
Bodies: 8 Bova. 6 East Lancs. 7 Irizar. 3 Plaxton.

A/c	Air conditioning	
	Vehicles suitable for disabled	
	Coach(es) with galley facilities	
wc	Coach(es) with toilet facilities	
	Seat belt-fitted vehicles	
R	Recovery service available (not 24 hr)	
R24	24hr recovery service	
	Replacement vehicle available	
T	Toilet-drop facilities available	
	Vintage vehicle(s) available	
	Open top vehicle(s)	

Ops incl: local bus services, school contracts
Livery: Electric Blue

HODGE'S COACHES (SANDHURST) LTD

100 YORKTOWN ROAD, SANDHURST GU47 9BH.
Tel: 01252 873131
Fax: 01252 874884.
E-mail: enquiries@hodges-coaches.co.uk
Web site: www.hodges-coaches.co.uk
Man Dir: P Hodge **Dir**: M Hodge, M Hodge
Fleet: 21 - 18 single-deck coach, 1 midicoach, 2 minicoach.
Chassis: 4 Bedford. 2 DAF, 1 MAN, 2 Toyota, 12 Volvo
Bodies: 10 Berkhof. 7 Caetano. 1 Duple. 3 Plaxton.
Ops incl: excursions & tours, private hire, continental tours, school contracts.
Livery: Blue/Gold

*HORSEMAN COACHES LTD

WHITLEY WOOD ROAD, READING RG1 8GG
Tel: 0118 975 3811
Fax: 0118 975 3515
E-mail: horsemancoaches@metronet.co.uk
Man Dir: Keith Horseman **Ops Dir**: James Horseman **Eng Man**: Derrick Holton
Fleet: 57 - 47 coach, 10 midicoach.
Chassis: 4 Dennis. 4 Iveco. 10 Toyota. 39 Volvo.
Bodies: 4 Beulas. 5 Berkhof. 10 Caetano. 15 Jonckheere. 15 Plaxton. 1 UVG. 7 other
Ops incl: local bus services, school contracts, excursions & tours, private hire, continental tours.
Livery: White with four-colour logo.

KINGFISHER MINI COACHES

357 BASINGSTOKE ROAD, READING RG2 0JA
Tel: 0118 931 3454
Prop: Kevin Pope
Fleet: 13 - 5 minibus, 8 minicoach
Chassis: incl. 6 Leyland. 4 Mercedes.
Ops incl: private hire. school contracts
Livery: White/Orange

*MEMORY LANE VINTAGE OMNIBUS SERVICES

78 LILLIBROOKE CRESCENT, MAIDENHEAD SL6 3XQ
Tel: 01628 825050
E-mail: admin@memorylane.co.uk
Web site: www.memorylane.co.uk
Prop: M J Clarke
Fleet: 6 - 4 double-deck bus, 2 single-deck bus
Chassis: 5 AEC. 1 Bristol
Bodies: 1 ECW. 1 MCW. 4 Park Royal.
Ops incl: private hire
Livery: Original operators

*NEWBURY & DISTRICT

169 NEW GREENHAM PARK, THATCHAM RG19 6HN
Tel: 01635 33855
Fax: 01635 821128
Dir: Simon Weaver
Fleet: 4 - 3 single-deck bus, 1 midibus.
Chassis: 1 Mercedes. 3 Volvo.
Bodies: 3 Wright. 1 Plaxton.
Ops incl: local bus services
Livery: White
Ticket System: Wayfarer 3

READING & WOKINGHAM COACHES

33 MURRAY ROAD, WOKINGHAM RG41 2TA
Tel: 0118 979 3983
Fax: 0118 979 4330
Props: Mark Way, Sharon Way.
Fleet: 10 - 8 coach, 2 minibus
Chassis: 1 Dennis. 1 Iveco. 1 Mercedes. 1 Setra. 1 Toyota. 5 Volvo.
Bodies: 1 Beulas. 2 Berkhof. 1 Caetano. 1 Ikarus. 1 Jonckheere. 1 Mercedes. 1 Setra. 2 Van Hool.
Ops incl: excursions & tours, private hire, school contracts, continental tours.
Livery: White

READING HERITAGE TRAVEL

PO BOX 147, READING RG1 6BD
Tel: 07850 220151
Prop/Tran Man: M J Russell
Fleet: 2 double-deck bus.
Chassis: 2 AEC
Bodies: 2 Park Royal
Ops incl: private hire
Livery: Red/Cream
Ticket System: Almex

READING TRANSPORT LTD

GREAT KNOLLYS STREET, READING RG1 7HH.
Tel: 0118 959 4000
Fax: 0118 957 5379
Recovery: 0118 958 5594
E-mail: info@reading-buses.co.uk.
Web site: www.reading-buses.co.uk
Fleetname: Reading Buses, Newbury Buses, Goldline Travel
Man Dir: Colin Thompson **Fin Dir**: James Carney **Ops Dir**: Sam Simpson
Goldline Man: Norman Fryer-Saxby
Newbury Ops Man: Mel Atkinson **Reading Ops Man**: Glynne Davies **Eng Man**: Mark Hodder **Personnel Man**: Caroline Anscombe
Fleet: 208 - 85 double-deck bus, 79 single-deck bus, 11 single-deck coach, 32 midibus, 1 midicoach.
Chassis: 56 DAF. 11 Dennis. 15 Leyland. 24 MCW. 58 Optare. 44 Scania.
Bodies: 17 East Lancs. 6 Irizar. 16 MCW. 117 Optare. 2 Park Royal. 6 Plaxton. 13 Roe. 5 Transbus. 5 Van Hool. 21 Wright.
Ops incl: local bus services, school contracts, excursions & tours, private hire,

continental tours.
Livery: Cream/Maroon
Ticket System: Wayfarer TGX150.

*TOP TRAVEL COACHES
See Hampshire

VINCE COACHES

AYRES HOUSE, AYRES LANE, BURGHCLERE RG20 9HG
Tel: 01635 278308
Prop: D L. Vince
Fleet: 5 coaches
Chassis/Bodies: 2 Berkhof. 3 Dennis.
Ops incl: private hire, school contracts.

*WEAVAWAY TRAVEL

169 NEW GREENHAM PARK, NEWBURY RG19 6HN
Tel: 01635 820028
Fax: 01635 821128
Dir: Simon Weaver
Fleet: 24 - 18 coach, 6 double-deck coach
Chassis: 8 Bova. 7 Scania. 9 Volvo.
Bodies: 8 Bova. 6 East Lancs. 7 Irizar. 3 Plaxton.
Ops incl: school contracts, private hire.
Livery: Electric Blue

WHITE BUS SERVICES

NORTH STREET GARAGE, WINKFIELD SL4 4TP
Tel: 01344 88262
Fax: 01344 886403
E-mail: reception@whitebus.co.uk
Dir: D. E. Jeatt
Fleet: 12 - 3 single-deck bus, 9 coach.
Chassis: include DAF, Bedford.
Bodies: Duple. Optare. Plaxton. Van Hool.
Ops incl: local bus services, school contracts, private hire.
Livery: White/grey skirt.
Ticket System: Wayfarer Saver, Setright

*WINDSORIAN COACHES

103 ARTHUR ROAD, WINDSOR SL4 1RU
Tel: 01753 860131
Fax: 020 8751 5054
Man Dir: Martin Cornell **Gen Man**: Gilbert Parsons
Fleet: 10 - 8 double-deck coach, 2 midicoach.
Chassis: 8 Dennis. 2 Mercedes.
Bodies: 8 Plaxton. 2 other.
Ops incl: school contracts, excursions & tours, private hire, continental tours.
Livery: White/Blue.

BRISTOL

*ABUS
104 WINCHESTER ROAD, BRISLINGTON, BRISTOL BS4 3NL
Tel: 0117 977 6126
E-mail: alan@abus.co.uk
Web site: www.abus.co.uk
Chmn/Man Dir: Alan Peters
Fleet: 20 - 17 double-deck bus, 3 midibus.
Chassis: 3 Bristol. 5 DAF. 1 Iveco. 8 Leyland. 2 Optare. 1 Scania.
Bodies: 7 Alexander. 3 ECW. 3 East Lancs. 6 Optare. 1 Reeve Burgess
Ops incl: local bus services
Livery: Cream/White/Maroon or Orange
Ticket System: Wayfarer 3

AZTEC COACH TRAVEL
6/8 EMERY ROAD, BRISLINGTON BS4 5PF
Tel: 0117 977 0314.
Fax: 0117 977 4431.
Man Dir: I. Fortune. **Fleet Eng**: D. Harvey.
Ops Man: P. Rixon.
Fleet: 15 - 13 midicoach, 2 minibus.
Chassis: 1 Freight Rover. 14 Mercedes.
Bodies: 2 Optare. 7 Reeve Burgess. 4 Autobus Classique.
Ops incl: excursions & tours, private hire, continental tours, school contracts.
Livery: White with diagonal red/orange stripes.

*BERKELEY COACH & TRAVEL
HAM LANE, PAULTON BS39 7PL
Tel: 01761 413196
Fax: 01761 416469
E-mail: mail@berkeleycoachandtravel.co.uk
Web site: www.berkeleycoachandtravel.co.uk
Fleet: 12 coach
Chassis: 12 Volvo
Bodies: 8 Plaxton. 4 Van Hool.
Ops incl: school contracts, private hire.
Livery: Silver/Blue

*BLAGDON LIONESS COACHES LTD
See Somerset

*BLUE IRIS COACHES
25 CLEVEDON ROAD, NAILSEA BS48 1EH
Tel: 01275 851121
Fax: 01275 856522
E-mail: tonys@blueiris.co.uk
Web site: www.blueiris.co.uk
Dirs: Philip Hatherall, Tony Spiller
Fleet: 15 - 2 single-deck bus, 7 single-deck coach, 6 minicoach.
Chassis: 2 Mercedes. 6 Scania. 6 Toyota. 1 Volvo.
Bodies: 1 Alexander. 6 Caetano. 1 Carlyle. 6 Irizar. 1 Plaxton.
Ops incl: private hire, local bus services, school contracts.
Livery: 2-tone Blue/White.
Ticket System: Setright

BRISTOL ELECTRIC RAILBUS LTD
HERON HOUSE, CHISWICK MALL, LONDON W4 2PR
Tel: 020 8995 3000
Fax: 020 8994 6060
Dir: James Skinner
Fleet: 1 tram.
Chassis/Body: Parry/Clayton

BUGLERS COACHES
100 SCHOOL ROAD, BRISLINGTON BS4 4NF
Tel: 0117 977 8759
E-mail: buglercoaches@yahoo.com
Web site: www.buglercoaches.co.uk
Dir: Bob Bugler
Fleet: 16 - 2 double-deck bus, 7 coach, 3 midicoach, 4 minibus
Chassis: Bristol, Dennis, Leyland, Mercedes, Optare, Volvo
Bodies: Alexander, Plaxton, other
Ops incl: local bus services, private hire
Livery: Yellow/Red/White

PETER CAROL PRESTIGE COACHING
BAMFIELD HOUSE, WHITCHURCH BS14 0XD
Tel: 01275 839839
Fax: 01275 835604
E-mail: charter@petercarol.co.uk
Web site: www.luxurycoach.co.uk
Gen Man: Peter Collis
Fleet: 12 - 10 coach, 2 double-deck coach.
Chassis: 2 Bova. 2 DAF. 2 MAN. 4 Neoplan. 1 Scania. 1 Toyota.
Bodies: 1 Berkhof. 2 Bova. 2 Caetano. 4 Neoplan. 1 Noge. 2 Van Hool.
Ops incl: excursions & tours, private hire, continental tours.
Livery: Dark Grey

*EAGLE COACHES
FIRECLAY HOUSE, NETHAM ROAD, ST GEORGE BS5 9PJ
Tel: 0117 955 7130
Fax: 0117 941 1107
E-mail: any@eagle-coaches.co.uk
Web site: www.eagle-coaches.co.uk
Fleet: 15 - 2 double-deck bus, 11 coach, 1 midicoach,1 minicoach
Chassis: 11 DAF. 1 Iveco. 1 Leyland. 1 Mercedes. 1 Scania.
Bodies: 2 Alexander. 1 Autobus. 1 Optare. 11 Van Hool.
Ops incl: school contracts, excursions & tours, private hire
Livery: Yellow

EASTVILLE COACHES LTD
15 ASHGROVE ROAD, REDLAND BS6 6NA
Tel: 0117 971 0657
Fax: 0117 971 5824.
Man Dir: T. Reece.
Fleet: 14 - 6 double-deck bus, 8 coach.
Chassis: 6 Bristol. 1 DAF. 7 Volvo.
Bodies: 6 ECW. 2 Plaxton. 6 Van Hool.
Ops incl: local bus services, school contracts, private hire, continental tours.
Livery: Myosotis Blue/White.

EUROTAXIS LTD
JORROCKS ESTATE, WESTERLEIGH ROAD, WESTERLEIGH BS37 8QH
Tel: 01454 320101
Fax: 01454 320011
E-mail: juan@euro-taxis.co.uk
Web site: www.euro-taxis.co.uk
Dirs: Juan Sanzo, Keith Sanzo, William Sanzo
Fleet: 89 - 4 double-deck bus, 10 single-deck bus, 10 coach, 15 midibus, 25 minicoach, 25 minicoach.
Chassis: 6 Dennis. 2 Iveco. 7 Leyland. 70 Mercedes. 1 Neoplan. 7 Optare. 4 Volvo.
Bodies: 1 Autobus. 4 East Lancs. 1 Jonckheere. 7 Leyland. 4 Mellor. 60 Mercedes. 1 Neoplan. 6 Optare. 7 Plaxton.10 Wadham Stringer.
Ops incl: local bus services, school contracts, private hire

FILER'S COACHES
STANTON WICK, PENSFORD BS39 4BZ.
Tel: 01761 490674, 490465.
Fax: 01761 490861.

FIRST IN BRISTOL
ENTERPRISE HOUSE, EASTON ROAD, BRISTOL BS5 0DZ
Tel: 0117 955 8211
Fax: 0117 955 1248
Web site: www.firstgroup.com
Man Dir: Tony Anthistle **Eng Dir**: Richard Noble **Fin Dir**: Mike Gahan **Ops Dir**: Jenny McLeod
Fleet: 314 - 133 double-deck bus, 44 single-deck bus, 124 midibus, 13 minibus.
Chassis: 115 Dennis. 91 Leyland. 19 Mercedes. 89 Volvo.
Bodies: 29 Alexander. 8 East Lancs. 35 Leyland. 70 Northern Counties. 102 Plaxton. 30 Roe. 40 Wright.

A/c	Air conditioning	
♿	Vehicles suitable for disabled	
🍴	Coach(es) with galley facilities	
wc	Coach(es) with toilet facilities	
▼	Seat belt-fitted vehicles	
R	Recovery service available (not 24 hr)	
R24	24hr recovery service	
✓	Replacement vehicle available	
T	Toilet-drop facilities available	
	Vintage vehicle(s) available	
	Open top vehicle(s)	

Ops incl: local bus services, school contracts.
Livery: First Bus Barbie 1+2
Ticket System: Wayfarer

GLENVIC OF BRISTOL LTD

THE OLD COLLIERY, STANTON WICK, PENSFORD BS39 4BZ
Tel: 01761 490116
Fax: 0117 907 7032
Dirs: Paul Holvey, Philip Holvey
Ops Man/Comp Sec: Paul Holvey
Eng: Nick Reed
Fleet: 13 - 4 double-deck bus, 5 coach, 4 minicoach
Chassis: 2 LDV. 7 Leyland. 2 Mercedes-Benz. 2 Volvo.

*GRAHAM'S COACHES OF BRISTOL

7 WYCK BECK ROAD, BRENTRY BS10 7JD
Tel/Fax: 0117 950 9398
Prop: Graham P Smith
Fleet: 8 - 5 double-deck bus, 3 midicoaches.
Chassis: 1 Bristol. 1 DAF. 1 Daimler. 2 Dennis. 1 Optare. 2 Volvo
Bodies: 2 Jonckheere. 1 Optare. 1 Van Hool. 4 other.
Ops incl: private hire, school contracts.

ARNOLD LIDDELL COACHES

89 JERSEY AVENUE, BRISLINGTON BS4 4QX.
Tel: 0117 977 2011.
Prop: Michael. Liddell. **Gen Man**: Arnold. Liddell. **Fleet Eng**: Robert Liddell
Fleet: 2 - 1 coach, 1 midicoach.
Chassis: 1 Leyland. 1 Mercedes.
Ops incl: excursions & tours, school contracts.
Livery: Blue/White.

MARTINS SELF DRIVE MINICOACH HIRE

GRINDELL ROAD GARAGE, 1 GRINDELL ROAD, REDFIELD BS5 9PG.
Tel: 0117 955 1042.
Fax: 0117 939 3383.
Fleet: 12 - 12 minibus.
Chassis: 12 Ford Transit.
Ops incl: Self Drive Minicoach Hire.

*NORTH SOMERSET COACHES

COATES ESTATE, SOUTHFIELD ROAD, NAILSEA BS48 1JN
Tel/Fax: 01275 859123
Prop: Graham Clements.
Fleet: 3 coach.
Chassis: 1 Dennis. 2 Volvo.
Bodies: 1 Berkhof. 1 Ikarus. 1 Plaxton.
Ops incl: school contracts, private hire.

PREMIER TRAVEL LTD
   R24

ALBERT CRESCENT, ST PHILIPS BS2 0SU
Tel: 0117 9300 5550
Fax: 0117 9300 5551
Man Dir: Glenn Bond
Fleet: 5 - 1 double-deck bus, 2 coach, 1 double-deck coach, 1 minicoach.
Chassis: 9 Bova. 1 DAF. 1 Freight Rover. 1 Leyland. 1 Volvo
Bodies: 1 Bova. 1 ECW. 2 Van Hool.
Ops incl: school contracts, continental tours, private hire.
Livery: White/Red with blue lettering.

SOUTH GLOUCESTERSHIRE BUS & COACH COMPANY

PEGASUS PARK, GYPSY PATCH LANE, PATCHWAY BS34 6QD
Tel: 0117 931 4340
Fax: 0117 979 9400

Man Dir: Roger Durbin **Gen Man**: Mike Owen **Wkshp Man**: Mark Wood **Sales Man**: Tony Laudie **Route Man**: Nathan Wrenn
Fleet: 99 - 26 double-deck bus. 26 single-deck bus. 22 coach. 1 double-deck coach. 9 midibus. 15 minibus.
Chassis: 10 Dennis. 35 Leyland. 15 Mercedes. 1 Toyota. 38 Volvo.
Bodies: 20 Alexander. 1 Caetano. 16 Northern Counties. 38 Plaxton. 6 Reeve Burgess. 12 Van Hool. 2 Wadham Stringer. 4 Wright.
Ops incl: local bus service, school contracts, excursions & tours, private hire, continental tours, express.
Livery: Blue/White.
Ticket system: Wayfarer 2

*SOMERBUS LTD
See Somerset

TURNERS COACHWAYS (BRISTOL) LTD

59 DAYS ROAD, ST PHILIPS BS2 0QS
Tel: 0117 955 9086
Fax: 0117 955 6948
E-mail: admin@turnerscoachways.co.uk
Web site: www.turnerscoachways.co.uk
Man Dir: A J Turner. **Private Hire Man**: E A Venn **Traf Man**: A Harvey
Fleet: 31 - 30 coach, 1 minicoach.
Chassis: 1 Mercedes. 7 Scania. 22 Volvo.
Bodies: 2 Berkhof. 7 Irizar. 12 Jonckheere. 9 Van Hool.
Ops incl: private hire

BUCKINGHAMSHIRE, MILTON KEYNES

AUTODOUBLE LTD
90 HAINAULT AVENUE, GIFFARD PARK, MILTON KEYNES MK14 5PE.
Tel: 01908 281350.
Fleetname: Starlight.
Fin Dir/Sec: N. A Gibbard.
Traf Man/Dir: K. G. Gibbard.
Fleet: 5 - 1 coach, 1 midibus, 3 minicoach.
Chassis: 2 Bedford. 1 Bristol. 2 Ford Transit.
Bodies: 1 ECW. 1 Plaxton. 2 Dormobile. 1 Tricentrol.
Ops incl: private hire, school contracts.
Livery: White/Burgundy.

*BRAZIERS MINI COACHES
17 VICARAGE ROAD, WINSLOW MK18 3BE
Tel: 01296 712201
Prop: Peter Brazier.
Fleet: 3 minicoach

Chassis: 3 LDV
Ops incl: private hire, school contracts.
Livery: White/Green/Gold

*CAROUSEL BUSES LTD

1 BAKER STREET, HIGH WYCOMBE HP11 2RX
Tel: 01494 533436
E-mail: enquiries@carouselbuses.com
Web site: www.carouselbuses.com
Man Dir/Co Sec: S Burns **Fin Dir**: J Robinson
Fleet: 41 - 22 double-deck bus, 19 single-deck bus
Chassis: 1 AEC. 6 DAF. 10 Dennis.3 Irisbus. 6 Leyland. 12 MCW. 3 Mercedes
Bodies: 3 East Lancs. 4 Leyland. 12 MCW. 3 Mercedes. 3 Northern Counties. 3 Optare. 1 Park Royal. 11 Plaxton. 1 Wright.

Ops incl: Local bus services, school contracts, private hire.
Livery: Red/Dark Red
Ticket system: Wayfarer 3

DERWENT TRAVEL

UNIT 11, PEMBROKE ROAD, STOCKLAKE, AYLESBURY HP20 1DB
Tel: 01296 415163
Fax: 01296 425938
Recovery: 07775 860511
Ptnrs: Diane Best, David Best **Man**: John Lake **Sec**: Barbara Nash
Fleet: 5 coach
Chassis/bodies: 5 Setra
Ops incl: excursions & tours, private hire, continental tours
Livery: Multicolour (same style)

*DRP TRAVEL
1 THE MEADWAY, LOUGHTON,
MILTON KEYNES MK5 8AN
Tel: 01908 394141
Mobile: 07979 364968
Web site: www.drptravel.co.uk
E-mail: drptravel@btinternet.com
Man: D R Pinnock
Fleet: 3 minicoach.
Chassis: 1 Iveco. 1 Optare. 1 Renault
Ops incl: school contracts, excursions and tours, private hire.

HOWLETTS COACHES

UNIT 2, STATION ROAD INDUSTRIAL ESTATE, WINSLOW MK18 3DZ
Tel: 01296 713201
Fax: 01296 715879
Prop: R. S. Durham
Fleet: 8 - 2 double-deck bus, 6 coach.
Chassis: 1 Bedford. 4 DAF. 2 MCW. 1 Setra.
Ops incl: private hire, continental tours, school contracts.
Livery: Brown/White.

*LANGSTON & TASKER
23 QUEEN CATHERINE ROAD, STEEPLE CLAYDON MK18 2PZ
Tel/Fax: 01296 730347
Ptnrs: Mrs J Langston, Mrs M A Fenner
Man: J Langston **Ops Man**: A P Price
Fleet: 19 - 13 single-deck coach, 6 minibus.
Chassis: 1 Bedford. 4 Dennis. 1 Iveco. 2 Leyland. 4 Mercedes. 1 Toyota. 6 Volvo.
Bodies: 1 Autobus. 2 Caetano. 3 Duple. 2 Jonckheere. 3 Mercedes. 6 Plaxton. 1 Transbus. 1 Wadham Stringer.
Ops incl: local bus services, school contracts, private hire
Livery: White/Red
Ticket system: Wayfarer

*MAGPIE TRAVEL
BINDERS INDUSTRIAL ESTATE, CRYERS HILL, HIGH WYCOMBE HP15 6LJ
Tel: 01494 715381
Prop: Martin Ash
Fleet: 17 - 3 single-deck bus, 5 coach, 2 midibus, 7 midicoach.
Chassis: 2 Dennis. 1 Leyland National. 12 Mercedes. 3 Volvo.
Ops incl: local bus services, school contracts, private hire.
Livery: White.
Ticket System: Almex

MK METRO LTD
UNIT 3, ARDEN PARK, OLD WOLVERTON, MILTON KEYNES MK12 5RN
Tel: 01908 225100
Fax: 01908 313553
Man Dir: J Peddle **Fin Dir**: Y Newey
Gen Man: M Heywood
Fleet: 89 - 4 double-deck bus, 82 single-deck bus, 3 midibus.

Chassis: 3 DAF. 24 Dennis. 26 Mercedes. 32 Optare. 1 Scania. 3 Volvo.
Bodies: 3 Alexander. 10 Caetano. 32 Optare. 37 Plaxton. 7 Wright.
Ops incl: local bus services, school contracts
Livery: Blue/Yellow.
Ticket System: Wayfarer 3
Part of Arriva plc

*MOTTS COACHES (AYLESBURY) LTD
GARSIDE WAY, STOCKLAKE, AYLESBURY HP20 1BH
Tel: 01296 398300
Fax: 01296 398386
E-mail: info@mottstravel.com
Web site: www.mottstravel.com
Fleetname: Motts Travel
Man Dir: M R Mott **Ops Dir**: C J Mott **Eng Dir**: I Scutt **Tours Dir**: C Joel **Traf Man**: H Shanks
Fleet: 43 - 4 double-deck bus, 5 single-deck bus, 25 coach, 2 double-deck coach, 5 midicoach, 2 minibus
Chassis: 6 Leyland. 3 MCW. 7 Mercedes. 1 Neoplan. 26 Volvo.
Bodies: 5 Alexander. 1 ECW. 1 Esker. 17 Jonckheere. 3 MCW. 1 Mellor. 1 Neoplan. 9 Plaxton. 1 Reeve Burgess. 1 Van Hool. 3 Sitcar.
Ops incl: local bus services, school contracts, excursions & tours, private hire, continental tours.
Livery: White/Yellow/Green.
Ticket System: Wayfarer.

PASSENGER TRANSPORT LOGISTICS LTD
MILTON KEYNES COACHWAY, BROOK FURLONG, MILTON KEYNES MK10 9AB.
Tel: 01908 676700.
Fax: 01908 694770.
Dir: M. E. Infanti. **Co Sec**: D. M. Infanti.
Gen Man: J. M. Lunt.
Fleet: 40 – 2 double-deck bus. 11 single-deck bus. 10 double-deck coach. 3 midicoach. 14 minicoach.
Chassis: 4 Bedford. 2 Daimler. 1 Ford Transit. 3 Freight Rover. 4 Mercedes-Benz.
Bodies: 3 Carlyle. 3 Mercedes-Benz. 4 Plaxton.
Ops incl: local bus services, school contracts, excursions & tours, private hire.
Livery: Blue/Silver.
Ticket System: AES.
Limousine hire and taxi service.

PAYNES COACHES & CAR HIRE LTD
6 BALMER CUT, BUCKINGHAM INDUSTRIAL ESTATE, BUCKINGHAM MK18 1UL.
Tel: 01280 813108, 817761.
Dirs: J. V. & K. R. Jeffs.
Fleet: 14 - 12 coach, 2 minicoach.
Chassis: Bedford. Ford. Leyland.
Bodies: 4 Caetano. 1 Duple. 2 Jonckheere.

3 Leyland. 1 Mercedes. 2 Optare. 1 Plaxton.
Ops incl: local bus services, excursions & tours, private hire, express, continental tours.
Livery: Green/Cream.
Ticket System: Almex/Wayfarer.
Subsidiary of Jeffs Coaches, Helmdon.

RED ROSE TRAVEL LTD
110 OXFORD ROAD, AYLESBURY HP19 2PB.
Tel: 01296 399500.
Fax: 01296 612196.
E-mail: redrose@showbus.com.
Web site: www.showbus.com/redrose
Dir: T. W. Khan. **Co Sec**: C. D. Day.
Fleet: 23 - 9 single-deck bus, 14 minibus.
Chassis: 6 Dennis. 1 Ford Transit. 2 Iveco. 2 Leyland. 8 Mercedes. 4 Optare.
Bodies: Caetano. East Lancs. Mellor. Optare. Plaxton. UVG.
Ops incl: local bus services, school contracts.
Livery: Red/Yellow.
Ticket System: Wayfarer.

ROBINSON'S COACHES
MANOR BUSINESS CENTRE, STEWKLEY, LEIGHTON BUZZARD LU7 0HR.
Tel: 01525 240264.
Fax: 01525 240050.
Fleet: 15 - 10 coach, 5 double-deck bus.
Ops incl: excursions & tours, private hire, continental tours.

*SOULS COACHES LTD
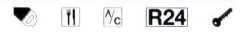
2 STILEBROOK ROAD, OLNEY MK46 5EA
Tel: 01234 711242
Fax: 01234 240130
Recovery: 07739 097775
E-mail: sales@souls-coaches.co.uk
Web site: www.souls-coaches.co.uk
Man Dir: David Soul **Sales Man**: Wendy Cheshire **Traf Man**: Neil McCormick
Wkshp Man: Drew Blunt
Fleet: 45 - 44 coach, 1 minicoach
Chassis: 1 DAF. 9 Dennis. 6 Setra. 1 Toyota. 28 Volvo.
Bodies: 1 Caetano. 5 Jonckheere. 33 Plaxton. 6 Setra.
Ops incl: local bus services, school contracts, excursions & tours, private hire, continental tours.

*WOOTTENS

THE COACH DEPOT, LYCROME ROAD, LYE GREEN, CHESHAM HP5 3LG
Tel: 01494 774411
Fax: 01494 784597
E-mail: info@woottens.co.uk
Web site: www.woottens.co.uk
Dirs: N H Woottens, M M Woottens **Ops Man**: M J Wootten
Traf Man: P Williams **Chief Eng**: R A Gomm

A/c	Air conditioning	♥	Seat belt-fitted vehicles
♿	Vehicles suitable for disabled	R	Recovery service available (not 24 hr)
🍴	Coach(es) with galley facilities		
wc	Coach(es) with toilet facilities	R24	24hr recovery service
✈	Replacement vehicle available	T	Toilet-drop facilities available
		🚌	Vintage vehicle(s) available
		🚍	Open top vehicle(s)

Buckinghamshire

Fleet: 21 - 3 double-deck bus, 4 single-deck bus, 14 coach.
Chassis: 1 Bristol. 6 Leyland. 14 Volvo.
Bodies: 1 Alexander. 1 Berkhof. 2 ECW. 1 East Lancs. 2 Leyland. 12 Plaxton. 1 Van Hool. 1 Willowbrook.
Ops incl: excursions and tours, continental tours, private hire, school contracts.
Livery: White with coloured swirls.
Ticket System: Wayfarer.

CAMBRIDGESHIRE, CITY OF PETERBOROUGH

ANDREWS COACHES

20 CAMBRIDGE ROAD, FOXTON CB2 6SH
Tel: 01223 873002
Fax: 01223 873036
E-mail: andrewscoaches@aol.com
Web site: www.andrewscoaches.co.uk
Prop: Andrew Miller
Fleet: 9 - 1 single-deck bus, 8 coach
Chassis: 1 AEC. 2 Bedford. 1 Ford. 4 Volvo. 1 Seddon.
Bodies: 1 Alexander. 1 Caetano. 7 Plaxton.
Ops incl: private hire, school contracts
Livery: White with Red/Blue arrows

*C & G COACHES

HONEYSOME LODGE, HONEYSOME ROAD, CHATTERIS PE16 6SB
Tel: 01354 692200
Fax: 01354 694433
E-mail: info@candgcoaches.co.uk
Web site: www.candgcoaches.co.uk
Prtnrs: C Day, G Ellwood, R Day **Ops Man**: C Smith
Fleet: 26 - 1 double-deck bus, 24 coach, 1 midicoach
Chassis: 4 Bedford. 1 Bristol. 1 Leyland. 1 MAN. 1 Neoplan. 13 Scania. 5 Volvo.
Bodies: 2 Duple. 1 ECW. 12 Irizar. 1 Neoplan. 8 Plaxton. 2 Van Hool.
Ops incl: school contracts, excursions & tours, private hire, continental tours
Livery: White/Red/Orange

COLLINS COACHES

UNIT 4, CAMBRIDGE ROAD INDUSTRIAL ESTATE, CAMBRIDGE CB4 6AZ
Tel: 01223 420462
Fax: 01223 424739
E-mail:
collinscoaches@sagehost.co.uk, office@collinscoaches.net
Ptnrs: C. R. Collins, R. T. Collins **Off Man**: Jacky Liptrot **Garage Man**: R D Curtis
Fleet: 19 - 3 coach, 3 midicoach, 13 minibus.
Chassis: 1 Bedford. 2 Dennis. 5 Ford Transit. 2 Freight Rover. 4 Iveco. 2 LDV.
Ops incl: excursions & tours, school contracts, private hire.
Livery: White/Orange

RON W DEW & SONS LTD

CHATTERIS ROAD, SOMERSHAM PE17 3DN.
Tel: 01487 740241.
Fax: 01487 740341.
E-mail: sales@dews-coaches.com
Web site: www.dews-coaches.com
Chmn: David Dew. **Ops Man**: Simon Dew.
Fleet: 10 - 3 single-deck bus, 7 single-deck coach.
Chassis: 2 Bedford, 1 DAF, 5 Scania, 2 Volvo.
Bodies: 2 Berkhof, 3 Irizar, 2 Van Hool.
Ops incl: excursions & tours, private hire, continental tours, school contracts.
Livery: Green/Grey.

EMBLINGS COACHES
BRIDGE GARAGE, GUYHIRN, WISBECH PE13 4ED.
Tel: 01945 450253.
Fax: 01945 450770
Man Dir: John Embling

*FENN HOLIDAYS

WHITTLESEY ROAD, MARCH PE15 0AG
Tel: 01354 653329
Fax: 01354 650647
E-mail: info@fennholidays.co.uk
Web site: www.fennholidays.co.uk
Man Dir: Peter Fenn **Dir**: Margaret Fenn
Fleet: 4 coach
Chassis: 2 Bova. 2 Van Hool
Bodies: 2 Bova. 2 Van Hool.
Ops incl: excursions & tours, private hire, continental tours
Livery: multicolour

FIRST CHOICE TRAVEL
9 LYTHEMERE, ORTON MALBORNE, PETERBOROUGH PE2 5NU.
Tel: 01733 753642.
Fleetname: First Choice.
Prop: D. Ely.
Fleet: 2 midibus.
Chassis: 1 Bedford. 1 Renault.
Bodies: 1 Marshall. 1 Wright.
Ops incl: local bus services, school contracts.
Livery: Maroon/Blue.
Ticket System: Setright.

*GRETTON'S COACHES

ARNWOOD CENTRE, NEWARK ROAD, PETERBOROUGH PE1 5YH
Tel: 01733 311008
Fax: 01733 319859
Prop: Roger Gretton
Fleet: 15 - 12 coach, 2 midicoach, 1 minicoach.
Chassis: 2 Bedford. 1 Mercedes. 11 Scania. 1 Volvo.
Bodies: 11 Plaxton, 4 Van Hool
Ops incl: school contracts, excursions & tours, private hire.
Livery: Silver/Red/Maroon

*GREYS OF ELY

41 COMMON ROAD, WITCHFORD, ELY CB6 2HY
Tel: 01353 662300
Fax: 01353 662412
E-mail: sales@greysofely.co.uk
Web site: www.greysofely.co.uk
Prop: D Grey **Co Sec**: R Grey **Ops Man**: C Covill
Fleet: 15 - 11 double-deck coach, 1 midibus, 3 midicoach.
Chassis: 11 Dennis. 3 Mercedes. 1 Fiat.
Bodies: 2 Berkhof. 1 Caetano. 13 Plaxton. 2 Euro
Ops incl: school contracts, private hire
Livery: Cream/Green

DEREK HIRCOCKS COACHES
THE OLD BARN, SCHOOL ROAD, UPWELL PE14 9EW
Tel: 01945 773461.
Fleetname: Upwell & District.
Prop: D. Hircock. **Eng**: W. Hircock.
Sec: Ms. C. Hircock.
Fleet: 7 coach.
Chassis: 4 AEC. 3 Leyland.
Ops incl: excursions & tours, private hire, school contracts.
Livery: Red/White/Blue.

HUNTINGDON & DISTRICT
STUKELEY ROAD, HUNTINGDON PE29 6HG
Tel: 01480 453159
Web site: www.huntsbus.co.uk
Ops Man: T Mead
Fleet: 30 - 15 double-deck bus, 13 single-deck bus, 2 coach

Chassis: 2 Dennis. 15 Leyland. 13 Volvo.
Bodies: 11 Alexander. 3 ECW. 6 Northern Counties. 2 Plaxton. 8 Wright.
Ops incl: local bus services.
Livery: Blue/Cream
Subsidiary Companies: part of Cavalier Travel, Lincolnshire.

JANS COACHES

23 TOWNSEND, SOHAM CB7 5DD
Tel: 01353 721344
Fax: 01353 721341
E-mail: janscoaches@aol.com
Dirs: Roland Edwards, Janet Edwards, Stuart Edwards
Fleet: 8 - 3 double-deck bus, 3 coach, 1 double-deck coach, 1 minicoach.
Chassis: 1 Dennis. 1 Iveco. 1 Leyland. 2 MAN. 2 MCW. 1 Neoplan.
Bodies: 1 Berkhof. 2 MCW. 3 Neoplan. 1 Northern Counties. 1 Indcar.
Ops incl: excursions & tours, private hire, continental tours, school contracts.
Livery: White.

*MIL-KEN TRAVEL LTD

11 LYNN ROAD, LITTLEPORT, ELY CB6 1QG
Tel: 01353 860705
Fax: 01353 863222
E-mail: milken@btconnect.com
Man Dir: Jason Miller **Fleet Eng**: Ian Martin
Gen Man: Mark Rogers
Fleet: 38 - 36 coach, 2 minibus.
Chassis: 2 Bedford. 6 DAF. 5 Dennis. 2 LDV. 23 Volvo.
Bodies: 3 Berkhof. 4 Duple. 3 Jonckheere. 23 Plaxton. 1 Willowbrook. 2 other.
Ops incl: private hire, continental tours, excursions & tours, school contracts.

*NEAL'S TRAVEL LTD

102 BECK ROAD, ISLEHAM CB7 5QP
Tel: 01638 780066
Fax: 01638 780011
E-mail: sales@nealstravel.com
Web site: www.nealstravel.com
Dirs: Bridget Paterson, Graham Neal, Lionel Neal, Nancy Neal
Fleet: 19 - 9 coach, 1 midibus, 7 midicoach, 2 minibus.
Chassis: 1 Iveco. 2 MAN. 9 Mercedes. 7 Volvo.
Bodies: 1 Indcar. 3 Jonckheere. 1 Mercedes. 1 Neoplan. 1 Noge. 3 Optare. 4 Plaxton. 2 Sunsundegui. 3 other.
Ops incl: local bus services, school contracts, private hire, excursions & tours, continental tours.
Livery: White/Blue, Silver/Blue
Ticket system: Wayfarer

D A PAYNE COACH HIRE

UNIT 2, FOUNDRY WAY, LITTLE END ROAD INDUSTRIAL ESTATE, EATON SOCON PE19 8JH.
Tel: 01480 473272.
Fax: 01480 211252
E-mail: david@dapayne.fsnet.co.uk
Web site: dapaynecoachhire.co.uk
Prop: D A Payne **Sec**: Mrs Carole Allen
Ops Man: R Wood
Fleet: 10 - 3 coach, 1 midibus, 1 midicoach, 2 minibus, 3 minicoach.
Chassis: include 3 Setra. 1 Toyota. 1 Volvo.
Bodies: include 1 Caetano. 1 Plaxton. 3 Setra..
Ops incl: school contracts, excursions & tours, private hire.

*PETERBOROUGH TRAVEL CONSULTANTS

12 BUCKLAND CLOSE, NETHERTON, PETERBOROUGH PE3 9UQ
Tel: 01733 267025
Fax: 01733 267025
E-mail: petertravelcon@aol.com
Props: Mrs P C Greeves
Fleet: 3 - 2 coach, 1 midicoach.
Chassis: 1 DAF. 2 Setra.
Ops incl: excursions & tours, school contracts, private hire, continental tours.
Livery: Blue/White/Red

PLANET TRAVEL

PLANET HOUSE, MEADOW DROVE, EARITH PE17 3QE.
Tel: 01487 843333.
Fax: 01487 843285.
Prop: D. J. Collier. **Ch Eng**: B. Turnock. **Co Acct**: M. Sloman. **Traf Man**: R. Birchenough. **Ops Man**: Mrs C. Stafford.
Fleet: 9 - 7 coach, 1 double-deck coach, 1 midicoach.
Chassis: 5 Bova. 1 Mercedes. 1 Scania. 2 Seddon.
Bodies: 1 Berkhof. 5 Bova. 2 Setra. 1 RH2000.
Ops incl: private hire, continental tours.

*ROBINSON KIMBOLTON

19 THRAPSTON ROAD, KIMBOLTON PE28 0HW
Tel: 01480 860581
E-mail: robinsoncharles@btconnect.com
Web site: www.robinsonkimbolton.co.uk
Man Dir: Charles Robinson
Fleet: 9 - 8 coach, 1 minibus
Chassis: 7 Dennis. 1 Scania. 1 Toyota.
Bodies: 3 Berkhof. 1 Caetano. 1 Duple. 3 Plaxton. 1 Van Hool.
Ops incl: private hire, school contracts.
Livery: Cream/Brown/Red

SEARLES AUTO SERVICES

10 GREAT NORTH ROAD, THORNHAUGH PE8 6HJ
Tel: 01780 783016
Fax: 01780 783016
Dir: Frank Searle
Fleet: 4 1 coach, 3 minibus
Chassis: 1 Bova. 2 Iveco. 1 Mercedes.
Bodies: 1 Bova. 2 Carlyle. 1 Mercedes-Benz
Ops incl: school contracts, private hire

SHAWS OF MAXEY

31 HIGH STREET, MAXEY PE6 9EF
Tel: 01778 342224
Fax: 01778 380378
Ptnrs: J. Duffelen R. E. Shaw, C. J. Shaw
Fleet: 23 - 1 single-deck bus, 19 coach, 2 midicoach, 1 minicoach.
Chassis: 8 Bedford. 1 Bova. 2 DAF. 1 Mercedes. 1 Renault. 1 Scania. 1 Toyota. 8 Volvo.
Bodies: 15 Plaxton. 1 Van Hool. 3 Jonckheere. 1 Bova. 1 Caetano. 1 Optare. 1 other.
Ops incl: local bus services, school contracts, excursions & tours, private hire, continental tours.
Livery: Blue/White

STAGECOACH CAMBRIDGE

100 COWLEY ROAD, CAMBRIDGE CB4 0DN
Tel: 01223 420544
Fax: 01223 420065
Web site: www.stagecoachbus.com
Man Dir: Andy Campbell **Com Dir**: Philip Norwell
Fleet: 205 - 98 double-deck bus, 88 single-deck bus, 11 coach, 8 minibus.
Chassis: 47 Dennis, 9 Leyland. 49 MAN. 8 Optare. 24 Transbus. 68 Volvo.
Bodies: 101 Alexander. 3 Leyland. 52 Northern Counties. 8 Optare. 17 Plaxton. 24 Transbus.
Ops incl: local bus services, school contracts.
Livery: Stagecoach 2000
Ticket system: Wayfarer 3

TOWLERS COACHES LTD

CHURCH ROAD, EMNETH PE14 8AA
Tel: 01945 583645
Fax: 01945 583645
E-mail: joanne@towlerscoaches.fsnet.co.uk
Dirs: Mark Towler, Wendy Shepherd, Anton Towler, Joanne Walton
Fleet: 7 - 3 double-deck bus, 3 coach, 1 double-deck coach
Chassis: 1 Bova. 1 Bristol. 3 Leyland. 1 Scania. 1 LAG-EOS.
Bodies: 1 Bova. 1 Duple. 1 ECW. 1 East Lancs. 1 Jonckheere. 1 Plaxton. 1 LAG EOS.

 Air conditioning	
Vehicles suitable for disabled	
Coach(es) with galley facilities	
Coach(es) with toilet facilities	
Seat belt-fitted vehicles	
Recovery service available (not 24 hr)	
R24 24hr recovery service	
Replacement vehicle available	
T Toilet-drop facilities available	
Vintage vehicle(s) available	
Open top vehicle(s)	

Ops incl: school contracts, excursions & tours, private hire.
Livery: Green/Cream/Orange

VICEROY OF ESSEX LTD
See Essex

WEBB'S

ST PETERS FARM, MIDDLE DROVE PE14 8JJ
Tel: 01945 430123
E-mail: webb-s-cant@fsbdial.co.uk
Prop: Barry Webb
Fleet: 3 - 1 midicoach,1 minicoach, 1 minibus.
Ops incl: local bus services

WHIPPET COACHES LTD

CAMBRIDGE ROAD, FENSTANTON PE18 9JB.
Tel: 01480 463792.
Fax: 01480 498534.
Web site: www.go-whippet.co.uk
Dirs: A. T. Lee, J. T. Lee, J. C. Lee, P. H. Lee, M. H. Lee.
Fleet: 49 - 20 double-deck bus, 6 single-deck bus, 20 coach, 3 minibus.
Chassis: Bedford, Leyland, Scania, Volvo.
Bodies: Duple, East Lancs, Leyland, Northern Counties, Park Royal, Plaxton, Van Hool, Alexander.
Ops incl: local bus service, school contracts, excursions & tours, private hire, express.
Livery: Blue/Cream with logo.
Ticket System: Almex Eurofare.

W & M TRAVEL

10 MAIN ROAD, PARSON DROVE, WISBECH PE13 4LF
Tel: 01945 700492
Fax: 01945 700964
Recovery: 01945 700942
Dir: W Norman
Fleet: 6 - 3 single-deck bus, 3 coach
Chassis: Bedford. DAF. Dennis. Scania.
Bodies: Berkhof. Duple. Plaxton. Marcopolo
Ops incl: local bus services, school contracts, excursions & tours, private hire.

CHESHIRE, HALTON & STOCKPORT

*ANGEL TRAVEL

108 GORSEY LANE, WARRINGTON WA2 7RY
Tel: 07090 741550
Fax: 01925 445591
E-mail: angeltravelwarrington@yahoo.co.uk
Dir: Richard Keane
Fleet: 3 minibus.
Chassis: LDV. Mercedes.
Ops incl: school contracts, private hire, excursions & tours.
Livery: Blue/White

*ANTHONYS TRAVEL

8 CORMORANT DRIVE, RUNCORN WA7 4UD
Tel: 01928 561460
Fax: 01928 561460
Emergency: 01928 576050
E-mail: anthonys@fsbdial.co.uk
Web site: www.anthonys-travel.co.uk
Partners: Richard Bamber, Anne Bamber, Anthony Bamber.
Fleet: 17 - 1 single-deck bus, 8 single-deck coach, 2 midicoach. 6 minicoach.
Chassis: 4 LDV. 1 MAN. 10 Mercedes. 2 Scania
Bodies: 1 Berkhof. 1 Irizar. 4 LDV. 2 Mercedes. 5 Neoplan. 2 Optare. 1 Setra. 1 other.
Ops incl: local bus services, school contracts, private hire, excursion & tours.
Livery: multi coloured

ARROWEBROOK COACHES
THE OLD COACH YARD, WERVIN ROAD, CROUGHTON CH2 4DA
Tel: 01244 382444
Fax: 01244 379777
Prop: A. G. Parsons

Ops Incl: local bus services
Livery: White/Green.

*BARRATT'S COACHES LTD

UNIT 15, MILLBANK WAY, SPRINGVALE INDUSTRIAL ESTATE, SANDBCH CW11 3GQ
Tel: 08450 625096
Fax: 08450 627728
Recovery: 07770 772080
E-mail: gilbarratt@aol.com
Web site: www.barrattscoaches.co.uk
Fleetname: Barratt's of Nantwich
Dir: G Barratt
Fleet: 16 - 14 coaches, 2 double-deck coach, 1 midibus, 1 midicoach
Chassis: Leyland. Neoplan. Volvo.
Bodies: Jonckheere. Neoplan. Plaxton. Van Hool.
Ops incl: local bus services, school contracts, excursions & tours, private hire, continental tours.
Livery: White.

BENNETT'S TRAVEL
ATHLONE ROAD, LONGFORD, WARRINGTON WA2 8JJ
Tel/Fax: 01925 415299.
Prop.: B. A. Bennett, D. B. Bennett.
Ops incl: local bus services
Livery: White/Blue.

BIRCHWOOD TRAVEL

106 NEW LANE, CROFT, WARRINGTON WA3 7JL.
Tel: 01925 767962.
Fax: 01925 767073.
Owner: B. Thompson.
Fleet: 8 - 1 single-deck bus, 2 coach, 5 minibus.
Chassis: 1 Bedford. 1 Ford. 3 Iveco. 3 Leyland.
Bodies: 2 Deansgate. 1 Mellor. 1 Dormobile. 1 Galaxy.
Ops incl: local bus services, school contracts, private hire.
Livery: White with Grey/Black stripe.

*A. & H. BOOTH LTD
See Greater Manchester

BOSTOCK'S COACHES
SPRAGG STREET GARAGE, CONGLETON CW12 1QH
Tel: 01260 273108
Fax: 01260 276338
E-mail: bostocks@holmeswood.uk.com
Web site: www.holmeswood.uk.com
Dirs: J F Aspinall, M Aspinall, C H Aspinall, D E Aspinall, M F Aspinall, M J Forshaw
Ops Man: M E Bostock **Tours Man**: J. Bostock-Gibson **Ch Eng**: M Boniface
Fleet: 40 - 3 double-deck bus, 33 coach, 1 double-deck coach, 2 midicoach, 1 minicoach.
Chassis: 1 Ayats. 1 Bova. 7 DAF. 6 Dennis. 2 Iveco. 4 Leyland. 4 MAN. 9 Scania. 6 Volvo.
Bodies: 1 Ayats. 1 Beulas. 2 Berkhof. 1 Bova. 3 Caetano. 2 ECW. 1 East Lancs. 4 Ikarus. 1 Indcar.1 Irizar. 6 Marcopolo. 8 Plaxton. 9 Van Hool.
Ops incl: local bus services, excursions & tours, private hire, continental tours, school contracts.
Livery: Green

H E BROWN & SONS

8 GREENFIELD ROAD, GREENFIELD FARM INDUSTRIAL ESTATE, CONGLETON CW12 4TR
Tel: 01260 275281
Fax: 01260 280955
Fleetname: Browns Coaches.
Prop: Dennis Brown

Fleet: 5 - 3 coach, 1 double deck coach, 1 midibus.
Chassis: 1 Leyland. 1 Neoplan. 1 Optare. 1 Volvo. 1 Van Hool
Bodies: 2 Duple. 1 Neoplan. 1 Optare. 1 Van Hool.
Ops incl: local bus services, school contract, private hire.
Livery: White/Red.
Ticket System: Setright.

*CHESTERBUS
STATION ROAD, CHESTER CH1 3AD
Tel: 01244 347452
Fax: 01244 347453
E-mail: hyslop@chesterbus.co.uk
Web site: www.chesterbus.co.uk
Man Dir: S Hyslop **Eng Dir**: M J Ridge
Fin Dir: R W Pointon **Traf Man**: J R Lee
Fleet: 82 - 20 double-deck bus, 7 open-top bus, 14 single-deck bus, 36 midibus, 5 minibus.
Chassis: 8 BMC. 7 Daimler. 22 Dennis. 15 Leyland. 4 Marshall. 5 Optare. 6 Scania. 5 VW.
Bodies: 4 Alexander. 8 BMC. 5 Constable. 5 East Lancs. 11 Marshall. 19 Northern Counties. 5 Optare. 17 Plaxton. 2 Roe. 6 Wright.
Ops incl: local bus services, school contracts.
Livery: Blue/Cream
Ticket System: Wayfarer TGX

DOBSON'S BUSES LTD
WINCHAM PARK, CHAPEL STREET, WINCHAM, NORTHWICH CW9 6DA
Tel/Fax: 01606 350200
Man Dir: I P Dobson **Ch Eng**: P J Dobson
Ops Man: R P Dobson **Co Sec**: R E Dobson
Fleet: 15 - 8 double-deck bus, 2 coach, 5 midibus.
Chassis: 2 Daimler. 2 Dennis. 1 Iveco. 6 Leyland. 2 Mercedes. 2 Peugeot.
Bodies: include: 1 Duple. 1 Marshall. 1 Mellor. 2 Plaxton. 2 Peugeot.
Ops Include: local bus services, school contracts, private hire
Ticket system: Datafare

EMMAS COACHES CYMRU
See Wales, Gwynedd

FIRST IN CHESTER & THE WIRRAL
669 NEW CHESTER ROAD, ROCK FERRY CH42 1PZ
Tel: 0151 645 8661
See Merseyside

*JOHN FLANAGAN COACH TRAVEL

2 REDDISH HALL COTTAGES, BROAD LANE, GRAPPENHALL, WARRINGTON WA4 3HS
Tel: 01925 266115
Fax: 01925 261100
Recovery: 01925 266115

E-mail: admin@flanagancoaches.co.uk
Web site: www.flanagancoaches.co.uk
Props: John Flanagan, Janette Flanagan
Co Sec: Sarah Ogden
Fleet: 7 - 3 coach, 1 midicoach, 3 minicoach.
Chassis: 1 Dennis. 1 Ford. 3 Mercedes. 2 Volvo.
Bodies: 1 Berkhof. 1 Esker. 2 Mercedes. 1 UVG. 1 Van Hool. 1 other.
Ops incl: private hire, school contracts, excursions and tours.
Livery: Red/Black/White

*HALTON BOROUGH TRANSPORT LTD
MOOR LANE, WIDNES WA8 7AF
Tel: 0151 423 3333
Fax: 0151 420 2362
E-mail:(anyone)@haltontransport.co.uk
Web site: www.haltontransport.co.uk
Fleetname: Halton Transport
Man Dir: Chris Adams **Eng Man**: Phil Matthews **Traf Man**: David Steadman
Ops Man: Barry Waterhouse **Fin Man**: Adele Cookson
Fleet: 61 single-deck bus
Chassis: 55 Dennis. 6 Leyland.
Ops incl: local bus services.
Livery: Red/Cream.
Ticket System: Wayfarer III

*HAPPY DAYS COACHES
See Shropshire

HULME HALL COACHES LTD
1 STANLEY ROAD, CHEADLE HULME SK8 6PL
Tel: 0161 486 1187
Fax: 0161 482 8125
E-mail: hulmehallcoaches@talk21.com
Web site: www.hulmehallcoaches.co.uk
Man Dir: D. Herald **Tran Man**: C. J. O'Neill
Traf Man: I Johnson **Fl Eng**: P Henshall
Fleet: 12 - 7 double-deck bus, 1 single-deck bus, 3 coach, 1 midibus.
Chassis: 6 Bristol. 1 Iveco. 1 Leyland. 1 Leyland National. 3 Volvo.
Bodies: 7 ECW. 1 East Lancs. 1 Mellor. 3 Plaxton.
Ops incl: local bus services, school contracts, private hire.
Livery: Red/Cream
Ticket System: Wayfarer

HUXLEY COACHES

GREAVES LANE EAST, THREAPWOOD, MALPAS SY14 7AS
Tel: 01948 770661
Fax: 01948 770459
Prop: Fred Huxley
Fleet: 16 - 11 coach. 5 midibus.
Ops incl: private hire, school contracts, excursions & tours, private hire,

continental tours.
Livery: Cream/Yellow/Brown

*LE-RAD COACHES & LIMOUSINES

THE BUNGALOW, 328 HYDE ROAD, WOODLEY SK6 1PF
Tel: 0161 430 2032
Recovery: 0770 314 5500
Prop: Jean Mycock
Fleet: 3 - 2 coach, 1 minicoach.
Chassis: 1 DAF. 1 Ford. 1 LDV.
Ops incl: private hire, excursions & tours, continental tours.

*ROY McCARTHY COACHES

THE COACH DEPOT, SNAPE ROAD, MACCLESFIELD SK10 2NZ
Tel: 01625 425060
Fax: 01625 619853
Senr Ptnr: Andy McCarthy
Fleet: 10 coach.
Chassis: 1 Bedford. 2 Dennis. 1 MAN. 6 Volvo.
Bodies: 1 Berkhof. 1 Caetano. 8 Plaxton.
Ops incl: school contracts, excursions & tours, private hire, continental tours.
Livery: Blue/Cream

MARPLE MINI COACHES
5 GROSVENOR ROAD, MARPLE SK6 6PR.
Tel: 0161 881 9111
Owner: G. W. Cross
Fleet: 2 minicoach
Chassis: Ford Transit, LDV.
Ops incl: school contracts, private hire.
Livery: White/Gold.

*MAYNE OF WARRINGTON
MAYNE COACHES LTD, BATTERSBY LANE, WARRINGTON WA2 7ET
Tel: 01925 445588
Fax: 01925 232300
E-mail: warrington@mayne.co.uk
Web site: www.mayne.co.uk
Chmn/Man Dir: S B Mayne **Dir/Gen Man**: R W Vernon **Dir/Asst Gen Man**: A Dykes
Co Sec: D Mayne **Traf Man**: J Drake **Ch Eng**: A Sutcliffe
Fleet: 30 - 4 double-deck bus, 26 coach.
Chassis: 2 Bova. 8 Leyland. 13 Scania. 7 Volvo.
Bodies: 2 Bova. 1 Duple. 4 East Lancs. 9 Irizar. 14 Plaxton.
Ops incl: local bus services, school contracts, private hire.

A/c	Air conditioning
	Vehicles suitable for disabled
	Coach(es) with galley facilities
wc	Coach(es) with toilet facilities
	Seat belt-fitted vehicles
R	Recovery service available (not 24 hr)
R24	24hr recovery service
	Replacement vehicle available
T	Toilet-drop facilities available
	Vintage vehicle(s) available
	Open top vehicle(s)

Livery: Red/Cream
Ticket system: Wayfarer

MEREDITHS COACHES LTD

LYDGATE, WELL STREET, MALPAS SY14 8DE
Tel: 01948 860405
Fax: 01948 860162
E-mail: info@merediths.f9.co.uk
Web site: www.meredithscoaches.co.uk
Dirs: J K Meredith, Mrs M E Meredith, D J Meredith **Co Sec**: Mrs Kirin Meredith
Ch Eng: C Bellis
Fleet: 16
Chassis: 1 Ford. 4 Leyland. 11 Volvo.
Bodies: 12 Plaxton. 2 Van Hool. 2 Wadham Stringer.
Ops incl: local bus services, school contracts, private hire.

MILLMAN'S COACHES

STATION YARD, GREEN LANE, PADGATE, WARRINGTON WA1 4JR
Tel: 01925 822298
Fax: 01925 813181
Prop: Eric Millman
Fleet: 8 coach
Chassis: 5 Leyland, 2 Volvo 1 other
Bodies: 1 Berkhof. 3 Duple, 3 Plaxton, 1 Van Hool.
Ops incl: local bus services, school contracts, excursions & tours, private hire.
Livery: Blue/White

MOORE'S COACHES LTD

53 REES CRESCENT, HOLMES CHAPEL CW4 7NL.
Tel/Fax: 01477 537004
Dirs: D. M. Moore, J. C. Moore.
Fleet: 4 coach.
Chassis: 1 Dennis. 1 Scania. 1 Volvo. 1 Van Hool.
Bodies: 1 Jonckheere. 1 Plaxton. 2 Van Hool.
Ops incl: excursions & tours, private hire, express, continental tours, school contracts.
Livery: Moore's Coaches/Nat. Express.

*NIDDRIE COACHES

THE GARAGE, LEVIN STREET, MIDDLEWICH CW10 9AS
Tel: 01606 832343
Fax: 01606 833449
E-mail: niddries@aol.com
Man Dir: R I Niddrie **Sec**: Miss F J Niddrie
Fleet: 4 coach
Chassis: 1 Bedford. 2 DAF. 1 Scania.
Bodies: 3 Plaxton. 1 Van Hool
Ops incl: excursions & tours, private hire, continental tours, school contracts.

Livery: Silver/Maroon

ROADLINER TRAVEL

102 VICTORIA STREET, CREWE CW1 2JT.
Tel/Fax: 01270 250292.
Fleetname: Worldflight Ltd
Dir: Keith Smedley.
Co Sec: Mrs J. Jones.
Fleet: 6 - 5 coach, 1 midicoach.
Chassis: 1 Mercedes. 5 Volvo.
Bodies: 2 Jonchkeere. 3 Plaxton
Ops incl: excursions & tours, private hire, school contracts.

*SELWYNS TRAVEL SERVICES

CAVENDISH FARM ROAD, WESTON, RUNCORN WA7 4LU
Tel: 01928 564515
Fax: 01928 591872
Recovery: 01928 572108
E-mail: sales@selwyns.co.uk
Web site: www.selwyns.co.uk
Man Dir: Selwyn A Jones **Gen Man**: Alan P Williamson **Co Sec/Acct**: Richard E Williams **Fleet Eng**: Cledwyn Owen
Fleet: 44 - 9 single-deck bus, 33 coach, 1 midibus, 1 minicoach.
Chassis: 31 DAF. 1 Caetano. 1 Dennis. 2 Mercedes. 1 Optare. 2 Volvo. 6 Tecnobus.
Bodies: 1 Caetano. 3 Ikarus. 2 Mercedes. 1 Optare. 6 Pantheon. 2 Plaxton. 27 Van Hool.
Ops incl: local bus services, school contracts, excursions & tours, private hire, express, continental tours.
Livery: White/Blue/Orange/Green
Ticket System: Wayfarer
See also Greater Manchester

SMITHS OF MARPLE LTD

72 CROSS LANE, MARPLE SK6 7PZ
Tel: 0161 427 2825
Fax: 0161 449 7731
E-mail: julie@smithsofmarple.fsnet.co.uk
Web site: www.smithsofmarple.fsnet.co.uk
Man Dir: Jason Hibbert. **Co Sec**: Julie Hibbert
Fleet: 6 - 1 double-deck bus, 3 coach, 2 midibus.
Chassis: 1 Bristol. 1 Irisbus. 2 Setra. 1 Toyota.
Bodies: 1 Beulas. 1 Caetano. 1 ECW. 1 Mellor. 2 Setra.
Ops incl: local bus services, school contracts, excursions & tours, private hire, continental tours.
Livery: White/Red, Green, Blue, Orange.

*W A SHEARINGS LTD
BARLEYCASTLE LANE, APPLETON, WARRINGTON WA4 4FR.
Tel: 01925 214600
Fax: 01925 262606
Ops Man: Chris Brown
See also W A Shearings Ltd, Greater Manchester.

JIM STONES COACHES
THE JAYS, LIGHT OAKS LANE, GLAZEBURY, WARRINGTON WA3 5LH
Tel/Fax: 01925 766465
E-mail: jimstones@ic24.net
Web site: www.jimstonescoaching.com
Ptnrs: J B Stones, Mrs J P Stones,
Gen Man: R Dyson
Fleet: 16 - single-deck bus.
Chassis: 12 Dennis. 4 Leyland.
Bodies: 1 DAB. 2 East Lancs. 13 Plaxton.
Ops incl: local bus services, school contracts
Livery: Blue/White
Ticket System: Almex, Wayfarer 3, Setright
Associated/Subsidiary Companies:

WARRINGTON BOROUGH TRANSPORT LTD

WILDERSPOOL CAUSEWAY, WARRINGTON WA4 6PT
Tel: 01925 634296
Fax: 01925 418382
Web site: www.warringtonboroughtransport.co.uk
Fleetname: Network Warrington
Man Dir: Nigel Featham **Fin Dir**: John Bannister **Ops Man**: Charlie Shannon
Eng Man: Damian Graham
Fleet: 115 - 34 double-deck bus, 69 midibus, 12 minibus.
Chassis: incl: Optare. Transbus. Volvo.
Bodies: incl: Wrightbus
Ops incl: local bus services, school contracts, private hire.
Livery: Red/Ivory
Ticket System: Wayfarer 3

WHITEGATE TRAVEL LTD

15 BEAUTY BANK, WHITEGATE, NORTHWICH CW8 2BP
Tel: 01606 882760
Fax: 01606 883356
Owner: K. Prince
Fleet: 12 minibus
Chassis: 1 Ford Transit. 2 Freight Rover. 2 Iveco. 2 Mercedes. 5 Leyland DAF.
Ops incl: local bus services, school contracts, private hire.
Livery: Yellow/White

CORNWALL

CARADON RIVIERA TOURS

THE GARAGE, UPTON CROSS,
LISKEARD PL14 5AX
Tel: 01579 362226.
Fax: 01579 362220
Prop: John K. Deeble.
Fleet: 39 - 6 single-deck bus, 28 coach,
1 midibus, 3 minicoach, 1 mincoach.
Chassis: 1 Bedford. 2 Bristol. 4 Dennis.
1 Freight Rover. 3 LDV. 26 Leyland. 2 MCW.
Bodies: 4 Alexander. 4 Duple. 4 East Lancs.
2 MCW. 4 Optare. 17 Plaxton. 1 UVG.
3 Wadham Stringer.
Ops incl: local bus services, school
contracts, excursions & tours, private hire.
Livery: Cream/Blue.
Ticket System: Setright.

DAC COACHES
  R24

RYLANDS GARAGE, ST ANNE'S
CHAPEL, GUNNISLAKE PL18 9HW
Tel: 01822 834571
Fax: 01822 833881
Recovery: 01822 833378
E-mail: dac.coaches@btconnect.com
Web site: www.daccoaches.co.uk
Dirs: Bernard Harding, Nick Smith
Fleet: 10 - 4 coach, 1 double-deck bus,
2 midibus, 3 minicoach.
Chassis: 1 Bedford. 1 Bristol. 1 Ford.
3 Mercedes. 1 Peugeot. 3 Volvo.
Bodies: Duple. ECW. 9 Plaxton. Van Hool.
Ops incl: local bus services, school
contracts, excursions & tours, private hire,
continental tours.
Livery: Blue/White/Red/Yellow.
Ticket System: Almex.

*DARLEY FORD TRAVEL

DARLEY FORD, LISKEARD
PL14 5AS
Tel: 01579 362272
Fax: 01579 363425
Owner: Albert J Deeble
Fleet: 8
Chassis: 2 Scania. 6 Volvo.
Bodies: include 1 Berkhof.
Ops incl: private hire, excursions & tours,
continental tours.
Livery: White

FIRST IN DEVON & CORNWALL
See Devon

*GROUP TRAVEL

DUNMERE ROAD GARAGE,
BODMIN PL31 2QN
Tel: 01208 77989
Fax: 01208 77989
E-mail: grouptravel@btinternet.com
Web site: grouptravelcoachhire.com
Dirs: Dawn Moon, David Benny
Fleet: 21 - 7 coach, 13 midibus, 1 minicoach.
Chassis: 1 Autosan. 1 Leyland. 1 MAN.
2 Marshall. 10 Mercedes. 1 Optare. 4 Volvo.
Bodies: 1 Caetano. 1 Jonckheere.
2 Marshall/MCV. 5 Mellor. 1
Optare. 3 Plaxton. 4 Reeve Burgess. 2 Van
Hool. 2 other.
Ops incl: local bus services, school
contracts, excursions & tours, private hire.
Livery: Silver/Turquoise + blue logo
Ticket system: Almex A90

O. J. HAMBLY & SONS LTD
THE GARAGE, PELYNT, LOOE
PL13 2JZ.
Tel: 01503 220660.
Gen Man: P. Hambly. **Ch Eng**: P. Yeo.
Sec: A. F. Hambly. **Traf Man**: P. Hambly.
Fleet: 8 - 6 coach, 2 minibus.
Chassis: 3 Bedford. 2 Mercedes. 3 Volvo.
Bodies: 1 Duple. 6 Plaxton. 1 Dormobile.
Ops incl: local bus services, school
contracts, excursions & tours, private hire.
Livery: Red/Cream.

HOOKWAYS JENNINGS
  R24

LANSDOWNE ROAD, BUDE
EX23 8BN.
Tel: 01288 352359
Fax: 01288 352140
E-mail: barry@hookways.com
Web site: www.hookways.com
Dir: Martin Hookway **Ops Man**:
Barry Coates.
Fleet: incl: coach, midibus, midicoach,
minibus
Chassis: 4 DAF. 6 Leyland. 4 MAN.
5 Mercedes. 1 Toyota. 28 Volvo. 1 Cummins.
Bodies: 1 Autobus. 1 Bova. 2 Caetano.
5 Duple. 2 Jonckheere. 3 Noge. 29 Plaxton.
1 Reeve Burgess. 2 LAG. 1 Sitcar. 2 Robin
Hood.
Ops incl: local bus services, school
contracts, excursions & tours, private hire,
continental tours.
Livery: Yellow/Purple/Blue.
Ticket System: Setright

HOPLEYS BUS & COACH

SUNIC, ROPE WALK, MOUNT
HAWKE, TRURO TR4 8DW.
Tel: 01209 890268.
Fax: 01209 890268.
Ptnrs: B. Hopley, D. R. Hopley, N. A. Hopley.
Fleet: 5 - 1 double-deck bus, 2 single-deck
bus, 2 coach.
Chassis: 1 Bedford. 1 Bristol. 3 Volvo.
Bodies: 1 Duple. 1 ECW. 1 Jonckheere.
1 Plaxton. 1 Wright.
Ops incl: local bus services, school
contracts, excursions & tours, private hire.
Livery: Red/White/Grey.
Ticket System: Wayfarer 3.

LISKEARD & DISTRICT OMNIBUS COMPANY LTD

HIGHER ST LUKES, BOLVENTOR,
LAUNCESTON PL15 7TP
Tel/Fax: 01566 86501
E-mail: cameldist@tesco.net
Ops Dir(Man): R Hobbs **Dir/Co Sec**:
C Hobbs
Fleet: 11 - 1 single-deck bus, 1 open-top
bus, 9 minibus
Chassis: incl: 1 AEC. 2 LDV.
Bodies: incl: 7 Mercedes. 1 Weymann.
Ops incl: local bus services, private hire,
school contracts.
Livery: White/Green
Ticket System: Almex

*MOUNTS BAY COACHES

4 ALEXANDRA ROAD, PENZANCE
TR18 4LY
Tel: 01736 363320
Fax: 01736 366985
Web site:
www.mountsbaycoaches.co.uk
Dir: Jeffrey Oxenham
Fleet: 10 coach, midicoach.
Chassis: Toyota. Volvo.
Bodies: Caetano. Duple. Van Hool.
Ops incl: school contracts, excursions &
tours, private hire.
Livery: Blue/White

*OTS MINIBUS & COACH HIRE
48 FORE STREET, CONSTANTINE,
FALMOUTH TR11 5AB
Tel: 01326 340703
Fax: 01326 340404
E-mail: salots@btinternet.com
Web site: www.otsfalmouth.co.uk
Prop: Stephen B Moore
Fleet: 4 - 1 coach, 1 midicoach, 1 minibus,
1 minicoach.
Chassis: 3 Mercedes. 1 Volvo.
Bodies: 2 Mercedes. 1 Plaxton. 1 Van Hool.
Ops incl: local bus services, school
contracts, private hire.
Livery: White with blue/brown stripe.
Ticket system: manual

PENMERE MINIBUS SERVICES

28 BOSMOOR ROAD, FALMOUTH
TR11 4PU
Tel/Fax: 01326 314165
E-mail:
enquiries@penmereminibus.co.uk
Web site: www.penmereminibus.co.uk
Man: Ben Moore
Fleet: 2 - 1 minibus, 1 minicoach.
Chassis: 2 Mercedes.
Ops incl: local bus services, school

Ac	Air conditioning
	Vehicles suitable for disabled
	Coach(es) with galley facilities
WC	Coach(es) with toilet facilities
	Seat belt-fitted vehicles
R	Recovery service available (not 24 hr)
R24	24hr recovery service
	Replacement vehicle available
T	Toilet-drop facilities available
	Vintage vehicle(s) available
	Open top vehicle(s)

contracts, private hire.
Livery: Blue/Brown stripes.
Ticket system: Manual

PRIMROSE COACHES OF CORNWALL

2 MARKET SQUARE, HAYLE TR27 4EA.
Tel: 01736 754788.
Fax: 01736 754788.
E-mail: wendy@primrose.co.uk
Web site:
www.primrosecfreeserve.co.uk
Prop: J. W. Runnalls.
Ops. Man: W. J. Runnalls.
Fleet: 5 - 4 coach, 1 midicoach.
Chassis: 1 Bedford, 1 Setra, 1 Toyota.
Bodies: 1 Caetano, 1 Neoplan, 1 Plaxton, 1 Setra, 1 Van Hool.
Ops incl: excursions & tours, private hire, continental tours, local bus services, school contracts.

*ROSELYN COACHES

MIDDLEWAY GARAGE, ST BLAZEY ROAD, PAR PL24 2JA
Tel: 01726 813737
Fax: 01726 813739
E-mail: info@roselyncoaches.co.uk
Dirs: Jonathan Ede, Karen Paramor **Ch Eng**: Graham Paramor **Ops Supervisor**: Richard Moon
Fleet: 37 - 10 double-deck bus, 26 coach, 1 minicoach.
Chassis: 2 Bova. 2 Bristol. 1 DAF. 1 Iveco. 8 Leyland. 1 Setra. 1 Toyota. 21 Volvo.
Bodies: 2 Bova. 2 Caetano. 4 ECW. 6 East Lancs. 1 Jonckheere. 14 Plaxton. 1 Setra. 7 Van Hool.
Ops incl: local bus services, school contracts, excursions & tours, private hire, continental tours.
Livery: Green/Gold
Ticket system: Setright

SUNSET COACHES

BRANE, PENZANCE TR20 8RB
Tel: 01736 810428
Props: Ian Topping
Fleet: 10 - 2 midibus, 1 midicoach, 6 minibus, 1 minicoach.
Chassis: 1 Iveco. 9 Mercedes.
Bodies: 2 Wadham Stringer. 8 other.
Ops incl: local bus services, school contracts, excursions & tours, private hire, continental tours.
Livery: Sky Blue

*TAVISTOCK COMMUNITY TRANSPORT

GREENLANDS, ST ANN'S CHAPEL, GUNNISLAKE PL18 9HW
Tel: 01822 833574
Fleetname: Tavistock Country Bus
Chmn: R Pike **Hon Sec**: K Potter **Hon Treas**: R Crosbie
Fleet: 1 minibus
Chassis: Iveco
Body: G M Coachwork.
Ops incl: local bus services, private hire.
Livery: Red/White
Ticket System: Wayfarer

TILLEY'S COACHES
THE COACH STATION, WAINHOUSE CORNER, BUDE EX23 0AZ.
Tel: 01840 230244.
Man Dir: Paul Tilley
Fleet: 12 coaches
Chassis: incl: 1 Irisbus
Bodies: incl: 1 Indcar
Livery: White/Cream/Maroon.

TRELEY MOTORS
ST BURYAN, PENZANCE TR19 6DZ
Tel: 01736 810322
Chmn: J Ley **Ops Man**: A J Ley **Co Sec**: A D Ley
Fleet: 2 - 1 coach, 1 minibus
Chassis/Body: 1 Dennis. 1 Mercedes.
Bodies: 1 Duple. 1 Olympus.
Ops incl: school contracts, excursions & tours, private hire
Livery: Blue/Cream

*TRURONIAN LTD

24 LEMON STREET, TRURO TR1 2LS
Tel: 01872 273453
Fax: 01872 222522
E-mail: enquiries@truronian.co.uk
Web site: www.truronian.com
Dirs: David Rabey, Geoff Rumbles **Gen Man**: Graham Gilbert **Fleet Eng**: Derek Beck **Ops Man**: Andrew Watmore
Coaching Man: Alan Cleave
Fleet: 65 - 8 double-deck bus, 38 single-deck bus, 11 coach, 3 articulated bus, 1 midibus, 3 minibus, 2 midicoach.
Chassis: 2 Autosan. 1 BMC. 1 Bristol. 21 Dennis. 4 Ford Transit. 7 Leyland. 4 Mercedes. 10 Optare. 13 Volvo.
Bodies: 1 BMC. 2 Caetano. 8 ECW. 10 Optare. 13 Plaxton. 20 Transbus. 1 Van Hool. 10 other.
Ops incl: local bus services, school contracts, excursions & tours, private hire, express, continental tours.
Livery: Red/Silver.
Ticket System: Almex A90

*WESTERN GREYHOUND LTD

WESTERN HOUSE, ST AUSTELL STREET, SUMMERCOURT, NEWQUAY TR8 5DR
Tel: 01637 871871
Fax: 01872 510150
E-mail:
enquiries@westerngreyhound.com
Web site: www.westerngreyhound.com
Man Dir: Mark Howard **Co Sec**: Mari Howarth **Dir**: Robin Orbell **Ops Man**: Brian James **Eng Man**: Steve Harris
Fleet: 59 - 3 coach, 7 double-deck bus, 2 open-top bus, 44 midibus, 3 heritage.
Chassis: 3 AEC. 2 Bristol. 2 Leyland. 44 Mercedes. 8 Volvo.
Bodies: 2 ECW. 5 East Lancs. 2 Leyland. 3 Park Royal. 44 Plaxton. 3 Van Hool.
Ops incl: local bus services, school contracts, excursions & tours, private hire.
Livery: Green/White
Ticket System: Wayfarer III

*WHEAL BRITON TRAVEL

MOOR COTTAGE, BLACKWATER, TRURO TR4 8ET
Tel: 01872 560281
Fax: 01872 560691
Prop: Stephen J Palmer
Fleet: 13 - 12 coach, 1 minibus.
Chassis: 2 Scania. 10 Volvo.
Bodies: 1 Jonckheere. 10 Plaxton. 1 Van Hool.
Ops incl: school contracts, excursions & tours, private hire, continental tours
Livery: Cream

F. T. WILLIAMS TRAVEL
DOLCOATH INDUSTRIAL PARK, DOLCOATH ROAD, CAMBORNE TR14 8RU
Tel: 01209 717152.
Fax: 01209 612511.
Prop: F. T. Williams.
Livery: White/Gold/Black.

CUMBRIA

*D K & N BOWMAN

BURTHWAITE HILL, BURTHWAITE, WREAY, CARLISLE CA4 0RT
Tel: 01697 473262
Fax: 01697 474800
E-mail: enquiries@bowmans-coaches.co.uk
Web site: www.bowmans-coaches.co.uk
Ptnrs: David K Bowman, Nora Bowman
Fleet: 8 coach.
Chassis: 4 AEC. 1 Bedford. 1 MAN. 2 Scania.
Bodies: 1 Irizar. 1 Jonckheere. 5 Plaxton. 1 other.
Ops incl: school contracts, excursions and tours, private hire.
Livery: Ivory/Red

*S H BROWNRIGG LTD

ENNERDALE HILL, EGREMONT CA22 2PN
Tel: 01946 820205
Fax: 01946 821919
Props: R J Cook, Mrs L Holliday, B P Marshall, Mrs D L Marshall
Fleet: 23 - 14 coach, 10 midibus, 3 minicoach
Chassis: 3 Ford. 4 Leyland. 9 Mercedes. 1 Scania. 1 Volkswagen. 9 Volvo.
Bodies: 1 Duple. 1 Mellor. 12 Plaxton. 1 Van Hool. 2 Wright. 10 other.
Ops incl: local bus services, school contracts, private hire.
Livery: Purple/White

CALDEW COACHES LTD

6 CALDEW DRIVE, DALSTON CA5 7NS
Tel/Fax: 01228 711690
E-mail: caldewcoachesltd@aol.com
Web site: www.caldewcoaches.co.uk
Dirs: H B McKerrell, Ann McKerrell, Bill Rogers **Co Sec**: Mandy Rogers
Fleet: 11 - 3 single-deck bus, 4 coach, 3 midicoach, 3 minicoach.
Chassis: 10 Mercedes. 1 Volvo.
Bodies: 6 Mercedes. 2 Plaxton. 1 Van Hool. 1 Eurocoach.
Ops incl: local bus services, school contracts, excursions & tours, private hire, continental tours.
Livery: White/Red
Ticket System: Almex.

CARR'S COACHES
CONTROL TOWER, THE AIRFIELD, SILLOTH CA7 4NS
Tel: 01697 331276
Fax: 01769 33823
Prop: A J Markley **Ch Eng**: Fred Gill
Fleet: 9 - 4 coach, 2 midibus, 1 midicoach, 2 minibus
Chassis: 1 Dennis. 3 Ford Transit.
1 Leyland. 2 Mercedes. 2 Scania.
Bodies: 2 Duple. 1 Optare. 2 Van Hool.
Ops incl: local bus services, school contracts, private hire.
Livery: Blue/White.

CLARKSON COACHWAYS LTD

UNIT 2B, ASHBURNER WAY, WALNEY ROAD INDUSTRIAL ESTATE, BARROW IN FURNESS LA14 5UZ
Tel: 01229 828022
Fax: 01229 828067
E-mail: info@clarksoncoachways.co.uk
Web site: www.clarksoncoachways.co.uk
Dirs: Susan Clarkson, Neil Clarkson
Fleet: 13 - 8 single-deck bus, 1 open-top bus, 3 midicoach, 1 minicoach.
Chassis: 5 Dennis. 1 Ford. 1 Leyland. 3 MAN. 1 Mercedes-Benz.
Bodies: 1 Alexander. 4 Berkhof. 3 Caetano. 1 Crest. 1 Marcopolo. 1 Optare.
Ops incl: school contracts, excursions & tours, private hire.
Livery: two-tone Green

COAST TO COAST PACKHORSE

WEST VIEW, HARTLEY, KIRKBY STEPHEN CA17 4JH
Tel: 01768 371680
Fax: 01768 371680
E-mail: packhorse@cumbria.com
Web site: www.cumbria.com/packhorse
Operator: J. Bowman.
Fleet: 3 minibus.
Chassis: 2 Ford Transit. 1 Freight Rover.
Ops incl: local bus services, school contracts, private hire.

CUMBRIA COACHES LTD
ALGA HOUSE, BRUNEL WAY, DURRANHILL INDUSTRIAL ESTATE, CARLISLE CA1 3NQ.
Tel: 01228 404300.
Fax: 01228 404309.
Dir: Dennis Smith, H. Humble
Ops Man: S. Hall.
Fleet: 12 - 8 coach, 4 double-deck coach.
Chassis: 2 Neoplan. 2 Setra. 8 Volvo.
Bodies: 4 Duple. 2 Jonckheere. 2 Neoplan. 2 Plaxton. 2 Setra.
Ops incl: excursions & tours, private hire, express, continental tours, school contracts.

*D & H TRAVEL LTD

66 STRAMONGATE, KENDAL LA9 4BD
Tel: 01539 730555
Fax: 01539 723181
Recovery: 07971 205314
Web site: www.dhtravel.co.uk
Dir: Derek Henderson **Ops Man**: John Robinson
Fleet: 15 - 2 single-deck bus, 3 single-deck coach, 6 midibus, 2 midicoach, 2 minicoach
Chassis: 5 Ford. 9 Mercedes. 1 Scania.
Bodies: 2 Ikarus. 1 Jonckheere. 6 Plaxton.
Ops incl: excursions & tours, private hire, continental tours, school contracts, local bus services.
Livery: White

DAGLISH COACHES

BECK LEA, PASTURE ROAD, ROWRAH, FRIZINGTON CA26 3XN
Tel/Fax: 01946 861940
E-mail: daglish.coaches@bobertd.demon.co.uk
Web site: www.daglishcoaches.co.uk
Dir: R. Daglish
Fleet: 13 - 10 coach, 1 double-deck coach, 2 minibus.
Chassis: 3 DAF. 1 Ford Transit. 1 LDV. 4 Leyland. 1 Leyland National. 1 MAN. 1 MCW. 1 Scania.
Ops incl: excursions & tours, private hire, school contracts.
Livery: Yellow/Blue/Red

GRAND PRIX COACHES

MAIN STREET, BROUGH CA17 4AY
Tel: 01768 341328
Web site: www.grand-prix-services.com
E-mail: allison@fsbdial.co.uk
Dirs: Frank Allison, Gilbert Allison, Michael Allison
Fleet: 18 - 4 single-deck bus, 8 coach, 1 midicoach, 4 minibus, 1 minicoach.
Chassis: 1 Bedford. 1 Bristol. 1 Ford Transit. 2 Freight Rover. 1 LDV. 1 MCW. 2 Mercedes. 1 Renault. 4 Volvo.
Bodies: 1 Autobus. 4 Duple. 4 Leyland. 1 MCW. 2 Mercedes. 4 Plaxton. 2 Van Hool.
Ops incl: local bus services, school contracts, excursions & tours, private hire, continental tours.
Livery: White/Blue
Ticket System: Wayfarer 3

JOHN HOBAN TRAVEL LTD
22 KING STREET, WORKINGTON CA14 4DJ
Tel: 01900 603579
Fax: 01900 605528
E-mail: johnhoban@aol.com
Ptnrs: John Hoban, Allison Hoban
Fleet: 6 minicoach, 4 midicoach.
Chassis/Bodies: 10 Mercedes
Ops incl: local bus services, private hire

A/c	Air conditioning
♿	Vehicles suitable for disabled
🍴	Coach(es) with galley facilities
WC	Coach(es) with toilet facilities
♦	Seat belt-fitted vehicles
R	Recovery service available (not 24 hr)
R24	24hr recovery service
✔	Replacement vehicle available
T	Toilet-drop facilities available
🚌	Vintage vehicle(s) available
🚍	Open top vehicle(s)

*IRVINGS COACH HIRE LTD

JESMOND STREET, CARLISLE
CA1 2DE
Tel: 01228 521666
Fax: 01228 521792
E-mail: office@irvings-coaches.co.uk
Web site: www.irvings-coaches.co.uk
Man Dir: Robert Irving **Dir**: Joan Harvey
Tours Dir: Amy Irving
Fleet: 9 coach.
Chassis: 3 DAF. 6 Volvo.
Bodies: 3 Bova. 1 Sunsundegui. 5 Van Hool.
Ops incl: excursions & tours, private hire, school contracts, express.
Livery: Orange/Black/White.

K & B TRAVEL LTD

THE ASHES, CLIBURN, PENRITH
CA10 3AL
Tel: 01768 865446
Fax: 01768 862715
E-mail: mail@kbtravel.freeserve.co.uk
Man Dir: G Lund **Dir**: Mrs B Bainbridge
Dir/Co Sec: Mrs T Lund
Fleet: 13 - 6 coach, 2 midicoach, 2 minibus, 1 minicoach, 1 midibus.
Chassis: 1 MAN. 5 Mercedes. 2 Neoplan. 4 Volvo.
Bodies: 1 Berkhof. 5 Mercedes. 2 Neoplan. 4 Van Hool.
Ops incl: local bus services, excursions & tours, private hire, school contracts, continental tours.
Livery: Blue with Green lettering

*LADYBIRD TRAVEL

22 CLIFTON COURT, WORKINGTON
CA14 3HR
Tel: 01900 61155
Fax: 01900 61155
E-mail: graham.ladybird@virgin.net
Web site: www.ladybirdtravel.com
Fleet: 16 - 11 coach, 2 midicoach, 3 minicoach.
Chassis: 5 DAF. 1 Dennis. 3 Iveco. 5 Mercedes. 1 Scania. 1 Volvo.
Bodies: 3 Beulas. 2 Duple. 1 Ikarus. 1 Marcopolo. 1 Plaxton. 3 Van Hool.
Ops incl: excursions & tours, private hire, school contracts.
Livery: White with red/black stripes

LAKES SUPERTOURS
1 HIGH STREET, WINDERMERE
LA23 1AF.
Tel: 01539 442751.
Fax: 01539 446026.
Dir: R. Minford, A. Dobson
Fleet: 9 minibus.
Chassis: 8 Renault. 1 Fiat.
Ops incl: excursions & tours.
Livery: White/Purple/Gold.

MESSENGERS COACHES LTD

STATION ROAD GARAGE,
ASPATRIA CA7 2AJ
Tel: 01697 320244
Fax: 01697 323900
Recovery: 016973 20244
Fleet: 12 - 11 coach, 1 minibus.
Chassis: 1 Bova. 1 Caetano. 2 Iveco. 5 Leyland. 3 Volvo.
Bodies: 2 Beulas. 1 Berkhof. 1 Caetano. 1 Duple. 7 Plaxton.
Ops incl: local bus services, school contracts, excursions & tours, private hire, continental tours.
Livery: Dual Blue/White

*MOUNTAIN GOAT LTD (incl PARK TOURS AND TRAVEL)

VICTORIA STREET, WINDERMERE
LA23 1AD
Tel: 015394 45161
Fax: 015394 45164
E-mail: enquiries@mountain-goat.com
Web site: www.mountain-goat.com
Dirs: Peter Nattrass, Stephen Broughton
Man: Sue Todd
Fleet: 16 minicoach
Chassis: 1 Ford Tourneo. 1 LDV. 14 Renault.
Ops incl: local bus services, excursions & tours, private hire, continental tours, school contracts.
Livery: Green/Red on White
Ticket system: Wayfarer

*REAYS COACHES LTD

STRAWBERRY FIELDS, SYKE
PARK, WIGTON CA7 9NE
Tel: 016973 49999
Fax: 016973 49900
E-mail: info@reays.co.uk
Web site: www.reays.co.uk
Dirs: C W Reay, N Reay **Ch Eng**: J M McGill **Ops Man**: C W Reay **Co Sec**: N Reay
Fleet: 33 - 5 single-deck bus, 17 coach, 1 double-deck coach, 5 midicoach, 4 minicoach.
Chassis: 10 DAF. 15 Mercedes. 2 Neoplan. 4 Scania. 2 Volvo.
Bodies: 6 Alexander. 10 Bova. 4 Irizar. 3 Mercedes. 2 Neoplan. 4 Optare. 4 Plaxton.
Ops incl: local bus services, school contracts, excursions & tours, private hire, continental tours.
Livery: White/Blue/Gold.

*ROBINSONS COACHES

STATION ROAD GARAGE, APPLEBY
CA16 6TX
Tel: 01768 351424
Fax: 01768 352199
Prop: S E Graham
Fleet: 9 - 5 coach, 4 minibus.
Chassis: 1 DAF. 2 Dennis. 3 LDV. 1 Mercedes. 2 Volvo.
Bodies: include: 1 Mercedes. 1 Plaxton. 1 UVG. 2 Van Hool. 1 Wadham Stringer.
Ops incl: local bus services, school contracts, excursions & tours, private hire.
Livery: White/Green

SIMS TRAVEL

HUNHOLME GARAGE, BOOT,
HOLMROOK CA19 1TF
Tel: 019467 23227
Fax: 019467 23158
E-mail: simstravel@hotmail.com
Ptnrs: J Andrew Sim, D Peter Sim
Fleet: 9 - 6 coach, 2 midicoach, 1 minicoach.
Chassis: 3 Mercedes. 1 Neoplan. 5 Volvo.
Bodies: 1 Autobus. 1 Berkhof. 1 Mercedes. 1 Neoplan. 2 Plaxton. 2 Van Hool. 1 Other.
Ops incl: excursions & tours, private hire, school contracts.
Livery: White/Red/Maroon.

*STAGECOACH NORTH WEST

BROADACRE HOUSE, 16-20
LOWTHER STREET, CARLISLE
CA3 8DA
Tel: 01228 597222
Fax: 01228 597888
E-mail: northwest.enquiries@stagecoachbus.com
Web site: www.stagecoachbus.com
Fleetname: Stagecoach Cumbria/Lancaster/Lancashire
Man Dir: Chris Bowles **Eng Dir**: P W Lee
Ops Dir: D M Ashworth **Com Dir**: C J Bowles
Fleet: 492 - 161 double-deck bus, 114 single-deck bus, 24 coach, 9 open-top bus, 73 midibus, 111 minibus.
Chassis: 1 Bristol. 91 Dennis. 67 Leyland. 16 MAN. 71 Mercedes. 2 Neoplan. 40 Optare. 204 Volvo.
Bodies: 306 Alexander. 4 Duple. 1 ECW. 10 Jonckheere. 20 Leyland. 2 Neoplan. 2 Northern Counties. 40 Optare. 2 Park Royal. 36 Plaxton. 69 Transbus.
Ops incl: local bus services, school contracts, excursions & tours, private hire, express.
Livery: Stagecoach - Blue/Red/Orange/White.
Ticket System: Wayfarer TGX

F W STAINTON & SON LTD

39 BURTON ROAD, KENDAL
LA9 7LJ
Tel: 01539 720156.
Fax: 01539 740287.
Fleetname: Staintons Olympic Holidays.
Man Dir: R. S. Stainton. **Ops Man**: C. J. Stainton. **Ch Eng**: I. M Stainton.
Fleet: 14 coach.
Chassis: 1 Mercedes, 7 Setra, 6 Volvo.
Ops incl: excursions & tours, private hire, continental tours.
Livery: Blue/Green/Silver.

STEVE'S OF AMBLESIDE LTD

GALAVA GATE, BORRANS ROAD,
AMBLESIDE LA22 0EN
Tel: 01539 433544.
Fax: 01539 432018.
Dir: S. A. Wise. **Sec**: Mrs E. Wise.
Fleet: 2 minibus.
Chassis: 1 Freight Rover. 1 Renault.

Ops incl: excursions & tours, private hire, school contracts. Livery: White.

*TITTERINGTON COACHES LTD

THE GARAGE, BLENCOW, PENRITH CA11 0DG
Tel: 01768 483228
Fax: 01768 483680
Web site:
www.titteringtoncoaches.co.uk
Ops Man: P Titterington **Ch Eng**: I Titterington **Tours Man**: C Titterington
Fleet: 14 coach
Chassis: 1 Iveco. 1 Leyland. 1 MAN. 1 Mercedes. 10 Volvo.
Bodies: 1 Beulas. 1 Duple. 4 Jonckheere. 2 Neoplan. 4 Plaxton. 2 Van Hool.
Ops incl: excursions & tours, private hire, continental tours, school contracts
Livery: Mustard/Brown/White

TOWER COACHES
THE GARAGE, BURNFOOT, WIGTON CA7 9HL
Tel: 01697 349600
Props: M D Sellars, Mrs T Sellars
Fleet: 5 - 2 coach, 2 midibus, 1 minibus.

Chassis: 1 DAF. 1 Leyland. 2 Mercedes. 1 Renault.
Bodies: 1 Alexander. 1 Holdsworth. 2 Plaxton. 1 Reeve Burgess.
Ops incl: local bus services, school contracts, private hire.
Livery: Dark Blue/Grey
Ticket System: Almex A

*THE TRAVELLERS CHOICE

BILLINGS ROAD, DALTON IN FURNESS LA13 0SA
Tel: 01229 824531
Fax: 01229 870515
Fleet: 10 - 9 coach, 1 midibus.
Chassis: 1 Leyland. 1 Mercedes. 8 Volvo.
Bodies: 1 Jonckheere. 8 Plaxton. 1 Reeve Burgess.
Ops incl: local bus services, school contracts, excursions & tours, private hire, continental tours, express.
Livery: White with blue/yellow/red stripe
Part of The Travellers Choice J Shaw & Son Ltd, Carnforth - *See Lancashire*

TUERS MOTORS LTD
BRIDGE HOUSE, MORLAND, PENRITH CA10 3AY

Tel: 01931 714224
Fax: 01931 714236
Fleet: 7 - 4 coach, 1 midicoach, 2 minicoach
Chassis: 1 AEC. 1 DAF. 1 Ford Transit. 1 Mercedes. 1 Toyota. 2 Volvo.
Bodies: 1 Caetano. 3 Plaxton. 2 Reeve Burgess. 1 Van Hool.
Ops incl: excursions & tours, private hire, school contracts, continental tours.
Livery: Cream/Red

WRIGHT BROS (COACHES) LTD
CENTRAL GARAGE, NENTHEAD, ALSTON CA9 3NP.
Tel: 01434 381200.
Fax: 01434 382089.
E-mail: wrightbros@btinternet.com
Chmn/Man Dir: J. G. Wright.
Dir: C. I. Wright.
Fleet: 12 - 10 coach, 2 double-deck coach.
Chassis: 5 Bedford. 2 Scania. 5 Volvo.
Bodies: 2 Jonckheere. 7 Plaxton. 2 Van Hool. 1 Ikarus.
Ops incl: local bus services, school contracts, private hire, continental tours.
Livery: Cream/Black/Gold.
Ticket System: Almex.

DERBYSHIRE

ANDREW'S OF TIDESWELL LTD
ANCHOR GARAGE, TIDESWELL SK17 8RB
Tel: 01298 871222
Fax: 01298 872412.
E-mail: info@andrews-of-tideswell.co.uk
Web site: www.andrews-of-tideswell.co.uk
Dirs: R. B. Andrew, P. D. Andrew.
Fleet: 18 - 2 double-deck bus, 11 coach, 2 double-deck coach, 2 midicoach, 1 minicoach.
Chassis: 2 Ford. 2 Leyland. 3 Mercedes. 1 Scania. 2 Setra. 8 Volvo.
Bodies: 2 Alexander. 3 Mercedes. 5 Plaxton. 2 Setra. 6 Van Hool.
Ops incl: excursions & tours, private hire, continental tours, school contracts
Livery: Cream/Ivory/Red flash.

ARRIVA DERBY LTD
ASCOT DRIVE, OFF LONDON ROAD, DERBY DE24 8ND
Tel: 01332 861500
Fax: 01332 861501
Fleetname: Arriva Serving Derby.

Prop: ARRIVA Midlands (*see Staffordshire*)
Man Dir: Catherine Mason
Fleet: 126 - 74 double-deck bus, 9 single-deck bus, 24 midibus, 19 minibus.
Chassis: 7 Daimler, 26 Dennis, 19 Mercedes, 3 Scania, 71 Volvo.
Bodies: Alexander, 31 East Lancs, Marshall, Northern Counties, Plaxton.
Ops incl: local bus services, school contracts, private hire.
Livery: Aquamarine/Cotswold Stone
Ticket System: Wayfarer II.

BAGNALLS COACHES
THE COACH STOP, GEORGE HOLMES WAY, SWADLINCOTE DE11 9DF
Tel: 01283 551964
Fax: 01283 552287
Dir/Ops Man: John Bagnall **Dir/Clerk**: Pat Bagnall **Dir/Ch Eng**: Karl Bagnall
Dir/Clerk: Gavin Bagnall
Fleet: 12 - single-deck bus, coach
Chassis: 12 Volvo
Bodies: 1 East Lancs. 1 Jonckheere. 1 Plaxton. 10 Van Hool.
Ops incl: local bus services, excursions & tours, private hire, school contracts.
Livery: various

BAKEWELL COACHES
24 MOORHALL, BAKEWELL DE45 1FP
Tel: 01629 813995

*BOWERS COACHES
ASPINCROFT GARAGE, CHAPEL-EN-LE-FRITH SK23 0NU
Tel: 01298 812204
Fax: 01298 816103
E-mail: kenny@bowerscoaches.co.uk
Web site: www.bowerscoaches.co.uk
Man Dir: Michael Bowers **Tran Man**: Kenny Duncan
Fleet: 34 - 7 single-deck bus, 6 coach, 19 midibus, 1 minibus. 1 van.
Chassis: 2 Dennis. 5 Leyland National. 1 MAN. 9 Mercedes. 10 Optare. 4 Scania. 1 Setra.
Bodies: 4 Alexander. 2 Irizar. 5 Leyland National. 10 Optare. 5 Reeve Burgess. 1 Setra. 3 Van Hool.
Ops incl: local bus services, school contracts, excursions & tours, private hire, continental tours.

A/c	Air conditioning
	Vehicles suitable for disabled
	Coach(es) with galley facilities
WC	Coach(es) with toilet facilities
	Seat belt-fitted vehicles
R	Recovery service available (not 24 hr)
R24	24hr recovery service
	Replacement vehicle available
T	Toilet-drop facilities available
	Vintage vehicle(s) available
	Open top vehicle(s)

*CLOWES COACHES

BARROWMOOR, LONGNOR
SK17 0QP
Tel: 01298 83292
Fax: 01298 83838
Ptnr: George Clowes
Fleet: 12 - 8 coach, 4 midibus.
Chassis: 4 DAF. 4 Mercedes. 3 Neoplan. 1 Scania.
Bodies: 3 Alexander. 3 Duple. 3 Neoplan. 1 Plaxton. 1 Smit.
Ops incl: local bus services, school contracts, excursions & tours, private hire.
Livery: Cream/Green/Red
Ticket system: individual tickets

COX'S OF BELPER
GOODS ROAD, BELPER DE56 1UU
Tel: 01773 822395
Fax: 01773 821157
E-mail: coxsofbelper@lineone.net
Prop: Bernard Bembridge
Fleet: 6 - 2 coach, 1 midicoach, 1 minibus, 1 minicoach, 1 midibus.
Chassis: 1 LDV. 3 Mercedes. 2 Volvo
Bodies: 1 Carlyle. 1 Jonckheere. 1 Mercedes. 1 VanHool. 2 conversions
Ops incl: excursions & tours, private hire, school contracts.
Livery: White/Blue

CRESSWELL'S COACHES (GRESLEY) LTD

3 SHORTHEATH ROAD, MOIRA, SWADLINCOTE DE12 6AL
Tel: 01283 217215
Fax: 01283 550043
Recovery: 01283 217215
E-mail: info@cresswellscoaches.com
Web site: www.cresswellscoaches.com
Man Dir: David Cresswell **Dir**: Jean Raynor
Ch Eng: Steve Lloyd **Tran Man**: John Collins
Fleet: 19 - 13 coach, 6 minicoach
Chassis: 4 Iveco. 6 Mercedes. 1 Optare. 9 Volvo.
Bodies: 4 Beulas. 2 Johckheere. 2 Marshall/MCV. 3 Mercedes. 1 Optare. 6 Plaxton. 1 Reeve Burgess. 1 Van Hool.
Ops incl: local bus services, school contracts, excursions & tours, private hire, continental tours.
Ticket System: Wayfarer

CRISTAL HIRE COACHES OF SWANWICK
19 CROMWELL DRIVE, SWANWICK DE55 1DB.
Tel: 01773 604932.
Prop: A. Hunt. **Co Sec**: Mrs Christine Hunt.
Fleet: 2 coach.
Chassis: 1 Bova. 1 Leyland.
Ops incl: excursions & tours, private hire, school contract.

DAWSON'S MINICOACHES

10 HOLLAND CLOSE, MORTON DE55 6HE
Tel: 01773 873149.
Prop: S. R. Dawson

Fleet: 4 - 2 minibus, 2 minicoach.
Chassis: 2 Ford Transit. 2 Freight Rover.
Ops incl: private hire, school contracts.
Livery: Grey/White/Blue stripe.

DERBY COMMUNITY TRANSPORT R24
MEADOW ROAD GARAGE, MEADOW ROAD, DERBY DE1 2BH
Tel: 01332 280738
Fax: 01332 203525
Chmn: Rev Graham Maskery **Sec**: K Johnson **Ops Man**: D Taylor
Fleet: 28 minibus
Chassis: LDV. Mercedes.
Bodies: Rohill. Swan.
Ops incl: local bus services, school contracts
Livery: Red/White

K&H DOYLE
190 NOTTINGHAM ROAD, RIPLEY DE55 3AY
Tel: 01773 745641
Prop: K Doyle.
Ops Incl: local bus services
Livery: Beige.

TIM DRAPER HOLIDAYS
SEVERN SQUARE, ALFRETON DE55 7BQ
Tel: 01773 830921
Fax: 01773 834401

*DUNN-LINE GROUP
See Nottinghamshire

'E' COACHES OF ALFRETON
1 MANOR COURT, RIDDINGS DE55 4DG
Tel: 01773 541222
Fax: 01629 825522
Owner: K. Bacon
Fleet: 5 - 2 midicoach, 3 minicoach.
Chassis: 3 Mercedes. 2 LDV.
Bodies: 2 Autobus. 3 Crest.
Ops incl: local bus service, school contract, excursions & tours, private hire.
Livery: Blue/White.

ENNIS COACHES
42 THE LIMES CLOSE, MATLOCK DE4 3DT
Tel: 01629 582397
E-mail: enniscoaches@yahoo.co.uk
Web site: www.geocities.com/enniscoaches
Fleet: 9 — 5 coaches, 2 single-decker buses, 2 minicoaches.
Chassis: 5 Bova, 2 Leyland, 1 MCW, Mercedes-Benz
Bodies: 1 Advanced, 1 Alexander, 5 Bova, 1 Leyland National, 1 MCW
Ops incl: private hire, school contracts

*FELIX BUS SERVICES LTD

157 STATION ROAD, STANLEY DE7 6FJ
Tel: 0115 932 5332
Fax: 0115 932 6096
Man Dir: G Middup **Ops Dir**: I Middup

Co Sec: C Middup
Fleet: 12 - 6 single-deck bus, 3 coach, 3 minibus.
Chassis: 1 Irisbus. 2 Leyland. 1 Mercedes. 2 Optare. 3 Scania. 2 Volvo.
Bodies: 2 Leyland. 2 Optare. 4 Plaxton. 3 Wright.
Ops incl: local bus services, school contracts, excursions & tours, private hire, continental tours.
Livery: Red/Gold
Ticket system: Wayfarer TGX

FLIGHTS HALLMARK
See West Midlands

GLOVERS COACHES LTD

MOOR FARM ROAD EAST, ASHBOURNE DE6 1MD
Tel/Fax: 01335 300043
E-mail: gloverscoaches@aol.com
Web site: www.gloverscoaches.co.uk
Dirs: Stephen Mason, Heather Mason
Fleet: 15 - 4 single-deck bus, 10 coach, 1 midibus.
Chassis: 1 Bedford. 2 Dennis. 3 Leyland. 9 Volvo.
Bodies: 5 Alexander. 1 Carlyle. 1 Duple. 8 Plaxton.
Ops incl: local bus serivces, school contracts, excursions & tours, private hire, continental tours.
Livery: Blue/Cream.
Ticket system: Wayfarer

GOLDEN GREEN LUXURY TRAVEL

GOLDEN GREEN GARAGE, LONGNOR SK17 0QP
Tel: 01298 83583.
Fax: 01298 83584
Props: John and Gill Worth
Fleet: 5 midicoach.
Chassis: 5 Mercedes.
Ops incl: school contracts, excursions & tours, private hire.

HARPUR'S COACHES
WINCANTON CLOSE, DERBY DE24 8NB
Tel: 01332 757677
Fax: 01332 757259
E-mail: harpurscoaches@tiscali.co.uk
Web site: www.harpurscoaches.co.uk
Man Dir: Nick Harpur
Fleet: 27 - 10 double-deck bus, 4 single-deck bus, 13 coach.
Chassis: 1 AEC. 2 Leyland. 9 MCW. 11 Volvo.
Bodies: 7 MCW. 1 Park Royal. 15 Plaxton.
Ops incl: school contracts, excursions & tours, private hire.
Livery: Cream/Brown

HARRISON'S TRAVEL
154 SOMERCOTES HILL, SOMERCOTES, ALFRETON DE55 4HU
Tel: 01773 833337

G & J HOLMES (COACHES) LTD
124A MARKET STREET, CLAY CROSS S45 9LY
Tel/Fax: 01246 863232.
Ops incl: local bus services

HENRY HULLEY & SONS LTD
DERWENT GARAGE, BASLOW DE45 1RP
Tel: 01246 582246
Fax: 01246 583161
E-mail: info@hulleys-of-baslow.co.uk
Web site: info@hulleys-of-baslow.co.uk
Fleetname: Hulleys of Baslow
Dirs: P Eades, R W Eades
Fleet: 19 - 11 single-deck bus, 5 coach, 2 minibus, 1 minicoach.
Chassis: 9 Dennis. 1 Leyland. 3 MAN. 3 Mercedes. 1 Optare. 1 Scania. 1 Volvo.
Bodies: 1 Caetano. 1 Leyland. 1 Marshall/MCV. 6 Optare. 8 Plaxton. 1 Reeve Burgess. 1 Van Hool.
Ops incl: local bus services, school contracts, private hire.
Livery: Buses: Cream/Blue; Coaches: White/Blue
Ticket System: Wayfarer 3

LEANDER TRAVEL
7 WORDSWORTH AVENUE, SWADLINCOTE DE11 0DZ
Tel/fax: 01283 213780
E-mail: pat@leandercoaches.co.uk
Web site: www.leandercoaches.co.uk
Fleetname: Leander Coaches
Prop: M. W. Bugden
Fleet: 4 coach, 1 minicoach.
Chassis: 3 DAF. 1 LDV. 1 Volvo.
Ops incl: excursions & tours, school contracts, continental tours.

*JOHNSON'S TOURS
See Nottinghamshire

KINCHBUS LTD
MANSFIELD ROAD, HEANOR DE75 7BG
Tel: 01775 536309
Web site: www.kinchbus.co.uk
Fleet: 35 - 8 double-deck bus, 9 single-deck bus, 18 minibus.
Chassis: 2 Dennis. 8 Leyland. 11 Mercedes. 11 Optare. 3 Volvo.
Ops incl: local bus services
Livery: Blue/Yellow
Ticket System: Wayfarer
Part of the Wellglade grop

*LITTLE TRANSPORT LTD
  R24
HALLAM FIELDS ROAD, ILKESTON DE7 4AZ
Tel: 0115 932 8581
Fax: 0115 932 5163
Recovery: 07919 020835
E-mail: enqiries@littletravel.co.uk
Web site: www.littletravel.co.uk
Fleetname: Little's Travel
Dirs: Steve Wells, Paul Wright
Fleet: 20 - 11 double-deck bus, 9 coach
Chassis: 3 Bova. 4 DAF. 5 Leyland. 2 Leyland National. 1 MCW. 4 Scania. 1 Volvo.
Bodies: 3 Bova. 5 East Lancs. 1 Ikarus. 6 Leyland. 2 Leyland National. 3 Van Hool.
Ops incl: excursions & tours, private hire, school contracts, local bus services, continental tours.
Livery: White
Ticket system: Almex

MACPHERSON COACHES LTD
THE GARAGE, HILL STREET, DONISTHORPE DE12 7PL
Tel: 01530 270226
Fax: 01530 273669
E-mail: travel@macphersoncoaches.co.uk
Web site: www.macphersoncoaches.co.uk
Man Dir: Neil MacPherson **Eng:** Colin Underwood **Sales Man:** Paul Krause
Traff Man: Russel Crosby
Fleet: 15 - 1 single-deck bus, 9 coach, 3 midibus, 1 midicoach, 1 minicoach.
Chassis: 1 Dennis. 7 Mercedes. 7 Setra.
Bodies: 1 Alexander. 1 Jonckheere. 1 Mercedes. 3 Plaxton. 7 Setra. 1 Strachans.
Ops incl: local bus services, school contracts, excursions & tours, private hire, continental tours.
Livery: Cream/Red
Ticket System: Wayfarer.

*MYKANN COACH HIRE
29 WARREN DRIVE, LINTON, SWADLINCOTE DE12 6QP
Tel: 01283 762673
Fleet: 2 coach
Chassis/bodies: 1 MAN. 1 Setra.
Bodies: 1 Jonckheere. 1 Setra.
Ops incl: private hire, school contracts.
Livery: White

NOTTS & DERBY TRACTION CO LTD
MANSFIELD ROAD, HEANOR DE75 7BG
Fleet: 49 - 5 double-deck bus, 32 single-deck bus, 12 minibus.
Chassis: 18 Dennis. 5 Leyland. 12 Mercedes. 3 Optare. 11 Volvo.
Livery: Blue/Green
Ticket System: Almex
(Part of the Wellglade Group)

PARKERS COACHES
41 LABURNUM ROAD, NEWHALL, SWADLINCOTE DE11 0NR.
Tel: 01283 550015.
Prop: W. A. Parker.
Fleet: 2 minibus.
Chassis: Ford Transit.
Ops incl: school contracts, private hire.
Livery: Blue/White.

RINGWOOD LUXURY COACHES
SPEEDWELL GARAGE, CROMPTON ROAD, SPEEDWELL INDUSTRIAL ESTATE, STAVELEY S43 3PG
Tel/Fax: 01246 476366
Prop: David T Brockbank
Fleet: 6 - 2 midicoach, 4 minicoach
Chassis: 5 Mercedes.
Bodies: 1 Caetano. 4 Mercedes. 1 Sitcar
Ops incl: school contracts, private hire

*SLACKS TRAVEL (K V & G L SLACK LTD)
THE TRAVEL CENTRE, LUMSDALE, MATLOCK DE4 5LB
Tel: 01629 582826
Fax: 01629 580519
E-mail: enq@slackscoaches.co.uk
Web site: www.slackscoaches.co.uk
Man Dir: G L Slack **Ch Eng:** R M Slack
Co Sec: D R Slack **Tran Man:** J Gough
Fleet: 19 - 15 coach, 2 midicoach, 2 minibus.
Chassis: 5 DAF. 3 Dennis. 2 Ford. 2 Ford Transit. 3 Iveco. 2 Mercedes. 1 Neoplan. 1 Scania. 1 Volvo.
Bodies: 1 Autobus. 3 Beulas. 1 Jonckheere. 1 Mercedes. 1 Neoplan. 5 Plaxton. 5 Van Hool.
Ops incl: excursions & tours, private hire, continental tours, school contracts

STAGECOACH EAST MIDLANDS
NEW STREET, CHESTERFIELD S40 2LQ
Tel: 01246 222018
Fax: 01246 232205
Web site: www.stagecoachbus.com
Fleetname: Stagecoach East Midlands
Man Dir: Paul Lynch **Ops Dir:** Richard Kay
Eng Dir: Mike Britten **Com Dir:** John Pope
Service Quality Man: John Curtis

A/c	Air conditioning	✔	Replacement vehicle available
♿	Vehicles suitable for disabled	T	Toilet-drop facilities available
🍴	Coach(es) with galley facilities		Vintage vehicle(s) available
wc	Coach(es) with toilet facilities		Open top vehicle(s)
♥	Seat belt-fitted vehicles		
R	Recovery service available (not 24 hr)		
R24	24hr recovery service		

Fleet: 502 - 193 double-deck bus, 76 single-deck bus, 33 single-deck coach, 126 midibus, 3 articulated coach, 71 minibus.
Chassis: 148 Dennis, 1 Ford, 117 Leyland, 71 Mercedes, 16 Optare, 2 Scania, 147 Volvo.
Bodies: 324 Alexander, 2 Duple, 15 ECW, 33 East Lancs, 13 Jonckheere, 33 Northern Counties, 17 Optare, 2 Park Royal, 58 Plaxton, 4 Van Hool, 1 Wadham Stringer.
Ops incl: local bus services, school contracts, private hire, express.
Livery: Stagecoach new.
Ticket System: ERG.

TM TRAVEL

FAN ROAD, STAVELEY S43 3PT
Tel: 01246 477331
Fax: 01246 281027
E-mail: info@tmtravel.co.uk
Web site: www.tmtravel.co.uk
Man Dir: Tim Watts **Tran Man:** Malcolm Watts **Ops Man:** Paul Hopkinson **Ch Eng:** John Burton
Fleet: 73 - 20 double-deck bus, 12 single-deck bus, 14 coach, 25 midibus, 2 midicoach.
Chassis: 8 DAF. 7 Dennis. 7 Leyland. 12 MCW. 14 Mercedes. 9 Optare. 1 Scania. 11 Volvo.
Bodies: 3 Alexander. 3 East Lancs. 1 Ikarus. 1 Jonckheere. 3 Leyland. 12 MCW. 1 Mellor. 1 Northern Counties. 12 Optare. 30 Plaxton. 4 UVG. 2 Van Hool. 1 Wright.
Ops incl: local bus services, school contracts, excursions & tours, continental tours, private hire.
Livery: Cream/Red/Maroon.
Ticket System: Wayfarer TGX150

TRENT BARTON
MANSFIELD ROAD, HEANOR DE75 7BG
Tel: 01773 536336
Tel: 01773 536333
Web site: www.trentbarton.co.uk
Chmn/Man Dir: B R King **Com Dir:** R F Morgan **Fin Dir:** G Sutton
Fleet: 286 - 279 single-deck bus, 7 coach.
Chassis: 51 Dennis. 8 Mercedes. 131 Optare. 75 Scania. 21 Volvo.
Bodies: 8 Irizar. 7 Northern Counties. 131 Optare. 72 Plaxton. 68 Wright.
Ops incl: local bus services.

VIKING TOURS & TRAVEL

UNIT 2, RYDER CLOSE, SWADLINCOTE DE11 9EU
Tel: 01283 217012
Fax: 01283 550685.
Fleetname: Viking
Gen Man: Graham Allen.
Ch Eng: Farrell Smith.
Fleet: 17 - 16 coach, 1 midicoach.
Chassis: 1 Bova, 1 MCW, 15 Volvo.
Bodies: 1 Bova. 1 ECW. 2 Jonckheere. 9 Plaxton. 4 Van Hool.
Ops incl: excursions & tours, private hire, express, continental tours, school contracts
Livery: Ocean Blue/Orange Band.

*WARRINGTON COACHES
THE COTTAGE, ILAM DE6 2AZ
Tel: 01335 350204
E-mail: info@warringtoncoaches.co.uk
Web site: www.warringtoncoaches.co.uk
Prop: Sheila Warrington
Fleet: 7 - 4 coaches, 3 minibus.
Chassis: 1 BMC. 2 Dennis. 3 Leyland. 1 Mercedes.
Bodies: 1 Autobus. 1 BMC. 3 Leyland.

2 Plaxton.
Ops incl: local bus services, school contracts, private hire
Livery: Red/Cream+Silver
Ticket system: Setright

ALBERT WILDE COACHES
40 BROOK STREET, HEAGE, BELPER DE56 2AF
Tel/fax: 01773 852374.
Dir: P Wilde.
Fleet: 5 coach.
Chassis/bodies: Bova.
Ops incl: excursions & tours, private hire, continental tours, school contracts.
Livery: Various.

WOODWARD'S COACHES LTD
100 HIGH STREET EAST, GLOSSOP SK13 8QF
Tel: 01457 852651
Fax: 01457 852234
Fleet: 6 - 4 coach, 2 minicoach
Chassis: 3 Dennis. 2 Freight Rover. 1 Volvo.
Bodies: Plaxton.
Ops incl: excursions & tours, private hire.
Livery: Blue/White

YESTERYEAR MOTOR SERVICES
10 LADY GATE, DISEWORTH, DERBY DE74 2QF
Tel/fax: 01332 810774
E-mail: yesteryear10@hotmail.com
Prop: D. J. Moores
Fleet: 2 - 1 single-deck bus, 1 coach.
Chassis: Bedford, Leyland.
Bodies: Duple, ECW.
Ops incl: private hire.
Livery: Green/Cream.
Ticket System: Bell Punch.

DEVON

*A B COACHES LTD

WILLS ROAD, TOTNES INDUSTRIAL ESTATE, TOTNES TQ9 5XN
Tel: 01803 864161
Fax: 01803 864008
E-mail: abcoaches@btconnect.com
Web site: www.abcoaches.com
Man Dir: Brian Smith **Dir/Co Sec:** Lynn Smith
Fleet: 11 coach.
Chassis: 3 DAF. 8 Dennis.
Ops incl: local bus services, school contracts, excursions & tours, private hire.
Livery: Cream/Red

ALANSWAY COACHES LTD
KING CHARLES BUSINESS PARK, OLD NEWTON ROAD, HEATHFIELD, NEWTON ABBOT TQ12 6UT
Tel: 01626 833664
Fax: 01626 835648
Web site: www.alansway.co.uk
Man Dir: Ms A Ellison
Fleet: 18 minibus.
Chassis: 14 Ford Transit. 4 Iveco.
Ops incl: local bus services, school contracts, private hire.
Livery: Orange/White.
Ticket System: Setright.

AXE VALLEY MINI TRAVEL
BUS DEPOT, 26 HARBOUR ROAD, SEATON EX12 2NA
Tel/Fax: 01297 625959
Fleetname: AVMT
Prop: Mrs F. M. Searle **Traf Man:** J. R. Paddon.
Fleet: 9 - 5 double-deck bus, 4 midibus.
Chassis: 1 Dodge. 2 Iveco. 1 Leyland. 4 MCW. 1 Optare.
Bodies: 1 Leyland. 1 Reeve Burgess. 4 MCW. 2 Dormobile. 1 Optare.
Ops incl: local bus services.
Livery: Maroon/White.
Ticket System: Wayfarer.

AYREVILLE COACHES

202 NORTH PROSPECT ROAD, PLYMOUTH PL2 2PR
Tel: 01752 605450.
Fax: 01752 219366.
E-mail: ayrevillecoaches@tinyonline.co.uk
Owner: M. J. Buley.
Fleet: 6 - 3 midicoach, 3 minibus.
Chassis: 1 Ford, 1 Iveco, 4 Mercedes.
Bodies: 2 Carlyle, 1 Reeve Burgess, 1 Devon Conversion, 2 Pilcher Green.
Ops incl: private hire, school contracts.
Livery: White.

BURNHAM PARK COACHES
20 BURNHAM PARK ROAD
PLYMOUTH PL3 5QD
Tel: 01752 703412

*CARMEL COACHES

STATION ROAD, NORTHLEW,
OKEHAMPTON EX20 3BN
Tel: 01409 221237
Fax: 01409 221226
E-mail: carmelcoaches@hotmail.com
Web site: www.carmelcoaches.co.uk
Prop: Tony Hazell.
Fleet: 19 - 3 single-deck bus, 12 coach, 4 minicoach.
Chassis: 1 Albion. 1 Bova. 2 DAF. 5 Dennis. 2 Marshall. 5 Mercedes. 1 Optare. 3 Scania. 1 Toyota.
Bodies: 2 Autobus. 1 Berkhof. 1 Bova. 1 Caetano. 2 Duple. 2 Irizar. 1 Marcopolo. 1 Marshall/MCV. 1 Optare. 2 Plaxton. 1 UVG. 3 Van Hool. 1 other.
Ops incl: local bus services, school contracts, excursions & tours, private hire, continental tours.
Livery: White
Ticket System: Almex

CLH TRAVEL
18 EUGENE ROAD, PAIGNTON
TQ3 2PQ
Tel: 01803 668900
Tran Man: Geoff Wilkins

DAISH'S TRAVEL
PARKHILL ROAD, TORQUAY
TQ1 2DY
Tel: 0870 902 1412
Web site: www.daishs.com
Fleet: 9 coach
Ops incl: excursions & tours, private hire, continental tours

DARTLINE COACHES

LANGDONS BUSINESS PARK,
CLYST ST MARY, EXETER EX5 1DR
Tel: 01392 872900
Fax: 01392 872909
E-mail: info@dartline-coaches.co.uk
Web site: www.dartlinecoaches.co.uk
Dir: D R P Hounslow **Man Dir**: D M Dart
Tran Man: M Lemin **Gen Man**: K Busby
Fleet: 38 - 21 coach, 5 midibus, 2 midicoach, 10 minicoach.
Chassis: 4 Bova. 2 DAF. 2 Dennis. 4 Iveco. 1 LDV. 12 Mercedes. 12 Volvo.
Bodies: 4 Bova. 1 Autobus. 2 Caetano. 2 Duple. 1 Jonckheere. 4 Marshall. 10 Mercedes. 8 Plaxton. 4 Van Hool. 2 Robin Hood.
Ops incl: local bus services, school contracts, excursions & tours, private hire, continental tours, express.
Livery: White/Green/Yellow.
Ticket System: Almex.
Owns Bow Belle of Devon.

DAWLISH COACHES LTD

SHUTTERTON INDUSTRIAL ESTATE,
DAWLISH EX7 0NH
Tel: 01626 862525
Fax: 01626 867167
Web site: www.dawlishcoaches.com
Dir: John Weaver
Fleet: 34 - 28 coach, 2 midibus, 4 midicoach.
Chassis: 13 Bova. 2 Iveco. 5 Mercedes. 10 Volvo. 2 other.
Bodies: 2 Beulas. 2 Berkhof. 13 Bova. 1 Caetano. 2 Duple. 1 Plaxton. 9 Van Hool.
Ops incl: local bus services, school contracts, private hire.
Livery: Red/Blue/White
Ticket System: Setright

*DOWN'S MOTORS & OTTER COACHES
1 MILL STREET, OTTERY ST MARY
EX11 1AB
Tel: 01404 812002
Tel: 01404 811128
Fleetname: Otter Coaches
Ptnrs: W M Down, A G Down, C P Down
Fleet: 10 - 9 coach, 1 midicoach.
Chassis: 3 Bedford. 1 Bova. 4 Dennis. 1 MAN. 1 Toyota.
Bodies: 1 Bova. 4 Caetano. 2 Duple. 3 Plaxton.
Ops incl: private hire, school contracts, excursions & tours.
Livery: Ivory/Red

EAST TEIGNBRIDGE COMMUNITY TRANSPORT
THE MANOR HOUSE, OLD TOWN
STREET, DAWLISH EX7 9AP
Tel: 01626 888890
Fax: 01626 889253
E-mail: etcta@lineone.net
Man: Jenny Connor **Coordinator**: Jan Green
Fleet: 3 minibus, 3 car.
Chassis: 1 Ford. 1 Ford Transit. 1 LDV. 1 Renault. 1 Fiat. 1 Volkswagen
Ops incl: school contracts, excursions and tours, private hire.

EASTWARD COACHES

1 BARLANDS WAY, DOLTON,
WINKLEIGH EX19 8QB
Tel: 01805 804659
Fax: 01805 804659
E-mail: eastwardcoaches@btopenworld.com
Web site: www.co.uk .com .net
Props: Karen Wonnacott, Nick Woolacott
Tran Man: Mike Yedermann
Fleet: 6 - 5 coach, 1 minibus.
Chassis: 1 AEC. 2 Bedford. 1 DAF. 1 Ford. 1 Freight Rover.
Bodies: 1 Carlyle. 4 Plaxton. 1 Van Hool.
Ops incl: school contracts, excursions & tours, private hire.

Livery: White with Green/Red stripes
Associated/Subsidiary Companies:
Peninsula Group

FILERS TRAVEL

SLADE LODGE, SLADE ROAD,
ILFRACOMBE EX34 8LB
Tel: 01271 863819
Fax: 01271 867281
E-mail: filers@filers.co.uk
Web site: www.filers.co.uk
Prop: Roy Filer **Off Man**: Christina King
Ch Eng: Jeffrey Chesters
Fleet: 17 - 11 coach, 1 midibus, 2 midicoach, 3 minibus.
Chassis: 4 Bova. 2 DAF. 1 LDV. 2 Mercedes. 1 Scania. 4 Volvo. 2 VW. 1 Beluga.
Bodies: 4 Bova. 2 Caetano. 2 Duple. 1 Irizar. 2 Mercedes. 1 Plaxton. 4 Van Hool. 1 Sitcar.
Ops incl: local bus services, excursions & tours, private hire, school contracts, continental tours.
Livery: White/Blue/Yellow
Ticket system: Almex

FIRST IN DEVON & CORNWALL

THE RIDE, CHELSON MEADOW,
PLYMOUTH PL9 7JT
Tel: 01752 495250
Fax: 01752 495225
Web site: www.firstgroup.com
Man Dir: Marc Reddy **Fin Dir**: John Mathias
Ops Dir: Ian Miller **Eng Dir**:
Karl Duncan **Comm Dir**: Richard White
Fleet: 386 - 70 double-deck bus, 20 single-deck bus, 45 coach, 7 open-top bus, 136 midibus, 108 minibus.
Chassis: 30 Bristol. 135 Dennis. 24 Leyland. 95 Mercedes. 15 Optare. 84 Volvo. 3 Other.
Bodies: 28 Alexander. 2 Carlyle. 3 Duple. 44 ECW. 10 East Lancs. 2 Irizar. 4 Leyland. 14 Marshall. 11 Northern Counties. 15 Optare. 206 Plaxton. 1 Reeve Burgess. 5 Transbus. 6 Van Hool. 23 Wright. 12 other.
Ops incl: local bus service, school contracts, excursions & tours, private hire, express.
Livery: various First liveries.
Ticket System: Almex Optima.

GARRETT COACHES LTD

3 STOKES CLOSE, NEWTON ABBOT
TQ12 3YY
Tel: 01626 366580
Fax: 01626 353733
E-mail: garrettcoach@tesco.net
Dir: P Garrett.

Fleet: 3 - 2 coach, 1 minibus.
Chassis/Bodies: 2 Bova. 1 Mercedes.
Ops incl: private hire, school contracts.
Livery: White

GOLD STAR COACHES

18 WOODVILLE ROAD, TORQUAY TQ1 1LP
Tel/Fax: 01803 200080
Prop: E Stirk
Fleet: 9 minicoach
Chassis: 2 Ford Transit. 5 LDV. 2 Mercedes.
Ops incl: private hire, school contracts
Livery: Green/Cream

GUSCOTT'S COACHES LTD

THE GARAGE, CROFT GATE, HALWILL EX21 5TL
Tel: 01409 221661
Fax: 01409 221435
Dirs: T Guscott, C D Guscott.
Fleet: 8 coach.
Chassis: 3 DAF. 2 Leyland. 3 Volvo.
Bodies: 1 Berkhof. 1 Duple. 1 LAG. 5 Plaxton.
Ops incl: local bus services, school contracts, private hire.
Livery: Cream/Blue/Red

*HEARD'S COACHES
FORE STREET, HARTLAND, BIDEFORD EX39 6BD
Tel: 01237 441233
Fax: 01237 441789
Dirs: D G, B W, G J, K M, J L Heard
Fleet: 18 coach
Chassis: 2 Dennis. 2 MAN. 1 Mercedes. 2 Scania. 11 Volvo.
Bodies: 1 Berkhof. 1 Caetano. 1 Duple. 2 Irizar. 1 Jonckheere. 1 Noge. 1 Plaxton. 8 Van Hool. 2 other.
Ops incl: school contracts, private hire
Livery: Blue/White.

HARDY TOURS
WILDER ROAD, ILFRACOMBE EX34 9AF
Tel: 01271 866455/863426
Web site: www.hardystours.co.uk

*HEMMINGS COACHES LTD

POWLERS PIECE GARAGE, PUTFORD, HOLSWORTHY EX22 7XW
Tel: 01237 451282
Fax: 01237 451920
E-mail: hemmingscoaches@aol.com
Props: Ken & Linda Hemmings.
Fleet: 7 - 6 coach, 1 midicoach.
Chassis: 1 DAF. 1 Leyland. 2 MAN. 2 Mercedes. 2 Toyota. 1 VW. 2 Volvo.
Bodies: 1 Bova. 2 Mercedes. 1 Neoplan. 1 Noge. 2 Plaxton.
Ops incl: excursions & tours, private hire, continental tours, school contracts, express.
Livery: White

*HILLS SERVICES LTD

THE GARAGE, STIBB CROSS, LANGTREE, TORRINGTON EX38 8LH
Tel: 01805 601203
Fax: 01805 601476
Recovery: 01805 601102
E-mail: hills.servicesltd@btinternet.com
Dirs: David J Hearn, Mrs M E Hearn
Fleet: 27 - 14 coach, 3 midibus,10 minibus.
Chassis: 4 DAF. 2 Ford Transit. 10 LDV. 3 Mercedes. 9 Volvo.
Bodies: 1 Bova. 5 Jonckheere. 1 Mellor. 2 Plaxton. 2 Reeve Burgess. 6 Van Hool.
Ops incl: excursions & tours, private hire, school contracts.

HOOKWAYS GREENSLADES

PEEK HOUSE, ANHOE TRADING ESTATE, VENNY BRIDGE, EXETER EX4 8JR.
Tel: 01392 469210
Fax: 01392 466036
Recovery: 01392 469210
E-mail: alistair@hookways.com
Web site: www.hookways.com
Dir: Martin Hookway **Ops Man**: Alistair Gray
Fleet: 50 - coach, midicoach, minibus, minicoach.
Chassis: 1 Bova. 4 DAF. 6 Leyland. 4 MAN. 5 Mercedes. 1 Toyota. 28 Volvo, 1 Cummins.
Bodies: 1 Autobus. 1 Bova. 2 Caetano. 5 Duple. 2 Jonckheere. 3 Noge. 29 Plaxton. 1 Reeve Burgess. 2 LAG. 1 Sitcar. 2 Robin Hood.
Ops incl: local bus services, school contracts, excursions & tours, private hire, continental tours.
Livery: Purple/Yellow/Blue.
Ticket System: Setright.

HOOKWAYS PLEASUREWAYS COACHES
MEETH EX20 3EP
Tel: 01837 810257
Fax: 01837 810066.
E-mail: barry@hookways.com
Web site: www.hookways.com
Dir: Martin Hookway **Ops Man**: Barry Coates
Fleet: incl: coach, midibus, midicoach, minicoach.
Chassis: 4 DAF. 6 Leyland. 4 MAN. 5 Mercedes. 1 Toyota. 28 Volvo. 1 Cummins.
Bodies: 1 Autobus. 1 Bova. 2 Caetano. 5 Duple. 2 Jonckheere. 3 Noge. 29 Plaxton. 1 Reeve Burgess. 2 LAG. 1 Sitcar. 2 Robin Hood.
Ops incl: local bus services, school contracts, excursions & tours, private hire, continental tours.
Livery: Purple/Yellow/Blue
Ticket system: Setright

IVYBRIDGE & DISTRICT COMMUNITY TRANSPORT

DOURO COURT, BROOK ROAD, IVYBRIDGE PL21 0LS.
Tel: 01752 690444.
Fleetname: Ivybridge Ring & Ride.
Co-ordinator: Mrs S. Jenkins.
Chmn: I. Martin.
Fleet: 1 minibus. **Chassis/Body**: LDV.
Ops incl: local bus services, private hire.

KINGDOM'S TOURS LTD

WESTFIELD GARAGE, EXETER ROAD, TIVERTON EX16 5NZ
Tel: 01884 252373
Fax: 01884 252646
Dirs: R. V. Kingdom, S. J. Kingdom (**Sec**)
Fleet: 27 - 11 coach, 3 midibus, 5 midicoach, 1 minibus, 7 minicoach.
Chassis: 2 DAF. 2 Iveco. 4 LDV. 10 Mercedes. 2 Scania. 7 Volvo.
Bodies: 2 Bova. 2 Irizar. 4 Leyland. 10 Mercedes. 7 Van Hool. 2 other.
Ops incl: local bus services, school contracts, excursions & tours, private hire, continental tours.
Livery: Cream/Red/Orange/White
Ticket System: Setright.

MID DEVON COACHES

STATION ROAD, BOW, CREDITON EX17 6JD
Tel/Fax: 01363 82200
E-mail: enquiries@mdcoaches.co.uk
Web site: www.mdcoaches.co.uk
Prop: K. J. Wills **Man**: Mrs L. A. Hamilton
Fleet: 22 - 18 single-deck coach, 2 minicoach, 2 minibus.
Chassis: 2 DAF. 3 Ford. 3 Ford Transit. 5 Leyland. 4 Scania. 2 Toyota. 2 Volvo.
Bodies: 2 Bova.. 2 Caetano. 1 Irizar. 2 Jonckheere. 10 Plaxton.
Ops incl: school contracts, excursions & tours, private hire, continental tours.
Livery: Green/Cream.

MOOR TO SEA
1 SOPHIA WAY, TOTNES ROAD, NEWTON ABBOT TQ12 1YW.
Tel/Fax: 01626 362002.
E-mail: moortosea@eurobell.co.uk
Owner/Operator: Robert Clifford.
Fleet: 1 midicoach.
Chassis: Volvo. **Body**: Plaxton.
Ops incl: private hire. **Livery**: White.

PARAMOUNT MINI-COACHES
6 VENN CRESCENT, HARTLEY, PLYMOUTH PL3 5PJ.
Tel: 01752 767255
Fax: 01752 767255
Prop: B. M. Couch
Fleet: 5 - 1 midicoach, 2 minibus, 2 minicoach.
Chassis: 2 Ford Transit. 1 Leyland. 2 Mercedes.
Ops incl: excursions & tours, private hire, school contracts.

PENINSULA GROUP
TREMATON DRIVE, ST PETER'S WAY, IVYBRIDGE PL21 0HT
Tel (office hrs): 01752 896471
Mobile/Direct: 07909 695438
Owner: Mike Yedermann
Touring Man: Brian Madge
Associated companies: Peninsula Drivers (see A-Z Driver Hire) Eastward Coaches (see above)

*PLYMOUTH CITYBUS LTD
1 MILEHOUSE ROAD, PLYMOUTH PL3 4AA
Tel: 01752 662271
Fax: 01752 567209
E-mail: md@plymouthbus.co.uk
Web site: www.citycoach.co.uk
Chmn: R Simmonds **Man Dir/Co Sec**: J Ackroyd **Eng Dir**: C Webster **Ops Dir**: P Smith **Fin Controller**: I Perring
Fleet: 177 - 22 double-deck bus, 79 single-deck bus, 14 coach, 1 open-top bus, 33 midibus, 28 minibus.
Chassis: 109 Dennis. 1 Leyland. 32 Mercedes. 35 Volvo.
Bodies: 15 Alexander. 8 Mercedes. 153 Plaxton/Transbus. 1 other.
Ops incl: local bus services, excursions & tours, private hire. continental tours, school contracts.

*POWELLS COACHES
2 BARRIS, LAPFORD EX17 6PT
Tel/Fax: 01363 83468
Ptnrs: J P Powell, D M Powell, W P Powell
Fleet: 7 coach.
Chassis: 3 Leyland. 1 MAN. 1 Mercedes. 2 Volvo.
Bodies: 1 Duple. 1 Jonckheere. 1 Mercedes. 1 Neoplan. 3 Plaxton.
Ops incl: excursions & tours, private hire, school contracts.
Livery: Yellow/Green/White

RADMORES TRAVEL
4 WOODFORD CRESCENT, PLYMPTON PL7 4QY
Tel/Fax: 01752 335391
Owner: John Williams **Man**: Sarah Hale
Fleetname: Radmores Coaches
Fleet: 5 - 1 double-deck bus, 2 midibus, 2 midicoach.
Chassis: 1 DAF. 1 Ford Transit. 1 Iveco. 1 Toyota.
Bodies: 1 Caetano. 1 Mellor. 1 Reeve Burgess.
Ops incl: local bus services, school contracts, excursions & tours, private hire.
Livery: Red/Gold

RAYS COACHES
88 KINGS TAMERTON ROAD, ST BUDEAUX PL5 2BW
Tel: 01752 369000

*REDWOODS TRAVEL
INDUSTRIAL PARK, HEMYOCK EX15 3SE
Tel: 01823 680288
Fax: 01823 681096
Recovery: 01823 680288
E-mail: info@redwoodstravel.fsnet.co.uk
Web site: www.redwoodstravel.com
Dirs: Paul J Redwood, Brian J Redwood
Fleet: 21 - 17 coach, 3 minibus, 1 midicoach.
Chassis: 2 DAF. 1 Iveco. 3 LDV. 3 MAN. 3 Scania. 9 Volvo.
Bodies: 1 Beulas. 2 Caetano. 3 Irizar. 2 Jonckheere. 2 Noge. 6 Plaxton. 2 Van Hool. 3 LDV.
Ops incl: school contracts, excursions & tours, private hire, continental tours
Livery: White/Red/Green (palm trees)

SEWARD COACHES
GLENDALE, DALWOOD, AXMINSTER EX13 7EJ
Tel/Fax: 01404 881343.
Ops Man: Richard M Seward **Joint Ptnr**: Ivy Ann Seward **Sec**: Catherine Seward
Fleet: 21 - 3 single-deck bus, 9 coach, 6 midicoach, 3 minibus
Chassis: 2 Bova. 6 Dennis. 1 Iveco. 2 Leyland. 1 Toyota. 3 MAN. 4 Mercedes. 1 Renault. 1 BMC.
Bodies: 2 Berkhof. 2 Bova. 3 Caetano. 1 Irisbus. 1 Mercedes. 1 Optare. 4 Plaxton. 2 Transbus. 1 BMC.
Ops incl: local bus services, school contracts, private hire.
Livery: Cream/Orange/Green

H. & A. SLEEP
STATION ROAD, BERE ALSTON PL20 7EW
Tel: 01822 840244.
Ptnrs: Mrs G. A. Sleep, R. G. Sleep.
Fleet: 6 coach.
Chassis: 4 Bedford. 2 Volvo.
Bodies: 3 Duple. 2 Plaxton. 1 Irizar.
Ops incl: local bus services, excursions & tours, private hire.
Livery: Maroon/Ivory.

STAGECOACH SOUTH WEST
BELGRAVE ROAD, EXETER EX1 2LB
Tel: 01392 439439
Tel: 01392 889727
Web site: www.stagecoachbus.com
Fleet name: Stagecoach in Devon
Man Dir: C G Hilditch **Eng Dir**: M Horide
Co Sec: A Withnall **Ops Dir**: R Stevens
Dirs: L B Warneford, M Griffiths
Fleet: 254 - 63 double-deck bus, 15 single-deck bus, 6 coach, 4 open-top bus, 86 midibus, 80 minibus.
Chassis: 72 Dennis. 5 Leyland. 50 Mercedes. 30 Optare. 11 Scania. 32 Transbus. 49 Volvo.
Bodies: 150 Alexander. 5 ECW. 1 East Lancs. 11 Northern Counties. 30 Optare. 51 Plaxton. 6 Wright.
Ops incl: local bus services, school contracts
Livery: Stagecoach UK bus livery - Blue/Red/Orange/White
Ticket System: Wayfarer 3.

*STREETS COACHWAYS LTD
THE OLD AERODROME, CHIVENOR, BARNSTAPLE EX31 4AY
Tel: 01271 815069
Fax: 01271 817333
E-mail: sandra@streetscoachways.co.uk
Dirs: S Street, H Street, S Popham
Fleet: 13 - 7 coach, 3 midicoach, 4 minibus
Ops incl: private hire.

*TALLY HO! COACHES
STATION YARD INDUSTRIAL ESTATE, KINGSBRIDGE TQ7 1ES
Tel: 01548 853081
Fax: 01548 853602
E-mail: info@tallyhocoaches.com
Web site: www.tallyhocoaches.com
Man Dir: Simon Wellington
Fleet: 45 - 3 double-deck bus, 6 single-deck bus, 25 coach, 8 midibus, 3 midicoach.
Chassis: 1 Bedford. 2 DAF. 7 Dennis. 3 Ford Transit. 2 LDV. 12 Leyland. 12 Mercedes. 3 Scania. 1 Toyota. 2 Volvo.
Bodies: 5 Alexander. 1 Caetano. 4 Duple. 3 Irizar. 1 Marshall. 1 Mercedes. 2 Optare. 17 Plaxton. 3 Reeve Burgess. 5 Van Hool. 1 Wadham Stringer.
Ops incl: local bus services, school contracts, private hire.
Ticket system: Almex

*TAVISTOCK COMMUNITY TRANSPORT
See Cornwall

*TAW & TORRIDGE COACHES LTD
incorporating LOVERINGS
GRANGE LANE, MERTON, OKEHAMPTON EX20 3ED
Tel: 01805 603400
Fax: 01805 603559
WEST DOWN COACH DEPOT, ILFRACOMBE EX34 8NU
Tel: 01271 863673
Fax: 01271 855540
E-mail: enquiries@tawandtorridge.co.uk
Web site: www.tawandtorridge.co.uk
Man Dir: Tony Hunt **Dir/Ops Man**: Mark Hunt **Dir/Co Sec**: Linda Hunt **Dir/Gen Man**: Chris Laughton **Dir**: Tracey Laughton
Fleet Eng: Chris Laughton
Fleet: 39 - 30 double-deck coach,

	Air conditioning
	Vehicles suitable for disabled
	Coach(es) with galley facilities
WC	Coach(es) with toilet facilities
	Seat belt-fitted vehicles
R	Recovery service available (not 24 hr)
R24	24hr recovery service
	Replacement vehicle available
T	Toilet-drop facilities available
	Vintage vehicle(s) available
	Open top vehicle(s)

Devon

2 midibus, 5 minibus, 2 midicoach
Chassis: 1 Bedford. 2 Bova. 1 Bristol.
6 Dennis. 1 Ford Transit. 4 LDV. 3 MAN.
1 Scania. 1 Toyota. 1 Van Hool. 19 Volvo.
Bodies: 2 Berkhof. 2 Bova. 1 Caetano.
2 Duple. 3 Jonckheere. 2 Neoplan.
14 Plaxton. 2 Van Hool. 5 Wadham Stringer.
Ops incl: school contracts, excursions & tours, private hire, continental tours.
Livery: Miami Blue/Silver

TOTNES & DARTMOUTH RING & RIDE
C/O RED CROSS CENTRE,
BABBAGE ROAD, TOTNES TQ9 5JA.
Tel: 01803 867878.
Co-ordinator: L. Clark.
Fleet: 3 minibus.
Chassis: 2 Ford Transit. 1 Peugeot.
Ops incl: local bus services, school contracts, excursions & tours, private hire.

TOWN & COUNTRY COACHES
UNIT 8B, SILVERLANDS ROAD,
DECOY INDUSTRIAL ESTATE,
NEWTON ABBOT TQ12 5ND
Tel: 01626 201052
Tran Man: Geoff Wilkins

TRATHENS TRAVEL SERVICES
BURRINGTON WAY, PLYMOUTH
PL5 3LS.
Tel: 01752 794545/790565
Fax: 01752 777931.

Chmn: D. I. Park. **Ch Eng**: P. Holmes.
Fin Dir: G. Donnachie. **Man Dir**:
M. Trathen. **Ops Man**: G. Masters.
Fleet: 50 - 15 coach, 35 double-deck coach.
Chassis: 5 MAN. 5 Neoplan. 40 Volvo.
Bodies: 5 Neoplan. 45 Van Hool.
Ops incl: express, continental tours.
Livery: White with Red and Yellow lining; National Express: White.
Subsidiary of Parks of Hamilton

*TURNERS TOURS
1 FORE STREET, CHULMLEIGH
EX18 7BT
Tel: 01769 580242
Fax: 01769 581281
E-mail: coaches@turnerstours.co.uk
Web site: www.turnerstours.co.uk
Dir: S Gilson
Fleet: 28 - coach, midibus, midicoach, minibus.
Chassis: 4 Dennis. 1 Dodge. 1 Freight Rover. 1 Mercedes. 21 Volvo.
Bodies: 4 Alexander. 1 Caetano.
5 Jonckheere. 2 Mercedes. 16 Plaxton.
Ops incl: local bus services, school contracts, excursions & tours, private hire, express, continental tours.
Livery: Cream.
Ticket System: Wayfarer.

*T. W. COACHES LTD
HACHE LANE, SOUTH MOLTON
EX36 3AG
Tel: 01769 572139
Fax: 01769 574182

Dirs: C Tearall, N Williams **Eng**: W Parker
Fleet: 16 coaches - 8 coach, 2 midibus, 5 midicoach, 1 minibus
Chassis: Dennis, Mercedes, Optare
Bodies: Mellor, Mercedes, Optare, Plaxton
Ops incl: local bus services, school contracts, excursions & tours, private hire, continental tours.
Livery: Blue

*W A SHEARINGS
BARTON HILL WAY, TORQUAY
TQ2 8JG
Tel: 01803 326016.
Fax: 01803 316059.
Depot Man: David Braund.
See also W A Shearings Ltd, Greater Manchester

WILLS MINI COACHES
2 LOWER UNION ROAD,
KINGSBRIDGE TQ7 1EF
Tel/Fax: 01548 852140.
Man Dir: E. G. Wills. **Dir/Co Sec**:
Mrs G. M. Wills.
Fleet: 5 minibus.
Chassis: 4 LDV. 1 Mercedes.
Ops incl: school contracts, private hire.

WOOD BROTHERS TRAVEL LTD
HAREWOOD GARAGE, BOSSELL
ROAD, BUCKFASTLEIGH TQ11 0AL.
Tel: 01364 643870.
Fax: 01364 643870.
Livery: Yellow/White.

DORSET, BOURNEMOUTH, POOLE

*BARRY'S COACHES LTD

9 CAMBRIDGE ROAD, GRANBY
INDUSTRIAL ESTATE, WEYMOUTH
DT4 9TJ
Tel: 01305 784850
Fax: 01305 782252
Fleet: 25 - 20 coach, 3 midicoach, 2 minicoach.
Chassis: 4 Dennis. 1 Iveco. 2 MAN.
9 Scania. 1 Toyota. 8 Volvo.
Bodies: 2 Berkhof. 1 Caetano. 8 Irizar.
2 Jonckheere. 2 Neoplan. 3 Plaxton.
1 Reeve Burgess. 5 Van Hool. 1 other.
Ops incl: school contracts, excursions & tours, private hire, continental tours.
Livery: white/blue/yellow

*BLUEBIRD COACHES (WEYMOUTH) LTD
450 CHICKERELL ROAD,
WEYMOUTH DT3 4DH
Tel: 01305 786262
Fax: 01305 766223

Recovery: 07771 561060
E-mail: martyn@bluebirdcoaches.com
Web site: www.bluebirdcoaches.com
Dir/Co Sec: Martyn Hoare **Dir/Ch Eng**: Stephen Hoare
Fleet: 22 - 20 coach, 1 midicoach, 1 minibus.
Chassis: 6 Bova. 2 DAF. 1 LDV. 3 Neoplan. 10 Volvo.
Bodies: 6 Bova. 1 Caetano. 3 Neoplan. 5 Plaxton. 6 Van Hool. 1 other.
Ops incl: school contracts, excursions & tours, private hire, express, continental tours.
Livery: White/Blue/Orange

*BOURNEMOUTH TRANSPORT LTD

YEOMANS WAY, BOURNEMOUTH
BH8 0BQ
Tel: 01202 636000
Fax: 01202 636001
E-mail: mail@yellowbuses.co.uk
Web site: www.yellowbuses.co.uk
Fleetname: Yellow Buses

Service Delivery Dir: D T Lott **Eng Dir**:
G Corrie **Fin Dir**: Mrs C Partridge.
Fleet: 118 - 65 double-deck bus, 36 single-deck bus, 14 coach, 3 open-top bus.
Chassis: 4 DAF. 55 Dennis. 4 Scania.
55 Volvo.
Bodies: 10 Alexander. 5 Caetano. 84 East Lancs. 5 Plaxton. 4 Van Hool. 10 Wright.
Ops incl: local bus services, school contracts, express.
Livery: bright Yellow
Ticket System: Wayfarer 3

COACH HOUSE TRAVEL
16 POUNDBURY WEST
INDUSTRIAL ESTATE,
DORCHESTER DT1 2PG
Tel: 01305 267644
Fax: 01305 260608
Prop: Les Watts. **Ops Man**: John Woollen.
Co Sec: Sarah Fursy Taylor **Ch Eng**: Phillip Watts
Fleet: 17 - 8 coach, 3 single-deck bus, 2 midicoach, 4 minibus.
Chassis: 4 DAF. 3 Dennis. 2 Iveco.
4 Mercedes. 4 Volvo.
Bodies: 1 Berkhof, 1 Bova. 3 LDV.

4 Marshall. 4 Plaxton. 1 Van Hool.
Ops incl: local bus services, school contracts, excursions & tours, private hire, continental tours.
Livery: Red/White with red/blue stripes.

CROSS COUNTRY HIRE

64 DORCHESTER ROAD, UPTON, POOLE BH16 5NS
Tel/Fax: 01202 624031
Prop: William G Sykes
Fleet: 1 minicoach.
Chassis: Toyota. **Body**: Caetano.
Ops incl: excursions & tours, private hire.

*DAMORY COACHES

UNIT 1, CLUMP FARM, SHAFTESBURY LANE, BLANDFORD FORUM DT11 7TD
Tel: 01258 452545
Fax: 01258 451930
E-mail: igray@damorycoach.co.uk
Local Man: I Gray **Man Dir**: Alex Carter
Eng Dir: Geoff Parsons **Ops Dir**: Andrew Wickham **Fin Dir**: Matt Dolphin
Fleet: 46 - 8 double-deck bus, 8 single-deck bus, 16 coach, 7 minibus, 1 midicoach, 6 minibus.
Chassis: 1 Bova. 8 Bristol. 10 DAF. 6 LDV. 1 Mercedes. 7 Optare. 13 Volvo.
Bodies: 1 Bova. 8 ECW. 3 Ikarus. 2 Northern Counties. 7 Optare. 13 Plaxton. 5 Van Hool. 7 other.
Ops incl: local bus services, school contracts, excursions & tours, private hire, continental tours.

*DORSET COUNTY COUNCIL PASSENGER TRANSPORT SECTION

EDUCATION TRANSPORT GARAGE, GROVE TRADING ESTATE, DORCHESTER DT1 1ST
Tel: 01305 224332
Fax: 01305 225166
E-mail: kevinrclarke@dorsetcc.gov.uk
Fleet: 8 - 4 70-seat, 4 53-seat
Chassis: 2 Dennis. 2 Cummins. 4 Scania.
Bodies: 4 Irizar. 4 Plaxton
Ops incl: school contracts, affiliated school and youth organisation day excursions

*EXCELSIOR COACHES LTD

CENTRAL BUSINESS PARK, BOURNEMOUTH BH1 3SJ
Tel: 01202 652222
Fax: 01202 652223
E-mail: coaches@excelsior-coaches.com
Web site: www.excelsior-coaches.com
Man Dir: Ken Robins
Fleet: 24 - 18 coach, 2 midicoach, 4 minicoach.

Chassis: 6 Mercedes. 18 Volvo
Bodies: 6 Caetano. 2 Esker. 2 Jonckheere. 4 Mercedes. 7 Plaxton. 3 Sunsundegui.
Ops incl: excursions & tours, private hire, express, continental tours.

MIKE HALFORD MINICOACHES

KISEM, NORTH MILLS, BRIDPORT DT6 3AH
Tel/Fax: 01308 421106
Prop: M. G. Halford
Ops incl: local bus services

*HOMEWARD BOUND TRAVEL

137 LYNWOOD DRIVE, WIMBORNE BH21 1UU
Tel: 01202 884491
Fax: 01202 885664
E-mail: enquiries@homewardboundtravel.co.uk
Web site: www.homewardboundtravel.co.uk
Prop: Louisa Fairhead
Fleet: 3 minicoaches
Chassis: 3 Renault
Ops incl: excursions & tours, private hire, continental tours.
Livery: Silver /Purple/Green

POWELLS COACHES

THORNFORD GARAGE, THORNFORD DT9 6QN
Tel: 01935 872390
Prop: C. Powell, Stella Powell.
Fleet: 3 - 2 coach, 1 midicoach.
Chassis: 2 Ford. 1 Volvo.
Bodies: 3 Plaxton.
Ops incl: local bus services, excursions & tours, private hire.
Livery: Red/White.
Ticket System: Setright.

RAMON TRAVEL

7 HARCOURT ROAD, BOSCOMBE BH5 2JG.
Tel: 01202 432690.
Fax: 01202 432690.
Owner/Ops: C. Rochester.
Fleet: 6 - 1 coach, 1 midicoach, 4 minibus.
Chassis: 1 Bedford. 4 Freight Rover.
Ops incl: excursions & tours, private hire, school contracts.

*ROADLINER PASSENGER TRANSPORT LTD

26 STOURPAINE ROAD, WEST CANFORD HEATH, POOLE BH17 9AT
Tel: 01202 385055
Fax: 01202 690370
Web site: www.roadliner.biz
Fleetname: Roadliner
Man Dir: Mark Self **Dir**: Mrs Joan Self
Co Sec: Nigel Hargreaves **Gen Man**: Mark Towers
Fleet: 11 - 6 coach, 1 double-deck coach, 1 midibus, 2 midicoach, 1 minicoach

Chassis: 3 Mercedes. 1 Optare. 6 Scania. 1 Volvo.
Bodies: 1 East Lancs. 5 Irizar. 4 Optare. 1 Plaxton.
Ops incl: local bus services, school contracts, excursions & tours, private hire, express, continental tours
Livery: Green/Black/Silver
Ticket system: Wayfarer

*SEA VIEW COACHES (POOLE) LTD

10 FANCY ROAD, POOLE BH12 4QZ
Tel: 01202 741439
Fax: 01202 740241
E-mail: coachhire@seaviewcoaches.com
Web site: www.seaviewcoaches.com
Man Dir: D K Tarr **Dir**: D E Tarr **Dir/Gen Man**: F J Catt
Fleet: 26 - 18 coach, 4 minibus, 2 midicoach. 2 minicoach.
Chassis: 5 DAF. 4 Ford. 2 Iveco. 11 MAN. 4 Mercedes.
Bodies: 3 Ayats. 2 Beulas. 9 Noge. 1 Optare. 3 Van Hool. 4 other.
Ops incl: school contracts, excursions & tours, private hire, continental tours.
Livery: Silver with Red/Blue waves

*SHAFTESBURY & DISTRICT MOTOR SERVICES LTD

UNIT 2, MELBURY WORKSHOPS, CANN COMMON, SHAFTESBURY SP7 0EB
Tel/Fax: 01747 854359
E-mail: rogerroutemaster@aol.com
Web site: www.sdbuses.co.uk
Dir: R Brown
Fleet: 15 - 3 double-deck bus, 2 single-deck bus, 6 coach, 1 midibus, 2 midicoach, 1 minicoach.
Chassis: 5 AEC. 2 Bristol. 1 DAF. 5 Leyland. 2 Volvo.
Bodies: 1 Alexander. 1 Berkhof. 1 Duple. 1 Ikarus. 1 Jonckheere. 1 MCW. 1 Optare. 4 Park Royal. 4 Plaxton.
Ops incl: local bus services, school contracts, private hire.
Livery: White/Green stripes (buses - Red)
Ticket System: Wayfarer II

SOUTH DORSET COACHES LTD

VICTORIA AVENUE INDUSTRIAL ESTATE, SWANAGE BH19 1AU.
Tel: 01929 423622.
Fax: 01929 427797.
E-mail: enquiries@southdorsetcoaches.co.uk
Web site: www.southdorsetcoaches.co.uk
Dirs: J. E. Sheasby, N. J. Sheasby.
Fleet: 10 coach.
Chassis: 2 Bedford. 6 Scania. 2 Volvo.
Bodies: 1 Jonckheere. 3 Plaxton. 6 Van Hool.
Ops incl: excursions & tours, private hire, continental tours, school contracts.

A/c	Air conditioning	
	Vehicles suitable for disabled	
	Coach(es) with galley facilities	
WC	Coach(es) with toilet facilities	
	Seat belt-fitted vehicles	
R	Recovery service available (not 24 hr)	
R24	24hr recovery service	
	Replacement vehicle available	
T	Toilet-drop facilities available	
	Vintage vehicle(s) available	
	Open top vehicle(s)	

Livery: Burgundy/Cream.

SOVE REIGN COACHES
See Devon

SOLENT COACHES
See Hampshire

*SOVEREIGN COACHES
PINE LODGE, SIDMOUTH ROAD, ROUSDON, LYME REGIS DT7 3RD
Tel: 01297 23000
Fax: 01297 22466
E-mail: rcksovereign@btinternet.com
Props: R A Keech, C M Keech **Ops Man:** R C Keech
Fleet: 9 - 5 midicoach, 4 minicoach.
Chassis: 2 LDV. 5 Mercedes. 2 Toyota.
Bodies: 2 Alexander. 2 Autobus. 2 Leyland. 1 Plaxton. 2 other.
Ops incl: school contracts, excursions & tours, private hire.
Livery: White.

SURELINE
UNIT 17, TRADECROFT INDUSTRIAL ESTATE, PORTLAND DT5 2LN
Tel: 01305 823039
Fax: 01305 822936
Web site: www.surelinebuses.co.uk
Dir: David Beaman **Ops Dir:** Bill Landucci
Ops incl: local bus services

WILTS & DORSET BUS COMPANY LTD

TOWNGATE HOUSE, 2-8 PARKSTONE ROAD, POOLE BH15 2PR
Tel: 01202 680888/673555
Fax: 01202 670244
E-mail: enquiries-poole@wdbus.co.uk
Web site: www.wdbus.co.uk

Man Dir: A Carter **Ops Dir:** A Wickham
Eng Dir: G Parsons
Fleet: 344 - 132 double-deck bus (incl. convertible open-top), 64 single-deck bus, 7 coach, 141 minibus.
Chassis: 25 Bristol. 96 DAF. 16 Leyland. 30 Mercedes. 156 Optare. 51 Volvo.
Bodies: 2 Duple. 35 ECW. 13 East Lancs. 30 Mercedes. 7 Northern Counties. 237 Optare. 11 Plaxton. 2 Roe. 3 Van Hool. 34 Wright.
Ops incl: local bus services, school contracts, private hire, express.
Livery: Red/White/Black Red/Blue
Ticket System: Wayfarer TGX
Part of the Go-Ahead Group

*YELLOW BUSES
See Bournemouth Transport above.

DURHAM

ALFA COACHES LTD

17 RAMSGATE, STOCKTON-ON-TEES TS18 1BS.
Tel: 01642 678066
Fax: 01642 673462
Fleetname: Gladwin Tours
Man Dir: P. Sawbridge. **Man:** M. Gladwin.
Co Sec: P. Sawbridge. **Ops Man:** D. Squire
Fleet: 8 coach
Chassis: DAF
Bodies: 5 Ikarus. 3 Van Hool.
Ops incl: excursions & tours, private hire, continental tours
Livery: Beige with Blue lettering

ALMAR TRAVEL
7 GLENAVON AVENUE, SOUTH PELAW DH2 2JL.
Tel: 0191 388 6752.
Fax: 0191 388 1777.
Prop: A. Rogers.
Fleet: 3 - 2 coach, 1 minicoach.
Chassis: 1 Mercedes. 2 Volvo.
Bodies: 1 Carlyle. 1 Plaxton. 1 Van Hool.
Ops incl: excursions & tours, private hire, continental tours.
Livery: Brown/Orange.

BEST WAY TRAVEL
21 CHARLTONS, SALTBURN TS12 3DA.
Tel: 01287 635573.
Co Sec: Ann Wakefield. **Business Man:** M. Wakefield. **Ops Man:** B. Wakefield.
Maintenance: C. Wakefield.
Fleet: 4 coach.
Chassis: 2 DAF. 2 Ford.
Ops incl: excursions & tours, private hire, continental tours, school contracts.
Livery: Bronze.

BROWNS OF DURHAM

1 LEESFIELD DRIVE, MEADOWFIELD, DURHAM DH7 8NG
Tel: 0191 373 4200
Fax: 0191 378 0393
Recovery: 0191 378 0393
E-mail: brownscoachesbv@aol.com
Dir: Ralph Brown
Fleet: 6 coach
Chassis: 1 Bova. 5 DAF.
Bodies: include LAG. EOS
Ops incl: excursions & tours, private hire, continental tours.

CLASSIC COACHES LTD

CLASSIC HOUSE, MORRISON ROAD, ANNFIELD PLAIN DH9 7RX
Tel: 01207 282288
Fax: 01207 282333
Recovery: 07736 178599
E-mail: sales@classic-coaches.co.uk
Web site: www.classic-coaches.co.uk
Man Dir: Ian Shipley **Ops Man:** Michael Harris **Tran Man:** John Snowball **Fleet Eng:** Eric Bowerbank
Fleet: 66 - 4 double-deck bus, 10 single-deck bus, 50 coach, 2 double-deck coach.
Chassis: 2 DAF. 1 Dennis. 4 MCW. 9 Mercedes. 12 Scania. 36 Volvo.
Bodies: 3 Berkhof. 7 Caetano. 12 Irizar. 4 MCW. 2 Neoplan. 26 Plaxton.
Ops incl: local bus services, school contracts, excursions & tours, private hire, continental tours
Livery: Red/Gold
Part of Tellings Golden Miller

COCHRANE'S
4 FARADAY ROAD, NORTH EAST INDUSTRIAL ESTATE, PETERLEE SR8 5AP.
Tel: 0191 586 2136.
Fax: 0191 586 5566.
Fleetname: Cochrane's Kelvin Travel.
Owner: I. P. Cochrane.
Fleet: 7 - 5 single-deck bus, 2 minicoach.
Chassis: 4 Bedford. 1 DAF. 1 Ford. 1 Freight Rover.
Bodies: 5 Plaxton. 2 others.
Ops incl: school contracts.
Livery: Orange/Black.
Ticket System: Setright.

COMPASS ROYSTON TRAVEL LTD

BOWESFIELD LANE INDUSTRIAL ESTATE, STOCKTON-ON-TEES TS18 3EG
Tel: 01642 606644
Fax: 01642 608617
Man Dir: G Walton **Trans Man:** M. Metcalfe
Fleet: 55 - double-deck bus, coach, midicoach.
Chassis: Bristol. Daimler. Ford. Leyland. Mercedes. Volvo.
Bodies: ECW. Jonckheere. Mercedes. Plaxton. Sunsundegui. Van Hool.
Ops incl: excursions & tours, private hire, express, continental tours, school contracts.
Livery: White with Red/Maroon stripe.

*DUNN-LINE (HOLDINGS) LTD
See Nottinghamshire

*DURHAM CITY COACHES LTD

BRANDON LANE, BRANDON, DURHAM DH7 8PG
Tel: 0191 378 0540
Fax: 0191 378 1985
E-mail: sales@durhamcitycoaches.co.uk
Web site: www.durhamcitycoaches.co.uk
Man Dir: Michael Lightfoot. **Co Sec**: Christine Lightfoot
Fleet: 14 - 10 coach, 3 minicoach, 1 midicoach.
Chassis: 1 Bova. 4 Mercedes. 9 Volvo.
Bodies: 1 Bova. 4 Jonckheere. 3 Mercedes. 4 Plaxton. 1 Van Hool. 1 other.
Ops incl: excursions & tours, private hire, continental tours, school contracts.
Livery: Black/Red/Gold

DURHAM TRAVEL SERVICES (DTS)

See Dunn-Line Group, Nottinghamshire

ENTERPRISE TRAVEL

14 BLOOMFIELD ROAD, DARLINGTON DL3 6SA
Tel/Fax: 01325 286924
E-mail: coachhire@aol.com
Web site: www.enterprisecoachhire.co.uk
Dirs: B R Brown, Mrs B M Brown
Fleet: 6 - 5 coach, 1 minibus.
Chassis: 1 Bedford. 1 DAF. 2 MAN. 2 Mercedes
Bodies: 2 Caetano. 1 Mercedes. 1 Plaxton. 1 Setra. 1 Van Hool.
Ops incl: private hire, school contracts, excursions & tours.
Livery: White with red/green reliefs.

GARDINERS TRAVEL

COULSON STREET, SPENNYMOOR DL16 7RS
Tel: 01388 814417
Fax: 01388 811466
E-mail: gardiners.travel@virgin.net
Man Dir: John Gardiner **Tran Man**: Harry Revel
Fleet: 8 - 6 coach, 2 midibus.
Chassis: 1 Iveco. 1 Leyland. 2 Optare. 4 Volvo.
Bodies: 1 Beulas. 1 Jonckheere. 2 Optare. 3 Plaxton. 1 Van Hool.
Ops incl: local bus services, school contracts, excursions & tours, private hire, continental tours.
Livery: Cream/Maroon
Ticket system: AES

 Air conditioning
 Vehicles suitable for disabled
Coach(es) with galley facilities
Coach(es) with toilet facilities

GARNETT'S COACHES

UNIT E1, ROMAN WAY INDUSTRIAL ESTATE, TINDALE CRESCENT, BISHOP AUCKLAND DL14 9AW.
Tel: 01388 604419.
Fax: 01388 609549.
Fleet Ops Man: Paul Garnett
Fleet: incl: coach
Chassis: incl: 4 Volvo.
Bodies: incl: 1 Sunsundegui.
Ops incl: excursions & tours, private hire, continental tours.
Livery: Yellow/Red/Black.

GRIERSONS COACHES

SEDGEFIELD ROAD GARAGE, FISHBURN, STOCKTON-ON-TEES TS21 4DD.
Tel: 01740 620209.
Fax: 01740 621243.
Prop: C. & D. Grierson.
Fleet: 20 - 5 double-deck bus, 6 single-deck bus, 4 coach, 1 midicoach, 4 minibus.
Chassis: 1 DAF. 1 Ford. 1 Ford Transit. 2 Freight Rover. 2 Mercedes. 1 Scania. 13 Volvo.
Bodies: 1 Carlyle. 3 Jonckheere. 2 Mercedes. 13 Plaxton. 1 Reeve Burgess. 1 Van Hool.
Ops incl: excursions & tours, private hire, express, continental tours.
Livery: Blue/Red.

HODGSONS COACHES

20 GALGATE, BARNARD CASTLE DL12 8BG.
Tel: 01833 630730.
Fax: 01833 630830.
Props: J. K. Hodgson, G. A. Hodgson.
Fleet: 6 - 2 coach, 1 midicoach, 3 minicoach.
Chassis: 1 Bedford. 1 Bova. 1 Leyland. 1 Mercedes.
Bodies: 1 Bova. 1 Plaxton. 1 Elme. 3 Concept Coach Craft.
Ops incl: local bus services, school contracts, excursions & tours, private hire, continental tours.

*HUMBLES COACHES

UP YONDER, ROBSON STREET, SHILDON DL4 1EB
Tel: 01388 772772
Fax: 01388 772211
Prop: Malcolm Humble **Tours Man**: Pam West
Fleet: 6 - 2 coach, 2 midicoach, 1 minibus.
Bodies: 4 Mercedes. 2 Plaxton.
Ops incl: excursions & tours, private hire.
Livery: Champagne/Maroon

 Seat belt-fitted vehicles
R Recovery service available (not 24 hr)
R24 24hr recovery service

J & C COACHES

COACH DEPOT, GROAT DRIVE, AYCLIFFE INDUSTRIAL PARK, NEWTON AYCLIFFE DL5 6HY.
Tel: 01325 312728.
Fax: 01325 320385.
Snr Ptnr: J. N. Jones.
Ptnrs: A. Jones, N. Jones, D. Jones.
Fleet: 10 - 6 coach, 1 midicoach, 3 minicoach.
Chassis: 4 DAF. 1 Dennis. 1 Ford Transit. 1 Freight Rover. 2 Mercedes. 1 Setra.
Bodies: 4 Bova. 1 Duple. 1 Leyland. 2 Mercedes. 1 Setra.
Ops incl: school contracts, excursions & tours, private hire, continental tours.
Livery: various

*JAYLINE BAND SERVICES LTD

UNIT 8A, KILBURN DRIVE, SEAVIEW INDUSTRIAL ESTATE, HORDEN SR8 4TQ
Tel: 0191 586 5787
Fax: 0191 586 5836
E-mail: jaylinetravel@hotmail.com
Web site: jaylinetravel.com
Prop: Jason Rogers **Dir**: Neil Tait
Fleet: 7 - 3 single-deck coach, 4 double-deck coach.
Chassis: 1 DAF. 5 Scania. 1 Volvo.
Bodies: 3 Berkhof. 1 Jonckheere. 3 Van Hool
Ops incl: private hire
Livery: Blue

*LEE'S COACHES LTD

MILL ROAD GARAGE, LITTLEBURN INDUSTRIAL ESTATE, LANGLEY MOOR DH7 8HE
Tel: 0191 378 0653
Fax: 0191 378 9086
E-mail: info@leescoaches.co.uk
Web site: www.leescoaches.co.uk
Dirs: Colin Lee, Jean Lee, Malcolm Lee
Fleet: 12 - 11 coach, 1 minibus.
Chassis: 1 Mercedes. 11 Volvo.
Bodies: 2 Berkhof. 4 Caetano. 1 Jonckheere. 1 Mercedes. 2 Plaxton. 2 Van Hool.
Ops incl: school contracts, excursions & tours, private hire, continental tours

MAUDES COACHES

REDWELL GARAGE, HARMIRE ROAD, BARNARD CASTLE DL12 8QJ
Tel: 01833 637341
Fax: 01833 631888
Prop: Stephen Maude
Fleet: 6 - 4 coach, 1 midicoach, 1 minicoach.
Chassis: 2 Mercedes. 4 Volvo.
Bodies: 1 Jonckheere. 2 Mercedes. 1 Plaxton. 2 Van Hool.
Ops incl: local bus services, school contracts, excursions & tours, private hire.
Livery: Red/White.

Replacement vehicle available
T Toilet-drop facilities available
 Vintage vehicle(s) available
Open top vehicle(s)

NORTON MINI TRAVEL
5 PLUMER DRIVE, NORTON TS20 1HF.
Tel: 01642 555832.
Owner: R. Spears.
Fleet: 2 minicoach.
Chassis: 1 Iveco, 1 Freight Rover.
Ops incl: private hire, school contracts.
Livery: White/Purple.

RICHARDSON COACHES
3 OXFORD ROAD, HARTLEPOOL TS25 5SS.
Tel/Fax: 01429 272235.
Man Dir/Ch Eng: T. Richardson.
Dir/Co Sec/Traf Man: D. Richardson.
Fleet: 8 coach.
Chassis: 1 DAF. 4 Leyland. 1 Mercedes. 1 Toyota. 1 Volvo.
Bodies: 1 Caetano. 1 Leyland. 1 Mercedes. 4 Plaxton. 1 Van Hool.
Ops incl: excursions & tours, private hire.
Livery: Green/Red/White.

ROBERTS TOURS

36 NORTH ROAD WEST, WINGATE TS28 5AP.
Tel: 01429 838268.
Fax: 01429 838228.
Web site: www.robertstours.com
Dirs: T. G. Roberts, D Roberts, C. A. Harper.
Fleet: 14 coach, 1 midibus.
Chassis: 5 Bova. 5 DAF. 2 Leyland 2 Volvo.
Bodies: 5 Bova. 8 Plaxton. 1 Wadham Stringer.
Ops incl: excursions & tours, private hire, express, school contracts.
Livery: Cream/Green.

*SCARLET BAND

WELFARE GARAGE, HIGH STREET, WEST CORNFORTH, FERRYHILL DL17 9LA
Tel: 01740 654247
Fax: 01740 656068
E-mail: sband@freeuk.com
Dirs: Arthur and Nancy Blenkinsop **Ops Man:** Andrew Dolan
Fleet: 22 - 7 coach, 15 midibus.
Chassis: 1 Bova. 2 Dennis. 5 Leyland. 1 Mercedes. 11 Optare. 1 Volvo.
Bodies: 1 Bova. 1 Marshall. 11 Optare. 7 Plaxton. 1 Van Hool. 1 Wright.
Ops incl: local bus services, school contracts, private hire.
Livery: White/Red/Yellow
Ticket System: Wayfarer III

SHERBURN VILLAGE COACHES
FRONT ST, SHERBURN VILLAGE DH6 1QY
Tel: 0191 372 1531.
Fax: 0191 386 1970.
Prop: J. Cousins.
Fleet: 6 - 3 coach, 1 midibus, 2 minicoach.
Chassis: 1 Leyland. 1 Mercedes. 2 Volvo.
Bodies: 2 Duple. 1 Plaxton. 2 Reeve Burgess. 1 Wadham Stringer.
Ops incl: local bus services, school contracts, excursions & tours, private hire.
Livery: Yellow/Red.
Ticket System: AES.

SNOWDON COACHES

SEASIDE LANE, EASINGTON SR8 3TW.
Tel: 0191 527 0535.
Fax: 0191 527 3280.
Prop: A. Snowdon. **Man:** G. Parkin.
Ch Eng: J. R. Main. **Sec:** V. Dowson.
Fleet: 16 coach.
Chassis: 1 Bova. 1 MAN. 14 Volvo.
Bodies: 1 Bova. 14 Plaxton. 1 Van Hool.
Ops incl: private hire, school contracts.
Livery: White with Pink reliefs.

STAGECOACH IN DARLINGTON, STAGECOACH IN HARTLEPOOL, STAGECOACH ON TEESIDE
See Stagecoach North East (Tyne & Wear)

STAGECOACH TRANSIT
CHIRCH ROAD, STOCKTON TS18 2HW
Tel: 01642 602112
Web site: www.stagecoachbus.com
Man Dir: John Conroy
Fleet: 207
Chassis: incl: Dennis. MAN. Mercedes. Scania. Volvo.
Bodies: Alexander. Leyland. Plaxton.
Ops incl: local bus services
Livery: Stagecoach

STANLEY TAXIS & MINICOACHES
THE BUS STATION, STANLEY DH9 0TD
Tel: 01207 237424.
Fax: 01207 233233.
E-mail: stanleytaxis@btinternet.com
Ptnr: Ian Scott.

TOWN & COUNTRY MOTOR SERVICES LTD
UNIT 2, HENSON ROAD, YARM ROAD BUSINESS PARK, DARLINGTON DL1 4QD.
Tel: 01325 489966.
E-mail: sales@townandcountrycoaches.co.uk
Web site: www.townandcountrycoaches.co.uk
Fleetname: Town & Country.
Man Dir: Philip Notman
Fleet: 3 - 1 single-deck bus, 1 midibus, 1 midicoach.
Chassis: 2 Leyland. 2 Mercedes.
Bodies: 1 Duple. 1 Marshall, 1 Plaxton.
Ops incl: local bus services, school contracts, private hire.
Livery: White/Blue.
Ticket System: Almex.

*PAUL WATSON TRAVEL

BRIDGE HOUSE, MOOR ROAD, STAINDROP DL2 3LF
Tel/Fax: 01833 660471
E-mail: paul@pwatsontravel.fslife.co.uk
Web site: www.paulwatsontravel.co.uk
Man Dir: Paul Watson,
Ops Man: Joanne Watson
Fleet: 4 - 2 single-deck coach, 1 midicoach, 1 midibus.
Chassis: 1 DAF. 1 Mercedes. 2 Volvo.
Bodies: 1 Autobus. 1 Jonckheere. 1 Plaxton. 1 LDV.
Ops incl: excursions & tours, private hire, continental tours, school contracts.

*WEARDALE MOTOR SERVICES LTD

STANHOPE DL13 2YQ
Tel: 01388 528235
Fax: 01388 526080
Dirs: Messrs Gibson
Fleet: 30 - 11 double-deck bus, 4 single-deck bus, 10 coach, 3 minibus, 1 minicoach, 1 midibus.
Chassis: Bova. DAF. Iveco. Leyland. MAN. MCW. Mercedes. Neoplan. Optare. Scania. Volvo.
Bodies: Alexander. Berkhof. Bova. ECW. Ikarus. MCW. Mercedes. Neoplan. Optare. Plaxton. Roe.
Ops incl: local bus services, excursions & tours, school contracts, private hire, express, continental tours.
Livery: Red/White
Ticket System: Wayfarer

EAST SUSSEX, BRIGHTON & HOVE

*AUTOPOINT COACHES

CAUSEWAY YARD, BODLE STREET, HAILSHAM BN27 4UA
Tel: 01323 832430
Fax: 01323 833434
E-mail: inf0@autopointcoaches.com
Web site: www.autopointcoaches.com
Dirs: B P Rodemark, G B J Rodemark, D Rodemark
Fleet: 13 - 2 single-deck bus, 4 coach, 5 midibus, 1 midicoach, 1 minibus.
Chassis: 1 Bedford. 2 Dennis. 1 Leyland. 1 Marshall. 5 Mercedes. 1 Optare. 2 Volvo.
Bodies: 1 Marshall. 1 Optare. 4 Plaxton. 1 Reeve Burgess. 1 Van Hool. 2 Wadham Stringer. 2 Wright. 1 other
Ops incl: local bus services, school contracts, private hire

*BARCROFT TOURS & EVENTS

60 QUEENS ROAD, HASTINGS TN34 1RE
Tel: 01424 200201
Fax: 01424 200206
Recovery: 07977 004371
E-mail: info@barcrofttours.com
Web site: www.barcrofttours.co.uk
Dir: Peter Warren
Fleet: 5 - 3 coach, 1 minibus, 1 midicoach
Chassis: 1 Ford Transit. 3 Mercedes. 1 Toyota.
Bodies: incl: 1 Caetano. 3 Setra.
Ops incl: school contracts, excursions & tours, private hire, continental tours.

*BRIGHTON & HOVE BUS & COACH CO

43 CONWAY STREET, HOVE BN3 3LT
Tel: 01273 886200
Fax: 01273 822073
E-mail: info@buses.co.uk
Web site: www.buses.co.uk
Fleetname: Brighton & Hove
Chmn: Chris Moyes OBE **Man Dir**: Roger French OBE **Fin Dir**: Phil Woodgate
Eng Dir: Tony Griffiths **Ops Dir**: Paul Williams
Fleet: 281 - 187 double-deck bus, 86 single-deck bus, 8 coach.
Chassis: 1 Bristol. 148 Dennis. 105 Scania. 27 Volvo.
Bodies: 7 Alexander. 5 Berkhof. 1 ECW. 143 East Lancs. 2 Irizar. 8 Marshall. 18 Optare. 76 Plaxton. 21 other.
Ops incl: local bus services, excursions & tours, private hire, continental tours.
Livery: Red/Cream
Ticket System: Wayfarer

BRIGHTONIAN COACHES
3 THE AVENUE, BRIGHTON BN2 4GF
Tel: 01273 696195
Props: Laurence R Walker, Susan M Walker
Fleet: 2 coach
Chassis: 2 Volvo.
Bodies: 1 Duple 1 Plaxton.
Ops incl: school contracts, private hire.
Livery: White

*C & S COACHES

STATION ROAD, HEATHFIELD TN21 8DF
Tel: 01435 866600
Fax: 01435 868264
E-mail: info@candscoaches.co.uk
Ptnrs: Chris Hicks, Geoff Shaw **Ch Eng**: Paul Matthews
Fleet: 37 - incl 1 double-deck coach, 1 midicoach.
Chassis: 20 DAF. 2 Leyland. 6 Scania. 9 Volvo.
Bodies: 2 Jonckheere. 6 Plaxton. 1 Reeve Burgess. 28 Van Hool.
Ops incl: school contracts, private hire.
Livery: White with red/black/grey graphics

*COASTAL COACHES
18 WEST POINT, NEWICK BN8 4NU
Tel: 01825 723024
E-mail: peterhjenkins@aol.com
Fleetname: Coastal
Owner: Peter Jenkins **Ops Man**: P Lockhart
Fleet: 10 single-deck bus.
Chassis: 9 Dennis. 1 Transbus.
Bodies: 9 Alexander. 1 Transbus.
Ops incl: local bus services
Livery: Green/White/Blue
Ticket System: Wayfarer 3

*CUCKMERE COMMUNITY BUS
THE OLD RECTORY, LITLINGTON BN26 5RB
Tel/Fax: 01323 870920
Web site: www.cuckmerebus.freeuk.com
Chmn: Mrs Beryl Smith **Organiser**: Philip Ayers **Hire Organiser**: Geoffrey Maynard
Sec: Susan de Angeli **Treasurer**: Andrew Cottingham
Fleet: 6 minibus
Chassis: 6 Mercedes.
Bodies: 2 Alexander. 1 Mellor. 1 other. 2 Constable
Ops incl: local bus services, excursions, private hire.
Livery: Green/Cream
Ticket system: Setright

*EASTBOURNE BUSES LTD
BIRCH ROAD, EASTBOURNE BN26 6PD
Tel: 01323 416416
Fax: 01323 643034
E-mail: mailbox@eastbournebuses.co.uk
Web site: www.eastbournebuses.co.uk
Man Dir: Steve Barnett
Fleet: 5 - 13 double-deck bus, 42 single-deck bus
Chassis: 26 DAF. 6 Dennis. 7 Leyland. 10 Optare. 6 Volvo.
Ops incl: local bus services, school contracts
Livery: base Blue with branding.
Ticket System: Wayfarer

*L J EDWARDS EXECUTIVE COACH HIRE

BELLBANKS CORNER, MILL ROAD, HAILSHAM BN27 2AH
Tel: 01323 440622
Fax: 01323 442555
E-mail: info@ljedwards.co.uk
Web site: www.ljedwards.co.uk
Prop: John Edwards
Fleet: 13 - 6 coach, 2 midicoach, 4 minibus, 1 minicoach
Chassis: 5 Bova. 1 Iveco. 1 Mercedes. 1 Toyota. 4 VW. 1 Volvo.
Bodies: 5 Bova. 2 Caetano. 1 Indcar. 1 Mercedes. 4 VW.
Ops incl: excursions & tours, private hire, continental tours, school contracts.
Livery: White/Red

*EMPRESS COACHES LTD

10/11 ST MARGARETS ROAD, ST LEONARDS-ON-SEA TN37 6EH
Tel/Fax: 01424 430621
E-mail: info@empresscoaches.com
Web site: www.empresscoaches.com
Dir: Stephen Dine
Fleet: 10 - 1 coach, 3 midibus, 6 midicoach.
Chassis: 1 Dennis. 3 Ford Transit. 2 Iveco. 3 Mercedes. 1 Omni.
Bodies: 1 Alexander. 2 Mellor. 1 Plaxton. 2 UVG. 1 Wadham Stringer. 3 other
Ops incl: school contracts, private hire.
Livery: White/Maroon

OCEAN COACHES
19 STONERY CLOSE, PORTSLADE BN41 2TD.
Tel/Fax: 01273 278385.
Web site: www.oceancoaches.net
E-mail: info@oceancoaches.net
Prop: Peter Woodcock.
Fleet: 1 coach.
Chassis: Volvo. **Body**: Ikarus.

A/c	Air conditioning
	Vehicles suitable for disabled
	Coach(es) with galley facilities
WC	Coach(es) with toilet facilities
	Seat belt-fitted vehicles
R	Recovery service available (not 24 hr)
R24	24hr recovery service
	Replacement vehicle available
T	Toilet-drop facilities available
	Vintage vehicle(s) available
	Open top vehicle(s)

Ops incl: private hire, school contracts.
Livery: Cream/Red.

*PAVILION COACHES

144 NEVILL AVENUE, HOVE
BN3 7NH
Tel: 01273 732405
Dir: P C Hammer
Fleet: double-deck bus, coach
Chassis: Leyland (RT). Volvo.
Bodies: Park Royal. Plaxton
Ops incl: excursions & tours, private hire, continental tours
Livery: White

R D H SERVICES

DITCHLING COMMON, DITCHLING, HASSOCKS BN6 8SG
Tel: 01444 257727
E-mail: info@rdhservices.co.uk
Web site: www.rdhservices.co.uk
Props: T M Hawthorne, D P Hunnisett
Ch Eng: M Wise
Fleet: 12 - 7 coach, 5 midicoach
Chassis: 4 Dennis. 4 Leyland. 2 Neoplan. 2 Volvo.
Bodies: 1 Ikarus. 1 Jonckheere. 2 Neoplan. 3 Plaxton. 1 Reeve Burgess. 4 Wadham Stringer.
Ops incl: private hire.
Livery: White/Orange/Blue.

RAMBLER COACHES

WESTRIDGE MANOR, WHITWORTH ROAD, HASTINGS TN37 7PZ
Tel: 01424 754881
Fax: 01424 751815
Ptnrs: C. Rowland, J. Goodwin.
Fleet: 38 - 5 single-deck bus, 26 coach, 1 midibus, 3 midicoach. 1 minicoach.
Chassis: 8 Bedford. 4 Dennis. 2 Leyland National. 5 Mercedes. 1 Scania. 18 Volvo.
Bodies: 5 Berkhof. 1 Duple. 2 Leyland National. 2 Optare. 17 Plaxton. 7 Van Hool.

1 Reeve Burgess. 1 Wadham Stringer. 1 Wright. 1 Hispano.
Ops incl: local bus services, school contracts, excursions & tours, private hire, continental tours.
Livery: Green/Black.
Ticket System: Wayfarer.

RENOWN COACHES

13 SEA ROAD, BEXHILL-ON-SEA TN40 1EE
Tel: 01424 211563
Fax: 01424 210744
Fleet: 18 - 4 double-deck bus, 4 single-deck bus, 10 coach
Chassis: 1 DAF. 1 Dennis. 11 Leyland. 1 Setra. 4 Volvo.
Bodies: 2 Caetano. 2 Duple. 6 Leyland. 1 Plaxton. 1 Reeve Burgess. 1 Setra. 4 Van Hool. 1 Wadham Stringer.
Ops incl: local bus services, school contracts, excursions & tours, private hire, continental tours.

STAGECOACH IN HASTINGS
BEAUFORT ROAD, SILVERHILL, ST LEONARDS ON SEA TN37 6PL
Tel: 01424 445600
Fax: 01424 435340
E-mail: enquiries.southeast@stagecoachbus.com
Web site: www.stagecoachbus.com/hastings
Man Dir: Paul Southgate **Ops Dir:** Neil Instrall **Eng Dir:** Keith Dyball
Fleet: 63 - 23 double-deck bus, 40 single-deck bus.
Chassis: 27 Dennis. 4 Leyland. 6 Scania. 26 Volvo
Bodies: 45 Alexander. 18 Northern Counties.
Ops incl: local bus services.
Livery: Stagecoach

SUSSEX PIONEER COACHES
3 THE AVENUE, BRIGHTON BN2 4GF.
Tel: 01273 696195.
Fax: 01273 696195.
Ptnrs: L. R. Walker, Mrs S. M. Walker.
Fleet: 3 coach.
Chassis: 3 Leyland.
Bodies: 1 Duple. 1 Plaxton. 1 Roe.
Ops incl: private hire.

*WARREN'S COACHES (KENT & SUSSEX) LTD

HIGH STREET, TICEHURST TN5 7AN
Tel: 01580 200226
Fax: 01580 201126
E-mail: contact@warrens.uk.com
Web site: www.warrens.uk.com
Man Dir: G R Fry **Dir/Co Sec:** M Fry
Fleet: 12 - 10 coach, 1 midicoach, 1 minicoach.
Chassis: 5 Iveco. 1 Mercedes. 1 Setra. 1 Toyota. 4 Volvo.
Ops incl: school contracts, private hire, excursions & tours, continental tours.
Livery: Primrose/Blue/Red

WISE COACHES LTD
74 HIGH STREET, HAILSHAM BN27 1AU
Tel: 01323 844321
Fax: 01323 845321
E-mail: info@wisecoaches.co.uk
Web site: www.wisecoaches.co.uk
Dirs: J S G Wise, J E Wise
Fleet: 4 coach.
Chassis: 3 DAF. 1 Iveco.
Bodies: 1 Beulas. 1 Ikarus. 1 Ovi. 1 Smit.
Ops incl: excursions & tours, private hire, continental tours, school contracts.
Livery: White/Red/Black.

EAST RIDING OF YORKSHIRE, CITY OF KINGSTON UPON HULL

*ABBEY COACHWAYS LTD
See main entry in North Yorkshire

ACKLAMS OF BEVERLEY
39 LADYGATE, BEVERLEY HU17 8BX
Tel: 01482 887666
Fax: 01482 874949
Web site: www.acklams-coaches-beverley.co.uk
Prop: Paul Acklam
Fleet: 10 - 5 coach, 2 midicoach, 3 minicoach.
Chassis: 2 DAF. 3 Dennis. 2 LDV. 2 Mercedes.

Bodies: 1 Optare. 6 Plaxton.
Ops incl: local bus services, school contracts, private hire.
Livery: Red/Grey

*ALPHA BUS & COACH CO

DAIRYCOATES INDUSTRIAL ESTATE, WILTSHIRE ROAD, HULL HU4 6PA
Tel: 01482 353941
Fax: 01482 353771
E-mail: scott.dunn.dunn-line.com
Web site: www.dunn-line.com
Partners: R A Dunn, A S Dunn, B K Geldart (Dir/Co Sec)

Fleet: 37 - 13 double-deck bus, 9 single-deck bus, 12 coach, 1 midibus, 2 minibus.
Chassis: 8 Dennis. 1 Ford Transit. 10 MAN. 9 Mercedes. 9 Volvo.
Bodies: 4 East Lancs. 10 MCW. 9 Mercedes. 1 Optare. 8 Plaxton. 5 other.
Ops incl: local bus services, school contracts, private hire, continental tours.
Livery: Purple/Silver
Ticket system: Almex

R DRURY COACHES

CARTER STREET, GOOLE DN14 6SL
Tel/Fax: 01405 763440
Dirs: Roland Drury, Richard Drury
Fleet: 5 coach, 1 midicoach
Chassis: 1 Toyota. 5 Volvo.

Bodies: 1 Caetano. 5 Plaxton.
Ops incl: local bus services, school contracts, private hire.
Livery: White/Green/Yellow

*EAST YORKSHIRE MOTOR SERVICES LTD

R24

252 ANLABY ROAD, HULL HU3 2RS
Tel: 01482 327142
Fax: 01482 212040
E-mail: admin@eyms.co.uk
Web site: www.eyms.co.uk
Chmn: P J S Shipp **Fin Dir:** Peter Harrison **Com Man:** Bob Rackley **Ch Eng:** D Heptinstall **Co Sec:** P Jenkinson **Coaching Man:** M Ellis
Fleet: 343 - 167 double-deck bus, 97 single-deck bus, 25 coach, 7 open-top bus, 34 midibus, 13 minibus.
Chassis: 1 AEC. 1 Bedford. 3 Bristol. 49 Dennis. 75 Leyland. 12 Leyland. 4 MCW. 34 Mercedes. 15 Optare. 147 Volvo.
Bodies: 44 Alexander. 7 Berkhof. 2 Caetano. 3 Duple. 12 ECW. 1 East Lancs. 9 Leyland. 5 MCW. 2 Mercedes. 1 Neoplan. 83 Northern Counties. 34 Optare. 113 Plaxton. 1 Willowbrook. 25 Wrightbus.
Ops incl: local bus services, school contracts, excursion & tours, private hire, express, continental tours.
Livery: Burgundy/Cream coaches-Riviera Blue/Primrose
Ticket System: Wayfarer TGX150

FRODINGHAM COACHES

MIDDLE STREET SOUTH, DRIFFIELD YO25 6PY
Tel: 0870 4430473
Fax: 01482 212040
E-mail: alan@frodinghamcoaches.co.uk
Web site: www.frodinghamcoaches.co.uk
Chmn: P J S Shipp **Fin Dir:** P Harrison **Man:** A Wilkinson
Fleet: 5 coach
Chassis: 1 MAN. 2 Mercedes. 1 Scania. 1 Volvo.
Bodies: 2 Mercedes. 1 Neoplan. 1 Plaxton. 1 Van Hool.
Ops incl: local bus services, school contracts, excursion & tours, private hire.
Livery: White/Blue/Grey
Part of East Yorkshire Motor Services

GREY DE LUXE COACHES

DAIRYCOTES INDUSTRIAL ESTATE, WILTSHIRE ROAD, HULL HU4 6PA.
Tel: 01482 571711.
Fax: 01482 353771.
Props: Craig Porteous, Jean Porteous.
See Alpha Coach Co, Hull.

BEN JOHNSON COACHES

THE GRANGE, CATFOSS LANE, BRANDESBURTON YO25 8EJ.
Tel: 01964 542475.
Fax: 01964 543982
Prop: Ben Johnson.
Fleet: 8 - 7 coach, 2 minibus.
Chassis: 1 DAF, 2 LDV. 2 Leyland. 1 Setra. 2 Volvo.
Bodies: 4 Plaxton. 1 Setra. 1 Van Hool.
Ops incl: local bus services, school contracts, private hire.

MANOR TRAVEL

2 MANOR DRIVE, MAIN STREET, BEEFORD YO25 8BB.
Tel: 01262 488431.

*NATIONAL HOLIDAYS

THE TRAVEL CENTRE, SPRINGFIELD WAY, ANLABY, HULL HU10 6RJ
Tel: 01482 569006
Fax: 01482 569003
E-mail: info@national-holidays.co.uk
Web site: www.national-holidays.co.uk
Ch Exec: John Slatcher **Dir:** Graham Rogers **Ops Man:** Adrian Hutchinson
Fleet: 81 coach
Chassis: 81 Volvo.
Bodies: 29 Jonckheere. 40 Plaxton. 12 Van Hool.
Ops incl: excursions & tours, private hire, continental tours.
Livery: White
(Subsidiary company of of WA Shearings)

*PEARSON COACHES LTD

9 HEADLANDS ROAD, ALDBROUGH HU11 4RR
Tel: 01964 527260 **Fax:** 01964 527774
E-mail: enquiries@pearsoncoaches.co.uk
Web site: www.pearsoncoaches.co.uk
Dirs: Mrs V Pearson, Mr C Pearson, Mr S Colley
Fleet: 10 - 5 coach, 4 minicoach. 1 midibus.
Chassis: 5 Volvo. 5 Mercedes
Bodies: 1 Autobus. 5 Van Hool. 4 other.
Ops incl: local bus services, school contracts, excursions & tours, private hire.
Livery: Pale Grey with Red/Burgundy stripe.
Ticket system: Wayfarer 2

COLLIN PHILLIPSON MINI-COACHES

1 HILLCREST, OUSEFLEET, GOOLE DN14 8HP
Tel: 01405 704394
Prop: Collin Phillipson **Tran Man:** Tracey Phillipson
Fleet: 1 minicoach
Chassis: 1 Mercedes
Bodies: 1 Excell
Ops incl: school contracts, private hire

STAGECOACH IN HULL

FOSTER STREET, HULL HU8 8BT
Tel: 01482 222333
Fax: 01482 217623
Web site: www.stagecoachbus.com
Dirs: as Stagecoach East Midland
Fleet: 132 - double-deck bus, single-deck bus, coach, midibus
Chassis: incl: 85 Dennis. 22 Volvo.
Bodies: incl: 22 Alexander. 28 Northern Counties. 14 Plaxton.
Ops incl: local bus services, express.
Livery: Stagecoach
Ticket system: Wayfarer 3.

SWEYNE COACHES

LONGSHORES, REEDNESS ROAD, SWINEFLEET DN14 8ER.
Tel: 01405 704263

WOLD TRAVEL

THE OLD FORGE, NORTH DALTON, DRIFFIELD YO25 9UY.
Tel: 01377 217461.
Fax: 01377 217810.
Dirs: D. Rowland, J. Rowland.
Fleet: 6 - 2 coach, 1 double-deck coach, 1 midicoach, 1 minicoach, 1 minibus.
Ops incl: excursions & tours, private hire, continental tours, school contracts.
Livery: Grey, Yellow with Red lines.

Air conditioning	
Vehicles suitable for disabled	
Coach(es) with galley facilities	
Coach(es) with toilet facilities	
Seat belt-fitted vehicles	
R Recovery service available (not 24 hr)	
R24 24hr recovery service	
Replacement vehicle available	
T Toilet-drop facilities available	
Vintage vehicle(s) available	
Open top vehicle(s)	

ESSEX

AMBASSADOR COACHES
AMBASSADOR HOUSE,
39 BOURNEMOUTH PARK ROAD,
SOUTHEND ON SEA SS2 5JH
Tel: 01702 315830
Props: M & D Murray

ANITAS COACH & MINIBUS HIRE LTD

ROOMS 4-5, AIRWAYS HOUSE,
FIRST AVENUE, STANSTED
AIRPORT CM24 1RY
Tel: 01279 681551
Fax: 01279 661771
E-mail: anitas.coaches@virgin.net
Web site: www.anitascoaches.com
Dirs: E A S Wheeler, Mrs V A Wyatt
Fleet: 7 - 5 coach, 1 midicoach, 1 minicoach.
Chassis: 2 DAF. 1 MAN. 1 Mercedes. 3 Volvo.
Bodies: 2 Bova. 4 Caetano. 1 Plaxton
Ops incl: school contracts, private hire, continental tours.

*APT COACHES LTD

27 RAWRETH INDUSTRIAL ESTATE,
RAWRETH LANE, RAYLEIGH SS6 9RL
Tel: 01268 783878
Fax: 01268 782656
E-mail: admin@aptcoaches.co.uk
Web site: www.aptcoaches.co.uk
Man Dir: Peter Thorn
Fleet: 13 - 1 double-deck bus, 11 coach, 1 midicoach.
Chassis: 2 Bova. 2 Leyland. 1 Mercedes. 5 Scania. 1 Setra. 1 Volvo.
Bodies: 1 Berkhof. 2 Bova. 1 Caetano. 3 Irizar. 1 Leyland. 2 Plaxton. 1 Setra. 2 Van Hool.
Ops incl: school contracts, excursions & tours, private hire, continental tours
Livery: White/Pink

*B J S TRAVEL
61A HIGH STREET, GREAT WAKERING SS3 0EF
Tel: 01702 219403
Fax: 01702 216472
Prop: Brian Snow
Fleet: 4 - 2 single-deck coach, 2 minicoach.
Chassis: 2 Mercedes. 1 Scania. 1 Volvo.
Bodies: 1 Berkhof. 1 Neoplan. 1 Reeve Burgess. 1 Other
Ops incl: school contracts, private hire.
Livery: White/Blue/Silver.

BLUE DIAMOND COACHES
37 HOLMES MEADOW, HARLOW CM19 5SG.
Tel: 01279 427524.
Fax: 01279 427525.
Prop: J. Robilliard. **Sec**: A. Robilliard.
Fleet: 4 - 1 coach, 2 minibus, 1 minicoach.
Chassis: 1 Bedford. 2 Freight Rover. 1 Toyota.
Bodies: 1 Caetano. 2 Carlyle. 1 Plaxton.
Ops incl: excursions & tours, private hire, continental tours, school contracts.
Livery: Blue/White.

BLUE TRIANGLE BUSES LTD
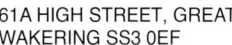
UNIT 3C, DENVER INDUSTRIAL ESTATE, RAINHAM RM13 9DD
Tel: 01708 631001/550743
Fax: 01708 522227
Web site: www.bluetrianglebuses.co.uk
Man Dir: Roger Wright
Fleet: 101 - 78 double-deck bus, 23 single-deck bus
Chassis: 8 AEC. 51 Dennis. 15 Leyland. 11 Leyland National. 23 MCW. 5 Volvo.
Bodies: 5 Alexander. 8 Caetano. 34 East Lancs. 6 Leyland. 23 MCW. 13 Park Royal. 20 Plaxton. 1 Saunders. 3 Weymann.
Ops incl: local bus services, excursions & tours
Livery: Red/Cream

*BORDACOACH
25B EASTWOOD ROAD, RAYLEIGH SS6 7JD
Tel: 01268 747608
Gen Man: D J Stubbington
Fleet: 1 coach.
Chassis: 1 Volvo
Bodies: 1 Van Hool.
Ops incl: school contracts, excursions & tours, private hire.
Livery: White

BRENTWOOD COACHES

79 WASH ROAD, HUTTON, BRENTWOOD CM13 1DL.
Tel: 01277 233144.
Fax: 01277 201386.
Prop: A. J. Brenson. **Ch Eng**: K. Wright.
Sec: Mrs P. Alexander. **Traf Man**: B. Pierce.
Fleet: 30 - 15 double-deck bus, 14 coach. 1 midibus.
Chassis: Daimler, Volvo.
Bodies: Caetano, Jonckheere, Plaxton.
Ops incl: excursions & tours, private hire, school contracts, continental tours.
Livery: White/Brown/Orange/Yellow.
Ticket System: Almex.

BURTONS COLCHESTER COACHWAYS
38 MAGDALEN ROAD, COLCHESTER RM17 5HJ
Tel: 01206 544449
Tel: 01206 766345
E-mail: colchester@burtons-bus.co.uk
Web site: www.burtonscoaches.com
Fleetname: Harris
Man Dir: Paul Cooper **Fleet Eng**: Steve Legate
Fleet: 24 - 10 double-deck bus, 18 single-deck bus, 4 coach, 2 minibus
Chassis: 2 DAF. 16 Dennis. 3 Leyland. 2 Mercedes. 11 Volvo.
Bodies: 3 ECW. 12 East Lancs. 2 Ikarus. 9 Plaxton. 8 Transbus. 2 Van Hool.

*C I COACHLINES

POOLS LANE, HIGHWOOD, CHELMSFORD CM1 3QL
Tel: 01245 248669
Fax: 01245 603534
E-mail: cicoachlines@btopenworld.com
Props: S Lodge, I Lodge, C Ferrier
Fleet: 4 coach
Chassis: 1 Iveco. 3 Volvo
Ops incl: private hire, school contracts

*C N ENTERPRISES LTD
9 BARTHOLOMEW DRIVE, HAROLD WOOD RM3 0WB
Tel/Fax: 01708 379700
E-mail: cnenterprise1@aol.com
ManDir: Colin Nossek **Dir**: Vena Nossek
Fleet: 1 coach.
Chassis: 1 Volvo.
Bodies: 1 Jonckheere.
Ops incl: excursions & tours, private hire.

CEDRIC COACHES
1 THE AVENUE, WIVENHOE CO7 9AH
Tel: 01206 824363
Fax: 01206 822253
Fleet: 27 - 12 double-deck bus, 10 coach, 2 double-deck coach. 1 minibus. 1 midicoach. 1 minicoach
Chassis: 3 Bova. 1 LDV. 12 Leyland. 1 Neoplan. 1 Scania. 3 Setra. 1 Toyota. 3 Volvo.
Bodies: 1 Berkhof. 3 Bova. 1 Caetano. 12 ECW. 1 Irizar. 1 Neoplan. 2 Plaxton. 3 Setra. 1 Van Hool.

CHADWELL HEATH COACHES
30 REYNOLDS AVENUE, CHADWELL HEATH RM6 4NT
Tel: 020 8590 7505
Fax: 020 8597 8883
Props: John Thompson, Lynn Thompson.
Fleet: 5 coach.
Chassis: 2 Leyland. 3 Volvo.
Bodies: 3 Berkhof. 1 Duple. 1 Plaxton.
Ops incl: excursions & tours, private hire, school contracts.
Livery: Country cream

CHARIOTS OF ESSEX LTD

THE COACH HOUSE, 1 ONE TREE HILL, STANFORD-LE-HOPE SS17 9NH
Tel: 01268 581444
Fax: 01268 581555
Man Dir: K T Flavin **Dir**: W J Collier
Fleet: 18 - 3 double-deck bus, 2 single-deck bus, 4 single-deck coach, 1 midicoach, 7 minibus, 1 minicoach.
Chassis: Bova. DAF. Freight Rover. Iveco. Mercedes. Toyota.
Bodies: Bova. Caetano. Marshall/MCV. MCW.

Ops incl: local bus services, school contracts, private hire, express.
Livery: Orange/Yellow
Ticket system: Wayfarer

*CLINTONA MINICOACHES

LITTLE WARLEY HALL LANE,
BRENTWOOD CM13 3HA
Tel: 01277 215526
Fax: 01277 200038
E-mail: enquiries@clintona.co.uk
Web site: www.clintona.co.uk
Ptnrs: Robin Staines, Barbara J Staines.
Fleet: 24 - 10 midibus, 8 midicoach, 3 minibus, 3 minicoach.
Chassis: 1 Ford Transit. 4 Iveco. 4 LDV. 15 Mercedes.
Ops incl: local bus services, school contracts, private hire.
Livery: White/Blue.
Ticket System: Wayfarer 3

*COOKS COACHES

607 LONDON ROAD, WESTCLIFF-ON-SEA SS0 9PE
Tel: 01702 344702
Fax: 01702 436887
Web site: www.cookscoaches.co.uk
Prop: W E Cook
Fleet: 12 - 10 coach, 2 minibus.
Chassis: 10 Bova. 2 Freight Rover.
Ops incl: excursions & tours, private hire, continental tours.
Livery: Red/White

*COUNTY COACHES

2 CRESCENT ROAD, BRENTWOOD CM14 5JR
Tel: 01277 201505
Fax: 01277 225918
E-mail: enquiries@countycoaches.com
Web site: www.countycoaches.com
Dirs: A R Pratt, R J Pratt, C A Jee, Mrs S M Best
Fleet: 12 - 11 coach, 1 midicoach.
Chassis: 1 Dennis. 1 Mercedes. 1 Toyota. 9 Volvo.
Bodies: 1 Berkhof. 3 Caetano. 2 Duple. 1 Jonckheere. 1 Mercedes. 1 Plaxton. 2 Van Hool. 1 other

CROWN COACHES

35 DANDIES DRIVE, EASTWOOD, LEIGH-ON-SEA SS9 5R4.
Tel/Fax: 01702 420201.
Owners: T. Cox, P. Cox.
Fleet: 8 - 3 coach, 1 midicoach, 4 minibus.
Chassis: 1 Bedford. 1 Bova. 1 DAF. 4 Iveco.
Bodies: 1 Bova. 4 Carlyle. 1 Duple. 1 Ikarus.
Ops incl: local bus services, excursions & tours, private hire.
Livery: Silver/Red/Orange/Grey stripes.
Ticket System: Wayfarer.

*CRUSADER HOLIDAYS

STEPHENSON ROAD WEST, CLACTON-ON-SEA CO15 4HP
Tel: 01255 431777
Fax: 01255 222683
E-mail: info@crusader-holidays.co.uk
Web site: www.crusader-holidays.co.uk
Chmn: Geoffrey Clarkson **Man Dir**: Michael Holden **Comm Dir**: Michael Drinkwater
Gen Man: Neil Pyemont
Fleet: 27 coach
Chassis/Bodies: 27 Setra
Ops incl: excursions & tours, continental tours, private hire
Livery: White/Blue

CUNNINGHAM CARRIAGE COMPANY

THE CARRIAGE HOUSE, FOBBING ROAD, CORRINGHAM SS17 9BG
Tel: 01375 676578.
Fax: 01375 679719.
Prop: Pat Cunningham **Junior Ptnr**: Sarah Cunningham
Fleet: 1 coach.
Chassis: 1 Scania.
Bodies: 1 Irizar.
Ops incl: private hire, express.
Livery: White
Ticket System: Setright.

DOCKLANDS BUSES LTD

See London

*DONS COACHES DUNMOW LTD

PARSONAGE DOWNS, GREAT DUNMOW CM6 2AT
Tel: 01371 872644
Fax: 01371 876055
Dirs: D T Hale, S D Harvey
Fleet: 16 - 2 double-deck bus, 10 coach, 2 midicoach, 2 minicoach.
Chassis: 1 Ayats. 6 Dennis. 2 Leyland. 2 Mercedes. 3 Neoplan. 2 Toyota.
Bodies: 2 Alexander. 1 Ayats. 2 Caetano. 2 Duple. 1 Marcopolo. 5 Neoplan. 3 Plaxton.
Ops incl: private hire, school contracts.

EDS MINIBUS & COACH HIRE

257 PRINCESS MARGARET ROAD, EAST TILBURY RM18 8SB
Tel/Fax: 01375 858049
Props: E Sammons, Mrs S Sammons
Fleet: 2 - 1 coach, 1 minibus.
Chassis/Body: MAN/Algarve
Ops incl: Private hire, excursions & tours

*ENSIGN BUS CO LTD

JULIETTE CLOSE, PURFLEET INDUSTRIAL PARK, PURFLEET RM15 4YF
Tel: 01708 865656
Fax: 01708 864340
E-mail: sales@ensignbus.com
Web-site: www.ensignbus.com
Chmn: Peter Newman **Dirs**: Ross Newman(**Sales**), Brian Longley (**Eng**), Steve Newman (**City Sightseeing**) **Com Dir**: Gary Nicholass **Eng Man**: Roger Jackson
Fleet (Purfleet): 36 - 24 double-deck bus, 8 single-deck bus, 1 coach, 4 open-top bus.
Chassis: 14 AEC. 1 Bristol. 2 Daimler. 6 Dennis. 12 MCW. 2 Volvo.
Bodies: 1 Ayats. 12 MCW. 1 Northern Counties. 11 Park Royal. 6 UVG. 2 Craven. 1 Weymann.
Ops incl: local bus services, private hire.
Livery: Blue/Silver
Ticket System: Almex A90

EXCALIBUR COACH TRAVEL

44 MOUNTVIEW CRESCENT, ST LAWRENCE BAY, SOUTHMINSTER CM0 7NR
Tel: 01621 779980
Fax: 01621 778928
E-mail: info@excaliburcoach.co.uk
Web site: www.excaliburcoach.co.uk
Prop: Trevor Wynn
Fleet: 3 minibus.
Chassis: 1 Ford Transit. 1 LDV.
Ops incl: private hire, school contracts.

EXCEL PASSENGER LOGISTICS LTD

AIRWAYS HOUSE, FIRST AVENUE, STANSTED AIRPORT NORTH CM24 1RY
Tel: 01279 681800
Fax: 01279 681900
E-mail: excelcoaches@hotmail.com
Man Dir: Graham Hayden **Fin Dir**: Lyn Watson
Fleet: 24 - 4 double-deck bus, 6 single-deck bus, 8 coach, 1 open-top bus, 9 midibus, 1 minibus, 1 minicoach.
Chassis: 2 Leyland. 11 Mercedes. 2 Scania. 14 Volvo.
Bodies: include: 6 Carlyle. 2 Irizar. 2 MCW. 8 Plaxton.
Ops incl: local bus services, private hire.

FARGO COACHLINES

ALLVIEWS, SCHOOL ROAD, RAYNE, BRAINTREE CM7 8SS
Tel: 01376 321817
Fax: 01376 551236
E-mail: fargocoachlines@btconnect.com
Prop: L J Smith

A/c	Air conditioning	◆	Seat belt-fitted vehicles	✦	Replacement vehicle available
♿	Vehicles suitable for disabled	R	Recovery service available (not 24 hr)	T	Toilet-drop facilities available
🍴	Coach(es) with galley facilities				Vintage vehicle(s) available
wc	Coach(es) with toilet facilities	R24	24hr recovery service	🚌	Open top vehicle(s)

Essex

Fleet: 30 - 12 double-deck bus, 11 single-deck coach, 2 double-deck coach, 4 midicoach, 1 minicoach.
Chassis: 3 DAF. 2 Daimler. 4 Dennis. 1 Freight Rover. 5 Leyland. 5 Mercedes. 2 Optare. 8 Scania.
Bodies: 5 Bova. 1 Irizar. 4 Leyland. 2 Optare. 1 Plaxton. 5 Van Hool. 2 other. 1 LDV Convoy.
Ops incl: private hire, school contracts.
Livery: White

FERRERS COACHES LTD

117B HULLBRIDGE ROAD, SOUTH WOODHAM FERRERS CM3 5LL
Tel: 01245 320456.
Dir: A. Read, G. Read.
Fleet: 4 - 2 coach, 2 minibus.
Chassis: 2 Dennis. 1 Ford Transit. 1 Freight Rover.
Ops incl: excursions & tours, private hire, school contracts.

FIRST ESSEX BUSES

WESTWAY, CHELMSFORD CM1 3AR
Tel: 01245 293400
Web site: www.firstgroup.com.
Man Dir: S W Smith **Eng Dir:** S Little **Fin Dir:** M Dolphin **Div Man N Essex:** L Berry **Div Man S Essex:** C McCormick
Fleet: 341 - 42 double-deck bus, 272 single-deck bus, 1 open-top double-deck bus, 17 midibus, 9 midicoach.
Chassis: 1 Bristol. 204 Dennis. 17 Leyland. 54 Mercedes-Benz. 38 Scania. 29 Volvo.
Bodies: 36 Alexander. 12 ECW. 21 East Lancs. 16 Marshall/MCV. 37 Northern Counties. 28 Optare. 136 Plaxton. 17 Transbus. 9 Wright.
Ops incl: local bus service, school contracts.
Livery: First Group - White/Blue/Magenta
Ticket System: Wayfarer

*FORDS COACHES

THE GARAGE, FAMBRIDGE ROAD, ALTHORNE CM3 6BZ
Tel: 01621 740326
Fax: 01621 742781
E-mail: info@fordscoaches.co.uk
Web site: www.fordscoaches.co.uk
Prop: Anthony A W Ford **Ch Eng:** Anthony W Ford
Fleet: 24 - 10 double-deck bus, 9 coach, 3 double-deck coach, 1 midicoach. 1 minicoach.
Chassis: 1 Ayats. 2 Bedford. 6 Dennis. 2 Iveco. 7 Leyland. 2 MAN. 1 Mercedes. 3 Scania.
Bodies: 2 Alexander. 1 Ayats. 1 Beulas. 2 Berkhof. 2 Caetano. 1 Duple. 7 ECW. 2 East Lancs. 1 Indcar. 1 Mellor. 1 Plaxton. 3 Van Hool.
Ops incl: local bus services, school contracts, excursions & tours, private hire.
Livery: White/Multi-colour stripe

GATWICK FLYER LTD
DANES ROAD, ROMFORD RM7 OHL
Tel: 01708 730555
Fax: 01708 751231
Web site: www.gatwickflyer.co.uk
Fleetnames: Gatwick Flyer, Avon Coaches

Fleet: 15 - 6 coach, 9 minicoach.
Ops incl: private hire, express.

GENIAL TRAVEL

43 PEACE ROAD, STANWAY, COLCHESTER CO3 0HL.
Tel/Fax: 01206 571513
Prop: Trevor Brookes
Fleet: 1 coach.
Chassis: 1 DAF
Body: 1 Van Hool
Ops incl: excursions & tours, private hire.
Livery: White/Blue/Yellow.

PETER GODWARD COACHES
4 EDWIN HALL VIEW, SOUTH WOODHAM FERRERS CM3 5QL
Tel: 01268 591834
Fax: 01268 591835
Prop: Peter Godward
Fleet: 12 - 8 single-deck coach, 1 double-deck coach, 1 midibus, 2 minicoach.
Chassis: 1 Ford Transit. 1 Mercedes-Benz. 6 Irisbus. 6 Iveco. 1 LDV. 1 Scania.
Ops incl: school contracts, excursions & tours, private hire, express, continental tours.

*GOLDEN BOY COACHES (JETSIE LTD)
See Hertfordshire

GOODWIN'S COACHES
ALWYNN, LONDON ROAD, BLACK NOTLEY, BRAINTREE CM7 8QQ
Tel: 01376 321096
Prop: A. M. Goodwin. **Sec:** I. B. Goodwin.
Fleet: 6 - 5 coach, 1 minibus.
Chassis: 3 Bedford. 2 Volvo.
Bodies: 1 Berkhof. 4 Plaxton. 1 Crystal.
Ops incl: excursions & tours, private hire.
Livery: White/Blue/Grey stripes.

GRAHAM'S
19 CHURCH ROAD, KELVEDON CO5 9JH
Tel: 01376 570150.
Fax: 01376 570657
Prop: G. Ellis.
Livery: White/Blue.

*HAILSTONE TRAVEL LTD

PLEASANT VIEW, DUNTON ROAD, LITTLE BURSTEAD CM12 9TZ
Tel: 01268 543543
Fax: 01268 543066
E-mail: info@hailstonetravel.co.uk
Web site: www.hailstonetravel.co.uk
Dirs: Mrs Tina Hailstone, Lawrence Hailstone
Fleet: midicoach, minicoach.
Chassis: Mercedes.
Ops incl: school contracts, private hire
Livery: White

HARRIS COACHES

DORSET ROAD, GRAYS RM17 5HJ
Tel: 01375 396677
E-mail: harris@burtons-bus.co.uk
Web site: www.burtonscoaches.com
Fleetname: Harris

Man Dir: Paul Cooper **Ops Man:** Steve Bolton **Fleet Eng:** Steve Legate
Fleet: 4 coach
Chassis: 4 Volvo.
Bodies: 2 Caetano. 2 Plaxton.
Ops incl: excursions & tours, private hire, continental tours.
Livery: Blue/Green on White base

*HEDINGHAM & DISTRICT OMNIBUSES LTD
WETHERSFIELD ROAD, SIBLE HEDINGHAM CO9 3LB
Tel: 01787 460621
Fax: 01787 462852
E-mail: services@hedingham.co.uk
Dirs: R J MacGregor, D R MacGregor
Fleet: 106 - 43 double-deck bus, 42 single-deck bus, 20 coach.
Chassis: 35 Bristol. 15 Dennis. 25 Leyland. 39 Volvo.
Bodies: 16 Alexander. 35 ECW. 1 East Lancs. 7 Leyland. 7 Northern Counties. 30 Plaxton. 4 Sunsundegui. 1 Willowbrook. 3 Wright.
Ops incl: local bus services, school contracts, excursions & tours, private hire.
Livery: Red/Cream.
Ticket System: Wayfarer 3

IMPERIAL BUS CO LTD
FROG ISLAND, FERRY LANE, RAINHAM RM13 9YN
Tel: 01708 550320
Man Dir: M Biddell
Fleet: 37 - 27 double-deck bus, 9 single-deck bus, 1 coach.
Livery: Green.

*KINGS COACHES

364 LONDON ROAD, STANWAY, COLCHESTER CO3 8LT
Tel: 01206 210312
Fax: 01206 213861
E-mail: andrew@kings-coaches.co.uk
Web site: www.kings-coaches.co.uk
Prop: Andrew Cousins
Fleet: 7 single-deck coach.
Chassis: 7 Bova.
Bodies: 7 Bova.
Ops incl: excursions & tours, private hire, continental tours.
Livery: Green/Cream

*KIRBYS COACHES (RAYLEIGH) LTD
PRINCESS ROAD, RAYLEIGH SS6 8HR
Tel: 01268 777777
Fax: 01702 202555
Dir: Edward Kirby **Co Sec:** Elizabeth Kirby
Fleet: 9 coach.
Chassis/bodies: 9 Setra.
Ops incl: excursions & tours, private hire, continental tours.
Livery: Lilac/Turquoise

LINKFAST LTD T/A S&M COACHES
93 ROSEBERRY AVENUE, BENFLEET SS7 4JF.

Tel/Fax: 01268 795763.
Props: B. W. Smith (Ch Eng), W. N. May (Sec).
Fleet: 10 - 9 double-deck bus, 1 coach.
Chassis: Daimler, Leyland.
Bodies: ECW, Northern Counties, Park Royal, Plaxton.
Ops incl: school contracts, private hire.
Livery: Mixed.

LODGE COACHES

THE GARAGE, HIGH EASTER, CHELMSFORD CM1 4QT
Tel: 01245 231262
Fax: 01245 231825
E-mail: lodgecoaches@btconnect.com
Web site: www.lodgecoaches.co.uk
Dirs: R C Lodge, A D Lodge, C J Lodge.
Fleet: 10 - 10 coach, 1 midicoach, 3 minibus, 1 minicoach, 1 vintage
Chassis: 3 Bedford. 1 Ford Transit. 3 Mercedes. 8 Scania. 1 Toyota.
Bodies: 1 Caetano, 2 Carlyle, 3 Duple. 1 Plaxton. 7 Van Hool, 2 other.
Ops incl: local bus services, school contracts, excursions & tours, private hire, continental tours.
Livery: Blue/Cream

MIKES COACHES
THE GRANARY, PIPPS HILL ROAD NORTH, CRAYS HILL, BASILDON CM11 2UJ.
Tel: 01268 525900.
Fax: 01268 453654.
Ptnrs: M. Orphan, D. Orphan, P. Brown.
Fleet: 6 - 5 coach, 1 midicoach.
Chassis: 2 Bedford. 1 DAF. 3 Volvo.
Bodies: 5 Plaxton. 1 Van Hool.
Ops incl: local bus services, school contracts, private hire.

W. H. NELSON (COACHES) LTD
THE COACH STATION, BRUCE GROVE, WICKFORD SS11 8BZ.
Tel: 01268 767870
Fax: 01268 735307
E-mail: info@nibsbus.com
Web site: www.nibsbus.com
Fleetname: Nelsons Independent Bus Services.
Ops incl: local bus services, school contracts
Livery: Yellow.

OLYMPIAN COACHES LTD

UNIT 9, BURNT MILL INDUSTRIAL ESTATE, ELIZABETH WAY, HARLOW CM20 2HT.
Tel: 01279 868868.
Fax: 01279 868867.
Dirs: C. Marino. **Co Sec:** Mrs D. K. Higgins.
Ops Dir: B. Gunton
Fleet: 40 - coach, minibus.

Ops incl: local bus services, school contracts, excursions & tours, private hire, continental tours.

P & M COACHES
74 CHURCHEND LANE, WICKFORD SS11 7JG.
Tel: 01268 763616.

PHILLIPS COACHES
117B HULLBRIDGE ROAD, SOUTH WOODHAM FERRERS CM3 5LL.
Tel/Fax: 01245 323039.
Prop: L. Phillips.
Fleet: 3 - 2 coach, 1 minibus.
Chassis: 1 Freight Rover. 2 Volvo.
Bodies: Plaxton. Van Hool.
Ops incl: excursions & tours, private hire, school contracts.
Livery: Cream/Maroon.

REGAL BUSWAYS LTD
ONGAR ROAD, CHELMSFORD CM1 3SR
Tel: 01702 291001
E-mail: info@regalbusways.com
Web site: www.regalbusways.com
Man Dir: Adrian McGarry **Ops Dir:** Lee Whitehead **Dir:** Mandy McGarry
Fleet: 14 - 4 double-deck bus, 9 single-deck bus, 1 double-deck coach
Chassis: 4 Dennis. 3 Leyland. 1 MCW. 2 Transbus. 4 Volvo.
Bodies: 1 Alexander. 2 ECW. 4 Marshall. 1 MCW. 4 Plaxton. 2 Transbus.
Ops incl: local bus services, private hire, school contracts.
Livery: Maroon/Cream
Ticket system: ERG

*RELIANCE LUXURY COACHES

54 BROOK ROAD, BENFLEET SS7 5JF
Tel/Fax: 01268 758426
Props: Martyn J Titchen, Patricia M Titchen
Fleet: 4 - 1 double-deck bus, 3 single-deck coach
Chassis: 1 Leyland. 3 Scania.
Bodies: 1 other. 3 Van Hool.
Ops incl: tours, private hire, school contracts.
Livery: Yellow/White/Orange/Red.

STALLION COACHES
STACEYS FARM BUNGALOW, BROOMFIELD, CHELMSFORD CM1 7HF.
Tel/Fax: 01245 443500.
Ptnrs: D. A. Brewster, Miss J. C. Pinkerton.
Fleet: 2 midicoach.
Chassis: 1 Mercedes. 1 Toyota.
Bodies: 1 Caetano. 1 Reeve Burgess.
Ops incl: school contracts, private hire.

STAN'S COACHES
THE COACH-HOUSE, BECKINGHAM ROAD, GREAT TOTHAM, MALDON CM9 8DY.
Tel: 01621 891959.
Fax: 01621 891365.
Prop: S. J. Porter.
Fleet: 6 - 5 coach, 1 minibus.
Chassis: 1 Bedford. 3 Bova. 1 Mercedes. 1 Volvo.
Bodies: 3 Bova. 1 Duple. 1 Mercedes. 1 Plaxton.
Ops incl: excursions & tours, private hire, continental tours.
Livery: White with Blue/Grey stripes.

STANSTED TRANSIT
OFFICE 17, BUILDING 44, STANSTED BUSINESS PARK, STANSTED AIRPORT CM24 1RY
Tel: 01229 681786
Prop: André Morris. **Co Sec:** Gillian Morris.
Ops Man: Sîan Morris. **Ch Eng:** Suzanne Morris.
Fleet: 33 - 5 double-deck bus, 22 single-deck bus, 6 midibus.
Chassis: 1 DAF, 12 Dennis, 1 Leyland National, 5 MCW. 7 Optare.
Bodies: 1 Alexander, 2 Caetano, 7 Leyland, 1 Leyland National, 5 MCW. 7 Optare. 7 Plaxton. 1 UVG. 2 Wright.
Ops incl: local bus services, school contracts, private hire.
Livery: White.
Ticket system: ERG.

*STEPHENSONS OF ESSEX LTD

RIVERSIDE INDUSTRIAL ESTATE, SOUTH STREET, ROCHFORD SS4 1BS
Tel: 01702 541511
Fax: 01702 549461
Web site: www.stephensonsofessex.com
E-mail: sales@stephensonsofessex.com
Man Dir: Bill Hiron **Fin Dir:** Lynn Watson
Ops Man: Lee Shuttleworth **Wkshp Man:** Tony Wright
Fleet: 36 - 19 double-deck bus, 9 single-deck bus, 8 coach.
Chassis: 8 Dennis. 19 Leyland. 8 Volvo.
Bodies: 4 Alexander.14 ECW. 1 Leyland. 1 Northern Counties. 16 Plaxton.
Ops incl: local bus services, school contracts, private hire, express.
Livery: White/Green
Ticket System: Wayfarer 3

SWALLOW COACH CO LTD

RAINHAM HOUSE, MANOR WAY, RAINHAM RM13 8RE.
Tel: 01708 630555.
Fax: 01708 555135.
Chmn: D. R. Webb. **Man Dir:** K. I. Webb.
Sec: Mrs. S. D. Webb.

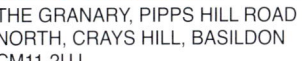

A/c	Air conditioning	✓	Replacement vehicle available
♿	Vehicles suitable for disabled	T	Toilet-drop facilities available
🍽	Coach(es) with galley facilities		Vintage vehicle(s) available
WC	Coach(es) with toilet facilities		Open top vehicle(s)
▼	Seat belt-fitted vehicles		
R	Recovery service available (not 24 hr)		
R24	24hr recovery service		

Fleet: 26 - 17 coach. 5 midicoach. 4 minicoach.
Chassis: 1 DAF. 1 Dennis. 1 Ford. 1 Ford Transit. 3 Freight Rover. 3 Leyland. 1 MAN. 2 Mercedes. 1 Setra. 1 Toyota. 11 Volvo.
Bodies: 5 Caetano. 1 Carlyle. 4 Jonckheere. 2 Mercedes. 6 Plaxton. 1 Setra. 2 Van Hool. **Ops incl:** Private hire.
Livery: Various.

T. F. MINI COACHES
1 SCRATTONS TERRACE, RIPPLE ROAD, BARKING IG11 0TY.
Tel: 020 8593 6205.
Fax: 020 8592 7182.
Man Dir: T. Farrugia.
Fleet: 7 midicoach.
Chassis: 7 Renault.
Ops incl: excursions & tours, private hire, airport transfer.

*TRUSTLINE SERVICES LTD
See Hertfordshire

VICEROY OF ESSEX LTD

12 BRIDGE STREET, SAFFRON WALDEN CB10 1BU.
Tel: 01799 508010
Fax: 01799 506106.
Web site: www.viceroycoaches.com
Fleet: 11 - coach, midibus, midibus, midicoach, minicoach, minibus.
Chassis: 1 Bedford. 1 DAF. 1 Dennis. 1 Leyland. 5 Mercedes. 2 Setra.
Bodies: 2 Duple. 2 Mercedes. 4 Plaxton. 2 Setra. 1 LAG.
Ops incl: local bus services, school contracts, excursions & tours, private hire.
Livery: White.
Ticket System: Wayfarer 3

*WALDEN TRAVEL LTD

126 THAXTED ROAD, SAFFRON WALDEN CB11 3BJ
Tel/Fax: 01799 516878

Man Dir: P B Blanchard **Non-exec Chmn:** J M Wilson **Non-exec Dirs:** D C Grimmett, J N Raynham
Fleet: 9 - 5 coach, 3 midibus, 1 minibus.
Chassis: 3 Dennis. 1 Ford. 1 Leyland. 3 Mercedes. 1 Volvo
Bodies: 1 Duple. 1 Jonckheere. 6 Plaxton. 1 other.
Ops incl: local bus services, school contracts, excursions & tours, private hire.
Livery: White
Ticket System: AEG

WEST'S COACHES LTD
198/200 HIGH ROAD, WOODFORD GREEN IG8 9EF
Tel: 020 8504 9747
Fax: 020 8559 1085
Man Dir: R West
Fleet: 16 coach.
Ops incl: excursions & tours, private hire, school contracts.
Livery: White with red/blue stripes

GLOUCESTERSHIRE

ALEXCARS LTD

LOVE LANE INDUSTRIAL ESTATE, CIRENCESTER GL7 1YG
Tel: 01285 653985
Fax: 01285 652964
E-mail: rod@alexcars.co.uk
Man Dir: Rod Hibberd **Dirs:** Jenny Jarvis, Barbara Hibberd **Tran Man:** Will Jarvis
Co Sec: Glyn Daye **Ch Eng:** Steve Hall
Fleet: 20 - 1 single-deck bus, 13 coach, 3 midicoach, 3 minicoach.
Chassis: 1 Bedford. 11 Dennis. 3 MAN. 2 Scania. 3 Toyota.
Bodies: 1 Berkhof. 5 Caetano. 1 Duple. 3 Irizar. 1 Noge. 3 Plaxton. 3 Wadham Stringer. 3 Marco Polo.
Ops incl: local bus services, school contracts, excursions & tours, private hire, continental tours.
Livery: Duo Blue
Ticket System: Almex

K. W. BEARD LTD

VALLEY ROAD, CINDERFORD GL14 2PD
Tel: 01594 823031
Fax: 01594 825965
E-mail: beardscoaches.co@btconnect.com
Ch Eng: A Baker **Co Sec:** Mrs M Beard.
Fleet: 10 - 9 coach, 1 midicoach.
Chassis: 1 Bedford. 2 Bova. 1 DAF. 2 Leyland. 1 Mercedes. 1 Setra. 2 Volvo.
Bodies: 2 Bova. 1 Jonckheere. 4 Plaxton. 1 Setra. 1 Van Hool. 1 Onyx.
Ops incl: local bus services, school contracts, excursions & tours, private hire, continental tours.
Livery: White/Blue
Ticket System: Setright.

*B. E. W. BEAVIS/BEAVIS HOLIDAYS
BUSSAGE GARAGE, BUSSAGE, STROUD GL6 8BA
Tel: 01453 882297
Fax: 01453 731019
E-mail: beavisholidays@btopenworld.com
Props/Ptnrs: Brian Beavis, Anita Baxter
Fleet: 8 - 5 coach, 1 midicoach, 1 minicoach, 1 minibus.
Chassis: 1 DAF. 4 Neoplan. 1 Scania. 1 Toyota. 1 Volkswagen.
Bodies: 1 Caetano, 1 Irizar, 4 Neoplan. 2 other.
Ops incl: excursions & tours, private hire, school contracts, continental tours.
Livery: Gold/Orange/Red/Yellow.

BENNETT'S COACHES
EASTERN AVENUE, GLOUCESTER GL4 7LP.
Tel: 01452 527809.
Fax: 01452 384448.
Prop: Peter Bennett
Fleet: 24 - 6 double-deck bus, 18 coach.
Chassis: incl: Bristol. DAF. Ford. Leyland. 4 Optare
Bodies: Duple. ECW. 4 Optare. Plaxton. Van Hool.
Ops incl: local bus services, excursions & tours, private hire, continental tours.
Livery: Blue/Grey/Orange.

*JAMES BEVAN (LYDNEY) LTD
THE BUS STATION, HAMS ROAD, LYDNEY GL15 5PE
Tel/Fax: 01594 842859
E-mail: bevanbus@tiscali.co.uk
Man Dir: James Bevan **Sec:** J Zimmerman
Eng Dir: M Zimmerman
Fleet: 8 - 5 coach, 2 midibus, 1 midicoach.
Chassis: 3 Dennis. 2 Optare. 3 Volvo.
Bodies: 2 Optare. 2 Plaxton. 1 Sunsundegui. 3 Wadham Stringer.
Ops incl: local bus services, school contracts, excursions & tours, private hire.
Livery: Silver/Grey
Ticket System: Wayfarer

CASTLEWAYS LTD
CASTLE HOUSE, GREET ROAD, WINCHCOMBE GL54 5PU
Tel: 01242 603715
Fax: 01242 604454
Web site: www.castleways.co.uk
Man Dir: John Fogarty **Co Sec:** Rowena McCubbin **Ch Eng:** Trevor Wood
Fleet: 12 - 2 single-deck bus, 9 coach, 1 midicoach
Chassis: 1 Dennis. 2 Leyland. 8 Mercedes. 1 Toyota.
Bodies: 1 Caetano. 1 Mercedes. 3 Plaxton. 6 Setra. 1 Transbus.
Ops incl: local bus services, private hire.
Livery: Blue/Silver
Ticket System: Wayfarer

COTTRELLS COACHES
MILL END, MITCHELDEAN GL17 0HP
Tel: 01594 542224
Fax: 01594 542740
Prop: Edgar R Cottrell
Fleet: 12 - 4 double-deck bus, 2 single-deck bus, 5 coach, 1 double-deck coach
Chassis: 1 Dennis. 4 Leyland. 4 MCW. 3 Volvo.
Bodies: 1 Alexander. 1 Duple. 4 MCW. 5 Plaxton. 1 Wadham Stringer.

EAGLE LINE TRAVEL
ANDOVERSFORD TRADING ESTATE, ANDOVERSFORD GL54 4LB
Tel: 01242 820535
Fax: 01242 820637
E-mail: brian@eaglelinetravel.co.uk
Web site: www.eaglelinetravel.co.uk
Man Dirs: Brian Davis Martin Davis Wayne Hodge **Ch Eng**: Tony Mezzone
Fleet: 22 - 10 coach, 2 double-deck coach, 2 midibus, 4 midicoach, 2 minicoach, 2 minibus.
Chassis: 2 DAF. 2 Dennis. 4 Ford Transit. 6 Mercedes. 1 Neoplan. 1 Scania. Setra.1 Toyota. 5 Volvo.
Bodies: 2 Autobus. 2 Berkhof. 1 Caetano. 2 Mercedes. 4 Ford Transit. 1 Neoplan. 2 Plaxton. 6 Van Hool. 2 VW.
Ops incl: school contracts, excursions & tours, private hire, continental tours.
Livery: Dark Blue/Silver/Silver Blue

EBLEY COACHES LTD
R24
UNIT 27, NAILSWORTH MILLS ESTATE, AVENING ROAD, NAILSWORTH GL6 0BS
Tel/Fax: 01453 839333
Dirs: C C Levitt, G A Jones.
Fleet: 19 - 6 double-deck bus, 7 coach, 5 minibus, 1 minicoach
Chassis: 6 Bristol. 5 DAF. 1 Leyland. 1 MAN. 6 Mercedes.
Bodies: 4 Alexander. 1 Duple. 6 ECW. 1 Plaxton. 2 Reeve Burgess. 5 Van Hool.
Ops incl: local bus services, school contracts, excursions & tours, private hire, continental tours.

DAVID FIELD
WHEATSTONE HOUSE, WATERY LANE, NEWENT GL18 1PY
Tel: 01531 820979
Prop/Ch Eng: David Field.
Fleet: 9 - 5 coach, 1 midibus, 3 midicoach.
Chassis: 1 Bedford. 1 DAF. 1 Dennis. 1 Iveco. 1 Leyland. 2 Mercedes. 1 Setra. 1 Toyota.
Ops incl: local bus services, school contracts,private hire.
Livery: Black/White.

Ticket System: Setright.

GRINDLES COACHES LTD
4 DOCKHAM ROAD, CINDERFORD GL14 2DD.
Tel: 01594 822110.
Fax: 01594 823189.
Man Dir: P. R. Grindle. **Co Sec:** W. H. R. Grindle.
Fleet: 7 coach.
Chassis: 3 Bedford. 1 Bova. 3 DAF.
Bodies: 1 Bova. 5 Plaxton. 1 Van Hool.
Ops incl: local bus services, private hire.

*MARCHANTS COACHES LTD
61 CLARENCE STREET GL50 3LB
Tel: 01242 257714
Fax: 01242 251360
E-mail: info@marchants-coaches.com
Web site: www.marchants-coaches.com
Man Dir: Roger Marchant **Dir/Ops Man**: Richard Marchant
Fleet: 24 -5 double-deck bus, 6 single-deck bus, 10 coach, 2 double-deck coach, 1 midicoach.
Chassis: 2 Bristol. 3 Leyland. 1 Mercedes. 2 Neoplan. 16 Volvo.
Bodies: 1 Alexander. 4 ECW. 4 Jonckheere. 2 Neoplan. 10 Plaxton. 3 Wright.
Ops incl: local bus services, school contracts, excursions & tours, private hire, continental tours.
Livery: Red/Gold
Ticket System: Wayfarer/Setright

*ROVER EUROPEAN TRAVEL LTD
THE COACH HOUSE, HORSLEY, STROUD GL6 0PU
Tel: 01453 832121
Fax: 01453 832722
E-mail: rovereuropean@compuserve.com
Man Dir: David Hand **Dir**: Carol Hand
Fleet: 11 - 10 coach, 1 midicoach
Chassis: 7 Bova. 3 Dennis. 1 Toyota.
Bodies: 1 Berkhof. 7 Bova. 1 Caetano. 1 Plaxton. 1 Wadham Stringer.
Ops incl: school contracts, excursions & tours, private hire, continental tours.
Livery: Cream base with Light Blue/Dark Blue/Orange.

*STAGECOACH WEST
3RD FLOOR, 65 LONDON ROAD, GLOUCESTER GL1 3HF
Tel: 01452 418630
Fax: 01452 304857
E-mail: enquiries@stagecoach-west.com
Web site: www.stagecoach-west.co.uk

Man Dir: I R Manning **Eng Dir**: P Sheldon
Ops Dir: S D V Thomas
Fleet: 242 - 75 double-deck bus, 36 single-deck bus, 3 coach, 112 midibus, 16 minibus.
Ops incl: local bus services, school contracts.
Livery: multicolour
Ticket System: Wayfarer 3

*STAGECOACH IN SOUTH WALES
See Torfaen

SWANBROOK TRANSPORT LTD
GOLDEN VALLEY, STAVERTON, CHELTENHAM GL51 0TE
Tel: 01452 712386
Fax: 01452 859217
E-mail: enquiries@swanbrook.co.uk
Web site: www.swanbrook.co.uk
Fleetname: Swanbrook Bus
Chmn: D J Thomas **Co Sec**: K J Thomas
Dir: Mrs K J West **Ch Eng**: G Hooper **Ops Man**: M Bowle
Fleet: 29 - 11 double-deck bus, 8 single-deck bus, 6 coach, 4 midibus.
Chassis: 2 Dennis. 1 Iveco. 5 Leyland. 8 MCW. 3 Mercedes. 5 Optare. 1 Scania. 4 Volvo.
Bodies: 3 Alexander. 1 Berkof. 1 East Lancs. 1 Irizar. 2 Marshall. 8 MCW. 5 Optare. 4 Plaxton. 4 Reeve Burgess.
Ops incl: local bus services, school contracts, private hire.
Livery: Blue/Purple
Ticket System: Wayfarer 2

F R WILLETTS & CO (YORKLEY) LTD
DEAN RISE, MAIN ROAD, PILLOWELL GL15 4QY
Tel: 01594 562511
Fax: 01594 564373
Man Dir: Geoff Willetts **Sec**: Sue Willetts
Fleet: 6 - 4 coach, 1 minicoach, 1 minibus.
Chassis: 1 Dennis. 1 Leyland. 2 Mercedes. 1 Setra. 1 Volvo.
Bodies: 1 Mercedes. 4 Plaxton. 1 Setra.
Ops incl: local bus services, school contracts, excursions & tours, private hire.
Livery: Red
Ticket System: Setright.

*MAL WITTS EXECUTIVE TRAVEL
1 YEW TREE COTTAGE, BRISTOL ROAD, HARDWICKE, GLOUCESTER GL2 4QZ
Tel/Fax: 01452 724072
E-mail: mal@malwittstravel.co.uk
Web site: www.malwittstravel.co.uk
Owners: Mal Witts, Lynn Witts
Fleet: 4 - 2 minicoach, 2 people carrier
Bodies: 2 Mercedes, 2 VW
Ops incl: private hire, continental tours.

A/c	Air conditioning
	Vehicles suitable for disabled
	Coach(es) with galley facilities
WC	Coach(es) with toilet facilities
	Seat belt-fitted vehicles
R	Recovery service available (not 24 hr)
R24	24hr recovery service
	Replacement vehicle available
T	Toilet-drop facilities available
	Vintage vehicle(s) available
	Open top vehicle(s)

Gloucestershire

GREATER MANCHESTER (BOLTON, BURY, OLDHAM, ROCHDALE, SALFORD, TAMESIDE, WIGAN)

*ADLINGTON TAXIS AND MINICOACHES
LODGE FARM, SANDY LANE, HORWICH BL6 6RS
Tel: 01204 697577
E-mail: frank@fjohnson7.wanado.co.uk
Fleet: 5 - 2 single-deck bus, 1 coach, 2 midicoach.
Chassis: 1 Bedford. 2 Freight Rover. 2 Iveco.
Ops incl: local bus services, private hire.
Ticket System: Wayfarer

ASHALL'S COACHES

612 ASHTON NEW ROAD, CLAYTON M11 4SG
Tel: 0161 231 7777
Fax: 0906 528 0920
Prop: D S Ashall
Fleet: 20 - 6 double-deck bus, 4 single-deck bus, 8 single-deck coach, 2 midicoach.
Chassis: 15 Dennis. 2 Mercedes. 1 Scania. 2 Volvo.
Bodies: 2 Duple. 2 Mellor. 6 Northern Counties. 2 Plaxton. 2 Transbus. 6 Wadham Stringer.
Ops incl: local bus services, school contracts, private hire.
Livery: Red
Ticket system: Wayfarer 2

BATTERSBY'S COACHES

73 BRIDGEWATER ROAD, WALKDEN M28 3AF
Tel/Fax: 0161 790 2842
Dirs: R W Griffiths, S. J. Griffiths
Fleet: 3 coach.
Chassis: 1 Leyland. 2 Setra.
Ops incl: private hire, school contracts.

BLUE BUS & COACH SERVICES LTD
See Lancashire

*BLUEBIRD BUS & COACH
ALEXANDER HOUSE, GREENGATE, MIDDLETON M24 1RU
Tel: 0161 653 1900
Fax: 0161 653 6602
Web site: www.bluebirdbus.co.uk
Gen Man: Michael T G Dunstan
Fleet: 40 single-deck bus.
Chassis: incl: 24 Dennis. 5 MAN. 1 Optare.
Bodies: incl: 12 Alexander. 3 Caetano. 11 East Lancs. 1 Marshall. 3 Wright.
Ops incl: local bus services.
Livery: two-tone Blue.
Ticket System: ERG

*A & H BOOTH LTD
 (with driver)
GROSVENOR GARAGE, DOWSON ROAD, HYDE SK14 5BN
Tel: 0161 368 2413
Dir: D Mycock
Fleet: 3 - 2 coach, 1 minicoach.
Chassis: 1 DAF. 1 Ford. 1 LDV.
Bodies: 1 Caetano. 1 Plaxton. 1 other.
Ops incl: private hire, continental tours.

R BULLOCK & CO (TRANSPORT) LTD

COMMERCIAL GARAGE, STOCKPORT ROAD, CHEADLE SK8 2AG
Tel: 0161 428 5265.
Fax: 0161 428 9074.
E-mail: bullockscoaches@talk21.com
Web site: www.bullockscoaches.co.uk
Fleet: 63 - double-deck bus, single-deck bus, coach, minibus
Livery: Red/White.

*BU-VAL BUSES LTD
UNIT 5, PARAGON INDUSTRIAL ESTATE, WALSDEN OL15 8QF
Tel: 01706 372787
Tel: 01706 372121
Man Dir: Martin Bull **Co Sec**: David Beames
Fleet: 20 midibus.
Chassis: 11 Dennis. 7 Marshall. 2 Optare.
Bodies: 2 Caetano. 7 Marshall/MCV. 2 Optare. 6 Plaxton. 2 Transbus. 1 UVG.
Ops incl: local bus services
Livery: White/Red
Ticket System: Wayfarer 386

LES BYWATER & SONS LTD

SPARTH BOTTOMS ROAD, ROCHDALE OL11 4HT.
Tel: 01706 648573.
Man Dir: M. T. Bywater. **Dir**: N. L. Bywater.
Fleet: 3 - 1 coach, 1 minibus, 1 minibus.
Chassis: 1 Dennis. 2 Iveco.
Bodies: 1 Duple. 2 Robin Hood.
Ops incl: private hire, school contracts.
Livery: White/Blue/Black.

CARSVILLE COACHES

51A HIGHER ROAD, URMSTON M41 9AP
Tel: 0161 748 2698
Fax: 0161 747 2694
E-mail: janetcarsville@hotmail.com
Man Dir: Dave Dickson
Fleet: 13 - 2 double-deck bus, 10 coach, 1 midicoach.
Chassis: 1 Bedford. 2 Ford. 4 Scania. 3 Volvo.
Bodies: 1 Caetano. 1 East Lancs. 1 Leyland. 1 Marcopolo. 5 Plaxton. 1 Van Hool.
Ops incl: private hire, excursions & tours, school contracts.
Livery: White/Purple.

*COACH OPTIONS LTD

768 MANCHESTER ROAD, CASTLETON, ROCHDALE OL11 3AW
Tel: 01706 712966
Fax: 01706 759996
E-mail: coach.options@freeuk.com
Prop: Paul R Stone
Fleet: 9 - 5 single-deck coach, 1 midicoach, 3 minibus.
Chassis: 2 Bova. 2 Ford Transit. 1 Irisbus. 1 Mercedes. 2 Scania.
Ops incl: excursions & tours, private hire, continental tours, school contracts.
Livery: Blue

COACHWAYS LTD

MANDALE PARK, CORPORATION ROAD, ROCHDALE OL11 4HJ
Tel: 01706 712321
Fax: 01706 632875
E-mail: coachhire@coachways.co.uk
Web site: www.coachways.co.uk
Man Dir: Edgar Oldman **Comm Dir**: Barry Drelincourt **Coach Man**: Ian Smithson
Fleet: 6 coach
Chassis: 1 Dennis. 5 Volvo.
Bodies: 3 Plaxton. 3 Sunsundegui.
Ops incl: school contracts, private hire, express.
Livery: White

CROPPER COACHES

316 BURY ROAD, TOTTINGTON BL8 3DT
Tel: 01204 885322.
Prop: L. Donnell.
Fleet: 7 minibus.
Chassis: 5 Ford Transit. 1 Freight Rover.
Ops incl: private hire, school contracts.

DAM EXPRESS
GROVE HOUSE, 27 MANOR STREET, ARDWICK GREEN M12 6HE.
Tel: 0161 273 1234.
Fax: 0161 274 4141.
Fleetname: Don Travel.
Prop/Ops Man: D. Francis.
Sales Man: W. Lee. **Co Sec**: Miss T. Wilding.
Fleet: 3 - 1 coach, 2 double-deck coach.
Ops incl: excursions & tours, private hire, express, continental tours.

ELITE SERVICES LTD

UNIT 6, ADSWOOD ROAD INDUSTRIAL ESTATE, ADSWOOD ROAD, STOCKPORT SK3 8LF.
Tel: 0161 480 0617.
Fax: 0161 480 3099.
Dirs: D R Nickson, A Roberts
Fleet: 10 - 8 coach, 2 double-deck coach.
Chassis: Ford. Leyland. Mercedes. Scania. Volvo.
Bodies: Duple. Jonckheere. Mercedes. Plaxton. Van Hool.
Ops incl: excursions & tours, private hire, continental tours, school contracts.
Livery: White/Purple.
(Part of the Elite Group)

*FINGLANDS COACHWAYS LTD

261 WILMSLOW ROAD, RUSHOLME, MANCHESTER M14 5LJ
Tel: 0161 224 3341
Fax: 0161 257 3154
E-mail: enquiry@finglands.co.uk
Web site: www.finglands.co.uk
Chmn: P J S Shipp **Dirs**: D Shurden, P Harrison **Fleet Eng**: T Jenkins **Coaching Man**: F Walton
Fleet: 55 - 45 double-deck bus, 10 coach
Chassis: 2 Dennis. 53 Volvo.
Bodies: 24 Alexander. 15 Northern Counties. 15 Plaxton. 1 Van Hool.
Ops incl: local bus services, school contracts, private hire.
Livery: White/Orange/Brown/Gold
Ticket System: Wayfarer TGX150

*FIRST IN MANCHESTER

WALLSHAW STREET, OLDHAM OL1 3TR
Tel: 0161 627 2929
Fax: 0161 627 5845
Fleetname: First
Man Dir: Ian Davies **Business Dir/Dep Man Dir**: Alan Pilbeam **Fin Dir**: Martin Wilson **Eng Dir**: Colin Stafford **Service Delivery Dir**: Robert Mason **Network Dir**: Simon Bennet
Fleet: 862 - 136 double-deck bus, 450 single-deck bus, 199 midibus, 34 articulated bus, 43 minibus.
Chassis: BMC. Dennis. Irisbus. Leyland. MCW. Mercedes. Optare. Scania. Volvo.
Bodies: BMC. ECW. East Lancs. Irisbus. Leyland. Marshall. Mercedes. Northern Counties. Optare. Scania. Transbus. Wright.
Ops incl: local bus services, school contracts, private hire.
Livery: First - Magenta/Blue & Grey/White
Ticket System: ERG TP4004

FREEBIRD

REVERS STREET GARAGE, WOODHILL BL8 1AQ
Tel: 0161 797 6633
Fax: 08712 773214
Recovery: 0161 797 6633
E-mail: info@freebirdcoaches.co.uk
Web site: www.freebirdcoaches.co.uk
Owner: Paul Dart **Man**: Rob Dart
Fleet: 15 - 6 coach, 4 midicoach, 5 minibus.
Chassis: 1 DAF. 1 Dennis. 2 Ford Transit. 3 LDV. 4 Mercedes. 4 Volvo.
Bodies: 1 Berkhof. 3 Plaxton. 2 Van Hool. 4 Balmoral.
Ops incl: excursions & tours, private hire, school contracts, continental tours.
Livery: White with maroon writing

HAYTON'S EXECUTIVE TRAVEL LTD

12 ACORN CLOSE, BURNAGE M19 2HS
Tel: 0161 223 3103
Fax: 0161 223 9528

Prop: Barry Hayton **Dir/Sec**: Barry A Hayton
Fleet: 17 - 3 double-deck bus, 3 single-deck bus, 10 coach, 1 midibus
Chassis: 3 MAN. 1 Neoplan. 1 Optare. 1 Setra. 10 Volvo.
Bodies: 2 East Lancs. 2 Jonckheere. 1 Noge. 2 Optare. 4 Plaxton. 1 Setra. 4 Van Hool.
Ops incl: local bus services, school contracts, excursions & tours, private hire, express, continental tours.
Livery: White

*HEALINGS INTERNATIONAL COACHES

251 HIGGINSHAW LANE, ROYTON, OLDHAM OL2 6HW
Tel: 0161 624 8975
Fax: 0161 652 0320
Ptnrs: Philip Healing, Richard Healing
Fleet: 7 - 5coach, 1 midicoach, 1 minicoach.
Chassis: 1 DAF. 1 Mercedes. 1 Scania. 1 Toyota. 1 Volvo. 2 Duple425
Ops incl: school contracts, excursions & tours, private hire, continental tours.
Livery: White with coloured decals

JONES EXECUTIVE COACHES LTD

THE COACH STATION, SHARP STREET, WALKDEN M28 3LX
Tel: 0161 790 9495
Fax: 0161 790 9400
Web site: www.jonesexecutive.co.uk
E-mail: simonjones@supanet.com
Man Dir: Simon Jones **Tran Man**: Peter Wragg
Fleet: 7 - 6 coach, 1 minicoach
Chassis: 2 DAF. 2 Iveco. 1 Mercedes. 1 Scania. 1 Volvo.
Bodies: 2 Beulas. 1 Duple. 1 Mercedes. 1 Plaxton. 2 Van Hool.
Ops incl: local bus services, school contracts, private hire.
Livery: Blue/Red/Gold

*LAMBS COACHES

2A BUXTON STREET, HAZEL GROVE, STOCKPORT SK7 4BB
Tel: 0161 456 1515
Fax: 0161 456 5011
E-mail: lambs139@aol.com
Man Dir: Geoff Lamb **Dir**: Graham Lamb
Fleet: 6 coach
Chassis: 1 Bova. 2 DAF. 2 Scania. 1 Volvo.
Bodies: 1 Bova. 5 Van Hool.
Ops incl: private hire, school contracts.
Livery: Blue/White

LENDOR MINI COACHES

17 VALLEY CLOSE, MOSSLEY OL5 0NH
Tel/Fax: 01457 832845
Prop: Leonard E Glynn
Fleet: 4 minibus
Chassis: 1 Ford Transit. 1 Iveco.

2 Mercedes.
Ops incl: private hire, school contracts.

MARPLE MINI COACHES

5 GROSVENOR ROAD, MARPLE SK6 6PR.
Tel: 0161 881 9111.
Owner: G. W. Cross.
Fleet: 2 minicoach.
Chassis: Ford Transit. LDV.
Ops incl: school contracts, private hire.
Livery: White/Gold.

*A MAYNE & SON LTD

ASHTON NEW ROAD, CLAYTON M11 4PD
Tel: 0161 223 2035
E-mail: coaches@mayne.co.uk
Web site: www.mayne.co.uk
Fleetname: Mayne of Manchester
Man Dir/Chmn: S B Mayne **Gen Man/Dir**: G R Thompson **Co Sec/Dir**: D Mayne **Ch Eng**: C Pannell **Comm Man**: A K Nuttall
Fleet: 58 - 26 double-deck bus, 13 single-deck bus, 19 coach.
Chassis: 4 Bova. 16 Dennis. 34 Scania.. 4 Volvo.
Bodies: 4 Bova. 20 East Lancs. 6 Irizar. 6 Marshall. 7 Northern Counties. 7 Plaxton. 2 UVG. 6 Wright.
Ops incl: local bus services, school contracts, excursions & tours, private hire.
Livery: Red/Cream
Ticket system: ERG/AES Prodata

METROLINK

SERCO METROLINK, METROLINK HOUSE, QUEENS ROAD, MANCHESTER M8 0RY
Tel: 0161 205 8685
Fax: 0161 205 8699
Web site: www.gmpte.co.uk
Man Dir: Phil Smith
Fleet: 28 - tram
Chassis: GEC Alstom
Bodies: Firema
Ops incl: tram service

*DAVID PLATT COACHES & MINITRAVEL OF LEES

8 THE WOODS, GROTTON, SADDLEWORTH, OLDHAM OL4 4LP
Tel/Fax: 0161 633 4845
Props: David Platt
Fleet: 2 - 1 coach, 1 minicoach.
Chassis: 1 Bedford. 1 Toyota.
Bodies: 1 Caetano. 1 Plaxton.
Ops incl: private hire.
Livery: Aqua/White

*SELWYNS TRAVEL SERVICES

BUILDING 77, TERMINAL 2, MANCHESTER AIRPORT M90 1QX
Tel: 0161 489 5720
Fax: 0161 499 9157

♨	Air conditioning
♿	Vehicles suitable for disabled
🍴	Coach(es) with galley facilities
wc	Coach(es) with toilet facilities
♥	Seat belt-fitted vehicles
R	Recovery service available (not 24 hr)
R24	24hr recovery service
🔧	Replacement vehicle available
T	Toilet-drop facilities available
🚌	Vintage vehicle(s) available
🚐	Open top vehicle(s)

E-mail: sales@selwyns.co.uk
Web site: www.selwyns.co.uk
Man Dir: Selwyn A Jones **Co Sec/Acct**: Richard E Williams **Fleet Eng**: Cledwyn Owen **Ops Man**: John Miller
Fleet: 18 - 7 coach, 2 midibus, 3 minicoach, 6 minicoach.
Chassis: 4 DAF. 1 Dennis. 9 Mercedes. 2 Optare. 2 Volvo.
Bodies: 1 Berkhof. 8 Mercedes. 2 Optare. 3 Plaxton. 4 Van Hool.
Ops incl: local bus services, school contracts, private hire.
Livery: White/Blue/Orange/Green
Ticket System: Wayfarer

SMITHS COACHES (MARPLE) LTD

72 CROSS LANE, MARPLE SK6 7PZ
Tel: 0161 427 2825.
Fax: 0161 449 7731.
Man Dir: J Hibbert
Fleet: 6 - 2 double-deck bus, 3 coach, 1 midibus.
Chassis: 2 Bristol. 2 Dennis. 1 Iveco. 1 Volvo.
Bodies: 1 Caetano. 2 ECW. 2 Neoplan.
Ops incl: local bus services, school contracts, excursions & tours, private hire, continental tours.
Livery: White/Orange-Rose.
(Part of the Elite Group)

SOUTH LANCS TRAVEL
UNIT 22/23, CHANTERS INDUSTRIAL ESTATE, ATHERTON M46 9BP
Tel: 01942 888893
Fax: 01942 894010
Man Dir: Martin Bott **Eng Dir**: D A Stewart
Tran Man: W Peach
Fleet: 50 - double-deck bus, single-deck bus, midibus
Chassis: incl: 2 Optare
Bodies: incl: 2 Optare
Ops incl: local bus services, tram service, school contracts
Livery: Yellow/Blue
Ticket System: Wayfarer 3

*STAGECOACH MANCHESTER
HEAD OFFICE, HYDE ROAD, MANCHESTER M12 6JS
Tel: 0161 273 3377
Fax: 0161 271 2594
E-mail: manchester.enquiries@stagecoachbus.com
Web site: www.stagecoachbus.com/manchester
Man Dir: M Threapleton **Ops Dir**: E Tasker.
Comm Dir: R A Cossins **Eng Dir**: D Roe
Ser Performance Man: A Wilson **Network Man**: J K Young **Mktng Man**: K Coventry
Personnel man: J E Crenigan
Fleet: 653 - 366 double-deck bus, 213 single-deck bus, 1 coach, 45 midibus, 33 minibus.
Chassis: 260 Dennis. 4 Iveco. 44 Leyland. 124 MAN. 33 Mercedes. 35 Scania. 158 Volvo.
Bodies: 443 Alexander. 20 Duple. 7 East Lancs. 1 Neoplan. 89 Northern Counties. 94 Plaxton. 4 other.
Ops incl: local bus services.
Livery: Blue/Orange/Red/White
Ticket System: ERG

STOTT'S TOURS (OLDHAM) LTD
144 LEES ROAD, OLDHAM OL4 1HT
Tel: 0161 624 4200.
Fax: 0161 628 2969.
Prop: A. Stott.
Ops incl: school contracts.
Livery: Cream/Red/Black.

VALES COACHES (MANCHESTER) LTD
49 BROUGHTON STREET, MANCHESTER M8 8AN
Tel: 0161 832 9445.
Fleetname: Vale of Manchester.
Dir: P. D. Green. **Dir/Sec**: G. L. Green
Fleet: 20 midibus.
Chassis: 20 Mercedes.
Bodies: 2 Alexander. 1 Carlyle. 13 Plaxton. 4 Reeve Burgess.
Ops incl: local bus services, private hire.
Livery: Blue/Cream
Ticket System: Wayfarer 2

VIKING COACHES
DOCTOR FOLD FARM, DOCTOR FOLD LANE, BIRCH, HEYWOOD OL10 2QE.
Tel: 01706 368999.
Fax: 01706 620011.
E-mail: viking@coaches76.freeserve
Web site: www.coach-day-trips
Owners: A. Warburton, Ms A. Warburton.
Fleet: 4 coach.
Chassis: Volvo. Iveco.
Bodies: Beulas. Plaxton. Van Hool.
Ops incl: excursions & tours, private hire, continental tours, school contracts.
Livery: Viking Ship.

*W A SHEARINGS LTD
MIRY LANE, WIGAN WN3 4AG
Tel: 01942 244246
Fax: 01942 824978
E-mail: coachhire@washearings.com
Web site: www.washearings.com
Chmn: Bernard Norman **ChExec**: John Slatcher **Fin Dir**: David Newbold
Ops Dir (Transport): Jimmy King **Fleet Eng**: Barry Mace
Fleet: 282 coach
Chassis: 282 Volvo.
Bodies: 73 Jonckheere. 81 Plaxton. 6 Sunsundegui. 122 Van Hool.
Ops incl: excursions & tours, private hire, continental tours.
Livery: Miami Blue or Gold

*WRIGLEY'S COACHES LTD

4 FIDDLERS LANE, IRLAM M44 6QE
Tel: 0161 775 2414
Fax: 0161 775 1558
E-mail: sales@wrigleyscoaches.com
Web site: www.wrigleyscoaches.com
Man Dir: Colin Wrigley **Co Sec/Dir**: Lesley Wrigley **Ops Man**: Alan Grice
Fleet: 8 - 1 double-deck bus, 4 coach, 2 double-deck coach, 1 minicoach.
Chassis: 1 Leyland. 2 MAN. 1 Neoplan. 1 Setra. 1 Toyota. 2 Volvo.
Bodies: 1 Alexander. 1 Caetano. 3 Neoplan. 1 Plaxton. 1 Setra. 1 Van Hool.
Ops incl: private hire, school contracts.
Livery: Blue/White

HAMPSHIRE

*AIRLYNX TRAVEL
THE SYCAMORES, OAKLEY ROAD, SOUTHAMPTON SO16 4LJ
Tel: 023 8039 9078
Fax: 023 8077 7724
Man Dir: Dominic Brown **Co Sec**: Michael Rudder **Ops Man**: Steven Gear
Fleet: 11 - 1 midicoach, 1 midibus, 8 minibus.
Chassis: 1 Dennis. 4 Ford Transit. 1 Mercedes. 5 Sprinter.
Ops incl: private hire, school contracts, local bus services.
Livery: Blue/Yellow

*ALTONIAN COACHES

THE DEPOT, MILL LANE TRADING ESTATE, ALTON GU34 2QJ
Tel: 01420 84839
Fax: 01420 84803
Dirs: R Turner, S P Austen **Ops Man**: M Jones **Ch Eng**: K Tillin
Fleet: 17 -11 coach, 3 minibus, 2 minibus, 1 minicoach.
Chassis: 1 DAF. 9 Dennis. 1 Ford Transit. 1 Leyland. 1 Mercedes. 1 Optare. 1 Renault. 2 Setra.
Bodies: 1 Autobus. 1 Caetano. 3 Duple. 1 Irizar. 4 Neoplan. 1 Optare. 2 Plaxton. 1 Reeve Burgess. 2 Van Hool. 1 Wadham Stringer.
Ops incl: local bus services, school contracts, excursions & tours, private hire, continental tours.
Livery: Orange (cream lettering)

AMK
MILL LANE, PASSFIELD, LIPHOOK GU30 7RP
Tel: 01428 751675
Fax: 01428 751677
E-mail: info@amkxl.com
Web site: www.amkxl.com
Ptnrs: K Moger, A Moger, S Moger.
Fleet: 78 - 65 minibus, 3 midibus, 10 minicoach.
Ops inc: local bus services, school contracts, excursions & tours, private hire.

*AMPORT & DISTRICT COACHES LTD
EASTFIELD HOUSE, AMESBURY ROAD, THRUXTON, ANDOVER SP11 8ED
Tel: 01264 772307
Fax: 01264 773020
E-mail: tedd@onetel.net
Dirs: P J Tedd, A M Tedd, N B Tedd
Fleet: 9 - 7 coach, 2 midicoach.
Chassis: 2 Mercedes. 2 Scania. 1 Setra. 4 Volvo.
Bodies: 1 Autobus. 3 Berkhof. 4 Plaxton. 1 Setra.
Ops incl: private hire, continental tours, school contracts.

Livery: White

*ANGELA COACHES LTD

OAKTREE HOUSE, LOWFORD, BURSLEDON SO31 8ES
Tel: 023 8040 3170
Fax: 023 8040 6487
E-mail: robert@angelacoaches.com
Web site: www.angelacoaches.com
Man Dir: M J Pressley **Co Sec**: Mrs H M Pressley **Ops Dir**: R J Pressley
Ch Eng: D Evans **Ops Man**: J Davies
Fleet: 9 - 3 coach, 1 midicoach, 5 minicoach.
Chassis: 5 Irisbus. 2 Mercedes. 2 Toyota.
Bodies: 4 Beulas. 1 Indcar. 4 other.
Ops incl: private hire, school contracts.
Livery: Maroon/White

AVENSIS COACH TRAVEL LTD t/a BUDDENS

29 PREMIER WAY, ABBEY PARK, ROMSEY SO51 9DQ
Tel: 01794 515260
Fax: 01794 512260
E-mail: sales@buddens-coaches.co.uk
Web site: www.buddens-coaches.co.uk
Dirs: Graham Humby, Simon Humby, Zak la Gumina
Fleet: 8 coach.
Chassis: 6 Scania. 2 Volvo.
Bodies: 2 Berkhof. 6 Irizar.
Ops incl: excursions & tours, private hire, continental tours.
Livery: Yellow/Purple

BYNGS INTERNATIONAL COACHES
1B ANGERSTEIN ROAD, NORTH END, PORTSMOUTH PO2 8HJ.
Tel: 023 9266 2223
Fax: 023 9267 8464
Dirs: Paul Grant, Trevor Grant. **Fleet Eng**: John Hampton.
Fleet: 40 - 1 single-deck bus, 37 coach, 1 midicoach, 1 minicoach.
Chassis: 10 Bova. 2 DAF. 2 Dennis. 4 Leyland. 4 Mercedes. 7 Scania. 1 Toyota. 10 Volvo.
Bodies: 10 Bova. 2 DAF. 2 Dennis. 4 irizar. 2 Jonckheere. 4 mercedes. 11 Plaxton. 7 Van Hool.
Ops incl: excursions & tours, private hire, school contracts.
Livery: Silver/Brown.

A. S. BONE & SONS
LONDON ROAD, HOOK RG27 9EQ
Tel: 01256 761388, 762106
Fleetname: Newnham Coaches
Man Dir: J. E. Bone. **Co Sec**: Mrs M. Bone.
Fleet: 5 - 3 double-deck bus, 2 single-deck bus.
Chassis: 1 Bristol. 2 Daimler. 2 Leyland National.
Ops incl: private hire.
Livery: Cream/Blue.

*BRIJAN TOURS LTD

THE COACH STATION, ABBEY MILL, BISHOPS WALTHAM SO32 1DH
Tel: 01489 892942
Fax: 01489 896361
Recovery: 01489 892942
E-mail: sales@brijantours.com
Man Dir: Brian Botley **Co Sec**: Janet Botley
Ops Man: Brian Bedford **Fleet Eng**: Colin Batten
Fleet: 24 - 7 double-deck bus, 7 coach, 7 midibus, 3 midicoach.
Chassis: 2 Bristol. 2 Dennis. 1 Iveco. 3 Leyland. 2 MCW. 9 Mercedes. 2 Scania. 3 Volvo.
Bodies: 2 Alexander. 3 Autobus. 2 ECW. 1 Irizar. 2 MCW. 1 Mellor. 1 Northern Counties. 1 Park Royal. 9 Plaxton. 1 Van Hool.
Ops incl: local bus services, school contracts, excursions & tours, private hire
Livery: coaches: Cream/Grey/Burgundy. Buses: Solent Blue Line livery
Ticket system: Wayfarer

*CLEGG & BROOKING COACHES
WHITE HORSE SERVICE STATION, MIDDLE WALLOP SO20 8DZ
Tel: 01264 781283
Fax: 01264 781679
E-mail: cleggandbrooking@btconnect.com
Dirs: Kevin Brooking, Jeanette Cook
Fleet: 10 - 1 double-deck bus, 6 coach, 1 midibus, 2 midicoach
Chassis: 3 Dennis. 1 Leyland. 1 Mercedes. 3 Scania. 2 Toyota. 1 Volvo.
Ops incl: local bus services, private hire, school contracts.
Livery: Blue/Grey

*COLISEUM COACHES LTD
BOTLEY ROAD GARAGE, WEST END, SOUTHAMPTON SO30 3JA
Tel: 023 8047 2377
Fax: 023 8047 6537
E-mail: info@coliseumcoaches.co.uk
Web site: www.coliseumcoaches.co.uk
Man Dirs: David Pitter, Kerry Pitter
Ch Eng: Dave Rowsell
Fleet: 12 coach.
Chassis: 12 MAN.
Bodies: 12 Neoplan
Ops incl: excursions & tours, private hire, continental tours.
Livery: Silver (Coliseum fleet); Red/White (Coliseum/Angela Holidays fleet)

A/c	Air conditioning	
	Vehicles suitable for disabled	
	Coach(es) with galley facilities	
wc	Coach(es) with toilet facilities	
	Seat belt-fitted vehicles	
R	Recovery service available (not 24 hr)	
R24	24hr recovery service	
	Replacement vehicle available	
T	Toilet-drop facilities available	
	Vintage vehicle(s) available	
	Open top vehicle(s)	

COOPERS COACHES
31-35 LAKE ROAD, WOOLSTON
SO19 9EB
Tel: 023 8039 3393
Fax: 023 8044 4929.
Prop: Stephen Cooper
Fleet: 8 - 5 coach, 2 minibus, 1 midicoach.
Chassis: 1 DAF. 1 Ford Transit. 1 LDV.
1 Mercedes. 4 Volvo.
Bodies: 1 Caetano. 1 Ikarus. 2 Plaxton.
1 Van Hool. 1 Robin Hood.
Ops incl: local bus services, school contracts, private hire.
Livery: Cream/Pine/Burgundy

RAY DUNN COACH TRAVEL

COACH HOUSE, 48 BRITANNIA GARDENS, HEDGE END SO30 2RP
Tel: 01489 797990
Fax: 01489 797990
E-mail: rdunncoachtravel@yahoo.co.uk
Prop: Ray Dunn **Ptnr**: Mrs Sally Dunn
Fleet: 9 - 7 coach, 2 minibus.
Chassis: 2 Ford Transit. 4 Mercedes. 3 Volvo.
Ops incl: local bus services, school contracts, private hire

EASSONS COACHES LTD

44 WODEHOUSE ROAD, ITCHEN SO19 2EQ
Tel: 023 8044 8153
Fax: 023 8044 1635
Dirs: R. A. Easson, D. H. Easson.
Fleet: 10 - 7 coach, 2 midicoach, 1 minibus.
Chassis: 3 Mercedes. 1 Neoplan. 3 Setra. 2 Volvo. 1 Van Hool.
Bodies: 1 Mercedes. 1 Neoplan. 2 Plaxton. 3 Setra. 1 Van Hool. 2 Robin Hood.
Ops incl: excursions & tours, private hire, continental tours.
Livery: Cream/Khaki Brown.

EMSWORTH & DISTRICT MOTOR SERVICES LTD

THE BUS GARAGE, CLOVELLY ROAD, SOUTHBOURNE PO10 8PE
Tel: 01243 378337
Fax: 01243 389424
E-mail: caren@emsworth+district.co.uk
Web site: www.emsworth+district.co.uk
Dirs: Paul Lea, Caren Austin, Marion Lea
Fleet: 8 - 3 double-deck bus, 1 midicoach, 2 minibus, 2 minicoach.
Chassis: 5 Bedford. 1 DAF. 1 Daimler. 4 Dennis. 1 Ford Transit. 9 Leyland. 1 MAN. 3 Mercedes. 1 Optare. 1 Van Hool.
Bodies: 1 Alexander. 1 Autobus. 1 Berkhof. 1 Carlyle. 2 Leyland. 2 Marshall. 1 MCW. 2 Mercedes. 1 Optare. 6 Plaxton. 6 Reeve Burgess. 5 Van Hool. 1 Wadham Stringer. 1 Chassis Developments.
Ops incl: local bus services, school contracts, excursions & tours, private hire, continental tours.

FIRST HAMPSHIRE & DORSET LTD
 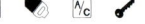
226 PORTSWOOD ROAD, SOUTHAMPTON SO17 2BE
Tel: 023 8058 4321
Fax: 023 8067 1448
Web site: www.firstgroup.com
E-mail: hampshire-dorset.csc@firstgroup.com
Man Dir: Richard Soper **Dep Man Dir**: Marc Reddy **Eng Dir**: David Toy **Fin Dir**: Ian Stone **Ops Dir**: Mike Smith **Ops Man**: Chris Bainbridge **Ops Eng**: Mike Britten
Comm Man: Kenneth Cobb
Fleet: 444 - 83 double-deck bus, 76 single-deck bus, 11 coach, 5 open-top bus, 179 midibus, 90 minibus.
Chassis: 7 Bristol. 177 Dennis. 36 Iveco. 32 Leyland. 67 Mercedes. 7 Optare. 26 Scania. 92 Volvo.
Bodies: 33 Alexander. 7 ECW. 26 East Lancs. 9 Leyland. 47 Marshall. 20 Northern Counties. 7 Optare. 124 Plaxton. 11 Roe. 1 Van Hool. 79 Wright. 80 other.
Ops incl: local bus services, school contracts, private hire

FLYGHT TRAVEL

3A SPUR ROAD, COSHAM PO6 3DY.
Tel: 023 9232 7703.
Fax: 023 9238 2900.
Chairm: J. Stewart. **Tran Man**: T. Byng.
Admin/Fin: Ms P. Stewart.
Fleet: 13 - 7 coach, 2 midibus, 1 midicoach, 2 minibus, 1 minicoach.
Chassis: 3 DAF. 2 MAN. 2 Mercedes. 1 Optare. 5 Scania.
Ops incl: excursions & tours, private hire, express, continental tours, school contracts.
Livery: White/Red Pegasus.

GEMINI TRAVEL SOUTHAMPTON LTD
MARCHWOOD INDUSTRIAL PARK, NORTH ROAD, MARCHWOOD SO40 4BL
Tel: 023 8066 0066
Fax: 023 8087 1308
Dirs: Ken Hatch, Mark Bennett **Gen Man**: Nigel Smith
Fleet: 10 - 2 single-deck coach. 4 midicoach, 4 minibus.
Chassis: 4 LDV. 4 Mercedes. 2 Volvo.
Bodies: 3 Optare. 2 Plaxton, 5 other.
Ops incl: private hire, school contracts.
Livery: White/Blue

HAYWDARDS COACHES
PO BOX 5626, BASINGSTOKE RG19 9AP
Tel: 01256 328832
Fax: 01635 821128
Dirs: Lyn Weaver, Simon Weaver
Fleet: 20 - 12 coach bus, 8 double-deck coach.
Chassis: 4 Bova. 4 Scania. 12 Volvo.
Bodies: 4 Bova. 8 East Lancs. 4 Ikarus. 4 Plaxton.
Ops incl: school contracts, private hire
Livery: Hiyo Silver

HELLYERS OF FAREHAM

FORT FAREHAM BUSINESS PARK, NEWGATE LANE, FAREHAM PO14 1AH
Tel: 01329 285432
Fax: 01329 235267
E-mail: info@hellyers-coaches.co.uk
Web site: www.hellyers-coaches.co.uk
Dir: Paul Grant **Dir/Co Sec**: Trevor Grant
Fleet Eng: Rob Ingram
Fleet: 38 - 1 single-deck bus, 37 coach.
Chassis: 8 Bova. 2 Dennis. 4 Leyland. 4 Mercedes. 4 Scania. 6 Setra. 1 Toyota. 9 Volvo.
Bodies: 8 Bova. 1 Caetano. 4 Ikarus. 1 Irizar. 3 Jonckheere. 4 Mercedes. 10 Plaxton. 6 Setra. 4 Van Hool.
Ops incl: excursions & tours, private hire, school contracts, express, continental tours.

HERRINGTON COACHES LTD

MANOR FARM, SANDLEHEATH ROAD, ALDERHOLT, FORDINGBRIDGE SP6 3EG
Tel: 01425 652842
Props: A G Herrington, Mrs J Herrington
Fleet: 6 - 3 coach, 3 minibus.
Chassis: 1 Dennis. 3 Mercedes. 2 Volvo.
Bodies: 1 Crest. 1 Jonckheere. 2 Mercedes. 1 Plaxton. 1 Van Hool.
Ops incl: local bus services, school contracts, private hire.
Livery: Grey/Red.

*HYTHE & WATERSIDE COACHES LTD
1A HIGH STREET, HYTHE SO45 6AG
Tel: 023 8084 4788
Fax: 023 8020 7284
E-mail: enquiries@watersidetours.co.uk
Web site: www.watersidetours.co.uk
Fleetname: Waterside Tours
Man Dir: Roy Barker **Dirs**: Pam Parker, Jackie Withey
Fleet: 7 - 4 coach, 1 minibus, 2 midicoach.
Chassis: 1 BMC. 1 Mercedes. 1 Toyota. 4 Volvo.
Bodies: 4 Berkhof. 1 Caetano. 2 other.
Ops incl: excursions & tours, private hire, continental tours, school contracts.
Livery: White/Burgundy/Gold.

LUCKETTS TRAVEL

BROADCUT, WALLINGTON, FAREHAM PO16 8TB
Tel: 01329 823755
Fax: 01329 823855
E-mail: info@lucketts.co.uk
Web site: www.lucketts.co.uk
Chmn: David Luckett **Joint Man Dirs**: Steven Luckett, Ian Luckett **Eng Dir**: Mark Jordan **Ops Man**: Tony Harper
Fleet: 33 - 29 coach, 2 double-deck coach, 2 minicoach.
Chassis: 1 DAF. 8 Dennis. 2 Neoplan. 18 Scania. 2 Toyota. 2 Volvo.
Bodies: 5 Berkhof. 1 Bova. 2 Caetano. 21 Irizar. 2 Neoplan. 4 Plaxton
Ops incl: excursions & tours, private hire,

continental tours, school contracts.
Livery: Grey/White/Orange

*MARCHWOOD MOTORWAYS (SOUTHAMPTON) LTD

200 SALISBURY ROAD, TOTTON
SO40 3PE
Tel: 023 8066 3700
Fax: 023 8066 7762
Dirs: D P Osborne, I C Osborne, S E Welbourn
Fleet: 55 - 22 single-deck bus, 18 coach, 3 double-deck coach, 4 midibus, 4 midicoach, 4 minibus.
Chassis: 1 Bova. 43 DAF. 3 Ford Transit. 4 Iveco. 1 MAN. 3 Toyota.
Bodies: 4 Caetano. 1 Duple. 7 Ikarus. 11 Optare. 10 Van Hool. 14 Wright. 7 other.
Ops incl: local bus services, school contracts, private hire.
Livery: Blue
Ticket system: Wayfarer

MERVYN'S COACHES

THE NEW COACH HOUSE,
INNERSDOWN, MICHELDEVER
SO21 3BW
Tel/Fax: 01962 774574
E-mail: mervynscoaches@btconnect.com
Web site: www.mervynscoaches.com
Ptnrs: Mervyn Annetts, Carol Annetts, Linda Porter, James Annetts.
Fleet: 6 - 4 coach, 1 midicoach, 1 minibus.
Chassis: 6 Bedford.
Chassis: 1 Duple. 4 Plaxton. 1 Churchill
Ops incl: local bus services, school contracts, excursions & tours, private hire.
Livery: Brown/Cream
Ticket System: Setright.

JOHN PIKE COACHES

77 SCOTT CLOSE, WALWORTH INDUSTRIAL ESTATE, ANDOVER
SP10 5NU.
Tel: 01264 334328.
Fax: 01264 334329.
Props: J. S. Pike, Jenny Pike, C. Pike, R. Pike.
Fleet: 15 - 4 double-deck bus, 5 coach, 2 midicoach, 4 minibus.
Chassis: Bristol. Ford Transit. Iveco. Mercedes. Volvo.
Bodies: Mercedes. Plaxton. ECW.
Ops incl: local bus services, school contracts, excursions & tours, private hire, continental tours.
Livery: White.
Ticket System: Setright.

*PRINCESS COACHES LTD

PRINCESS COACHES GARAGE,
BOTLEY ROAD, WEST END,
SOUTHAMPTON SO30 3HA
Tel: 023 8047 2150
Fax: 023 8039 9944
E-mail: princesscoaches@aol.com
Web site: www.princesscoaches.com
Dirs: Y B Barfoot, D K Brown, P A Brown
Fleet: 16 - 12 coach, 2 double-deck coach, 1 minibus. 1 minicoach.
Chassis: 1 Ford. 14 Scania. 1 Toyota.
Bodies: 2 Berkhof. 1 Caetano. 8 Irizar. 4 Jonckheere. 1 other.
Ops incl: private hire, school contracts, continental tours.
Livery: White with multi-coloured flashes

*SEAVIEW SERVICES LTD
See Isle of Wight

SOLENT BLUE LINE

BARTON PARK, EASTLEIGH
SO50 6RR
Tel: 023 8061 4459
Fax: 023 8061 4234
E-mail: enquiries@solentblueline.com
Web site: www.solentblueline.com
Chmn: S G Linn **Man Dir:** P J Stockley
Service Delivery Dir: R S Dorr **Fin Dir:** A R Hiles **Comm Man:** P C Curtis
Fleet: 72 - 45 double-deck bus, 19 single-deck bus, 2 open-top bus, 6 midibus.
Chassis: 2 Bristol. 24 Dennis. 6 Iveco. 20 Leyland. 20 Volvo.
Bodies: 5 Alexander. 22 ECW. 18 East Lancs. 14 Leyland. 2 Marshall/MCV. 4 Mellor. 7 Northern Counties. 2 Reeve Burgess. 12 Transbus.
Ops incl: local bus services
Livery: Blue
Ticket System: Wayfarer 3

*SOLENT COACHES LTD

BROOKSIDE GARAGE, CROW LANE, RINGWOOD BH24 3EA
Tel: 01425 473188
Fax: 01425 473669
Recovery: 0784 326 6720/1
E-mail: enquiries@solentcoaches.co.uk
Web site: www.solentcoaches.co.uk
Man Dir/Co Sec: John Skew **Dir/Ch Eng:** Paul Skew.
Fleet: 9 - 7 coach, 1 minibus, 1 midicoach.
Chassis: 1 Mercedes. 6 Scania. 1 SETRA. 1 Toyota.
Bodies: 1 Caetano. 2 Irizar. 1 Mercedes. 1 Setra. 4 Van Hool.
Ops incl: excursions & tours, private hire, continental tours, school contracts.
Livery: White/Blue

STAGECOACH HAMPSHIRE

BUS STATION, FESTIVAL PLACE,
CHURCHILL WAY, BASINGSTOKE
RG21 7HZ
Tel: 01256 464501
Fax: 01256 811931
Man Dir: Andrew Dyer. **Eng Dir:** Richard Alexander. **Fin Dir:** Martin Stoggell. **Div Man:** Matthew Callow.
Fleet: 150 - 47 double-deck bus. 86 single-deck bus. 17 minibus.
Chassis: 4 Bristol, 53 Dennis, 16 Leyland, 15 Mercedes, 2 Optare. 60 Volvo.
Bodies: 138 Alexander. 4 ECW. 2 Optare. Plaxton.
Ops incl: local bus services, school contracts.
Livery: Blue/Red/Orange
Ticket System: Wayfarer.

STAGECOACH HANTS & SURREY

HALIMOTE ROAD, ALDERSHOT
GU11 1NJ
Tel: 01256 464501.
Man Dir: Andrew Dyer. **Eng Dir:** Richard Alexander. **Fin Dir:** Martin Stoggell. **Div Man:** Philip Medlicott.
Fleet: 80 - 13 double-deck bus, 43 single-deck bus, 24 minibus.
Chassis: 37 Dennis. 6 Leyland. 24 Mercedes. 13 Volvo.
Bodies: Alexander. Plaxton.
Ops incl: local bus services, school contracts.
Livery: Blue/Red/Orange
Ticket System: Wayfarer

*SUMMERFIELD COACHES LTD

247 ALDERMOOR ROAD,
ALDERMOOR, SOUTHAMPTON
SO16 5NU
Tel: 023 8077 8717
Fax: 023 8032 0327
E-mail: summerfield@tcp.co.uk
Man Dir: Tracey Ralph **Chmn/Dir:** Colin Ralph **Ops Man:** Dave Wheeler
Fleet: 9 - 5 coach, 2 minibus, 2 minicoach.
Chassis: 2 LDV. 1 MAN. 1 Mercedes. 1 Toyota. 4 Volvo.
Bodies: 1 Berkhof. 3 Caetano. 2 Leyland. 2 Plaxton. 1 other.
Ops incl: school contracts, private hire, excursions & tours, continental tours.
Livery: Green/Gold

*TEST VALLEY TRAVEL
See Wiltshire

*TOP TRAVEL COACHES

169 NEW GREENHAM PARK,
BASINGSTOKE RG19 6HN
Tel: 01256 397270
Fax: 01635 821128
Dirs: Simon Weaver
Fleet: 24 - 18 coach bus, 6 double-deck coach.
Chassis: 8 Bova. 7 Scania. 9 Volvo.
Bodies: 8 Bova. 6 East Lancs. 7 Irizar. 3 Plaxton.

♨	Air conditioning	💺	Seat belt-fitted vehicles	🔧	Replacement vehicle available
♿	Vehicles suitable for disabled	R	Recovery service available (not 24 hr)	T	Toilet-drop facilities available
🍴	Coach(es) with galley facilities	R24	24hr recovery service	🚌	Vintage vehicle(s) available
wc	Coach(es) with toilet facilities				Open top vehicle(s)

Ops incl: school contracts, private hire
Livery: Electric Blue

VISION TRAVEL INTERNATIONAL LTD

12 BUNTING GARDENS, COWPLAIN, WATERLOOVILLE PO8 9UN

Tel: 023 9235 9168
Fax: 023 9236 1253
Recovery: 023 9259 1940
E-mail: visiontravels@aol.com
Web site: www.visiontravel.co.uk
Dirs: Peter R Sharpe, David J Sharpe, Rebecca Simmons
Fleet: 13 - 11 coach, 1 midicoach, 1 minibus
Chassis: 2 DAF. 1 Leyland. 2 MAN. 2 Mercedes. 5 Scania.

Bodies: 5 Ikarus. 1 Leyland. 2 Mercedes. 1 Neoplan.
Ops incl: school contracts, excursions & tours, private hire, continental tours.

HEREFORDSHIRE

BOWYER'S COACHES
QUARRY GARAGE, PETERCHURCH HR2 0TF.
Tel: 01981 550206.
Prop: Fernley C. Anning, Anthony H. Anning.
Fleet: 9 - 5 coach, 4 minibus.
Chassis: Bedford. LDV.
Ops incl: private hire, school contracts.
Livery: White/Red.

BROMYARD OMNIBUS COMPANY
STREAMHALL GARAGE, LINTON TRADING ESTATE, BROMYARD HR7 4QL
Tel: 01885 482782
Fax: 01885 482127
Prop: Martin Perry **Fleet Eng**: Michael Simcock
Fleet: 11 - 6 single-deck bus, 3 coach, 1 midibus, 1 minicoach.
Chassis: 1 Bedford. 2 Leyland. 2 Mercedes. 4 Optare. 1 Volvo. 1 Trojan.
Bodies: 2 Autobus. 1 Caetano. 1 Duple. 4 Optare. 2 Plaxton. 1 Trojan.
Ops incl: local bus services, school contracts, privte hire.
Livery: Red/Cream
Ticket System: Wayfarer Saver

COACH COMPANIONS LTD
MAGNOLIA HOUSE, 12 ST BOTOLPH'S GREEN, LEOMINSTER HR6 8ER
Tel: 01568 620279
Fax: 01568 616906
E-mail: enquiries@coachcompanions.co.uk
Web site: www.coachcompanions.co.uk
Dir: Richard Asghar-Sandys
Fleet: 1 midicoach.
Chassis: 1 Mercedes.
Bodies: 1 other.
Ops incl: private hire.
Livery: White

*D R M BUS AND CONTRACT SERVICES
THE COACH GARAGE, BROMYARD HR7 4NT
Tel: 01885 483219
Prop: David R. Morris

Fleet: 9 single-deck bus
Chassis: 3 Scania. 6 Volvo.
Bodies: 2 Alexander. 3 East Lancs. 1 Leyland National. 3 Omnicity.
Ops incl: local bus services, school contracts.
Livery: Blue/Silver-White
Ticket System: Wayfarer 3

GOLDEN PIONEER TRAVEL
BRANDON, REDHILL, HEREFORD HR2 8BH
Tel: 01432 274307
Fax: 01432 275809
Prop: Bryan Crockett **Dir**: J Crockett.
Fleet: 5 coach, 1 minicoach.
Chassis: incl. 1 Scania. 1 Toyota.
Bodies: 2 Beulas. 1 Mercedes. 1 Van Hool.
Ops incl: school contracts, excursions & tours, private hire, continental tours.
Livery: Black/Gold/Red/Green

*GOLD STAR TRAVEL
See Worcestershire

*P. W. JONES COACHES
HILBROY GARAGE, BURLEY GATE, HEREFORD HR1 3QL
Tel: 01432 820214
Fax: 01432 820521
Recovery: 01432 820214
E-mail: coaches@p.w.jones.com
Owner: Philip W Jones
Fleet: 18 - 16 single-deck coach, 1 midicoach, 1 minicoach.
Chassis: 1 Bedford. 1 Bova. 13 Dennis. 1 MAN. 1 Mercedes. 1 Neoplan. 1 Toyota.
Bodies: 1 Bova. 1 Caetano. 1 uple. 1 Marcopolo. 1 Neoplan. 14 Plaxton.
Ops incl: excursions & tours private hire, continental tours, school contracts., express
Livery: White/Blue

*LUGG VALLEY PRIMROSE TRAVEL LTD
THE NEW BUS STATION, WESTBURY STREET, LEOMINSTER HR6 8PX
Tel: 01432 344341
Fax: 01432 356206
Man Dir: Mrs E Sankey **Sec**: Mrs E Sankey
Ops Man: J E Hodges **Eng**: Paul Bird
Fleet: 25 - 15 single-deck bus, 10 coach.
Chassis: 1 Bedford. 1 BMC. 6 Dennis. 1 Marshall. 10 Optare. 1 Scania. 5 Volvo.

Bodies: 1 Berkhof. 1 BMC. 3 Carlyle. 1 Irizar. 1 Jonckheere. 1 Marshall. 10 Optare. 7 Plaxton.
Ops incl: local bus services, school contracts, excursions & tours, private hire, continental tours.
Livery: Cream/Green/Orange
Ticket System: Wayfarer

*M & S COACHES OF HEREFORDSHIRE LTD
CROFTWELL HOUSE, KIMBOLTON, LEOMINSTER HR6 0HD
Tel: 01568 612803
Dir: Maurice Peruffo
Fleet: 7 - 4 midicoach, 3 minicoach.
Chassis: 4 Mercedes. 2 Toyota. 1 Volvo.
Bodies: 2 Caetano. 2 Mercedes. 1 Optare. 1 Van Hool. 1 other.
Ops incl: school contracts, private hire

NEWBURY COACHES
LOWER ROAD TRADING ESTATE, LEDBURY HR8 2DJ.
Tel: 01531 633483.
Fax: 01531633650.
Livery: Blue/White.

SARGANTS BROS LTD
MILL STREET, KINGTON HR5 3AL
Tel/Fax: 01544 230481
E-mail: mike@sargantsbros.com
Web site: www.sargantsbros.com
Prop: Michael Sargant
Fleet: 29 - 1 double-deck bus, 2 single-deck bus, 6 single-deck coach, 10 midibus, 1 midicoach, 9 minibus.
Chassis: 4 Bedford, 1 DAF, 1 Dodge, 4 Ford Transit, 1 LAG, 2 Leyland, 7 Mercedes, 4 Optare, 2 Renault, 1 Volvo, 2 Talbot.
Bodies: 1 Alexander, 2 Jonckheere, 7 Optare, 6 Plaxton, 2 Reeve Burgess, 2 PMT, 1 LAG, 1 Cymric, 2 Freeway, 4 Ford. 1 Renault.
Ops incl: local bus services, school contracts, private hire.
Livery: Red
Ticket System: Wayfarer

SMITHS MOTORS (LEDBURY) LTD
COACH GARAGE, HOMEND, LEDBURY HR8 1BA.
Tel: 01531 632953.

Dirs: F. W. B. Sterry, M. Sterry.
Fleet: 11 - 8 coach, 2 midicoach, 1 minibus.
Chassis: 3 Bedford. 1 Ford. 1 Iveco.
4 Leyland. 2 Mercedes.
Bodies: 1 Caetano. 3 Duple. 3 Plaxton.
2 Van Hool. 1 PMT. 1 Devon.
Ops incl: local bus services,
continental tours.
Livery: White with Green/Blue/Red stripe.
Ticket System: Setright.

*STAGECOACH IN SOUTH WALES
See Torfaen

*YEOMANS CANYON TRAVEL LTD
21-23 THREE ELMS TRADING ESTATE, HEREFORD HR4 9PU.
Tel: 01432 356201
Fax: 01432 356206
E-mail: nigelyeomans@aol.com
Dirs: N. D. & G. H. Yeomans **Sec**:
S. M. T. Yeomans **Traf Man**: N. Yeomans.
Fleet: 37 - 11 single-deck bus, 24 coach, 2 minibus.
Chassis: 2 BMC. 11 Dennis. 2 Ford Transit.

2 Leyland. 1 Neoplan. 5 Optare. 2 Scania.
1 Transbus. 11 Volvo.
Bodies: 2 Berkhof. 2 BMC. 4 Duple.
2 Leyland. 1 Marcopolo. 1 Neoplan.
5 Optare. 11 Plaxton. 2 Van Hool. 7 other.
Ops incl: local bus services, school contracts, excursions & tours, private hire, express, continental tours.
Livery: Cream
Ticket System: Wayfarer

HERTFORDSHIRE

ABBEY TRAVEL LTD

58 BURYMEAD ROAD, HITCHIN SG5 1RT
Tel: 01462 421777/421888
Fax: 01462 421999
E-mail: rich@abbeytravel.co.uk
Web site: www.abbeytravel.co.uk
Man Dir: Peter Malyon **Dir**: Patricia Malyon
Co Man: Richard Window.
Co Sec: Leigh Featherstone
Fleet: 14 - 2 single-deck bus, 8 coach,
1 midibus, 2 minibus, 1 minicoach.
Chassis: 1 Dennis. 1 Ford Transit.
4 Mercedes. 1 Peugeot. 7 Volvo.
Bodies: 1 Berkhof. 1 Duple. 2 Jonckheere.
1 Mercedes. 4 Plaxton. 3 Reeve Burgess.
1 Van Hool. 1 Peugeot.
Ops incl: excursions & tours, private hire, continental tours, school contracts.
Livery: White/Blue.

ACE TRAVEL
11 MAYFLOWER GARDENS, BISHOPS STORTFORD CM23 4PA
Tel: 07774 251851
Fax: 01279 658056
Dir: Frank Gowen
Fleet: 1 coach.
Chassis: 1 Scania.
Body: 1 Irizar.
Ops incl: excursions & tours, private hire.
Livery: Blue

ALPHA PERSONALISED TRAVEL LTD
300 HIGH ROAD, LEAVESDEN WD25 7EB
Tel/Fax: 01923 202052.
Chmn: G. Picton. **Man Dir**: D. Green.
Co Sec: J. Foster.
Fleet: 3 - 1 midicoach, 2 minibus.
Chassis: 2 Ford Transit. 1 Toyota.
Bodies: 1 Caetano.
Ops incl: excursions & tours, private hire, continental tours.
Livery: Blue/Orange/White.

*A R TRAVEL LTD
40 PERRY GREEN, HEMEL HEMPSTEAD HP2 7ND
Tel: 01442 408093
Fax: 01442 389899
Recovery: 07710 379873
E-mail: artravelltd@hotmail.com
Web site: www.artravelltd.co.uk
Man Dir: Terry Hill
Fleet: 3 minibus
Chassis: 2 Mercedes. 1 VW.
Bodies: 2 Optare. 1 other.
Ops incl: excursions & tours, continental tours, private hire,school contracts.
Livery: White

ANITAS COACH & MINIBUS HIRE LTD
See Essex.

CANTABRICA COACH HOLIDAYS
9 ELTON WAY, WATFORD WD25 8HH
Tel: 01923 230526
Fax: 01923 817066
Fleet: 20
Chassis: 1 Freight Rover. 3 Mercedes. 16 Volvo.
Ops incl: excursions & tours, private hire, continental tours.
Livery: Blue/Red.
Coach wash, workshop facilities.

*CHAMBERS COACHES (STEVENAGE) LTD
38 TRENT CLOSE, STEVENAGE SG1 3RT
Tel: 01438 352920
Fax: 01462 486616

E-mail: chamberscoaches@btconnect.com
Web site: www.chamberscoaches.com
Dirs: Cyril Chambers, M R Chambers, Mrs S M Chambers **Co Sec**: Mrs D C Tidey.
Fleet: 17 - 12 single-deck coach, 3 midicoach, 2 minicoach
Chassis: Dennis. Ford. Leyland. Volvo.
Bodies: Caetano. Leyland. Marcopolo. Transbus.
Ops incl: private hire
Livery: White/Red/Blue

GALLEON TRAVEL LTD
THE GARAGE, FILLETS FARM, STANSTEAD ROAD, HUNSDON SG12 8QA
Tel: 01920 870700
Fax: 01279 877079
E-mail: galleontravel@btopenworld.com
Web site: www.galleontravel.com
Man Dir: Helen Bowden **Ops Dir**: Mark Bowden
Fleet: 4 - 2 coach, 2 double-deck coach
Chassis: 3 Scania. 1 Volvo.
Bodies: 1 Berkhof. 1 East Lancs. 2 Irizar.
Ops incl: school contracts, private hire, continental tours.
Livery: White.

*GOLDEN BOY COACHES (JETSIE LTD)
JOHN TERENCE HOUSE, GEDDINGS ROAD, HODDESDON EN11 0NT
Tel: 01992 465747
Fax: 01992 450957
E-mail: sales@goldenboy.co.uk
Web site: www.goldenboy.co.uk
Joint Man Dirs: G A McIntyre, T P McIntyre
Tran Man: G Jaikens **Ch Eng**: P Murdoch
Fleet: 33 - 2 single-deck bus, 17 coach, 12 midicoach, 2 minicoach.

Chassis: 2 Dennis. 14 Mercedes. 17 Volvo.
Bodies: 2 Alexander. 2 Crest. 1 Euro.
9 Plaxton. 2 Sitcar. 17 Van Hool.
Ops incl: local bus services, private hire, school contracts.
Livery: Black/Red/Gold.
Ticket System: Wayfarer

GRAVES COACHES & MINIBUSES
134 WINFORD DRIVE DRIVE, BROXBOURNE EN10 6PN
Tel/Fax: 01992 445556
E-mail: m.graves@btinternet.com
Prop: Michael Graves
Fleet: 2 -1 minicoach, 1 minibus
Chassis: 1 Mercedes. 1 Toyota.
Bodies: 1 Caetano. 1 Mercedes.
Ops incl: private hire, school contracts.

GROVE COACHES
101 MANDEVILLE ROAD, HERTFORD SG13 8JL
Tel: 01992 583417
Fleetname: Pride of Hertford
Driver/operator: R A Bowers
Fleet: 1 coach.
Chassis: Volvo. **Body**: Plaxton.
Ops incl: private hire, school contracts.
Livery: Brown/Orange

KENZIES COACHES LTD

6 ANGLE LANE, SHEPRETH SG8 6QH
Tel: 01763 260288
Fax: 01763 262012
Fleet: 25 coach.
Chassis: 2 Bedford. 1 Scania. 22 Volvo.
Bodies: 6 Plaxton. 19 Van Hool.
Ops incl: private hire, school contracts.

*LITTLE JIM'S
1 CASTLE STREET, BERKHAMSTED HP4 2BQ
Tel: 01442 870029
Fax: 01442 877217
E-mail: littlejimbuses@aol.com
Prop: James H Petty
Fleet: 2 - 1 midibus, 1 midicoach.
Chassis: 2 Mercedes.
Bodies: 2 Mercedes.
Ops incl: local bus services, excursions & tours, private hire.
Livery: Variable.
Ticket System: Almex

*MARSHALLS COACHES LLP
See London

*MASTER TRAVEL COACHES

9-11 PEARTREE FARM, WELWYN GARDEN CITY AL7 3UW
Tel: 01707 334040
Fax: 01707 334366
E-mail: mastertravel@btclick.com
Web site: www.master-travel.co.uk
Ptnrs: R J Goulden, S Goulden
Fleet: 14 - 3 single-deck bus, 4 coach, 3 midicoach, 4 minibus.
Chassis: 1 BMC. 5 Dennis. 3 Iveco. 2 LDV. 2 Mercedes. 1 Neoplan. 1 Optare.

Bodies: 1 Berkhof. 1 BMC. 2 Marcopolo. 2 Mercedes. 1 Neoplan. 1 Optare. 6 other.
Ops incl: school contracts, private hire, continental tours.
Livery: White/Blue.

MINIBUS SERVICES
773 ST ALBANS ROAD, WATFORD WD25 9LA
Tel: 01923 219107
Fax: 01923 219108
E-mail: minibusservices@btconnect.com
E-mail: www.minibusservices.uk.com
Prop: Russell Crowson
Fleet: 5 - 1 coach, 2 minibus, 2 midicoach
Chassis: 1 Iveco. 1 LDV. 1 Mercedes.1 Renault. 1 Volvo.
Bodies: include Plaxton
Ops incl: school contracts, private hire, excursions & tours

PARKSIDE TRAVEL

PARADISE WILDLIFE PARK, WHITE STUBBS LANE, BROXBOURNE EN10 7QA
Tel: 01992 444477
Fax: 01992 465441
Fleetname: Parkside Travel
Dirs: P C Sampson, G F Sampson
Fleet: 7 minibus.
Chassis: 7 Ford Transit.
Ops incl: school contracts, private hire.
Livery: Light Blue

*PROVENCE PRIVATE HIRE LTD
HEATH FARM LANE, ST ALBANS AL3 5AE
Tel: 01727 864988
Fax: 01727 855275
E-mail: office@pphcoaches.com
Web site: www.pphcoaches.com
Dirs: A. K. Hayes, R. F. Hayes
Ch Eng: D. Higgins
Fleet: 30 - 3 double-deck bus, 23 coach, 1 double-deck coach, 1 minibus, 1 midicoach, 1 minicoach.
Chassis: 1 Bedford. 1 DAF. 5 Dennis. 1 Ford Transit. 4 Leyland. 2 MCW. 1 Mercedes. 8 Scania. 1 Toyota. 4 Volvo. 1 other.
Bodies: 2 Caetano. 1 Duple. 4 East Lancs. 4 Irizar. 2 MCW. 1 Mercedes. 3 Neoplan. 9 Plaxton. 2 UVG. 1 Van Hool. 2 Wadham Stringer. 1 other.
Ops incl: excursions & tours, private hire, continental tours, school contracts.
Livery: Yellow.

*REG'S COACHES LTD

C/O FOXHOLES FARM, LONDON ROAD, HERTFORD SG13 7NT
Tel: 01992 586302
Fax: 01992 586302
E-mail: regscoaches@btconnect.com
Web site: www.regscoaches.co.uk
Man Dir: T Hunt **Dir**: Mrs B Hunt **Ch Eng**: W Parlow
Fleet: 15 - 2 single-deck bus, 12 coach, 1 midicoach.
Chassis: 9 Dennis. 1 Mercedes. 5 Volvo.

Bodies: 1 Optare. 10 Plaxton. 1 Transbus. 2 Van Hool. 1 Wright.
Ops incl: local bus services, school contracts, excursions & tours, private hire.
Livery: Black/Green/Orange
Ticket System: Wayfarer 2/Almex

*REYNOLDS DIPLOMAT COACHES
285 LOWER HIGH STREET, WATFORD WD17 2HY
Tel: 01923 296877
Fax: 01923 210020
E-mail: enquiries@reynoldscoaches.com
Web site: www.reynoldscoaches.com
Props: Richard Reynolds, Susan Reynolds
Ops Dir: Christopher Barker
Fleet: 18 - 13 coach, 3 double-deck coach, 2 midibus.
Chassis: 1 MAN. 3 Mercedes. 3 Scania. 3 Setra. 7 Volvo.
Bodies: 1 Caetano. 7 Jonckheere. 3 Neoplan. 1 Optare. 3 Setra. 3 Van Hool.
Ops incl: excursions & tours, private hire, continental tours, school contracts.
Livery: Gold

*RICHMOND'S COACHES
THE GARAGE, BARLEY, ROYSTON SG8 8JA
Tel: 01763 848226
Fax: 01763 848105
E-mail: postbox@richmonds-coaches.co.uk
Web site: www.richmonds-coaches.co.uk
Dirs: David Richmond, Michael Richmond, Andrew Richmond **Sales & Mktg Man**: Rick Ellis **Asst Ops Man**: Craig Ellis **Ch Eng**: Patrick Granville **Exc & Tours Man**: Natalie Richmond
Fleet: 26 - 19 single-deck coach, 1 midicoach, 6 midibus.
Chassis: 6 Bova. 2 DAF. 1 Dennis. 5 Mercedes. 2 Optare. 10 Volvo.
Bodies: 1 Berkhof. 6 Bova. 2 Optare. 4 Plaxton. 12 Van Hool. 1 other.
Ops incl: local bus services, school contracts, excursions & tours, private hire, express, continental tours.
Livery: Chocolate/Cream

RONSWAY COACHES
  R24
FIRBANK WAY, LEIGHTON BUZZARD LU7 4YP
Tel: 01442 242641
Fax: 01525 850967
Recovery: 01525 375301
E-mail: info@marshalls-coaches.co.uk
Web site: www.marshalls-coaches.co.uk
Props: G R Marshall, S J Marshall **Ops Man**: Ian White **Fleet Eng**: Nick Aris
Fleet: 22 - 1 double-deck coach, 20 coach, 1 midicoach.
Chassis: 4 Dennis. 6 Iveco. 1 Mercedes. 1 Neoplan. 10 Volvo.
Bodies: 6 Beulas. 1 Ikarus. 6 Jonckheere. 1 Mercedes. 1 Neoplan. 7 Plaxton.
Ops incl: private hire, school contracts, local bus services.
Livery: Blue multicoloured

*SHIRE COACHES

PO BOX 862, ST ALBANS AL1 9BT
Tel: 01772 832519
Fax: 01727 832548
E-mail: shirecoaches@btconnect.com
Web site: www.shirecoaches.co.uk
Ptnrs: Lynda Maney, Michael Maney
Fleet: 10 coach - 8 coach, 2 minibus.
Chassis: 1 Ayats. 1 Ford. 1 Mercedes. 6 Scania. 1 Volvo.
Bodies: incl 1 UVG
Ops incl: school contracts, excursions & tours, private hire, continental tours.
Livery: Purple/Silver

SIMMONDS COACHES LTD

9 BROADWATER AVENUE, LETCHWORTH SG6 3HE.
Tel: 01462 684729.
Fax: 01462 683879.
Garage: NORTON WAY NORTH, LETCHWORTH
Tel: 01462 683879 (night 01462 730517).
Dirs: M. J. Simmonds, B. J. Simmonds, S. M. Simmonds.
Fleet: 12 - 1 double-deck bus, 7 coach, 2 midicoach, 2 minicoach.
Chassis: 1 Daimler. 1 MAN. 2 Mercedes. 1 Toyota. 7 Volvo.
Bodies: 1 Caetano. 2 Optare. 1 Park Royal. 4 Plaxton. 4 Van Hool.
Ops incl: local bus services, school contracts, excursions & tours, private hire.
Livery: Fawn/Orange/Brown.
Ticket System: Setright.

SMITH BUNTINGFORD

CLAREMONT, BALDOCK ROAD, BUNTINGFORD SG9 9DJ
Tel/Fax: 01763 271516
Prop: Graham H Smith **Fleet Eng**: Stewart C Smith
Fleet: 6 minicoach.
Chassis: 1 Ford Transit. 3 Mercedes. 1 Renault. 1 Vauxhall
Bodies: 1 Autobus. 1 Courtside. 1 Ford. 1 Mellor. 1 Stanford.
Ops incl: private hire, school contracts
Livery: White/Orange

G. A. SMITHS COACHES LTD

THE GARAGE, WIGGINTON HP23 6EJ
Tel: 01442 823163.
Fax: 01442 824799.
Dirs: G. A. Smith (**Man Dir**), Mrs S. N. Smith, J. Smith.
Fleet: 8 - 6 coach, 1 midicoach, 1 minicoach. **Chassis**: 2 Mercedes. 6 Volvo.
Bodies: 2 Mercedes. 1 Plaxton. 1 Reeve Burgess.
Ops incl: local bus services, excursions & tours, private hire, continental tours.
Livery: Red/Cream.

SOUTH MIMMS TRAVEL LTD

21 GOWERFIELD, SOUTH MIMMS EN6 3NT.
Tel: 01707 660664
Fax: 01923 859396.
E-mail: info@southmimmstravel.com
Web site: www.southmimmstravel.co.uk
Man Dir: S. J. Griffiths.
Fleet: 10 coach.
Chassis: incl: Dennis, MCW, Neoplan, Volvo.
Bodies: incl: Berkhof, Bova, MCW, Neoplan, Plaxton.
Ops incl: school contracts, excursions & tours, private hire, continental tours.
Livery: Red/Black/Gold

SULLIVAN BUSES LTD

FIRST FLOOR, DEARDS HOUSE, ST ALBANS ROAD, POTTERS BAR EN6 3NE
Tel: 01707 646803
Fax: 01707 646804
E-mail: admin@sullivanbuses.com
Web site: www.sullivanbuses.com
Man Dir: Dean Sullivan
Fleet: 36 - 26 double-deck bus, 10 single-deck bus
Chassis: 3 AEC. 11 Leyland. 9 MCW. 10 Transbus. 2 Volvo.
Bodies: 7 Caetano. 1 Carlyle. 2 East Lancs. 11 Leicester. 9 MCW. 3 Park Royal. 3 Plaxton.
Ops incl: local bus services
Livery: Red
Ticket system: Wayfarer TGX

*TATES COACHES

44 HIGH STREET, MARKYATE AL3 8PA
Tel: 01582 840297
Fax: 01582 840014
E-mail: tates-coaches@fsbdial.co.uk
Web site: www.tates-coaches.co.uk
Dirs: Alan Tate (**Com Sec**), Tony Tate, Stephen Tate
Fleet: 10 - 1 single-deck bus, 9 coach
Chassis: 1 Bova. 2 DAF. 1 Dennis. 1 Mercedes. 1 Neoplan. 4 Scania.
Bodies: 1 Bova. 1 Caetano. 2 Hispano. 4 Irizar. 1 Neoplan. 1 Wadham Stringer.
Ops incl: school contracts, excursions & tours, private hire, continental tours.
Livery: Cream/Blue/Orange

TERRY'S COACHES

45 HOMEFIELD ROAD, HEMEL HEMPSTEAD HP2 4BZ
Tel: 01442 265850
Dirs: Terry Bunyan, Shirley Bunyan.
Fleet: 5 - 1 midibus, 2 midicoach, 2 minicoach.
Chassis: 1 Iveco. 1 LDV. 2 Mercedes.
Bodies: 1 Leicester. 2 Optare. 2 other.

Ops incl: school contracts, private hire.
Livery: Blue/White

*TIMEBUS TRAVEL

See London

*TRUSTLINE

THE COACH HOUSE, FOXHOLES, LONDON ROAD, HERTFORD SG13 7NT
Tel: 01922 503343
Fax: 01992 503515
Recovery: 01922 503707
E-mail: trustlineservices@talk21.com
Man Dir: Helen Bowden **Ops Dir**: Mark Bowden **Fleet Eng**: Derek Collier
Admin Man: V Chessman
Fleet: 20 - 5 double-deck bus, 15 single-deck bus
Chassis: 14 Dennis. 4 Leyland. 1 MAN. 1 MCW.
Ops incl: local bus services
Livery: Yellow/Red/Blue
Ticket System: Almex A90

UNICORN COACHES LTD

PO BOX 45, HATFIELD AL9 5LD
Tel: 01707 269003
Tel: 01707 260039
E-mail: stsunicorn@aol.com
Web site: www.unicorncoaches.com
Man Dir: Mrs J E Pleshette **Gen Man**: S T Saltmarsh
Fleet: 2 minibus.
Chassis: 2 Ford Transit.
Ops incl: school contracts, private hire.
Livery: Red/White

UNO LTD

GYPSY MOTH AVENUE, HATFIELD BUSINESS PARK, HATFIELD AL10 9BS
Tel: 01707 255764
Fax: 01707 255761
Web site: www.universitybus.co.uk
Man Dir: Bill Hilton
Fleet: 42 single-deck bus.
Chassis: 4 Bluebird, 8 DAF, 19 Dennis, 1 Leyland, 1 Marshall, 4 Mercedes, 3 Optare.
Bodies: 4 Bluebird, 1 Mercedes, 1 East Lancs, 1 Leyland, 5 Marshall, 2 Northern Counties, 4 Optare, 1 Reeve Burgess, 20 Wright.
Ops incl: local bus services, school contracts.
Livery: Pink/Purple.
Ticket System: Wayfarer 3 Inform.

LEN WRIGHT BAND SERVICES LTD

9 ELTON WAY, WATFORD WD2 8HH.
Tel: 01923 238611.
Fax: 01923 230134.
E-mail: lwbs1@aol.com
Web site: www.lenwright.co.uk

A/c	Air conditioning
	Vehicles suitable for disabled
	Coach(es) with galley facilities
wc	Coach(es) with toilet facilities
	Seat belt-fitted vehicles
R	Recovery service available (not 24 hr)
R24	24hr recovery service
	Replacement vehicle available
T	Toilet-drop facilities available
	Vintage vehicle(s) available
	Open top vehicle(s)

Ops Dir: L. Collins.
Fleet: 13 - 6 coach, 5 double-deck coach (all sleeper), 2 minibus.
Chassis: 1 Bova. 2 Mercedes. 4 Scania. 6 Volvo.
Bodies: 1 Bova. 2 Irizar. 2 Jonckheere. 2 Plaxton. 4 Van Hool. 2 Autobus.
Ops incl: specialist private hire.
Livery: Grey.

ISLE OF WIGHT

AWAY DAYS

56 WILTON ROAD, SHANKLIN PO37 7BZ
Tel: 01983 862774
Fax: 01983 864315
E-mail: awaydays@supanet.com
Website: www.awaydaysiowco.uk
Props: Roy Townend, Hedda Townend
Fleet: 3 coach
Chassis: 2 Iveco. 1 Scania.
Bodies: 2 Beulas. 1 Berkhof.
Ops incl: school contracts, excursions & tours, private hire, continental tours.
Livery: White with orange lettering and multi-coloured kite.

GANGES COACHES

77 PLACE ROAD, COWES PO31 7AE
Tel: 01983 296666
Fax: 01983 296666
Prop: John Gange
Fleet: 9 - 4 coach, 3 midicoach, 1 minibus, 1 minicoach.
Chassis: 1 AEC. 1 Bedford. 1 Ford. 1 Leyland. 3 Mercedes. 1 Renault. 1 Peugeot/Talbot
Bodies: 2 Duple. 1 Mercedes. 3 Plaxton. 3 other.
Ops incl: private hire
Livery: Red/Cream and Blue/Cream

GRAND HOTEL TOURS LTD (KIM'S COACHES)

GRAND HOTEL, CULVER PARADE, SANDOWN PO36 8QA.
Tel: 01983 402236.
Fax: 01983 406784.
Fleetname: Grand Tours.
Prop: R. J. H. & M. A. Hayter.
Sec: Mrs Marilyn Gerrard. **Traf Man**: G. Worrall. **Gen Man**: R. H. J. Hayter.
Fleet: 3 coach.
Chassis: DAF. Dennis. Scania.
Bodies: Duple. Van Hool. LAG.
Ops incl: excursions & tours, private hire.
Livery: Yellow/White.

ISLAND COACH SERVICES LTD

UNIT D10, SPITHEAD BUSINESS CENTRE, NEWPORT ROAD, SANDOWN PO36 9PH
Tel: 01983 408080
Fax: 01983 408808
Website: www.islandcoachservices.co.uk
E-mail: info@islandcoachservices.co.uk
Dir: R J Long **Tran Man**: D Draper
Fleet: 11 coach
Chassis: 1 DAF. 1 Dennis. 1 Mercedes. 8 Volvo.
Bodies: 2 Caetano. 2 Jonckheere. 1 Mercedes. 1 Neoplan. 3 Plaxton. 2 Van Hool.
Ops incl: excursions & tours, private hire, continental tours, school contracts.
Livery: Blue flash/White.

ISLE OF WIGHT COUNTY TRANSPORT DEPARTMENT

21 WHITCOMBE ROAD, NEWPORT PO30 1YS
Tel: 01983 823784.
Fax: 01983 825818.
Fleetname: Wightbus.
Tran Man: A. A. Morris. **Ops Man**: J. Lamb.
Fleet: 27 - 1 double-deck bus, 13 single-deck bus, 2 coach, 11 midibus.
Chassis: 13 Dennis. 1 Ford. 2 Leyland. 11 Mercedes.
Bodies: 2 Caetano. 1 Duple. 1 ECW. 1 Reeve Burgess. 15 Wadham Stringer. 1 Wright. 1 LCB. 1 Mellor. 1 Steedrive. 2 Withey.
Ops incl: local bus services, school contracts, excursions & tours, private hire.
Livery: White with Orange and Blue stripes.
Ticket System: Setright.

KARDAN TRAVEL LTD

490 NEWPORT ROAD, COWES PO31 8QU
Tel/Fax: 01983 520995
E-mail: info@kardan.co.uk
Web site: www.kardan.co.uk
Dir: R L Hodgson
Fleet: 5 coach
Chassis: 1 Leyland. 2 Setra. 2 Volvo.
Bodies: 3 Plaxton. 2 Setra.
Ops incl: private hire
Livery: Yellow/White

*SEAVIEW SERVICES LTD

SEAFIELD GARAGE, COLLEGE FARM ESTATE, FAULKNER LANE, SANDOWN PO36 9AZ
Tel: 01983 407070
Fax: 01983 407045
Recovery: 0773 923 7361
E-mail: mail@seaview-services.com
Web site: www.seaview-services.com
Chmn: P Robinson **Man Dirs**: A Robinson, Mrs M Robinson **Ops Man**: Karen Heathfield **Ch Eng**: Peter Brand
Co Tour Man: Mairi Robinson
Fleet: 11 - 10 coach, 1 min icoach.
Chassis: 2 Iveco. 1 Toyota. 8 Volvo.
Bodies: 2 Beulas. 2 Caetano. 7 Van Hool.
Ops incl: excursions & tours, private hire, continental tours, express, school contracts.
Livery: Green/Red

*THE SOUTHERN VECTIS OMNIBUS CO LTD

NELSON ROAD, NEWPORT PO30 1RD
Tel: 01983 522456
Fax: 01983 524961
Recovery: 01983 821135
E-mail: a.white@southernvectis.com
Web site: www.islandbuses.info
Man Dir: Alex Carter **Gen Man**: Alan White
Ops Dir: Andrew Wickham **Eng Dir**: Geoff Parsons **Ops Man**: Mick Poole **Comm Man**: Marc Morgan-Huws
Fleet: 85 - 49 double-deck bus, 25 single-deck bus, 2 coach, 8 open-top bus, 1 midibus.
Chassis: 6 Bristol. 27 Dennis. 1 Iveco. 25 Leyland. 26 Volvo.
Bodies: 15 Alexander. 2 Duple. 6 ECW. 16 Leyland. 1 Marshall. 28 Northern Counties. 9 Plaxton. 2 Reeve Burgess. 6 UVG.
Ops incl: local bus services, school contracts, excursions and tours, private hire.
Livery: Green/Red/Blue/Orange-Yellow.
Ticket system: Wayfarer

*WIGHTROLLERS

UNIT D10, SPITHEAD BUSINESS CENTRE, NEWPORT ROAD, SANDOWN PO36 9PH
Tel: 01983 404028
Fax: 01983 404772
E-mail: wightrollers@supanet.co.uk
Web site: www.wightrollers.com
Dirs: P Steele, T Steele **Ops Man**: C Steele
Ch Eng: C Steele
Fleet: 14 coach
Chassis: 1 DAF. 2 Dennis. 2 MAN. 3 Mercedes. 6 Volvo.
Bodies: 3 Caetano. 2 Duple. 4 Jonckheere. 2 Plaxton. 3 Van Hool.
Ops incl: excursions & tours, private hire, continental tours.
Livery: Burgundy/Pink

*JOHN WOODHAMS VINTAGE TOURS
GROVE ROAD, RYDE PO33 3LH
Tel/Fax: 01983 812147
E-mail: vintagetours@btconnect.com
Web site: www.vintagetours.net

Prop: John Woodhams
Fleet: 2 midicoach.
Chassis: 2 Bedford.
Bodies: 2 Duple.
Ops incl: excursions & tours, private hire

KENT

*ARRIVA SOUTHERN COUNTIES
INVICTA HOUSE, ARMSTRONG ROAD, MAIDSTONE ME15 9TG
Tel: 01622 697000
Fax: 01622 697001
Web site: www.arriva.co.uk
Man Dir: Heath Williams **Eng Dir**: Tony Ward **Fin Dir**: Beverley Lawson. **Comm Dir**: Kevin Hawkins
Fleet: 633 - 174 double-deck bus, 402 single-deck bus, 32 minibus, 1 midibus, 24 coach.
Chassis: 101 DAF. 302 Dennis. 50 Leyland. 3 MCW. 25 Mercedes. 7 Optare. 13 Scania. 132 Volvo.
Bodies: 26 Alexander. 1 Duple. 36 East Lancs. 2 Ikarus. 9 Leyland. 3 MCW. 6 Mercedes. 90 Northern Counties. 7 Optare. 262 Plaxton. 76 Transbus. 10 Van Hool. 4 Wadham Stringer. 101 Wright.
Ops incl: local bus services, school contracts, excursions & tours, express, continental tours, private hire.
Livery: Blue/Cream.
Ticket System: Wayfarer 3 & TGX150

*ASM COACHES
8 THE OAZE, WHITSTABLE CT5 4TQ
Tel: 01227 280254
Fax: 01227 280467
E-mail: asm.coaches@virgin.net
Props: Steven R Morrish, Alison Morrish.
Fleet: 2 minicoach
Chassis: 2 Mercedes.
Ops incl: school contracts, private hire, continental trips.
Livery: Purple/White

AUTOCAR BUS & COACH SERVICES LTD
64 WHETSTED ROAD, FIVE OAK GREEN, TONBRIDGE TN12 6RT
Tel: 01892 833830
Fax: 01892 836977
Dir: Eric Baldock **Fleet Eng**: Ray Tompsett
Fleet: 8 - 4 single-deck bus, 2 coach, 1 double-deck coach, 1 midicoach.
Chassis: 1 DAF. 1 Dennis. 4 Leyland. 1 Mercedes. 1 Scania.
Bodies: 1 Alexander. 1 Duple. 2 East Lancs. 2 Plaxton. 1 Wadham Stringer. Wright.
Ops incl: local bus services, school contracts, private hire.

Livery: White/Purple (two shades)
Ticket System: Wayfarer 2

BEXLEY COACHLINES
25 OLDFIELD ROAD, BEXLEYHEATH DA7 4DX
Tel: 020 8302 7551.
Web site: www.bexleycoach.co.uk
Gen Man: Glyn Matthews.
Fleet: 5 coach.
Chassis: 1 AEC. 2 Dennis. 2 Volvo.
Bodies: 5 Plaxton.
Ops incl: excursions & tours, private hire.
Livery: Green/Cream.

*BRITANNIA COACHES
HOLLOW WOOD ROAD, DOVER CT17 0UB
Tel: 01304 228111
Fax: 01304 215350
E-mail: enq@britannia-coaches.co.uk.
Web site: www.britannia-coaches.co.uk.
Ptnrs: Barry Watson, Danny Lawson.
Fleet: 30 minicoach.
Chassis/bodies: 20 Mercedes. 10 Renault.
Ops incl: private hire, school contracts, excursions & tours.

BROWNS COACHES
OAKTREE COTTAGE, MANOR POUND LANE, BRABOURNE, ASHFORD TN25 5LG.
Tel: 01303 813555
Fax: 01303 812070
Prop: Patrick Browne
Fleet: 4 - 3 coach, 1 minibus.
Chassis: 1 LDV. . 3 Volvo.
Ops incl: school contracts, private hire

*BUZZLINES
UNIT G1, LYMPNE INDUSTRIAL PARK, LYMPNE CT21 4LR
Tel: 01303 261870
Fax: 01303 230093
Recovery: 07767 475625
E-mail: sales@buzzlines.co.uk

Web site: www.buzzlines.co.uk
Dir: Mrs K Busbridge **Man Dir**: N. P. Busbridge **Eng Man**: D Lange
Ops Man: G Creasey
Fleet: 56 - 2 single-deck bus, 28 coach, 3 double-deck coach, 3 midicoach, 15 minbus, 5 people carrier.
Chassis: 1 Dennis. 4 Ford Transit. 11 Mercedes. 11 Neoplan. 8 Scania. 2 Seat. 7 Setra. 4 Toyota. 5 Volvo. 3 Volkswagen.
Bodies: 4 Caetano. 4 Ford Transit. 6 Irizar. 11 Neoplan. 7 Setra. 11 Mercedes. 5 Volvo. 3 Volkswagen. 2 Seat. 2 PTS.
Ops incl: local bus services, school contracts, excursions & tours, private hire, continental tours.
Livery: Metallic blue.

CENTRAL MINI COACHES
177 LOWER ROAD, DOVER CT17 0RE.
Tel/Fax: 01304 823030.
Prop: P. Hull.
Fleet: 6 - 5 minibus, 1 minicoach.
Chassis: 3 Bedford. 1 Mercedes. 1 Renault.
Ops incl: private hire, school contracts.

CHALKWELL COACH HIRE & TOURS
195 CHALKWELL ROAD, SITTINGBOURNE ME10 1BJ
Tel: 01795 423983
Fax: 01795 431855
E-mail: coachhire@chalkwell.co.uk
Web site: www.chalkwell.com
Man Dir: Chris Eglinton **Ops Man**: Roland Eglinton
Fleet: 31 - 18 coach, 3 midibus, 6 midicoach, 4 minicoach.
Chassis: 9 Dennis. 1 Iveco. 3 LDV. 9 Mercedes. 9 Volvo.
Bodies: 5 Alexander. 1 Caetano. 18 Plaxton. 2 UVG. 1 Wadham Stringer.
Ops incl: local bus services, school contracts, excursions & tours, private hire, express, continental tours.
Livery: White/Red/Black
Ticket System: Almex A90

Ac Air conditioning
   Vehicles suitable for disabled
   Coach(es) with galley facilities
wc Coach(es) with toilet facilities
   Seat belt-fitted vehicles
R Recovery service available (not 24 hr)
R24 24hr recovery service
   Replacement vehicle available
T Toilet-drop facilities available
   Vintage vehicle(s) available
   Open top vehicle(s)

Isle of Wight / Kent

*CRAKERS COACHES

52 BIRDWOOD AVENUE, DEAL
CT14 9SF
Tel/Fax: 01304 362002
Prop: Alfred Craker
Fleet: 1 coach.
Chassis: 1 Volvo.
Bodies: 1 Van Hool.
Ops incl: private hire
Livery: Cream/Red

*CROSSKEYS COACHES

CROSSKEYS BUSINESS PARK,
CAESARS WAY, FOLKESTONE
CT19 4AL
Tel: 01303 272625
Fax: 01303 274085
E-mail: coachire@crosskeys.uk.com
Web site: www.crosskeys.uk.com
Prop: A Johnson
Fleet: 19 - 2 single-deck bus, 14 coach, 3 minicoach.
Chassis: 1 Bedford. 9 Bova. 2 Leyland National. 1 Mercedes.
Bodies: 9 Bova. 2 Leyland National. 3 Plaxton.
Ops incl: local bus services, school contracts, excursions & tours, private hire, continental tours.
Livery: Orange

*ALAN DAWNEY HOLIDAYS
   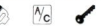
UNIT 6, TRANSIT WORKS, POWER STATION ROAD, HALFWAY, SHEERNESS ME12 3AD
Tel/Fax: 01795 662688
E-mail: dawneyholidays@aol.com
Dirs: Alan Dawney, Carole Dawney
Fleet: 9 - 3 coach, 6 minicoach.
Chassis: 1 MAN. 2 Volvo.
Bodies: include - 3 Caetano.
Ops incl: excursions & tours, private hire, continental tours.
Livery: White/Green/Yellow

EASTONWAYS LTD
MANSTON ROAD, RAMSGATE
CT12 6HJ
Tel: 01843 588944
Fax: 01843 582300
E-mail: ele@eastonways.demon.co.uk
Web site: www.eastonways.demon.co.uk
Chmn/Co Sec E. L. Easton.
Man Dir: D. Austin **Dir**: Y. M. Easton.
Ops Man: S. Lee. **Eng**: E. Easton.
Fleet: 15 - 2 double-deck coach, 8 single-deck bus, 3 coach, 2 midicoach.
Chassis: 2 Bristol. 1 DAF. 1 Optare. 2 Toyota. 1 Volvo.
Bodies: 1 Caetano. 1 Duple. 2 Northern Counties. 8 Optare. 1 Van Hool.
Ops incl: local bus services, school contracts, private hire.
Livery: Coaches: Blue/Silver. Buses: Red.
Ticket System: Wayfarer.

*EUROLINK FOKESTONE

GREATWORTH, CANTERBURY ROAD, ETCHINGHILL, FOLKESTONE CT18 8BS
Tel: 01303 862767
Fax: 01303 862484
E-mail: eurolinkfolkestone@email.com
Ptnrs: Andy Williams, Lyn Williams
Fleet: 9 - 4 midicoach, 5 minibus.
Chassis: 1 Ford Transit. 2 MAN. 4 Mercedes. 1 Renault. 1 Toyota.
Bodies: 3 Caetano. 1 Esker. 1 Mercedes. 1 Optare. 3 other.
Ops incl: school contracts, private hire.

FARLEIGH COACHES
ST PETERS WORKS, HALL ROAD, WOULDHAM, ROCHESTER ME1 3XL
Tel: 01634 201065.
Fax: 01634 660350.
Prop: J. M. Smith.
Livery: White/Yellow/Red/Black.

FERRYMAN TRAVEL
RECTORY LANE NORTH, LEYBOURNE ME19 5HD.
Tel/Fax: 01732 843396
Fleet: 4 minibus.
Chassis: 3 DAF. 1 Ford Transit.
Ops incl: school contracts, excursions & tours, private hire, continental tours.

*G & S TRAVEL

14 PYSONS ROAD, RAMSGATE CT12 6TS
Tel: 01843 591105.
Fax: 01843 596274.
E-mail: malc@pysons.freeserve.co.uk
Dirs: Shirley Rimmer, George Rimmer, Malcolm Wood **Ch Eng**: Robert Maunder
Fleet: 12 - 9 coach, 1 minibus, 2 midicoach.
Chassis: 1 LDV. 2 Toyota. 8 Volvo. 1 Van Hool
Bodies: 5 Caetano. 5 Plaxton. 1 Van Hool. 1 other.
Ops incl: school contracts, excursions & tours, private hire, continental tours.
Livery: White.

JAYCREST LTD
14 BAYFORD ROAD, SITTINGBOURNE ME10 3AD
Tel: 01795 438400
Fleet: 22 - 1 single-deck bus, 3 coach, 18 midibus
Ops incl: local bus services

KENT COACH TOURS LTD

THE COACH STATION, MALCOLM SARGENT ROAD, ASHFORD TN23 6JW
Tel/Recovery: 01233 627330
Fax: 01233 612977
Web site: www.kentcoachtours.co.uk
Dirs: David Farmer, Ann Farmer, Andrew Farmer (**Co Sec**), Brian Farmer (**Ch Eng**)
Fleet: 13 - 1 single-deck bus, 7 coach, 5 minibus.
Chassis: 1 MAN. 5 Mercedes. 1 Optare. 7 Volvo.
Bodies: 1 Optare. 12 Plaxton.
Ops incl: local bus services, school contracts, excursions & tours, private hire.
Livery: Blue
Ticket System: Wayfarer

KENT COUNTY COUNCIL

COMMERCIAL SERVICES, PASSENGER SERVICES, FORSTAL ROAD, AYLESFORD ME20 7HB
Tel: 01622 605935.
Fax: 01622 790338.
Tran Man: Darien Goodwin. **Ops Contr**: Roger Faunch. **Asst Ops Contr**: Mick Curd.
Fleet: 48 - 2 double-deck bus, 12 single-deck bus, 4 coach, 2 midibus, 1 midicoach, 27 minibus.
Chassis: 5 Dennis. 27 Iveco. 4 Leyland. 3 Mercedes. 4 Optare. 1 Volvo.
Bodies: 1 Alexander. 1 Caetano. 7 Leicester. 2 Leyland. 4 Optare. 6 Plaxton. 27 Euromotive.
Ops incl: local bus services, school contracts, private hire.
Livery: Red on White.
Ticket System: Almex.

*THE KINGS FERRY TRAVEL GROUP
THE TRAVEL CENTRE, GILLINGHAM ME8 6HW
Tel: 01634 377577
Fax: 01634 370656
E-mail: sales@thekingsferry.co.uk
Web site: www.thekingsferry.co.uk
Chmn: P O'Neill **Man Dir**: S O'Neill **Dir**: V Broster **Group Comm Man**: D Elford
Group Ops Man: I Fraser
Fleet: 74 - 2 double-deck bus, 3 single-deck bus, 54 coach, 7 double-deck coach, 1 open-top bus, 2 midicoach, 5 minicoach.
Chassis: 1 Bova. 1 DAF. 2 Iveco. 1 Leyland. 8 Mercedes. 1 Neoplan. 37 Scania. 5 Setra. 19 Volvo.
Bodies: 19 Berkhof. 1 Bova. 1 Caetano. 1 Castrosua. 2 East Lancs. 3 Hispano. 2 Indcar. 10 Irizar. 1 Leyland. 1 Mercedes. 1 Neoplan. 4 Plaxton. 5 Setra. 5 Sunsundegui. 11 Van Hool. 4 other.
Ops incl: local bus services, school contracts, excursions & tours, private hire, express, continental tours.
Livery: Yellow with green stripe

*KINGSMAN INTERNATIONAL TRAVEL
57 BRAMLEY AVENUE, FAVERSHAM ME13 8LP
Tel: 01795 531553
Fax: 01795 536798
E-mail: jonathanamancini@tiscali.co.uk
Prosp: J A Mancini, J Mancini
Fleet: 8 - 4 single-deck bus, 3 coach, 1 midicoach.
Chassis: 6 Mercedes. 3 Neoplan.
Bodies: 4 Mercedes. 3 Neoplan. 2 Plaxton.
Ops incl: local bus services, excursions & tours, private hire, continental tours.

*LOGANS TOURS LTD

1 AND 2 THE COTTAGES,
NORTHFLEET GREEN DA13 9PT
Tel: 01474 833876
Fax: 01474 832038
E-mail: dave@loganstours.co.uk
Web site: www.loganstours.co.uk
Dir: David Logan
Fleet: 2 coach.
Chassis: 1 Dennis. 1 Raba.
Bodies: 1 Caetano. 1 Ikarus.
Ops incl: excursions & tours, private hire, continental tours
Livery: Pink/White

NEW ENTERPRISE COACHES
CANNON LANE, TONBRIDGE
TN9 1PP.
Tel: 01732 355256.
Fax: 01732 357716.
Prop: Arriva Southern Counties.
Gen Man: Chris Lawrence.
Eng Man: Andy Weber.
Fleet: 24 - 5 double-deck bus, 2 single-deck bus, 17 coach.
Chassis: 8 DAF. 3 Leyland. 4 MCW. 3 Scania. 6 Volvo.
Bodies: 2 Caetano. 3 Duple. 4 MCW. 1 PMT. 11 Plaxton. 1 Reeve Burgess. 3 Van Hool.
Ops incl: local bus services, school contracts, excursions & tours, private hire, continental tours.
Livery: White/Red/Blue.
Ticket System: Wayfarer II.

*NU-VENTURE COACHES LTD
UNIT 2F, DEACON TRADING ESTATE, FORSTAL ROAD,
AYLESFORD ME20 7JN
Tel: 01622 882288
Fax: 01622 718070
Web site: www.nu-venture.co.uk
Dir: D Quick **Co Sec**: N Kemp
Fleet: 37 - 10 double-deck bus, 12 single-deck bus, 4 coach, 11 midibus.
Chassis: Dennis. Leyland. MAN. Mercedes. Optare. Scania. Transbus.
Bodies: Alexander. East Lancs. Irizar. Leyland. Marcopolo. Marshall. Optare. Plaxton. Transbus. UVG. Van Hool.
Ops incl: local bus services, school contracts, private hire, excursions & tours.
Livery: White/Blue/Red
Ticket System: Wayfarer 3.

*POYNTERS COACHES LTD
WYE COACH DEPOT, WYE
TN25 5BX.
Tel: 01233 812002
Fax: 01233 813210
Recovery: 07770 874631
E-mail: poyntercoaches@aol.com
Dir: B. J. Poynter. **Ch Eng**: B. J. Poynter
Fleet: 14 - 1 double-deck bus, 6 single-deck bus, 5 coach, 1 double-deck coach.
Chassis: 2 Bova. 4 DAF. 4 Dennis. 1 Leyland. 1 Mercedes. 2 Neoplan. 2 Optare. 2 Volvo.
Bodies: 1 Berkhof. 2 Bova. 2 East Lancs. 1 Leyland. 2 Neoplan. 3 Plaxton. 1 Van Hool
Ops incl: local bus services, school contracts, excursions & tours, private hire, continental tours
Livery: White/Yellow/Red
Ticket System: Wayfarer

R. K. F. TRAVEL

19 COBB CLOSE, STROOD ME2 3TY
Tel/Fax: 01634 715897.
Dir: Ray Fraser.
Fleet: 2 minibus.
Chassis: 1 LDV, 1 VW.
Ops incl: private hire.

*THE RAINHAM COACH CO
1A SPRINGFIELD ROAD,
GILLINGHAM ME7 1YJ
Tel/Fax: 01634 852020
Recovery: 07850 657653
E-mail: sales@rainhamcoach.co.uk
Web site: www.rainhamcoach.co.uk
Senr Ptnr: David Graham **Ptnr**: Chris Graham **Ops Man**: Alan Lorenston
Fleet Eng: Geoff Baldock
Fleet: 19 - 4 midicoach, 1 minibus, 14 minicoach.
Chassis/Bodies: 4 Ford Transit. 12 Mercedes. 1 Optare. 2 other.
Ops incl: school contracts, private hire, excursions & tours, continental tours.
Livery: Magenta/Grey on white base.

REDROUTE BUSES
GRANBY COACHWORKS, GROVE ROAD, NORTHFLEET DA11 9AX
Tel: 01474 353896
Web site: www.redroutebus.com
Fleet: 25 - 14 double-deck bus, 3 single-deck bus, 1 coach, 7 minibus.
Ops incl: local bus services
Livery: Red

REGENT COACHES

UNIT 16, ST AUGUSTINES BUSINESS PARK, WHITSTABLE
CT5 2QJ
Tel: 01227 794345
Fax: 01227 795120
E-mail: info@regentcoaches.com
Web site: www.regentcoaches.co.uk
Ptnrs: Paul Regent, Kerry Regent **Tran Mans**: Colin MacDonald, Kenneth Bishop
Traff Assistant: Sam Regent **Fleet Eng**: Robert Wildish
Fleet: 25 - 8 minibus, 10 midicoach, 7 minicoach.
Chassis: 4 Iveco. 5 LDV. 12 Mercedes. 4 Renault.
Ops incl: local bus services, school contracts, private hire.
Livery: White/Red/Orange
Ticket system: Almex Electronic

ROUNDABOUT BUSES LTD

3 HATHERLEY ROAD, SIDCUP
DA14 4BH.
Tel/Fax: 020 8302 7551.
E-mail: info@roundaboutbuses.co.uk
Web site: www.roundaboutbuses.co.uk
Man Dir: Glyn Matthews.
Fleet: 6 - 1 single-deck bus, 1 minibus.
Chassis: 1 AEC. 2 Iveco. 5 Leyland.
Bodies: 3 ECW. 1 Marshall. 1 Park Royal. 1 Roe. 1 Robin Hood.
Ops incl: local bus services, school contracts.
Livery: Green/Cream.
Ticket System: Wayfarer.

SCOTLAND & BATES
HEATH ROAD, APPLEDORE
TN26 2AJ
Tel: 01233 758325.
Fax: 01233 758611.
E-mail: info@scotlandandbates.co.uk
Web site: www.scotlandandbates.co.uk
Ptnrs: D C R Bates, R M Bates, G A Bates.
Fleet: 17 coach.
Chassis: 1 Bedford. 16 Volvo.
Bodies: 6 Plaxton. 11 Van Hool.
Ops incl: local bus services, school contracts, private hire
Livery: Cream/Brown/Orange

SEATH COACHES
FIELDINGS, STONEHEAP ROAD,
EAST STUDDAL CT15 5BU
Tel/Fax: 01304 620825.
Owner: P. Seath.
Fleet: 4 coach.
Chassis: Ford. Iveco. Leyland. Volvo.
Bodies: Caetano. Plaxton
Ops incl: school contracts, private hire.
Livery: Pink/White/Beige.

*SKINNERS OF OXTED
See Surrey

SMITHS CONTINENTAL TRAVEL

THE COACH STATION,
KING STREET, BRENZETT
TN29 9UD
Tel: 01797 344228
Fax: 01797 344248
Man Dir: Dave Smith **Ops Man**: Steve Rees
Ch Eng: F C Ovenden
Fleet: 17 - 16 coach, 1 double-deck coach.
Chassis: 1 DAF. 9 Leyland. 7 Scania.
Bodies: 2 Jonckheere. 11 Plaxton. 4 Van Hool.
Ops incl: local bus services, school contracts, excursions & tours, private hire, continental tours.
Livery: Blue/White
Ticket system: Wayfarer

A/c	Air conditioning
♿	Vehicles suitable for disabled
🍴	Coach(es) with galley facilities
WC	Coach(es) with toilet facilities
🪑	Seat belt-fitted vehicles
R	Recovery service available (not 24 hr)
R24	24hr recovery service
🔧	Replacement vehicle available
T	Toilet-drop facilities available
🚌	Vintage vehicle(s) available
🚐	Open top vehicle(s)

SOUTHNOR COACHES
91 DARTFORD ROAD, DARTFORD DA1 3ES.
Tel/Fax: 01322 228963.
Owner: D. Hucker.
Fleet: 2 - 1 coach, 1 minibus.
Chassis: Volvo. **Body:** Plaxton.
Ops incl: excursions & tours, private hire, continental tours.

SPOT HIRE TRAVEL
STATION APPROACH, BEARSTED RAILWAY STATION, MAIDSTONE ME14 4PH
Tel: 01622 738932
Fax: 01622 630406
Prop: Roger Young
Fleet: 11 - 6 coach, 1 midicoach, 4 minicoach.
Chassis: 5 Mercedes. 6 Volvo.
Bodies: 2 Autobus. 1 Jonckheere. 2 Mercedes. 5 Plaxton. 1 Van Hool.
Ops incl: school contracts, private hire.
Livery: Cream

STAGECOACH IN EAST KENT & HASTINGS

BUS STATION, ST GEORGE'S LANE, CANTERBURY CT1 2SY
Tel: 01227 828103
Fax: 01227 828150
Web site: www.stagecoachbus.com
Ch Exec: Brian Souter **Man Dir UK Bus:** L Warneford **Group Fin Dir:** M Griffiths **Co Sec:** A Whitnall **Man Dir:** Paul Southgate **Ops Dir:** Neil Instrall **Eng Dir:** Keith Dyball
Fleet: 302 - 143 double-deck bus, 45 single-deck bus, 17 coach, 45 midibus, 52 minibus.
Chassis: 48 Dennis. 3 Dodge. 1 Ford. 4 Ford Transit. 43 Leyland. 9 MAN. 52 Mercedes. 44 Scania. 106 Volvo.
Bodies: 182 Alexander. 4 Leyland. 7 Leyland. 74 Northern Counties. 40 Plaxton. 3 Wadham Stringer. 3 Wright.
Ops incl: local bus services, express.
Livery: Stagecoach (Blue,Orange,White,Red); National Express (White).
Ticket System: ERG/Wayfarer.

STREAMLINE
WEST STATION APPROACH, MAIDSTONE ME16 8RJ
Tel: 01622 750000
Fax: 01622 752978
E-mail: ron.parker@streamlinetaxis.co.uk
Man Dir: Ron Parker
Fleet: 5 - 1 coach, 2 minibus, 2 midicoach.
Chassis/Bodies: 2 Mercedes. 2 Plaxton. 1 Setra.
Ops include: excursions & tours, private hire, continental tours
Livery: Silver with blue writing

TANGNEY TOURS
PILGRIM HOUSE, STATION COURT, BOROUGH GREEN TN15 8AF
Tel: 01732 885688.
Fax: 01732 886885.
Propr: P. J. Tawney. **Ops Man:** S. L. Hedley
Fleet: 5 - 4 single-deck coach, 1 midicoach.
Chassis: 4 Setra.
Bodies: 1 Caetano. 4Setra.
Ops incl: excursions & tours, private hire, continental tours.

*THOMSETT'S COACHES

50 GOLF ROAD, DEAL CT14 6QB
Tel/Fax: 01304 374731
E-mail: thomsettcoaches@efsmail.net
Prop: S. J. Thomsett
Fleet: 5 - 4 coach, 1 midicoach.
Chassis: 1 MAN. 3 Scania.
Bodies: 1 Caetano. 2 Plaxton. 2 Van Hool.
Ops incl: school contracts, private hire.

TIM'S TRAVEL

THE COACH STATION, DORSET, SHEERNESS ME12 1LT
Tel: 01634 265511
Fax: 01634 370656
Recovery: 01634 265508
Fleetname: The Kings Ferry
Chmn: Peter O'Neill **Man Dir:** Steven O'Neill **Eng Man:** Danny Elford **Group Ops Man:** Ian Fraser
Fleet: 13 - 11 coach, 2 double-deck coach.
Chassis: 1 DAF. 4 Mercedes. 2 Scania. 6 Volvo.
Bodies: 1 Berkhof. 1 Caetano. 4 Mercedes. 6 Plaxton. 1 Van Hool.
Ops incl: local bus services, school contracts, excursions & tours, private hire, express.
Livery: Green

TRACKS VEHICLE SERVICES LTD
THE FLOTS, BROOKLAND, ROMNEY MARSH TN29 9TG
Tel: 01797 344164
Fax: 01797 344135
E-mail: info@tracks-travel.com
Web site: tracks -travel.com
Man Dir: Andrew Toms.
Fleet: 6 coach.
Chassis: DAF. Mercedes. Scania. Setra.
Bodies: Caetano. Jonckheere. Mercedes. Setra..
Ops incl: continental tours.
Livery: White

THE TRAVEL LINK

THE TRAVEL CENTRE, EASTCOURT LANE, GILLINGHAM ME8 6HW
Tel: 01634 265503
Fax: 01634 370656
E-mail: sales@thetravellink.co.uk
Web site: www.thetravellink.co.uk
Chmn: P O'Neill **Man Dir:** S O'Neill **Dir:** V Broster **Group Eng Man:** D Elford **Group Ops Man:** I Fraser **Fin Dir:** S Huis
Fleet: 18 - 2 double-deck bus, 12 single-deck coach, 3 double-deck coach, 1 minicoach.
Chassis: 1 Ayats. 3 DAF. 1 Mercedes. 11 Scania. 4 Volvo.
Bodies: 1 Ayats. 2 Berkhof. 2 East Lancs. 2 Irizar. 1 Mercedes. 7 Plaxton. 5 Van Hool.
Ops incl: local bus services, school contracts, excursions & tours, private hire, express, continental tours.
Livery: Yellow with green stripe

*TRAVELMASTERS

DORSET ROAD INDUSTRIAL ESTATE, DORSET ROAD, SHEERNESS ME12 1LT
Tel: 01795 66066
Fax: 01795 660033
E-mail: sales.travel@btconnect.com
Dirs: T Lambkin, C Smith
Fleet: 7 - 2 double-deck bus, 3 coach, 1 midicoach, 1 minibus.
Chassis: 1 Bristol. 2 Mercedes. 3 Volvo.
Ops incl: school contracts, private hire.
Livery: White/Blue/Yellow

TRAVEL RITE

THE TRAVEL CENTRE, EASTCOURT LANE, GILLINGHAM ME8 6HW
Tel: 01634 265511
Fax: 01634 370656
Recovery: 01634 265508
E-mail: sales@travelrite.co.uk
Web site: www.travelrite.co.uk
Fleetname: The Kings Ferry

The Grasshopper Inn
(A25) Moorhouse, Nr. Westerham, Kent
13TH CENTURY TUDOR INN WITH 21ST CENTURY HOSPITALITY
Coffee, Drinks, Lunch or Dinner Stops
Kent/Surrey's Best Carvery
We welcome Coach Parties
Complimentary meal/refreshments for the driver with each coach party.
Massive car park with coach bays. Situated South of London, within 10 minutes of the M25 (jnct. 5 & 6)
Phone our friendly staff to make a booking.
Tel: 01959 563136
E-mail: info@grasshopperinn.co.uk
Website: www.grasshopperinn.co.uk

Chmn: Peter O'Neill **Man Dir**: Steven O'Neill **Eng Man**: Danny Elford **Group Ops Man**: Ian Fraser
Fleet: 7 - 5 coach, 1 double-deck coach, 1 minibus.
Chassis: 1 DAF. 1 Mercedes. 5 Scania.
Bodies: 2 Berkhof. 2 Irizar. 1 Mercedes. 1 Plaxton. 1 Van Hool.
Ops incl: school contracts, private hire.
Livery: Yellow

VIKING MINICOACHES

UNIT 1, LYSANDER CLOSE, PYSONS ROAD INDUSTRIAL ESTATE, BROADSTAIRS CT10 2YJ
Tel/Fax: 01843 860876
Fax: 01843 866975
Prop: Paul Troke
Fleet: 7 - 2 midicoach, 5 minibus.
Chassis/bodies: 2 Iveco. 1 LDV. 2 Mercedes. 1 Renault. 1 Toyota. 1 Caetano
Ops incl: school contracts, private hire.

WALLIS LIMOUSINES

46A VALLEY ROAD, BROMLEY BR2 0HD
Tel: 09741 467905
Fax: 020 8466 0490
E-mail: info@wallislimousines.com

Dir: Stephen Wallis
Fleet: single-deck bus
Chassis: Leyland
Ops incl: local bus services, school contracts.
Livery: White/Blue
Ticket system: Wayfarer

*WARREN'S COACHES (KENT & SUSSEX) LTD
See East Sussex

*WESTERHAM COACHES
See Surrey

LANCASHIRE (BLACKBURN, DARWEN, BLACKPOOL, WIGAN)

*ADLINGTON TAXIS & MINICOACHES
See Greater Manchester

*ALFA TRAVEL

EUXTON LANE, CHORLEY PR7 6AF
Tel: 0845 130 5777
Fax: 0845 130 3777
E-mail: req@alfatravel.co.uk
Web site: www.alfatravel.co.uk
Fleetname: Alfa Travel
Man Dir: Paul Sawbridge **Fin Dir**: Peter Sawbridge **Head of Tour Ops**: Neil McMurdy **Ops Man**: Tom Smith
Fleet: 34 coach
Chassis: 10 DAF. 19 Dennis. 5 Volvo.
Bodies: 10 Ikarus. 24 Plaxton.
Ops incl: excursions & tours, private hire, continental tours.
Livery: Cream

J & F ASPDEN (BLACKBURN) LTD

LANCASTER STREET, BLACKBURN BB2 1UA.
Tel: 01254 52020.
Fax: 01254 57474.
Fleetname: Aspdens Coaches.
Fleet: 14 - 1 double-deck bus, 13 coach.
Chassis: 1 Bristol. 13 Leyland.
Bodies: 5 Duple. 1 Northern Counties. 8 Plaxton.
Ops incl: school contracts, excursions & tours, private hire, continental tours.
Livery: Yellow/Black.
Subsidiary of Holmeswood Coaches

BATTERSBY SILVER GREY COACHES

THE COACH STATION, MIDDLEGATE, WHITE LUND BUSINESS PARK, MORECAMBE LA3 3PE
Tel: 01524 380000
Fax: 01524 380800
E-mail: sales@battersbys.co.uk
Web site: www.battersbys.co.uk
Chmn: J A Harrison **Man Dir**: M R Harrison
Sec: M F Harrison
Fleet: incl. coach, midicoach, midibus.
Chassis: Mercedes, Volvo.
Bodies: Plaxton.
Ops incl: local bus services, excursions & tours, private hire, continental tours, school contracts.
Livery: White

*BLACKBURN BOROUGH TRANSPORT LTD

INTACK, BLACKBURN BB1 3JD.
Tel: 01254 51112
Fax: 01254 662637
E-mail: info@blackburntransport.co.uk
Web site: www.blackburntransport.co.uk
Fleetname: Blackburn Transport
Chmn: Cllr James Shorrock **Man Dir**: Michael Morton. **Fin Dir/Co Sec**: Ted Buckley **Fleet Eng**: Glenn Dearden
Fin Man: Jan Lundie
Fleet: 109 - 59 double-deck bus. 20 single-deck bus. 30 midibus.
Chassis: 21 Dennis. 50 Leyland. 14 Optare.
23 Volvo.
Bodies: 6 Alexander. 34 ECW. 13 East Lancs. 9 Leyland. 8 Northern Counties. 15 Optare. 10 Plaxton. 1 Roe. 12 Wright.
Ops incl: local bus services, school contracts, private hire.
Livery: two-tone Green/Cream/Yellow
Ticket System: Almex Optima.

BLACKPOOL TRANSPORT LTD

RIGBY ROAD, BLACKPOOL FY1 5DD
Tel: 01253 473001
Fax: 01253 473101
E-mail: directors@blackpooltransport.com
Web site: www.blackpooltransport.com
Fleetname: MetroCoastlines
Man Dir: Steve Burd **Eng Dir**: Bill Gibson
Ops Dir: David Eaves **Fin Dir**: Allan Leach
Business Development Man: Liz Esnouf
Human Res Man: Annie Nancollis
Fleet: 229 - 72 double-deck bus, 39 single-deck bus, 46 midibus, 72 tram.
Chassis: 30 DAF. 18 Dennis. 48 Leyland. 55 Optare. 6 Volvo.
Bodies: 10 ECW. 44 East Lancs. 15 Northern Counties. 85 Optare. 3 Roe. (also 8 Optare Solos jointly owned by Blackpool Borough Council and Lancashire County Council)
Ops incl: local bus services, tram services, school contracts, private hire.
Livery: Yellow plus route branded route colours.
Ticket System: Almex A90

Air conditioning	Replacement vehicle available
Vehicles suitable for disabled	Toilet-drop facilities available
Coach(es) with galley facilities	Vintage vehicle(s) available
Coach(es) with toilet facilities	Open top vehicle(s)
Seat belt-fitted vehicles	
Recovery service available (not 24 hr)	
R24 24hr recovery service	

BLUE BUS AND COACH SERVICES LTD

MOOR LANE BUS STATION, BLACK HORSE STREET, BOLTON BL1 1SY
Tel: 01204 388125
Fax: 01204 396257
Web site: www.blue-bus.co.uk
Man Dir: Roger Jarvis **Ops Mans**: Ian Laing, Ben Jarvis **Fleet Eng**: John Nixon
Comm Man: Andrew Jarvis
Fleet: 98 - 16 double-deck bus, 53 single-deck bus, 2 coach, 10 midibus, 17 minibus.
Chassis:16 DAF. 33 Dennis. 14 Leyland. 5 MAN. 5 Mercedes. 15 Optare. 10 Volvo.
Bodies: 24 Alexander. 2 Duple. 17 East Lancs. 10 Ikarus. 3 Leyland. 15 Optare. 22 Plaxton. 6 Wright.
Ops incl: local bus services, school contracts, private hire.
Livery: two-tone Blue
Ticket System: ERG TP4000
Part of Arriva North West

*BRADSHAWS TRAVEL

46 WESTBOURNE ROAD, KNOTT END ON SEA FY6 0BS
Tel: 01253 810058
Prop: Mrs Jill Swift
Fleet: 6 - 5 coach, 1 minibus.
Chassis: 1 Dennis. 3 Leyland. 1 Mercedes. 1 Volvo.
Bodies: 1 Berkof. 1 Duple. 1 Mercedes. 3 Plaxton.
Ops incl: private hire, school contracts.
Livery: White.
Ticket System: Almex

BURNLEY & PENDLE

QUEENSGATE BUS DEPOT, COLNE ROAD, BURNLEY BB10 1HH
Tel: 01282 427778
Web site: www.burnleyandpendle.co.uk
Prop: Blazefield Holdings Ltd.
Chmn: Giles Fearnley. **Man Dir**: Stuart Wilde. **Dir (Lancs)**: George Scrymgeour.
Fleet: 72 - double-deck buses, single-deck buses.
Chassis: Dennis, Leyland, Mercedes-Benz, Volvo.
Bodies: Alexander, ECW, Northern Counties, Plaxton, Wright.
Livery: Red/Cream.
Ticket System: ERG.
Part of the Blazefield group which is owned by Transdev

*COACH OPTIONS

See Greater Manchester

COLRAY COACHES

14 PRESTBURY AVENUE, BLACKPOOL FY4 1PT
Tel: 01253 349481
Dirs: Geoffrey Shaw, V Shaw
Fleet: 4 - coach, midibus, midicoach.
Chassis: 1 Mercedes. 1 Setra. 2 Toyota. 1 Volvo.
Bodies: 1 Caetano. 1 Mercedes. 1 Plaxton. 1 Setra
Ops incl: excursions & tours, school contracts, private hire, continental tours.
Livery: White/Blue

EAVESWAY TRAVEL LTD

BRYN SIDE, BRYN ROAD, ASHTON-IN-MAKERFIELD WN4 8BT
Tel: 01942 727985
Fax: 01942 271234
E-mail: sales@eaveswaytravel.com
Web site: www.eaveswaytravel.com
Man Dir: Mike Eaves **Dir**: Phil Rogers.
Fleet: 20 coach
Chassis: 12 DAF. 8 MAN.
Bodies: 20 Van Hool.
Ops incl: excursions & tours, private hire.
Livery: Silver/Blue/Green.

JOHN FISHWICK & SONS

GOLDEN HILL GARAGE, LEYLAND PR25 3LE.
Tel: 01772 421207.
Fax: 01772 622407.
E-mail: enquiries@fishwicks.co.uk
Web site: www.fishwicks.co.uk
Dir: J. C. Brindle. **Dir**: J. F. Hustler. **Ch Eng**: J. Cave. **IT Man**: A Clenshaw **Coach Man**: A Aldam.
Fleet: 47 - 7 double-deck bus, 31 single-deck bus, 8 coach, 1 minibus.
Chassis: 12 DAF. 4 Dennis. 5 EOS. 15 Leyland. 8 Leyland National. 2 Mercedes.
Bodies: 6 Alexander. 2 ECW. 8 Leyland. 9 Leyland National. 1 Plaxton. 1 Reeve Burgess. 7 Van Hool. 8 Wright.
Ops incl: local bus services, school contracts, excursions & tours, private hire, continental tours.
Livery: Green.
Ticket System: Wayfarer.

FLIGHTS HALLMARK

See West Midlands

FOCUS COACHES LTD

UNIT 4, LONGTON BUSINESS PARK, MUCH HOOLE PR4 5LE
Tel: 01772 616699
Fax: 01772 616677
E-mail: darrencritchley@aol.com
Web site: www.focuscoaches.co.uk
Man Dir: Darren J Critchley **Co Sec**: Lisa Lee
Fleet: 24 - 11 double-deck bus, 2 single-deck bus, 9 coach, 2 midicoach
Chassis: 1 Bristol. 1 Daimler. 9 Leyland. 2 Mercedes. 9 Volvo.
Bodies: 2 Alexander. 1 ECW. 9 Northern Counties. 1 Optare. 3 Plaxton. 7 Van Hool. 1 Sitcar.
Ops incl: school contracts, excursions & tours, private hire, continental tours.
Livery: White/Purple/Pink/Gold.
Ticket System: Wayfarer/Almex

FRASER EAGLE

R24

THE COACH HOUSE, SHUTTLEWORTH MEAD, BUSINESS PARK, PADIHAM BB12 7NG
Tel: 01254 231100
Fax: 01254 350575
Recovery: 01254 232700
E-mail: howard.tyrer@frasereagle.co.uk
Web site: www.frasereagle.com
Fleetname: Fraser Eagle Coaching
Chmn: Alan Dyson **Dir**: Kevin Dean
Principal: Howard Tyrer
Fleet: 18
Chassis: 8 DAF. 1 MAN. 2 Mercedes. 2 Scania. 5 Volvo.
Bodies: 3 Bova. 3 Neoplan. 12 Van Hool.
Ops incl: school contracts, excursions & tours, private hire, express, continental tours.
Livery: Green front/Blue rear/White slash with Eagle in middle.

*FREEBIRD

R

REVERS STREET GARAGE, WOODHILL, BURY BL8 1AQ
Tel: 0161 797 6633
Fax: 08712 773124
E-mail: info@freebirdcoaches.co.uk
Web site: www.freebirdcoaches.co.uk
Owner: Paul Dart **Man**: Rob Dart **Tran Man**: Jason Taylor
Fleet: 15 - 3 single-deck bus, 6 coach, 2 midicoach, 4 minibus.
Chassis: 2 DAF. 2 Dennis. 2 Ford Transit. 3 Irisbus. 2 LDV. 2 Volvo
Bodies: 1 Beulas. 1 Berkhof. 1 Caetano. 1 Marcopolo. 2 Optare. 1 Plaxton. 1 Van Hool. 7 other.
Ops incl: excursions & tours, private hire, school contracts, continental tours.
Livery: White.

GPD TRAVEL

27 HARTFORD AVENUE, HEYWOOD OL10 4XH
Tel: 01706 622297
Fax: 01706 361494
Web site: www.gpdtravel.freeserve.co.uk
E-mail: gary@gpdtravel.freeserve.co.uk
Props: Gary Dawson, Janine Dawson
Fleet: 7 - 3 coach, 2 minicoach. 2 midibus.
Chassis: 2 DAF. 4 Mercedes. 1 Volvo.
Bodies: 1 Autobus, 1 Caetano. 2 Plaxton.
Ops incl: school contracts, excursions & tours, private hire, continental tours.
Livery: Red/Gold stripes.

G-LINE COACHES

48 ST PATRIC'S ROAD SOUTH, ST ANNES-ON-SEA FY8 1XW
Dir: G Bradshaw
Fleet: coach
Chassis: incl: Volvo
Bodies: incl: Plaxton
Ops incl: excursions & tours.
Livery: White/Brown

JEFF GRIFFITHS COACHES

22 MYERSCOUGH AVE, ST ANNES-ON-SEA FY8 2HY
Tel: 01253 714230
Fax: 01253 640560
E-mail: jeff-griffiths@comserve.com
Dir: Jeff Griffiths
Fleet: coach
Chassis: Volvo.

Bodies: Plaxton
Ops incl: excursions & tours, private hire.
Livery: White

GRIMSHAWS, RIGBY'S, KIRKHAM'S

THE COACH CENTRE, MOORFIELD INDUSTRIAL ESTATE, MOORFIELD DRIVE, ALTHAM, ACCRINGTON BB5 5WG
Tel: 01254 388866
Fax: 01254 232505
Web site: www.thecoachcentre.co.uk
Co Sec/Dir: D. Moorhouse **Engs/Dirs**: M. Mellor, K. Hoyle **Traffic/Dir**: A M. Knowles
Fleet: 23 - 20 coach, 1 midicoach, 2 minicoach
Chassis: 3 Leyland. 3 Mercedes. 3 Scania. 14 Volvo.
Bodies: 1 Autobus. 4 Duple. 2 Neoplan. 7 Plaxton. 9 Van Hool.
Ops incl: school contracts, excursions & tours, private hire, continental tours.
Livery: Blue/Orange/Red
Ticket system: Almex

*HEALINGS INTERNATIONAL COACHES
See Greater Manchester

HODDER MOTOR SERVICES LTD

3 ALDERFORD CLOSE, CLITHEROE BB7 2QP
Tel: 01200 422473
Fax: 01200 422590
E-mail: hodder@talk21.com
Dir: Paul Hodgson **Co Sec**: Janice Hodgson.
Fleet: 1 coach
Chassis: Volvo.
Body: Jonckheere.
Ops incl: private hire, excursions & tours.
Livery: Green/Blue/White

HOLMESWOOD COACHES LTD

SANDY WAY, HOLMESWOOD, ORMSKIRK L40 1UB
Tel: 01704 821245
Fax: 01704 822090
E-mail: sales@holmeswood.uk.com
Web site: www.holmeswood.uk.com
Dirs: J F Aspinall, M Aspinall, D G Aspinall, C H Aspinall, M F Aspinall, M J Aspinall
Fleet: 134 - 18 double-deck bus, 97 coach, 2 double-deck coach, 1 midibus, 10 midicoach, 6 minicoach.
Chassis: 2 Ayats. 1 Bova. 18 DAF. 17 Dennis. 10 Irisbus/Iveco. 14 Leyland. 16 MAN. 2 Mercedes. 22 Scania. 32 Volvo.
Bodies: 5 Alexander. 1 Autobus. 2 Ayats. 4 Beulas. 7 Berkhof. 1 Bova. 8 Caetano.

3 ECW. 5 East Lancs. 9 Ikarus. 2 Irizar. 5 Jonckheere. 21 Marcopolo. 1 Neoplan. 4 Northern Counties. 25 Plaxton. 25 Van Hool. 6 Indcar.
Ops incl: local bus services, school contracts, excursions & tours, private hire, continental tours.
Livery: Green
Ticket system: Wayfarer

J & Y COACHES

9 MILLTHORNE AVENUE, CLITHEROE BB7 2LE.
Tel/Fax: 01200 426269.
Web site: www.uk-coachtours.co.uk
Ptnrs: J. Robinson, Yvonne Robinson.
Fleet: 1 coach. **Chassis/body**: Setra.
Ops incl: excursions & tours, private hire, continental tours.
Livery: Blue/White.

*JACKSONS COACHES

JACKSON HOUSE, BURTON ROAD, BLACKPOOL FY4 4NW
Tel: 01253 792222
Fax: 01253 792222
Ptnr: J P Jackson
Fleet: 6 coach.
Chassis: 3 DAF. 1 Scania. 2 Volvo.
Bodies: 4 Plaxton. 2 Van Hool.
Ops incl: school contracts, private hire, excursions & tours.
Livery: White/Blue.
Ticket System: Setright

KIRKBY LONSDALE COACH HIRE

TWENTY ACRES, MOOR END, HUTTON ROOF, CARNFORTH LA6 2PF
Tel: 01524 272239
E-mail: sutton@klchbbfree.co.uk
Dirs: J M Sutton, S J Sutton
Fleet: 18 - 4 coach, 5 midibus, 2 midicoach, 7 minibus, 2 minicoach.
Chassis: 1 Cannon. 4 DAF. 12 Mercedes. 4 Optare.
Bodies: 1 Alexander. 1 Caetano. 1 Leicester. 2 Marshall/MCV. 5 Optare. 4 Plaxton. 1 UVG. 2 Van Hool.
Ops incl: local bus services, school contracts, excursions & tours, private hire.
Livery: buses: Maroon/White coaches: White/Blue/Maroon
Ticket System: Wayfarer

LANCASHIRE UNITED
MANNER SUTTON STREET, BLACKBURN BB1 5DT.
Tel: 01254 260661
Web site: www.lancashireunited.co.uk
Prop: Blazefield Holdings Ltd
Chairman: Giles Fearnley. **Man Dir**: Stuart Wilde. **Dir (Lancs)**: George Scrymgeour.
Fleet: 131 - 45 double-deck buses, 68 single-deck buses, 18 minibuses.
Chassis: Dennis, Leyland, Mercedes-Benz, Optare, Volvo.

Bodies: Alexander, Berkhof, East Lancs, National, Northern Counties, Plaxton, Wright.
Livery: Blue/Cream.
Ticket System: ERG.
Part of the Blazefield group which is owned by Transdev

LENDOR TAXIS & LUXURY MINICOACH TRAVEL
See Greater Manchester

McLAUGHLIN'S TOURS

UNIT 1A PORTA CABIN, FACTORY LANE, PENWORTHAM PR1 9TZ
Tel/Fax: 01772 749358
Prop: Anthony McLaughlin
Fleet: 7 - 4 coach, 3 minibus.
Chassis: 2 Leyland, 3 Volvo.
Bodies: 3 Mercedes.
Ops incl: local bus services, school contracts, excursions & tours, continental tours.
Livery: Blue/White/Yellow.
Ticket System: Almex

*NORTHERN BLUE

UNIT 7, DEAN MILL, PLUMBE STREET, BURNLEY BB11 3AG
Tel: 01282 456351
Fax: 01282 439386
Web site: www.northernblue.co.uk
Man Dir: Philip Beaumont **Sec**: Michael Robinson **Engineer**: Lee Welton
Fleet: 54 - 18 double-deck bus, 14 single-deck bus, 1 coach, 21 midibus
Chassis: 1 Dennis. 2 Leyland. 21 Optare. 18 Scania. 12 Volvo.
Bodies: 21 Alexander. 1 Caetano. 5 East Lancs. 21 Optare. 5 Plaxton. 1 other
Ops incl: local bus services, school contracts, express, private hire.
Livery: Blue/White.
Ticket System: Wayfarer TGX

*NORTH WEST COACHES & LIMOS
  R24

HILLHOUSE INTERNATIONAL BUSINESS PARK, WEST ROAD, THORNTON CLEVELEYS FY5 4DQ
Tel: 01253 855000
Fax: 01253 859009
Recovery: 07850 500015
E-mail: stewart.farrel@tiscali.co.uk
Web site: www.northwestcoaches.co.uk
Owner/Operator: Stuart J Farrell **Ops Man**: Paul Portisman **Head Fitter**: John Keen
Fleet: 18 - 1 double-deck coach, 3 coach, 2 midibus, 5 midicoach, 7 minibus.
Chassis: 1 DAF. 1 Iveco. 5 Mercedes. 1 Neoplan. 8 Renault. 2 Volvo.
Ops incl: local bus services, excursions & tours, school contracts, private hire

---

A/c	Air conditioning
♿	Vehicles suitable for disabled
🍴	Coach(es) with galley facilities
WC	Coach(es) with toilet facilities
💺	Seat belt-fitted vehicles
R	Recovery service available (not 24 hr)
R24	24hr recovery service
✔	Replacement vehicle available
T	Toilet-drop facilities available
🚌	Vintage vehicle(s) available
	Open top vehicle(s)

OLYMPIA TRAVEL

44 ARGYLE STREET, HINDLEY WN2 3PH
Tel: 01942 522282
Fax: 01942 254666
E-mail: olympia@coach-hire.net
Web site: www.olympiatravel.co.uk
Props: Joseph Lewis, Shaun Lewis.
Fleet: 18 - 12 coach, 4 midicoach, 2 minibus.
Chassis: 1 Bedford. 6 Dennis. 1 Ford Transit. 1 LDV. 5 Volvo.
Bodies: 5 Duple. 2 Jonckheere. 2 Mercedes. 4 Plaxton. 1 Reeve Burgess.
Ops incl: local bus services, school contracts, private hire, continental tours.
Livery: White with blue stripes

*PRESTON BUS LTD

221 DEEPDALE ROAD, PRESTON PR1 6NY
Tel: 01772 253671
Fax: 01772 555840
Recovery: 01772 253671
E-mail: peter.bell@prestonbus.co.uk
Web site: www.prestonbus.co.uk
Man Dir: Peter Bell **Ops Dir:** John Asquith **Eng Dir:** Jack Hornby. **Fin Dir:** Margaret Ingram
Fleet: 119 - 54 double-deck bus, 16 single-deck bus, 1 coach, 48 minibus.
Chassis: 18 Dennis. 52 Leyland. 48 Optare. 1 Volvo.
Bodies: 12 Alexander. 1 ECW. 24 East Lancs. 28 Leyland. 5 Northern Counties. 48 Optare. 1 Van Hool.
Ops incl: local bus services, school contracts, excursions & tours, private hire.
Livery: Blue/Cream
Ticket System: Wayfarer TGX150

REDLINE COACHES
83 BISHAM AVENUE, LEYLAND PR5 3QE.
Tel: 01772 611612.
Fax: 01772 611613.
Prop: R. G. H. & S. R. Nuttall.

*REEVES COACH HOLIDAYS

34 MONKS DRIVE, WITHNELL, CHORLEY PR6 8SG.
Tel/Fax: 01254 830545
E-mail: info@reevescoachholidays.com
Web site: www.reevescoachholidays.com
Prop: John E Reeves
Fleet: 1 coach.
Chassis/body: Setra.
Ops incl: excursions & tours, private hire, continental tours.
Livery: White/Purple/Red

*ROBINSONS HOLIDAYS

PARK GARAGE, GREAT HARWOOD BB6 7SP
Tel: 01254 889900
Fax: 01254 884708
E-mail: sales@robinsons-holidays.co.uk
Web site: www.robinsons-holidays.co.uk
Dirs: D D Lord, J E Bannister (**Sec**), J McMillan **Ops Man:** C Skeen **Engineer:** P Godwin **Off man:** B Cooke **Sales Man:** G Holdsworth
Fleet: 17 - 15 coach, 2 minibus.
Chassis: 1 DAF. 4 MAN. 10 Volvo.
Bodies: 3 Jonckheere. 4 Noge. 7 Plaxton. 1 Van Hool.
Ops incl: excursions & tours, private hire, continental tours, school contracts.
Livery: Blue

ROSSENDALE TRANSPORT LTD

35 BACUP ROAD, RAWTENSTALL BB4 7NG
Tel: 01706 212337
Fax: 01706 229515
Web site: www.rossendalebus.co.uk
E-mail: info@rossendalebus.co.uk
Man Dir: Edgar Oldham **Comm Dir:** Barry Drelincourt
Fleet: 107 - 15 double-deck bus, 92 single-deck bus.
Chassis: 43 Dennis. 5 Leyland. 4 Mercedes. 23 Optare. 26 Volvo. 6 other.
Ops incl: local bus services, school contracts, private hire, express, continental tours.
Livery: White/Red/Cream.
Ticket System: Wayfarer TGX

SANDGROUNDER COACHES
28 WARWICK STREET, SOUTHPORT PR8 5ES
Tel: 01704 541194
Recovery: 07734 003464
E-mail: gerry@dohe.wanadoo.co.uk
Dirs: Gerald Doherty, John Fairbank
Fleet: 3 coaches.
Chassis: 2 DAF. 1 Mercedes.
Ops incl: school contracts, excursions & tours, private hire.

*STAGECOACH NORTH WEST
See Cumbria

*THE TRAVELLERS CHOICE

THE COACH & TRAVEL CENTRE, SCOTLAND ROAD, CARNFORTH LA5 9RQ
Tel: 01524 720033
Fax: 01524 720044
E-mail: info@travellerschoice.co.uk
Web site: www.travellerschoice.co.uk
Chmn: R. Shaw **Man Dirs:** J Shaw, D Shaw **Co Sec:** P Shaw **Dir:** M Shaw
Fleet: 28 - 20 coach, 1 double-deck coach, 6 midicoach, 1 minicoach.
Chassis: 1 Ford Transit. 6 Mercedes. 1 Neoplan. 20 Volvo.
Bodies: 16 Jonckheere. 6 Mercedes. 1 Neoplan. 5 Sunsundegui.
Ops incl: local bus services, school contracts, excursions & tours, private hire, continental tours, express.
Livery: White with blue/yellow/red stripe

R. S. TYRER & SON
51 CHORLEY ROAD, HEATH CHARNOCK, CHORLEY PR6 9JT.
Tel: 01257 480979.
Fax: 01257 480951.
Props: Ms S. Buckle, G. Buckle.
Fleet: 3 - 2 coach, 1 minibus.
Chassis: 1 Leyland. 1 Mercedes. 1 Volvo.
Bodies: 1 Plaxton. 1 Van Hool.
Ops incl: excursions & tours, private hire, continental tours, school contracts, .

TYRER TOURS

THE COACH HOUSE, SHUTTLEWORTH MEAD, BUSINESS PARK, PADIHAM BB12 7NG
Tel: 01254 611123
Fax: 01254 350575
Recovery: 01254 232700
E-mail: howard.tyrer@frasereagle.co.uk
Web site: www.tyrercoaching.com
Chmn: Alan Dyson **Dir:** Kevin Dean
Principal: Howard Tyrer
Fleet: 13 - 11 coach, 1 midicoach.
Chassis: 10 DAF. 2 Mercedes.
Bodies: 1 Neoplan. 1 Plaxton. 10 Van Hool.
Ops incl: school contracts, excursions & tours, private hire, express, continental tours.
Livery: White with Blue/Red lettering

VISCOUNT CENTRAL COACHES LTD

6 DEAN MILL, PLUMBE STREET, BURNLEY BB11 2AG
Tel: 01282 439371
Fax: 01282 421386
Web site: www.viscountcentral.co.uk
Man Dir: Philip Beaumont
Fleet: 10 - 7 coach, 1 minicoach.
Chassis: 3 Iveco.1 Toyota. 4 Volvo.
Bodies: 3 Beulas. 1 Caetano. 4 Van Hool.
Ops incl: private hire

*YELLOW ROSE COACHES

WEST LEA, DIXON'S FIELD, CRAG BANK, CARNFORTH LA5 9JN
Tel: 01524 735853
E-mail: www.yellowrosecoaches.co.uk
Web site: yellowrosecoaches@tiscali.co.uk
Dirs: G Brocken(**Co Sec**), Mrs C M Brocken
Fleet Eng: C R Ardis
Fleet: 5 - 2 coach, 1 midicoach, 1 minibus, 1 minicoach.
Chassis: 1 MAN. 2 Mercedes. 2 Volvo.
Bodies: 1 Caetano. 1 Mellor. 1 Mercedes. 2 Van Hool.
Ops incl: excursions & tours, private hire, school contracts.
Livery: Yellow/White
Ticket System: Almex.

LEICESTERSHIRE, CITY OF LEICESTER, RUTLAND

ARRIVA MIDLANDS
PO BOX 613, LEICESTER LE4 8BT
Tel: 0116 264 0400
Fax: 0116 260 5605
Web site: www.arriva.co.uk
Man Dir: Catherine Mason **Fin Dir:** John Barlow **Eng Dir:** Richard Dyball **Ops Dirs:** Stuart McIntosh, John Marrow **Eng Dir:** Jason Chalk
Fleet: 650 - double-deck bus, single-deck bus, coach, midibus.
Chassis: 46 DAF. 58 Dennis. 21 Leyland. 99 Mercedes. 58 Scania. 49 Volvo.
Bodies: Alexander. ECW. East Lancs. Leicester. Leyland. Northern Counties. Optare. Plaxton. Reeve Burgess.
Ops incl: local bus services, school contracts, private hire, express.
Livery: Aquamarine/Cotswold Stone
Ticket System: Wayfarer

ASMAL COACHES
70 KEDLESTONE ROAD, LEICESTER LE5 5HW
Tel/Fax: 0116 249 0443
Man Dir: Mehboob M. Asmal.

AUSDEN CLARK LTD

DYSART WAY, LEICESTER LE1 2JY
Tel: 0116 262 9492
Fax: 0116 251 5551
Man Dir: Paul Ausden-Clark.
Dir: Danny Smith. **Co Sec:** Susan Ward.
Fleet: 32 - 1 double-deck bus, 24 coach, 1 double-deck coach, 6 minicoach.
Chassis: 13 Bedford. 1 Leyland. 6 Mercedes. 11 Scania. 1 Volvo.
Ops incl: local bus services, school contracts, excursions & tours, private hire, continental tours.

BAILISS TOURS
21 ODSTONE ROAD, BARTON-IN-THE-BEANS CV13 0DF.
Tel: 01455 290253.
Fax: 01455 292700.
Prop: G. Treadwell.
Fleet: 1 coach. **Chassis:** DAF.
Body: Duple.
Ops incl: excursions & tours, private hire, continental tours.
Livery: Blue/Cream.

*CONFIDENCE BUS & COACH HIRE
30 SPALDING STREET, LEICESTER LE5 4PH
Tel: 0116 276 2171
Fax: 0116 276 2171
E-mail: confidencebus@btclick.com
Web site: www.confidencebus.co.uk
Dirs: K M Williams, A P Williams, S S Williams, C A Dalby **Ch Eng:** M Crawford
Fleet: 32 - 19 double-deck coach, 13 coach.

Chassis: 1 AEC. 28 Leyland. 3 Volvo.
Bodies: 1 Duple. 12 ECW. 2 East Lancs. 1 Optare. 1 Park Royal. 11 Plaxton. 3 Roe. 1 Van Hool.
Ops incl: local bus services, school contracts, private hire.
Livery: Buses: Black/Grey, Coaches: Black/Red.
Ticket System: Setright

COUNTY MINI COACHES
31 EDENHURST AVENUE, LEICESTER LE3 2PH.
Tel/Fax: 0116 289 7205.
Owner: F. Bradshaw.
Fleet: 3 - 2 midicoach, 1 minibus.
Chassis: 1 DAF. 1 Freight Rover. 1 Iveco.
Ops incl: school contracts, private hire.

COUNTRY HOPPER
213 MELBOURNE ROAD, IBSTOCK LE67 6NQ
Tel: 01530 260888

*DUNN-LINE GROUP
See Nottinghamshire

FIRST LEICESTER

ABBEY PARK ROAD, LEICESTER LE4 5AH.
Tel: 0116 251 6691.
Fax: 0116 253 8270.
Man Dir: I. Humphreys. **Eng Dir:** C. Stafford. **Fin Dir:** J. Hollis. **Gen Man Ops:** C. Lara.
Fleet: 116 - double-deck bus, single-deck bus, coach, midibus, minibus.
Chassis: Bristol. Dennis. Mercedes. Optare. Scania. Volvo.
Bodies: 8 Alexander. 71 East Lancs. 10 Marshall. 20 Northern Counties. 19 Optare. 3 Plaxton. 11 Wright.
Ops incl: local bus services, school contracts, excursions & tours, private hire, express, continental tours.
Livery: Multicoloured.
Ticket System: Wayfarer 3

BRYAN GARRATT/COACHMASTER

RMC YARD, THURMASTON FOOTPATH, HUMBERSTONE LANE, LEICESTER LE4 9JU
Tel: 0116 276 7228
Fax: 0116 246 1338
Prop: Bryan A Garratt
Fleet: coach, midicoach.
Chassis: Dennis. Leyland. Scania. Toyota. Volvo.
Ops incl: school contracts, excursions & tours, private hire.
Livery: White/Blue/Red.

*HYLTON & DAWSON
18 CHESTNUT ROAD, GLENFIELD, LEICESTER LE3 8DB
Tel: 0116 233 0222
Fax: 0116 233 1011
E-mail: hyltonadrian@yahoo.co.uk
Web site: www.hyltonanddawson.co.uk
Prop: A. E. Hylton.
Fleet: 3 coach.
Chassis: 2 Bedford. 1 Dennis.
Bodies: 3 Duple.
Ops incl: school contracts, private hire.
Livery: Maroon/Cream/Grey.

PAUL JAMES COACHES

UNIT 5, GRANGE FARM BUSINESS PARK, GRANGE ROAD, HUGGLESCOTE LE67 2BT
Tel: 01530 832399
Fax: 01530 836128
E-mail: info@pauljamescoaches.co.uk
Web site: www.pauljamescoaches.co.uk
Man Dir: P. O'Brien **Coaching Man:** D Wood
Fleet: 35 - single-deck bus, coach, midibus.
Chassis: incl: 3 Bedford. 2 Bova. 1 Dennis. 2 Leyland. 6 Mercedes. 6 Optare. 1 Setra. 6 Volvo.
Bodies: incl: 5 Alexander. 1 Autobus. 2 Bova. 6 Optare. 10 Plaxton. 2 Van Hool.
Ops incl: excursions & tours, private hire, local bus services, school contracts, continental tours.
Livery: Ivory
Ticket System: Wayfarer 3

MACPHERSON COACHES LTD
See Derbyshire

NESBIT BROS LTD

BURROUGH ROAD, SOMERBY, MELTON MOWBRAY LE14 2PP.
Tel: 01664 454284.
Fax: 01664 454106.
Dirs: I. Foster, J. Townsend.
Ch Eng: J. Townsend. **Sec:** E. Tomes.
Ops Man: I. Foster.
Fleet: 13 coach.
Chassis: 1 AEC. 1 Leyland. 11 Volvo.
Bodies: 6 Duple. 7 Plaxton.
Ops incl: school contracts, excursions & tours, private hire.
Livery: Blue/Cream.
Ticket System: Setright.

	Air conditioning		Seat belt-fitted vehicles		Replacement vehicle available
	Vehicles suitable for disabled	R	Recovery service available (not 24 hr)	T	Toilet-drop facilities available
	Coach(es) with galley facilities				Vintage vehicle(s) available
wc	Coach(es) with toilet facilities	R24	24hr recovery service		Open top vehicle(s)

*NIGEL JACKSON TRAVEL

5 NEW ZEALAND LANE,
QUENIBOROUGH LE7 3FU
Tel: 0116 276 9456
Fax: 0116 276 1969
Owner: Nigel Jackson.
Fleet: 7 - 3 double-deck bus, 3 coach,
1 midicoach
Chassis: 1 Bristol. 1 Dennis. 2 Leyland.
1 MCW. 1 Scania. 1 Toyota.
Bodies: 1 Caetano. 1 Duple. 1ECW.
1 MCW. 1 Northern Counties. 2Plaxton.
Ops incl: school contracts, private hire,
continental tours.
Livery: Blue/Red

RELIANT COACHES LTD

MILL LANE, HEATHER LE67 2QE.
Tel: 01530 260468.
Fax: 01530 263685.
Man Dir: M. Stannard. **Traf Man**: B. Moors.
Dir: M. Bishop. **Ops Dir**: H. King.
Co Sec: J. Highton.
Fleet: 17 - 16 coach, 1 midicoach.
Chassis: 2 Bedford. 4 Bova. 4 DAF.
1 Mercedes. 6 Volvo.
Bodies: 4 Bova. 8 Caetano. 1 Duple.
3 Plaxton. 1 Coach Kraft.
Ops incl: excursions & tours, private hire,
express, continental tours.
Livery: Bachelor Blue/Larkspur Blue.

*ROBERTS COACHES LTD

THE LIMES, MIDLAND ROAD,
HUGGLESCOTE LE67 2FX
Tel: 01530 817444
Fax: 01530 817666
E-mail: info@robertscoaches.co.uk
Web site: www.robertscoaches.co.uk
Man Dir: Jonathan Hunt
Fleet: 26 - 11 double-deck bus, 10 coach,
3 open-top bus, 1 minibus, 1 minicoach.
Chassis: 1 LDV. 2 Leyland. 10MCW.
1 Mercedes. 3 Scania. 9 Volvo.
Bodies: 2 East Lancs. 2 Jonckheere.
10 MCW. 1 Plaxton. 8 Van Hool. 2 other.
Ops incl: local bus services, school
contracts, excursions & tours, private hire,
continental tours
Livery: Gold.

SCHOFIELD TRAVEL LTD

PRINCE WILLIAM ROAD,
LOUGHBOROUGH LE11 0GU.
Tel: 01509 611045
Fax: 01509 611012
Man Dir: E. B. Mee **Dir/Ch Eng**:
K. W. Greasley. **Gen Man**: R. A. Schofield.
Fleet: 6 - 4 coach, 2 midicoach.
Chassis: 1 Bedford. 2 Bova. 2 DAF. 1 Ford.
Bodies: 2 Bova. 4 Plaxton.
Ops incl: school contracts, private hire,
express.
Livery: Blue/Pale Grey.

TRAVEL-WRIGHT

64 ROCKHILL DRIVE,
MOUNTSORREL LE12 7DT.
Tel: 0116 230 2887.
Fax: 0116 230 2223.
E-mail: trwright@demon.co.uk
Dir: C. Wright.
Fleet: 5 minibus.
Chassis: 1 DAF. 2 Mercedes. 2 VW.
Bodies: 2 Crystals. 2 VW. 1 Advanced.
Ops incl: private hire, school contracts.

WEST END/RUTLAND TRAVEL

COACH & BUS CENTRE, DIXON
DRIVE, OFF LEICESTER ROAD,
MELTON MOWBRAY LE13 0BS
Tel: 01664 563498
Fax: 01664 568568
Fleetname: Romdrive
Man Dirs: John Penniston, Peter Penniston
Fleet: 23 - 1 single-deck bus, 11 coach,
8 midibus, 2 minibus, 1 minicoach.
Chassis: 1 Dennis. 11 Mercedes. 1 Scania.
3 Setra. 4 Volvo.
Bodies: 4 Alexander. 2 Jonckheere.
5 Mercedes. 7 Plaxton. 1 Reeve Burgess.
3 Setra. 1 Wadham Stringer.
Ops incl: local bus services, school
contracts, excursions & tours, private hire,
continental tours.
Livery: Red/Blue/White
Ticket System: Wayfarer 3

WIDE HORIZON

48 COVENTRY ROAD, BURBAGE,
HINCKLEY LE10 2HP
Tel: 01455 615915
Fax: 01455 230767
Ptnrs: Reg Clarke, Jon Clarke.

Fleet: 16 - 9 double-deck bus, 7 coach
Chassis: 1 Bova. 3 DAF. 1 Dennis.
1 Leyland. 1 MAN. 1 Mercedes. Neoplan.
1 Scania. 1 Volvo.
Bodies: 2 Berkhof. 1 Bova. 2 Plaxton.
2 Setra.
Ops incl: local bus services, excursions &
tours, school contracts, private hire,
continental tours.
Livery: White

PAUL S WINSON COACHES LTD

 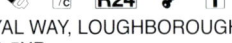

ROYAL WAY, LOUGHBOROUGH
LE11 5XR
Tel: 01509 232354
Fax: 01509 265110
Recovery: 01509 237999
Web site: www.winsoncoaches.co.uk
E-mail: sales@winsoncoaches.co.uk
Chmn: Paul Winson **Ch Eng**:
Paul B Winson **Dir**: Mrs M A Winson
Ops Man: Anthony J Winson
Fleet: 28 - 6 double-deck bus, 18 coach,
4 minibus.
Chassis: 4 Bova. 1 DAF. 3 Dennis.
6 Leyland. 7 Mercedes. 8 Volvo.
Bodies: 1 Autobus. 4 Bova. 1 Caetano.
3 Jonckheere. 2 Northern Counties.
12 Plaxton. 3 Roe.
Ops incl: local bus services, school
contracts, excursions & tours, private hire,
continental tours.
Livery: Red/White/Blue.
Ticket system: Wayfarer

WOODS COACHES LTD

211 GLOUCESTER CRESCENT,
WIGSTON LE18 4YH
Tel: 0116 278 6374
Fax: 0116 247 7819
E-mail: sales@woods-coaches.co.uk
Web site: woods-coaches.com
Dirs: Mark Wood, Kevin Brown **Mktg Exec**:
Alison Trunkfield **Eng Dir**: Ian Trigg
Fleet: 32 - 14 single-deck bus, 18 midibus
Chassis: 18 Mercedes. 14 Volvo.
Bodies: 8 Alexander. 1 Caetano. 1 Duple.
1 Marshall. 1 Mellor. 1 Mercedes.
19 Plaxton.
Ops incl: local bus services, excursions &
tours, private hire, continental tours.
Livery: Blue base – orange/yellow/white
relief
Ticket System: Wayfarer.

LINCOLNSHIRE

BRYLAINE TRAVEL LTD
291 LONDON ROAD, BOSTON PE21 7DD
Tel: 01205 364087.
Fax: 01205 359504.
Dirs: Brian W Gregg, Elaine R Gregg
Co Sec: Susan E Bradshaw **Eng Dir**: Brian P Gregg **Ops Dir**: Malcolm P Wheatley
Fleet: 34 - 6 double-deck bus, 19 single-deck bus, 9 midibus.
Chassis: 6 DAF. 4 Dennis. 6 Leyland. 2 MCW. 3 Mercedes. 10 Optare. 3 Scania.
Bodies: 4 Alexander. 6 Ikarus. 2 Leyland. 4 Marshall. 2 MCW. 1 Mercedes. 2 Northern Counties. 10 Optare. 3 Paladin
Ops incl: local bus services, school contracts.
Livery: Blue/White.
Ticket System: Wayfarer 3.

J W CARNELL LTD
72 BRIDGE ROAD, SUTTON BRIDGE PE12 9UA.
Tel: 01406 350482.
Fax: 01406 350600.
E-mail: carnellcoaches@ukonline.co.uk
Dirs: John Grindwood, Mervyn Emmet
Fleet: 22 - 3 double-deck bus, 16 coach, 2 midicoach, 1 minicoach.
Chassis: 2 Bedford. 1 Bova. 2 DAF. 5 Leyland. 1 MAN. 3 MCW. 2 Toyota. 6 Volvo.
Bodies: 1 Bova. 3 Caetano. 8 Duple. 3 MCW. 6 Plaxton. 1 Van Hool.
Ops incl: local bus services, school contracts, excursions and tours.
Livery: Silver/Red/Orange.
Ticket system: Setright.

CAVALIER TRAVEL
SEAGATE ROAD, LONG SUTTON PE12 9AD.
Tel: 01406 362518
Fax: 01406 362418
Props: A. D. Ladbrook, C. J. Boor. **Man Dir**: Dennis Upton
Fleet: 40 double deck/single deck buses
Livery: Blue
Ops incl: local bus services, school contracts

*CROPLEY COACHES
MAIN ROAD, FOSDYKE, BOSTON PE20 2BH
Tel: 01205 260226
Fax: 01205 260246
Web site: www.cropleycoach.co.uk
E-mail: enquiries@cropleycoach.co.uk
Dirs: J R Cropley, Mrs S R Cropley
Fleet: 12 coach.
Chassis: 1 Setra, 11 Volvo.
Bodies: 1 Jonckheere. 7 Plaxton. 1 Setra. 3 Sunsundegui
Ops incl: school contracts, excursions & tours, private hire, continental tours.

Livery: White

*DELAINE BUSES LTD
8 SPALDING ROAD, BOURNE PE10 9LE
Tel: 01778 422866
Fax: 01778 425593
Web site: www.delainebuses.com
Chmn: I Delaine-Smith **Man Dir**: A Delaine-Smith **Dirs**: M Delaine-Smith, K Delaine-Smith **Sec**: Mrs B P Tilley
Fleet: 20 - 14 double-deck bus, 6 single-deck bus.
Chassis: 4 Leyland. 16 Volvo.
Bodies: 2 Duple. 14 East Lancs. 2 Northern Counties. 2 Wright.
Ops incl: local bus services, school contracts.
Livery: Light Blue/Dark Blue/Ivory.
Ticket System: Almex A90

*DUNN-LINE (HOLDINGS) LTD
See Nottinghamshire

EAGRE COACHES LTD

CROOKED BILLET STREET, MORTON, GAINSBOROUGH DN21 3AG
Tel: 01427 612098
Fax: 01427 811340
Man Dir: Rob Eaglen **Ch Eng**: M Thrower
Tours Man: Ann Lee
Fleet: 8 coaches
Chassis: incl: Irisbus. MAN.
Bodies: incl: Beulas. Noge. Marcopolo.
Ops incl: excursions & tours, private hire, continental tours
Livery: Multicolours

*W H FOWLER & SONS (COACHES) LTD
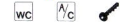

155 DOG DROVE SOUTH, HOLBEACH DROVE, SPALDING PE12 0SD
Tel: 01406 330232
Fax: 01406 330923
E-mail: andrew@fowlerstravel.com
Web site: www.fowlerstravel.com
Fleetname: Fowlers Travel
Man Dir: John Fowler **Sec**: Jackie Fowler
Dir: Andrew Fowler
Fleet: 18 - 6 double-deck bus, 2 single-deck bus, 10 coach.
Chassis: 1 DAF. 1 Leyland. 16 Volvo.
Bodies: 2 Alexander. 1 Duple. 2 Jonckheere. 4 Marshall. 9 Plaxton.
Ops incl: local bus services, school contracts, excursions & tours, private hire.
Livery: Cream/Orange/Red
Ticket System: Wayfarer.

*GRAYSCROFT BUS SERVICES LTD
15A VICTORIA ROAD, MABLETHORPE LN12 2AY
Tel/Fax: 01507 473236
E-mail: grayscroft.buses@btinternet.com
Web site: www.grayscroft.co.uk
Dirs: C W Barker, N Barker, N W Barker
Fleet: 15 - 5 double-deck bus, 8 coach, 2 midibus.
Chassis: 2 Leyland. 1 Mercedes. 1 Neoplan. 1 Optare. 10 Volvo.
Bodies: 1 Alexander. 1 Caetano. 3 Jonckheere. 1 Neoplan. 3 Northern Counties. 1 Optare. 1 Park Royal. 2 Plaxton. 3 Van Hool.
Ops incl: local bus services, school contracts, excursions & tours, private hire, express, continental tours.
Livery: White/Blue/Orange
Ticket system: Setright/Wayfarer

PHIL HAINES COACHES
RALPHS LANE, FRAMPTON WEST, BOSTON PE20 1QU.
Tel/Fax: 01205 722359.
Props: N. A. & F. E. Haines.

*HODSON COACHES LTD

CHAPEL LANE, NAVENBY LN5 0ER
Tel: 01522 810262
Fax: 01522 810793
E-mail: sales@hodsoncoaches.co.uk
Web Site: www.hodsoncoaches.co.uk
Dirs: S Carter, J Carter.
Fleet: 15 - 1 single-deck bus, 6 coach, 1 midicoach, 7 minicoach.
Chassis: 8 Mercedes. 5 Setra. 2 VW.
Ops incl: local bus services, school contracts, excursions & tours, private hire, express, continental tours.
Livery: Cream/Purple/Maroon.
Ticket system: Almex

*F HUNT COACH HIRE LTD
2/3 WEST STREET, ALFORD LN13 9DG
Tel/Fax: 01507 463000
E-mail: hunts@huntstravel.fsnet.co.uk
Web site: www.hunts-coaches.co.uk
Fleetname: Hunts Travel
Dirs: Michael Hunt, Charles Hunt, Dave Eales
Fleet: 19 - 1 double-deck bus, 5 single-deck bus, 10 coach, 3 midibus.
Chassis: 3 Dennis. 1 Leyland. 3 Mercedes. 1 Optare. 11 Volvo.
Bodies: 2 Alexander. 3 Mercedes. 1 Optare. 10 Van Hool. 3 Wright.
Ops incl: local bus services, school contracts, excursions & tours, private hire, express, continental tours.
Livery: White/Red/Grey
Ticket System: Almex

Air conditioning	Replacement vehicle available
Vehicles suitable for disabled	Toilet-drop facilities available
Coach(es) with galley facilities	Vintage vehicle(s) available
Coach(es) with toilet facilities	Open top vehicle(s)
Seat belt-fitted vehicles	
Recovery service available (not 24 hr)	
24hr recovery service	

R KIME & CO LTD
3 SLEAFORD ROAD, FOLKINGHAM, SLEAFORD NG34 0SB
Tel: 01529 497251
Fax: 01529 497554
Fleetname: Kimes Coaches.
Man Dir: Paul Brown
Fleet: 20 - 10 double-deck bus, 6 single-deck bus, 3 coach, 1 midicoach.
Chassis: 4 DAF. 12 Leyland. 1 Mercedes. 3 Volvo.
Bodies: 2 Alexander. 12 Leyland. 3 Northern Counties. 1 Optare. 2 Plaxton.
Ops incl: local bus services, school contracts, excursions & tours, private hire.
Livery: Cream/Green
Ticket System: Almex

STAGECOACH LINCOLNSHIRE
PO BOX 15, DEACON ROAD, LINCOLN LN2 4JB
Tel: 01522 522255
Fax: 01522 538229
Web site: www.stagecoachbus.com
Man Dir: Gary Nolan **Eng&Ops Dir**: D B Bradley
Fleet: 272 - 100 double-deck bus, 145 single-deck bus, 4 open-top bus, 20 midibus, 3 minibus.
Chassis: incl: DAF. Dennis. Mercedes. Optare. Renault. Scania. 80 Volvo.
Bodies: incl: Alexander. East Lancs. Optare. Plaxton. Wright.
Ops incl: local bus services, school contracts
Livery: Green/Yellow/White; Blue/Yellow/Red
Ticket System: Almex.
Part of Stagecoach

MEMORY LANE COACHES

ELM HOUSE, OLD BOLINGBROKE, SPILSBY PE23 4HF
Tel: 01790 763394
Prop: John B Dorey
Fleet: 5 - 3 coach, 2 midicoach.
Chassis: 2 Bedford. 1 Iveco. 1 Leyland. 1 Mercedes.
Bodies: 1 Carlyle. 3 Duple. 1 Plaxton.
Ops incl: school contracts, private hire.

Livery: White/Green/Red.

*MILLMAN COACHES
See North Lincolnshire

PC COACHES OF LINCOLN LTD

17 CROFTON ROAD, ALLENBY TRADING ESTATE, LINCOLN LN3 4NL
Tel: 01522 533605
Fax: 01522 560402
E-mail: pctravel@aol.com
Web site: www.pc-coaches.co.uk
Man Dir: P C Smith **Off Man**: S Pickering
Wkshp Man: D Longmate
Fleet: 57 - double-deck bus, single-deck bus, coach, midicoach, minibus.
Chassis: incl: Mercedes. Optare. Scania.
Bodies: incl: East Lancs. Irizar. Optare. Plaxton. Van Hool. 1 Wright
Ops incl: local bus services, school contracts, private hire, excursions & tours, continental tours.
Livery: White/Orange/Maroon.
Ticket System: Wayfarer.

*PULFREYS COACHES
271 HARLAXTON ROAD, GRANTHAM NG31 7SL
Tel: 01476 564144
Dir: A Pulfrey.
Fleet: 3 - 2 coach, 1 midicoach.
Chassis: 1 Dennis. 1 Iveco. 1 Mercedes.
Bodies: 1 Beulas. 2 Plaxton.
Ops incl: local bus, school contracts, excursions & tours, private hire, continental tours.
Livery: Blue/Yellow
Ticket System: Wayfarer

ROADCAR
See Lincolnshire Road Car

ROY PHILLIPS
69 STATION ROAD, RUSKINGTON NG34 9DF
Tel: 01526 832279

Prop: R Phillips.
Fleet: 6 coach.
Chassis: 1 Leyland. 5 Volvo.
Bodies: 3 Plaxton. 3 Van Hool.
Ops incl: private hire, school contracts.

SMITHS COACHES, CORBY GLEN
THE GREEN, CORBY GLEN NG33 4NR.
Tel: 01476 550285.
Fax: 01476 550032.
Ptnrs: H. J. and Mary J. Smith.
Fleet: 7 - 5 coach, 1 double-deck coach, 1 minibus.
Chassis: 1 Bedford. 1 Bova. 1 Ford. 1 Freight Rover. 2 MAN. 1 Mercedes.
Bodies: 1 Bova. 1 Carlyle. 1 Duple. 2 MAN. 1 Neoplan. 1 Plaxton.
Ops incl: excursions & tours, private hire, continental tours, school contracts.
Livery: Blue/White.

TOURMASTER COACHES LTD
See Lincolnshire

*TRAVELPATH 3000
PO BOX 32, GRANTHAM NG31 7JA
Tel: 01476 570187
Fax: 01476 572718
E-mail: info@travelpath-uk.com
Web site: www.travelpath3000.com
Ops Man: Jon Brown
Ops incl: continental tours

*TRANSLINC

JARVIS HOUSE, 157 SADLER ROAD, LINCOLN LN6 3RS
Tel: 01522 503400
Fax: 01522 503422
E-mail: logistics@translinc.co.uk
Web site: www.translinc.co.uk
Man Dir: Brian West **Sales & Mktg Dir**: John Soulby **Dir of Logistics**: Carole Smith
Fleet: 250 - single-deck bus, coach, midibus, minibus, minicoach, midicoach.
Ops incl: school contracts, excursions & tours, private hire, express.

LONDON

This section includes those operators in the London postal areas, as well as operators who have asked to appear under this heading. Other operators within Greater London with a non-London postal address, eg Kingston, Surrey; Bromley, Kent; Enfield, Middlesex, etc, may be found under their respective postal counties.

AA, KNIGHTS OF THE ROAD

WREN ROAD, SIDCUP DA14 4NA
Tel: 020 8309 7741
Prop: J. V. H. Knight. **Ch Eng**: D. Knight
Fleet: 10 - 6 coach, 2 double-deck coach, 2 minicoach.
Chassis: 6 DAF. 2 Mercedes. 2 Volvo.
Bodies: 6 Bova. 2 Jonckheere. 2 Mercedes.
Ops incl: excursions & tours, private hire, continental tours, school contracts.
Livery: Cream/Beige.

ACE TRAVEL
See Hertfordshire

AIRLINKS
HEATHROW COACH CENTRE, SIPSON ROAD, WEST DRAYTON UB7 0HN
Tel: 020 8990 6300
Fax: 020 8997 3626
Man Dir: Bill Cahill. **Fin Dir**: Richard Smith.
Dir of Eng: Steve Perks.
Fleet: 329 - includes 19 double-deck bus.
Chassis: 76 DAF. 54 Dennis. 3 MAN. 57 Mercedes. 16 Scania. 12 Toyota. 111 Volvo.
Bodies: 14 Alexander. 32 Berkhof. 15 Caetano. 6 Cobus. 17 East Lancs. 8 Jonckheere. 2 LDV. 11 Frank Guy. 16 Mercedes. 2 Northern Counties. 6 Optare. 99 Plaxton. 13 UVG. 32 Van Hool. 36 Wright.
Ops incl: local bus services, excursions & tours, private hire, express.
Livery: Various.
Subsidiary of National Express

ANDERSON TRAVEL LTD /LONDON MINI-COACHES
178A TOWER BRIDGE ROAD, LONDON SE1 3LS
Tel: 020 7403 8118
Fax: 020 7403 8421
E-mail: sales@andersontravel.co.uk
Web site: www.andersontravel.co.uk
Group Man Dir: Mark Anderson **Gen Man**: Stephen Lee **Tran Mans**: Peter Gilbert, David Phillips
Fleet: 24 - 17 coach, 4 midicoach, 3 minibus
Chassis: 12 Bova. 10 Mercedes. 2 Toyota.
Bodies: 12 Bova. 2 Caetano. 5 Mercedes. 5 Setra.
Ops incl: excursions & tours, private hire, continental tours.
Livery: White/Green, Silver/Red

ANGEL MOTORS (EDMONTON) LTD
1 CONSTABLE CRESCENT, LONDON N15 4QZ

Tel: 020 8808 2000
Fax: 020 8808 0008
Fleet: 19 - 17 coach, 2 minicoach.
Livery: White/Blue/Yellow.

*ARMCHAIR COACHES LTD
27A SPRING GROVE ROAD, HOUNSLOW TW3 4BE
Tel: 020 8568 6227
Fax: 020 8847 2649
E-mail: tours@armchair.co.uk
Web site: www.armchair.co.uk
Gen Man: Tim Miles **Ops Man**: David Attfield **Ch Eng**: Graham Bessant
Fleet: 12
Chassis: 3 Bova. 9 Volvo.
Bodies: 2 Bova. 9 Van Hool.
Ops incl: excursions & tours, private hire, express, continental tours.
Livery: Orange/White
(Part of the Comfort Delgro Corporation)

ARRIVA LONDON
16 WATSONS ROAD LONDON N22 7TZ
Tel: 020 8271 0101
Web site: arriva.co.uk
Man Dir: Mark Yexley
Fleet: 1460 - incl: double-deck bus, single-deck bus, 157 articulated bus.
Chassis: incl: DAF. Dennis. Mercedes. Volvo.
Bodies: incl: Alexander. Mercedes. Plaxton. Wright
Ops incl: local bus services, excursions & tours, private hire.
Livery: Red

*BACK ROADS TOURING CO LTD
14A NEW BROADWAY, LONDON W5 2XA.
Tel: 020 8566 5312
Fax: 020 8566 5457
E-mail: info@backroadstouring.co.uk
Web site: www.backroadstouring.co.uk
Man Dir: Bruce Cherry **Fin Dir**: Erika Harcz
Ops Dir: Alex Newmann
Fleet: 22 minibus
Chassis/Bodies: 16 Mercedes. 6 Renault
Ops incl: excursions & tours, private hire, continental tours.
Livery: White

BEXLEY COACHLINES
See Kent

BIG BUS COMPANY
GROSVENOR GARDENS HOUSE, 35-37 GROSVENOR GARDENS, LONDON SW1W 0BS
Tel: 020 7233 8722
Fax: 020 7233 8766
E-mail: pgriffith@bigbustours.com
Web site: www.bigbustours.com
Man Dir: R P Maybury **Exec Dir**: E M Maybury **Eng**: D V Maybury **Bus Dev**: P Waterman **Ops**: M Forde
Fleet: 155 - 79 double-deck bus, 76 open-top bus.
Chassis: 4 AEC. 16 Dennis. 59 Leyland.
Ops incl: private hire, excursions & tours.

BLUEWAYS GUIDELINE COACHES LTD
49 WINDERS ROAD, LONDON SW11 3HE
Tel: 020 7228 3515
Fax: 020 7228 0290
E-mail: blueways@clara.co.uk
Web site: www.bluewaysguideline.co.uk
Dirs: Philip Bruton, Janet Bruton, Thomas McKechnie.
Fleet: 6 - 4 coach. 2 minicoach.
Chassis: 1 Mercedes. 3 Scania. 2 Toyota
Bodies: 2 Caetano. 3 Irizar. 1 Mercedes.
Ops incl: excursions & tours, private hire, continental tours, school contracts.
Livery: 2 White/two-tone Blue, 2 White, 2 England sponsors.

*BRENTONS OF BLACKHEATH
GREENWICH HIGH ROAD, LONDON SE10 8JL
Tel: 020 820 2020
Fax: 020 692 4932
E-mail: davee@brentonsofblackheath.co.uk
Web site: www.brentonsofblackheath.co.uk
Prop: C Clark **Coach Man**: D Eaton
Ch Eng: I Powell
Fleet: 14 - 11 coach, 1 midicoach, 2 minicoach.
Chassis: 2 Dennis. 5 Leyland. 3 Mercedes. 5 Volvo.
Bodies: 1 Berkhof 2 Duple. 3 Mercedes. 7 Plaxton. 1 Van Hool.
Ops incl: private hire, school contracts, excursions and tours.
Livery: Red/Cream/Grey

A/c	Air conditioning
♿	Vehicles suitable for disabled
🍽	Coach(es) with galley facilities
wc	Coach(es) with toilet facilities
♥	Seat belt-fitted vehicles
R	Recovery service available (not 24 hr)
R24	24hr recovery service
🔑	Replacement vehicle available
T	Toilet-drop facilities available
	Vintage vehicle(s) available
🚌	Open top vehicle(s)

BRYANS OF ENFIELD

19 WETHERLEY ROAD, ENFIELD EN2 0NS.
Fax: 020 8366 0062.
Owner: B. Nash.
Fleet: 6 - 3 double-deck bus, 1 single-deck bus, 1 coach, 1 double-deck coach.
Chassis: 1 AEC. 1 DAF. 2 Daimler. 1 Leyland. 1 MCW.
Bodies: 1 ECW. 2 MCW. 2 Park Royal. 1 Van Hool.
Ops incl: school contracts, private hire.
Livery: Red.

CENTAUR TRAVEL MINICOACHES

188 HALFWAY STREET, SIDCUP DA15 8DJ.
Tel: 020 8300 3001.
Fax: 020 8302 5959.
Man Dir: M. Sims. **Ch Eng**: R. Raison.
Ops Man: Kay Priestley.
Fleet: 14 - 2 midicoach, 5 minibus, 7 minicoach.
Chassis: 7 Freight Rover. 2 Mercedes. 5 Renault.
Ops incl: private hire, school contracts.

*CALL-A-COACH
See Surrey

*CAVALIER TRAVEL SERVICES

ARMCHAIR HOUSE, COMMERCE ROAD, BRENTFORD TW8 8LZ
Tel: 0845 125 9379
Fax: 020 8758 1914
E-mail: bookings@cavaliercoaches.com
Web site: www.cavaliercoaches.com
Dirs: Andrew W Pagan, Denise H Pagan
Fleet: 12 - 4 coach, 5 midicoach, 2 minicoach. 1 people carrier.
Chassis: 3 Irisbus. 1 Mercedes. 2 Neoplan. 3 Optare. 1 Scania. 1 Toyota.
Bodies: 3 Beulas. 1 Caetano. 1 Esker. 2 Neoplan. 3 Optare. 1 Van Hool.
Ops incl: private hire, excursions & tours
Livery: White/Blue

CHALFONT LINE LTD

4 PROVIDENCE ROAD, WEST DRAYTON UB7 8HJ
Tel: 01895 459540
Fax: 01895 459549
E-mail: holidays@chalfont-line.co.uk
Web site: www.chalfont-line.co.uk
Chmn: Terry Reynolds **Dir**: Tim Parsons
Tran Man: Tom Barrett
Ch Eng: Dave Stockford
Fleet: 75 - 3 single-deck bus, 2 coach, 70 minibus.
Chassis: 1 Ford Transit. 12 Leyland. 6 Mercedes. 3 Optare. 50 Renault. 2 Volvo.
Bodies: include 2 Van Hool
Ops incl: local bus services, excursions & tours, private hire, continental tours, school contracts.
Livery: White/Green

CHERRY BRIAR LTD

SUPREME HOUSE, STOUR WHARF, STOUR ROAD, LONDON E3 2NT
Tel: 020 8985 8888
Fax: 020 8936 8444
Man Dir: Clifford Humphreys **Ops Man/Co Sec**: Helen Humphreys **Ch Eng**: B Raif.
Fleetname: Channel Coachways
Fleet: 5 - 4 coach. 1 midicoach.
Chassis: Scania. Toyota.
Bodies: Caetano. Irizar.
Ops incl: school contracts, excursions & tours, private hire, continental tours.
Livery: White/Red/Blue.

CITYCIRCLE UK LTD

95 CROMWELL ROAD, LONDON SW7 4JJ
Tel: 020 8561 2112
Fax: 020 8561 2010
Web site: www.citycircleuk.com
Dir: Neil Pegg **Ops Man**: Mike Fletcher
Fleet: 17 coach
Chassis: 7 MAN. 10 Setra.
Bodies: 7 Neoplan. 10 Setra.
Ops incl: excursions & tours, private hire, continental tours.
Livery: White/Red/Grey

CLARKES OF LONDON

KANGLEY BRIDGE ROAD, LONDON SE26 5AT
Tel: 020 8778 6697
Fax: 020 8778 0389
E-mail: info@clarkescoaches.co.uk
Web site: www.clarkescoaches.co.uk
Man Dir: Mrs D Newman **Comm Dir**: J Devacmaker **Fin Dir**: S Reeve.
Fleet: 57 - 53 coach, 4 minicoach.
Chassis: 20 Setra. 15 Scania . 4 Toyota. 18 Volvo.
Bodies: 4 Caetano. 15 Irizar. 10 Jonckheere. 20 Setra. 8 Mistral.
Ops incl: excursions & tours, private hire, express, continental tours.
Livery: Green/Silver.

COLLINS COACHES LTD

UNIT 6, WATERSIDE TRADING CENTRE, TRUMPERS WAY, LONDON W7 2QD
Tel: 020 8843 2145
Fax: 020 8843 2375
E-mail: collinscoaches@aol.com
Web site: www.collins-coaches.co.uk
Man Dir: Eric Collins **Sec**: Pauline Collins
Dir: Alfred Collins
Fleet: 9 coach.
Chassis: 9 Volvo.
Bodies: 4 Jonckheere. 4 Plaxton. 1 Van Hool.
Ops incl: private hire, school contracts.
Livery: Red/White.

CONISTON COACHES LTD

88 CONISTON ROAD, BROMLEY BR1 4JB.
Tel/Fax: 020 8460 3432
Web site: www.conistoncoaches.co.uk

Dir: Richard Smock
Fleet: 5 coach
Chassis: 5 Volvo
Bodies: 1 Caetano. 4 Plaxton.
Ops incl: excursions & tours, private hire, continental tours, school contracts.
Livery: White/Red.

COUNTY COACHES
See Essex

DAVID CORBEL OF LONDON LTD

6 CAMROSE AVENUE, EDGWARE HA8 6EG
Tel: 020 8952 1300.
Fax: 020 8952 8641
E-mail: corbeloflondon@aol.com
Dir: Robert Whelan
Fleet: 9 coach
Chassis: 4 Dennis. 1 Setra. 4 Volvo.
Bodies: 4 Plaxton. 1 Setra. 4 UVG.
Ops incl: school contracts, private hire.
Livery: Pink/Blue.

*CROWN COACHES

68 CANON ROAD, BICKLEY BR1 2SP
Tel: 020 8313 3020
Fax: 020 8464 2375
Fleet: 5 - 4 coach, 1 minibus.
Chassis: incl: 1 Ford Transit.
Bodies: incl: 2 Mercedes. 1 Setra. 1 Van Hool.
Ops incl: excursions & tours, private hire, continental tours.

CROYDON TRAMLINK

TRAMTRACK CROYDON LTD, COOMBER WAY, CROYDON CR0 4TQ
Tel: 020 8665 9695
Fax: 020 8665 7347
Web site: www.tfl.gov.uk/trams
Ops Man: John Ryman **Head of Safety**: C Tomlinson
Fleet: 24 Tram
Chassis/bodies: Bombardier
Ops incl: local tram services
Livery: Red/White

CRYSTALS COACHES LTD

HORTENSIA ROAD, LONDON SW10 0QP.
Tel: 020 7376 3015
Fax: 020 7376 3019
Ops Man: G. Betts.
Fleet: 30 - 15 minibus, 15 minicoach.
Chassis: Ford Transit. Freight Rover. Mercedes.
Ops incl: local bus services, school contracts, private hire.

DANS MINI-BUS HIRE LTD

ROYAL FOREST COACH HOUSE, 109 MAYBANK ROAD, LONDON E18 1EZ.
Tel: 020 8505 8833.
Fax: 020 8519 1937.
Man Dir: D. J. Brown. **Dir**: S. A. Brown.
Fleet: 43 mini/midicoaches.

Chassis: 19 Ford Transit. 24 Mercedes.
Bodies: 24 Mercedes. 7 Optare. 5 Reeve Burgess. 1 Ford.
Ops incl: school contracts, excursions & tours, private hire, continental tours.

DOCKLANDS BUSES LTD

FACTORY ROAD, LONDON
E16 2EW
Tel: 020 7474 8130
E-mail: docklandsbuses@aol.com
Web site: www.docklandsbuses.co.uk
Dir: F Cheroomi
Fleet: 27 - 14 single-deck bus, 5 coach, 3 midicoach, 5 minibus
Ops incl: local bus services, school contracts, excursions & tours, private hire

EALING COMMUNITY TRANSPORT LTD
97 BOLLO LANE, LONDON W3 8QN
Tel: 020 8753 7810
Web site: www.ectgroup.co.uk
Pass Ops Dir: Anna Whitty
Fleet: 28 - 13 single-deck bus, 15 minibus
Ops incl: local bus services
Livery: Red/Yellow

*P & J ELLIS LTD
UNIT 3, RADFORD ESTATE, OLD OAK LANE, LONDON NW10 6UA
Tel: 020 8961 1141
Fax: 020 8965 5995
E-mail: enquiries@pjellis.co.uk
Web-site: www.pjellis.co.uk
Dir: Matthew Ellis
Fleet: 12 coach.
Chassis: 12 Volvo.
Bodies: 12 Jonckheere.
Ops incl: excursions & tours, private hire, continental tours.

*ELTHAM EXECUTIVE CHARTER LTD

21-23 CROWN WOODS WAY, LONDON SE9 2NL
Tel: 020 8850 2011
Fax: 020 8850 5210
E-mail: enquiries@eec-minicoaches.co.uk
Web site: www.eec-minicoaches.co.uk
Dirs: Ray Lawrence, Jill Lawrence, Fiona Lawrence
Fleet: 6 - 3 midicoach, 1 minibus, 2 minicoach
Chassis: 1 Ford. 5 Iveco.
Bodies: 3 Indcar. 1 Optare. 2 other
Ops incl: private hire.
Livery: White with blue&gold graphics

EMPRESS MOTORS LTD

3 CORBRIDGE CRESCENT, LONDON E2 9DS.
Tel: 020 7739 5454
Fax: 020 7729 0237
E-mail: info@empresscoaches.co.uk
Web site: www.empresscoaches.co.uk
Fleetmane: Empress of London
Man Dir: P D Stanton **Co Sec**: T A Stanton
Dir: L M R Stanton **Op Mans**: J C Stanton, M E Stanton
Fleet: 18 - 13 coach, 3 midicoach, 2 minibus
Chassis/Bodies: 1 Caetano. 1 Jonckheere. 1 Mercedes. 1 Optare. 13 Plaxton. 1 Toyota.
Ops incl: private hire.
Livery: Cream/Maroon.

EXCALIBUR COACHES

1A BRABOURN GROVE, LONDON SE15 2BS
Tel: 020 7358 1441
Fax: 020 7358 1661
E-mail: garbyzacca@aol.com
Web site: www. excaliburcoaches.com
Man Dir: Garby Zacca **Ch Eng**: C Patel
Fleet: 12 coach.
Chassis: 2 Iveco. 10 Scania.
Bodies: 2 Beulas. 10 Irizar.
Ops incl: excursions & tours, private hire, express, continental tours, school contracts.
Livery: Blue

FIRST LONDON & BERKSHIRE

3RD FLOOR, MACMILLAN HOUSE, PADDINGTON STATION, LONDON W2 1TY
Tel: 020 7298 7300
Fax: 020 7706 8789
Web site: www.firstgroup.co.uk
Man Dir: Tony Wilson. **Ops Dir**: Adrian Jones.
Fleet: 1204 - 699 double-deck bus, 12 single-deck bus, 476 midibus, 15 minibus, 2 open-top bus.
Chassis: 59 AEC. 924 Dennis. 21 Leyland. 24 MCW. 24 Mercedes. 149 Volvo.
Bodies: 67 Alexander. 3 Carlyle. 49 East Lancs. 1 Leyland. 450 Marshall. 30 MCW. 14 Mercedes. 89 Northern Counties. 59 Park Royal. 429 Plaxton. 2 Reeve Burgess. 11 Wright.
Ops incl: local bus services, school contracts, private hire.
Livery: Red with Yellow/Grey stripes.
Ticket System: Prestige (TfL).

FLIGHTS HALLMARK
See West Midlands

FOREST COACHES
THE COACH HOUSE, NELSON STREET, LONDON E6 2QA.
Tel: 020 8472 5954.
Fax: 020 8472 6098.

FORESTDALE COACHES LTD
68 VINEY BANK, COURTWOOD LANE, FORESTDALE, ADDINGTON CR0 9JT
Tel/Fax: 020 8651 1359
Chmn/Man Dir: V Holub **Co Sec**: Mrs P R Holub
Fleet: 1 coach.
Chassis/Body: Bova.
Ops incl: excursions & tours, private hire
Livery: Red/Gold

*GOLDENSTAND (SOUTHERN) LTD

13 WAXLOW ROAD, LONDON NW10 7NY
Tel: 020 8961 9974/5
Fax: 020 8961 9949
Web site: www.goldenstand.co.uk
Chmn: J Chivrall **Sec**: J Kemp
Fleet: 8 - 5 coach, 3 minibus.
Chassis: 3 LDV. 5 Scania.
Bodies: 5 Jonckheere. 3 Leyland
Ops incl: school contracts, private hire, excursions & tours
Livery: Red/White

THE GOLD STANDARD
94A HORSENDEN LANE NORTH, GREENFORD UB6 7QH
Tel: 020 8795 0075.
Fax: 020 8900 9630.
E-mail: paul@luxuryminicoaches.co.uk
Web site: www.luxuryminicoach.co.uk
Prop: Paul Grant
Fleet: 1 minicoach.
Chassis: Optare.
Ops incl: excursions & tours, private hire.

*A GREEN COACHES LTD
357A HOE STREET, LONDON E17 9AP
Tel: 020 8520 1138
Fax: 020 8520 1139
E-mail: agreencoaches357@aol.com
Dirs: Keith Richards, Janis Grover (**Tran Man**)
Fleet: 5 coach.
Chassis: 1 Scania. 4 Volvo. 1 Setra.
Ops incl: private hire, school contracts.
Livery: Orange/Yellow/Green/White

*HAILSTONE TRAVEL
See Essex

Air conditioning	Seat belt-fitted vehicles
Vehicles suitable for disabled	Recovery service available (not 24 hr)
Coach(es) with galley facilities	
Coach(es) with toilet facilities	24hr recovery service
	Replacement vehicle available
	Toilet-drop facilities available
	Vintage vehicle(s) available
	Open top vehicle(s)

*HEARNS COACHES

801 KENTON LANE, HARROW WEALD HA3 6AH
Tel: 020 8954 0444
Fax: 020 8954 5959
E-mail: ged@hearns-coaches.co.uk
Web site: www.hearns-coaches.co.uk
Man Dir: R J Hearn **Ops Man**: Ged Newham
Fleet: 38 - 35 coach, 2 minicoach, 1 midicoach.
Chassis: 1 Iveco. 3 Mercedes. 2 Neoplan. 20 Scania. 9 Setra. 1 Volvo.
Bodies: 3 Beulas. 20 Irizar. 3 Mercedes. 2 Neoplan. 9 Setra.
Ops incl: private hire

*JOHN HOUGHTON LUXURY MINI COACHES

2 ELGAR AVENUE, LONDON W5 3JU
Tel: 020 8567 0056
Fax: 020 8567 5781
E-mail: jrhoughten@connectfree.co.uk
Web site: www.luxury-mini-coaches.co.uk
Prop: John Houghton **Co Sec**: Marlene Houghton
Fleet: 3 minicoach.
Chassis/bodies: Mercedes.
Ops incl: private hire.

*HOUNSLOW MINI COACHES

2 VINEYARD ROAD, HIGH STREET, FELTHAM TW13 4HQ.
Tel: 020 8890 8429
Fax: 020 8893 1736
Web site:
www.hounslowminicoaches.co.uk
E-mail:
hounslowminicoaches@btconnect.com
Fleet: 19 - 3 midicaoch, 4 minibus, 4 minicoach, 8 people carrier.
Chassis: 2 Ford Transit, 1 Iveco. 5 LDV. 7 Mercedes. 1 Toyota.
Bodies: 1 Caetano. 3 Mellor. 4 Mercedes. 5 Optare. 3 other.
Ops incl: school contracts, private hire.

HOUSTON'S OF LONDON

83 GLADESMORE ROAD, LONDON N15 6TL.
Tel/Fax: 020 8800 4576.
Prop: H. Jones.
Fleet: 2 coach. **Chassis**: Leyland.
Ops incl: school contracts, excursions & tours, private hire.

IMPACT OF LONDON

7-9 WADSWORTH ROAD, GREENFORD UB6 7JZ
Tel: 020 8579 9922
Fax: 020 8840 4780.
E-mail: info@impactgroup.co.uk
Web site: www.impactgroup.co.uk
Dir: A Hill **Gen Man**: A. Palmer.
Engs: H Louis, L. Singh.
Fleet: 44 - 14 coach, 20 midicoach, 10 minibus.
Chassis: 2 Bova. 2 Dennis. 10 LDV.

20 Mercedes. 10 Volvo.
Bodies: 7 Berkhof. 2 Bova. 1 Caetano. 2 Mellor. 24 Mercedes. 3 Optare. 3 Plaxton. 2 Van Hool.
Ops incl: excursions & tours, private hire, express, continental tours, school contracts.
Livery: White.

INTERNATIONAL COACH LINES LTD

19 NURSERY ROAD, THORNTON HEATH CR7 8RE.
Tel: 020 8684 2995.
Fax: 020 8689 3483.
Dir: Mrs S. Bailey.
Fleet: 18 - 3 double-deck bus, 1 single-deck bus, 10 coach, 4 minicoach.
Ops incl: excursions & tours, private hire, express, continental tours.
Livery: Blue/White.

ISLEWORTH COACHES
See Middlesex

THE KINGS FERRY
See Kent

LEWIS TRAVEL UK PLC

2-10 DENHAM STREET, LONDON SE10 0RY
Tel: 020 8858 0031
Fax: 020 8858 7631
E-mail: sales@lewistravel.co.uk
Dir: T Legnor-Lewis **Gen Man**: J Harpic
Fleet: 29 - 20 coach, 4 midibus, 3 minibus, 2 minicoach.
Chassis: 1 Ayats. 1 Bova. 4 DAF. 3 Dennis. 4 Mercedes. 2 Neoplan. 2 Scania. 1 Setra. 6 Transbus. 6 Volvo.
Bodies: 1 Ayats. 1 Bova. 1 Duple. 4 Ikarus. 3 Irizar. 1 Jonckheere. 2 Mercedes. 1 Neoplan. 7 Plaxton. 1 Setra. 4Transbus. 3 Van Hool.
Ops incl: local bus services, school contracts, excursions & tours, private hire, continental tours.
Livery: incl. Red

LINK LINE COACHES LTD

1 WROTTESLEY ROAD, LONDON NW10 5XA.
Tel: 020 8965 2221.
Fax: 020 8961 3680.
E-mail: info@linkline-coaches.co.uk
Web site: wwwlinkline-coaches.co.uk
Man Dir: T. J. Russell.
Fleet: 10 - 7 single-deck bus, 3 coach.
Chassis: 6 Dennis. 1 Mercedes. 3 Volvo.
Bodies: 8 Caetano. 1 Optare. 1 Plaxton.
Ops incl: private hire, continental tours, school contracts.

THE LITTLE BUS COMPANY

HOME FARM, ALDENHAM ROAD, ELSTREE WD6 3AZ
Tel: 020 8953 0202
Fax: 020 8953 9553
E-mail: enquiry@littlebus.co.uk
Web site: www.littlebus.co.uk
Fleet: includes single deck coach, midicoach, minibus, minicoach
Chassis: LDV. Leyland. Mercedes.

Bodies: Mercedes.
Prop: Jeremy Reese
Fleet: 7 minibus.
Chassis: 5 LDV. 2 Ford Transit.
Ops incl: school contracts, private hire.

LONDON BUSES LTD t/a EAST THAMES BUSES

ASH GROVE, MARE STREET, LONDON E8 4RH
Tel: 020 7241 7220.
Fax: 020 7241 7239.
Fleet Name: East Thames Buses.
Man Dir: Alan Barrett **Fin Dir**: David Bowen. **Eng. Dir**: Gary Filbey. **Gen Man**: Norman Priestly.
Fleet: 128 - 77 double-deck bus. 51 single-deck bus.
Chassis: 12 DAF, 15 Dennis. 10 Optare. 14 Scania. 77 Volvo.
Bodies: 40 East Lancs. 10 Optare. 21 Plaxton. 3 Wright.
Ops incl: local bus services.
Livery: Red.
Ticket System: Prestige
Part of Transport for London

*LONDON CENTRAL BUS CO LTD

18 MERTON HIGH STREET, LONDON SW19 1DN
Tel: 020 8545 6100
Fax: 020 8545 6101
Web site: www.go-ahead-london.com
Fleet Name: London Central
Ch Exec: David Brown **Eng Dir**: Phil Margrave **Fin Dir**: Paul Reeves
Ops Dir: John Trayner
Fleet: 675 - 455 double-deck bus, 157 single-deck bus, 63 articulated bus.
Chassis: 8 AEC. 23 DAF. 133 Dennis. 63 Mercedes. 448 Volvo.
Bodies: 46 Alexander. 17 East Lancs. 20 Marshall. 63 Mercedes. 50 Northern Counties. 8 Park Royal. 280 Plaxton. 113 Transbus. 78 Wright.
Ops incl: local bus services, school contracts, excursions & tours, private hire.

*LONDON GENERAL TRANSPORT SERVICES LTD

18 MERTON HIGH STREET, LONDON SW19 1DN
Tel: 020 8545 6100
Fax: 020 8545 6101

Web site: www.go-ahead-london.com
Fleet Name: London General
Ch Exec: David Brown **Eng Dir**: Phil Margrave **Fin Dir**: Paul Reeves
Ops Dir: John Trayner
Fleet: 623 - 449 double-deck bus, 143 single-deck bus, 31 articulated bus.
Chassis: 199 Dennis. 31 Mercedes. 393 Volvo.
Bodies: 52 East Lancs. 31 Mercedes. 139 Plaxton. 199 Transbus. 202 Wright.
Ops incl: local bus services, school contracts, excursions & tours, private hire.

*LONDON UNITED BUSWAYS LTD
See Middlesex

LUXURY MINI COACH

94A HORSENDEN LANE,
GREENFORD UB6 7QH
Tel: 020 8795 0075.
Fax: 020 8900 9630.
E-mail: paul@luxuryminicoach.co.uk
Web site: www.luxuryminicoach.co.uk
Dir: Paul Grant
Fleet: minicoaches.
Ops incl: private hire.

*MARTINS COACHES

THE GAS WORKS, 709 OLD KENT ROAD, LONDON SE15 1JZ
Tel: 020 7732 1000
Fax: 020 7732 1011
E-mail: info@martinscoachesco uk
Web site: www.martinscoaches.co.uk
ManDir: Steve Martin **Dirs**: Terry Martin, Anne Martin **Transport**: Dave Carter **Eng**: Andy Carter
Fleet: 17 - 9 coach, 6 midicoach, 2 minicoach
Chassis: 7 Dennis. 10 Mercedes
Bodies: 2 Optare. 13 Plaxton. 2 other.
Ops incl: school contracts, excursions & tours, private hire, continental tours.
Livery: White/Mauve/Gold

*MARSHALLS COACHES LLP

FIRBANK WAY, LEIGHTON BUZZARD LU7 4YP
Tel: 020 7837 6663
Fax: 01525 850967
Recovery: 01525 375301
E-mail: info@marshalls-coaches.co.uk
Web site: www.marshalls-coaches.co.uk
Props: G Marshall, Mrs S Marshall **Ops Man**: Ian White **Fleet Eng**: R Winters
Fleet: 21 - 19 coach, 1 double-deck coach, 1 midicoach.
Chassis: 4 Dennis. 2 Iveco. 1 Mercedes. 1 Neoplan. 1 Scania. 12 Volvo.
Bodies: 2 Beulas. 1 Caetano. 1 Ikarus. 5 Jonckheere. 1 Mercedes. 1 Neoplan. 10 Plaxton.
Ops incl: private hire, school contracts, local bus services.
Livery: Blue/Multicoloured.

*METROLINE
See Middlesex

MINI-BUS SHUTTLE SERVICE

68 LUPUS STREET, LONDON SW1V 3EH.
Tel: 020 7821 1157.
Fax: 020 7834 6748.
Prop: Kaye Stoyles. **Man**: R. Stoyles.
Fleet: 16 minibus.
Ops incl: school contracts, excursions & tours, private hire.

*M&M COACHLINES
See Middlesex

M T P CHARTER COACHES

39 GROSVENOR ROAD, LONDON E11 2EW
Tel/Fax: 020 8989 0211
Prop: M Powis
Fleet: 2 - 1 coach, 1 mdnicoach.
Chassis/bodies: 1 Setra. 1 Caetano.
Ops incl: private hire, excursions & tours, continental tours.
Livery: White

NEW BHARAT COACHES LTD

1A PRIORY WAY, SOUTHALL UB2 5EB
Tel: 020 8574 6810
Fax: 020 8813 9555
E-mail: admin@newbharat.co.uk
Web site: www.newbharat.co.uk
Dir: Surjit Singh Dhaliwal **Ch Eng**: Alan Littlemore
Fleet: 4 coach
Chassis: 4 Volvo
Ops incl: school contracts, excursions & tours, private hire, express, continental tours.
Livery: Red/Yellow/Blue on white base.

NEWBOURNE COACHES

FIRBANK WAY, LEIGHTON BUZZARD LU7 4YP
Tel: 020 7837 6663
Fax: 01525 850967
Web site: www.marshalls-coaches.co.uk
E.mail: info@marshalls-coaches.co.uk
Props: G R Marshall, S J Marshall
Ops Man: Ian White **Ch Eng**: Nick Aris
Fleet: 22 - 20 coach, 1 double-deck coach, 1 midicoach
Chassis: 4 Dennis. 6 Iveco. 1 Mercedes. 1 Neoplan. 10 Volvo.
Bodies: 6 Beulas. 1 Ikarus. 6 Jonckheere. 1 Mercedes. 1 Neoplan. 7 Plaxton.
Ops incl: private hire, school contracts, local bus services.
Livery: Blue/Multicoloured.

THE ORIGINAL LONDON TOUR

JEWS ROW, LONDON SW18 1TB
Tel: 020 8877 1722
Fax: 020 8877 1968
E-mail: info@theoriginaltour.com
Web site: www.theoriginaltour.com
Fleet: 94 - 24 double-deck bus, 70 open-top bus.
Chassis: 2 Dennis. 13 Leyland. 41 MCW. 14 Volvo.
Bodies: 13 Alexander. 41 MCW. 2 Northern Counties. 14 Transbus.
Ops incl: local bus services.
Livery: Red/Cream

Ticket system: Almex/Wayfarer
Subsidiary of Arriva

*REDWING COACHES

10 DYLAN ROAD, LONDON SE24 0HL
Tel: 020 7733 1124
Fax: 020 7733 5194
E-mail: redwing@redwing-coaches.co.uk.
Web site: www.redwing-coaches.co.uk.
Man Dir: Paul Campana **Ops Man**: Barry Nunn **Gen Man**: John Fowler **Ch Eng**: Robbie Hodgekiss **Sales & Mktg**: Keith Payne **Reservations**: Jef Johnson
Fleet: 45 - 43 coach, 2 midicoach.
Chassis: 20 Iveco. 11 Mercedes. 14 Setra.
Bodies: 20 Beulas. 11 Caetano. 14 Setra
Ops incl: excursions & tours, private hire, continental tours.
Livery: Red/Cream

*SILVERDALE LONDON LTD

UNIT 3, RADFORD ESTATE, OLD OAK LANE, LONDON NW10 6UA
Tel: 020 8961 1812
Fax: 020 8961 5677
Email: silverdalelondon@aol.com
Web site: www.silverdalelondon.com
Dir: Robert Green **Tran Man**: Richard Cassell
Fleet: 14 - coach, midibus.
Chassis: 1 Dennis. 1 MAN. 2 Mercedes. 10 Volvo.
Bodies: 10 Caetano. 1 Marcopolo. 2 Optare. 1 Plaxton.
Ops incl: school contracts, excursions & tours, private hire, express, continental tours.
Livery: White/Red

*SOUTHGATE & FINCHLEY COACHES LTD

231A COLNEY HATCH LANE, LONDON N11 3DG
Tel: 020 8368 0040
Fax: 020 8361 1934
Web site: www.coaches.org.uk
Man Dir: M. P. Rice. **Dirs**: Mrs V. M. Rice (Co Sec), P. M. Rice, Mrs E. B. Scrivens.
Fleet: 23 coach.
Chassis: 23 V.olvo.
Bodies: 23 Plaxton
Ops incl: school contracts, excursions and tours, private hire
Livery: Yellow/Blue/Orange

*STAGECOACH LONDON

2 CLEMENTS ROAD, ILFORD IG1 1BA
Tel: 020 8695 3420
Fax: 020 8477 7200
E-mail: pr.london@stagecoachbus.com

Air conditioning	Seat belt-fitted vehicles	Replacement vehicle available
Vehicles suitable for disabled	Recovery service available (not 24 hr)	Toilet-drop facilities available
Coach(es) with galley facilities		Vintage vehicle(s) available
Coach(es) with toilet facilities	24hr recovery service	Open top vehicle(s)

Web site:
www.stagecoachbus.com/london
Man Dir: Nigel Barrett **Eng Dir**: Peter Sumner **Ops Dir**: Barry Beckham **Ser Perf Man**: Richard Franklin **HR Dir**: Sarah Rennie **Mktg & Comm Man**: Paul Owens **Communications Man**: Ben Franklin
Fleet: 1344 - 957 double-deck bus, 29 single-deck bus, 7 coach, 6 double-deck coach, 77 articulated bus, 268 midibus.
Chassis: 29 AEC. 13 DAF. 1193 Dennis. 1 Leyland. 77 Mercedes. 16 Scania. 15 Volvo.
Bodies: 1145 Alexander. 5 Jonckheere. 77Mercedes. 6 Northern Counties. 13 Optare. 30 Park Royal. 52 Plaxton. 16 Wright.
Ops incl: local bus services, excursions & tours, private hire.

*TELLINGS GOLDEN MILLER COACHES LTD

ENSIGN CLOSE, HEATHROW AIRPORT, HOUNSLOW TW6 2PQ
Tel: 020 8757 4700
Fax: 020 8757 4718
E-mail: sales@telling.co.uk
Web site:
www.tellingsgoldenmiller.co.uk
Chmn: Stephen Telling **Group Ops Dir**: Richard Telling **Fin Dir/Co Sec**: Basil Taylor **Ops Dir**: Paul Cowell **Eng Man**: Ian Foster
Fleet: 75 - 58 coach, 14 minicoach, 3 minicoach.
Chassis: 2 Iveco. 15 Mercedes. 3 Setra. 2 Toyota. 53 Volvo.
Bodies: 2 Beulas. 6 Caetano. 3 Mercedes. 59 Plaxton. 3 Setra. 2 Van Hool.
Ops incl: school contracts, excursions & tours, private hire, express, continental tours.
Livery: White/Blue/Yellow

F E THORPE & SONS LTD

UNIT 5, FOURTH WAY, WEMBLEY HA9 0LH
Tel: 020 8998 1155
Man Dir: F. Thorpe. **Dir**: J. Thorpe.
Fleet: 106 - 84 single-deck bus, 19 double-deck bus, 3 minibus
Chassis: 60 Dennis. 15 MCW. 3 Mercedes. 28 Volvo.
Bodies: 2 Alexander. 28 East Lancs. 15 MCW. 60 Plaxton. 1 Wadham Stringer.
Livery: Red/Yellow
Ops incl: local bus services, school contracts
(Subsidiary of Metroline)

*TIMEBUS TRAVEL

7 BOLEYN DRIVE, ST ALBANS AL1 2BP
Tel: 01727 866248
Web site: www.timebus.co.uk
Fleetname: Timebus
Prop: David Pring
Fleet: 12 - 8 double-deck bus, 2 single-deck bus, 2 open-top bus
Chassis: 11 Aec. 1 Leyland.
Bodies: 2 MCW. 9 Park Royal. 1 other.
Ops incl: private hire
Livery: Red with grey lining

TOMORROWS TRANSPORT

GIBBS STORAGE, GIBBS ROAD, LONDON N18 3PU
Tel: 020 8807 4555
Fax: 020 8807 4603
Prop: V A Daniels
Fleet: 3 - 2 coach, 1 midicoach
Chassis: 1 DAF. 1 Leyland. 1 Toyota.
Bodies: 1 Caetano. 1 Duple. 1 Van Hool.
Ops incl: private hire

*TRAVEL LONDON LTD

301 CAMBERWELL NEW ROAD, LONDON SE5 0TF
Tel: 020 7805 3500
Fax: 020 7805 3510
Web site: www.travellondonbus.co.uk
Man Dir: Paul McGowan **Ops Dir**: Bill Weatherley **Eng Dir**: Steve Hamilton
Fin Dir: Ross Hanley
Fleet: 433 - 198 double-deck bus, 223 single-deck bus, 12 midibus
Chassis: Dennis. Optare. Mercedes. Volvo.
Bodies: Alexander. Wright. East Lancs. Plaxton. Caetano.
Ops incl: local bus services
Livery: Red (London), Red and white (Surrey CC)
Ticket system: Wayfarer, Almex
(Subsidiary of National Express Group)

WALLIS LIMOUSINES

See Kent

*WESTBUS COACH SERVICES LTD

27A SPRING GROVE ROAD, HOUNSLOW TW3 4BE
Tel: 020 8572 6348
Fax: 020 8570 2234
Recovery: 020 8572 6348
E-mail: reservations@westbus.co.uk
Web site: www.westbus.co.uk
Gen Man: Tim Miles **Ops Man**: Chris Shaw **Ch Eng**: Graham Bessant
Chassis: 15 DAF. 4 Mercedes. 2 Setra. 5 Volvo.
Bodies: 2 Berkhof. 1 Hispano. 5 Plaxton. 2 Setra. 1 Sitcar. 15 Van Hool.
Ops incl: private hire, continental tours, excursions & tours, school contracts.
Livery: Red/Cream
(Part of the Comfort Delgro Corporation)

WESTWAY COACH SERVICES

7A RAINBOW INDUSTRIAL ESTATE, STATION APPROACH, RAYNES PARK, LONDON SW20 0JY
Tel: 020 8944 1277.
Fax: 020 8947 5339.
E-mail: david@westway-coaches.co.uk
E-mail:
www.westwaycoachservices.com
Prop: David West. **Gen Man**: Arthur Richardson.
Fleet: 16 - 7 coach, 7 double-deck coach, 2 midicoach.
Chassis: 2 Mercedes. 14 Volvo
Bodies: 6 Jonckheere. 1 Plaxton. 6 Van Hool. 2 other.
Ops incl: school contracts, excursions & tours, private hire, continental tours.
Livery: Blue/Orange.

WINGS LUXURY TRAVEL LTD

WEST LONDON COACH CENTRE, HAYES UB3 4QT
Tel: 020 8573 8388
Fax: 020 8573 7773
Web site: www.wingstravel.co.uk
E-mail: info@wingstravel.co.uk
Gen Man: Bill Gritt
Fleet: 17 - 7 midicoach, 4 minicoach, 6 exec. minicoach.
Chassis/Bodies: Mercedes. East Lancs. Optare. Setra.
Ops Incl: school contracts, excursions and tours, private hire.

MERSEYSIDE (ST HELENS, KNOWSLEY, LIVERPOOL, SEFTON, WIRRAL)

A1A LTD
373 CLEVELAND STREET, BIRKENHEAD CH41 4JW.
Tel: 0151 650 1616
Fax: 0151 650 0007
Web site: www.a1atravel.co.uk
Props: John and Barbara Ashworth
Fleet: 26 - 7 single-deck bus, 8 midibus, 11 minibus.
Chassis: 7 Dennis. 8 LDV. 1 Mazda. 5 Mercedes. 1VW.
Ops incl: local bus services, school contracts, private hire.
Livery: White/Blue

*A.2.B TRAVEL UK LTD

PRENTON WAY, NORTH CHESHIRE TRADING ESTATE, PRENTON CH43 3DU
Tel: 0151 609 0600
Fax: 0151 609 0601
Dirs: G Evans, D Evans
Fleet: 15 - 3 single-deck coach, 2 midicoach, 10 minicoach.
Chassis: 2 Iveco. 10 LDV. 1 MAN. 1 Mercedes.
Bodies: incl: 1 Beulas. 1 Caetano. 1 Plaxton.
Ops incl: school contracts, private hire, excursions & tours.
Livery: Silver

AINTREE COACHLINE
11 CLARE ROAD, BOOTLE L20 9LY.
Tel: 0151 922 8630.
Fax: 0151 933 6994.
Livery: Red/Cream.
Owns Helms of Eastham.

ARRIVA NORTH WEST AND WALES
73 ORMSKIRK ROAD, AINTREE L9 5AE.
Tel: 0151 522 2880
Fax: 0151 525 9556
Web site: www.arriva.co.uk
Man Dir: Bob Hind **Eng Dir**: Malcolm Gilkerson
Fleet: 1325 - 181 double-deck bus, 890 single-deck bus, 2 coach, 10 open-top bus, 234 midibus, 8 minibus.
Chassis: 1 Bristol. 135 DAF. 553 Dennis. 74 Leyland. 4 MCW. 104 Mercedes. 15 Neoplan. 10 Optare. 98 Scania. 331 Volvo.
Bodies: 89 Alexander. 5 Carlyle. 9 ECW. 136 East Lancs. 5 Ikarus. 8 Leyland. 64 Marshall. 4 MCW. 1 Mellor. 15 Neoplan. 194 Northern Counties. 10 Optare. 471 Plaxton. 2 Van Hool. 2 Wadham Stringer. 2 UVG. 308 Wright.
Ops incl: local bus services, school contracts.
Livery: Arriva Blue/Cream
Ticket System: Wayfarer TGX150GB

G. ASHTON COACHES
WATERY LANE, ST HELENS WA9 3JA
Tel: 01744 733275
Fax: 01744 454122
Prop: George Ashton
Fleet: 8 coach
Chassis/bodies: 1 Ford. 4 Scania. 2 Duple. 1 Caetano.
Ops incl: excursions & tours, private hire, continental tours.

AVON COACH AND BUS COMPANY
10 BROOKWAY, NORTH CHESHIRE TRADING ESTATE, PRENTON CH43 3DT.
Tel: 0151 608 8000.
Fax: 0151 608 9955.
Prop: L. W. Smith.
Tran/Ops Man: P. Harwood.
Fleet: 10 - 7 double-deck bus, 2 single-deck bus, 1 coach.
Chassis: 1 Bedford. 2 Daimler. 4 Leyland. 2 Leyland National. 1 Volvo.
Ops incl: local bus services, school contracts, excursions & tours, private hire.
Livery: Cream with Blue and Gold stripe.
Ticket System: Wayfarer.

BLUELINE COACHES
54 STATION ROAD, MAGHULL L31 3DB.
Tel/Fax: 0151 526 8888.
Prop: C. P. Carr.
Fleet: 12 - 3 coach, 4 midicoach, 5 minicoach.
Ops incl: private hire, school contracts.

CUMFY COACHES
49 MILL LANE, SOUTHPORT PR9 7PL.
Tel: 01704 227321.
Fax: 01704 505781.
Prop: M. R. Vickers. **Admin**: Mrs P. Lyon.
Fleet: 12 - 1 midicoach, 3 minibus, 8 minicoach.
Chassis: 1 Bedford. 3 Dodge. 1 Iveco. 1 Mercedes. 5 Renault.
Bodies: 1 Duple. 1 Wright. 3 Reeve Burgess. 6 van conversions.
Ops incl: excursions & tours, private hire, school contracts.

FIRST IN CHESTER & THE WIRRAL
659 NEW CHESTER ROAD, ROCK FERRY CH42 1PZ
Tel: 0151 645 8661
Web site: www.firstgroup.com
Area Ops Man: Peter Walch
Fleet: 203 double-deck bus, single deck bus, coach, midibus.
Ops incl: local bus services

*FIVE STAR GROUP TRAVEL

SNAPE GATE, FOXS BANK LANE, LIVERPOOL L35 3SS
Tel: 0151 481 0000
Fax: 0151 493 9999
E-mail: phil@fivestar.freeserve.co.uk
Web site: www.fivestartravel.co.uk
Prop: Phil Riley
Fleet: 3 coach.
Chassis: 3 DAF.
Bodies: 3 Bova.
Ops incl: excursions & tours, private hire, continental tours.
Livery: White

*FORMBY COACHWAYS LTD
38 STEPHENSON WAY, FORMBY L37 8EG
Tel: 01704 834448
Fax: 01704 878820
Fleetname: Freshfield Coaches.
Man Dir: K W Bradley **Sec**: D A Bradley
Fleet: 1 minicoach.
Chassis/bodies: Mercedes.
Ops incl: school contracts, private hire.
Livery: Green/Silver

HAPPY AL'S COACHES
40 CLEVELAND STREET, BIRKENHEAD L41 8EQ
Tel: 0151 653 0053
Fax: 0151 670 0509
E-mail: dan@happyals.com
Web site: www.happyals.com
Fleetname: Happy Al's
Owner: T. A. Cullinan. **Ops Man**: M. Cullinan
Fleet: 51 - 39 double-deck bus, 3 single-deck bus, 8 coach, 1 double-deck coach.
Chassis: 20 Bristol. 3 DAF. 5 Dennis. 14 Leyland. 6 Leyland National. 1 Neoplan. 3 Volvo.
Bodies: 5 Alexander. 2 ECW. 2 Ikarus. 14 Leyland. 6 Leyland National. 1 Neoplan. 2 Optare. 4 Van Hool. 3 others.
Ops incl: local bus services, school contracts, excursions & tours, private hire, express, continental tours.
Livery: Multi-coloured.
Ticket System: Wayfarer 3.

- Air conditioning
- Vehicles suitable for disabled
- Coach(es) with galley facilities
- Coach(es) with toilet facilities
- Seat belt-fitted vehicles
- R Recovery service available (not 24 hr)
- R24 24hr recovery service
- Replacement vehicle available
- T Toilet-drop facilities available
- Vintage vehicle(s) available
- Open top vehicle(s)

*HARDINGS TOURS LTD

60 ST JOHNS ROAD, HUYTON
L36 5SY
Tel: 0151 489 1228
Fax: 0151 480 2030
Web site: www.hardingstours.co.uk
Man Dir: Selwyn A Jones **Ops Man**: Ken Pickavance **Fleet Eng**: Cledwyn Owen
Fleet: 13 - 11 coach, 1 minibus, 1 minicoach
Chassis: 1 Caetano. 2 Mercedes. 8 Scania. 2 Volvo.
Bodies: 1 Berkhof. 1 Caetano. 7 Irizar. 2 Mercedes. 2 Van Hool.
Ops incl: school contracts, excursions & tours, private hire, continental tours.
Livery: White/Red/Orange/Yellow.

K G & R HATTON
ST HELENS CENTRAL STATION YARD, SHAW STREET, ST HELENS WA10 1DQ
Fleetname: Hattons Travel, Nip on Transport.
Prop: K.G. & R. Hatton.
Livery: Red/White.

LIVERPOOL CITY COACHES/CITY BUS
99-103 STANHOPE STREET, LIVERPOOL L8 5RE.
Tel: 0151 708 6201.
Fax: 0151 708 7201.
Prop: J. Bleasdale.
Fleet: 13 - 2 double-deck bus, 6 single-deck bus, 2 coach, 1 midibus, 2 minibus.
Chassis: 2 Bristol. 1 Ford Transit. 1 Freight Rover. 4 Leyland. 5 Leyland National.
Bodies: 2 ECW. 1 Leyland. 5 Leyland National. 1 Optare. 2 Plaxton.
Ops incl: local bus services, private hire.
Livery: Blue/White.
Ticket System: Wayfarer.

*MAYPOLE COACHES

SPENCERS LANE, MELLING
L31 1HB
Tel: 0151 547 2713
Fax: 0151 548 2849

Prop: John Donnelly
Fleet: 23 - 10 double-deck bus, 10 coach, 2 midicoach, 1 minibus.
Chassis: 10 Leyland. 2 Mercedes. 1 Optare. 10 Volvo.
Bodies: 5 Ikarus. 2 Jonckheere. 10 Leyland. 2 Mercedes. 1 Optare. 2 Van Hool.
Ops incl: school contracts, excursions & tours, private hire, express, continental tours.
Livery: White.
Ticket System: ERG

GAVIN MURRAY & ELLISONS COACHES
QUEENS GARAGE, 61 BOUNDARY ROAD, ST HELENS WA10 2LX.
Tel: 01744 22882.
Fax: 01744 24402.
Dirs: A. Magowan, M. Magowan.
Fleet: 10 coach.
Chassis: 6 Bova. 3 Mercedes. 1 Volvo.
Bodies: 6 Bova. 3 Neoplan. 1 Van Hool.
Ops incl: private hire.
Livery: White/Red/Yellow.

DAVID OGDEN COACHES
BAXTERS LANE, SUTTON, ST HELENS WA9 3DH
Tel/Recovery: 01744 606176
Fax: 01744 850903
E-mail: ogdenssutton@btconnect.com
Web site: www.davidogdenholidays.co.uk
Dirs: David Ogden, Carol Ogden.
Fleet: 19 - 2 single-deck bus, 14 coach, 3 minibus.
Chassis: 16 DAF. 2 Ford Transit. 1 Mercedes.
Bodies: 3 Ikarus. 3 Plaxton. 10 Van Hool.
Ops incl: excursions & tours, private hire, express, continental tours.
Livery: Red/White/Blue.

SANDGROUNDER COACHES
See Lancashire

STAGECOACH MERSEYSIDE
GILMOSS GARAGE, EAST LANCASHIRE ROAD, LIVERPOOL L11 0BB
Tel: 0151 330 6200
Web site: www.stagecoachbus.com
Fleet: 173 - double-deck bus, single-deck bus, midibus
Chassis: MCW, Leyland, Optare, Dennis Scania.
Bodies: MCW, Park Royal, Plaxton, Marshall, Optare
Ops incl: local bus services

STAGECOACH MERSEYSIDE
GILMOSS GARAGE, EAST LANCASHIRE ROAD, LIVERPOOL L11 0BB
Tel: 0151 330 6204
Web site: www.stagecoachbus.com
Fleet: 173 - includes single-deck bus, double-deck bus.
Ops incl: local bus services

SUPERTRAVEL OMNIBUS LTD
STC HOUSE, SPEKE HALL ROAD, SPEKE L24 9HD
Tel: 0151 486 3994
Fax: 0151 448 1216
Man Dir: Graham Bolderson.
Fleetname: Supertravel Minicoaches
Fleet: 37 - 28 single-deck bus, 6 midicoach, 2 minibus, 1 minicoach.
Chassis: 24 Dennis. 1 LDV. 8 Mercedes-Benz. 3 Optare.
Bodies: 2 Alexander. 1 Marshall/MCV. 1 MCW. 3 Mercedes. 5 Optare. 23 Plaxton. 2 other.
Ops incl: local bus services, school contracts, private hire.

MIDDLESEX

ALLIED COACHLINES LTD

THE BULLS BRIDGE CENTRE, NORTH HYDE GARDENS, HAYES UB3 4QT
Tel: 020 8573 2626
Fax: 020 8561 6636
E-mail: sales@alliedcoachlines.co.uk
Web site: www.alliedcoachlines.co.uk
Dirs: R & R Charles
Fleet: 7 coach.
Chassis: 5 Mercedes. 2 Setra

Bodies: 5 Mercedes. 2 Setra.
Ops incl: private hire.

*ARMCHAIR PASSENGER TRANSPORT CO LTD
See London

ARON COACHLINES LTD

THE BULLS BRIDGE CENTRE, NORTH HYDE GARDENS, HAYES UB3 4QT

Tel: 020 8569 2949
Fax: 020 8561 2829
E-mail: sales@aroncoachlines.co.uk
Web site: www.aroncoachlines.co.uk
Dirs: S. Robinson, R. Charles
Fleet: 6 - 4 coach, 2 minibus.
Chassis: 6 Mercedes.
Bodies: 6 Mercedes.
Ops incl: private hire.

ASHFORD LUXURY COACHES
373 HATTON ROAD, FELTHAM TW14 9QS
Tel: 020 8890 6394
Fax: 020 8751 5054
Web site: www.ashfordluxurycoaches.co.uk
Man Dir: Martin Cornell
Fleet: 10 - 1 single-deck bus, 6 coach, 2 midicoach, 1 minicoach.
Chassis: 7 Dennis. 3 Mercedes.
Bodies: 3 Mellor. 7 Plaxton.
Ops incl: private hire, school contracts, local bus services.

BEECHES TRAVEL
23 POWDER MILL LANE, TWICKENHAM TW2 6EE.
Tel/Fax: 020 8898 7048.
Prop: C. Miller.
Fleet: 4 minicoach.
Chassis: Ford Transit. Freight Rover.
Ops incl: school contracts, excursions & tours, private hire.
Livery: White/Yellow.

BESSWAY TRAVEL
16 TINTERN WAY, WEST HARROW HA2 0SA.
Tel: 020 8422 3128.
Prop: Michael Heffernan.
Fleet: 6 - 1 coach, 3 midicoach, 2 minicoach.
Chassis: 1 Dennis. 5 Mercedes.
Bodies: 5 Autobus. 1 UVG.
Ops incl: private hire, school contracts.

CABIN COACHES
1 PARSONAGE CLOSE, HAYES UB3 2LZ
Tel: 020 8573 1100
Fax: 020 8573 8604
E-mail: cabincoaches@aol.com
Props: P Martin
Fleet: 5 - 4 coach, 1 midicoach.
Chassis: 1 Dennis. 1 Mercedes. 1 Scania. 2 Setra.
Bodies: 1 Duple. 1 Mercedes. 2 Setra. 1 Van Hool.
Ops incl: excursions & tours, school contracts, private hire.
Livery: White

*CALL-A-COACH
See Surrey

*CAVALIER TRAVEL SERVICES
See London

*CARAVELLE COACHES
9 CHESTNUT AVENUE, EDGWARE HA8 7RA
Tel/Fax: 020 8952 4025
Dir: H Lawrence.
Fleet: 2 - 1 midibus, 1 minibus.

Chassis: 1 Iveco. 1 Mercedes.
Ops incl: school contracts, private hire.

CHALFONT COACHES OF HARROW LTD
200 FEATHERSTONE ROAD, SOUTHALL UB2 5AQ
Tel: 020 8843 2323
Fax: 020 8574 0939
E-mail: chalfont.coaches@btopenworld.com
Web site: www.chalfontcoaches.co.uk
Man Dir: C J Shears **Dirs**: I Shears, M Shears **Ops Man**: P Williams **Ch Eng**: R Arents **Co Sec**: G Shears
Fleet: 18 - 15 coach, 1 midicoach, 2 minibus.
Chassis: 2 LDV. 1 Mercedes. 15 Volvo.
Bodies: 3 Autobus. 15 Van Hool.
Ops incl: school contracts, excursions & tours, private hire, express, continental tours.
Livery: Mauve/White

CITY CIRCLE UK LTD
See London

CUMFI-LUX COACHES
69 CORWELL LANE, HILLINGDON UB8 3DE.
Tel: 020 8561 6948
Fax: 020 8569 3809.
Prop: N. R. Farrow (**Traf Man**).
Sec: Mrs T. K. Lovell.
Fleet: 3 - 1 coach, 1 minibus, 1 minicoach.
Chassis: 2 Mercedes. 1 Scania
Ops incl: excursions & tours, private hire.
Livery: Orange/White (coach); White (minibuses).

*FALCON TRAVEL
123 NUTTY LANE, SHEPPERTON TW17 0RQ
Tel: 01932 787752
Fax: 01932 785521
Fleet: 6 - 5 coach, 1 midicoach.
Chassis: 1 Mercedes. 5 Volvo.
Bodies: 5 Van Hool. 1 other.
Ops incl: private hire, school contracts.
Livery: White/Black/Crimson

THE GOLD STANDARD
94A HORSENDEN LANE NORTH, GREENFORD UB6 7QH.
Tel: 020 8795 0075.
Fax: 020 8900 9630.
Owner/driver: P. Grant.
Fleet: 1 minicoach.
Chassis: Mercedes. **Body**: Soroco.
Ops incl: excursions & tours, private hire, continental tours.

HAMILTON OF UXBRIDGE
589-591 UXBRIDGE ROAD, HAYES END UB4 8HP
Tel: 01895 232266
Fax: 01895 810454.

Ops Man: D. L. Bennett.
Fleet: 10 - 8 coach, 2 double-deck coach.
Chassis: 10 MAN.
Bodies: 5 Ayats. 4 Noge. 1 Marco Polo
Ops incl: private hire, express, continental tours.

*HEARNS COACHES
See London

HOUNSLOW COMMUNITY TRANSPORT
9 MONTAGUE ROAD, HOUNSLOW TW3 1JY.
Tel: 020 8572 8204.
Fax: 020 8572 0997
E-mail: haightim@aol.com
Ch Officer: Tim Haigh **Flt Co-ord**: Steve Cann
Fleet: 9 minibus

*HOUNSLOW MINI COACHES
See London

*VIC HUGHES & SON LTD
61 FERN GROVE, FELTHAM TW14 9AY
Tel: 020 8831 0770
Fax: 020 8831 0660
Man Dir: V B Hughes.
Co Sec: Mrs V. Hughes. **Dir**: K. Hughes.
Fleet: 21 - 4 midicoach, 5 minibus, 12 ambulance.
Chassis: Ford, Mercedes.
Ops incl: school contracts, excursions & tours, private hire.
Livery: White/Black.

IMPACT OF LONDON
See London

ISLEWORTH COACHES
UNITS 4/5, PHOENIX DISTRIBUTION PARK, PHOENIX WAY, HESTON TW5 9NB
Tel: 020 8754 0800
Fax: 020 8754 8080
E-mail: kevin@isleworthcoaches.co.uk
Web site: www.isleworthcoaches.co.uk
Dir: Kevin Wick
Fleet: 4 coach.
Chassis: incl: Volvo. Irisbus.
Bodies: incl: Plaxton. ElMundo.
Ops incl: private hire.
Livery: Blue with red relief.

J & D EURO TRAVEL
58 WEALD LANE, HARROW HA3 5EX.
Tel: 020 8861 1829, 8933 2961.
Fax: 020 8424 2585.
Sole Trader: J. T. Thomas.

A/c	Air conditioning
♿	Vehicles suitable for disabled
🍴	Coach(es) with galley facilities
WC	Coach(es) with toilet facilities
♥	Seat belt-fitted vehicles
R	Recovery service available (not 24 hr)
R24	24hr recovery service
✂	Replacement vehicle available
T	Toilet-drop facilities available
🚌	Vintage vehicle(s) available
🚐	Open top vehicle(s)

Fleet: 9 - 2 coach, 1 midicoach, 4 minibus, 2 minicoach.
Chassis: 1 Bedford. 1 DAF. 1 Ford. 1 Ford Transit. 1 Freight Rover. 1 Iveco. 1 Mercedes. 1 Renault. 1 Volvo.
Bodies: 1 Alexander. 1 Carlyle. 1 Jonckheere. 1 Leyland. 1 Van Hool. 2 Pentiplan.
Ops incl: school contracts, excursions & tours, private hire, continental tours.
Livery: Black/White.

*LEOLINE TRAVEL

UPPER SUNBURY ROAD, HAMPTON TW12 2DW
Tel: 020 8941 3370
Fax: 020 8941 3272
E-mail: daveleoline@aol.com
Web site: www.leolinetravel.co.uk
Prop: David Baker **Ops Man:** Judy Dale
Fleet: 6 - 5 coach, 1 minibus.
Chassis: 1 Iveco. 1 Toyota. 4 Volvo.
Bodies: 1 Beulas. 1 Caetano. 2 Jonckheere. 2 Van Hool.
Ops incl: excursions & tours, private hire, school contracts.
Livery: Dark Blue/Orange

*LONDON UNITED BUSWAYS LTD

BUSWAYS HOUSE, WELLINGTON ROAD, TWICKENHAM TW2 5NX
Tel: 020 8400 6600
Fax: 020 8977 0390
Web site: www.lonutd.co.uk
Dirs: C Beaumont, L Birchley, R C Casling, A McGill, D A Lott, F X Perin, P Wren, P Gillespie, K S Chadra, K Fuller
Fleet: double-deck bus, single-deck bus.
Chassis: 502 Dennis. 64 Scania. 190 Volvo.
Bodies: 235 Alexander. 119 East Lancs. 399 Plaxton.
Ops Incl: local bus services, private hire
Livery: TfL

LUXURY MINI COACH

94A HORSENDEN LANE, GREENFORD UB6 7AH
Tel: 020 8795 0075.
Fax: 020 8900 9630.

Web site: www.luxuryminicoach.co.uk
Dir: Paul Grant
Fleet: minicoaches.
Ops incl: private hire.

*M&M COACHLINES

33 HITHERWELL DRIVE, HARROW WEALD HA3 6JD
Tel: 020 8863 2085
Fax: 020 8861 6175
Prop: M C Burcombe **Sec/Prop:** Mrs M M Burcombe **Ch Eng:** N Bassett
Fleet: 1 coach.
Chassis: Scania.
Body: Berkhof.
Ops incl: private hire, excursions & tours, continental tours.

MCH MINIBUSES

126-127 WATERLOO ROAD, UXBRIDGE UB8 2QZ
Tel: 01895 230643.
Fax: 01895 234891.
Web site: mch-coaches.co.uk
E-mail: info@mch-coaches.co.uk
Dirs: P. N. Webber (**Tran Man**), E. Gavin.
Fleet: 32 - 5 coach, 10 midibus, 17 minibus.
Chassis: 29 Mercedes. 3 Neoplan.
Bodies: 27 Autobus. 2 Mercedes. 3 Neoplan.
Ops incl: private hire, school contracts,
Livery: White.

*METROLINE TRAVEL LTD

66 COLLEGE ROAD, HARROW HA1 1BE
Tel: 020 8218 8888
Fax: 020 8218 8899
E-mail: info@metroline.co.uk
Web site: www.metroline.co.uk
Chief Exec Off: Jaspal Singh **Ch Op Officer:** Sean O'Shea **Fin Dir:** David Donelly **Dir Safety Standards:** Eddie Ledwith **Eng Dir:** Russell Hargrave
Fleet: 1203 - 750 double-deck bus, 425 single-deck bus, 20 coach, 1 open-top bus, 7 midibus.
Chassis: 3 AEC. 931 Dennis. 2 MCW. 7 Optare. 260 Volvo.

Bodies: 145 Alexander. 80 Marshall. 2 MCW. 16 Northern Counties. 7 Optare. 3 Park Royal. 903 Plaxton. 47 Transbus.
Ops incl: local bus services, school contracts, private hire.
Livery: Red/Blue.
Ticket System: Wayfarer (London Buses spec).

SUNBURY COACHES

204A CHARLTON ROAD, SHEPPERTON TW17 0RG.
Tel: 01932 785153.
Fax: 01932 761923.
Dir: P. Jones.
Fleet: 5 coach.
Chassis: Irisbus, Leyland, Volvo.
Bodies: Berkhof, Beulas, Jonckheere.
Ops incl: excursions & tours, private hire.
Livery: White/Turquoise.

*TELLINGS GOLDEN MILLER COACHES LTD
See London

VENTURE TRANSPORT (HENDON) (1965) LTD

307 PINNER ROAD, HARROW HA1 4HG.
Tel: 020 8427 0101.
Fax: 020 8427 1707.
Ops incl: private hire
Subsidiary of Hearns Coaches

*WESTBUS COACH SERVICES LTD
See London

*WILTAX BUSES LTD
See Surrey

NORFOLK

AMBASSADOR TRAVEL (ANGLIA) LTD

JAMES WATT CLOSE, GAPTON HALL INDUSTRIAL ESTATE, GREAT YARMOUTH NR31 0NX
Tel: 01493 440350
Fax: 01493 440367
Recovery: 01493 440350
Man Dir: M C Green **Dep Ops Man:** M Pleasants **Ops Man:** B Picton
Co Sec: B Digman
Fleet: 58 - 16 single-deck bus, 42 coach
Chassis: 1 DAF. 2 Dennis. 1 Iveco. 5 Leyland. 3 Mercedes. 5 Scania. 41 Volvo.
Bodies: 2 Caetano. 2 Irizar. 4 Jonckheere. 4 Optare. 35 Plaxton. 2 Sunsundegui. 4 Van Hool. 7 Wright.
Ops incl: local bus services, school contracts, private hire, express, continental tours.
Livery: White.
Ticket System: Setright/Wayfarer.

*ANGLIAN COACHES LTD
See Suffolk

CHENERY TRAVEL

THE GARAGE, DICKLEBURGH, DISS IP21 4NJ
Tel: 01379 741221
Fax: 01379 740728
Recovery: 01379 741656
E-mail: julia@chenerytravel.co.uk

Web site: www.chenerytravel.co.uk
Dir: Mrs P Garnhem **Gen Man**: Mrs J M McGraffin
Fleet: 20 coach.
Chassis: 1 Bedford. 1 Leyland. 18 Setra.
Bodies: 1 Duple. 1 Plaxton. 18 Setra.
Ops incl: school contracts, excursions & tours, private hire, express, continental tours.
Livery: Silver/Blue.

*COACH SERVICES LTD

CROXTON ROAD, THETFORD
IP24 1AG
Tel: 01842 752226
Fax: 01842 750498
E-mail: glyn@coachservicesltd.co.uk
Fleet: 28 - 19 coach. 4 midibus. 1 midicoach. 2 minibus. 2 minicoach.
Chassis: 2 Bova. 2 DAF. 2 Dennis. 1 Ford transit. 1 LDV. 1 Leyland. 2 Mercedes. 3 Optare. 3 Scania. 2 VW. 9 Volvo.
Bodies: 2 Bova. 3 Irizar. 7 Jonckheere. 3 Optare. 5 Plaxton. 1 Transbus. 3 Van Hool. 4 other.
Ops incl: local bus services, school contracts, excursions & tours, private hire
Ticket System: Almex.

*CRUSADER HOLIDAYS
See Essex

*D-WAY TRAVEL
See Suffolk

*EASTONS COACHES

THE OLD COACH HOUSE,
STRATTON STRAWLESS,
NORWICH NR10 5LR
Tel: 01603 754253
Fax: 01603 754133
E-mail: admin@eastonsholidays.co.uk
Web site: www.eastonsholidays.co.uk
Dirs: Robert Easton, Derek Easton
Fleet: 11 - 1 single-deck bus, 10 coach.
Chassis: 2 Bova. 4 DAF. 1 Dennis. 1 Irisbus. 1 Optare. 2 Volvo.
Bodies: 1 Beulas. 2 Bova. 1 Duple. 1 Optare. 1 Plaxton. 5 Van Hool.
Ops incl: local bus services, excursions & tours, school contracts, private hire, continental tours.
Livery: Purple
Ticket System: Almex.

EUROSUN COACHES

THORPE MARKET ROAD, UNIT 1,
GREENWAYS, SOUTH REPPS
NR11 8NQ.
Tel: 01263 834483
Fax: 01263 834482
E-mail: eurosuncoaches@hotmail.com
Web site: www.eurosun.net
Ch Eng: Adam Goffin **Sales & Mktg**

Man: Tony Porter **Dirs**: Phil Overy, Jack Overy
Fleet: 19 - 16 coach, 3 double-deck coach.
Chassis: 7 DAF. 4 Leyland. 3 MAN. 2 Mercedes. 5 Neoplan.
Bodies: 3 Bova. 2 Leyland. 5 Neoplan. 6 Plaxton. 2 Van Hool. 1 other.
Ops incl: school contracts, excursions & tours, private hire, continental tours.
Livery: Red and Gold

*FARELINE COACH SERVICES
See Suffolk

*FIRST EASTERN COUNTIES BUSES LTD

ROUEN HOUSE, ROUEN ROAD,
NORWICH NR1 1RB
Tel: 01603 760076
Fax: 01603 615439
E-mail: contactus.fec@firstgroup.com
Web site: www.firstgroup.com
Man Dir: Keith Andrews **Fin Dir**: David Marshall **Ops/Com Dir**: Philip Seago
Eng Dir: Jon Smith
Fleet: 325 - 69 double-deck bus, 216 single-deck bus, 40 coach.
Chassis: 3 AEC. 121 Dennis. 44 Leyland. 60 Scania. 97 Volvo.
Bodies: 67 Alexander. 2 Duple. 5 ECW. 2 East Lancs. 11 Leyland. 3 Marshall. 10 Northern Counties. 3 Park Royal. 183 Plaxton. 1 Roe. 79 Wright.
Ops incl: local bus services, private hire, express.
Livery: First Group
Ticket System: Wayfarer 3

FREESTONES COACHES

GREEN LANE, BEETLEY NR20 4DL.
Tel: 01362 860236.
Fax: 01362 860276.
Dir: B. Feeke.

GRANGEWOOD TRAVEL

GRANGEWOOD, CHAPEL ROAD,
POTTER HEIGHAM NR29 5LS.
Tel: 01692 670944.
Prop: Phil Burgin.
Fleet: 1 minibus.
Chassis: 1 Toyota.
Ops incl: private hire.

*D&H HARROD (COACHES) LTD

BUS STOP, CASTLE ROAD,
WORMEGAY, KING'S LYNN
PE33 0SG
Tel: 01553 840492
Fax: 01553 841318
E-mail: harrod.coaches@eidosnet.co.uk
Web site: www.harrodcoachesltd.co.uk
Man Dir: David Reeve **Co Sec**: Jennifer Reeve **Ch Eng**: Derek Harrod.
Fleet: 12 coach

Chassis: 3 Dennis. 1 Iveco. 8 Volvo.
Bodies: 4 Jonckheere. 1 Plaxton. 3 Van Hool. 2 Wadham Stringer. 2 other.
Ops incl: local bus services, school contracts, excursions & tours, private hire, continental tours.
Livery: White

*KONECTBUS LTD

7 JOHN GOSHAWK ROAD, DEREHAM
NR19 1SY
Tel: 01362 851210
Fax: 01362 851215
E-mail: enquiries@konectbus.co.uk
Web site: www.konectbus.co.uk
Dirs: Julian Patterson, Steve Challis
Fleet: 31 - 5 double-deck bus, 26 single-deck bus.
Chassis: 11 DAF. 1 Leyland National. 19 Optare.
Bodies: 1 Leyland National. 25 Optare. 5 Wright.
Ops incl: local bus services
Livery: Blue/Yellow/Grey

*MATTHEWS COACHES

WESTGATE STREET GARAGES,
SHOULDHAM, KING'S LYNN
PE33 0BN
Tel: 01366 347220
Fax: 01366 347293
E-mail: matthewscoaches@aol.com
Man Dir: J P Lloyd
Fleet: 6 - 5 coach, 1 minibus
Chassis: 2 DAF. 3 Dennis. 1 LDV.
Bodies: 1 Berkhof. 1 Leyland. 2 Plaxton. 2 Van Hool.
Ops incl: local bus servcies, school contracts, excursions & tours, private hire.
Livery: White/Blue

*NORFOLK GREEN

HAMLIN WAY, KINGS LYNN
PE31 6HA
Tel: 01553 776980
Fax: 01553 770891
E-mail: enquiries@norfolkgreen.co.uk
Web site: www.norfolkgreen.co.uk
Man Dir: Ben Colson **Co Sec**: Keith Shayshutt **Fleet Eng**: Nigel Firth **Ops Man**: Richard Pengelly **Accountant**: Simon Carr
Fleet: 41 - 7 single-deck bus, 34 coach.
Chassis: 4 Dennis. 1 MAN. 17 Mercedes. 19 Optare.
Bodies: 7 Alexander. 1 Marshall. 19 Optare. 14 Plaxton.
Ops incl: local bus services
Livery: two-tone Green/White
Ticket System: Wayfarer TGX

PEELINGS COACHES

THE GARAGE, CLAY HILL,
TITTLESHALL, KING'S LYNN
PE32 2RQ
Tel/Fax: 01328 701531
E-mail: jr@peelingscoaches.fsnet.co.uk
Prop: Jonathan Joplin **Ch Eng**: Jonathan Sayer

A/c	Air conditioning
	Vehicles suitable for disabled
	Coach(es) with galley facilities
WC	Coach(es) with toilet facilities
	Seat belt-fitted vehicles
R	Recovery service available (not 24 hr)
R24	24hr recovery service
✓	Replacement vehicle available
T	Toilet-drop facilities available
	Vintage vehicle(s) available
	Open top vehicle(s)

Norfolk

Fleet: 6 - coach.
Chassis: 1 Bedford. 1 DAF. 1 Dennis. 1 Van Hool. 2 Volvo.
Bodies: 4 Plaxton. 2 Van Hool.
Ops incl: local bus services, school contracts, excursions & tours, private hire, express.
Livery: White
Ticket System: Setright

*REYNOLDS COACHES OF CAISTER
THE GARAGE, ORMESBY ROAD, CAISTER-ON-SEA NR30 5QJ
Tel: 01493 720312/720050
Fax: 01493 721512
E-mail: reynolds.coaches@gtyarmouth.co.uk
Web site: www.reynolds-coaches.co.uk
Prop: Charles Reynolds
Fleet: 16 - 12 coach, 3 midicoach, 1 minibus.
Chassis: 1 Bedford. 3 DAF. 4 Dennis. 1 Ford Transit. 1 MAN. 1 Mercedes. 1 Scania. 1 Setra. 3 Volvo.
Bodies: 2 Caetano. 6 Plaxton. 1 Reeve Burgess. 1 Setra. 5 Van Hool.
Ops incl: school contracts, excursions & tours, private hire, continental tours.
Livery: Blue/Grey/Yellow.

*SANDERS COACHES
HEATH DRIVE, HEMPSTEAD ROAD INDUSTRIAL ESTATE, HOLT NR25 6ER
Tel: 01263 712800
Fax: 01263 710920
Website: www.sanderscoaches.com
Dir: Charles Sanders
Fleet: 85 - 8 double-deck bus, 24 single-deck bus, 36 coach, 14 midibus, 2 minicoach, 1 minibus.
Chassis: 10 Bedford. 43 DAF. 7 Dennis. 4 Leyland. 17 Mercedes. 2 Setra. 2 Volvo.

Bodies: 3 Duple. 4 ECW. 17 Ikarus. 2 Neoplan. 4 Northern Counties. 14 Optare. 20 Plaxton. 7 Reeve Burgess. 2 Setra. 12 Van Hool.
Ops incl: local bus services, school contracts, excursions & tours, private hire, continental tours.
Livery: Yellow/Blue/Orange
Ticket System: Wayfarer 3

*H SEMMENCE & CO LTD
34 NORWICH ROAD, WYMONDHAM NR18 0NS
Tel: 01953 602135
Fax: 01953 605867
E-mail: sales@semmence.co.uk
Web site: www.semmence.co.uk
Chairm: R H Green **Man Dir**: Sean Green
Co Sec: Mark Green **Tran Man**: Brian Lafferty **Eng Man**: Kevin Hughes
Fleet: 30 - 26 coach, 4 minicoach.
Chassis: 15 Dennis. 4 Mercedes. 1 Scania. 10 Volvo.
Ops incl: local bus services, school contracts, excursions & tours, express, private hire
Livery: White
Ticket System: Wayfarer

*SIMONDS COACH & TRAVEL
ROSWALD HOUSE, OAK DRIVE, DISS IP22 4GX
Tel: 01379 647300
Fax: 01379 647350
Recovery: 01379 647300
E-mail: martyn@simonds.co.uk
Web site: www.simonds.co.uk
Chmn: D O Simonds **Man Dir**:
M S Simonds **Dirs**: R S Simonds, A Tant
Acc Man: S Moyse **Comm Man**: A Burrows
Ops Man: C Cummins
Fleet: 43 - 6 single-deck bus, 30 coach,

6 midibus, 1 minicoach.
Chassis: 1 DAF. 4 Dennis. 1 Leyland. 7 Mercedes. 2 Transbus. 28 Volvo.
Bodies: 1 Optare. 26 Plaxton. 2 Transbus. 14 Van Hool.
Ops incl: local bus services, school contracts, excursions & tours, private hire, continental tours.
Livery: White/Green/Red/Gold leaves
Ticket system: Wayfarer TGX

*SPRATTS COACHES LTD
THE GARAGE, WRENINGHAM, NORWICH NR16 1AZ
Tel: 01508 489262
Fax: 01508 489404
E-mail: sprattscoaches@aol.com
Web site: www.sprattscoaches.co.uk
Dirs: Richard Spratt, Christine Bilham **Ops Man**: Mark Benham
Fleet: 11 - 8 coach, 2 midicoach, 1 minibus.
Chassis: 1 Bedford. 1 Bova. 2 MAN. 1 Mercedes. 5 Scania. 1 Volvo.
Bodies: 1 Autobus. 2 Berkhof. 1 Bova. 1 Caetano. 1 Duple. 5 Van Hool.
Ops incl: private hire, school contracts, excursions and tours.
Livery: White

*SUNBEAM COACHES LTD
WESTGATE STREET, HEVINGHAM, NORWICH NR10 5NH
Tel/Fax: 01603 754211
E-mail: sunbeamcoaches@aol.com
Man Dir: G M Coldham **Dir**: J M Cole
Ch Eng: G J Coldham
Fleet: 7 - 6 coach, 1 minicoach.
Chassis: 2 Dennis. 2 MAN. 1 Toyota. 2 Volvo.
Bodies: 1 Caetano. 2 Neoplan. 3 Plaxton. 1 Van Hool.
Ops incl: school contracts, private hire, excursions & tours.
Livery: White with Orange/Blue/Yellow

NORTH & NORTH EAST LINCOLNSHIRE

APPLEBYS COACHES
CONISHOLME, LOUTH LN11 7LT
Tel: 01472 355 964
E-mail: sales@expertcoaches.co.uk
Web site: www.applebyscoaches.co.uk
Fleet: 14 coach
Ops incl: excursions & tours, continental tours.

EMMERSON COACHES LTD
BLUESTONE LANE, IMMINGHAM DN40 2EL.
Tel: 01469 578166
Fax: 01469 575278
Web site:
www.emmersoncoaches.ukf.net

Dirs: Alan Brumby, O. M. Stocks, Allen Stocks.
Fleet: 12 - 11 coach, 1 minibus.
Chassis: 1 Bedford. 1 DAF. 1 Ford. 2 MAN. 3 Mercedes. 1 Scania. 3 Volvo.
Bodies: 2 Duple. 1 Ikarus. 1 Jonckheere. 2 Mercedes. 4 Plaxton. 1 other.
Ops incl: school contracts, private hire.
Livery: Cream with orange and brown stripes.

BEN GEORGE TRAVEL LTD
BRICKHILLS, BROUGHTON, BRIGG DN20 0BZ
Tel: 01652 654681
Fax: 01652 350396
Dirs: S & J Easton
Fleet: 31 - 5 double-deck bus, 7 coach,

1 double-deck coach, 1 midicoach, 3 minibus.
Chassis: 3 AEC. 3 Bedford. 1 Bristol. 1 Daimler. 1 Dennis. 2 Leyland. 2 MAN. 3 Mercedes. 1 Neoplan.
Bodies: 1 Alexander. 3 Duple. 1 Jonckheere. 2 Leyland. 3 Mercedes. 1 Neoplan. 3 Plaxton.
Ops incl: local bus services, school contracts, excursions & tours, private hire, continental tours.
Livery: Red/White/Blue

EXPERT COACH SERVICES LTD
2 PASTURE STREET, GRIMSBY DN31 1QD
Tel: 01472 350650
Fax: 01472 351926

E-mail: sales@expertcoaches.co.uk
Web site: www.expertcoaches.co.uk
Man Dir: L A Harniess **Dir**: C J Cator
Fleet: 2 coach
Chassis: 2 Scania.
Bodies: 1 Berkhof. 1 Plaxton.
Ops incl: excursions & tours, private hire, continental tours.
Livery: Blue/White.

HOLLOWAY COACHES LTD
COTTAGE BECK ROAD,
SCUNTHORPE DN16 1TP.
Tel: 01724 282277, 281177.
Fax: 01724 289945.
Dirs: F. S. Holloway (**Man Dir**),
P. A. Holloway.
Fleet: 14 - 7 double-deck bus, 6 coach, 1 minicoach.
Chassis: 1 Bedford. 2 Dennis. 11 Leyland.
Bodies: 7 Alexander. 6 Plaxton. 1 other.
Ops incl: excursions & tours, express.
Livery: Red/White/Blue.

*HORNSBY TRAVEL SERVICES LTD

51 ASHBY HIGH STREET,
SCUNTHORPE DN16 2NB
E-mail: office@hornsbytravel.co.uk
Web site: www.hornsbytravel.co.uk
Man Dir: R Hornsby **Dir/Gen Man/Co Sec**: N J Hornsby **Eng Dir**: P Gawley
Fleet: 31 - 5 double-deck bus, 10 single-deck bus, 9 coach, 6 midibus, 1 midicoach.
Chassis: 5 DAF. 11 Dennis. 3 Leyland.

2 MCW. 4 Mercedes. 1 Renault. 3 Transbus. 2 Volvo.
Bodies: 1 Alexander. 2 ECW. 1 Ikarus. 2 MCW. 1 Northern Counties. 1 Optare. 15 Plaxton. 3 Transbus. 5 Wright.
Ops incl: local bus services, excursions & tours, private hire, school contracts
Livery: Silver/Blue.
Ticket System: Almex

*MILLMAN COACHES

17 WILTON ROAD, HUMBERSTON, GRIMSBY DN36 4AW
Tel/Fax: 01472 210297
E-mail: enquiries@millmancoaches.co.uk
Web site: www.millmancoaches.co.uk
Ptnrs: M Millman, D Millman, A J Millman
Fleet: 8 - 5 single-deck coach, 2 midicoach, 1 minibus.
Chassis: 1 Dennis. 4 Leyland. 1 Mercedes. 2 Volvo.
Bodies: 2 Duple. 2 Jonckheere. 1 Mercedes. 3 Plaxton.
Ops incl: private hire, school contracts.
Livery: White/Blue/Yellow

*RADLEY COACH TRAVEL

50 WRAWBY STREET, BRIGG
DN20 8JB
Tel: 01652 653583
Fax: 01652 656020
E-mail: enquiries@radleytravel.co.uk
Web site: www.radleytravel.co.uk
Owner: Kevin Radley.

Fleet: 2 coach
Chassis: 2 Scania.
Bodies: 2 Irizar.
Ops incl: excursions & tours, private hire, continental tours.
Livery: Gold/Maroon

*SHERWOOD TRAVEL
19 QUEENS ROAD, IMMINGHAM
DN40 1QR
Tel: 01469 571140
Fax: 01469 574937
E-mail: enquiries@sherwoodtravel.co.uk
Web site: www.sherwoodtravel.co.uk
Dirs: Stuart Oakland, Jane Oakland, Lucy Oakland
Chassis: Dennis. Ford Transit. Mercedes.
Ops incl: school contracts, excursions & tours, private hire.

SOLID ENTERTAINMENTS

46 WELLOWGATE, GRIMSBY
DN32 0RA.
Tel: 01472 349222.
Fax: 01472 362275.
Prop: S. J. Stanley.
Fleet: 2 - 1 coach, 1 minibus.
Chassis: 1 Scania.
Bodies: 1 Irizar.
Ops incl: excursions & tours, private hire, continental tours.
Livery: Black.

NORTH YORKSHIRE, YORK

*ABBEY COACHWAYS LTD
MEADOWCROFT GARAGE, LOW STREET, CARLTON DN14 9PH
Tel: 01405 860337
Fax: 01405 869433
Dirs: Mrs L E Baker, S J Stockdale.
Fleet: 5 coaches.
Chassis: 1 Scania. 4 Volvo.
Bodies: 1 Duple. 1 Jonckheere. 3 Plaxton.
Ops incl: private hire.
Livery: Blue/White.

G. ABBOTT & SONS

AUMANS HOUSE, LEEMING, NORTHALLERTON DL7 9RZ
Tel: 01677 422858/422571
Fax: 01677 424971

Fleetname: Abbotts of Leeming
Ptnrs: David C Abbott, Clifford G Abbot.
Fleet: 61 - 1 double-deck bus, 3 single-deck bus, 50 coach, 6 midibus, 1 minicoach.
Chassis: 2 Bedford. 6 DAF. 6 Ford Transit. 1 Iveco. 10 Leyland. 3 Optare.
Bodies: 1 Caetano. 6 Duple. 10 Irizar. 3 Optare. 20 Park Royal. 10 Van Hool.
Ops incl: local bus services, school contracts, excursions & tours, private hire, express, continental tours.

ALTERNATIVE TRAVEL
53 NAPIER CRESCENT,
SCARBOROUGH YO12 4HX
Tel/Fax: 01723 863885.
Prop: Malcolm Chambers
Fleet: 2 - 1 coach, 1 minicoach
Chassis: 1 Mercedes. 1 Volvo.
Bodies: 2 Optare. 1 Plaxton.
Ops incl: private hire, school contracts

*H ATKINSON & SONS (INGLEBY) LTD
NORTHALLERTON DL6 3LN
Tel: 01609 882212
Fax: 01609 882222
E-mail: h.atkinson@eurotelonline.com
Web site: www.atkinsoncoaches.co.uk
Dirs: D Atkinson, R Atkinson **Co Sec**: M T Atkinson
Fleet: 12 - 1 double-deck bus, 9 coach, 1 double-deck coach, 1 midicoach
Chassis: 3 Irisbus.1 Leyland. 2 Setra. 6 Volvo.
Bodies: 2 Beulas. 2 Berkhof. 2 Jonckheere. 1 Leyland. 1 Marcopolo. 1 Plaxton. 2 Setra. 1 other.
Livery: Maroon/Cream

A/c	Air conditioning	
	Vehicles suitable for disabled	
	Coach(es) with galley facilities	
wc	Coach(es) with toilet facilities	
	Seat belt-fitted vehicles	
R	Recovery service available (not 24 hr)	
R24	24hr recovery service	
	Replacement vehicle available	
T	Toilet-drop facilities available	
	Vintage vehicle(s) available	
	Open top vehicle(s)	

BALDRY'S COACHES

LEYLANDII, SELBY ROAD, HOLME-ON-SPALDING-MOOR YO43 4HB.
Tel: 01430 860992.
Prop: A. Baldry.
Fleet: 9 - 8 coach, 1 midicoach.
Chassis: 1 AEC. 1 Bedford. 5 Ford.
Ops incl: school contracts, excursions & tours, private hire.
Livery: Two-tone Green.

*BARNARD CASTLE COACHES (BURRELLS)

SOUTH VIEW GARAGE, NEWSHAM, RICHMOND DL11 7RA
Tel: 01833 621302/621494
Fax: 01833 621431
E-mail: qlburrell@hotmail.com
Dirs: Mrs Marlene Burrell, Alan Burrell, Mrs Sandra Burrell
Fleet: 5 - 4 coach, 1 minibus.
Chassis: 1 Mercedes. 4 Volvo.
Bodies: 1 Plaxton. 3 Van Hool. 1 other.
Ops incl: school contracts, excursions & tours, private hire, continental tours.
Livery: Yellow/White

BEECROFT COACHES

POST OFFICE, FEWSTON HG3 1SG.
Tel/Fax: 01943 880206.
Prop: D. Beecroft.
Fleet: 6 - 3 coach, 1 midicoach, 2 minibus.
Chassis: 1 DAF. 1 Dodge. 2 Freight Rover. 1 Scania. 1 Volvo.
Bodies: 1 Alexander. 1 Bova. 3 Carlyle. 1 Duple. 1 Plaxton. 1 Van Hool.
Ops incl: local bus services, school contracts, excursions & tours, private hire, continental tours.
Livery: Green/Orange/White.

BIBBY'S OF INGLETON

NE0W ROAD, INGLETON LA6 3NU.
Tel: 01524 241330
Fax: 01524 242216
E-mail: bibbys_travel@talk21.com
Man Dir: P Bibby **Co Sec**: Mrs S Holcroft
Ch Eng: M Stephenson.
Fleet: 22 - 17 coach, 5 minibus.
Chassis: 17 DAF. 3 LDV. 3 Mercedes.
Bodies: 6 Ikarus. 3 LDV. 2 Mercedes. 4 Plaxton. 7 Van Hool. 1 Ovi.
Ops incl: school contracts. excursions & tours, private hire, continental tours.
Livery: Blue/Grey/Red with white stripes.

BOTTERILLS

HIGH STREET GARAGE, THORNTON DALE YO18 7QW
Tel: 01751 474210
E-mail: botterills@hotmail.com
Web site: www.botterills.org.uk
Fleet: 4 minibus
Chassis/bodies: 4 Mercedes
Ops incl: local bus services, private hire.
Livery: White with black/gold lettering

*EDDIE BROWN TOURS LTD

BAR LANE, ROECLIFFE, BOROUGHBRIDGE, YORK YO51 9LS
Tel: 01423 321240
Fax: 01423 326213
E-mail: enquiries@eddiebrowntours.com
Web site: www.eddiebrowntours.com
Ops Dir: P Brown, D Brown **Gen Man**: P Joyce
Fleet: 40 - 32 coach, 6 midibus, 2 midicoach
Chassis: 1 Dennis. 5 Mercedes. 1 Neoplan. 2 Scania. 2 Setra. 1 Toyota. 28 Volvo.
Bodies: Autobus. Neoplan. Plaxton. Setra. Van Hool.
Ops incl: school contracts, excursions & tours, private hire, continental tours.
Livery: White/Orange/Red/Maroon

CHARTER COACH LTD

THE CONTROL TOWER OFFICES, THE AIRFIELD, TOCKWITH YO26 7QF
Tel: 01423 359655.
Fax: 01423 359459.
E-mail: expert.coaches@btinternet.com
Dir: Antoni LaPilusa

COASTAL & COUNTRY COACHES LTD

THE GARAGE, FAIRFIELD WAY, STAINSACRE INDUSTRIAL ESTATE, WHITBY YO22 4PU.
Tel: 01947 602922.
Fax: 01947 600830
E-mail: enquiries@coastalandcountry.co.uk
Web site: www.coastalandcountry.co.uk
Fleet: 16 - 13 coach, 1 open-top bus. 2 minicoach.
Chassis: 1 Bedford. 1 Bristol. 2 Dennis. 5 Leyland. 2 Mercedes. 6 Volvo.
Bodies: 1 Duple. 1 ECW. 1 Jonckheere. 10 Plaxton. 1 Reeve Burgess. 2 Van Hool. 1 Adamson
Ops incl: local bus services, school contracts, excursions & tours, private hire.
Livery: White and two blues.

*COLLINS COACHES

CLIFFE SERVICE STATION, YORK ROAD, CLIFFE, SELBY YO8 6NN
Tel: 01757 638591
Fax: 01757 630196
E-mail: collins@coaches.hotmail.co.uk
Web site: www.collinscoaches.co.uk
Prop: Alan Collins.
Fleet: 5 - 4 coach, 1 midicoach
Chassis: 1 Mercedes. 4 Volvo.
Ops incl: school contracts, private hire.
Livery: White

COUNTRYSIDE BUS SERVICES

SOUTH GOWLAND, GOWLAND LANE, CLOUGHTON, SCARBOROUGH YO13 0DU
Tel: 01723 870790
Fax: 01273 870790
Tran Man: Piers Turner **Ptnr**: Mrs Jasmin M Turner.
Fleet: 2 minibus.
Chassis/bodies: 2 LDV
Ops incl: local bus services, school contracts.
Livery: White/Yellow/Blue

JOHN DODSWORTH (COACHES) LTD

WETHERBY ROAD, BOROUGHBRIDGE YO5 9HS.
Tel: 01423 322236.
Fax: 01423 324682.
Dir: John Dodsworth.
Fleet: 17 - 10 coach, 2 midicoach, 1 minicoach.
Chassis: 3 Mercedes. 12 Volvo.
Bodies: 10 Plaxton. 2 Reeve Burgess. 1 Onyx.
Ops incl: excursions & tours, private hire, continental tours, school contracts.
Livery: Cream/Orange.

FIRST YORK

7 JAMES STREET, YORK YO10 3HH
Tel: 01904 883000
Fax: 01904 883056
Web site: www.firstgroup.com
Man Dir: Jonathan May
Fleet: 100 - 12 double-deck bus, 86 single-deck bus, 2 midibus.
Chassis: 98 Volvo, 2 Optare
Bodies: 12 Alexander. 2 Optare. 86 Wright.
Ops incl: local bus services, school contracts.
Livery: Grey/Magenta/Blue.
Ticket System: Wayfarer.

*R HANDLEY & SONS LTD

NORTH ROAD, MIDDLEHAM, LEYBURN DL8 4PJ
Tel: 01969 623216
Fax: 01969 624546
Recovery: 01969 623216
Fleetname: Handleys Coaches
Dirs: M K Anderson, J Anderson, E Bowes.
Fleet: 12 - 8 coach, 4 minicoach.
Chassis: 1 Ford Transit. 1 LDV. 4 Leyland. 2 Mercedes. 3 Scania. 1 Volvo.
Bodies: 1 Berkhof. 2 Mercedes. 5 Plaxton. 2 Van Hool. 2 other.
Ops incl: local bus services, private hire, school contracts, excursions & tours.
Livery: Black/White/Grey

*HARGREAVES COACHES
 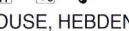

BRIDGE HOUSE, HEBDEN, SKIPTON BD23 5DE
Tel: 01756 752567
Fax: 01756 753768
E-mail: hargreaves.coaches@ukonline.co.uk
Prop: A C Howick
Fleet: 7 - coach, double-deck coach, midicoach, minibus, midibus.
Chassis: 1 LDV. 2 MAN. 3 Mercedes. 1 Scania.
Bodies: 1 Berkhof. 1 LDV. 2 Neoplan. 1 Noge. 2 Optare.
Ops incl: school contracts, excursions &

tours, private hire, continental tours.
Livery: Pink/Silver-Grey/White

HARROGATE & DISTRICT TRAVEL LTD

PROSPECT PARK, BROUGHTON WAY, STARBECK, HARROGATE HG2 2NY
Tel: 01423 884020
Fax: 01423 885670
Web site:
www.harrogateanddistrict.co.uk
www.the36.co.uk
Fleetname: Harrogate & District.
Chmn: G R Fearnley **Man Dir:** Dave Alexander
Fleet: 66 - 8 double-deck bus, 45 single-deck bus, 13 coach.
Chassis: 13 Dennis. 6 Leyland. 47 Volvo.
Bodies: 7 Alexander. 4 Northern Counties. 13 Plaxton. 42 Wright.
Ops incl: local bus services, school contracts.
Livery: Red/Cream.
Ticket System: Wayfarer 3
Part of the Blazefield group which is owned by Transdev

HOPWOOD COACHES

22 MAIN STREET, ASKHAM BRYAN YO23 3QU
Tel: 01904 707394
Dirs: P Hopwood, Mrs D A Hopwood, R C Baker, Mrs A J Baker
Fleet: 3 coach.
Chassis: 3 Dennis.
Bodies: 2 Duple. 1 Plaxton.
Ops incl: school contracts, private hire.

*INGLEBY'S LUXURY COACHES LTD
24 HOSPITAL FIELDS ROAD, FULFORD ROAD, YORK YO10 4DZ
Tel: 01904 637620
Fax: 01904 612944
Dir: C Ingleby **Fleet Eng:** R Atkinson
Ops: A Evans
Fleet: 12 - 8 coach, 2 midicoach, 2 minibus.
Chassis: 1 Bova. 1 Dennis. 4 Mercedes. 6 Volvo.
Bodies: 1 Bova. 2 Mercedes. 2 Plaxton. 1 Sitcar. 6 Van Hool.
Ops incl: private hire.
Livery: Blue/Cream

J. R. TRAVEL
36 CALF CLOSE, HAXBY YO3 3NS.
Tel: 01904 766233.
Ptnrs: R. Flatt, J. Smith.
Fleet: 10 - 3 double-deck bus, 3 coach, 4 double-deck coach.
Chassis: 3 Daimler. 3 Mercedes. 4 Neoplan.
Bodies: 1 East Lancs. 2 Neoplan. 2 Northern Counties. 2 Plaxton. 3 Taz.

Ops incl: local bus services, school contracts, excursions & tours, private hire, continental tours.
Livery: White with green/red stripes.

KINGS LUXURY COACHES
FERRY ROAD, MIDDLESBROUGH TS2 1PL.
Tel: 01642 243687.
Prop: K. E. King.
Fleet: 5 - 2 double-deck bus, 3 coach.
Chassis: 2 Scania. 3 Setra.
Bodies: 1 Jonckheere. 3 Setra. 1 Van Hool.
Ops incl: private hire, continental tours.
Livery: Yellow/White.

METRO COACHES
51 LANGLEY AVENUE, THORNABY TS17 7HG.
Tel: 01642 643322.
Fax: 01642 805639.
Prop: Michael Dales.
Fleet: 4 - 3 coach, 1 midibus.
Chassis: 2 Leyland, 1 Volvo.
Bodies: include 1 Mercedes.
Ops incl: private hire, school contracts.
Livery: Blue/white.

PERRY'S COACHES

RICCAL DRIVE, YORK ROAD INDUSTRIAL PARK, MALTON YO17 6YE.
Tel: 01653 690500
Fax: 01653 690800
Web site: www.perrystravel.com
E-mail: info@perrystravel.com
Ptnrs: D J Perry (**Gen Man/Ch Eng**) Mrs A Holtby (**Co Sec**)
Fleet: 19 - 11 coach, 6 midicoach, 2 minicoach.
Chassis: 1 Dennis. 7 Mercedes. 1 Toyota. 9 Volvo.
Bodies: 1 Caetano. 2 Crest. 1 Jonckheere. 9 Plaxton. 3 Van Hool. 2 Sitcar.
Ops incl: local bus services, school contracts, excursions & tours, private hire, continental tours.
Livery: Red/White.

*PROCTERS COACHES (NORTH YORKSHIRE) LTD
TUTIN ROAD, LEEMING BAR INDUSTRIAL ESTATE, LEEMING BAR, NORTHALLERTON DL7 9UJ
Tel: 01677 425203
Fax: 01677 426550
E-mail:
enquiries@procterscoaches.co.uk
Web site: www.procterscoaches.co.uk
Man Dir: Kevin Procter **Fleet Eng:** Philip Kenyon **Tran Man:** Andrew Fryatt
Fleet: 56 - 31 coach, 1 double-deck coach, 2 midicoach, 22 minibus.
Chassis: 1 DAF. 5 Dennis. 1 Ford Transit. 1 Leyland. 13 Mercedes. 9 Optare. 1 Setra. 1 Van Hool. 23 Volvo.

Bodies: 1 Alexander. 1 Autobus. 5 Berkhof. 3 Jonckheere. 1 Mercedes. 9 Optare. 29 Plaxton. 1 Setra. 3 Transbus. 2 Van Hool. 1 Wright.
Ops incl: local bus services, school contracts, private hire, continental tours.
Livery: White
Ticket System: Wayfarer 3

*RELIANCE MOTOR SERVICES
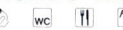
RELIANCE GARAGE, YORK ROAD, SUTTON-ON-THE-FOREST, YORK YO61 1ES.
Tel/Fax: 01904 768262
Prop: John H Duff
Fleet: 10 - 4 double-deck bus, 3 single-deck bus, 2 coach, 1 midicoach.
Chassis: 1 DAF. 1 Dennis. 8 Volvo.
Bodies: 1 Alexander. 2 East lancs. 2 Plaxton. 1 Van Hool. 4 Wright.
Ops incl: local bus services, school contracts, private hire.
Livery: Cream/Green
Ticket System: Wayfarer.

*RONDO TRAVEL

LEVENS HALL PARK, LUND LANE, KILLINGHALL, HARROGATE HG3 2BG
Tel: 01423 526800
Fax: 01423 527800
E-mail: sales@rondotravel.co.uk
Web site: www.rondotravel.co.uk
Man Dir: J D Bullock **Duty Man:** M A Wilson **Traff Man:** N T Chatterton
Fleet: 3 coach
Chassis: 1 Scania, 2 Setra
Bodies: 2 Setra, 1 Van Hool
Ops incl: private hire, excursions & tours, continental tours.
Livery: Red/Gold.

SCARBOROUGH & DISTRICT

BARRY'S LANE, SCARBOROUGH YO12 4HA
Tel: 01723 500064
Fax: 01723 370064
E-mail: sd@eyms.co.uk
Web site: www.eyms.co.uk
Chmn: P J S Shipp **Fin Dir:** P Harrson
Com Man: R Rackley **Eng&Ops Man:** R Graham
Ops incl: local bus services, school contracts, excursions & tours, private hire, express, continental tours.
Livery: Burgundy/Cream
Ticket system: Wayfarer TGX150
A division of East Yorkshire Motor Services Ltd

	Air conditioning		Seat belt-fitted vehicles		Replacement vehicle available
	Vehicles suitable for disabled	R	Recovery service available (not 24 hr)	T	Toilet-drop facilities available
	Coach(es) with galley facilities				Vintage vehicle(s) available
WC	Coach(es) with toilet facilities	R24	24hr recovery service		Open top vehicle(s)

SIESTA INTERNATIONAL HOLIDAYS

158 LINTHORPE ROAD, MIDDLESBROUGH TS1 3RB
Tel: 01642 227711
Fax: 01642 225067
Web site: www.siestaholidays.co.uk
Dir: Paul R Herbert **Co Sec**: Julie Marsh
Fleet Man: Brian Watson
Fleet: 14 - 3 coach, 10 double-deck coach, 1 minibus.
Chassis: 1 DAF. 1 Ford Transit. 12 Scania.
Bodies: 12 Berkhof. 1 Bova.
Ops incl: excursions & tours, private hire, continental tours.
Livery: Blue.

*JOHN SMITH & SONS LTD

R24

THE AIRFIELD, DALTON, THIRSK YO7 3HE
Tel: 01845 577250
Fax: 01845 577752
E-mail: sarah@johnsmithandsons.net
Web site: www.johnsmithandsons.net
Dirs: A N Smith, J G Smith, J Smith, A J Smith (**Ch Eng**), I Smith (**Ops Man**)
Fleet: 24 - 1 double-deck bus, 2 single-deck bus, 11 coach, 4 midibus, 2 midicoach, 2 minibus, 2 minicoach.
Chassis: 1 Bedford. 7 DAF. 1 Ford. 2 Ford Transit. 3 Leyland. 1 MAN. 5 Mercedes. 3 Neoplan.
Bodies: 3 Duple. 2 Mercedes. 3 Neoplan. 5 Plaxton. 1 Reeve Burgess. 2 UVG. 4 Van Hool.
Ops incl: local bus services, school contracts, excursions & tours, private hire, continental tours.
Livery: Green/Cream/Gold
Ticket system: Wayfarer

*STEPHENSONS OF EASINGWOLD LTD
MOOR LANE INDUSTRIAL ESTATE, THOLTHORPE, YORK YO61 1SR
Tel: 01347 838990
Fax: 01347 830189
E-mail: sales@stephensonsofeasingwold.co.uk
Web site: www.stephensonsofeasingwold.co.uk
Dirs: Harry Stephenson, David Stephenson
Gen Man: Jonathan Hill

Fleet: 35 - 9 double-deck bus, 5 single-deck bus, 20 coach, 1 minibus.
Chassis: 1 Bristol. 4 DAF. 1 Ford Transit. 6 Leyland. 1 Leyland National. 1 Optare. 21 Volvo.
Bodies: 1 Caetano. 2 Duple. 6 leyland. 1 Leyland National. 1 MCW. 1 Optare. 21 Plaxton. 1 Van Hool. 1 Wright.
Ops incl: local bus services, school contracts, private hire.
Livery: Cream with orange-red stripes
Ticket system: Wayfarer

STEVE STOCKDALE COACHES (t/a Validford Ltd)

76 GREEN LANE, SELBY YO8 9AW
Tel: 01757 703549
Fax: 01757 210956
Dirs: S. Stockdale, J. Stockdale
Dir/Co Sec: Julie O'Neill
Fleet: 6 - 2 double-deck bus, 4 coach
Chassis: 2 Bedford. 2 Bristol. 2 Leyland.
Bodies: 2 Alexander. 2 Duple. 2 Plaxton.
Ops incl: local bus services, school contracts, private hire.
Livery: Red/White.
Ticket System: Almex.

*THORNES INDEPENDENT LTD

THE COACH STATION, HULL ROAD, HEMINGBROUGH, SELBY YO8 6QG
Tel: 01757 630777
Fax: 01757 630666
Man Dir: Philip Thornes **Ch Eng**: Steve Cotton **Co Sec**: Christine Thornes.
Fleet: 16 - 2 double-deck bus, 1 single-deck bus, 11 coach, 2 midibus.
Chassis: 1 Bedford. 1 Bristol. 1 DAF. 2 Dennis. 1 Ford Transit. 1 Leyland. 1 Leyland/Beadle.1 Mercedes. 6 Volvo. 1 Seddon.
Bodies: 1 Beadle. 1 Duple. 3 East Lancs. 1 Harrington. 1 Optare. 7 Plaxton. 1 Van Hool.
Ops incl: local bus services, school contracts, excursions & tours, private hire, continental tours, wedding transport.
Livery: Blue/Grey
Ticket System: Wayfarer Saver

*TOP LINE TRAVEL OF YORK LTD
23 HOSPITAL FIELDS ROAD, FULFORD INDUSTRIAL ESTATE, YORK YO10 4EW
Tel: 01904 655585
Fax: 01904 655587

E-mail: toplinetravel@aol.com
Web site: www.toplinetravelofyork.co.uk, www.yorktourbuses.co.uk
Man Dir: Peter Dew **Dir/Co Sec**: Susan Dew.
Fleet: 18 - 16 double-deck bus, 1 single-deck bus, 1 midibus.
Chassis: 1 DAF. 1 Dennis. 5 Leyland. 10 MCW. 1 Optare.
Bodies: 2 Alexander. 3 East Lancs. 10 MCW. 2 Optare. 1 Wright.
Ops incl: local bus services, school contracts, excursions & tours, private hire.
Livery: Blue/Yellow (Top Line), Red (City Sightseeing), Green/Cream (Guide Friady),
Ticket System: Almex A90

WINN BROS
8 MILL HILL CLOSE, BROMPTON DL6 2QP.
Tel: 01609 773520.
Fax: 01609 775234.

WISTONIAN COACHES
PLANTATION GARAGE, CAWOOD ROAD, WISTOW YO8 0XB.
Tel: 01757 269303.
Props: John Firth, Gordon Firth.
Fleet: 3 coach, 1 midicoach.
Chassis: 1 Bedford. 3 Volvo. **Bodies**: 4 Plaxton.
Ops incl: school contracts, private hire.
Livery: Cream, Red/Orange/Yellow stripes.

YORKSHIRE COASTLINER LTD
BUS STATION, RAILWAY STREET, MALTON YO17 7NR.
Tel: 01653 692556.
Fax: 01653 695341.
Web site: www.yorkshirecoastliner.co.uk
Prop: Blazefield Holdings Ltd.
Ops Man: Brian Kneeshaw.
Fleet: 19 - 12 double-deck bus, 7 single-deck bus.
Chassis: 26 Volvo.
Bodies: 11 Alexander. 1 Northern Counties. 3 Plaxton. 13 Wright.
Ops incl: local bus services.
Livery: Cream/Blue.
Ticket System: Wayfarer 3
Part of the Blazefield group which is owned by Transdev

NORTHAMPTONSHIRE

ALEC HEAD
R24
LUTTON, PETERBOROUGH PE8 5NE
Tel: 01832 272546
Fax: 01832 273077
Web site: www.alecheadcoaches.co.uk
Ptnrs: A M Head, Mrs J Head, Mrs S J Johns
Fleet: 39 - 7 double-deck bus, 10 single-deck bus, 15 coach, 4 double-deck coach, 1 open-top bus, 1 midicoach, 1 minicoach.
Chassis: 24 Bedford. 7 Dennis. 4 Iveco. 1 Leyland. 2 MAN. 2 Mercedes. 7 Scania. 1 Toyota. 5 Volvo.
Bodies: 7 Alexander. 4 Ayats. 1 Caetano. 2 Marcopolo. 4 MCW. 2 Neoplan.
Ops incl: local bus services, school contracts, excursions & tours, private hire, continental tours.

*GEOFF AMOS COACHES LTD
THE COACH STATION, WOODFORD ROAD, DAVENTRY NN11 3PL
Tel: 01327 260522
Fax: 01327 262883
E-mail: sales@geoffamos.co.uk
Web site: www.geoffamos.co.uk
Fin Dir: Shirley Smith **Tran Man**: Brian Amos **Ops Man**: Brian Ellard **Ch Eng**: Kevin Wilson
Fleet: 23 - 8 double-deck bus, 7 single-deck bus, 7 coach, 1 midicoach
Chassis: 5 Dennis. 10 Leyland. 4 MAN. 1 Mercedes. 1 Optare. 2 Volvo.
Bodies: 3 Berkhof. 1 Caetano. 8 ECW. 5 Marshall. 1 Mercedes. 1 Optare. 2 Plaxton. 2 Sunsundegui.
Ops incl: local bus services, school contracts, private hire, continental tours.
Livery: buses: Yellow, coaches: Metallic
Ticket system: Wayfarer

BASFORDS COACHES LTD

HIGH STREET, GREENS NORTON NN12 8BA.
Tel: 01327 350493.
Dirs: J. V. & K. R. Jeffs.
Fleet: 15 - 3 double-deck bus, 12 single-deck bus.
Chassis: 3 Bedford. 1 Ford. 3 Leyland. 8 Volvo.
Bodies: 6 Caetano. 4 Duple. 2 Jonckheere. 3 Leyland National.
Ops incl: school contracts, excursions & tours, private hire, continental tours.
Livery: Red/White/Green.
Ticket System: Bellgraphic.
Subsidiary of Jeffs Coaches Ltd.

*L F BOWEN T/A YORKS COACHES
SHORT LANE, COGENHOE NN7 1LE
Tel: 01604 890210
Fax: 0870 990 9524
Recovery: 01604 890210
E-mail: yorksta@yorks-travel.co.uk
Web site: www.yorkstravel.com
Fleetname: Yorks Coaches
Chmn: A H Moseley **Ch Exec**: K Lower
Man Dir (coaching): R Lyng **Eng Man**: D Hoy **Traf Man**: N G Tetley
Fleet: 29 - 26 coach, 1 minicoach, 2 minibus.
Chassis: 2 Bova. 3 Dennis. 2 LDV. 10 MAN. 1 Neoplan. 3 Scania. 3 Setra. 1 Toyota. 4 Volvo.
Ops incl: local bus services, excursions & tours, school contracts, private hire, express, continental tours.
Livery: Silver
Ticket System: Almex

BRITTAINS COACHES LTD
SOUTHBRIDGE, COTTON END, NORTHAMPTON NN4 8BS.
Tel: 01604 765708.
Fax: 01604 700481.
Dirs: W. J. Cunningham, Mrs P. M. Brittain, Mrs J. Cunningham.
Co Sec: Miss C. Brittain. **Off Man**: M. Kelly.
Fleet: 7 - 3 double-deck bus, 4 coach.
Chassis: 3 Bristol. 2 DAF. 2 Scania.
Bodies: 3 Alexander. 2 Caetano. 2 Van Hool.
Ops incl: private hire.
Livery: White with Black lettering.

*BUCKBY'S COACHES
3 FOX STREET, ROTHWELL, KETTERING NN14 6AN
Tel: 01536 710344
Tel: 01536 712244
Prop: Minesh Uka.
Fleet: 7 - 1 single-deck bus, 5 coach, 1 minicoach.
Chassis: 2 Bedford. 2 Dennis. 1 Mercedes. 2 Volvo.
Bodies: 1 Duple. 6 Plaxton.
Ops incl: local bus services, school contracts, excursions & tours, private hire, continental tours.

COOPERS COACHES
FOX STREET, ROTHWELL NN14 6AN
Tel: 01536 710227
Fax: 01536 712244.
Ptnrs: H F Cooper, J Hochrath
Fleet: 1 coach.
Chassis: 1 Dennis.
Body: 2 Plaxton.
Ops incl: school contracts, private hire.

Livery: White with blue/red flash

COUNTRY LION (NORTHAMPTON) LTD
87 ST JAMES MILL ROAD, NORTHAMPTON NN5 5JP
Tel: 01604 754566
Fax: 01604 755800
Dirs: J S F Bull, A J Bull
Fleet: 40
Chassis: 1 Bristol. 5 Dennis. 4 Iveco. 7 Mercedes. 2 Scania. 16 Volvo.
Bodies: 4 Alexander. 4 Beulas. 2 East Lancs. 2 Irizar. 1 Jonckheere. 1 Optare. 19 Plaxton. 1 Van Hool. 2 Wadham Stringer. 3 other.
Ops incl: local bus services, school contracts, private hire.
Livery: White/Yellow/Orange/Brown.
Ticket System: Almex.

FIRST NORTHAMPTON
ST JAMES' ROAD, NORTHAMPTON NN5 5JD
Tel: 01604 751431.
Man Dir: I. Humphreys **Fin Dir**: A Bhimani
Fleet: 75 - 42 double-deck bus, 24 single-deck bus, 5 coach, 4 minibus.
Chassis: 3 Bristol. 9 MCW. 4 Renault. 6 Scania. 45 Volvo.
Bodies: Alexander, East Lancs, Northern Counties, Wright.
Ops incl: local bus services, school contracts, private hire.
Livery: Cream/Red.
Ticket System: Wayfarer 3

*GOODE COACHES
47 BURFORD AVENUE, BOOTHVILLE, NORTHAMPTON NN3 6AF
Tel: 01604 862700
Prop: David Goode **Tran Man**: Andrew Wall
Fleet: 4
Chassis: 4 Leyland.
Bodies: 3 Plaxton. 1 Van Hool.
Ops incl: school contracts, private hire.
Livery: Cream/Maroon.

J. C. S. COACHES
2 THE JAMB, CORBY NN17 1AY
Tel: 01536 202660
Props: Jaqueline Burton, Michael Burton
Fleet: 7 - 5 coach, 2 midicoach.
Chassis: 5 DAF. 2 Mercedes.
Bodies: 1 Autobus. 3 Bova. 2 Caetano. 1 Marshall.
Ops incl: excursions & tours, private hire, school contracts.
Livery: Silver

	Air conditioning		Seat belt-fitted vehicles		Replacement vehicle available
	Vehicles suitable for disabled	R	Recovery service available (not 24 hr)	T	Toilet-drop facilities available
	Coach(es) with galley facilities				Vintage vehicle(s) available
wc	Coach(es) with toilet facilities	R24	24hr recovery service		Open top vehicle(s)

J. R. J. COACHES

24 STALBRIDGE WALK, CORBY NN18 0DT.
Tel: 01536 200317.
Fax: 01536 394387.
Prop: J. D. Judge.
Fleet: 6 - 3 coach, 1 midicoach, 2 minibus.
Chassis: 1 Bedford. 1 Ford Transit. 1 Mercedes.
Bodies: 1 Caetano. 1 Carlyle. 1 Duple. 1 Mercedes.
Ops incl: local bus services, school contracts, excursions & tours, private hire.

JEFFS COACHES LTD

HIGH STREET, GREENS NORTON NN12 8BA.
Tel: 01327 350493
Fax: 01327 353538.
Dir: K. R. Jeffs **Man**: I R Higham.
Fleet: 14 - 3 double-deck bus, 11 coach.
Fleet: 1 Bedford. 3 Leyland . 10 Volvo.
Bodies: 1 Alexander. 8 Caetano. 1 Duple. 2 ECW. 1 Jonckheere. 1 Plaxton.
Ops incl: school contracts, excursions & tours, private hire, continental tours.
Livery: White /Red/Green.
(Subsidiary of L F Bowen Ltd, West Midlands)

R B TRAVEL

ISHAM ROAD, PYTCHLEY NN4 1EW
Prop: Roger Bull
Tel/Fax: 01536 791066
Fleet: 10 coach
Chassis: 6 DAF. 4 MAN.
Bodies: 2 Plaxton. 8 Van Hool.

MARTINS COACHES
6 HAZEL ROAD, KETTERING NN16 7AL.
Prop: G. H. Martin.

*RODGER'S COACHES LTD

102 KETTERING ROAD, WELDON NN17 3GG
Tel: 01536 200500
Fax: 01536 407407
E-mail: rodgerscoaches@hotmail.com
Props: Jim Rodger, Linda Rodger
Fleet: 13 - 5 double-deck bus, 6 single-deck bus, 2 double-deck coach.
Ops incl: private hire, school contracts, excursions & tours, continental tours.

*SOUL BROTHERS
See: Buckinghamshire

*STAGECOACH EAST

ROTHERSTHORPE AVENUE, NORTHAMPTON NN4 8UT
Tel: 01604 702112
Fax: 01604 701807
Web site: www.stagecoachbus.com
Fleetnames: Stagecoach in Bedfordshire, Stagecoach in Northamptonshire
Man Dir: James Freeman, **Ops Dir**: Michelle Hargreaves **Eng Dir**: Lee Sheldon
Fleet: 338 - 127 double-deck bus, 4 single-deck bus, 39 coach, 91 midibus, 77 minibus.
Chassis: 113 Dennis. 44 Leyland. 35 Mercedes. 42 Optare. 5 Scania. 99 Volvo
Bodies: 228 Alexander. 5 East Lancs. 21 Northern Counties. 42 Optare. 42 Plaxton.
Ops incl: local bus services, school contracts.
Livery: Stagecoach
Ticket System: ERG

NORTHUMBERLAND

*ADAMSON'S COACHES

8 PORLOCK TOWER, NORTHBURN CHASE, CRAMLINGTON NE23 3TT
Tel/Fax: 01670 734050
Recovery: 07721 633351
Prop: Allen Mullen **Ch Eng**: Paul Mullen **Co Sec**: Mrs Wendy Mullen
Fleet: 4 coach
Chassis: 4 DAF
Bodies: 4 Van Hool
Ops incl: excursions & tours, private hire
Livery: Cream/White

*HENRY COOPER
See Tyne & Wear

CRAIGGS TRAVEL EUROPEAN

1 CENTRAL AVENUE, AMBLE, MORPETH NE65 0NQ
Tel/Fax: 01665 710614
E-mail: classicalholiday@aol.com
Web site: www.coachhireandholidays.co.uk
Props: J Craiggs, I C Craiggs **Co Sec**: L C Craiggs **Eng**: I C Craiggs
Fleet: 4 coach.
Chassis: 1 Leyland. 2 Setra. 1 Volvo.
Bodies: 2 Plaxton. 2 Setra.
Ops incl: excursions & tours, private hire,

continental tours.
Livery: Red

*GO NORTH EAST
See Tyne & Wear.

*HILLARYS COACHES

20 CASTLE VIEW, PRUDHOE NE42 6NG
Tel/Fax: 01661 832560
Props: L Hillary, V Hillary
Fleet: 5 - 1 coach. 3 midicoach, 1 minibus.
Chassis/Bodies: 1 DAF. 1 MAN. 3 Mercedes.
Ops incl: local bus services, school contracts, excursions & tours, private hire.

LONGSTAFF'S COACHES

UNIT 107, AMBLE INDUSTRIAL ESTATE, AMBLE, MORPETH NE65 0PE
Tel: 01665 713300
Fax: 01665 710987
Man Dir: Frederick Longstaff **Co Sec**: Alison Longstaff **Ops Man**: Frederick Longstaff
Fleet: 9 - 7 coach, 1 midicoach
Chassis: 1 Leyland. 1 Mercedes. 1 Neoplan. 7 Volvo
Bodies: 1 Jonckheere. 1 Neoplan.

3 Plaxton. 3 Van Hool. 1 other
Ops incl: local bus services, excursions & tours, private hire, continental tours, school contracts.
Livery: Blue/Cream/Yellow.

ROWELL COACHES

3B DUKES WAY, PRUDHOE NE42 6PQ
Tel: 01661 832316
Fax: 01661 834485
E-mail: sales@rowellcoaches.co.uk
Web site: www.rowellcoaches.co.uk
Dirs: Mrs Gardiner, Mrs B Gardiner
Fleet: 10 coach
Chassis: 6 Bova. 4 Duple.
Ops incl: school contracts, excursions & tours, private hire.
Livery: White

SERENE TRAVEL

86A FRONT STREET EAST, BEDLINGTON NE22 5AB.
Tel: 01670 829636.
Fax: 01670 827961.
Web site:
www.yell.co.uk/sites/serenetravel
Man Dir: Mrs C. E. Fielding. **Flt Eng**: G. J. Balsdon. **Co Sec**: D. A. Fielding.

Fleet: 17 - 7 single-deck bus, 6 coach, 2 midicoach, 2 minibus.
Chassis: 1 AEC. 2 Bedford. 1 Ford Transit. 1 Iveco. 3 Leyland. 6 Leyland National. 2 MCW. 1 Volvo.
Bodies: 2 Carlyle. 2 Duple. 6 Leyland National. 2 Optare. 4 Plaxton. 1 Burlingham.
Ops incl: local bus services, school contracts, excursions & tours, private hire, express.
Livery: Blue/Cream.
Ticket System: Wayfarer II.

TARGET TRAVEL GROUP LTD

STATION ROAD, CRAMLINGTON NE23 9DL.
Tel: 01670 712244, 0191 261 1126
Fax: 01670 734794
E-mail: enquiries@target-group.co.uk
Website: www.target-group.co.uk
Dir: J. Reed.
Fleet: 6 - 2 coach, 1 midibus, 1 minibus, 2 minicoach.
Chassis: 1 DAF. 1 Ford Transit. 1 LAG. 1 MCW. 2 Mercedes.
Bodies: 1 Duple. 2 Mercedes. 1 LAG. 1 Plaxton. 1 Ford Transit.
Ops incl: local bus services, school contracts, excursions & tours, private hire, express, continental tours.
Livery: Red.
Ticket System: Almex

*TRAVELSURE

25 MAIN STREET, SEAHOUSES NE68 7RE.
Tel: 01665 720907
Fax: 01665 721381
E-mail: travelsure@travelsure.co.uk
Web site: www.travelsure.co.uk
Owner: Barrie Patterson **Dir:** Karen Patterson
Fleet: 28 - 1 double-deck bus, 2 single-deck bus, 11 coach, 1 double-deck coach, 4 midibus, 5 midicoach, 2 minibus, 2 minicoach.
Chassis: 1 Bova. 2 DAF. 3 Dennis. 2 Iveco. 2 LDV. 4 Leyland. 3 MCW. 5 Mercedes. 3 Scania. 1 Setra. 2 VW. 1 Volvo.
Bodies: 2 Beulas. 1 Berkhof. 1 Bova. 1 Caetano. 1 Duple. 1 East Lancs. 1 Esker. 1 Irizar. 1 Leicester. 3 MCW. 2 Plaxton. 1 Reeve Burgess. 1 Setra. 1 Transbus. 2 Van Hool. 8 other.
Ops incl: local bus services, school contracts, excursions & tours, private hire, continental tours.
Livery: Blue.
Ticket System: Wayfarer

TYNEDALE GROUP TRAVEL

TOWNFOOT GARAGE, HALTWHISTLE NE49 0EJ.
Tel: 01434 322944.
Fax: 01434 322955.
E-mail: admin@tynedalegrouptravel.co.uk
Web site: www.tynedalegrouptravel.co.uk
Ptnr: Andy Sinclair.
Fleet: 6 - 1 single-deck coach, 3 midibus, 2 midicoach.
Chassis: 5 Mercedes. 1 Volvo.
Bodies: 4 Plaxton, 1 Van Hool, 1 other.
Ops incl: local bus servcices, school contracts, excursions & tours, private hire, continental tours.

*TYNE VALLEY COACHES LTD

ACOMB, HEXHAM NE46 4QT
Tel: 01434 602217
Fax: 01434 604150
Dirs: H. D. Weir, K. M. Weir.
Fleet: 18 - 1 single-deck bus, 17 coach.
Chassis: 1 DAF. 13 Leyland. 4 Volvo.
Bodies: 6 Duple. 1 Optare. 10 Plaxton. 1 Van Hool.
Ops incl: local bus services, school contracts, private hire
Livery: Blue/Silver
Ticket System: AES

NOTTINGHAMSHIRE, NOTTINGHAM

BAILEY'S COACHES LTD

EEL HOLE FARM, LONG LANE, WATNALL NG16 1HY.
Tel: 0115 968 0141
Fax: 0115 968 1101.
Dirs: T. Bailey (**Gen Man & Traf Man**), Mrs J. Bailey (**Sec**).
Ch Eng: G. Payne.
Fleet: 10 - 2 double-deck bus, 6 coach 2 double-deck coach.
Chassis: Bristol. DAF. Duple. Volvo.
Bodies: 10 Duple. 3 Others.
Ops incl: local bus services, school contracts, excursions & tours, private hire, continental tours.
Livery: White with Yellow/Brown/Orange stripes.

*BUTLER BROTHERS COACHES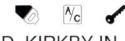

60 VERNON ROAD, KIRKBY IN ASHFIELD NG17 8ED

Tel: 01623 753260
Fax: 01623 754581
E-mail: butlerscoaches@btconnect.com
Dirs: Robert Butler, Anita Butler, James Butler.
Fleet: 9 - 1 double-deck bus, 7 coach, 1 midicoach.
Chassis: 2 DAF. 3 Dennis. 1 Leyland. 2 MAN. 1 Volvo.
Bodies: 1 Berkhof. 2 Caetano. 1 East Lancs. 2 Plaxton. 3 Van Hool.
Ops incl: school contracts, excursions & tours, private hire, continental tours.
Livery: Dual Blue
Ticket System: Wayfarer

*DUNN-LINE (HOLDINGS) LTD

BEECHDALE ROAD, BEECHDALE, NOTTINGHAM NG8 3EU

Tel: 0115 916 9000
Fax: 0115 942 0578
E-mail: scot.dunn@dunn-line.com
Web site: www.dunn-line.com
Dirs: R A Dunn, A S Dunn J T Moore, B K Geldart (**Co Sec**)
Fleet: 160 - 40 double-deck bus, 28 single-deck bus, 65 coach, 1 open-top bus, 23 midibus, 3 minibus.
Chassis: 1 Bova. 8 Dennis. 2 Ford Transit. 3 Leyland National. 5 MAN. 27 MCW. 24 Mercedes. 10 Optare. 13 Scania. 67 Volvo.
Bodies: 3 Alexander. 2 Autobus. 5 Caetano. 14 East Lancs. 8 Irizar. 1 Jonckheere. 3 Leyland National. 6 MCV/Marshall. 27 MCW. 4 Mellor. 3 Northern Counties. 10 Optare. 47 Plaxton. 10 Sunsundegui. 3 Transbus. 9 Van Hool. 5 other.
Ops incl: local bus services, school contracts, private hire, express, continental tours.
Livery: Purple/Silver
Ticket System: Wayfarer 3

A/c	Air conditioning	✓	Replacement vehicle available
♿	Vehicles suitable for disabled	T	Toilet-drop facilities available
🍴	Coach(es) with galley facilities		Vintage vehicle(s) available
WC	Coach(es) with toilet facilities	🚌	Open top vehicle(s)
♥	Seat belt-fitted vehicles		
R	Recovery service available (not 24 hr)		
R24	24hr recovery service		

*EDWARDS CAR & COACH HIRE EAST MIDLANDS

91 COLLEGE STREET, LONG EATON NG10 4GE
Tel: 0115 973 5202
Fax: 0115 973 5202
E-mail: info@ljedwards.co.uk
Web site: www.ljedwards.co.uk
Prop: John Edwards
Fleet: 2 - 1 coach, 1 minicoach.
Chassis: 1 Iveco. 1 Toyota.
Bodies: 1 Beulas. 1 Caetano.
Ops incl: excursions & tours, private hire, express, continental tours.
Livery: Silver

GOSPEL'S COACHES

27 ASCOT DRIVE, HUCKNALL NG15 6JA
Tel: 0115 963 3894
Dirs: T Gospel, G Gospel, G T Gospel
Fleet: 4 - 2 double-deck bus, 2 coach.
Chassis: 2 Leyland. 2 Volvo.
Bodies: 1 Alexander. 1 Northern Counties. 2 Plaxton.
Ops incl: excursions & tours, private hire, school contracts.
Livery: White/Blue.

*HENSHAWS COACHES

57 PYE HILL ROAD, JACKSDALE NG16 5LR
Tel: 01773 607909
Prop: Paul Henshaw
Fleet: 6 - 5 coach, 1 midicoach
Chassis: Bova, DAF, Leyland, MAN, Mercedes
Bodies: Bova, Duple, Hispano, Noge, Van Hool.
Ops incl: excursions & tours, private hire, school contracts, continental tours.
Livery: Cream/Orange/Brown

*JOHNSON'S BROS TOURS

R24

GREEN ACRES, HODTHORPE, WORKSOP S80 4XR
Tel: 01909 721847
Fax: 01909 722886
E-mail: enquiries@johnsonstours.co.uk
Web site: www.johnsonstours.co.uk
Dir: Tony Johnson **Ops**: Lee Johnson
Ch Eng: Antony Johnson
Fleet: 98 - 40 double-deck bus, 10 single-deck bus, 40 coach, 1 double-deck coach, 3 midibus, 2 midicoach, 3 minicoach.
Chassis: 1 Bova. 1 DAF. 2 Ford. 2 Ford Transit. 7 Irisbus. 7 Iveco. 1 LDV. 40 MCW. 20 Mercedes. 5 Neoplan. 1 Optare. 3 Scania. 1 Toyota. 5 Transbus. 10 Volvo.
Bodies: 1 Autobus. 5 Beulas. 2 Berkhof. 1 Bova. 40 ECW . 3 Irizar. 3 Jonckheere. 5 Neoplan. 5 Van Hool.
Ops incl: local bus services, school contracts, excursions & tours, private hire, continental tours, express.
Livery: Blue faded.

JUMBO MINI COACHES
338 THE WELLS ROAD, NOTTINGHAM NG3 3AA.
Tel: 0115 958 4730.
Owner: J. Talbot.
Fleet: 2 minibus. **Chassis**: 2 LDV.
Ops incl: school contracts, private hire.
Livery: White/Blue.

K & S COACHES

21 CLIFTON GROVE, MANSFIELD NG18 4HY.
Tel/Fax: 01623 656768.
Prop: K. & Sue Burnside.
Fleet: 4 - 1 midicoach, 3 minicoach.
Chassis/bodies: Ford Transit. Mercedes. Renault. Talbot.
Ops incl: school contracts, excursions & tours, private hire.
Livery: White/Red/Grey.

*KETTLEWELL (RETFORD) LTD

GROVE STREET, RETFORD DN22 6LA
Tel: 01777 860360
Fax: 01777 710351
Chmn: A J Kettlewell **Man Dir**: P C Kettlewell **Dir**: C C Kettlewell **Senior Officer**: M Burton **Ops Man**: T Bradley
Fleet: 18 - 2 double-deck coach, 15 coach, 1 minicoach.
Chassis: 1 Leyland. 1 Mercedes. 2 Neoplan. 12 Scania. 1 Volvo.
Bodies: 1 East Lancs. 10 Irizar. 1 Jonckheere. 1 Mercedes. 2 Neoplan. 1 Plaxton.
Ops incl: school contracts, excursions & tours, private hire, continental tours.
Livery: White/Yellow.

MARSHALLS OF SUTTON-ON-TRENT
11 MAIN STREET, SUTTON-ON-TRENT NG23 6PF.
Tel: 01636 821138
Fax: 01636 822227
Web site: www.marshallscoaches.co.uk
Prop: J. A. Marshall. **Flt Eng**: P. J. Marshall
Ops Man: K G Tagg
Fleet: includes double-deck bus, single-deck bus, coach, midibus, midicoach.
Chassis: Dennis. Leyland. MAN. Mercedes. Optare. Transbus. Volvo.
Bodies: Alexander. Berkhof. Caetano. East Lancs. Northern Counties. Optare. Plaxton. Transbus. Van Hool.
Ops incl: local bus services, school contracts, excursions & tours, private hire, continental tours.
Livery: Blue/Cream.
Ticket System: Almex

MAUN CRUSADER TOURS

NEW CROSS HOUSE, 8-10 MANSFIELD ROAD, SUTTON-IN-ASHFIELD NG17 4GR.
Tel: 01623 555621.
Fax: 01623 555671.
Dirs: R. A. Read (**Gen Man/Traf Man**), N. G. Barks (**Sec**). **Ch Eng**: S. Palmer.
Fleet: 17 - 8 double-deck bus, 8 single-deck bus. 1 midicoach.
Chassis: 3 DAF, 1 Daimler. 5 Dennis. 2 Leyland. 1 MAN. 1 Mercedes. 4 Integral.
Bodies: 1 Alexander. 1 Caetano. 6 Duple. 1 East Lancs. 1 Jonckheere. 1 Marco Polo. 4 Northern Counties. 1 Plaxton. 1 SC.
Ops incl: private hire, continental tours, school contracts.
Livery: Multi-coloured.

C. W. MOXON LTD

MALTBY ROAD, OLDCOTES, WORKSOP S81 8JN.
Tel: 01909 730345.
Fax: 01909 733670.
Web site: www.moxons-tours.co.uk
Fleetname: Moxons Coaches.
Dirs: Mrs L. Marlow, Mrs M. Moxon, **Co Sec**: Mrs J. Holder, **Ch Eng**: M. Marlow.
Fleet: 15 - 3 double-deck bus, 12 coach.
Chassis: 2 Bedford. 3 Bristol. 7 DAF. 2 Leyland. 1 Iveco.
Bodies: 2 Bova. 1 Duple. 3 MCW. 5 Plaxton. 3 Van Hool. 1 Eos.
Ops incl: excursions & tours, private hire, continental tours, school contracts.
Livery: Cream/Red.

*NOTTINGHAM CITY TRANSPORT

LOWER PARLIAMENT STREET, NOTTINGHAM NG1 1GG
Tel: 0115 950 5745
Fax: 0115 950 4425
E-mail: travelcentre@nctx.co.uk
Web site: www.nctx.co.uk
Chmn: Cllr Brian Parbutt **Man Dir**: Mark Fowles **Eng Dir**: Barry Baxter **Fin Dir**: Rob Hicklin **Mktg Dir**: Nicola Tidy **HR Dir**: Mick Leafe **Comm Man**: Barrie Burch
Fleet: 337 - 155 double-deck bus, 94 single-deck bus, 5 articulated bus, 83 midibus.
Chassis: 55 Dennis. 110 Optare. 142 Scania. 54 Volvo.
Bodies: 13 Alexander. 219 East Lancs. 1 Northern Counties. 110 Optare. 7 Plaxton. 11 Wright.
Ops incl: local bus services

NOTTINGHAM EXPRESS TRANSIT

LAWRENCE HOUSE, TALBOT STREET, NOTTINGHAM NG1 5NT
Tel: 0115 915 6600
Web site: www.thetram.net, www.nottinghamcity.gov.uk, www.nottinghamexpresstransitco.uk, www.netphasetwo.com
Concession Co: Arrow Light Rail (Bombardier, Carillion, Transdev, Nottingham City Transport, Innisfree, CDC Projects)
Fleet: 15 tram
Chassis/bodies: Bombardier
Ops incl: tram service
Livery: Green/White

*PATRON TRAVEL

GLEBE COTTAGE, 1 FOSSE WAY, FLINTHAM NG23 5LH
Tel: 01636 525725
Fax: 01636 525731
Prop: Ron Todd
Fleet: 3 - 1 double-deck bus, 2 coach.
Chassis: 1 Leyland. 2 Volvo

Bodies: 1 Alexander. 2 Jonckheere.
Ops incl: continental tours, private hire, school contracts.
Livery: Cream

PEGASUS COACHWAYS LTD

GROVE STREET, RETFORD
DN22 6LA.
Tel: 01777 860360.
Fax: 01777 710351.
Chmn: A. J. Kettlewell. **Man Dir**: P. C. Kettlewell. **Dir**: C. C. Kettlewell. **Tours Man**: M. Burton
Fleet: 9 coach
Chassis: 9 Scania.
Bodies: 9 Irizar.
Ops incl: excursions and tours, continental tours.
Livery: White/Yellow

REDFERN COACHES (MANSFIELD) LTD

LINDLEY STREET, MANSFIELD
NG18 1QE
Tel: 01623 27653
Fax: 01623 25787
E-mail: enquiries@johnsontours.co.uk
Web site: www.johnsontours.co.uk
Fleet: 29 - 18 double-deck bus, 4 single-deck bus, 4 coach, 1 midibus, 1 midicoach, 1 minicoach.
Chassis: 18 Bristol. 1 Ford. 1 Freight Rover. 1 Scania. 2 Volvo.
Bodies: include 2 Irizar.
Ops incl: local bus services, excursions & tours, private hire, express, continental tours, school contracts.
Livery: Green/Faded Green/Gold
Subsidiary of Johnsons Tours (Derbyshire)

SILVERDALE TOURS LTD

LITTLE TENNIS STREET SOUTH, NOTTINGHAM NG2 4EU
Tel: 0115 912 1000
Fax: 0115 912 1558
Dir: John Doherty
Fleet: 50 - mainly coach.
Chassis: mainly Volvo
Bodies: includes Plaxton
Ops incl: private hire, express, school contracts.

SKILLS MOTOR COACHES

BELGRAVE ROAD, BULWELL
NG6 8LY
Tel: 0115 977 0080
Fax: 0115 977 7439
Recovery: 0115 977 7424
E-mail: enquiry@skillsholidays.co.uk
Web site: www.skillsholidays.co.uk
Man Dir: Nigel Skill **Eng Man**: Steve Robinson **Fin Dir**: Simon Skill
Fleet: 29 - 2 double-deck coach, 24 coach, 2 midibus, 1 midicoach.
Chassis: 1 Leyland. 6 MAN. 10 Mercedes. 12 Volvo.
Bodies: 4 Jonckheere. 1 Leyland. 1 Mercedes. 1 Plaxton. 14 Setra. 8 Van Hool.
Ops incl: school contracts, excursions & tours, private hire, continental tours.
Livery: Green/Black.

SPENCERS COACHES

20 THORNHILL DRIVE, BOUGHTON, NEWARK NG22 9JG
Tel: 01623 860394
Dir: R Spencer
Fleet: 2 midicoach.
Chassis: 2 Mercedes.
Bodies: 2 Plaxton
Ops incl: school contracts, private hire
Livery: Cream/Green

F T TAGG COACHES

QUARRY YARD, SUTTON-IN-ASHFIELD NG17 1BQ
Tel/Fax: 01623 554458
E-mail: ft.taggcoaches@virgin.net
Props: F T Derbyshire, Mrs D J Derbyshire
Fleet: 3 coach.
Chassis: 1 DAF. 1 MAN. 1 Scania.
Bodies: 1 Irizar. 2 Van Hool.
Ops incl: excursions & tours, private hire, continental tours.
Livery: White with red and blue

TRANSIT EXPRESS TRAVEL

UNIT 7, EVANS BUSINESS PARK, RADMARSH ROAD, LENTON, NOTTINGHAM NG7 2GN
Tel: 0115 970 2900
Fax: 0115 970 5515
Fleetname: Transit Express
Prop: G M Crosby

Fleet: 9 - 1 single-deck bus, 3 coach, 2 midicoach, 2 minibus, 1 minicoach.
Chassis: 2 Ford. 4 Ford Transit. 2 Leyland. 1 MAN.
Bodies: 1 Caetano. 1 Carlyle. 2 Duple. 3 Ford. 1 Plaxton. 1 Reeve Burgess.
Ops incl: school contracts, excursions and tours, private hire.
Livery: Blue/White

*TRAVEL WRIGHT LTD

BRUNEL BUSINESS PARK, JESSOP CLOSE, NEWARK NG24 2AG
Tel: 01636 703813
Fax: 01636 674641
E-mail: info@travelwright.fsnet.co.uk
Web site: www.travelwright.co.uk
Dirs: T D Wright, Mrs M Wright, D C Wright, C A Wright, Mrs P J Allen(**Co Sec**), D Walker(**Ch Eng**)
Fleet: 30 - 1 double-deck bus, 7 single-deck bus, 21 coach, 1 midibus.
Chassis: 9 Dennis. 8 MAN. 8 Mercedes. 1 Neoplan. 1 Optare. 1 Scania. 2 Volvo.
Bodies: 1 Alexander. 2 Berkhof. 8 Caetano. 1 Marshall/MCV. 3 Neoplan. 1 Noge. 1 Optare. 9 Plaxton. 1 Reeve Burgess. 3 Van Hool.
Ops incl: local bus services, school contracts, excursions & tours, private hire, continental tours.
Livery: Fawn with red/brown trim
Ticket System: Wayfarer

UNITY COACHES

BECK GARAGE, CLAYWORTH DN22 9AG.
Tel: 07777 817556.
Ptnrs: F. Marriott, Mrs J. Marriott.
Livery: Blue/Grey/Cream.

*WALLIS COACHWAYS

BRAIL WOOD ROAD, BILSTHORPE NG22 8SP
Tel: 01623 870655
Fax: 01623 870655
Prop: Stephen Wallis
Fleet: 3 - 1 coach, 1 midibus, 1 midicoach.
Chassis: incl 1 Setra.
Bodies: incl. 1 Caetano.
Ops incl: local bus services, school contracts, excursions & tours, private hire
Livery: White with cocktail glass logo
Ticket system: Almex

OXFORDSHIRE

BAKERS COMMERCIAL SERVICES
UNIT 5A, ENSTONE BUSINESS PARK, ENSTONE OX7 4NP
Tel: 01608 677415/6
Fax: 01608 677150
E-mail: enquiries@bakerscoaches.co.uk
Web site: www.bakerscoaches.co.uk
Prop: Mike Baker **Ops Man**: Dave Goodall
Ch Eng: Dave Nappin
Fleet: 12 - 11 coach, 1 minibus, 2 minicoach.
Chassis: 6 Dennis. 3 Mercedes. 5 Volvo.
Bodies: 1 Berkhof. 1 Caetano. 11 Plaxton.
Ops incl: local bus services, school contracts, excursions & tours, private hire, continental tours.
Livery: Red on White.

BANBURYSHIRE ETA LTD
UNIT 17, BEAUMONT BUSINESS CENTRE, BEAUMONT CLOSE, BANBURY OX16 7TN
Tel: 01295 263777
Fax: 01295 273086
E-mail: bcta@msn.com
Fleetname: Cherwell District Dial-A-Ride
Fleet: 3 minibus
Chassis/Bodies: 2 Mercedes. 1 Peugeot
Ops incl: local bus services, private hire

*BLUNSDON'S COACH TRAVEL
R24
73 GROVE ROAD, BLADON OX20 1RJ
Tel: 01993 811320
Fax: 01993 811416
E-mail: blunsdons-coaches@merlyn73.wanadoo.co.uk
Dirs: Merlyn H Blunsdon, Michael A Blunsdon
Fleet: 5 coach
Chassis: 5 Dennis.
Bodies: 2 Neoplan. 3 Plaxton.
Ops incl: private hire, school contracts, excursions & tours
Livery: White with Red/Green.

CHARLTON-ON-OTMOOR SERVICES
THE GARAGE, CHARLTON-ON-OTMOOR OX5 2UQ.
Tel: 01865 331249.
Fax: 01865 316189.

*CHENEY COACHES LTD
THORPE MEAD, BANBURY OX16 4RZ
Tel: 01295 254254
Fax: 01295 271990
E-mail: travel@cheneycoaches.co.uk
Web site: www.cheneycoaches.co.uk
Chmn: Graham Peace **Man Dir**: Mark Peace **Co Sec**: Shirley Peace **Dir**: Andrew Peace **Fleet Eng**: Tony Pioteowski
Fleet: 51 - 3 double-deck bus, 2 single-deck bus, 34 coach, 1 midibus, 11 minibus.
Chassis: 2 DAF. 1 Dennis. 1 Dodge. 6 Ford Transit. 1 Freight Rover. 9 Leyland. 2 Leyland National. 1 MAN. 4 Mercedes. 1 Neoplan. 23 Volvo.
Bodies: 1 Berkhof. 4 Caetano. 2 Duple. 11 Jonckheere. 3 Leyland. 2 Leyland National. 4 Mercedes. 1 Neoplan. 8 Plaxton. 6 Van Hool.
Ops incl: local bus services, school contracts, private hire
Livery: White
Ticket system: Wayfarer

*GRAYLINE COACHES (HARTWOOL) LTD
R24
STATION APPROACH, BICESTER OX26 6HU
Tel: 01869 246461
Fax: 01869 240087
E-mail: sales@grayline.co.uk
Web site: www.grayline.co.uk
Dirs: A Gray, B Gray
Fleet: 16 - 8 coach, 8 midicoach.
Chassis: 1 Bedford. 3 Dennis. 3 Iveco. 1 MAN. 5 Mercedes. 3 Optare.
Bodies: 3 Beulas. 1 Caetano. 1 Hispano. 1 Mercedes. 1 Neoplan. 3 Optare. 5 Plaxton.
Ops incl: school contracts, local bus services, private hire, continental tours.
Livery: White/Red/Blue
Ticket System: Wayfarer

HEYFORDIAN TRAVEL LTD
R24
MURDOCK ROAD, BICESTER OX26 4PP.
Tel: 01869 241500.
Fax: 01869 360011.
E-mail: info@heyfordian.co.uk
Web site: www.heyfordian.co.uk
Chmn: J. T. Smith **Man Dir**: R. D. Smith.
Tech Dir: A. M. Smith **Sales Dir**: J. J. Smith. **Chief Eng**: D. F. James.
Fleet: 85 - 4 double-deck bus, 11 70 coach, 2 double-deck coach, 3 minibus. 3 minicoach.
Chassis: 8 Bova. 8 DAF. 2 Dennis. 27 Leyland. 1 MAN. 4 Optare. 20 Scania. 15 Volvo.
Bodies: 7 Alexander. 8 Bova. 4 Caetano. 31 Jonckheere. 2 Neoplan. 4 Optare. 25 Plaxton. 4 Van Hool.
Ops incl: local bus services, school contracts, excursions & tours, private hire, continental tours.
Livery: White/Red/Orange/Black.
Ticket System: Wayfarer.

McLEANS COACHES
UNIT 5, TWO RIVERS INDUSTRIAL ESTATE, STATION LANE, WITNEY OX28 6BH.
Tel: 01993 771445.
Fax: 01993 779556
Dirs: Roger Alder, Mark Hepden
Fleet: 18 - 14 coach. 4 midicoach.
Chassis: MAN. Mercedes. Neoplan. Volvo.
Bodies: incl. Sunsundegui
Ops incl: local bus services, school contracts, excursions & tours, private hire.
Livery: White/Red.

*THE OXFORD BUS COMPANY
COWLEY HOUSE, WATLINGTON ROAD, OXFORD OX4 6GA
Tel: 01865 785410
Fax: 01865 711745
E-mail: info@oxfordbus.co.uk
Web site: www.oxfordbus.co.uk
Man Dir: Philip Kirk **Eng Dir**: Ray Woodhouse **Ops Dir**: Louisa Weeks **Fin Dir**: Helen Le Fevre
Fleet: 150 - 20 double-deck bus, 80 single-deck bus, 38 coach, 12 midibus.
Chassis: 32 Dennis. 27 Mercedes. 12 Scania. 79 Volvo.
Bodies: 20 Alexander. 12 Irizar. 6 Jonckheere. 27 Mercedes. 54 Plaxton. 31 Wright.
Ops incl: local bus services, express.
Livery: Red (city services), Blue (Airline): Green (Espress & park&ride)
Ticket System: Wayfarer TGX150

*OXFORD INTERNATIONAL
169 NEW GREENHAM PARK, BASINGSTOKE RG19 6HN
Tel: 01865 770778
Fax: 01635 821128
Dirs: Simon Weaver
Fleet: 124 - 10 coach bus, 2 double-deck coach.
Chassis: 2 Bova. 8 DAF. 2 Volvo.
Bodies: 2 Bova. 2 East Lancs. 8 Van Hool.
Ops incl: school contracts, private hire
Livery: Electric Blue

PEARCES PRIVATE HIRE
TOWER ROAD INDUSTRIAL ESTATE, BERINSFIELD, WALLINGFORD OX10 7LN
Tel: 01865 340560.
Fax: 01865 341582.
Props: Clive Pearce, Martin Pearce.
Fleet: 12 - 8 coach, 2 midicoach, 2 minicoach.
Chassis: 1 Bova. 6 Dennis. 2 Mercedes. 1 Scania. 2 Toyota.
Bodies: 1 Bova . 2 Caetano. 2 Neoplan. 6 Plaxton. 1 Van Hool.
Ops incl: school contracts, excursions and tours, private hire.
Livery: Yellow/White

PLASTOWS COACHES
R24
134 LONDON ROAD, WHEATLEY OX33 1JH
Tel: 01865 872270
Fax: 01865 875066
Recovery: 01865 872270
Owner: Barbara Plastow
Fleet: 9 coach.
Chassis: Dennis. Volvo.
Bodies: Jonckheere. Plaxton.
Ops incl: excursions & tours, private hire, continental tours, school contracts.
Livery: White /Orange/Yellow

STAGECOACH IN OXFORDSHIRE

HORSEPATH ROAD, COWLEY
OX4 2RY
Tel: 01865 772250
Fax: 01865 747879
E-mail: oxford.enquiries@stagecoachbus.com
Web site: www.stagecoachbus.com/www.oxfordtube.com
Man Dir: Martin Sutton **Service Delivery Dir**: Paul O'Callaghan
Fleet: 179 - 26 double-deck bus, 63 single-deck bus, 28 double-deck coach, 25 minibus, 33 midibus.
Chassis: 18 Dennis. 72 MAN. 25 Mercedes. 28 Transbus. 36 Volvo.
Bodies: 123 Alexander. 28 Jonckheere. 28 Transbus.
Ops incl: local bus services, express.
Livery: Stagecoach
Ticket system: Wayfarer 3

*TAPPINS COACHES

COLLETT ROAD, DIDCOT OX11 7ET
Tel: 01235 819393
Fax: 01235 816464
Recovery: 01235 819393
E-mail: coaches@tappins.co.uk
Web site: www.tappins.co.uk
Fleet: 69 - 1 double-deck bus, 3 single-deck bus, 50 coach, 1 double-deck coach, 2 minicoach, 12 open top double-deck bus.
Chassis: 12 Leyland. 1 Neoplan. 2 Toyota. 54 Volvo.
Bodies: 11 Alexander. 2 Caetano. 1 East lancs. 1 MCW. 1 Neoplan. 28 Plaxton. 25 Van Hool.
Ops incl: school contracts, excursions & tours, private hire, express, continental tours.
Livery: Orange/Black

*WORTHS MOTOR SERVICES LTD

ENSTONE, CHIPPING NORTON
OX7 4LQ
Tel: 01608 677322
Fax: 01608 677298
E-mail: worths.coaches@ukonline.co.uk
Web site: www.worthscoaches.co.uk
Dirs: Richard Worth, Paul Worth **Ch Eng**: Mike Florey
Fleet: 23 - 2 double-deck bus, 3 single-deck bus, 18 coach.
Chassis: 2 Dennis. 2 Leyland. 1 Mercedes. 18 Volvo.
Bodies: 1 Berkhof. 2 Jonckheere. 1 Mercedes. 2 Northern Counties. 17 Plaxton.
Ops incl: local bus services, school contracts, continental tours, private hire.
Livery: Silver/Blue
Ticket System: Wayfarer 3.

SHROPSHIRE

ASTONS OF NEWPORT
STATION GARAGE, NEWPORT
TF10 7EN
Tel/Fax: 01952 811285
Dirs: E. H. Aston, J. E. Aston, P. T. H. Aston
Fleet: 4 - 1 single-deck bus, 2 coach, 1 minibus.
Chassis: 2 Bedford. 1 Ford Transit. 1 Renault
Bodies: 1 Duple. 1 Northern Counties. 1 Plaxton. 1 Ford.
Ops incl: school contracts, private hire.

*BOULTONS OF SHROPSHIRE LTD

SUNNYSIDE, CARDINGTON,
CHURCH STRETTON SY6 7JZ
Tel: 01694 771226
Fax: 01694 771296
Dirs: M Boulton, Miss G Brough
Fleet: 18 - 6 single-deck bus, 5 coach, 4 midicoach, 1 minibus, 2 midibus.
Chassis: DAF. Ford Transit. Mercedes. Optare.
Bodies: Alexander. BMC. Bova. Leyland. Mercedes. Optare.
Ops incl: local bus services, school contracts, excursions & tours, private hire, continental tours.

Livery: Cream/Orange/Brown
Ticket System: Microfare

A T BROWN (COACHES) LTD
81 TRENCH ROAD, TELFORD
TF2 6PF
Tel: 01952 605331
Fax: 01952 608011
E-mail: atbrowncoaches@aol.com
Web site: www.atbrowncoaches.co.uk
Dirs: Nina Macleod, Ewen Macleod
Fleet: 12 - 10 coach, 2 midicoach
Chassis: 9 DAF. 1 Dennis. 2 Mercedes.
Bodies: 1 Autobus. 3 Caetano. 1 Ikarus. 5 Plaxton. 2 Van Hool.
Ops incl: school contracts, private hire, excursions & tours.
Livery: Sky Blue/Navy

*BUTTERS COACHES LTD

VILLAGE ROAD, CHILDS ERCALL,
MARKET DRAYTON TF9 2DG
Tel: 01952 840216
Fax: 01952 840498
E-mail: butterscoaches@btopenworld.com
Dirs: L A Mackintosh, E D Mackintosh, R D Taylor, K L Taylor, B B Managh.

Fleet: 9 - 8 coach, 1 minibus.
Chassis: 4 DAF. 2 Dennis. 1 LDV. 1 Leyland. 1 Volvo.
Bodies: 1 Duple. 1 Jonckheere. 1 Leyland. 1 UVG. 5 Van Hool.
Ops incl: local bus services, school contracts, excursions & tours, private hire.
Livery: Blue/White
Ticket system: Wayfarer

CARADOC COACHES

UNIT 3, CROSSWAYS INDUSTRIAL ESTATE, CHURCH STRETTON
SY6 6PQ
Tel/Fax/Recovery: 01694 724522
Prop: G Gough
Fleet: 9 - 2 coach, 2 midicoach, 4 minibus, 1 minicoach
Chassis: 1 Iveco. 4 LDV. 1 Leyland. 1 Mercedes. 1 Toyota. 1 Volvo.
Bodies: 1 Caetano. 1 Mercedes. 3 Plaxton. 4 other.
Ops incl: local bus services, school contracts, excursions & tours, private hire.

*COURTESY TRAVEL
See West Midlands

❄	Air conditioning
♿	Vehicles suitable for disabled
🍴	Coach(es) with galley facilities
WC	Coach(es) with toilet facilities
●	Seat belt-fitted vehicles
R	Recovery service available (not 24 hr)
R24	24hr recovery service
✔	Replacement vehicle available
T	Toilet-drop facilities available
🚌	Vintage vehicle(s) available
🚐	Open top vehicle(s)

*ELCOCK REISEN

THE MADDOCKS, MADELEY, TELFORD TF7 5HA
Tel: 01952 585712
Fax: 01952 582577
Web site: www.elcockgroup.co.uk
Dirs: J C Elcock, J H Elcock, J D Ashley
Ops Man: Mark Perkins
Fleet: 36 - 28 coach, 4 midicoach, 4 minicoach.
Chassis: 8 Mercedes. 28 Volvo.
Bodies: 1 Esker. 34 Plaxton. 1 Van Hool.
Ops incl: school contracts, excursions & tours, private hire, continental tours.
Livery: Silver/Red/Gold

*HAPPY DAYS COACHES

LITTLE GREEN, BRONINGTON, WHITCHURCH SY13 3HQ
Tel: 01948 780269
Fax: 01948 780271
E-mail: info@happydayscoaches.co.uk
Web site: www.happydayscoaches.co.uk
Dirs: Huw Austin, Neil Austin, Richard Austin
Fleet: 20 - single-deck bus, coach, midicoach, minicoach.
Chassis: 1 DAF. 1 Neoplan. 6 Scania. 12 Volvo.
Bodies: 1 Irizar 1 Neoplan. 8 Plaxton. 10 Van Hool.
Ops incl: local bus services, school contracts, excursions & tours, continental tours, private hire, express.
Livery: White with rising sun

HOLMES GROUP TRAVEL

CHAPEL HOUSE, 6 STAFFORD ROAD, NEWPORT TF10 7LY
Tel: 01952 820477
Fax: 01952 270607
Fax: 07831 258084
Dir: C Holmes
Fleet: 3 - coach
Chassis: includes 1 Mercedes, 1 Volvo.
Bodies: 1 Mercedes. 1 Plaxton.
Ops incl: excursions & tours, private hire.
Livery: White with flag emblem

HORROCKS

IVY HOUSE, BROCKTON, LYDBURY NORTH SY7 8BA.
Tel: 01588 680364
Prop: A P Horrocks
Fleet: 9 - 2 double-deck bus, 2 single-deck bus, 5 midibus.
Chassis: 1 Bedford. 1 Bristol. 1 Daimler. 1 Dodge. 1 LDV. 4 Mercedes. 1 Volvo.
Ops incl: school contracts, private hire
Livery: White/Blue

*LAKESIDE COACHES LTD

THE COACH CENTRE, ELLESMERE BUSINESS PARK, OSWESTRY ROAD, ELLESMERE SY12 0EW
Tel: 01691 622761
Fax: 01691 623694
E-mail: mailbox@lakesidecoaches.co.uk
Web site: www.hiremeacoach.co.uk
Chmn: John Davies **Co Sec**: Dorothy Davies **Gen Man**: Neal Hall
Fleet: 18 - 14 coach, 3 midicoach, 1 minicoach
Chassis: 1 DAF. 4 Dennis. 2 Mercedes. 3 Toyota. 8 Volvo.
Bodies: 5 Caetano. 1 Mercedes. 1 Optare. 10 Plaxton. 1 Van Hool.
Ops incl: local bus services, excursions & tours, private hire, school contracts continental tours.
Livery: Green/White
Ticket system: Almex

*LONGMYND TRAVEL LTD

THE COACH DEPOT, LEA CROSS, SHREWESBURY SY5 8HX
Tel: 01743 861999
Fax: 01743 861901
E-mail: info@longmyndtravel.co.uk
Dirs: T G Evans, F J Evans, V Sheppard-Evans, D M Sheppard.
Fleet: 22 - 19 coach, 2 midicoach, 1 minibus
Chassis: 2 DAF. 1 Iveco. 1 Mercedes. 1 Toyota. 17 Volvo.
Bodies: 1 Berkhof. 2 Bova. 2 Caetano. 16 Jonckheere.
Ops incl: school contracts, private hire.
Livery: Red/White

MYTTON TRAVEL

MYTTON DINGLE, STIPERSTONES, MINSTERLEY SY5 0LZ
Tel: 01743 791309/ 01588 520358
Prop: D J Bradbury
Fleet: 8
Chassis: 2 Ford Transit . 4 LDV. 1 Freight Rover. 1 Mercedes. .
Ops incl: school contracts, private hire.
Livery: White with yellow/red stripes

M &B COACHES & MINIBUSES

UNIT 22, HADLEY PARK INDUSTRIAL ESTATE, TELFORD TF1 2PY
Tel: 01952 251125
Fax: 01952 619619
Mobile: 07812 178163
Prop: Brian Bull
Fleet: 6 - 5 midicoach. 1 coach
Chassis: 1 Dennis. 1 DAF. 4 Mercedes.
Bodies: 1 Duple. 1 LDV. 3 Mercedes. 1 Robin Hood.
Ops incl: school contracts, private hire.
Livery: Red (metallic) with gold and silver letters

M & J TRAVEL

COACH GARAGE, NEWCASTLE, CRAVEN ARMS SY7 8QL.
Tel: 01588 640273.
Prop: W. M. Price.
Fleet: 13 - 7 coach, 1 midicoach, 5 minibus.
Chassis: 4 Bedford. 2 Dennis. 1 Toyota. 1 Talbot.
Bodies: 1 Caetano. 2 Duple. 4 Plaxton.
Ops incl: school contracts, excursions & tours, private hire, continental tours.
Livery: White/Black/Gold.
Ticket System: Setright.

M P MINICOACHES

14 REDBURN CLOSE, KETLEY BANK TF2 0EE
Tel: 01952 415607
Fax: 01952 619188
E-mail: mpminicoaches@hotmail.co.uk
Prop: Mark Perkins
Fleet: 2 minicoach.
Chassis/bodies: 2 Mercedes.
Ops incl: school contracts, private hire.
Livery: Two-tone Blue

*MINSTERLEY MOTORS SERVICES LTD
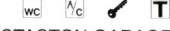

STIPERSTONES, MINSTERLEY, SHREWSBURY SY5 0LZ
Tel: 01743 791208
Fax: 01743 790101
E-mail: john@minsterley-motors.co.uk, minsterley-motors@i12.com
Web site: www.minsterley-motors.co.uk
Man Dir: John Jones
Fleet: 40 - 6 single-deck bus, 32 coach, 2 midicoach.
Chassis: 6 Bedford. 2 Bova. 1 Dennis. 2 Mercedes. 9 Scania. 20 Volvo.
Bodies: 8 Berkhof. 2 Bova. 3 Duple. 12 Jonckheere. 2 Mercedes. 7 Plaxton. 2 Sunsundegui. 4 Wright.
Ops incl: local bus services, school contracts, excursions & tours, private hire, continental tours.
Livery: Blue/Dark Blue/White
Ticket system: Wayfarer

*N. C. B. MOTORS LTD

EDSTASTON GARAGE, WEM SY4 5RF
Tel: 01939 232379
Fax: 01939 234892
E-mail: mail@ncb-motors.co.uk
Dirs: D N Brown, P R Brown.
Fleet: 15 coach
Chassis: 15 Volvo.
Bodies: 1 Duple. 5 Jonckheere. 9 Plaxton.
Ops incl: private hire, school contracts.
Livery: Brown/Cream.

*OWENS COACHES

36 BEATRICE STREET, OSWESTRY SY11 1QG
Tel: 01691 652126
Fax: 01691 670047
E-mail: info@owenstravel.co.uk
Web site: www.owenstravel.co.uk
Dirs: F G Owen, M Owen
Fleet: 22 - incl: 2 single-deck bus, coach,
Chassis: 2 Ayats. 1 Bova. 1 DAF. 2 Dennis. 2 Iveco. 2 MAN. 1 Mercedes. 2 Toyota. 7 Volvo. 2 BMC.
Bodies: 2 Ayats. 1 Beulas. 2 Berkhof. 2 BMC. 1 Bova. 3 Caetano. 1 Duple. 1 Jonckheere. 2 Marcopolo. 5 Plaxton. 1 Van Hool.
Ops incl: local bus services, excursions & tours, private hire, continental tours, school contracts.

R & B TRAVEL
PLEASANT VIEW, KNOWLE, LUDLOW SY8 3NE.
Tel/Fax: 01584 890770.
Prop: A T Radnor, L Radnor.
Fleet: 11 - midibus,
Chassis: 2 Bedford. 2 Leyland DAF. 1 Ford Transit. 2 VW. 1 Iveco. 2 Volvo.
Bodies: Duple. Optare. Plaxton. Robin Hood. Wright.
Ops incl: Local bus services, school contracts, private hire, excursions & tours.
Livery: Silver/Red/Orange/White

RIVERSIDE COACHES
HEATH HILL, DAWLEY TF4 2JU
Tel: 01952 505490
Fax: 01952 505590
Prop: K H Pollen
Fleet: 13 - included 2 double-deck buses, 1 double-deck coach
Chassis: includes - Bristol. Ford. Volvo.
Ops Incl: private hire, school contracts
Livery: Blue/Silver and Blue/White

SHROPSHIRE COUNTY COUNCIL
INTEGRATED TRANSPORT UNIT, 107 LONGDEN ROAD, SHREWSBURY SY3 9DS.
Tel: 01743 245300
Fax: 01743 253279
E-mail: peter.ralphs@shropshire-cc.gov.uk
Web site: www.shropshireonline.gov.uk
Fleetname: Fleet Operations
Ch Exec: Carolyn Downs **Gen Man Transp**: Adrian Millard **Fleet Ops Off**: Peter Ralphs.
Fleet: 55 - 1 single-deck bus, 51 minibus, 2 midicoach, 1 midibus.
Chassis: 1 Ford Transit. 30 Iveco. 13 LDV. 8 Mercedes. 1 Optare. 2 Renault.
Ops incl: local bus services, school contracts.
Livery: White
Ticket system: Almex

WORTHEN TRAVEL   R24 T
STATION ROAD, LITTLE MINSTERLEY SY5 OBW
Tel: 01743 792622
Fax: 01743 791053
Recovery: 01743 792622
E-mail: jackie@worthentravel.freeserve.co.uk
Prop: D A Pye **Gen Man**: C L Robinson
Sec: J Davies
Fleet: 20 - 2 single-deck bus, 15 coach, 3 minibus.
Chassis: 5 DAF. 1 Ford Transit. 7 other.
Bodies: 3 Caetano. 4 Leyland. 3 Van Hool.
Ops incl: local bus services, school contracts, excursions & tours, private hire, express, continental tours.
Livery: White/Blue
Ticket system: Wayfarer 2

SOMERSET (ALSO BATH & N E SOMERSET, N SOMERSET)

A1 TRAVEL
80 HIGHFIELD ROAD, YEOVIL BA21 4RJ
Tel/Fax: 01935 477722
Web site: www.a1travelservices.com
Dir: Ian Watson
Fleet: 5 - 2 midibus, 3 minibus.
Chassis: 1 Ford. 2 Freight Rover. 2 LDV. 1 Mercedes. 1 Setra.
Bodies: include 1 Plaxton. 1 Setra.
Ops incl: school contracts, private hire.

*ARLEEN COACH HIRE & SERVICES LTD
14 BATH ROAD, PEASEDOWN ST JOHN, BATH BA2 8DH
Tel: 01761 434625
Fax: 01761 436578
E-mail: arleen.coach-hire@virgin.net
Web site: www.arleen.co.uk
Senior Dir: A W Spiller **Co Sec**: Mrs M K Spiller **Dir**: A A Spiller **Off Man**: Mrs C M Spiller **Ops Man**: J C Spiller **Ch Eng**: K T Spiller
Fleet: 25 - 20 single-deck bus, 2 midicoach, 3 minibus.
Chassis: incl 3 Bedford. 4 DAF. 1 LDV. 2 MAN. 3 Mercedes. 2 Neoplan. 1 Optare. 1 Volvo.
Bodies: incl: 1 Autobus. 1 Berkhof. 1 Bova. 3 Mercedes. 2 Neoplan. 1 Optare. 2 Plaxton. 3 Van Hool. 1 Wadham Stringer.
Ops incl: school contracts, excursions & tours, private hire, continental tours.
Livery: Red/White/Blue

AXE VALE COACHES
BIDDISHAM, AXBRIDGE BS26 2RD
Tel: 01934 750321
Fax: 01934 750334
Ptnrs: A L Bailey, C P Bailey (**Ops**), J Bailey
Ch Eng: J Bailey
Fleet: 12 - 10 coach, 1 midicoach, 1 minibus.
Chassis: 7 Bova. 2 DAF. 1 Ford. 1 LDV. 1 Mercedes.
Bodies: incl: 7 Bova. 1 Leyland. 3 Plaxton.
Ops incl: local bus services, school contracts, excursions & tours, private hire, express, continental tours.
Livery: White
Ticket system: Setright

BAKERS COACHES   R24
8 BUCKLAND ROAD, YEOVIL BA21 5EA.
Tel: 01935 428401.
Fax: 01935 410423
Recovery: 01935 428401
Dirs: S Baker, A Palmer
Fleet: 13 - 9 coach, 1 midicoach, 3 minibus.
Chassis: 1 Bova. 6 DAF. 1 Mercedes.
Bodies: 1 Bova. 1 Jonckheere. 2 Van Hool.
Ops incl: school contracts, excursions & tours, private hire, continental tours.
Livery: Red/White

BAKERS DOLPHIN COACH TRAVEL
48 LOCKING ROAD, WESTON-SUPER-MARE BS23 3DN
Tel: 01934 635635.
Fax: 01934 641162.
E-mail: coach.hire@bakersdolphin.com
Web site: www.bakersdolphin.com
Chmn: John Baker **Man Dir**: Tim Newcombe **Ch Eng**: Mark Vearncombe
Mktg Dir: Amanda Harrington **Ops Dir**: Max Fletcher **Ops Man**: Chris Rubery **Fin Controller**: Steve Hunt
Fleet: 75 - 68 single-deck coach, 3 double-deck coach, 1 midicoach, 2 minibus, 1 minicoach
Chassis: 4 Bedford. 1 Bova. 1 Dennis. 5 Iveco. 2 LDV. 15 Leyland. 2 Mercedes. 45 Volvo.
Bodies: 5 Beulas. 1 Bova. 3 Jonckheere. 2 LDV. 1 Mercedes. 1 Optare. 34 Plaxton. 28 Van Hool.
Ops incl: local bus services, excursions & tours, private hire, express, continental tours, school contracts.
Livery: Blue/White/Green/Yellow.
Ticket System: Setright

A/c	Air conditioning	
	Vehicles suitable for disabled	
	Coach(es) with galley facilities	
wc	Coach(es) with toilet facilities	
	Seat belt-fitted vehicles	
R	Recovery service available (not 24 hr)	
R24	24hr recovery service	
	Replacement vehicle available	
T	Toilet-drop facilities available	
	Vintage vehicle(s) available	
	Open top vehicle(s)	

Somerset

BATH BUS COMPANY
1 PIERREPONT STREET, BATH
BA1 1LB.
Tel: 01225 330444.
Fax: 01225 330727.
E-mail: hq@bathbuscompany.com
Web site: www.bathbuscompany.com
Chmn: Peter Newman **Man Dir**: Martin Curtis. **Dir**: Dr. Mike Walker. **Eng Dir**: Collin Brougham-Field. **Co Sec/Dir**: Rob Bromley.
Com Dir: Keith Tazewell.
Fleet: 11 double-deck bus, 7 single-deck bus, 3 minibus.
Chassis: 1 AEC, 6 Bristol, 6 Dennis, 3 Leyland-DAB, 3 Leyland, 3 MCW. 4 Mercedes.
Bodies: 1 Alexander. 6 ECW. 1 Leyland. 3 MCW. 1 Park Royal. 3 Plaxton. 4 Wright.
Ops incl: local bus services, excursions & tours, private hire.
Livery: Red/Primrose.
Ticket System: Wayfarer/BBC punch system.
Subsidiary of Ensignbus

*BERKELEY COACH AND TRAVEL
See Bristol

*BERRY'S COACHES (TAUNTON) LTD
CORNISHWAY WEST, NEW WELLINGTON ROAD, TAUNTON TA1 5NA
Tel: 01823 331356
Fax: 01823 322347
E-mail: info@berryscoaches.co.uk
Web site: www.berryscoaches.co.uk
Dirs: S A Berry, P I Berry
Fleet: 29 coach.
Chassis: 29 Volvo.
Bodies: incl: 10 Van Hool.
Ops incl: local bus services, school contracts, excursions & tours, private hire, express, continental tours.
Livery: White/Red/Orange

*BLAGDON LIONESS COACHES LTD
MENDIP GARAGE, STREET END, BLAGDON BS40 7TL
Tel: 01761 462250
Fax: 01761 463237
Dir: T M Lyons **Gen man**: M A Lyons
Fleet: 3 - 2 coach, 1 minibus
Chassis: 1 Bova. 1 Leyland. 1 Mercedes
Bodies: 1 Bova. 2 Plaxton.
Ops incl: local bus services, excursions & tours, private hire, school contracts.
Livery: White
Ticket System: Wayfarer

*BLUE IRIS COACHES
See Bristol

*CENTURION TRAVEL LTD
WEST ROAD GARAGE, WELTON, RADSTOCK BA3 2TP
Tel: 01761 417272
Web site: www.centuriontravel.co.uk
Man Dir: Martin Spiller **Dirs**: Steven Spiller, Darren Spiller **Sec**: Hazel Spiller

Fleet: 21 - 17 coach, 1 minibus, 3 minicoach.
Chassis: 3 Bedford. 2 Bova. 4 DAF. 3 Dennis. 2 Leyland. 5 Mercedes. 1 Scania.
Bodies: 1 Autobus. 2 Bova. 1 Caetano. 5 Duple. 1 Irizar. 2 Jonckheere. 1 Marcopolo. 2 Optare, 3 Plaxton, 2 Van Hool
Ops incl: private hire, continental tours.
Livery: Red/Cream/Burgundy.

CLAPTON COACHES
1 HAYDON ESTATE, RADSTOCK BA3 3RD
Tel: 01761 431936
Fax: 01761 431935
E-mail: claptonholidays@btconnect.com
Dirs: S C Lippet, M C Lippet, C Higgs
Fleet: 12 - 6 coach, 6 minicoach.
Bodies: 2 Beulas. 4 Bova.
Ops incl: excursions & tours, private hire, continental tours.
Livery: Lilac

*COOKS COACHES
VICTOR HOUSE, GREENHAM BUSINESS PARK, WELLINGTON TA21 0LR
Tel: 01823 672247
Fax: 01823 673101
E-mail: landylines@aol.com
Web site: www.cookscoaches-somerset.co.uk
Man Dir: Paul Landymore
Ops Dir: Nigel Billinger.
Fleet: 60 - 21 single-deck bus, 1 coach, 8 midicoach, 12 midibus, 14 minibus, 4 minicoach.
Chassis: 1 Dennis. 1 Iveco. 16 LDV. 21 Mercedes. 21 Optare.
Bodies: 4 Alexander. 3 Autobus. 1 Berkhof. 21 Optare. 9 Plaxton. 2 UVG. 1 Wadham Stringer.
Ops incl: local bus services, school contracts, private hire.
Livery: White with Red/Blue
Ticket System: Almex Optima

*COOMBS TRAVEL
SEARLE CRESCENT, WESTON-SUPER-MARE BS23 3YX
Tel: 01934 428555
Fax: 01934 428559
E-mail: coombscoaches@aol.com
Man Dir: B. F. Coombs **Ops Man**: Mrs J Carroll **Sec**: Mrs M Lillie **Traf Man**: C Winser **Ch Eng**: J. J. Ellis
Fleet: 38 - 1 double-deck bus, 14 coach, 4 midibus, 1 midicoach, 6 minibus, 12 minicoach.
Chassis: 3 Dennis. 10 Ford Transit. 6 LDV. 3 Leyland. 6 Mercedes. 8 Scania. 1 Toyota.
Bodies: 1 Autobus. 3 Irizar. 10 Plaxton. 3 Van Hool
Ops incl: local bus services, school contracts, excursions & tours, private hire.
Livery: Yellow/White

FIRST SOMERSET & AVON LTD
R24
OLDMIXON CRESCENT, WESTON-SUPER-MARE BS24 9AY
Tel: 01934 620122
Fax: 01934 415859

Recovery: 0117 955 4442
Web site: www.firstgroup.com
Man Dir: Tony Anthistle **Fin Dir**: Mike Gahan
Fleet: 460 - 85 double-deck bus, 10 articulated single-deck bus, 106 single-deck bus, 8 coach, 124 midibus, 127 minibus.
Ops incl: local bus services, school contracts, excursions & tours, express, private hire.
Livery: First
Ticket System: Wayfarer

*HUTTON COACH HIRE
95 MOORLAND ROAD, WESTON-SUPER-MARE BS23 4HS
Tel: 01934 618292
Fax: 01934 641362
E-mail: hutton-coach-hire.co.uk
Owner: John Lawrence **Man**: Wendy Dover
Fleet: 4 - 2 coach, 1 minibus, 1 midicoach.
Chassis: 1 Dennis. 1 MAN. 1 Mercedes. Volvo.
Ops incl: private hire, school contracts.
Livery: Maroon with orange/green logo

*NITEFLIGHT BUS LEASING
THE BUS DEPOT, TWEED ROAD, CLEVEDON BS21 6RR
Tel/Fax: 01275 876543
Fax: 01275 340280
E-mail: chris@niteflitebussing.co.uk
Web site: www.niteflitebusleasing.co.uk
Owner: M D C Langson
Fleet: 9 - 1 coach, 8 double-deck coach.
Bodies: 2 Berkhof. 1 Irizar. 1 Jonckheere. 1 Neoplan. 4 Van Hool.
Ops incl: continental tours, private hire
Livery: Blue

*QUANTOCK MOTOR SERVICES LTD
UNIT 13A, TAUNTON TRADING ESTATE, NORTON FITZWARREN TA2 6RX
Tel: 01823 251140
Fax: 01823 251833
E-mail: sales@quantockmotorservices.co.uk
Web site: www.quantockmotorservices.co.uk
Man Dir: Steve Morris, Liz Ranson **Fleet Eng**: Paul Smith **Ops Man**: Jon Pratt
Fleet: 55 - 15 double-deck bus, 30 single-deck bus, 10 single-deck coach, 7 open-top bus.
Chassis: incl: 7 Bristol. 2 Daimler. 16 Leyland.
Ops incl: local bus services, private hire, school contracts.
Livery: Red
Ticket system: Wayfarer

*RIDLERS LTD
JURY ROAD GARAGE, DULVERTON TA22 9EJ
Tel: 01398 323398
Fax: 01398 324398
E-mail: info@ridlers.co.uk
Dirs: G Ridler, S L Ridler **Ops Man**:

M E Jamieson
Fleet: 14 - 13 coach, 1 midicoach.
Chassis: 1 Bedford. 4 Dennis. 1 Iveco. 3 Leyland. 4 Scania. 1 Toyota.
Bodies: 1 Berkhof. 1 Caetano. 5 Duple. 1 Irizar. 4 Plaxton. 2 Van Hool.
Ops incl: local bus services, school contracts, continental tours, private hire
Livery: White/Red/Silver.
Ticket system: Almex

D. W. SKELTON
90 BROADWAY, CHILTON POLDEN TA7 9EQ.
Tel: 01278 722066.
Fax: 01278 722608.
Fleetname: Skelton Tours.
Prop: D. W. Skelton.
Fleet: 3 coach.
Chassis: 1 Ford. 2 MAN.
Bodies: 1 Neoplan. 1 Plaxton. 1 MAN.
Ops incl: excursions & tours, private hire, continental tours.
Livery: Black/Green/Gold.

*SMITH'S COACHES (B.E. & G.W. SMITH)
BYFIELDS, PYLLE BA4 6TA.
Tel: 01749 830126
Fax: 01749 830888
Prop: Graham Smith
Fleet: 14 coach.
Chassis: 3 Bedford. 3 Leyland. 8 Volvo.
Bodies: 14 Plaxton.
Ops incl: school contracts, private hire.
Livery: Maroon/Cream

*SOMERBUS LTD
64 BROOKSIDE, PAULTON, BRISTOL BS39 7YR
Tel/Fax: 01761 415456
Web site: www.somerbus.co.uk
E-mail: somerbus@tinyworld.co.uk
Man Dir: Tim Jennings
Fleet: 5 - 1 single-deck bus, 4 midibus.
Chassis: 1 Dennis. 2 Mercedes. 2 Optare.
Bodies: 1 Marshall. 3 Optare. 1 other.
Ops incl: local bus services, school contracts
Livery: Orange/White
Ticket system: Wayfarer

*SOUTH WEST COACHES LTD/SOUTH WEST TOURS LTD
SOUTHGATE ROAD, WINCANTON BA9 9EB
Tel: 01963 33124
Fax: 01963 31599

E-mail: info@southwestcoaches.co.uk
Web site: www.southwestcoaches.co.uk
Man Dir: A M Graham **Co Sec**: S Graham
Comm Dir: S Caine **Eng Man**: K Jeffrey
Ops Man: J A Hiscock **Tours Man**: D Green
Fleet: 69 - 8 single-deck bus, 33 coach, 7 midibus, 3 midicoach, 18 minibus.
Chassis: 3 Bedford. 1 DAF. 1 Dennis. 14 Ford Transit. 1 Iveco. 2 LDV. 13 Leyland. 11 Mercedes. 1 Optare. 5 Setra. 15 Volvo. 2 VW.
Bodies: Duple. East Lancs. Leyland. Marshall. Mercedes. Plaxton. Setra. Van Hool. Wadham Stringer.
Ops incl: local bus services, school contracts, excursions & tours, private hire, continental tours.
Livery: Blue/White/Red
Ticket System: Pay Cell/Setright

STONES OF BATH
LOWER BRISTOL ROAD, BATH BA2 3DR
Tel: 01225 422267
Fax: 01225 442209
E-mail: stonescoaches@compuserve.com
Senior Ptnr: D G Stone, **Ops Man**: C G Stone, **Ch Eng**: S M Stone, **Sec/Fin**: Mrs N R Russell
Fleet: 13 - 10 double-deck coach, 3 midicoach
Chassis: DAF. Neoplan. Scania. Toyota.
Bodies: Bova. Irizar. Neoplan. Van Hool.
Ops incl: excursions & tours, school contracts, private hire, continental tours.
Livery: Cream/Red

*TAYLORS COACH TRAVEL LTD

PLOT 10, BRYMPTON WAY, LYNX WEST TRADING ESTATE, YEOVIL BA20 2HP
Tel: 01935 427556
Fax: 01935 423177
Recovery: 01935 423177
E-Mail: taylorscoachtravel@tintinhull.fsword.co.uk
Web site: www.taylorscoachtravel.co.uk
Chmn: D D J Elliott **Co Sec**: Mrs T R Elliott
Man Dir: D Porter **Ops Dir**: D Kirkland
Fleet: 41 - 30 coach, 7 midicoach, 4 minibus.
Chassis: 2 Autosan. 2 Bova. 4 BMC. 2 DAF.

2 Dennis. 3 Irisbus. 2 Iveco. 2 LDV. 6 Leyland. 1 Mercedes. 14 Volvo.
Bodies: 2 Autosan. 3 Alexander. 4 BMC. 2 Bova. 2 Duple. 1 Indcar. 2 Leyland. 1 Mercedes. 6 Plaxton. 1 Reeve Burgess. 13 Van Hool. 1 Wadham Stringer. 3 Vehixel.
Ops incl: local bus services, private hire, school contracts, excursions & tours, continental tours
Livery: White/Gold and burgundy stripes
Ticket system: Wayfarer

TRAVELINE   R24
SUMMERLAND CAR PARK, MINEHEAD TA24 5BN.
Tel: 01643 704774, 821883.
Fax: 01643 821883.
Dirs: D. C. & P. A. Grimmett.
Fleet: 1 coach. **Chassis/Body**: Bova.
Ops incl: excursions & tours, private hire, continental tours.

*VISTA COACHWAYS
9 GRAITNEY CLOSE, CLEEVE, BRISTOL BS49 4NJ
Tel: 01934 832074
E-mail: terry@vistacoach.co.uk
Web site: www.vistacoach.co.uk
Prop: T P Jones
Fleet: 5 - 1 coach, 2 midibus, 2 midicoach.
Chassis: 1 Bedford. 1 Bristol. 2 Iveco. 1 Mercedes.
Bodies: 2 Mellor. 2 Plaxton. 1 PMT.
Ops incl: local bus services, private hire.
Livery: Cream with green/red
Ticket system: Wayfarer

WEBBER BUS
BRUE AVENUE, COLLEY LANE INDUSTRIAL ESTATE, BRIDGWATER TA6 5LT
Tel: 0800 096 3039
Fax: 01278 455250
Web site: www.webberbus.com
Dirs: D J Webber, D A Webber, T Gardner, E Gardner.
Fleet: 29 - 15 coach, 2 midicoach, 10 minibus, 2 minicoach.
Chassis: 1 Bova. 2 DAF. 5 Ford Transit. 7 LDV. 1 Neoplan. 1 Scania. 6 Volvo.
Bodies: 2 Bova. 1 Caetano. 4 Duple. 1 Mellor. 1 Neoplan. 5 Plaxton. 2 Van Hool. 8 other.
Ops incl: local bus services, school contracts, excursions & tours, private hire, continental tours.

- Air conditioning
- Vehicles suitable for disabled
- Coach(es) with galley facilities
- Coach(es) with toilet facilities
- Seat belt-fitted vehicles
- R Recovery service available (not 24 hr)
- R24 24hr recovery service
- Replacement vehicle available
- T Toilet-drop facilities available
- Vintage vehicle(s) available
- Open top vehicle(s)

SOUTH YORKSHIRE

*ANDERSON COACHES LTD

4 HOLLY BANK AVENUE,
SHEFFIELD S12 2BL
Tel: 0114 239 9231
Fax: 01709 364750
Fleet: 5 - 3 coach, 2 minibus.
Chassis: 2 Dennis. 1 Ford Transit. 1 LDV. 1 Neoplan.
Ops incl: excursions & tours, private hire

ASHLEY TRAVEL LTD
t/a GRANT & McALLIN
8A STATION ROAD, MOSBOROUGH,
SHEFFIELD S19 5AD.
Tel: 0114 251 1234.
Fax: 0114 251 1900.
Dirs: R. Atack (**Gen Man/Traf Man**),
T. F. Atack (**Ch Eng/Sec**).
Fleet: 3 coach.
Chassis: 1 Bedford. 2 Volvo.
Bodies: 3 Plaxton.
Ops incl: excursions & tours, private hire.
Livery: Turquoise/Blue/White.

BARNSLEY & DISTRICT TRACTION CO
WAKEFIELD ROAD, BARNSLEY
S71 1NU
Tel: 01226 299288
Fax: 01226 779079
Gen Man: K Allison
Fleet: 43 single-deck bus.
Chassis: 19 DAF. 24 Volvo.
Bodies: 23 Alexander. 1 East Lancs. 19 Optare.
Ops incl: local bus services.

BILLIES COACHES LTD

C/O W GORDON & SONS,
CHESTERTON ROAD, EASTWOOD
TRADING ESTATE, ROTHERHAM
S65 1SU
Tel: 01709 363913
Fax: 01709 830570
Dir: D Gordon
Fleet: 1 coach
Chassis/Bodies: 1 Bova
Ops Incl: school contracts, excursions & tours, private hire
Livery: Red/ivory

BUCKLEYS

STONEHAVEN, GATEHOUSE LANE,
AUCKLEY, DONCASTER DN9 3EJ
Tel: 01302 770379.
Man Dir: Richard Buckley.
Fleet: 2 double-deck coach.
Chassis/Bodies: Mercedes/Neoplan.
Ops incl: excursions & tours.

*BURDETTS COACHES LTD
8 STATION ROAD, MOSBOROUGH,
SHEFFIELD S20 5AD
Tel: 0114 248 2341
Fax: 0114 247 5733
Dir: F. Burdett
Fleet: 12 coach.
Chassis: 2 Leyland. 10 Volvo.
Bodies: 2 Plaxton. 10 Van Hool.
Ops incl: private hire

BYRAN COACHES LTD

31 SUSSEX STREET, SHEFFIELD
S4 7YY
Tel/Fax: 0114 270 0060
Dir/Owner: Julie Scott **Dir**: Dennis Heaton
Fleet: 6 - 3 minibus, 3 minicoach.
Chassis: 1 Ford. 4 Mercedes.
Bodies: include 1 Setra.
Ops incl: school contracts, excursions & tours, private hire.
Livery: White/Jade/Black.

*CLARKSONS HOLIDAYS
See West Yorkshire

COOPERS TOURS LTD

ALDRED CLOSE, NORWOOD
INDUSTRIAL ESTATE, KILLAMARSH
S21 2JH
Tel: 0114 248 2859.
Fax: 0114 248 3867.
E-mail: sales@cooperstours.co.uk
Web site: www.cooperstours.co.uk
Dirs: Alan Cooper, Graham Cooper.
Fleet: 8 coach.
Chassis: 1 AEC. 2 Leyland. 1 MAN. 3 Volvo.
Bodies: 2 Berkhof. 4 Plaxton. 2 Van Hool.
Ops incl: excursions & tours, private hire, continental tours.
Livery: Yellow/White.

COSY COACHES
5 MEYNELL WAY, KILLAMARSH,
SHEFFIELD S21 1HG
Tel: 0114-248 9139
E-mail: enquiries@cosycoach.co.uk
Web site: www.cosycoach.co.uk
Fleet: 1 Bedford/Duple vintage coach

ELLENDERS COACHES

71 HURLFIELD AVE, SHEFFIELD
S12 2TL.
Tel: 0114 264 1837.
Ptnrs: Mrs P. J. D. Ellender, C. S. Ellender.
Fleet: 2 coach.
Chassis: Volvo. **Bodies**: Jonckheere.
Ops incl: excursions & tours, private hire, continental tours, school contracts.

*EXPRESSWAY COACHES

DERWENT WAY, WATH ON
DEARNE, ROTHERHAM S63 6EX
Tel: 01709 877797
Fax: 01709 879919
E-mail: expresswaycoaches@btconnect.com
Web site: www.expresswaycoaches.co.uk
Dirs: Peter Regan, Liam Regan
Fleet: 15 - 4 coach 5 midicoach, 6 minibus.
Chassis: 1 MAN. 12 Mercedes. 2 Volvo.
Bodies: 1 Neoplan. 1 Noge. 2 Plaxton. 2 Transbus. 9 Other.
Ops incl: private hire, continental tours, school contracts, excursions & tours.
Livery:)range/Yellow/White

FIRST SOUTH YORKSHIRE

MIDLAND ROAD, ROTHERHAM
S61 1TF.
Tel: 01709 566000
Fax: 01709 566063
E-mail: enquiries@firstgroup.com
Web site: www.firstgroup.com
Man Dir: Bob Hamilton **Eng Dir**: John Clayton **Comm Dir**: Brandon Jones **Ops Dir**: Dennis Hajdukiewicz
Fleet: 623 - 151 double-deck bus, 318 single-deck bus, 112 midibus, 42 minibus.
Chassis: 111 Dennis. 30 Mercedes. 12 Optare. 12 Scania. 458 Transbus.
Bodies: 164 Alexander. 134 Northern Counties. 12 Optare. 113 Plaxton. 200 Wright.
Ops incl: local bus services
Livery: FirstGroup corporate livery
Ticket System: Wayfarer 3

L. FURNESS & SONS
THOMPSON HILL, HIGH GREEN,
SHEFFIELD S30 4JU.
Tel: 0114 284 8365.
Ptnrs: G. Furness, A. Furness.
Ch Eng: P. Hayes.
Fleet: 8 - 7 coach 1 minicoach.
Chassis: 3 DAF. 3 Ford. 1 Leyland. 1 Mercedes.
Bodies: 1 Duple. 7 Plaxton.
Ops incl: excursions & tours, private hire.
Livery: Red/Cream.

*GEE-VEE TRAVEL
173 DONCASTER ROAD,
BARNSLEY S70 1UF
Tel: 01226 287403
Fax: 01226 284783
Fleet: 14 - 12 coach, 2 minibus.
Chassis: 12 Bova. 2 Mercedes.
Bodies: 2 Bova. 2 Mercedes.
Ops incl: excursions & tours, private hire, continental tours.

W GORDON & SONS
EASTWOOD TRADING ESTATE,
CHESTERTON ROAD, ROTHERHAM
S65 1SU
Tel: 01709 363913
Fax: 01709 830570
Dir: D Gordon
Fleet: 16 coach
Chassis: 2 Dennis. 1 Mercedes. 12 Volvo.
Bodies: incl: 15 Plaxton.
Ops incl: school contracts, excursions & tours, private hire, express.
Livery: Red/Ivory

GRAYS LUXURY TRAVEL
30-32 SHEFFIELD ROAD, HOYLAND
COMMON S74 0DQ.
Tel: 01226 743109.

Fax: 01226 749430.
E-mail: stephen@grays-travel.co.uk
Web site: www.grays-travel.co.uk
Man Dir: S. Gray. **Ch Eng:** P. Winter.
Fleet: 10 - 7 coach 1 midicoach, 1 minibus, 1 minicoach.
Chassis: 1 Bova. 6 DAF. 2 Dennis. 1 Toyota.
Bodies: 1 Berkhof. 1 Caetano. 2 Duple. 6 Plaxton.
Ops incl: excursions & tours, private hire, school contracts.
Livery: White/Blue/Yellow.

HAGUES COACHES
C/O W GORDON & SONS, CHESTERTON ROAD, EASTWOOD TRADING ESTATE, ROTHERHAM S65 1SU
Tel: 01709 382912
Fax: 01709 382570
Ops incl: excursions & tours.

HEATON'S OF SHEFFIELD

46 CANTERBURY CRESCENT, FULWOOD, SHEFFIELD S10 3RX
Tel/Fax: 0114 230 9184
Fleet: 10 - 4 coach, 2 midicoach, 4 minicoach.
Chassis: 1 Ford. 4 Mercedes. 5 Setra.
Bodies: 4 Mercedes. 1 Plaxton. 5 Setra.
Ops incl: school contracts, excursions & tours.
Livery: White.

HOGG EUROPEAN COACHES
50 DOVERCOURT ROAD, SHEFFIELD S2 1UA.
Tel: 0114 272 0895.
Prop: A. Hogg.
Fleet: 1 coach.
Chassis: DAF. **Body:** Moseley.
Ops incl: excursions & tours, continental tours.
Livery: Blue/Blue.

ISLE COACHES
97 HIGH STREET, OWSTON FERRY DN9 1RL
Tel: 01427 728227.
Props: J. & C. Bannister.
Ch Eng: E. Scotford. **Sec:** Jill Bannister.
Fleet: 12 - 2 double-deck bus, 3 single-deck bus, 6 coach 1 minibus.
Chassis: 2 Daimler. 1 Ford. 4 Leyland. 3 Leyland National. 1 Mercedes. 1 Volvo.
Bodies: 1 Alexander. 1 Duple. 3 Leyland National. 4 Plaxton. 1 Reeve Burgess. 1 Roe. 1 Van Hool.
Ops incl: local bus services, excursions & tours, private hire.
Livery: Blue/Cream.
Ticket System: Almex.

JEMS TRAVEL
23 STANWOOD CRESCENT, STANNINGTON S6 5JA
Tel: 0800 298 1938.

Fax: 0114 233 5329.
E-mail: info@jemstravel.co.uk
Prop: Malcolm S Mallender.
Fleet: 1 minibus.
Chassis: 1 LDV
Bodies: 1 other
Ops incl: school contracts, private hire.

*JOHNSON'S TOURS
See Nottinghamshire

K. M. MOTORS LTD

WILSON GROVE, LUNDWOOD, BARNSLEY S71 5JS
Tel: 01226 245564
Fax: 01226 213004
Man Dir: Keith Meynell
Fleet: 10 - 8 coach, 1 minicoach, 1 midicoach.
Chassis/bodies: incl: 2 Bova. 1 Mercedes. 4 Scania.
Ops incl: excursions & tours, continental tours, private hire.
Livery: Gold/Maroon/White.

LADYLINE
47 BERNARD STREET, RAWMARSH S62 5NR.
Tel: 01709 522422.
Fax: 01709 525558.
Owner: C. B. Goodridge.
Fleet: 6 coach.
Chassis: 2 AEC. 3 Bova. 1 DAF.
Bodies: 3 Bova. 1 Caetano. 2 Plaxton.
Ops incl: local bus services, school contracts, excursions & tours, private hire, continental tours.
Livery: Blue/White.

LEON MOTOR SERVICES LTD
FINNINGLEY DN9 3DE.
Tel: 01302 770273.
Fax: 01302 770483.
Traf Man: E. McGuinness.
Fleet: 38 - 19 double-deck bus, 10 single-deck bus, 9 coach.
Chassis: Dennis, Leyland.
Bodies: Alexander, Duple, East Lancs, ECW, Northern Counties, Plaxton, Optare, Van Hool.
Ops incl: local bus services, excursions & tours, express, continental tours.
Livery: Blue/Cream.
Ticket System: Almex, A90
Subsidiary of Mass Transit

*MALCYS
27 BOYNTON ROAD, SHIRECLIFFE, SHEFFIELD S5 7HJ
Tel: 0800 298 1938.
Fax: 0114 242 0885
E-mail: malcystravel@aol.com
Dir: Malcolm S Mallender
Fleet: 2 minibus.
Chassis: 1 Iveco. 1 LDV.
Bodies: 1 Mellor. 1other.
Ops incl: school contracts, excursions & tours, private hire.

WALTER MARTIN COACHES

57 OLD PARK AVENUE, GREENHILL, SHEFFIELD S8 7DQ
Tel: 0114 274 5004
Prop: John Martin, June Martin.
Fleet: 3 coach.
Chassis: 3 Volvo.
Ops incl: excursions & tours, private hire.

MARTINS COACHES
58 ARUNDEL ROAD, CHAPELTOWN, SHEFFIELD S35 2RD.
Tel: 0114 246 0111.

MASS TRANSIT

HOUGHTON ROAD, THE NORTH ANSTON TRADING ESTATE, ANSTON, SHEFFIELD S25 4JJ.
Tel: 01909 550480.
Fax: 01909 550486.
E-mail: masseng@aol.com
Man Dir: M. Strafford.
Fleet: 45 double-deck bus.
Chassis: 3 Dennis, 42 Leyland.
Bodies: 3 Alexander. 42 Leyland.
Ops incl: local bus services, school contracts, private hire.
Livery: Red/White/Green.
Ticket System: Wayfarer.
Also offers a complete maintenance/refurbishment service to bus and coach operators.

MAYFIELD COACHES
172 AUGHTON ROAD, AUGHTON, SHEFFIELD S26 3XE
Tel: 0114 287 2622
Fax: 0114 287 5003
E-mail: info@mayfieldtravel.co.uk
Web site: www.mayfieldtravel.co.uk

MOSLEYS TOURS

LEES HALL ROAD, THORNHILL LEES, DEWSBURY WF12 9EQ.
Tel: 01226 382243.
Fax: 01924 458665.
Dirs: A. Gath-Bragg, J. R. Bragg. **Gen Man:** P. R. Emerton.
Fleet: 3 - 2 coach, 1 midicoach.
Chassis: 1 Dennis, 1 Leyland, 1Volvo.
Ops incl: school contracts, private hire, continental tours, excursions and tours, express
Livery: Grey/Cream.

NIELSEN TRAVEL SERVICE

23 WINN GROVE, MIDDLEWOOD, SHEFFIELD S6 1UW
Tel/Fax: 0114 234 2961
E-mail: niel@nielsentravel.co.uk
Web site: www.nielsentravel.co.uk
Fleet: 2 minibus
Chassis: 2 Mercedes.

Ops incl: school contracts, private hire, excursions & tours

COLLIN PHILLIPSON
1 HILLCREST, OUSEFLEET, GOOLE DN14 8HP.
Tel: 01405 704394.
Prop: C. Phillipson. **Traf Man:** Miss T. Phillipson.
Fleet: 1 minicoach.
Chassis: Mercedes.
Bodies: Autobus Classique.
Ops incl: excursions & tours, private hire.
Livery: White.

*JOHN POWELL TRAVEL
UNIT 2, 6 HELLABY LANE, HELLABY INDUSTRIAL ESTATE, ROTHERHAM S66 8HN
Tel: 01709 700900
Fax: 01709 701521
Recovery: 0870 6008787, 07770 566599
E-mail: ianpowell@powellsbus.co.uk
Props: John Powell, Pauline Powell, Ian Powell, Jane Powell **Man:** Lynn Oliver
Ch Eng: Ian Slater **Recovery Eng:** Paul Roddison
Fleet: 30 - 7 double-deck bus, 14 single-deck bus, 7 coach, 2 minicoach
Chassis: 1 BMC. 12 Dennis. 2 Leyland. 5 MCW. 2 Mercedes. 1 Setra. 7 Volvo.
Bodies: 2 Leyland. 5 MCW. 2 Mercedes. 12 Plaxton. 1 Setra. 8 Wright.
Ops incl: local bus services, school contracts, excursions & tours, private hire
Livery: Blue/Orange/Yellow.
Ticket System: Wayfarer 3

ROEVILLE TOURS LTD
APEX HOUSE, CHURCH LANE, ADWICK-LE-STREET DN6 7DY.
Tel: 01302 330330.
Fax: 01302 330204.
Dirs: W. A. & S. M. Scholey. **Ch Eng:** N. G. Haxby. **Gen Man:** P. G. Haxby.
Fleet: 7 - 1 double-deck bus, 4 coach 2 minibus. Also nine taxis able to carry disabled passengers.
Chassis: 1 AEC. 1 DAF. 2 Ford. 1 Leyland. 1 Mercedes. 1 Scania.
Bodies: 1 Duple. 1 Mercedes. 3 Plaxton. 1 Reeve Burgess. 1 Roe.
Ops incl: local bus services, excursions & tours, private hire, continental tours.
Livery: Green/Blue/White.
Ticket System: Almex.
Subsidiary of Wilfreda Beehive.

*ROYLES TRAVEL

114 TUNWELL AVENUE, SHEFFIELD S5 9FG
Tel: 0114 245 4519
Fax: 0114 257 8585
E-mail: info@roylestravel.co.uk
Web site: www.roylestravel.co.uk
Ptnrs: Ricky Eales, Roy Eales.
Fleet: 2 coach.
Chassis: 1 Bova. 1 Iveco.
Bodies: 1 Beulas. 1 Bova.
Ops incl: excursions & tours.

SLEIGHTS COACHES
87 STATION STREET, SWINTON S64 8PZ.
Tel: 01709 584561.
Fax: 01709 582016.
Owner: J. Sleight.
Fleet: 3 coach.
Chassis: DAF. **Bodies:** Jonckheere.
Ops incl: excursions & tours, private hire, continental tours, school contracts.
Livery: Orange/Cream.

STAGECOACH SHEFFIELD
GREEN LANE DEPOT, ECCLESFIELD S35 9WY
Tel: 0114 246 5555
Fax: 0114 257 0343
Fleet: 119 – double-deck bus, single-deck bus, coach, midibus.
Chassis: DAF. Dennis. Leyland. Leyland National. MCW. Optare. Volvo.
Bodies: Alexander. East Lancs. Leyland National. MCW. Optare. Plaxton.
Ops incl: local bus services, school contracts.
Livery: Stagecoach

STAGECOACH SUPERTRAM
NUNNERY DEPOT, WOODBURN ROAD, SHEFFIELD S9 3LS
Tel: 0114 275 9888
Fax: 0114 279 8120
Web site: www.supertram.com
Man Dir: A Morris
Fleet: 25 tramcars
Chassis/bodies: Siemens
Ops incl: tram services.
Livery: White/Orange/Red

*SWIFTS HAPPY DAYS TRAVEL

HAPPY DAYS, THORNE ROAD, BLAXTON DN9 3AX
Tel/Fax: 01302 770999
Ptnrs: S J Swift, J E Swift
Fleet: 3 coach.
Chassis: 3 DAF.
Bodies: 3 Van Hool.
Ops incl: private hire.
Livery: Red/White/Blue

*TRAVELGREEN COACHES
CANDA LODGE, HAMPOLE BALK LANE, SKELLOW, DONCASTER DN6 8LF
Tel: 01302 722227
Owner: Dave Green
Fleet: 5 - 2 midicoach, 3 minicoach.
Chassis: 5 Mercedes.
Bodies: 2 Esker. 3 Optare.
Ops incl: private hire, continental tours.
Livery: Maroon/White

WILFREDA BEEHIVE

APEX HOUSE, CHURCH LANE, ADWICK-LE-STREET DN6 7AY
Tel: 01302 330330

Fax: 01302 330204
E-mail: sales@wilfreda.co.uk
Web site: www.wilfreda.co.uk
President: W A Scholey **Man Dir/Co Sec:** S M Scholey **Dirs:** R Haxby, N Haxby **Ops Man:** Ian Kaye **Mktg Man:** P Scholey **Ch Eng:** P Whitaker
Fleet: 38 - 7 double-deck bus, 10 single-deck bus, 15 coach, 3 midibus, 1 minicoach, 2 minibus.
Chassis: 4 BMC. 3 Bristol. 2 Chrysler. 2 Dennis. 74 Mercedes. 1 Neoplan. 10 Optare. 9 Scania.
Bodies: 4 BMC. 5 East Lancs. 7 Irizar. 2 Mercedes. 1 Neoplan. 5 Plaxton. 11 Optare
Ops incl: local bus services, school contracts, excursions & tours, private hire, continental tours.
Livery: Blue/White/Yellow.
Ticket System: Wayfarer.

WILKINSONS TRAVEL
2 REDSCOPE CRESCENT, KIMBERWORTH PARK, ROTHERHAM S61 3LX
Tel: 01709 553403
Fax: 01709 550550
Owner: M. D. Wilkinson.
Fleet: 9 - 2 coach 3 minibus, 4 minicoach.
Chassis: AEC. Volvo.
Bodies: Berkhof. Duple. Ikarus. Jonckheere.
Ops incl: excursions & tours, private hire, continental tours, school contracts.

WILLIAMSONS OF ROTHERHAM
19 VICTORIA STREET, CATCLIFFE S60 5SJ.
Tel: 01709 366856.
Fax: 01709 828241.
Prop: P. Williamson.
Fleet: 3 coach.
Chassis: 1 Bedford. 1 DAF. 1 Leyland.
Bodies: 1 Duple. 1 Leyland. 1 Van Hool.
Ops incl: school contracts, excursions & tours, private hire, continental tours.
Livery: White.

WILSON'S COACHES
PLOT 5, BANKWOOD LANE INDUSTRIAL ESTATE, ROSSINGTON, DONCASTER DN11 0PS.
Tel: 01302 866193
Recovery: 07836 757618
Dir: E Wilson
Fleet: 3 coach.
Chassis: 3 Volvo.
Bodies: 1 Ikarus. 2 Van Hool.
Ops incl: excursions & tours, private hire.

STAFFORDSHIRE

ACE TRAVEL
10 BIDDULPH PARK, IRONSTON ROAD, BURNTWOOD WS7 8LG.
Tel: 01543 279068.
Prop: G. E. Elson.
Fleet: 1 midicoach. **Chassis:** Toyota.
Ops incl: excursions & tours, private hire, continental tours, school contracts.

ARRIVA MIDLANDS LTD
DELTA WAY, CANNOCK WS11 3XB.
Tel: 01543 466123.
Fax: 01543 570900.
Web site: www.arriva.co.uk
Fleetname: Arriva Serving the North Midlands.
Man Dir: Catherine Mason **Fin Dir:** M. G. Doyle. **Eng Dir:** B. J. Baxter. **Com Dir:** K. J. Belfield. **Ops Dir:** J. Morrow.
Fleet: 386 - 19 double-deck bus, 289 single-deck bus, 78 midibus.
Chassis: 38 DAF. 151 Dennis. 44 Leyland. 78 Mercedes. 2 Optare. 24 Scania. 49 Volvo.
Bodies: Alexander. Carlyle. ECW. East Lancs. Leyland. Marshall. Northern Counties. Optare. Plaxton. Reeve Burgess. Wright.
Ops incl: local bus services, school contracts.
Livery: Aquamarine/Cotswold Stone.
Ticket System: Wayfarer 3.

*BAKERS COACHES
SPRING GROVE, CONGLETON ROAD, BIDDULPH ST8 7RQ
Tel: 01782 522101
Fax: 01782 513106
E-mail: sales@bakerscoaches.com
Web site: www.bakerscoaches.com
Man Dir: Philip Baker **Ch Eng:** Steve Marsh
Ops Mans: Nigel Whalley, David Machin
Fleet: 41 - 8 single-deck bus, 18 coach, 13 midibus, 2 midicoach.
Chassis: 6 DAF. 14 Mercedes. 5 Scania. 16 Volvo.
Bodies: 3 Caetano. 4 Irizar. 13 Marshall/MCV. 15 Plaxton. 6 Wright.
Ops incl: local bus services, school contracts, excursions & tours, private hire, continental tours.
Livery: Duo-green/White
Ticket System: Wayfarer

BENNETTS TRAVEL (CRANBERRY) LTD
CRANBERRY, COTES HEATH ST21 6SQ.
Tel: 01782 791468
Prop/Gen Man: J. P. McDonnell.
Fleet: 27
Chassis: Bedford. Ford Transit. Leyland. Mercedes.
Bodies: Mercedes. Plaxton.
Ops incl: local bus services, excursions & tours, private hire.
Livery: Blue/White

*L F BOWEN LTD
104 MARINER, TAMWORTH B79 7UL
Tel: 01827 300000
Fax: 01827 300009
Web site: www.bowenstravel.co.uk
Man Dir: Rob Lyng **Ops Man:** Colin Rowe
Ch Eng: Kevin Morgan **Traf Man:** Tony York
Fleet: 27 - 26 coach, 1 minicoach.
Chassis: 10 MAN, 14 Scania, 1 Toyota. 2 Volvo.
Bodies: 1 Caetano, 14 Irizar, 2 Marcopolo. 8 Noge, 2 Plaxton.
Ops incl: private hire, express, continental tours.
Livery: Silver

M BOYDON & SONS
ASHBOURNE ROAD, WINKHILL, LEEK ST13 7PP
Tel: 01538 308255
Fax: 01538 308849
E-mail: lynton@boydons.freeserve.co.uk
Fleetname: Boydons Coaches.
Ptnrs: R M Boydon, G M L Boydon
Man: L Boydon **Ch Eng:** G N Boydon.
Fleet: 16 - 14 coach, 2 midicoach.
Chassis: 2 DAF. 4 Dennis. 7 Leyland. 1 Toyota. 2 Volvo.
Bodies: 1 Caetano. 5 Duple. 1 Jonckheere. 7 Plaxton. 1 Van Hool. 1 other.
Ops incl: local bus services, school contracts, excursions & tours, private hire.
Livery: Maroon/Gold
Ticket system: Wayfarer

*TERRY BUSHELL TRAVEL

13 DERBY STREET, BURTON-ON-TRENT DE14 2LA
Tel/Fax: 01283 538242
Prop: Terry Bushell
Fleet: 4 - 3 coach, 1 minicoach.
Chassis: 2 Volvo. 2 Mercedes.
Bodies: 1 Jonckheere. 1 Mercedes. 1 Neoplan. 1 Van Hool.
Ops incl: excursions & tours, private hire, continental tours.
Livery: Red/Gold/Orange

*CHASE BUS SERVICES
See West Midlands

COPELAND TOURS (STOKE-ON-TRENT) LTD
R24
UTTOXETER ROAD, MEIR, STOKE-ON-TRENT ST3 6HE.
Tel: 01782 324466
Fax: 01782 319401
Recovery: 01782 324466
E-mail: mb@copelandtours.co.uk
Web site: www.copelandtours.co.uk
Chmn/Man Dir: J E M Burn **Dir:** Mrs P Burn **Ch Eng:** J C Burn **Co Sec:** J E M Burn
Fleet: 26 - 1 single-deck bus, 22 coach, 2 midibus, 1 midicoach.
Chassis: 1 AEC. 14 DAF. 1 Dennis. 7 Leyland. 1 MAN. 2 Mercedes.
Bodies: 1 Duple. 1 Jonckheere. 1 Marshall. 17 Plaxton. 4 Van Hool. 2 Wadham Stringer.
Ops incl: local bus services, school contracts, excursions & tours, private hire, express, continental tours.
Livery: Blue-Blue/Orange.
Ticket System: Wayfarer.

CRUSADE TRAVEL LTD
THE COACHYARD, PINFOLD LANE, PENKRIDGE ST19 5AS
Tel/Fax: 01785 714124
E-mail: enquiries@crusade-travel.com
Web site: www.crusade-travel.com
Dir: J P McDonnell **Co Sec:** Mrs J McDonnell
Fleet: 6 - 3 coach, 1 midicoach, 2 minibus.
Chassis: 1 Dennis. 2 Mercedes. 1 Toyota. 2 Volvo.
Bodies: 1 Caetano. 1 Jonckheere. 1 Plaxton. 1 Van Hool. 2 Central Conversions.
Ops incl: school contracts, private hire.

D & G COACH AND BUS LTD
MOSSFIELD ROAD, OFF ANCHOR ROAD, LONGTON ST3 5BW
Tel: 01782 332337
Fax: 01782 337864
E-mail: dreeves@dgbus.co.uk
Man Dir: D Reeve **Fleet Eng:** M Johnson
Depot Eng: K Mitchell
Fleet: 49 - 14 coach, 35 midibus.
Chassis: 10 Dennis. 1 Ford. 33 Mercedes. 5 Optare.
Bodies: 7 Alexander. 2 Carlyle. 3 East Lancs. 1 Marshall. 6 Optare. 12 Plaxton. 2 Reeve Burgess. 1 Wadham Stringer. 4 Wright. 11 other.
Ops incl: local bus services, school contracts.
Livery: Cream/Blue
Ticket system: Wayfarer

*D H CARS OF DENSTONE LTD
9 HAWTHORN CLOSE, DENSTONE, UTTOXETER ST14 5HB
Tel: 01889 590819
Fax: 01889 591888
Dir: Donald Handley **Sec:** Alison Williams
Fleet: 2 - 1 coach, 1 midicoach.

Air conditioning	Seat belt-fitted vehicles	Replacement vehicle available
Vehicles suitable for disabled	**R** Recovery service available (not 24 hr)	**T** Toilet-drop facilities available
Coach(es) with galley facilities		Vintage vehicle(s) available
Coach(es) with toilet facilities	**R24** 24hr recovery service	Open top vehicle(s)

Chassis: 1 Bova. 1 Mercedes.
Bodies: 1 Bova. 1 Van Conversions.
Ops incl: private hire
Livery: White

D R M MINIBUS & COACH TRAVEL
43 HIGH STREET, CHASE TERRACE WS7 8LR.
Tel: 01543 410223 (day),
01543 276655 (night).
Fax: 01543 416223.
Prop: D. R. Morgan.
Fleet: 8 - 6 coach, 2 minibus.
Chassis: 3 Bedford. 1 DAF. 1 Ford Transit. 1 Freight Rover. 1 Leyland. 1 Volvo.
Bodies: 3 Duple. 2 Plaxton. 1 LAG.
Ops incl: school contracts, excursions & tours, private hire, express, continental tours.
Livery: White/Silver.

*DUNN-LINE GROUP
See Nottinghamshire

EAGLE TRAVEL
3A NEWPORT ROAD, STAFFORD ST16 2HH
Tel: 01785 220777
Fax: 01785 220666
Recovery: 07931 828762
E-mail: mikegilmore@btconnect.com
Dirs: M W Gilmore, D E Kaminski
Fleet: 11 - 3 coach, 3 midibus, 5 minibus.
Chassis: 1 DAF. 4 LDV. 3 Mercedes. 1 Talbot. 2 Volvo.
Bodies: incl: 3 Alexander. 2 Duple. 1 LAG.
Ops incl: private hire, school contracts.
Livery: Gold eagle/Burgundy and Gold stripes and lettering

FIRST POTTERIES
ADDERLEY GREEN GARAGE, DIVIDY ROAD, STOKE-ON-TRENT ST3 0AJ
Tel: 01782 592500
Fax: 01782 592541
Man Dir: Ken Poole **Comm Dir**: David Astill **Punctuality Man**: Phil Kelsall **Ops Man (Newcastle/Crewe)**: Howard Berry **Ops Man (Birkenhead)**: Colin Pierce

HAPPY DAYS COACHES

GREYFRIARS COACH STATION, GREYFRIARS WAY, STAFFORD ST16 2SH
Tel: 01785 229797.
Fax: 01785 229791
Recovery: 07973 940555
E-mail: info@happydayscoaches.co.uk
Web site: www.happydayscoaches.co.uk
Man Dir: Brian Austin **Dirs**: Neil Austin, Huw Austin, Richard Austin.
Fleet: 32 - 30 coach, 2 minicoach.
Chassis: Leyland. Mercedes. Scania. Volvo.
Bodies: Plaxton. Van Hool.
Ops incl: excursions & tours, private hire, express, continental tours, school contracts.
Livery: White with rising sun motif

HOLLINSHEAD COACHES LTD
WHARF ROAD, BIDDULPH ST8 6AQ.
Tel: 01782 512209.
Man Dir: David Haydon
Fleet: 10 coach
Chassis: 1 DAF. 2 Leyland. 7 Volvo.
Ops incl: school contracts, excursions & tours, private hire

*JOSEPHS MINI COACHES
171 CRACKLEY BANK, CHESTERTON, NEWCASTLE-UNDER-LYME ST5 7AB
Tel: 01782 564944
Dir: Joseph Windsor
Fleet: 2 minicoach.
Chassis/bodies: 2 Mercedes.
Ops incl: private hire
Livery: White/Red

LEONS COACH TRAVEL (STAFFORD) LTD
DOUGLAS HOUSE, TOLLGATE, BEACONSIDE, STAFFORD ST16 3EE
Tel: 01785 244575
Fax: 01785 258444
E-mail: info@leons.co.uk
Web site: www.leons.co.uk
Chmn: L H Douglas **Co Sec**: S Douglas
Dirs: R L Douglas, A O Douglas
Fleet: 21 - 18 coach, 2 midicoach, 1 minicoach.
Chassis: 6 Bova. 3 Mercedes. 8 Scania. 4 Setra.
Bodies: 6 Bova. 3 Irizar. 3 Mercedes. 4 Setra. 5 Van Hool.

MOORLAND BUSES
WESTON SERVICE STATION, WESTON COYNEY ST3 6QB.
Tel: 01782 334202.
Prop: A Titterton.
Ops incl: local bus services
Livery: Blue/White.

PARAGON TRAVEL LTD
THE GARAGE, SPATH ST14 5AE
Tel: 01889 569899
Fax: 01889 563518
Recovery: 01889 569899
E-mail: phil@paragontravel.co.uk
Web site: www.paragontravel.co.uk
Dir: P L Smith **Ops Man**: www.paragontravel.com
Fleet: 14 coach
Chassis: 1 Leyland. 1 Mercedes. 2 Scania. 10 Volvo
Bodies: 1 Alexander. 3 Jonckheere. 4 Plaxton. 6 Van Hool.
Ops incl: local bus services, school contracts, excursions & tours, continental tours, private hire.
Livery: White with Blue/Red lettering.
Ticket system: Setright

PARRYS INTERNATIONAL TOURS LTD
LADYWOOD GREEN, CHESLYN HAY WS6 7QX
Tel: 01922 414576.
Fax: 01922 413416
E-mail: info@parrys-international.co.uk
Web site: www.parrys-international.co.uk
Man Dir: David Parry
Fleet: 11 coach.
Chassis: 11 Neoplan.
Bodies: 11 Neoplan.
Ops incl: excursions & tours
Livery: Red/Gold

*PLANTS LUXURY TRAVEL
167 TEAN ROAD, CHEADLE ST10 1LS
Tel: 01538 753561
Fax: 01538 757025
E-mail: julie.plant@plantsluxurytravel.co.uk
Web site: www.plantsluxurytravel.co.uk
Ptnrs: T J Plant, M P Plant
Fleet: 6 - 1 coach, 2 midicoach, 3 minicoach.
Chassis: 1 LDV. 5 Mercedes.
Bodies: 2 Optare. 2 Onyx. 2 Unvi.
Ops incl: private hire, excursions & tours, school contracts.
Livery: Silver with Burgundy/Gold/Mustard stripes

F PROCTER & SON LTD
DEWSBURY ROAD, FENTON ST4 2HS.
Tel: 01782 846031.
Fax: 01782 744732.
Dirs: R Walker, J Walker.
Fleet: 16
Chassis: 2 Bova. 5 DAF. 1 Iveco. 6 Leyland. 2 Scania.
Ops incl: local bus services, school contracts, excursions & tours, private hire.
Livery: Blue/White
Ticket System: Wayfarer

ROBIN HOOD TRAVEL LTD
HIGHWAY GARAGE, MACCLESFIELD ROAD, LEEK ST13 8PS
Tel: 01538 306618
Fax: 01538 306079
Dir: R Eyre
Fleet: 10 - 9 single-deck bus, 1 minibus.
Chassis: incl: Bova.
Ops incl: private hire
Livery: Green/Gold

*SHIRE TRAVEL INTERNATIONAL LTD
UNIT 4:02 CANNOCK ENTERPRISE CENTRE, WALKERS RISE, HEDNESFORD WS12 0QU
Tel/Fax: 01543 871605
E-mail: hire@shiretravel.co.uk
Web site: www.shiretravel.co.uk
Dir: Robert Garrington **Co Sec**: Michelle Rogers
Fleet: 9 - 5 coach, 2 midicoach,

2 minicoach.
Chassis: 2 Leyland. 6 Mercedes. 1 Scania.
Ops incl: private hire, school contracts, excursions & tours, continental tours.
Livery: White/Red/Gold with England flag

*STANWAYS COACHES
  R24

UNIT 1, THE OLD GASWORKS INDUSTRIAL ESTATE, HARDINGSWOOD ROAD, KIDSGROVE ST7 1EF
Tel: 01782 786232
Fax: 01782 786040
Recovery: 07976 425829
E-mail: stanwayscoaches@yahoo.co.uk
Dirs: David Elliot, Paul Richman, David Finney
Fleet: 9 - 8 coach, 1 midicoach.
Chassis: 2 DAF. 2 Dennis. 1 mercedes. 4 Volvo.
Bodies: 1 Berkhof. 2 Jonckheere. 2 Plaxton. 2 Van Hool. 2 other.
Ops incl: excursions & tours, private hire, continental tours, school contracts.

*STODDARDS LTD

GREENHILL GARAGE, LEEK ROAD, CHEADLE ST10 1JF
Tel: 01538 752253
Fax: 01538 750375
Man Dir: Judith Myatt **Chmn**: Brian Stoddard **Ops/Ch Exec**: Paul Stoddard
Fleet: 6 - 2 single-deck bus, 4 coach.
Chassis: 6 DAF
Bodies: 6 Bova.

Ops incl: excursions & tours, private hire, school contracts.
Livery: Silver/Blue

*SWIFTSURE TRAVEL (BURTON UPON TRENT) LTD

3 GUILD STREET, BURTON-UPON-TRENT DE14 1NA.
Tel: 01283 512974
Fax: 01283 516728
E-mail: info@swiftsure-travel.co.uk
Web site: www.swiftsure-travel.co.uk
Man Dir: Richard Hackett **Co Sec**: Kathy Hackett **Dirs**: Brian Kershaw, Julian Peddle
Fleet: 7 - 4 coach, 2 midicoach, 1 minicoach.
Chassis: 1 Bova. 2 DAF. 1 LDV. 1 Mercedes. 1 Scania. 1 Toyota.
Bodies: 1 Autobus. 1 Bova. 1 Caetano. 1 Irizar. 1 Van Hool. 1 other.
Ops incl: local bus services, excursions & tours, express, private hire, continental tours.
Livery: White/Blue/Green
Ticket system: Setright

*WARRINGTON COACHES
See Derbyshire

WARSTONE MOTORS LTD
THE GARAGE, LANDYWOOD WS6 6AD.
Tel: 01922 414141.
Fleetname: The Green Bus Service.
Dir: G. Martin

Fleet: 25 - 3 double-deck bus, 18 single-deck bus, 4 minibus.
Chassis: Leyland, Mercedes.
Bodies: Alexander. Carlyle. Duple. East Lancs. Massey. Roe.
Ops incl: local bus services.
Livery: Green/Cream.
Ticket System: Wayfarer.

WINTS COACHES

MONTANA, WETTON ROAD, BUTTERTON ST13 7ST
Tel/Fax: 01538 304370
Props: Andrew Wint, Maxine Wint.
Fleet: 10 - 8 coach, 2 minicoach.
Chassis: 1 DAF. 1 Dennis. 6 Mercedes. 1 Optare. 1 Volvo.
Bodies: 1 Bova. 6 Mercedes. 1 Neoplan. 1 Optare. 1 Plaxton.
Ops incl: school contracts, excursions & tours, private hire, continental tours.

J. P. A. WORTH R24
GOLDEN GREEN GARAGE, LONGNOR SK17 0QP.
Tel: 01298 83583.
Fleet: 2 - 1 midicoach, 1 minicoach.
Chassis: 1 Leyland. 1 Mercedes.
Ops incl: school contracts, private hire.

SUFFOLK

*ANGLIAN BUS & COACH LTD

BECCLES BUSINESS PARK, BECCLES NR34 7TH
Tel: 01502 711109
Fax: 01502 711161
E-mail: andrew@angliancoaches.co.uk
Web site: www.anglianbus.co.uk
Fleet: 55 - 5 double-deck bus, 8 single-deck bus, 9 single-deck coach, 33 minibus.
Chassis: 2 Leyland. 36 Mercedes. 9 Optare. 8 Volvo.
Bodies: 1 ECW. 3 East Lancs. 7 Mercedes. 1 Northern Counties. 9 Optare. 31 Plaxton. 1 Van Hool. 2 Wadham Stringer.
Ops incl: local bus services, school contracts.

Livery: Yellow with blue stripes
Ticket System: Wayfarer 3

IAN BALDRY PUBLIC TRANSPORT SERVICES

43 CAGE LANE, FELIXSTOWE IP11 9BJ
Tel: 01394 672344
E-mail: ic.baldry@talk21.com
Man Dir: Ian Baldry

*BEESTONS (HADLEIGH) LTD R24

LONG BESSELS, HADLEIGH, IPSWICH IP7 5DB
Tel: 01473 823243
Fax: 01473 823608

Recovery: 07769 978191
E-mail: info@beestons.co.uk
Web site: www.beestons.co.uk
Man Dir: P Munson **Co Sec**: S Munson
Ops Man: T Munson
Fleet: 39 - 10 double-deck bus, 4 single-deck bus, 16 coach, 1 midibus, 8 minibus.
Chassis: 7 Leyland. 6 Mercedes. 3 Optare. 14 Scania. 9 Volvo.
Bodies: 2 Alexander. 1 ECW. 6 East Lancs. 1 Leyland. 3 Optare. 8 Plaxton. 14 Van Hool. 4 Wright.
Ops incl: local bus services, school contracts, excursions & tours, private hire, continental tours.
Livery: coach - Gold/Black, bus - Blue/White
Ticket System: Wayfarer 3

Air conditioning	Replacement vehicle available
Vehicles suitable for disabled	Toilet-drop facilities available
Coach(es) with galley facilities	Vintage vehicle(s) available
Coach(es) with toilet facilities	Open top vehicle(s)
Seat belt-fitted vehicles	
Recovery service available (not 24 hr)	
R24 24hr recovery service	

BURTONS COACHES LIMITED

DUDDERY HILL, HAVERHILL CB9 8DR
Tel: 01440 420512
Fax: 01440 713287
E-mail: hire@burtons-bus.co.uk
Web site: www.burtoncoaches.com
Fleetname: Burtons
Chmn: Stephen Telling **Man Dir**: Paul Cooper **Fleet Eng**: Steve Legate
Fleet: 66 - 9 double-deck bus, 16 single-deck bus, 30 coach, 10 midibus, 1 midicoach.
Chassis: 3 Bova. 16 Dennis. 1 Iveco. 3 Leyland. 10 Mercedes. 33 Volvo.
Bodies: 5 Alexander. 1 Beulas. 3 Bova. 15 Caetano. 3 ECW. 3 East Lancs. 36 Plaxton
Ops incl: local bus services, school contracts, excursions & tours, private hire, express, continental tours.
Livery: Blue/Yellow on white base.
Ticket system: Almex A90

H C CHAMBERS & SON LTD

HIGH STREET, BURES CO8 5AB
Tel: 01787 227233
Fax: 01787 227042
Recovery: 07770 886834
E-mail: info@chamberscoaches.co.uk
Web site: www.chamberscoaches.co.uk
Fleet: 25 - 13 double-deck bus, 2 single-deck bus, 7 coach, 3 minibus
Chassis: 3 DAF. 4 Leyland. 2 MAN. 3 Mercedes. 13 Volvo.
Bodies: 5 Alexander. 4 East Lancs. 2 Jonckheere. 4 Marshall. 4 Northern Counties. 2 Plaxton. 4 Van Hool.
Ops incl: local bus services, excursions & tours, private hire.
Livery: Red
Ticket System: Wayfarer

*D-WAY TRAVEL

GREENWAYS, THE STREET, EARSHAM, BUNGAY NR35 2TZ
Tel: 01986 895375
Fax: 01986 891110
E-mail: david@dwaytravel.com
Web site: www.dwaytravel.com
Prop: David Thompson
Fleet: 8 - 6 coach, 1 minibus, 1 midicoach.
Chassis: 1 Ford Transit. 6 MAN. 1 Mercedes.
Bodies: incl: 6 MAN. 1 Robin Hood.
Ops incl: school contracts, excursions & tours, private hire.

*FARELINE BUS & COACH SERVICES

OLD ROSES, SYLEHAM ROAD, WINGFIELD, EYE IP21 5RF
Tel: 01379 668151
Mobile: 07850 940445
Prop: Jeff Morss
Fleet: 1 coach
Chassis: 1 Bedford.
Body: 1 Plaxton
Ops incl: local bus services, school contracts, excursions & tours, private hire.
Livery: Blue/Cream

Ticket System: Setright Mk 3

*FORGET-ME-NOT (TRAVEL) LTD

CHAPEL ROAD, OTLEY, IPSWICH IP6 9NT
Tel: 01473 890268
Fax: 01473 890748
E-mail: sales@forgetmenot-travel.co.uk
Web site: www.forgetmenottravel.co.uk
Fleetname: Soames
Dirs: A F Soames, Mrs M A Soames, A M Soames **Ch Eng**: A M Soames
Fleet: 17 - 16 coach, 1 midicoach.
Chassis: 1 Mercedes. 16 Volvo.
Bodies: 1 Esker. 1 Jonckheere. 13 Plaxton. 2 Van Hool.
Ops incl: private hire, school contracts.
Livery: three-tone Blue

*GALLOWAY EUROPEAN COACHLINES

DENTERS HILL, MENDLESHAM IP14 5RR
Tel: 01449 766323
Fax: 01449 766241
E-mail: coach@galloway-travel.co.uk
Man Dirs: David Cattermole **Traf man**: G Calver
Fleet: 35 - 1 double-deck bus, 1 single-deck bus, 27 coach, 4 minicoach, 2 minibus.
Chassis: 1 Bedford. 24 DAF. 1 Dennis. 1 Iveco. 1 Leyland. 6 Mercedes. 1 Scania.
Bodies: 1 Autobus. 1 Beulas. 1 ECW. 3 Ikarus. 2 Optare. 7 Plaxton. 1 UVG. 19 Van Hool.
Ops incl: local bus services, school contracts, excursions & tours, private hire, express, continental tours.
Livery: White
Ticket System: Setright/Wayfarer.

*GEMINI TRAVEL

UNIT 20, STERLING COMPLEX, FARTHING ROAD, IPSWICH IP1 5AP
Tel: 01473 462721
Fax: 01473 462731
E-mail: info@geminiofipswich.co.uk
Web site: www.geminiofipswich.co.uk
Dir: Ed Nicholls **Co Sec**: Keith Nicholls
Traff Man: Stacey Middlemas **Dir**: Neville Jephcote
Fleet: 10 - 5 single-deck bus, 4 midicoach, 1 minibus
Chassis: 1 BMC. 1 LDV. 8 Mercedes.
Bodies: 1 BMC. 3 Optare. 3 Plaxton. 2 Reeve Burgess
Ops incl: local bus services, excursions & tours, private hire, school contracts

*HARLEQUIN TRAVEL

77 LANERCOST WAY, IPSWICH IP2 9DP
Tel: 01473 407408
E-mail: paul.lewis80@ntlworld.com
Web site: www.harlequin-travel.co.uk
Dirs: P D Lewis, Mrs L M Lewis
Fleet: 3 - 2 midicoach, 1 minibus.
Chassis: 2 Mercedes. 1 Peugeot
Bodies: incl: 1 Autobus. 1 Plaxton.
Ops incl: school contracts, private hire

Livery: Maroon/White

*IPSWICH BUSES LTD

7 CONSTANTINE ROAD, IPSWICH IP1 2DL.
Tel: 01473 232600
Fax: 01473 232062
E-mail: info@ipswichbuses.co.uk
Web site: www.ipswichbuses.co.uk
Fleet: 95 - 28 double-deck bus, 1 open-top bus, 48 single-deck bus, 18 midibus.
Chassis: 16 DAF. 23 Dennis. 16 Leyland. 34 Optare. 3 Scania. 3 Volvo.
Bodies: 3 Alexander. 38 East Lancs. 10 Leyland. 43Optare. 1 Roe.
Ops incl: local bus services, school contracts, excursions & tours, private hire.
Livery: Green/White
Ticket System: Wayfarer TGX150

*LAMBERT'S COACHES (BECCLES) LTD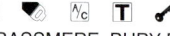

UNIT 4A, MOOR BUSINESS PARK, BECCLES NR34 7TQ
Tel: 01502 717579
Fax: 01502 711209
E-mail: office@lambertscoaches.co.uk
Web site: www.lambertscoaches.co.uk
Man Dir: David Reade
Fleet: 11 coach.
Chassis: 1 Bedford. 4 DAF. 2 Leyland. 4 Volvo.
Bodies: 7 Plaxton. 4 Van Hool.
Ops incl: private hire, school contracts.
Livery: Blue/White

*MIL-KEN TRAVEL LTD

GRASSMERE, BURY ROAD, KENTFORD, NEWMARKET CB8 7PZ
Tel: 01638 750201
Fax: 01638 750439
E-mail: milkenkentford@btconnect.com
Man: Mark Rogers **Man Dir**: Jason Miller
Fleet Man: Ian Martin
Fleet: 38 - 36 coach, 2 minibus.
Chassis: 2 Bedford. 6 DAF. 5 Dennis. 2 LDV. 23 Volvo.
Bodies: 3 Berkhof. 4 Duple. 3 Jonckheere. 23 Plaxton. 1 Willowbrook. 2 other.
Ops incl: private hire, excursions & tours, continental tours, school contracts.

MINIBUS & COACH HIRE

LINGS FARM, BLACKSMITHS LANE, FORWARD GREEN, EARL STONHAM IP14 5ET.
Tel: 01449 711117.
Fax: 01449 711977.
Owner: Mrs L. J. Eustace.
Fleet: 11 - 3 coach, 8 minibus.
Chassis: 3 Bedford, 1 Iveco. 6 LDV. 1 Nissan.
Bodies: Plaxton.
Ops incl: local bus services, school contracts, excursions & tours, private hire.

MULLEYS MOTORWAYS LTD

STOW ROAD, IXWORTH IP31 2JB.
Tel: 01359 230234
Fax: 01359 232451

E-mail: enquiries@mulleys.co.uk
Web site: www. mulleys.co.uk
Dir/Co Sec: Jayne D Munson **Dir**: David J Munson
Fleet: 39 - 4 double-deck bus, 26 coach, 2 double-deck coach, 3 midicoach, 4 midibus.
Chassis: 4 Iveco. 8 Leyland. 4 Mercedes. 7 Scania. 4 Setra. 12 Volvo.
Bodies: 1 Alexander. 3 Beulas. 2 Duple. 4 ECW. 11 Jonckheere. 11 Plaxton. 4 Setra. 6 Van Hool. 2 Indcar. 1 Euro Coach.
Ops incl: local bus services, school contracts, excursions & tours, private hire.
Livery: Orange/Silver.
Ticket System: Wayfarer.

*B R SHREEVE & SONS LTD

BELLE COACHES, RIVERSIDE ROAD, LOWESTOFT NR33 0TU
Tel: 01502 564384
Fax: 01502 532009

E-mail: info@bellecoaches.co.uk
Web site: www.bellecoaches.co.uk
Fleetname: Belle Coaches.
Dirs: Ken Shreeve, Robert Shreeve, John Shreeve **Co Sec**: Sue Speed **Tran Man**: Alan White **Tours Man**: David Dickinson
Fleet: 41 - 38 coach, 3 midicoach
Chassis: 2 Bedford. 4 DAF. 3 MAN. 2 Mercedes. 11 Scania. 10 Setra. 1 Toyota. 8 Volvo.
Bodies: 3 Berkhof. 1 Caetano. 1 Duple. 11 Plaxton. 13 Setra. 11 Van Hool. 1 other.
Ops incl: local bus services, school contracts, excursions & tours, private hire, continental tours.
Livery: Blue/Yellow

SQUIRRELL'S COACHES

OLD MILL GARAGE, HITCHAM, IPSWICH IP7 7NF.
Tel/Fax: 01449 740582.
Dir: Richard Squirrell.

Fleet: 7 - 5 coach, 2 midicoach.
Chassis: 2 Leyland. 1 MAN. 2 Mercedes. 2 Volvo.
Bodies: 1 Duple. 1 Mercedes. 2 Plaxton. 1 Reeve Burgess. 4 Van Hool.
Ops incl: local bus services, school contracts, private hire.
Livery: Silver/Blue.
Ticket System: Setright.

THOMPSON'S REMOVALS & COACH HIRE

DORMICK HOUSE, NEW STREET, FRAMLINGHAM IP13 9RF.
Tel: 01728 723403.
Prop: M. A. Rogers, D. J. Rogers (Sec).
Fleet: 3 coach.
Chassis: 1 Ford. 2 Volvo.
Bodies: 1 Duple. 2 Jonckheere.
Ops incl: local bus services, excursions & tours, private hire, continental tours.
Livery: Blue/White.

SURREY

*ANNTONY MINIBUSES

33 GASSIOT WAY, SUTTON SM1 3AZ
Tel: 020 8715 2517
Prop: D Pickett
Fleet: 1 minibus
Ops incl: excursions & tours

ARRIVA SURREY & WEST SUSSEX

FRIARY BUS STATION, GUILDFORD GU1 4YP
Tel: 01483 505693
Fleetname: Arriva serving Guildford & West Surrey.
Acting Man Dir: Kevin Hawkins
Eng Dir: I. Tarran. **Fin Dir**: Ms E. Limm.
Gen Man: R. Thornton.
Fleet: 59 - 3 double-deck bus, 56 single-deck bus.
Chassis: 29 DAF. 39 Dennis.
Bodies: East Lancs. Plaxton. Wright.
Ops incl: local bus services.
Livery: Aquamarine and Stone.
Ticket System: Wayfarer 3

*BANSTEAD COACHES LTD

1 SHRUBLAND ROAD, BANSTEAD SM7 2ES.
Tel: 01737 354322
Fax: 01737 371090
Recovery: 01737 354322
E-mail: sales@bansteadcoaches.co.uk
Web site: www.bansteadcoaches.co.uk

Man Dir: D C Haynes **Dir/Co Sec**: Mrs C J Haynes **Dir**: M C Haynes.
Fleet: coach.
Chassis: Bedford. Dennis. Mercedes.
Bodies: Berkhof. Mercedes. Plaxton.
Ops incl: school contracts, private hire.
Livery: Pink/White

BUSES4U

EAST SURREY RURAL TRANSPORT PARTNERSHIP, TANDRIDGE DISTRICT COUNCIL, STATION ROAD EAST, OXTED RH8 0BT
Tel: 01730 815518
Web site: www.buses4u.org.uk

*CALL-A-COACH

CAPRI HOUSE, WALTON-ON-THAMES KT12 2LY
Tel: 01932 223838
Fax: 01932 269109
Web-site: call-a-coach.org, call-a-coach.org.uk, call-a-coach.net
E-mail: call-a-coach@aol.com
Owner: Arthur Freakes **Tran Man**: Clive Bennett, L Freakes
Fleet: 9 - 3 coach, 1 midicoach, 5 minicoach.
Chassis: 3 DAF. 5 LDV. 1 Mercedes.
Ops incl: school contracts, excursions & tours, private hire.

CARS INTERNATIONAL A. C. T.

4 WYCHWOOD CLOSE, ASH GU12 6RA.
Tel: 01252 328774.
Fax: 01252 332337.
Prop: G. Hawkins. **Traf Man**: J. Baker.
Fleet: 3 coach.
Chassis: 1 Leyland. 2 Setra.
Bodies: 1 Leyland. 2 Setra.
Ops incl: excursions & tours, private hire, continental tours, school contracts.

CENTRA PASSENGER SERVICES

UNIT 4B, CANAL BRIDGE INDUSTRIAL ESTATE, BYFLEET ROAD, NEW HAW KT15 3JE
Tel: 01932 859 250
Ops incl: private hire
(Subsidiary of Central Parking Systems Of UK Ltd)

*CHEAM COACHES

11 FREDERICK CLOSE, CHEAM SM1 2HY
Tel: 01372 742527
Fax: 01372 742528
E-mail: cheamco@aol.com
Web site: www.cheamcoaches.co.uk
Props: Michael Mower, Lise Cyr-Mower
Fleet: 6 - 2 coach, 4 minibus.
Chassis: 4 Mercedes. 1 Setra. 1 Volvo.
Bodies: 1 Jonckheere. 4 Mercedes. 1 Setra.

A/c	Air conditioning	
♿	Vehicles suitable for disabled	
🍴	Coach(es) with galley facilities	
wc	Coach(es) with toilet facilities	
🔻	Seat belt-fitted vehicles	
R	Recovery service available (not 24 hr)	
R24	24hr recovery service	
✓	Replacement vehicle available	
T	Toilet-drop facilities available	
	Vintage vehicle(s) available	
	Open top vehicle(s)	

Ops incl: private hire, school contracts

*CHIVERS COACHES LTD

13A ROSS PARADE, WALLINGTON SM6 8QG
Tel: 020 8647 6648
Fax: 020 8647 6649
E-mail: chivlyn@aol.com
Dirs: Miss M Chivers, Mrs L Lucas, Mrs P Chivers
Fleet: 4 - 2 coach, 1 midicoach, 1 minibus.
Chassis: 1 LDV. 1 Mercedes. 2 Volvo.
Bodies: 1 Leyland. 2 Van Hool. 1 other.
Ops incl: private hire, school contracts.
Livery: White with blue graphics

COUNTRYLINER COACH HIRE LTD

GB HOUSE, WESTFIELD ROAD, GUILDFORD GU1 1RR
Tel: 01483 506919
Fax: 01483 306395
E-mail: info@countryliner-coaches.com
Web site: www.countryliner-coaches.co.uk
Dirs: R Hodgetts, R Belcher, B King **Gen Man**: N Natcher **Ops Mans**: M Lambley, M Chadwick, J Rees
Fleet: 40 - 5 double-deck bus, 21 single-deck bus, 10 coach, 2 double-deck coach, 1 midibus, 1 midicoach.
Chassis: 2 DAF. 19 Dennis. 6 Leyland. 5 Mercedes. 1 Neoplan. 2 Optare. 5 Volvo.
Bodies: 1 Alexander. 1 Caetano. 1 Duple. 5 ECW. 1 Ikarus. 1 Neoplan. 2 Optare. 21 Plaxton. 2 Van Hool. 5 other.
Ops incl: local bus services, school contracts, excursions & tours, private hire.
Livery: Green/White.
Ticket System: Wayfarer 2

*CRUISERS LTD

UNIT M, KINGSFIELD BUSINESS CENTRE, REDHILL RH1 4DP
Tel: 01737 770036
Fax: 01737 770046
E-mail: info@cruisersltd.co.uk
Web site: www.cruisersltd.co.uk
Dir: M Walter
Fleet: 35 - 9 coach, 3 midibus, 3 minicoach, 20 minibus.
Chassis: Dennis, Ford Transit, Iveco, LDV, Mercedes, Renault, Volvo.
Bodies: Optare, Plaxton, UVG, Wadham Stringer
Ops incl: local bus services, private hire.
Livery: metallic various

*EPSOM COACHES GROUP

BLENHEIM ROAD, EPSOM KT19 9AF
Tel: 01372 731700
Fax: 01372 731740
Recovery: 01372 731727
E-mail: enquiries@epsomcoaches.com
Web site: www.epsomcoaches.com
Fleetname: Epsom Coaches, Quality Line
Chmn: R B Richmond **Man Dir**: A J Richmond **Comm Dir**: S R Whiteway **Ch Eng**: P Mabbott **Bus Services Man**: G Wernham **Ops Mans**: P Minnette, J Ball
Fleet: 73 - 16 single-deck bus, 20 coach, 35 midibus, 1 minicoach.
Chassis: 27 Dennis. 1 Iveco. 11 Mercedes. 21 Optare. 15 Setra. 3 Volvo. 1 VW
Bodies: incl: 5 East Lancs. 3 Jonckheere.
Ops incl: local bus services, excursions & tours, private hire, express, continental tours.
Livery: Coach: Red/Cream. Bus: Red
Ticket system: Prestige

*FARNHAM COACHES

ODIHAM ROAD, FARNHAM GU10 5AE
Tel: 01252 724010
Fax: 01252 724350
Dirs: Mrs E G Newman, Mrs C Newman, D K Newman, M G Newman, A J Halliday
Ops Man: C S West
Fleet: 11 coach
Chassis: 2 MAN. 4 Setra. 5 Volvo.
Bodies: 5 Plaxton. 4 Setra. 2 Neoplan.
Ops incl: excursions & tours, private hire, school contracts, continental tours.
Livery: Red/Cream

FERNLEAF COACHES

7 MARTIN GROVE, MORDEN SM4 5AJ.
Tel: 020 8715 1839.
Fax: 020 8543 0722.
Owners: K. J. Leigh, L. M. Leigh.
Fleet: 4 - 2 coach, 2 minicoach.
Ops incl: excursions & tours, private hire, continental tours.

*G J TRAVEL LTD

STATION APPROACH, GUILDFORD STREET, CHERTSEY KT16 9BQ
Tel: 01932 560196
Fax: 01460 66967
Dirs: S G Adams, Mrs B Adams.
Fleet: 6 - 2 minibus, 4 midicoach.
Chassis/bodies: 1 LDV. 5 Mercedes.
Ops incl: school contracts, private hire.

GALES COACHES LTD

SPRINGFARM ROAD, CAMELSDALE, HASLEMERE GU27 3RH.
Tel: 01428 643837.
Fax: 01428 658809.
Dir: J. P. Pirard. **Co Sec**: R. L. Pirard.
Fleet: 5 - 3 coach, 2 midicoach.
Chassis: 1 Mercedes. 1 Toyota. 3 Volvo.
Bodies: 1 Caetano. 3 Jonckheere. 1 Plaxton.
Ops incl: private hire, school contracts.
Livery: White/Red/Gold.

*HARDINGS COACHES

WELLWOOD, WELLHOUSE LANE, BETCHWORTH RH3 7HH
Tel: 01737 842103
Fax: 01737 842831
Dirs: D Harding, S Harding
Fleet: 12 - 6 coach, 3 midicoach. 3 minicoach.
Chassis: 1 MAN. 5 Mercedes. 6 Volvo.
Bodies: 2 Berkhof. 1 Autobus. 1 Caetano. 2 Esker. 2 Jonckheere. 1 Optare. 3 Plaxton.
Ops incl: private hire
Livery: White/Red/Orange

HARWOOD COACHES

51 ELLESMERE ROAD, WEYBRIDGE KT13 0HW.
Tel: 01932 842073, 227272.
Prop: G. A. Harwood.
Fleet: 5 coach.
Chassis: 2 Bedford. 3 Volvo.
Bodies: 2 Duple. 3 Van Hool.
Ops incl: private hire.
Livery: Beige/Red/Brown.

HILLS

129 BURWOOD ROAD, HERSHAM KT12 4AN
Tel: 01932 254795
Fax: 01932 222671
Dir: D Hill
Fleet: 6 - 4 coach, 1 minicoach, 1 minibus.
Chassis: 1 DAF. 1 Iveco. 1 Mercedes. 1 Toyota. 2 Volvo.
Bodies: 1 Beulas 1 Bova 1 Caetano 1 Mercedes
Ops incl: school contracts, private hire

K-VALLEY MINI-COACHES

WOODPECKERS, CARLTON ROAD, WOKING GU21 4HE.
Tel: 01483 769462.
Mobile: 0771 368 1207.
Fax: 01483 769462.
Prop: F. E. Trotman.
Fleet: 1 minibus.
Chassis/body: DAF.
Ops incl: private hire.

MAYDAY TRAVEL

UNIT 8, MILL LANE TRADING ESTATE, MILL LANE, CROYDON CR0 4AA
Tel: 020 8680 5111
Web site: www.coachhirelondon.co.uk
Fleet: coach, midibus, minibus.
Ops incl: private hire, excursions & tours.
Livery: White/Blue

M&E COACHES

11 VAUX CRESCENT, HERSHAM KT12 4HE.
Tel: 01932 244664.
Prop/Gen Man: M. W. Oram.
Sec: Mrs A. E. Oram.
Fleet: 3 coach.
Chassis: 1 MAN. 2 Mercedes.
Ops incl: school contracts, excursions & tours, private hire.
Livery: Blue/White.

MERTON COMMUNITY TRANSPORT

JUSTIN PLAZA 3, SUITE 3, LONDON ROAD, MITCHAM CR4 4BE
Tel: 020 8648 7727
E-mail: mertonct@ukonline.co.uk

PICKERING COACHES

12 HAYSBRIDGE COTTAGES, WHITE WOOD LANE, SOUTH GODSTONE RH9 8JN.
Tel/Fax: 01342 843731.
Props: R. Pickering, Ms D. Pickering.
Fleet: 5 coach.
Chassis: Volvo.
Bodies: 2 Duple. 1 Jonckheere. 2 Plaxton.
Ops incl: private hire, school contracts.

RANGER TRAVEL
PO BOX 805, SOUTH CROYDON CR8 2XY.
Tel: 020 8673 0077.
Fleet: 5 - 3 coach, 1 midibus, 1 minibus.
Chassis: 1 Bedford. 1 DAF. 1 LDV. 1 MCW. 1 Volvo.
Bodies: 1 Leicester. 1 MCW. 2 Plaxton. 1 Van Hool.
Ops incl: private hire.
Livery: White

*SAFEGUARD COACHES LTD

RIDGEMOUNT GARAGE, GUILDFORD PARK ROAD, GUILDFORD GU2 7TH
Tel: 01483 561103
Fax: 01483 455865
E-mail: sales@safeguardcoaches.co.uk
Web site: www.safeguardcoaches.co.uk
Dirs: Mrs E G Newman, Mrs C Newman, D K Newman, M G Newman, A J Halliday
Ops Man: C S West
Fleet: 24 - 7 single-deck bus, 15 coach, 2 midicoach.
Chassis: 1 AEC. 6 Dennis. 3 Mercedes. 4 Optare. 10 Volvo.
Bodies: 1 Carlyle. 1 Hispano. 1 Northern Counties. 4 Optare. 12 Plaxton. 4 Van Hool. 1 other.
Ops incl: local bus services, school contracts, private hire, excursions & tours, continental tours.
Livery: Red/Cream.
Ticket System: Almex A90

*SKINNERS OF OXTED

15 BARROW GREEN ROAD, OXTED RH8 0NJ
Tel: 01883 713633
Fax: 01883 730079
E-mail: info@skinnerstravel.co.uk
Web site: www.skinnerstravel.co.uk
Dirs: Stephen Skinner, Deborah Skinner.
Fleet: 14 - 11 coach, 1 midicoach, 2 minicoach.
Chassis: 2 Dennis. 1 MCW. 2 Mercedes.
1 Neoplan. 6 Setra. 2 Volvo.
Bodies: 2 Duple. 1 Neoplan. 2 Optare. 2 Plaxton. 1 Reeve Burgess. 6 Setra.
Ops incl: excursions & tours, private hire, school contracts, continental tours.

*SOUTH COAST MOTOR SERVICES LTD

PO BOX 1029, CROYDON CR9 6AA
Tel: 0701 0708 767
Fax: 0701 0709 767
E-mail: enquiries@southcoastmotorservices.co.uk
Web site: www.southcoastmotorservices.co.uk
Dirs: Peter Staveley, Alan Elliott, Tim Baker, Graham Burtenshaw, Tim Robbins
Fleet: 3 - 1 double-deck, 1 open-top bus, 1 coach
Chassis: 3 Leyland
Ops incl: private hire, excursions & tours
Livery: Green/Cream

SUNRAY TRAVEL LTD

79 ASHLEY RD, EPSOM KT18 5BN
Tel: 01372 740400
Web site: www.sunraytravel.co.uk
Dir: Noel Millier
Fleet: 7 coach
Chassis: 3 Dennis. 1 Leyland. 3 Volvo
Bodies: include: 2 Carlyle. 4 Plaxton
Ops incl: local bus services, school contracts, excursions & tours, private hire, continental tours.
Livery: Blue with yellow/orange/red sun rays

*SURELINE COACHES

UNIT 8, MARTLANDS INDUSTRIAL ESTATE, SMARTS HEATH LANE, MAYFORD GU22 0RQ
Tel: 01483 234649
Fax: 01483 236464
E-mail: sureline@btclick.com
Prop: J McCracken
Fleet: 12 - 3 single-deck bus, 7 coach, 2 minibus.
Chassis: 7 Bova. 2 Dennis. 1 Iveco. 2 Mercedes.
Bodies: 7 Bova. 1 Marshall/MCV. 1 Plaxton. 2 Reeve Burgess.
Ops incl: local bus services, excursions & tours, private hire, school contracts, continental tours.
Livery: White
Ticket system: Wayfarer Saver

*SUTTON COMMUNITY TRANSPORT

HALLMEAD DAY CENTRE, ANTON CRESCENT, COLLINGWOOD ROAD, SUTTON SM1 2NT
Tel: 020 8644 6001
Fax: 020 8644 2247
Ch Exec: Turner Duff **Ops Man**: Malcolm Sailing **Chmn**: P Hewitt **Dirs**: D Mason, P Bloxham, Judith Pratt, Tony Pattison, Inger Wilson, Pam Wilson, Lal Hussain MBE
Fleet: 15 minibus.
Chassis/bodies: Ford Transit. Iveco. VW. LDV. Mercedes.
Ops incl: school contracts, excursions & tours, private hire.
Livery: White with purple logo

*TELLINGS GOLDEN MILLER COACHES LTD
See Middlesex

*EDWARD THOMAS & SON

442 CHESSINGTON ROAD, WEST EWELL KT19 9EJ
Tel: 020 8397 4276
Fax: 020 8397 5276
E-mail: edwardthomasandson@btconnect.com
Owner: Ivan Thomas **Ch Eng**: Manny Seager **Ops Man**: Neil Seager
Acc: Sharman Grey
Fleet: 24 - 4 double-deck bus, 20 coach
Chassis: Leyland. Volvo.
Ops incl: local bus services, school contracts, private hire.
Livery: Green/Cream

TRINGWOOD TRAVEL

TRINGWOOD, 28 NEW ZEALAND AVENUE, WALTON ON THAMES KT12 1PT
Tel: 01932 242900.
Fax: 01932 252829.
E-mail: tringwood.travel@virgin.net
Props: Jean Bell
Fleet: 1 minicoach.
Chassis: 1 Mercedes
Ops incl: excursions & tours, private hire.
Livery: White/Green/Gold.

W H MOTORS
See West Sussex.

*WESTERHAM COACHES

15 BARROW GREEN ROAD, OXTED RH8 ONJ
Tel: 01883 713633
Fax: 01883 730079
Ptnrs: Stephen Skinner, Deborah Skinner.
Fleet: 14 - 11 coach, 1 midicoach, 2 minicoach.
Chassis: 2 Dennis. 1 MCW. 2 Mercedes. 1 Neoplan. 6 Setra. 2 Volvo.
Bodies: 2 Duple. 1 Neoplan. 2 Optare. 2 Plaxton. 1 Reeve Burgess. 6 Setra.
Ops incl: excursions & tours, private hire, school contracts, continental tours.

- Air conditioning
- Vehicles suitable for disabled
- Coach(es) with galley facilities
- Coach(es) with toilet facilities
- Seat belt-fitted vehicles
- Recovery service available (not 24 hr)
- R24 24hr recovery service
- Replacement vehicle available
- Toilet-drop facilities available
- Vintage vehicle(s) available
- Open top vehicle(s)

*WILTAX BUSES LTD

UNIT 4A, CANAL BRIDGE INDUSTRIAL ESTATE, BYFLEET ROAD, ADDLESTONE KT15 3JE
Tel: 01932 856655
Fax: 01932 858101
E-mail: info@wiltaxbuses.com
Web site: www.wiltaxbuses.com
Dir: L Bainbridge **Gen Man**: M Gilbert **Ops Man**: N Glaskin
Fleet: 12 - 8 double-deck bus, 1 single-deck bus, 2 coach, 1 open-top bus.
Chassis: 1 DAF. 1 MAN. 5 MCW. 1 Volvo.
Bodies: incl: 4 Leyland
Ops incl: local bus services, school contracts, private hire, excursions & tours
Livery: Poppy Red
Ticket System: Almex A90/Wayfarer

TYNE & WEAR

*A & J COACHES OF WASHINGTON CO LTD

6 SKIRLAW CLOSE, GLEBE VILLAGE, WASHINGTON NE38 7RE
Tel: 0191 417 2564
Fax: 0191 415 4672
E-mail: jean@ajcoaches.fsnet.co.uk
Dir: Ian Ashman **Co Sec**: Jean Ashman
Fleet: 1 coach
Chassis: 1 Volvo
Bodies: 1 Plaxton
Ops incl: school contracts, private hire.
Livery: White/Blue

*A LINE COACHES
UNIT 1, PELAW INDUSTRIAL ESTATE, GATESHEAD NE10 0UW
Tel/Fax: 0191 495 2424
E-mail: les@a-linecoaches.co.uk
Web site: www.a-linecoaches.co.uk
Ptnrs: D C Annis, L B Annis **Sec**: Mrs S Reay **Wkshp**: B Jennings, S King
Fleet: 8 - 2 single-deck bus, 2 coach, 4 midibus.
Chassis: 1 DAF. 4 Dennis. 1 Leyland. 1 Mercedes. 1 Optare.
Bodies: 1 Duple. 1 Leyland. 1 Mellor. 1 Optare. 2 Plaxton. 1 Van Hool. 1 Wright.
Ops incl: local bus services, school contracts, excursions & tours, private hire, continental tours.
Livery: Red/White
Ticket System: AES 2000

ALTONA COACH SERVICES & TRAVEL CONSULTANT
UNIT K4, SKILLION BUSINESS CENTRE, GREEN LANE, FELLING NE10 0QW.
Tel: 0191 469 2193.
Fax: 0191 469 3025.
Fleetname: Altona Travel.
Prop: A. C. Hunter. **Ops Man**: A. I. Hunter.
Office Man: R. Dudding.
Fleet: 9 - 5 coach, 2 midicoach, 2 minicoach.
Chassis: 1 DAF. 1 Dennis. 2 Mercedes. 1 Toyota. 3 Volvo.
Bodies: 2 Caetano. 2 Duple. 1 LAG.

2 Plaxton. 1 Robin Hood. 1 Bus Craft Impala.
Ops incl: excursions & tours, private hire, continental tours.
Livery: Two tone Blue and Orange.

ARRIVA NORTH EAST
ADMIRAL WAY, DOXFORD INTERNATIONAL BUSINESS PARK, SUNDERLAND SR3 3XP
Tel: 0191 520 4200
Fax: 0191 520 4222
Web site: www.arriva.co.uk
Man Dir: S. L. Noble **Eng Dir**: J Greaves
Fin Dir: Mrs S Richardson **Ops Dir**: I McInroy **Comm Dir**: Mrs L Esnouf
Fleet: 650 - 117 double-deck bus, 326 single-deck bus, 8 coach, 199 minibus.
Chassis: DAF. Dennis. Iveco. Leyland. MCW. MAN. Mercedes. Optare. Scania. Transbus. Volvo.
Bodies: Alexander. ECW. East Lancs. Ikarus. Leyland. MCW. Mercedes. Northern Counties. Optare. Plaxton. Transbus. Van Hool. Wright.
Ops incl: local bus services, school contracts, private hire, express.
Livery: Aquamarine/Stone
Ticket System: Wayfarer 3

*ROWLANDS GILL TAXIS & COACHES

1 THORNLEY VIEW, ROWLANDS GILL NE39 1QL
Tel: 01207 543118
Prop: David Murphy
Fleet: 7 - 2 midibus, 2 minibus, 1 midicoach, 2 minicoach.
Chassis: 5 Ford Transit. 1 LDV. 1 Mercedes.
Ops incl: shool contracts, private hire

*CAMPBELLS COACHES
37 MORPETH AVENUE, SOUTH SHIELDS NE34 0SF
Tel: 0191 455 4295
Prop: Gordon Campbell
Fleet: 1 coach
Chassis: 1 Bedford
Body: 1 Duple
Ops incl: excursions & tours, private hire

*COACHLINERS OF TYNESIDE

16 BRANDLING COURT, SOUTH SHIELDS NE34 8PA
Tel/Fax: 0191 427 1515
Prop: John Dorothy
Fleet: 2 midicoach
Chassis: 2 Mercedes.
Bodies: 2 Plaxton.
Ops incl: school contracts, excursions & tours, private hire.
Livery: White with red stripes

*HENRY COOPER COACHES

LANE END GARAGE, ANNITSFORD NE23 7BD
Tel: 0191 250 0260
Fax: 0191 250 1820
E-mail: ggpam@tiscali.co.uk
Ptnrs: Graham Greaves
Fleet: 8 - 1 single-deck bus, 7 coach
Chassis: 1 Leyland. 7 Volvo.
Ops incl: school contracts, private hire, excursions & tours, continental tours.

DERWENT COACHES LTD
MORRISON ROAD, ANNFIELD PLAIN DH9 7RX
Tel: 0191 488 7248.
Fax: 01207 281333.
E-mail: derwentc@aol.com
Man Dir: I. Shipley. **Dir**: A. Fox.
Comm Exec: D. Allan.
Garage Foreman: B. Thurgood.
Fleet: 10 coach.
Chassis: Volvo.
Bodies: 5 Plaxton. 5 Van Hool.
Ops incl: local bus services, school contracts, excursions & tours, private hire, express, continental tours.
Livery: White, Red & Blue.
Ticket System: Almex.

ERB SERVICES LTD

HANNINGTON PLACE, BYKER, NEWCASTLE UPON TYNE NE6 1JU
Tel: 0191 224 0002
Fax: 0191 224 0030
Man Dir: Edmund Brown(snr)

Dirs: Edmund Brown(jnr), David Brown
Fleet: 12 - 2 coach, 1 midibus, 3 midicoach, 6 minibus
Chassis: 10 Mercedes. 2 Optare.1 Volvo
Bodies: 10 Mercedes. 2 Optare. 1 Van Hool.
Ops incl: school contracts, excursions & tours, private hire
Livery: White/Maroon

*GO NORTH EAST
117 QUEEN STREET, GATESHEAD NE8 2UA
Tel: 0191 420 5050
Fax: 0191 420 0225
E-mail: customerservices@gonortheast.co.uk
Web site: www.simplygo.co.uk
Man Dir: Peter Huntley **Ops Dir**: K Carr
Fin Dir: G C McPherson
Comm Dir: M P Harris
Fleet: 716 - 170 double-deck bus, 222 single-deck bus, 18 coach, 4 articulated bus, 147 midibus, 155 minibus.
Chassis: 110 DAF. 260 Dennis. 25 Leyland. 5 MCW. 38 Optare. 87 Scania. 26 Transbus. 165 Volvo.
Bodies: 28 Alexander. 13 Caetano. 2 ECW. 30 East Lancs. 49 Marshall/MCV. 5 MCW. 94 Northern Counties. 101 Optare. 142 Plaxton. 68 Transbus. 184 Wright.
Ops incl: local bus services, school contracts.
Livery: Red/Blue/Yellow
Ticket System: Wayfarer 3

*JIM HUGHES COACHES LTD
WEAR STREET, LOW SOUTHWICK, SUNDERLAND SR5 2BH
Tel: 0191 548 9600
Fax: 0191 549 3728
Man Dir: James Hughes **Dir**: Valerie Hughes **Co Sec**: Jean Fisher **Ch Eng**: Stephen McGuinness
Fleet: 7 - 6 coach, 1 minicoach.

Chassis: 1 Mercedes. 6 Volvo.
Bodies: 3 Plaxton. 1 Reeve Burgess. 3 Van Hool.
Ops incl: private hire, continental tours.
Livery: Cream

*KINGSLEY COACHES
PENSHAW WAY, PORTOBELLO INDUSTRIAL ESTATE, BIRTLEY DH3 2SA
Tel: 0191 492 1299
Fax: 0191 410 9281
E-mail: accounts@kingsleycoaches.co.uk
Owner: David Kingsley (senior) **Co Sec**: Eileen Kingsley **Eng**: David Kingsley (junior)
Fleet: 22 - 11 double-deck bus, 1 double-deck coach, 8 coach, 2 minicoach.
Chassis: 1 Dennis. 1 Freight Rover. 6 Leyland. 12 MCW. 1 Mercedes. 1 Volvo.
Bodies: 1 Berkhof. 2 Duple. 1 Leyland. 12 MCW. 4 Plaxton. 1 Reeve Burgess. 1 Van Hool.
Ops incl: school contracts, excursions & tours, private hire, continental tours
Livery: Blue/White.
Ticket System: Wayfarer 3

PRIORY MOTOR COACH CO LTD
59 CHURCHWAY, NORTH SHIELDS NE29 0AD.
Tel: 0191 257 0283.
Man Dir: S. H. Lee. **Eng**: G. Hatley.
Fleet: 8 coach.
Chassis: Bedford.
Bodies: 2 Duple. 6 Plaxton.
Ops incl: excursions & tours, private hire, school contracts.

*REDBY BUS & COACH
STRATTONS GARAGE, HENDON ROAD, SUNDERLAND SR2 8NT

Tel: 0191 514 2294
E-mail: jean@redbycoaches.com
Man Dir: Jean Stratton **Dir**: Neil Stratton
Fleet: double-deck bus, single-deck bus, coach, double-deck coach, open-top bus, midibus, midicoach, minicoach, minibus.
Chassis: Dennis. Ford Transit. Mercedes. Scania. Volvo.
Bodies: Alexander. Caetano. Jonckheere. Leyland. Mercedes. Optare. Plaxton.
Ops incl: local bus services, excursions & tours, school contracts, private hire, express, continental tours.
Livery: White/Red/Black

ROWELL COACHES
See Northumberland

*STAGECOACH NORTH EAST
WHEATSHEAF, SUNDERLAND SR5 1AQ
Tel: 0191 567 5251
Fax: 0191 566 0202
E-mail: infonortheast@stagecoachbus.com
Web site: www.stagecoachgroup.com
Man Dir: John Conroy **Ops Dir**: Nigel Winter **Eng Dir**: David Kirsopp **Com Dir**: Robin Knight
Fleet: 564 - 72 double-deck bus, 295 single-deck bus, 176 midibus, 21 minibus.
Chassis: 166 Dennis. 18 Leyland. 159 Marshall. 21 Mercedes. 14 Scania. 176 Volvo. 10 Designline.
Bodies: 517 Alexander. 2 Jonckheere. 12 Northern Counties. 23 Plaxton. 10 other
Ops incl: local bus services, school contracts.
Livery: Stagecoach (White/Blue/Orange/red)
Ticket System: ERGsystem4000

TYNE VALLEY
See Northumberland

WARWICKSHIRE

CATTERALLS OF SOUTHAM
74 COVENTRY STREET, SOUTHAM CV47 0EA
Tel: 01926 813840/3192
Fax: 01926 813915
Recovery: 01926 817442
E-mail: paul@travelcatteralls.co.uk
Web site: www.travelcatteralls.co.uk
Dir: Paul Catterall **Tran Man**: Stan Griffin
Eng: Paul Rhodes **Garage Man**: Dave Ould
Operations (Tours): Maureen Allison
Admin: Richard Wilderspin
Fleet: 20 - 16 coach, 3 double-deck coach, 1 midicoach
Chassis: 3 MAN. 2 Mercedes. 2 Scania. 13 Volvo.
Bodies: 1 Irizar. 3 Jonckheere.

1 Marcopolo. 2 Noge. 10 Plaxton. 1 Setra. 2 Van Hool.
Ops incl: local bus services, school contracts, excursions & tours, private hire, continental tours.
Livery: Blue/Yellow stripes on White

*CHAPEL END COACHES
WILSON HOUSE, 3 OASTON ROAD, NUNEATON CV11 6JX
Tel: 024 7635 4588
Fax: 024 7635 6406
Web site: www.chapelendcoaches.co.uk
E-mail: cecoaches@ukonline.co.uk
Chmn: Malcolm Wilson **Man Dir**: Ian Wilson **Dir/Sec**: Mrs Tracey Wilson
Fleet: 12 coaches.

Chassis: 2 Dennis. 1 Scania. 9 Volvo.
Bodies: 4 Caetano. 4 Plaxton. 4 Van Hool.
Ops incl: local bus services, excursions & tours, private hire, continental tours, school contracts.
Livery: White/Red/Black

L. S. COURT LTD
RED HILL, FILLONGLEY CV7 8DA
Tel: 01676 540282
Fax: 01676 541110
Dirs: G Purchase, Mrs J Purchase. **Co Sec**: J Purchase **Ch Eng**: D Purchase
Fleet: 14 - 2 double-deck bus, 1 single-deck bus, 7 coach, 3 midicoach, 1 minibus
Chassis: 1 Bedford. 1 Iveco. 3 Leyland. 2 MCW. 4 Mercedes. 3 Scania.
Bodies: 1 Beulas. 1 Jonckeere. 2 MCW.

❄ Air conditioning	💺 Seat belt-fitted vehicles	✓ Replacement vehicle available
♿ Vehicles suitable for disabled	R Recovery service available (not 24 hr)	T Toilet-drop facilities available
🍴 Coach(es) with galley facilities	R24 24hr recovery service	🚌 Vintage vehicle(s) available
WC Coach(es) with toilet facilities		Open top vehicle(s)

4 Mercedes. 3 Plaxton. 3 Reeve Burgess.
1 Van Hool.
Ops incl: local bus services, school contracts, private hire.

*MIKE DE COURCEY TRAVEL LTD
See West Midlands.

LEWIS'S COACHES
CENTRAL GARAGE, PAILTON
CV23 0QE.
Tel: 01788 832261.
Fax: 01788 832558.
Prop: N. E. Lewis.
Fleet: 13 coach.
Chassis: Dennis. Ford. Iveco.
Bodies: Plaxton.
Ops incl: excursions & tours, private hire, continental tours, school contracts.
Livery: Multi colour.

MARTIN'S OF TYSOE
20 OXHILL ROAD, MIDDLE TYSOE
CV35 0SX
Tel: 01295 680642.
Prop: Martin Thomas.

SKYLINERS LTD
19 BOND STREET, NUNEATON
CV11 4NX.
Tel: 024 7632 5682
Fax: 024 7635 4626
E-mail: haydn@skyliners.co.uk
Dir: Haydon J. Dawkins
Fleet: 1 double-deck coach.
Body: Neoplan.
Ops incl: excursions & tours, private hire, continental tours.

*STAGECOACH IN WARWICKSHIRE
RAILWAY TERRACE, RUGBY
CV21 3HS
Tel: 01788 562036
Fax: 01788 566094
E-mail: warks.enquiries@stagecoachbus.com
Web site: www.stagecoachbus.com/warwickshire
Man Dir: Phil Medlicot **Eng Dir**: Mike Bishop
Fleet: 181 - 39 double-deck bus, 43 single-dek bus, 11 coach, 49 midibus, 39 minibus.
Chassis: 35 Dennis. 17 Leyland.
13 Mercedes. 26 Neoplan. 90 Volvo.

Bodies: 107 Alexander. 9 ECW.
11 Jonckheere. 3 Northern Counties.
26 Optare. 20 Plaxton. 4 Transbus. 1 Wright.
Ops incl: local bus services, school contracts, express
Livery: Stagecoach corporate livery
Ticket System: ERG

*WAINFLEET COACHES
OASTON ROAD, NUNEATON
CV11 6JX
Tel: 024 7638 3243
Fax: 024 7638 3160
Dir: K Clifford **Eng**: D Ridgway.
Fleet: 11 coach
Chassis: 11 Volvo.
Bodies: 11 Plaxton.
Ops incl: local bus services, school contracts, excursions & tours, private hire, express.
Livery: Green/Cream

WEST MIDLANDS

*ADAMS TOURS
75 SANDBANK, BLOXWICH
WS3 2HL
Tel: 01922 406469
Fax: 01922 406469
Ptnr: David Adams
Fleet: 8 - 4 coach, 2 midicoach, 2 minibus.
Chassis: 4 DAF. 4 Mercedes.
Bodies: 2 Autobus. 1 Mellor. 1 Plaxton.
4 Van Hool.
Ops incl: private hire, school contracts, excursions & tours
Livery: Cream/Green/Orange

*B B COACHES LTD
22 VICTORIA AVENUE,
HALESOWEN B62 9BL
Tel: 0121 422 4501
Fax: 0121 602 2040
Dirs: Barbara, Mick
Fleet: 2 coach.
Chassis: 2 Volvo
Bodies: 2 Plaxton
Ops incl: excursions & tours, private hire.

BEACON COACHES
24 CHICHESTER GROVE,
CHELMSLEY WOOD B37 5RZ.
Tel: 0121 783 2221
Fax: 0121 680 2582
E-mail: enquiries@beaconcoaches.co.uk
Web site: www.beaconcoaches.co.uk
Fleet: 6 - 2 double-deck coach,
1 midicoach, 1 minicoach, 2 minibus.

Chassis: 1 MAN, 2 Scania, 1 Toyota. LDV.
Bodies: 3 Jonckheere.
Ops incl: excursions & tours, private hire, school contracts, continental tours.
Livery: White /Red/Grey.

THE BIRMINGHAM COACH COMPANY LTD
CROSS QUAYS BUSINESS PARK,
HALLBRIDGE WAY, TIPTON ROAD,
TIVIDALE, OLDBURY B69 3HY.
Tel: 0121 557 7337
Fax: 0121 520 4999
E-mail: enquiries@birmingham-coach.co.uk
Web site: www.birmingham-coach.co.uk
Man Dir: John Craggs **Traff Dir**: G H Howle
Ops Dir: Nigel Eggleton **Eng Dir**: Colin James
Fleet: 109 - 78 single-deck bus, 31 coach.
Chassis: 26 DAF. 53 Dennis. 1 Leyland.
10 Optare. 16 Scania. 3 Volvo.
Bodies: 1 Jonckheere. 28 Nothern Counties. 10 Optare. 27 Plaxton. 1 Transbus. 20 Van Hool. 14 Wright.
Ops incl: local bus services, school contracts, private hire, express.
Part of the Go-Ahead Group

*BIRMINGHAM INTERNATIONAL COACHES
10 FORTNUM CLOSE, TILE CROSS,
BIRMINGHAM B33 0JT
Tel/Fax: 0121 783 4004
E-mail: birminghamintl@btconnect.com

Web site: www.birminghaminternationalcoaches.co.uk
Dirs: A Watkiss, M Watkiss, N Watkiss
Co Sec: M Watkiss
Fleet: 10 - 9 coach, 1 midicoach.
Chassis: incl: 9 Bova.
Bodies: incl: 1 Caetano.
Ops incl: excursions & tours, private hire, continental tours, school contracts.
Livery: Dark Silver/Red

*COURTESY TRAVEL
2 WOODFIELD AVENUE,
SHREWSBURY SY3 8HT
Tel: 01743 358209
E-mail: courtesy@tiscali.co.uk
Prop: John Amies.
Fleet: 2 - 1 minicoach, 1 midicoach.
Chassis: 1 Mercedes. 1 Renault
Bodies: 1 Optare. 1 other.
Ops incl: excursions & tours, private hire.
Livery: Blue/White

DEN CANEY COACHES LTD
THE COACH STATION, 182 STONE HOUSE LANE, BARTLEY GREEN,
BIRMINGHAM B32 3AH
Tel: 0121 427 2078
Fax: 0121 427 8905
Dirs: D. Stevens, Mrs W. Caney, M. Stevens
Ch Eng: A Doggett **Ops Man**: J Clarke
Administrator: Mrs D Johnston
Fleet: 13 - 10 coach, 3 minicoach.
Chassis: 2 Dennis. 2 Leyland. 3 Toyota.
5 Volvo.
Bodies: 3 Caetano. 9 Plaxton. 1 Van Hool.
Ops incl: excursions & tours, private hire,

school contracts.
Livery: White/Yellow/Beige/Green

CHAUFFEURS OF BIRMINGHAM

CREST HOUSE, 7 HIGHFIELD ROAD, EDGBASTON, BIRMINGHAM B15 3ED.
Tel: 0121 456 3355.

*CHASE BUS SERVICES

UNIT 17, ZONE 3, BURNTWOOD BUSINESS PARK, BURNTWOOD WS7 3FS
Tel: 01543 686960
Fax: 01543 686432
Web site: www.chase-coaches.co.uk
Chmn: G H Dodd **Dir**: A G Dodd **Ops Man**: E Faulkner **Ch Eng**: D Russon
Fleet: 32 - 31 single-deck bus, 1 midibus.
Chassis: 1 DAF. 3 Dennis. 1 LDV. 27 Leyland National.
Bodies: 1 Ikarus. 27 Leyland National. 3 UVG. 1 other.
Ops incl: local bus services
Livery: Orange/Brown/White
Ticket System: Almex A90

*CLARIBEL COACHES

10 FORTNUM CLOSE, TILE CROSS, BIRMINGHAM B33 0JT
Tel: 0121 789 7878
Fax: 0121 785 0967
Dirs: A Watkiss, M Watkiss, N Watkiss, M Watkiss
Fleet: 21 - 1 double-deck bus, 20 single-deck bus.
Chassis: 14 DAF. 1 Dennis. 6 Optare.
Ops incl: local bus services, school contracts, private hire, excursions & tours
Livery: Blue/White.
Ticket System: Wayfarer 3

N N CRESSWELL

See Worcestershire

DAIMLER

99 SAREHOLE ROAD, HALL GREEN, BIRMINGHAM B28 8ED.
Tel: 0121 778 2837.
Fax: 0121 702 2843.
Prop: Roy Picken
Fleet: 1 coach.
Chassis/Body: Neoplan.
Ops incl: excursions & tours, continental tours.
Livery: White/Burgundy.

*MIKE DE COURCEY TRAVEL LTD

ROWLEY DRIVE, COVENTRY CV3 4FG
Tel: 024 7630 2656
Fax: 024 7663 9176

E-mail: coaches@decourceytravel.com
Web site: www.decourceytravel.com
Fleetname: Travel De Courcy
Man Dir: Mike de Courcey **Co Sec**: M B de Courcey **Gen Man**: Bob Wildman **Fleet Eng**: Neville Collins **Ops Man**: John Browns **Services Man**: Mick Rossiter
Business Dev Man: A de Courcey
Fleet: 70 - 24 double-deck bus, 30 single-deck bus, 12 coach, 3 minibus, 1 vintage.
Chassis: 1 Daimler. 8 Dennis. 1 LDV. 1 Leyland. 22 MAN. 24 MCW. 2 Mercedes. 10 Volvo.
Bodies: 4 Alexander. 4 Caetano. 2 Carlyle. 4 Jonckheere. 1 Leyland National. 2 Marcopolo. 22 Marshall/MCV. 24 MCW. 1 Northern Counties. 4 Plaxton. 3 Van Hool.
Ops incl: local bus services, school contracts, excursions & tours, private hire, express, continental tours.
Livery: White/Blue/Orange.
Ticket System: Wayfarer 3 & TGX

DIRECT COACH TOURS

68 BERKELEY ROAD EAST, HAY MILLS, BIRMINGHAM B25 8NP
Tel: 0121 772 0664.
Fax: 0121 773 8649.
Tours Man: Brian Bourne.
Fleet: 7 - 6 coach, 1 midicoach.
Chassis: 1 Toyota. 6 Volvo.
Bodies: 1 Caetano. 6 Plaxton.
Ops incl: excursions & tours, private hire.

FLIGHTS HALLMARK

FLIGHTS COACH STATION, LONG ACRE, BIRMINGHAM B7 5JJ
Tel: 0121 322 2222
Fax: 0121 322 2224
E-mail: sales@flightshallmark.com
Web site: www.flightshallmark.com
Fleetname: Flights & Hallmark
Chmn: Stuart Lawrenson **Ops Dir**: Paul Churchman **Head of Ops**: Simon Dunn
Fleet: 68 - 14 single-deck bus, 51 single-deck coach, 3 midicoach.
Chassis: 16 Dennis. 10 MAN. 3 Mercedes. 3 Scania. 2 Toyota. 34 Volvo.
Bodies: 2 Caetano. 1 Irizar. 1 Jonckheere. 2 Mercedes. 9 Neoplan. 48 Plaxton. 2 Sunsundegui. 1 Van Hoo/EOSl. 2 Wright.
Ops incl: local bus services, school contracts, excursions & tours, private hire, express, continental tours.
Livery: Silver

*ENDEAVOUR COACHES LTD

30 PLUME STREET, ASTON, BIRMINGHAM B6 7RT
Tel: 0121 326 4994
Fax: 0121 326 4999
Dirs: J Mitchell, G Mitchell, D Mitchell
Fleet: single-deck coach, midibus.
Chassis: 1 Bova. 1 DAF. 1 MAN. 5 Volvo.
Bodies: 1 B`ova. 1 Marcopolo. 2 Plaxton. 5 Van Hool.

Ops incl: excursions and tours, school contracts, express.

*EUROLINERS

1631 BRISTOL ROAD SOUTH, REDNAL, BIRMINGHAM BH45 9UA
Tel: 0121 453 5151
Fax: 0121 453 5504
E-mail: info@euroliners.co.uk
Web site: www.euroliners.co.uk
Prop: Tony Armstrong **Gen Man**: Glen Styles
Fleet: 16 - 4 coach, 6 midicoach, 6 minicoach.
Chassis: 16 Mercedes.
Bodies: incl: 4 Esker. 6 Mercedes.
Ops incl: local bus services, school contracts, private hire, continental tours.

GLIDER TRAVEL

13 HILLSIDE, BROWNHILLS WS8 7AE.
Tel/Fax: 01543 375801.
Owner: S. J. Mealey.
Fleet: 1 coach.
Chassis: Volvo. **Body**: Jonckheere.
Ops incl: excursions & tours, private hire.
Livery: Cream/Red.

*GOODE'S COACHWAYS OF WEDNESBURY

150 CRANKHALL LANE, WEDNESBURY WS10 0ED
Tel: 0121 556 0706
Fax: 0121 505 1619
E-mail: info@goodebus.com
Web site: www.goodebus.com
SeniorPtnr/CEO: P W Goode. **Ops/Ptnr**: K Goode **Tran Man**: G McGowan **Fleet Man**: M Eaton
Fleet: 11 - 9 coach. 1 midicoach. 1 minicoach.
Chassis: 1 Mercedes. 9 Volvo. 1 Toyota. .
Bodies: 1 Caetano, 3 Jonckheere, 1 Optare. 5 Plaxton, 1 Van Hool.
Ops incl: excursions & tours, private hire, continental tours.

GRAY'S TRAVEL OF COVENTRY

12 MONMOUTH CLOSE, MOUNT NOD, COVENTRY CV5 7JA.
Tel/Fax: 024 7647 4481.
Prop: E. Gray. **Chassis**: Bedford.
Fleet: 3 coach.
Ops incl: local bus services, school contracts, private hire.
Livery: Name Black with Red shadow; Black/Red stripes.
Ticket System: Setright.

HAPPY WANDERER TRAVEL

17 COLLEGE ROAD, HANDSWORTH WOOD, BIRMINGHAM B20 2HU.
Tel: 0121 554 2533.
Fax: 0121 523 5068

West Midlands

Senior Ptnr: Mrs E. M. G. Charnock **Ptnr**: J. R. Charnock.
Fleet: 1 coach.
Chassis: Volvo
Body: Plaxton
Ops incl: excursions & tours, private hire.
Livery: Yellow/Black

*HARDINGS INTERNATIONAL

OXLEASOW ROAD, REDDITCH
B98 0RE
Tel: 01527 525200
Fax: 01527 523800
E-mail: john@hardingscoaches.com
Web site: www.hardingscoaches.co.uk
Man Dir: John Dyson
Co Sec: Malcolm Playford
Fleet: 36 - 6 single-deck bus, 25 coach, 5 midicoach.
Chassis: 6 DAF. 5 Leyland. 8 Mercedes. 17 Scania.
Bodies: 2 Berkhof. 1 East Lancs. 1 Ikarus. 11 Irizar. 7 Mercedes. 3 Plaxton. 1 Reeve Burgess. 10 Van Hool.
Ops incl: local bus services, school contracts, excursions & tours, private hire, continental tours

J. R. HOLLYHEAD INTERNATIONAL

32 CROSS STREET, WILLENHALL
WV13 1PG.
Tel: 01902 607364.
Fax: 01902 609772.
Owner: J. R. Hollyhead.
Fleet: 5 coach.
Chassis: 2 Bova. 3 Volvo.
Bodies: 2 Bova. 3 Plaxton.
Ops incl: excursions & tours, private hire, express, continental tours.
Livery: White.

JOHNSONS (HENLEY) LTD

LIVERIDGE HOUSE, LIVERIDGE HILL, HENLEY-IN-ARDEN B95 5QS
Tel: 01564 797000
Fax: 01564 797050
Recovery: 01564 797040
E-mail: info@johnsonscoaches.co.uk
Web site: www.johnsonscoaches.co.uk
Dirs: P G Johnson, J R Johnson, J M Johnson **Ch Eng**: J Lawrence
Traf Man: M Fox
Fleet: 55 - 15 single-deck bus, 37 coach, 3 minicoach.
Chassis: 37 Bova. 3 Toyota.
Bodies: 37 Bova. 1 Ikarus. 1 Marshall/MCV. 2 Mercedes. 7 Optare. 4 Wright.
Ops incl: local bus services, school contracts, excursions & tours, private hire, continental tours.
Livery: Yellow/White with Blue stripe
Ticket system: Wayfarer
Bodies: 28 Bova. 1 Irizar. 1 Leyland. 2 Mercedes. 8 Plaxton.
Ops incl: school contracts, excursions & tours, private hire, continental tours.
Livery: Yellow/Blue/White.
Ticket System: Setright.

*JOSEPHS MINI COACHES
See Staffordshire

KEN MILLER TRAVEL
   R24

10 CHURCHILL ROAD, SHENSTONE WS14 0LP
Tel: 01827 60494
Fax: 01827 60494
Recovery: 07976 303951
E-mail: ken.m.traveluk@amserve.net
Fleetname: Ken Miller Recovery
Prop: Ken Miller
Fleet: 2 single-deck bus, 2 minibus.
Chassis: LDV. Volvo.
Ops incl: school contracts, private hire, express, continental tours.
Livery: Blue/Silver
Ticket system: Wayfarer.

KINGSNORTON COACHES

40 BISHOPS GATE, NORTHFIELD, BIRMINGHAM B31 4AJ
Tel: 0121 550 8519
Fax: 0121 501 6554
Web site: www.kingsnortoncoaches.co.uk
Props: Richard Egan, Malcolm Stanley
Fleet: 15 - 2 coach, 13 minibus.
Ops incl: school contracts, excursions & tours, private hire.

KINGSWINFORD COACHWAYS
  **R24**

HIGH STREET, PENSNETT, BRIERLEY HILL DY6 8XB
Tel: 01384 401626
Fax: 01384 401580
Recovery: 07831 148222
Dir: C J Wood **Ch Eng**: R J Lamsdale
Ops Man: B A J Probert
Fleet: 9 - 7 coach, 1 midibus, 1 midicoach.
Chassis: 3 Bedford. 4 Volvo.
Ops incl: school contracts, private hire, excursions & tours.
Livery: White/Yellow/Green.

*LAKESIDE COACHES LTD
See Shropshire

LUDLOWS OF HALESOWEN LTD

COOMBS ROAD, HALESOWEN B62 8AA.
Tel: 0121 559 7506.
Fax: 0121 561 4503.
Dirs: Mrs P. C. Ludlow, A. S. Ludlow.
Fleet: 32 - 22 single-deck bus, 7 coach, 2 minibus, 1 minicoach.
Chassis: 8 Dennis. 11 Leyland National. 2 Mercedes. 5 Scania. 4 Volvo. 2 Irizar.
Bodies: 2 Duple. 11 Leyland National. 2 Plaxton. 3 Van Hool. 9 Wright.
Ops incl: local bus services, school contracts, excursions & tours, private hire, continental tours.
Livery: Base White and multi-colour.
Ticket System: Wayfarer 3

MEADWAY PRIVATE HIRE LTD

MEADWAY COACHES, 28-32 BERKELEY ROAD, HAY MILLS, BIRMINGHAM B25 8NG
Tel: 0121 773 8389
Fax: 0121 693 7171
Fleet: single-deck bus, coach, midicoach, minibus.
Chassis: Bedford. Dennis. Leyland. Mercedes. Transbus. Volvo.
Bodies: Caetano. Leyland. Mercedes. Plaxton. Transbus.
Ops incl: private hire, school contracts.

*NASH COACHES LTD

83 RAGLAN ROAD, SMETHWICK B66 3TT
Tel: 0121 558 0024
Fax: 0121 558 0907
E-mail: info@nashscoaches.co.uk
Web site: www.nashscoaches.co.uk
Dirs: I F Powell, Miss L P K Powell, G S Powell
Fleet: 10 - 8 coach, 1 midicoach, 1 people-carrier.
Chassis: 5 Mercedes. 2 Scania. 1 Toyota. 1 Volvo.
Bodies: 1 Caetano. 2 Neoplan. 3 Setra. 3 Van Hool.
Ops incl: excursions & tours, private hire, express, continental tours, school contracts.
Livery: Grey/Blue/Red

NATIONAL EXPRESS LTD

ENSIGN COURT, 4 VICARAGE ROAD, EDGBASTON, BIRMINGHAM B15 3ES.
Tel: 0121 625 1122.
Fax: 0121 456 1397.
E-mail: reception@nationalexpress.co.uk
Web site: www.nationalexpress.com
Fleetname: National Express.
Ch Exec: D Wormwell
Chassis: Volvo. **Body**: Plaxton.
Ops incl: express.
Livery: White/Blue.
Ticket System: Pre-sale National Express, Wayfarer.

NEVILLE'S TOURS

4 HARLAND ROAD, SUTTON COLDFIELD B74 4DA
Tel: 0121 308 6942
Prop: Mrs J Neville
Ops incl: excursions & tours, private hire

NEWBURY TRAVEL

NEWBURY LANE, OLDBURY B69 1HF
Tel: 0121 552 3262
Fax: 0121 552 0230
E-mail: newburytravel@aol.com
Web site: www.newburytravel.co.uk
Man Dir: David Greenhouse **Ch Eng**: Chris Phillips
Fleet: 11 - 5 coach, 3 midicoach, 3 minicoach.
Chassis: 1 Ford Transit. 2 LDV. 3 Mercedes. 5 Volvo.
Bodies: 1 Berkhof. 3 Mercedes. 4 Van Hool.
Ops incl: school contracts, private hire.
Livery: White

NORTH BIRMINGHAM BUSWAYS LTD
38 WOOD LANE, ERDINGTON, BIRMINGHAM B24 9QL
Tel: 0121 377 8554.
Fax: 0121 377 7456
Web site: www.northbhambusways.co.uk
Chmn: Patrick Lane **Fin Dir:** Ken Daniels.
Ops Dir: David Wall. **Eng Man:** Les Watts.
Admin Man: Andrew Moore.
Fleet: 29 - 23 double-deck bus. 3 single-deck bus. 1 trainer. 1 recovery vehicle. 1 exhibition.
Chassis: 22 Leyland, 4 Dennis.
Bodies: 8 East Lancs. 2 Alexander. 15 Northern Counties. 1 Reeve Burgess.
Ops incl: local bus services, school contracts, private hire.
Livery: Green/Cream.
Ticket System: Wayfarer.

PATHFINDER MASONS (FHW) LTD
29 BILSTON LANE, WILLENHALL WV13 2QF.
Tel: 01902 606382.
Fax: 01902 605033.
Man Dir: A Winkle **Dir:** Mrs A Arnold
Co Sec: Mrs J Winkle
Fleet: 11 - 10 single-deck bus, 1 minicoach.
Chassis: 2 Dennis. 4 Ford. 1 Toyota. 4 Volvo.
Ops incl: excursions & tours, private hire, express, school contracts.
Livery: Maroon/Grey

PEOPLE'S EXPRESS
PO BOX 7161, WEST BROMWICH B70 0FF
Tel: 0121 505 3245
Fax: 0121 505 2096
E-mail: enquiries@petestravel.co.uk
Web site: www.petestravel.co.uk.
Fleetnames: Pete's Travel, Britannia Travel
Props: Peter Jones, Kevin Jones.
Fleet: 105
Chassis: Dennis, Volvo, Mercedes, Ford Transit, MCW, Dodge.
Bodies: Plaxton, Alexander, Wright, MCW, Carlyle, Mellor.
Ops incl: local bus services, school contracts, private hire.
Livery: Yellow.

*PRE METRO OPERATIONS LTD
21 WOODGLADE CROFT, KINGS NORTON, BIRMINGHAM B38 8TD
Tel: 0121 243 9906
Fax: 0121 243 9906 or 01384 569171
E-mail: premetro@aol.com
Web site: www.parrytech.com
Dirs: P R Evans, G J Lusher, J P M Parry MBE, A Wenban-Smith
Fleet: 1 light rail vehicle, 1 minibus
Chassis/Bodies: incl: 1 Parry PeopleMover 50
Ops incl: ultra-light rail service

*PROSPECT COACHES WEST LTD
81 HIGH STREET, LYE, STOURBRIDGE DY9 8NG
Tel: 01384 895436
Fax: 01384 898654
E-mail: sales@prospectcoaches.co.uk
Web site: www.prospectcoaches.co.uk
Man Dir: Geoffrey J O Watts **Sales Dir:** Mrs Roslynd A D Hadley **Ops Dir:** D Price
Fleet: 30 coach.
Chassis: 5 DAF. 24 Dennis. 1 Neoplan.
Bodies: 11 Duple. 1 Neoplan. 18 Plaxton.
Ops incl: school contracts, private hire.
Livery: Silver/Blue

HARRY SHAW
MILL HOUSE, MILL LANE, BINLEY, COVENTRY CV3 2DU.
Tel: 024 7665 0650
Fax: 024 7663 5684
E-mail: john@harryshaw.co.uk
Web site: www.harryshaw.co.uk
Fleet: 15 coach
Chassis: 1 Scania, 3 Setra, 11 Volvo
Ops incl: local bus services, excursions & tours, school contracts, private hire, continental tours.
Livery: Orange

SHEN CARE VOLUNTARY TRANSPORT
330 GREEN MEADOW ROAD, SELLY OAK, BIRMINGHAM B29 4EE.
Tel/Fax: 0121 476 1816.
Man: J. McKernan.
Fleet: 5 minibus.
Chassis: 1 Ford Transit. 1 Iveco. 3 Leyland.
Services for elderly/less abled.

SILVERLINE LANDFLIGHT LTD
ARGENT HOUSE, VULCAN ROAD, SOLIHULL B91 2JY
Tel: 0121 711 7799
Fax: 0121 709 0556
E-mail: silverline@landflight.co.uk
Web site: www.landflight.co.uk
Man Dir: Malcolm Breakwell **Co Sec:** Jim Fell **Bus Dev Dir:** Danny Matthews.
Ops Dir: Richard Knott **Eng Man:** Roger Nolan
Fleet: 13 - 2 single-deck bus, 6 coach, 5 midicoach.
Chassis: 4 MAN. 2 Mercedes. 2 Neoplan. 2 Optare. 1 Scania. 4 Toyota.
Bodies: 2 Caetano. 1 Irizar. 2 Neoplan. 2 Noge. 4 Optare.
Ops incl: local bus services, excursions & tours, private hire, continental tours.
Livery: Silver/Blue

*T. N. C. COACHES
257 CHESTER ROAD, CASTLE BROMWICH B36 0ET
Tel: 0121 747 5722
Fax: 0121 747 5722
Dirs: N T Cunningham, K M Cunningham.
Fleet: 5 - 2 coach, 3 minibus.
Chassis: 1 DAF. 1 Leyland. 3 LDV.
Bodies: Duple. Van Hool.
Ops incl: school contracts, excursions & tours, private hire.

*TERRY'S COACH HIRE
21 PANDORA ROAD, WALSGRAVE, COVENTRY CV2 2FU
Tel/Fax: 024 7636 2975
E-mail: enquiries@terrys-coaches.co.uk
Web site: www.terrys-coaches.co.uk
Prop: T C Hall **Ch Eng:** J Hall
Ch Sup: S G Hall **Ch Ops:** L Hall
Fleet: 10 - 2 single-deck bus, 6 coach, 1 double-deck coach, 1 midicoach.
Chassis: 2 Dennis. 1 Leyland. 1 MAN. 1 Optare. 1 Toyota. 4 Volvo.
Bodies: 2 Caetano. 1 Leyland. 1 Neoplan. 1 Noge. 3 Plaxton. 2 Van Hool.
Ops incl: excursions & tours, private hire, continental tours, school contracts.
Livery: Gold

THE TRANSPORT MUSEUM, WYTHALL
See Worcestershire

TIMELINE TRAVEL
See Greater Manchester

*TRAVEL WEST MIDLANDS
51 BORDESLEY GREEN, BIRMINGHAM B9 4BZ
Tel: 0121 254 7200
Fax: 0121 254 7277
Web site: www.travelwm.co.uk
Ch Exec: Denis Wormwell **Fin Dir:** Peter Coates **Eng Dir:** Jack Henry
Fleet: 1,687 - 978 double-deck bus, 31 articulated bus, 613 single-deck bus, 65 minibus.
Chassis: 21 DAF. 360 Dennis. 13 Leyland. 283 MCW. 288 Mercedes. 91 Optare. 620 Volvo. 11 Scania.
Bodies: 412 Alexander. 13 Leyland. 283 MCW. 288 Mercedes. 112 Optare. 102 Plaxton. 466 Wright. 11 Scania.
Ops incl: local bus services, school contracts, private hire.
Livery: Red/White/Blue
Ticket System: Wayfarer 3.
Associated companies: Travel Dundee, Travel London

MIDLAND METRO
METRO CENTRE, POTTERS LANE, WEDNESBURY WS10 0AR
Tel: 0121 502 2006
Fax: 0121 556 6299
Web site: www.centro.org.uk
Fleet: 16 articulated tramcars
General Manager: Fred Roberts
Chassis/Bodies: Ansaldo
Ops incl: tram service
Part of Travel West Midlands

A/c	Air conditioning
♿	Vehicles suitable for disabled
🍴	Coach(es) with galley facilities
wc	Coach(es) with toilet facilities
♥	Seat belt-fitted vehicles
R	Recovery service available (not 24 hr)
R24	24hr recovery service
✓	Replacement vehicle available
T	Toilet-drop facilities available
🚌	Vintage vehicle(s) available
🚐	Open top vehicle(s)

*W A SHEARINGS LTD
BAYTON ROAD, EXHALL CV7 9EJ.
Tel: 024 7664 4633.
Fax: 024 7636 0304.
Gen Man: Carol Carpenter.
See also W A Shearings Ltd, Greater Manchester.

WEST MIDLANDS SPECIAL NEEDS TRANSPORT
218-220 WINDSOR STREET, NECHELLS, BIRMINGHAM B7 4NE
Tel: 0121 333 3107
Fax: 0121 333 3345
E-mail: enquiries@wmsnt.org
Web site: www.wmsnt.org
Ch Exec: E B Connor **Ops Man**: D Rogers
Co Sec: J Frater
Fleet: 260 minibus.
Chassis: 260 Volkswagen.
Bodies: 260 Concept.
Ops incl: local bus services, school contracts.
Livery: Red/White/Blue Blue/Yellow
Ticket system: manual/receipts

*WHITTLE COACH & BUS LTD
See Worcestershire

*WICKSONS TRAVEL
COPPICE ROAD, BROWNHILLS WS8 7DG
Tel: 01543 372247
Fax: 01543 374271
Web site: www.wicksons.co.uk
Fleet: 11 - 8 coach, 1 midibus, 2 midicoach
Chassis: 5 DAF. 1 MAN. 1 Mercedes. 4 Volvo

Bodies: 1 Autobus. 1 Noge. 9 Van Hool.
Ops incl: school contracts, excursions & tours, private hire, continental tours.
Livery: White/Blue/Orange

*WINDSOR-GRAY TRAVEL
186 GRIFFITHS DRIVE, WEDNESFIELD, WOLVERHAMPTON WV11 2JR
Tel: 01902 722392
Fax: 01902 722339
E-MAIL: grahamwgt@hotmail.co.uk
Owner: Graham Williams
Fleet: 2 midicoach.
Chassis: 1 Bedford.1 Toyota.
Bodies: 1 Plaxton. 2 Caetano.
Ops incl: school contracts, private hire, excursions & tours.
Livery: Blue/White/Red
(COACHES HAVE TABLES, EXTRA LEGROOM, LUGGAGE BOOT)

YARDLEY TRAVEL LTD
68 BERKELEY ROAD EAST, HAY MILLS, BIRMINGHAM B25 8MP **Tel**: 0121 772 3700.
Fax: 0121 773 8649
Dirs: R A Meddings, R W Meddings, W J A Meddings
Fleet: 9 - 8 coach, 1 midicoach
Chassis: 1 Toyota. 8 Volvo.
Bodies: 2 Caetano. 7 Plaxton.
Ops incl: excursions & tours, private hire.
Livery: White/Yellow/Black.

*YOUNGS OF ROMSLEY
MALVERN VIEW, DAYHOUSE BANK, ROMSLEY, HALESOWEN B62 0EU
Tel/Fax: 01562 710717
Prop: R Young
Fleet: 3 - 1 coach, 2 minibus.
Chassis: 2 Mercedes. 1 Volkswagen.
Bodies: incl: 2 Mercedes
Ops incl: excursions & tours, private hire, continental tours.
Livery: Bronze

*ZAK'S BUS & COACH SERVICES LTD/BIRMINGHAM COACH SERVICES/CHASE COACHES
ZAK'S DEPOT, SHADY LANE, GREAT BARR, BIRMINGHAM B44 9ER
Tel: 0121 360 2862
Fax: 0121 360 2862
Recovery: 07973 939103
E-mail: e-mail@zaksbuses.com
Web site: www.zaksbuses.com
Man Dir: Matt Lawton **Fin Dir**: Chris Hart
Snr Ops Man: Steve Elms **Ch Eng**: Graham Woodall
Fleet: 46 - 24 single-deck bus, 14 coach, 12 minibus.
Chassis: 30 Dennis. 9 LDV. 1 MAN. 1 Neoplan. 1 Setra. 8 Volvo.
Bodies: 4 Caetano. 1 Duple. 1 Neoplan. 2 Plaxton. 1 Setra. 6 Van Hool.
Ops incl: local bus services, school contracts, excursions & tours, private hire, express, continental tours
Livery: various
Ticket System: Wayfarer TGX

WEST SUSSEX

ARUN COACHES/FAWLTY TOURS
1 NORFOLK TERRACE, HORSHAM RH12 1DA.
Tel: 01403 272999.
Fax: 01403 272777.
Prop/Ch Eng: H. Miller.
Fleet: 4 coach.
Chassis: 1 AEC. 1 Bristol. 2 Hestair/Duple.
Bodies: 2 Duple. 1 ECW. 1 Plaxton.
Ops incl: private hire.
Livery: Red/Gold.

CHARIOTS OF CRAWLEY
12 FURNACE DRIVE, FURNACE GREEN, CRAWLEY RH10 6JA
Tel: 01293 513371
Prop: B D Cullip
Fleet: 1 midicoach.
Chassis: Iveco.
Ops incl: private hire.

C. L. COACHES
UNIT 13, CHARTWELL ROAD, LANCING BN15 8TU.
Tel: 01903 752555
Fax: 01903 752777
Man Dir: D Brown **Dir**: G Brown, D Brown
Man: H Ticehurst.
Fleet: 15 - 1 double-deck bus, 14 coach
Chassis: 15 Volvo
Bodies: 1 Alexander. 14 Plaxton
Ops incl: private hire, school contracts.
Livery: Cream/Green/Grey

COMPASS TRAVEL
FARADAY CLOSE, WORTHING BN13 3RB
Tel: 01903 690025
Fax: 01903 690015
E-mail: office@compass-travel.co.uk
Web site: www.compass-travel.co.uk
Fleetname: Compass Bus

Man Dir: Chris Chatfield **Ops Man**: Bryan Constable **Eng Dir**: Malcolm Gallichan
Fleet: 43 - 14 single-deck bus, 6 coach, 15 midibus, 5 midicoach, 3 minibus
Chassis: 2 DAF. 14 Dennis. 14 Mercedes. 9 Optare. 4 Volvo.
Bodies: 4 Alexander. 3 Autobus. 2 Ikarus. 2 Jonckheere. 14 Optare. 10 Plaxton. 2 Van Hool. 6 other.
Ops incl: local bus services, school contracts, private hire.
Livery: White/Burgundy.
Ticket System: Almex.

CRAWLEY LUXURY
STEPHENSON WAY, THREE BRIDGES RH10 1TN.
Tel: 01293 521002
Fax: 01293 522450
E-mail: crawleylux@aol.com
Fleetname: Crawley Luxury Coaches.
Dirs: David Brown, Darren Brown, Gavin Brown **Ops Mans**: Stephen Burse,

Howard Ticehurst
Fleet: 37 - 2 double-deck bus, 35 coach.
Chassis: 37 Volvo.
Bodies: 2 Alexander. 1 Duple.
1 Jonckheere. 33 Transbus.
Ops incl: private hire, school contracts.
Livery: Cream/Green/Grey.

*METROBUS LTD

WHEATSTONE CLOSE, CRAWLEY
RH10 9UA
Tel: 01293 449192
Fax: 01293 404281
Web site: www.metrobus.co.uk
Man Dir: Alan Eatwell **Dep Man Dir**: Kevin Lavender **Ops Dir**: Kevin Carey **Eng Dir**: Dominic Moorhouse **Ops Eng**: Les Bishop
Fleet: 391 - 134 double-deck bus, 255 single-deck bus, 2 minibus.
Chassis: 1 AEC. 193 Dennis. 1 Leyland. 2 Mercedes. 3 Optare. 160 Scania. 31 Volvo.
Bodies: 11 Alexander. 22 Caetano. 153 East Lancs. 2 Koch. 1 Leyland. 1 Marcopolo. 8 Marshall/MCV. 14 Northern Counties. 5 Optare. 1 Park Royal. 90 Plaxton. 46 Scania. 38 Transbus.
Ops incl: local bus services
Ticket system: Wayfarer

*PAVILION COACHES

See East Sussex

R D H SERVICES
See East Sussex

RICHARDSON TRAVEL LTD

RUSSELL HOUSE, BEPTON ROAD, MIDHURST GU29 9NB
Tel: 01730 813304
Fax: 01730 815985
E-mail: ast@richardson-travel.co.uk
Web site: www.richardson-travel.co.uk
Dirs: R W Richardson, C Richardson
Fleet: 14 - 7 double-deck bus. 7 single-deck coach.
Chassis: 14 Volvo.
Bodies: 5 Alexander. 2 East Lancs. 7 Plaxton.
Ops incl: local bus services, school contracts, excursions & tours, private hire, continental tours.
Livery: Blue

*ROADMARK TRAVEL LTD

UNIT 1, WISTON BUSINESS PARK, LONDON ROAD, ASHINGTON
RH20 3DJ
Tel: 01903 893400
Fax: 01903 893700
E-mail: coaches@roadmarktravel.co.uk
Web site: www.roadmarktravel.co.uk
Man Dir: Mark Anderson **Co Sec**:

Les Anderson **Dir**: David Coster
Fleet: 3 - 2 coach, 1 open-top bus
Chassis: incl: 2 Neoplan
Bodies: 1 Leyland. 2 Neoplan
Ops incl: excursions & tours, private hire, continental tours.
Livery: White/Blue

*RUTHERFORDS INTERNATIONAL

BRAMFIELD HOUSE, CHURCH LANE, EASTERGATE, CHICHESTER
PO20 3UZ
Tel: 01243 543673
Fax: 01403 782028
Owner: G R Bell
Fleet: coach
Chassis: Leyland. Neoplan. Scania.
Bodies: Irizar. Noge. Plaxton
Ops incl: private hire, school contracts.
Livery: White

*SOUTHDOWN PSV LTD

SILVERWOOD, SNOW HILL, COPTHORNE RH10 3EN
Tel: 01342 719619
Fax: 01342 719617
E-mail: busops@southdownpsv.co.uk
Web site: www.southdownpsv.co.uk
Man Dir: S J Swain **Eng Dir**: S Stanford
Fin Dir: P Larking **Ops Dir**: G Wood
Fleet: 18 - 5 double-deck bus, 13 single-deck bus.
Chassis: 6 DAF. 11 Dennis. 1 Leyland.
Bodies: 3 Alexander. 1 East Lancs. 1 Leyland. 1 Optare. 12 Plaxton.
Ops incl: local bus services, school contracts
Livery: White/Blue/Turquoise
Ticket System: Wayfarer TGX150

STAGECOACH (SOUTH) LTD

BUS STATION, SOUTHGATE, CHICHESTER PO19 8DG
Tel: 01243 536161
Fax: 01243 528743
E-mail: enquiries.south@stagecoachbus.com
Web site: www.stagecoachbus.com
Fleetnames: Stagecoach in Hampshire, Stagecoach in Hants & Surrey, Stagecoach in the South Downs, Stagecoach in Portsmouth
Man Dir: Andrew Dyer **Eng Dir**: Richard Alexander **Ops Dir**: Philip Medlicott
Fleet: 471 – 115 double-deck bus, 54 single-deck bus, 7 coach, 7 double-deck coach, 229 midibus, 59 minibus.
Chassis: 16 AlexanderDennis. 177 Dennis. 32 Leyland. 53 Mercedes. 6 Optare. 39 Transbus. 148 Volvo.
Bodies: 16 AlexanderDennis. 294 Alexander. 5 Berkhof. 1 ECW. 3 Mercedes. 31 Northern Counties. 6 Optare. 76 Plaxton. 39 Transbus.
Ops incl: local bus services, school contracts, private hire, express.
Livery: Stagecoach standard

Ticket system: Wayfarer

*SUSSEX COUNTRY COACH HIRE

TERMINAL BUILDING, SHOREHAM AIRPORT BN43 5FF
Tel: 01273 465500
Fax: 01273 453040
E-mail: sxcountry@tiscali.co.uk, sussex-country@tiscali.co.uk
Man Dir: Tony Wright **Sec**: Mary Keats
Fleet: 4 - 2 coach, 1 midicoach, 1 minibus
Chassis: 1 LDV. 1 Mercedes. 2 Volvo
Bodies: incl: 1 Plaxton. 1 Van Hool. 1 other
Ops incl: private hire, school contracts, excursions & tours.
Livery: Blue/Green/Yellow on White

*W+H MOTORS

KELVIN WAY, CRAWLEY RH10 9SF
Tel: 01293 510220
Fax: 01293 513263
Recovery: 01293 548111
E-mail: coach@wandhgroup.co.uk
Web site: www.wandhgroup.co.uk
Man Dir: G M Heron **Co Sec**: Peter Phillips
Fleet: 14 - coach, double-deck coach, minicoach, midicoach.
Chassis: 1 Iveco. 1 Leyland. 6 MAN. 6 Volvo.
Bodies: 2 Jonckheere. 1 Marshall/MCV. 3 Noge. 6 Sunsundegui. 1 Van Hool. 1 Wadham Stringer.
Ops incl: excursions & tours, private hire, school contracts, continental tours, express.
Livery: White/Blue

*WESTRINGS COACHES LTD

3 CHURCH ROAD, EAST WITTERING, CHICHESTER
PO20 8PS
Tel: 01243 672411
Fax: 01243 671366
E-mail: westringscoaches@btconnect.com
Web site: www.westringscoaches.co.uk
Ptnrs: W J Buckland **Co Sec**: T S West
Fleet: 7 - 2 single-deck bus, 4 coach, 1 midicoach.
Chassis: 1 Dennis. 3 Scania. 1 Toyota, 2 Volvo.
Bodies: 1 Alexander. 1 Caetano. 1 East Lancs. 3 Jonckheere. 1 Plaxton.
Ops incl: school contracts, excursions & tours, private hire, continental tours.

*WOODS TRAVEL LTD

PARK ROAD, BOGNOR REGIS
PO21 2PX
Tel: 01243 868080
Fax: 01243 871667
Man Dir: R Elsmere **Dirs**: T Shaw-Morton, K Elsmere **Co Sec**: M Elsmere **Traf Man**: G Hawkes **Tours man**: D Kirkby-Bott
Fleet: 15 - 14 coach, 1 midicoach.
Chassis: 14 DAF. 1 Mercedes.

A/c	Air conditioning	✓	Replacement vehicle available
	Vehicles suitable for disabled	T	Toilet-drop facilities available
	Coach(es) with galley facilities	R	Recovery service available (not 24 hr)
	Coach(es) with toilet facilities		Vintage vehicle(s) available
♥	Seat belt-fitted vehicles		Open top vehicle(s)
R24	24hr recovery service		

Bodies: 14 Bova. 1 Mercedes
Ops incl: excursions & tours, private hire, continental tours, school contracts
Livery: Red/White/Blue.

WORTHING COACHES [wc]
117 GEORGE V AVENUE,
WORTHING BN11 5SA.
Tel: 01903 505805
Prop: Lucketts of Fareham

Fleet: 7 coach.
Chassis: Volvo.
Bodies: 5 Plaxton. 2 Van Hool.
Ops incl: excursions & tours, private hire, continental tours.
Livery: Red/White/Yellow

YELLOWLINE TOURS LTD
34 TRULEIGH ROAD, UPPER BEEDING BN44 3JR.

Tel: 01903 813428.
Fax: 01243 829840.
Dir: Miss K. Fisher. **Co Sec**: G. Hanton.
Fleet: 1 coach.
Chassis: Leyland. **Body**: Plaxton.
Ops incl: excursions & tours, private hire.
Livery: Yellow/Black/White.

WEST YORKSHIRE, BRADFORD, CALDERDALE

ACRON TRAVEL [wc]
102 NEWLAITHES ROAD,
HORSFORTH LS18 4SY
Tel: 0113 258 8923.
Fax: 0113 250 8204.
Fleetname: Travel Team.
Ptnrs: G. Navey, C. A. Goodmill
Fleet: 8 coach.
Chassis: 3 DAF. 1 MAN. 1 Neoplan. 2 Scania. 1 Volvo.
Bodies: 1 Berkhof. 1 Jonckheere. 2 LAG. 1 Neoplan. 3 Van Hool.
Ops incl: private hire, continental tours.
Livery: White with Blue splash.

*ANDERSON'S COACHES
[wc]
HOLMFIELD HOUSE,
STRANGLANDS LANE,
FERRYBRIDGE WF11 8SD
Tel: 01977 552980
Fax: 01977 557823
E-mail: info@andersons-coaches.co.uk
Web site: www.andersons-coaches.co.uk
Prop: Paul Anderson.
Fleet: 3 - 2 coach, 1 midibus.
Chassis: 1 Mercedes. 2 Setra.
Bodies: include 2 Setra.
Ops incl: excursions & tours, private hire, continental tours
Livery: Champagne/Salmon.

*ARRIVA YORKSHIRE LTD
24 BARNSLEY ROAD, WAKEFIELD WF1 5JX
Tel: 01924 231300
Fax: 01924 200106
Web site: www.arrivabus.co.uk
Man Dir: Philip M Stone **Eng Dir**: Philip Cummins **Fin Dir**: David Cocker **Ops Dir**: Paul Adcock
Fleet: 379 - 125 double-deck bus, 251 single-deck bus, 3 minibus.
Chassis: 129 DAF. 127 Dennis. 38 Leyland. 1 Mercedes. 2 Optare. 82 Volvo.
Bodies: 197 Alexander. 22 ECW. 20 East Lancs. 26 Ikarus. 1 Mercedes. 15 Northern Counties. 42 Optare. 38 Plaxton. 1 UVG. 17 Wright.
Ops incl: local bus services, express.
Livery: Blue/Cream
Ticket System: Wayfarer III

B & H TOURS [wc]
52 WILSON AVENUE, MIRFIELD WF14 9AT.
Tel/Fax: 01924 497067.
Prop: Barbara Armitage.
Fleet: 1 coach. **Chassis/Body**: Bova.
Ops incl: excursions & tours, private hire, continental tours.
Livery: Cream/Brown.

B & J TRAVEL
3 SANDY LANE, MIDDLESTOWN, WAKEFIELD WF4 4PW.
Tel: 01924 263334.
Prop: J. S. Bendle.
Fleet: 2 coach.
Chassis: DAF. Volvo.
Bodies: Jonckheere. Plaxton.
Ops incl: school contracts, excursions & tours, private hire.
Livery: Red/White/Blue.

BRITANNIA TRAVEL
[wc]
113 WESTON LANE, OTLEY LS21 2DX.
Tel/Fax: 01943 465591
Prop: A. Broome, Mrs S. Eastwood.
Fleet: 1 coach.
Chassis: Iveco. **Body**: Beulas.
Ops incl: excursions & tours, private hire, continental tours.
Livery: Silver/Red/Blue.

*BROWNS COACHES (SK) LTD
[wc]
WHITE APRON STREET, SOUTH KIRKBY WF9 3HQ
Tel: 01977 644777
Fax: 01977 643210
E-mail: browns.sk@speed-mail.co.uk
Web site: www.brownscoaches.com
Fleetname: Browns
Man Dir: Mrs J M Brown **Co Sec**: Miss M Brown **Gen Man**: A Griffith **Eng Dir**: D Brown **Ops Man**: S Covell
Fleet: 16 - 5 coach, 7 midicoach, 4 minibus.
Chassis: 2 Ford Transit. 3 Iveco. 8 Mercedes. 3 Scania.
Bodies: 2 Beulas. 1 Esker. 3 Irizar. 3 Plaxton. 7 other.
Ops incl: private hire, school contracts, continental tours.
Livery: Red/White/Blue

*CLARKSONS HOLIDAYS
[wc]
52 DONCASTER ROAD, SOUTH ELMSALL, PONTEFRACT WF9 2JN
Tel: 01977 642385
Fax: 01977 640158
E-mail: info@clarksoncoaches.co.uk
Web site: www.clarksoncoaches.co.uk
Chmn: Ken Clarkson **Dir/Co Sec**: JohnHancock **Dir**: Paul Clarkson
Fleet: 9 - 7 coach, 1 minicoach, 1 midicoach.
Chassis: 4 Mercedes. 5 Neoplan.
Bodies: 5 Mercedes. 4 Neoplan.
Ops incl: excursions & tours, continental tours.
Livery: Blue

DALESMAN
[wc]
VICTORIA ROAD, GUISELEY LS20 8DG
Tel: 01943 870228
Fax: 01943 878227
E-mail: dalesman@lineone.net
Fleet: 14 - 8 coach, 3 midicoach, 3 minicoach.
Chassis: 8 DAF. 6 Mercedes.
Bodies: 3 Autobus. 3 Mercedes. 8 Van Hool.
Ops incl: school contracts, excursions & tours, private hire, continental tours.
Livery: White/Blue

*DEWHIRST COACHES LTD
[wc]
THORNCLIFFE ROAD, BRADFORD BD8 7DD
Tel/Fax: 01274 481208
Recovery: 01274 633520
Dirs: S & D Dewhirst
Fleet: 6 - 3 double-deck bus, 3 coach.
Chassis: 2 DAF. 2 MAN. 1 Scania. 1 Volvo.
Bodies: 1 Alexander. 2 East Lancs. 3 Van Hool.
Ops incl: excursions & tours, private hire, school contracts, continental tours.
Livery: Blue/White

FIRST BRADFORD
BOWLING BACK LANE, BRADFORD BD4 8SP
Tel: 01274 734833
Fax: 01274 736768

E-mail: contact.us@firstgroup.com
Web site: www.firstgroup.com
Man Dir: Ian Davies
Fleet: includes double-deck bus, single-deck bus, minibus.
Chassis: Leyland. Leyland National. Optare. Volvo.
Bodies: Alexander. Leyland. Leyland National. Optare. Wright.
Ops incl: local bus services, school contracts.
Ticket System: Wayfarer

FIRST HALIFAX

SKIRCOAT ROAD, HALIFAX HX1 2RF.
Tel: 01422 305426
Fax: 01422 346323
Web site: www.firstcalderline.co.uk.
Man Dir: Mick Herdman **Ops Dir**: Graham Riley **Comm Dir**: Nigel Winter **Fin Dir**: Christine Haigh, **Eng Dir**: Mark Hargreaves, **Ops Man**: Adrian Arthur.
Fleet: 221 - 85 double-deck bus, 109 single-deck bus, 27 minibus.
Chassis: 2 Bluebird. 60 Dennis. 51 Leyland. 16 MCW. 27 Mercedes. 65 Volvo.
Bodies: Alexander. Bluebird. ECW. MCW. Optare. Plaxton. Roe. Wright.
Ops incl: local bus services, school contracts.
Livery: FirstGroup.
Ticket System: Wayfarer 3.

FIRST IN HUDDERSFIELD

OLD FIELDHOUSE LANE, HUDDERSFIELD HD2 1AG.
Tel: 01484 426313
Fax: 01484 431214
Web site: www.firsthuddersfield.co.uk.
Div Dir: Ian Davies **Man Dir**: Mark Herdman
Comm Dir: Nigel Winter
Fleet: 160 - 48 double-deck bus. 103 single-deck bus. 9 minibus.
Chassis: 99 Dennis. 17 Leyland. 9 Mercedes. 31 MCW. 4 Scania.
Bodies: MCW. Northern Counties. Plaxton. Roe.
Ops incl: local bus services, school contacts.
Livery: White/Magenta/Blue
Ticket System: Wayfarer.

FIRST IN LEEDS

KIRKSTALL ROAD, LEEDS LS3 1LH.
Tel: 0113 245 1601
Fax: 0113 242 9721
Web site: www.firstgroup.com www.firstleeds.co.uk
Fleetname: First in Leeds
Div Dir: Ian Davies
Fleet: 487 - 268 double-deck bus, 182 single-deck bus, 15 articulated bus, 22 minibus.
Chassis: 84 Dennis. Ford Transit. 33 MCW. 8 Mercedes. 14 Optare. 65Leyland. 150 Scania. 133 Volvo.
Bodies: Alexander. MCW. Optare. Plaxton. Roe. Wright.
Ops incl: local bus services, school contacts.
Livery: FirstGroup

Ticket System: Wayfarer 3.

GAIN TRAVEL EXPERIENCE LTD

6 FAIR ROAD, WIBSEY, BRADFORD BD6 1QN.
Tel: 01274 603224.
Fax: 01274 678274.
Web site: www.gaintravel.co.uk
E-mail: gaintravel@clara.co.uk
Fleet: 7 - 6 coach, 1 minibus.
Chassis: 6 MAN.
Bodies: 6 Van Hool.
Ops incl: excursions & tours, continental tours, private hire.

*STANLEY GATH COACHES LTD

LEES HALL ROAD, THORNHILL LEES, DEWSBURY WF12 9EQ.
Tel: 01924 466766
Fax: 01924 458665
E-mail: info@stanleygath.co.uk
Web site: www.stanleygath.co.uk
Man Dir: A Gath-Bragg **Gen Man**: P R Emerton.
Fleet: 13 - 12 coach, 1 midicoach.
Chassis: 1 DAF. 1 LDV. 11 Volvo.
Ops incl: excursions & tours, private hire, continental tours, school contracts, express.
Livery: Grey/Cream.

GLENWAY COACHES (HALIFAX)

LEES HALL ROAD, THORNHILL LEES, DEWSBURY WF12 9EQ.
Tel: 01422 823244.
Fax: 01924 458665.
Dirs: J. R. Bragg, A. Gath-Bragg. **Gen Man**: P. R. Emerton.
Fleet: 4 - 2 single-deck coach, 1 double-deck coach, 1 minicoach.
Chassis: 1 LDV. 1 Neoplan. 2 Volvo.
Ops incl: excursions & tours, private hire, school contracts, express, continental tours.
Livery: Grey/Cream

J D GODSON

3 SANDBED LANE, CROSSGATES LS15 8JH
Tel: 0113 264 6166.
Fax: 0113 390 9669.
E-mail: godsonscoaches@hotmail.com
Man Dir: David Godson
Fleet: 8
Chassis: 2 Bova. 3 DAF. 3 Volvo
Bodies: 2 Bova. 1 Caetano. 5 Plaxton.
Ops incl: school contracts, private hire.
Livery: Pink/White/Brown

G. W. GOULDING

64 THE RIDGEWAY, KNOTTINGLEY WF11 0JS.
Tel: 01977 672265, 672059.

Fax: 01977 670276.
Fleetname: B. Goulding.
Prop: G. W. Goulding.
Fleet: 5 - 3 coach, 1 midicoach, 1 minicoach.
Chassis: 1 Bristol. 1 Leyland. 1 Toyota. 2 Volvo.
Bodies: 1 Caetano. 4 Plaxton.
Ops incl: excursions & tours, private hire, continental tours.
Livery: White with Red/Yellow/Blue stripes.

GRA-CAR COACHES

THE GARAGE, FEATHERSTONE LANE, FEATHERSTONE WF7 6AN.
Tel: 01977 791950.
Fleet: 2 - 1 single-deck bus, 1 coach.
Chassis: DAF. Leyland.
Ops incl: local bus services, excursions & tours, private hire.

CENTRAL GARAGE

STANSFIELD ROAD, TODMORDEN OL14 5DL
Tel/Fax: 01706 813909
Man Dir: D P Guest **Dir**: Mrs A L Guest
Rec Man: A. J. Gledhill.
Fleet: 2 minibus.
Chassis/bodies: 2 Mercedes.
Ops incl: private hire, school contracts, excursions & tours.

HOWIE'S OF ROBERTTOWN

194 ROBERTTOWN LANE, ROBERTTOWN, LIVERSEDGE WF15 7LF
Tel/Fax: 01924 400386.
Props: D. Howie, Susan Howie.
Fleet: 1 coach. **Chassis/Body**: Bova.
Ops incl: excursions & tours, private hire.
Livery: Cream/Purple/Gold.

ILLINGWORTH COACHES

UPPER WARRENGATE, WAKEFIELD WF1 4DT
Tel: 01924 373085
Fax: 01924 274110
Dirs: G Illingworth, P Illingworth
Fleet: 3 coach.
Chassis: 3 Scania.
Bodies: 3 Irizar
Ops incl: excursions & tours, private hire, continental tours.
Livery: White

*INDEPENDENT COACHWAYS LTD

LOW FOLD GARAGE, NEW ROAD SIDE, HORSFORTH LS18 4DR
Tel: 0113 258 6491
Fax: 0113 259 1125
E-mail: independentcoachways@yahoo.co.uk
Web site: www.independentcoachways.co.uk
Dirs: P & C Thornes, **Gen Man**: Barry

	Air conditioning		Seat belt-fitted vehicles		Replacement vehicle available
	Vehicles suitable for disabled	R	Recovery service available (not 24 hr)	T	Toilet-drop facilities available
	Coach(es) with galley facilities				Vintage vehicle(s) available
	Coach(es) with toilet facilities	R24	24hr recovery service		Open top vehicle(s)

Rennison M Inst TA **Traf Man**: Seaward
Ch Eng: Peter Foster
Fleet: 9 - 1 single-deck bus, 8 coach
Chassis: 1 DAF. 8 Volvo.
Bodies: 1 Optare. 7 Plaxton. 1 Van Hool.
Ops incl: private hire, excursions & tours.
Livery: Blue/Grey

KEIGHLEY & DISTRICT

CAVENDISH HOUSE,
91-93 CAVENDISH STREET,
KEIGHLEY BD21 3DG
Tel: 01535 603284
Fax: 01535 610065
Web site:
www.keighleyanddistrict.co.uk
Fleet name: The Zone
Chmn: G R Fearnley
Fleet: 103 - 40 double-deck bus, 63 single-deck bus.
Chassis: Dennis. Volvo.
Bodies: Alexander. Plaxton. Wright.
Ops incl: local bus services, school contracts
Livery: Blue/White, Blue/Red
Part of the Blazefield group which is owned by Transdev

*J J LONGSTAFF & SONS LTD

64 DAISY HILL, DEWSBURY
WF13 1LH
Tel: 01924 463124
Fax: 01924 430345
Web site: www.longstaffofmirfield.com
Fleetname: Longstaff of Mirfield
Co Sec: Mrs S Kaye
Fleet: 6 - 2 single-deck bus, 4 coach.
Chassis: 6 Volvo.
Bodies: 4 Van Hool. 2 Wright.
Ops incl: local bus services, school contracts, excursions & tours, private hire, express, continental tours.
Livery: Blue/Grey/White.

*A. LYLES & SON

63 COMMONSIDE, BATLEY
WF17 6LA
Tel: 01924 464771
Fax: 01924 469267
Senior Ptnr: Terence Lyles
Ptnr: Howard Lyles.
Fleet: 6 - 5 coach. 1 midicoach.
Chassis: 1 DAF. 1 Dennis. 4 MAN.
Bodies: 1 Duple. 1 Indcar. 1 Optare. 3 Van Hool
Ops incl: local bus services, school contracts, excursions & tours, private hire, continental tours.
Livery: Beige/Brown/Red

*DAVID PALMER COACHES LTD

THE TRAVEL OFFICE, WAKEFIELD
ROAD, NORMANTON WF6 2BT
Tel: 01924 895849
Fax: 01924 897750
E-mail:
info@davidpalmercoaches.co.uk
Web site:
www.davidpalmercoaches.co.uk
Dirs: Andrew Palmer, Lisa Palmer, David Palmer, Margaret Palmer.

Fleet: 7 - 4 coach, 1 midicoach, 2 minibus.

Chassis: 2 DAF. 1 LDV. 2 MAN.
1 Mercedes. 1 Toyota.
Bodies: incl 1 Mercedes. 4 Van Hool.
Ops incl: excursions & tours, private hire, continental tours.
Livery: Silver

PAUL'S TRAVEL
R24

31 ST JOHN'S ROAD,
HUDDERSFIELD HD1 5DX
Tel: 01484 454040.
Fax: 01484 300900.
Prop: P. Singh.
Fleet: 40 - 2 single-deck bus, 6 coach,
1 midibus, 1 midicoach, 30 minibus.
Chassis: 3 Bova. 2 DAF. 5 Ford Transit.
3 Iveco. 3 LDV. 2 Leyland. 15 Mercedes.
6 Optare. 1 Volvo.
Bodies: 3 Bova. 2 Leyland. 15 Mercedes.
6 Optare. 1 Plaxton.
Ops incl: local bus services, school contracts, excursions & tours, private hire, continental tours.

PULLMAN DINER

THE HAWTHORNES, GREAT
NORTH ROAD, KNOTTINGLEY
WF11 0BS
Tel: 07860 302018
Fax: 07860 677554
Web site: www.pullmandiner.co.uk
Prop: Michael Hartley
Fleet: 1 coach
Chassis: 1 MAN
Bodies: 1 Van Hool.
Ops incl: excursions & tours, private hire, continental tours

RED ARROW COACHES LTD

ASPLEY HOUSE, LINCOLN STREET,
HUDDERSFIELD HD1 6RX.
Tel: 01484 420993.
Fax: 01484 540409.
E-mail: info@redarrowcoaches.co.uk
Web site: www.redarrowcoaches.co.uk
Dirs: Steven R. Moore, Suichwant Singh.
Fleet: 10 - 9 coach, 1 midicoach.
Chassis: 1 Ayats. 2 Bova. 2 DAF. 1 Dennis.
2 MAN. 2 Scania.
Bodies: 1 Ayats. 2 Bova. 1 Caetano.
2 Plaxton. 4 Van Hool.
Ops incl: excursions & tours, private hire, continental tours, school contracts.

*JOHN RIGBY TRANSPORT & TRAVEL

SPRINGWELL MILLS, 231
BRADFORD ROAD, BATLEY
WF17 6JL
Tel: 01924 485151
E-mail: rigbytransport@hotmail.co.uk
Web site: www.johnrigby.co.uk
Prop: John Rigby **Tran Man**: Steve Clayton

Fleet: 8 - 5 coach, 2 midicoach,
1 minicoach.
Chassis: 2 DAF. 1 Dennis. 2 MAN.
1 Mercedes. 2 Volvo.
Bodies: 3 Caetano. 1 Marcopolo.
1 Mercedes. 1 Plaxton. 2 Van Hool.
Ops incl: private hire, school contracts.
Livery: White

ROLLINSON SAFEWAY LTD

65 HALL LANE, LEEDS LS12 1PQ
Tel: 0113 231 1355
Fax: 0113 231 1344
Man Dir: Paul Rollinson. **Dir**: Peter Rollinson. **Contracts Man**: M. J. Joyce.
Fleet: 72 minibus.
Chassis: 1 Fiat. 3 Ford Transit. 3 Iveco.
20 Mercedes. 45 Renault.
Ops incl: private hire, school contracts.
Livery: Brown/Gold.

ROPERS COACHES

69 DUCKWORTH LANE, BRADFORD
BD9 5EX
Tel: 01274 487973
Fax: 01274 543430
Dir: Vera Roper.
Fleet: 1 coach.
Chassis: 1 DAF
Body: 1 Bova.
Ops incl: excursions & tours, private hire, continental tours.
Livery: Blue/Silver.

ROSS TRAVEL

THE GARAGE, ALLISON STREET,
FEATHERSTONE WF7 6BB
Tel: 01977 792106
Fax: 01977 690109
Web Site: www.rosstravelgroup.co.uk
Props: Peter Ross, Mary Ross.
Fleet: 17 - 9 single-deck bus, 6 coach,
1 midicoach, 1 minibus.
Chassis: 3 DAF. 1 LDV. 1 MAN.
7 Mercedes. 4 Optare. 1 Scania.
Bodies: 1 Bova. 1 Jonckheere. 1 Leyland.
4 Optare. 5 Plaxton. 1 Setra. 3 Van Hool.
Ops incl: local bus services, excursions & tours, private hire, school contracts, continental tours.
Livery: Red/White.
Ticket System: Wayfarer.

*STEELS LUXURY COACHES

61 MAIN STREET, ADDINGHAM
LS29 0PD
Tel: 01943 830206
Fax: 01943 831499
E-mail: info@steelscoaches.co.uk
Web site: www.steelscoaches.co.uk
Dir: Tim Steel **Co Sec**: Jane Steel
Fleet: 9 - 4 coach, 4 midicoach,
1 minicoach.
Chassis: 1 Dodge. 5 Mercedes. 3 Volvo.
Bodies: 1 Duple. 2 Jonckheere. 2 Optare.
2 Plaxton. 2 other.
Ops incl: excursions & tours, private hire, school contracts.
Livery: White/Red/Black

E STOTT & SONS LTD

COLNE VALE GARAGE, SAVILE
STREET, MILNSBRIDGE,
HUDDERSFIELD HD3 4PG
Tel: 01484 460463
Fax: 01484 461463

E-mail: carl/markstott@stottscoaches.co.uk
Web site: www.stottscoaches.co.uk
Dirs: Mark Stott, Carl Stott
Fleet: 25 - 4 single-deck bus, 10 coach, 1 midicoach, 10 minibus.
Chassis: 4 Leyland. 11 Mercedes. 10 Volvo.
Bodies: 4 Leyland. 10 Reeve Burgess. 1 Optare. 1 Plaxton.
Ops incl: local bus services, school contracts, excursions & tours, private hire, continental tours.
Livery: White/Red/Black/Silver
Ticket System: Wayfarer

*STRINGERS PONTEFRACT MOTORWAYS

102 SOUTHGATE, PONTEFRACT WF8 1PN
Tel: 01977 600205
Fax: 01977 704178
E-mail: ms@stringerscoaches.fsnet.co.uk
Ptnrs: Sydney Stringer, Mark G Stringer
Tran Man: Mark S Stringer **Sec**: Sonia Stringer **Ch Eng**: Chris Palmer
Fleet: 11 - 6 single-deck bus, 4 coach, 1 midicoach.
Chassis: 1 Mercedes. 6 Optare. 4 Volvo.
Bodies: 6 Optare. 1 Plaxton. 4 Van Hool.
Ops incl: local bus services, school contracts, excursions & tours, private hire.
Livery: Red/Black/White
Ticket system: Almex

T & S TRAVEL

INDUSTRIAL ESTATE, SOUTH KIRKBY, PONTEFRACT WF9 3NR.
Tel: 01977 644992.
Fax: 01977 608652.
Ptnrs: Mrs L. Stevenson, J. Tebbett.
Fleet: 9 - 4 midicoach, 5 minibus.
Chassis: 2 Ford Transit. 1 Freight Rover. 1 MCW. 3 Mercedes.
Ops incl: local bus services, excursions & tours.

*TETLEYS MOTOR SERVICES LTD

76 GOODMAN STREET, LEEDS LS10 1NY
Tel: 0113 276 2276
Fax: 0113 276 2277
E-mail: sales@tetleyscoaches.com
Web site: www.tetleyscoaches.com
Man Dir: Ian Tetley **Ch Mechanic**: David Leach **Ops Man**: Steve Cunniff
Fleet: 12 - 13 coach. 1 minicoach.
Chassis: 2 Dennis. 1 Renault. 10 Volvo.
Bodies: 9 Plaxton. 3 Van Hool. 1 other.
Ops incl: local bus services, private hire, school contracts, express.
Livery: Blue on White

TWIN VALLEY COACHES

INDUSTRIAL ROAD, SOWERBY BRIDGE HX6 2RA.
Tel/Fax: 01422 833358.
Dirs: D Pilling, E Pilling.
Fleet: 5 - 2 coach, 2 midicoach, 1 minicoach.
Chassis: 2 Dennis. 1 LDV. 1 MAN. 2 Mercedes.
Bodies: 1 Caetano. 2 Optare. 1 Plaxton.
Ops incl: private hire, school contracts.
Livery: Green/White.

*W A SHEARINGS LTD

MILL LANE, NORMANTON WF6 1RF
Tel: 01977 603088
Fax: 01977 603114
Ops Man: Martin Guy
See also W A Shearings Ltd, Greater Manchester

WAKEFIELD TUTORIAL SCHOOL

COMMERICIAL STREET, MORLEY LS27 8HY
Tel: 0113 257 6165, 253 4033.
Fleetname: W. T. S. Travel.
Dirs: R. Favell (**Gen Man/Traf Man**), J. A. Crosby. **Sec**: S. Kelson.
Fleet: 1 minicoach.
Chassis: Freight Rover. **Body**: Concept.
Ops incl: excursions & tours, private hire.
Livery: White with Red/Green stripe.

*WELSH'S COACHES LTD

FIELD LANE, UPTON, PONTEFRACT WF9 1BH
Tel: 01977 643873
Fax: 01977 648143
E-mail: info@welshscoaches.com
Web site: www.welshscoaches.com
Dirs: John Welsh, Judy Welsh
Fleet: 7 - 5 coach, 2 minicoach.
Chassis: 2 Mercedes. 5 Setra.
Bodies: 2 Mercedes. 5 Setra.
Ops incl: excursions & tours, continental tours.
Livery: White/Red/Green

*W T S MINICOACHES

49 PRIESTHORPE ROAD, FARSLEY, LEEDS LS28 5JR
Tel: 0113 257 6165
Web site: www.wyco.net/wts
Prop: R Favell
Fleet: 1 minibus.
Chassis: 1 LDV
Ops incl: school contracts, private hire, excursions & tours.
Livery: Green/White

WILTSHIRE

ADRAINS OF BRINKWORTH

THE COACH YARD, THE COMMON, BRINKWORTH SN15 5DX
Tel: 01666 510874
Recovery: 07831 303295
Prop: Adrain Griffiths **Ops Man**: Colin Minchin
Fleet: 8 - 3 single-deck bus, 4 coach, 1 minibus.
Chassis: 1 LDV. 2 Leyland. 3 Mercedes. 2 Volvo.
Bodies: 7 Plaxton. 1 Reeve Burgess.
Ops incl: local bus services, school contracts, private hire.
Livery: White/Blue/Yellow

Ticket system: Wayfarer

*ANDYBUS AND COACH LTD (ANDREW JAMES QUALITY TRAVEL)

UNIT 6, WHITEWALLS, EASTON GREY, MALMESBURY SN16 0RD
Tel: 01666 825655
Fax: 01666 825651
E-mail: ajcoaches@netcentral.co.uk
Web site: www.andrew-james.co.uk, www.andybus.co.uk
Man Dir: Andrew James
Fleet: 18 - 3 coach, 5 single-deck bus, 9 midibus, 1 midicoach.
Chassis: 2 Bova. 1 DAF. 4 Dennis. 1 Leyland. 2 MAN. 1 Marshall. 5 Mercedes. 1 Toyota. 1 Transbus.
Bodies: 2 Bova. 1 Caetano. 1 East Lancs. 1 Ikarus. 1 Optare. 9 Plaxton. 1 Transbus.
Ops incl: local bus services, school contracts, private hire.
Livery: Cream/Orange, Yellow/Black
Ticket System: Wayfarer

APL TRAVEL

PEAR TREE COTTAGE, CRUDWELL SN16 9ES
Tel/Fax: 01666 577774
Prop: A.P. Legg

Ac	Air conditioning
	Vehicles suitable for disabled
	Coach(es) with galley facilities
WC	Coach(es) with toilet facilities
	Seat belt-fitted vehicles
R	Recovery service available (not 24 hr)
R24	24hr recovery service
	Replacement vehicle available
T	Toilet-drop facilities available
	Vintage vehicle(s) available
	Open top vehicle(s)

*BARNES COACHES

UNIT E, WOODSIDE ROAD, SOUTH MARSTON BUSINESS PARK, SWINDON SN34 4AQ
Tel: 01793 821303
Fax: 01793 828486
E-mail: travel@barnescoaches.co.uk
Web site: www.barnescoaches.co.uk
Fleet: 24 coach
Chassis: 8 Bova. 16 Volvo.
Bodies: 2 Berkhof. 8 Bova. 2 Plaxton. 12 Van Hool
Ops incl: local bus services, excursions & tours, school contracts, private hire, continental tours
Livery: Green

*BEELINE (R & R) COACHES LTD

BISHOPSTROW ROAD, WARMINSTER BA12 9HQ
Tel: 01985 213503
Fax: 01985 213922
Dirs: M N Hayball, A D Hayball **Gen Man**: N Ennis
Fleet: 32 - 22 coach, 6 midicoach, 4 minibus.
Chassis: 4 LDV. 12 Mercedes. 16 Volvo.
Bodies: 2 Optare. 26 Plaxton. 4 other.
Ops incl: local bus services, school contracts, private hire
Livery: Beige/White
Ticket system: Setright

*BELLS LUXURY COACHES

162 CASTLE STREET, SALISBURY SP1 3UA.
Tel: 01722 339422
Fax: 01722 412681
Man Dir: A Carter **Eng Dir**: G Parsons
Man: Chris Mills **Ops Dir**: A Wickham.
Fleet: 9 - 1 midicoach, 2 minicoach, 6 single-deck coach..
Chassis: 1 DAF. 1 Dennis. 2 Mercedes. 4 Volvo. 1 Toyota.
Bodies: 1 Caetano. 1 Jonckheere. 4 Plaxton. 1 Van Hool. 2 other.
Ops incl: excursions & tours, private hire, school contracts, continental tours.
Livery: Green/Cream.

BETTER MOTORING SERVICES

104A SWINDON ROAD, STRATTON-ST MARGARET SN3 4PT
Tel: 01793 823747
Fax: 01793 831898
Fleetname: B.M.S. Coaches.
Prop: D G Miles **Eng**: M J Hopkins **Sec**: Mrs M Mulhern
Fleet: 10 - 8 midicoach, 2 minicoach.
Chassis: 1 Ford. 9 Mercedes.
Bodies: 5 Autobus. 2 Mellor. 1 Optare. 1 Ford. 1 Onyx.
Ops incl: school contracts, excursions & tours, private hire, continental tours.
Livery: Coffee/Cream

C BODMAN & SONS

88 HIGH STREET, WORTON, DEVIZES SN10 5RU
Tel: 01380 722393
Fax: 01380 721969
Ptnrs: R J Bodman, D N Bodman, C J Bodman, K G Heath **Tran Man**: C J Bodman **Ops Man**: G Carter
Fleet: 41 - 21 single-deck bus, 19 coach, 1 minibus.
Chassis: 1 Bedford. 22 Dennis. 1 Iveco. 1 LDV. 3 Leyland. 2 Mercedes. 4 Optare. 6 Volvo.
Bodies: 3 Alexander. 3 Berkhof. 16 Carlyle. 2 Marshall. 1 Mellor. 4 Optare. 9 Plaxton. 2 UVG. 1 Wadham Stringer.
Ops incl: local bus services, school contracts, excursions & tours, private hire.

CHANDLERS COACH TRAVEL

158 CHEMICAL ROAD, WEST WILTS TRADING ESTATE, WESTBURY BA13 4JN
Tel: 01373 824500
Fax: 01373 824300
E-mail: info@chandlerscoach.co.uk
Web site: www.chandlerscoach.co.uk
Prop: Margaret l'Anson **Fleet Eng**: Christopher l'Anson
Fleet: 10 - 9 coach, 1 minibus.
Chassis: 1 Renault. 9 Volvo.
Bodies: 4 Plaxton. 1 Renault. 5 Van Hool.
Ops incl: school contracts, excursions & tours, private hire, continental tours.
Livery: White/Burgundy/Gold

COACHSTYLE LTD

HORSDOWN GARAGE, NETTLETON, CHIPPENHAM SN14 7LN
Tel/Fax: 01249 782224
Owners: Andrew Jones, Mrs A L Jones
Fleet: 15 - 2 single-deck bus, 13 coach.
Chassis: 4 DAF. 3 Leyland. 1 Scania. 6 Volvo.
Bodies: 3 Berkhof. 1 Caetano. 2 Duple. 3 Jonckheere. 2 Mercedes. 3 Van Hool.
Ops incl: local bus services, school contracts, excursions & tours, private hire, continental tours.

CROSS COUNTRY COACHES

BLACKFORD LANE, CASTLE EATON SN6 6LE
Tel: 01285 810000
Fax: 01285 810142
E-mail: sales@crosscountrycoaches.com
Dir: B. Telford.
Fleet: 12 - 5 double-deck bus, 5 coach, 1 double-deck coach, 1 vintage.
Chassis: 1 Bedford, 5 DAF. 5 Daimler. 1 Setra.
Ops incl: local bus services, excursions & tours, private hire, continental tours, school contracts.

*ELLISON'S COACHES

THE GARAGE, HIGH ROAD, ASHTON KEYNES, SWINDON SN6 6NX
Tel: 01285 861224
Fax: 01285 862115
E-mail: sales@ellisonscoaches.co.uk
Web site: www.ellisonscoaches.co.uk
Man Dir: A A Ellison
Fleet: 18 coach
Chassis: Bedford. Dennis. MAN. Mercedes. Neoplan.
Bodies: Duple. Neoplan. Plaxton
Ops incl: local bus services, excursions & tours, school contracts, private hire, continental tours.
Livery: White/Yellow/Blue/Red

*FARESAVER BUSES

THE COACH YARD, VINCENTS ROAD, BUMPERS FARM INDUSTRIAL ESTATE, CHIPPENHAM SN14 6QA
Tel: 01249 444444
Fax: 01249 448844
E-mail: sales@faresaver.co.uk
Web site: www.faresaver.co.uk
Prop: J V Pickford **Ops Man**: D J Pickford
Eng Man: J M Pickford **Traf Man**: D Beard
Fleet: 60 - 30 midibus, 30 midicoach
Chassis: Mercedes.
Bodies: Alexander. Marshall. Plaxton. Wadham Stringer.
Ops incl: local bus services, school contracts, private hire.
Livery: White/Mauve.
Ticket System: Wayfarer 3

G-LINE MINICOACHES

15 BROAD TOWN ROAD, BROAD TOWN, SWINDON SN4 7RB.
Tel/Fax: 01793 814336.
E-mail: gline@btinternet.com
Chmn: P. McGarry. **Man Dir**: N. McGarry.
Service Dir: J. McGarry.
Tpt Man: N. McGarry.
Fleet: 30 - 4 minicoach, 26 midicoach
Chassis: 4 Ford Transit. 2 Iveco. 10 LDV. 5 Mercedes.
Ops incl: private hire, school contracts.

R. J. HARLEY

119 LONDON ROAD, MARLBOROUGH SN8 1LH.
Tel: 01672 52786.
Fleetname: Harley Travel.
Prop: R. J. Harley.
Gen Man/Traf Man: A. M. Harley.
Fleet: 2 minicoach. **Chassis**: 2 Ford Transit.
Ops incl: local bus services, school contracts, private hire.
Livery: Green/Red.
Ticket System: Setright.

*HATTS COACHES

FOXHAM, CHIPPENHAM SN15 4NB
Tel: 01249 740444
Fax: 01249 740447
E-mail: info@hattstravel.co.uk
Web site: www.hattstravel.co.uk
Man Dir: A C Hillier **Traf Mans**: A Bridgman,

P Turner **Ch Eng**: M Henderson **Tours & Hols, Ops**: Miss A Marsh, Miss K Dixon **Group Travel**: Mrs M Nelson
Fleet: 32 - 5 single-deck bus, 19 coach, 1 midibus, 2 midicoach, 3 minibus, 2 minicoach.
Chassis: 4 DAF. 1 Iveco. 1 Leyland. 5 MAN. 8 Mercedes. 3 Scania. 1 Toyota. 9 Volvo.
Bodies: 3 Autobus. 1 Ayats. 1 Beulas. 3 Berkhof. 3 Irizar. 1 Mellor. 4 Plaxton. 2 Reeve Burgess. 13 Van Hool. 1 Wadham Stringer.
Ops incl: local bus services, excursions & tours, private hire, continental tours, school contracts.
Livery: multi
Ticket System: Setright.

HI-DECK EUROCRUISERS

4 REEVES PLACE, WESTBURY BA13 4TH
Tel: 0800 328 2453
Web site!: www.hideck.co.uk
Fleet: single-deck and double-deck coach
Chassis: incl: Neoplan
Ops incl: private hire, excursions.
Livery: Cream
Ticket system: Wayfarer

ANDREW JAMES QUALITY TRAVEL

FERRIS FARM, OLIVEMEAD LANE, DAUNTSEY SN15 4JF
Tel: 01666 505585
Fax: 01666 504647
E-mail: ajcoach@netcentral.co.uk
Web site: www.andrew-james.co.uk
Fleet: 18 - 12 single-deck bus, 4 coach, 1 midicoach, 1 minicoach.
Chassis: 2 Bova. 1 Dennis. 1 Dodge. 3 Iveco. 1 MAN. 6 Mercedes. 1 Neoplan. 1 Optare. 2 Renault.
Bodies: 2 Bova. 2 Duple. 1 ECW. 1 Neoplan. 3 Optare. 3 Plaxton. 1 Reeve Burgess. 1 Wadham Stringer.
Ops incl: local bus services, school contracts, private hire.
Livery: Yellow/Cream.
Ticket system: Wayfarer

KINGSTON COACHES

162 CASTLE STREET, SALISBURY SP1 3UA
Tel: 01722 337311
Fax: 01722 412681
Man: C Mills **Ops Man**: S Hursthouse
Fleet: 4 coach.
Chassis: 2 DAF. 1 Dennis. 1 Volvo.
Bodies: 3 Plaxton. 1 Van Hool.
Ops incl: private hire, continental tours, school contracts.
Livery: Red/Cream
(Subsidiary of Wilts & Dorset)

*LEVER'S COACHES

162 CASTLE STREET, SALISBURY SP1 3UA
Tel: 01722 417229
Fax: 01722 412681
Man: C Mills **Asst Man**: I Bassindale
Fleet: 6 - 5 coach, 1 midicoach.
Chassis: 3 DAF. 1 Dennis. 1 Mercedes. 1 Volvo.
Bodies: 1 Autobus. 1 Jonckheere. 1 Plaxton. 3 Van Hool.
Ops incl: local bus services, school contracts, private hire.
Livery: Cream/Blue.
Ticket system: Almex

MANSFIELD'S COACHES
27 FINCHDALE, COVINGHAM, SWINDON SN3 5AL.
Tel/Fax: 01793 525375.
Prop: R. E. Mansfield. **Man**: A. Mansfield.
Tran Man: P. Mansfield.
Sec: Mrs M. S. Mansfield.
Fleet: 6.
Chassis: 3 MAN. 2 Mercedes. 1 Toyota.
Ops incl: excursions & tours, private hire, express, school contracts.
Livery: Yellow/Green/Red.
Ticket System: Setright.

PEWSEY VALE COACHES

HOLLYBUSH LANE, PEWSEY SN9 5BB
Tel/Fax: 01672 562238
E-mail: pewseyvalecoaches@aol.com
Dirs: Andrew Thorne, Dawn Thorne, Anne Thorne
Fleet: coach, minicoach.
Chassis: Bova. Leyland. Mercedes. Volvo.
Bodies: Bova. Plaxton. Van Hool.
Ops incl: local bus services, school contracts, excursions & tours, private hire, continental tours
Livery: White/Blue/Red
Ticket system: Almex

ROBIN'S COACHES

TREDENA, FORD, CHIPPENHAM SN14 8RR
Tel/Fax: 01249 782574
E-mail: info@robinscoaches.co.uk
Web site: robinscoaches.co.uk
Ptnrs: Robin Smith, D. P. Smith.
Fleet: 3 - 2 coach, 1 minibus.
Chassis: 2 Renault. 2 Volvo.
Bodies: 1 Berkhof. 1 Plaxton.
Ops incl: school contracts, excursions & tours, private hire, continental tours.
Livery: White/Blue/Pink

SEAGER'S COACHES LTD

AUDLEY ROAD, CHIPPENHAM SN14 0EN.
Tel: 01249 654949

Fax: 01249 462006
E-mail: seagerscoaches@hotmail.com
Web site: www.seagers-coaches.co.uk
Dirs: Ms J Seager, T Woods, A Watts, Ms A Truscott
Fleet: 19 - 1 coach, 14 minibus, 2 midicoach
Chassis: 1 DAF. 9 Ford Transit. 4 Iveco. 3 LDV. 2 Mercedes.
Ops incl: private hire, school contracts.
Livery: White

STAGECOACH WEST
See Gloucestershire

SWINDON VINTAGE OMNIBUS SOCIETY
10 FRASER CLOSE, NYTHE, SWINDON SN3 3RP
Tel: 01793 526001.
Chairm: M. Naughton. **Sec**: D. Nicol. **Treas**: D. Mundy.
Fleet: 1 double-deck bus.
Chassis: 1 Daimler.
Bodies: 1 Weymann.

*TEST VALLEY TRAVEL LTD

BANISTER BARN, NEWTON LANE, WHITEPARISH SP5 2QQ
Tel: 01794 884555
Man Dir: J M Norman **Co Sec**: Mrs A N Norman
Fleet: 4 - 2 midicoach, 2 minibus.
Chassis/bodies: 1 Ford Transit. 3 LDV.
Ops incl: private hire, school contracts.
Livery: White with Green/Gold relief.

*THAMESDOWN TRANSPORT

BARNFIELD ROAD, SWINDON SN2 2DJ
Tel: 01793 428400
Fax: 01793 428405
Recovery: 01793 428432
E-mail: customerservices@thamesdown-transport.co.uk
Web site: www.thamesdown-transport.co.uk
Chmn: Cllr Steve Allsopp **Man Dir**: Paul Jenkins **Eng Dir**: Nigel Mason
Fin Controller/Co Sec: Cliff Connor
Ops Dir: David Burch
Fleet: 113 - 28 double-deck bus, 85 single-deck bus.
Chassis: 21 Daimler. 82 Dennis. 10 Scania.
Bodies: 14 Alexander. 6 ECW. 7 East Lancs. 1 Northern Counties. 75 Plaxton. 10 Wright.
Ops incl: local bus services, school contracts.
Livery: Blue/White
Ticket System: Wayfarer.

*TOURIST COACHES LTD

162 CASTLE STREET, SALISBURY
SP1 3UA
Tel: 01722 338359
Fax: 01722 412681
Man Dir: A Carter **Ops Dir**: A Wickham
Eng Dir: G Parsons **Man**: C Mills **Ops Man**: S Hursthouse
Fleet: 32 - 21 coach, 4 midibus, 3 midicoach, 2 minicoach, 2 minibus
Chassis: 9 DAF. 5 Dennis. 2 LDV. 5 Mercedes. 3 Optare. 1 Toyota. 7 Volvo.
Bodies: 1 Autobus. 1 Caetano. 2 Ferqui. 1 Mercedes. 3 Optare. 11 Plaxton. 1 Reeve Burgess. 8 Van Hool. 5 other.
Ops incl: local bus services, school contracts, excursions & tours, private hire, continental tours
Livery: Orange/Cream.
Ticket System: Setright.

WILTS & DORSET BUS CO LTD
See Dorset.

*ASTONS COACHES
   R24
CLERKENLEAP, BROOMHALL, WORCESTER WR5 3HR
Tel: 01905 820201
Fax: 01905 829249
E-mail: info@astons-coaches.co.uk
Web site: www.astons-coaches.co.uk
Man Dir: T W Halford **Dir**: R J Conway
Tran Man: M Wells **Sales & Mktg Man**: A Thornber
Fleet: 29 - 2 double-deck bus, 17 coach, 6 midicoach, 3 minibus, 1 minicoach.
Chassis: 2 Dennis. 1 LDV. 6 Mercedes. 1 Optare. 12 Scania. 5 Volvo.
Bodies: 1 Berkhof. 3 Irizar. 1 Jonckheere. 1 Optare. 4 Plaxton. 9 Van Hool. 1 Wright.
Ops incl: local bus services, school contracts, private hire, continental tours.
Livery: White/Purple
Ticket system: ERG

*N N CRESSWELL

WORCESTER ROAD, EVESHAM WR11 4RA
Tel: 01386 48655
Fax: 01386 48656
Props: Mrs Mary Shephard, Mrs Sue Everatt **Ch Eng**: W G Fairbrother
Fleet: 20 - 16 coach, 3 minibus, 1 minicoach.
Chassis: 8 Bedford. 7 Dennis. 5 Mercedes.
Bodies: 20 Plaxton
Ops incl: local bus services, school contracts, private hire.
Livery: Wessex Bus/White
Ticket System: Setright.

*DUDLEY'S COACHES
POPLAR GARAGE, ALCESTER ROAD, RADFORD, WORCESTER WR7 4LS
Tel: 01386 792206
E-mail: info@dudleys-coaches.co.uk
Web site: www.dudleys-coaches.co.uk
Dir: C Dudley
Fleet: 20 - 19 coach, 1 minibus.
Chassis: 3 Dennis. 1 Leyland. 1 VW. 15 Volvo.
Bodies: 1 Jonckheere. 13 Plaxton. 5 Van Hool. 1 other.
Ops incl: local bus services, school contracts, excursions & tours, private hire
Livery: Green/Cream.

FIRST WYVERN
HERON LODGE, LONDON ROAD, WORCESTER WR5 2EU.
Tel: 01905 359393.
Fax: 01905 351104.
Fleet: 240 - 119 single-deck bus, 7 coach, 114 minibus.
Chassis: Dennis. Leyland. Mercedes. Optare. Volvo
Bodies: Alexander. Leyland. Marshall. Optare. Plaxton. Wright
Ops incl: local bus services, school contracts.
Livery: White/Magenta/Blue
Ticket System: Wayfarer

*GOLD STAR TRAVEL
COOKSEY LODGE FARM, UPTON WARREN, BROMSGROVE B61 9HD
Tel/Fax: 01527 861685
Prop: Mrs Dorothy Homer.
Fleet: 1 single-deck bus
Chassis/Bodies: 1 Volvo/Van Hool.
Ops incl: private hire, excursions and tours.
Livery: White/Gold

*HARDINGS INTERNATIONAL
OXLEASOW ROAD, REDDITCH B98 0RE
Tel: 01527 525200
Fax: 01527 523800
E-mail: john@hardingscoaches.com
Web site: www.hardingscoaches.co.uk
Man Dir: John Dyson
Co Sec: Malcolm Playford
Fleet: 36 - 6 single-deck bus, 25 coach, 5 midicoach.
Chassis: 6 DAF. 5 Leyland. 8 Mercedes. 17 Scania.
Bodies: 2 Berkhof. 1 East Lancs. 1 Ikarus. 11 Irizar. 7 Mercedes. 3 Plaxton. 1 Reeve Burgess.10 Van Hool.
Ops incl: local bus services, school contracts, excursions & tours, private hire, continental tours

HARRIS EXECUTIVE TRAVEL
58 MEADOW ROAD, CATSHILL, BROMSGROVE B61 0JL
Tel: 01527 872857
Fax: 01527 872708
E-mail: steve@harriscoaches.fsnet.co.uk
Dirs: J G Harris, S W Harris
Fleet: 7 - 6 coach, 1 mdnicoach.
Chassis: 7 Mercedes.
Bodies: 1 Caciamali. 6 Neoplan
Ops incl: excursions & tours, private hire, continental tours.
Livery: White/Red/Orange/yellow

J B C MALVERNIAN TOURS
NEWTOWN ROAD TRAVEL CENTRE, NEWTOWN ROAD, MALVERN WR14 1PJ.
Tel: 01684 575082.
Fax: 01684 568870.
Fleetname: Jones Bros Coaches
E-mail: info@malverncoaches.co.uk
Web site: www.malverncoaches.co.uk
Prop: M. A. Crump. **Gen Man**: Michael Yates. **Ch Eng**: A. Jackson.
Fleet: 11 - 10 coach, 1 midicoach.
Chassis: 2 Bova. 1 DAF. 2 Dennis. 2 Leyland. 1 MAN. 1 Toyota. 2 Volvo.
Bodies: 2 Bova. 3 Duple. 3 Plaxton. 1 Van Hool.
Ops incl: local bus services, school contracts, excursions & tours, private hire, continental tours.
Livery: Off-white/Orange.

KESTREL COACHES
UNITS 1&2, BARRACKS ROAD, SANDY LANE, STOURPORT-ON-SEVERN DY13 9QB
Tel/Fax: 01299 829689
Prop: M Wood.
Fleet: 10 - 4 coach, 3 midicoach, 3 minibus.
Chassis: 1 Bedford. 2 Bova. 1 DAF. 1 LDV. 2 Mercedes. 2 Toyota. 1 Citroën.
Bodies: 2 Bova. 3 Caetano. 1 Leyland. 2 Mercedes. 1 Van Hool. 1 Relay
Ops incl: local bus services, school contracts, private hire.
Livery: White
Ticket System: Almex

*THE TRANSPORT MUSEUM, WYTHALL
THE TRANSPORT MUSEUM, CHAPEL LANE, WYTHALL B47 6JX
Tel: 01564 826471
E-mail: enquiries@bammot.org.uk
Web site: www.bammot.org.uk

Trustees: David Taylor, Paul Gray, Philip Ireland, Malcolm Keeley
Fleet: 7 - 4 double-deck bus, 3 single-deck bus.
Chassis: 3 BMMO. 2 Bristol. 1 Daimler. 1 Guy.
Bodies: 3 BMMO. 2 ECW. 2 MCW.
Ops incl: local bus services, excursions & tours, private hire.
Livery: various
Ticket System: Setright

*WHITTLE COACH & BUS LTD

FOLEY BUSINESS PARK,
STOURPORT ROAD,
KIDDERMINSTER DY11 7QL
Tel: 01562 820002
Fax: 01562 820027
E-mail: webenquiries@whittlecoach.co.uk
Web site: www.whittlecoach.co.uk
Chmn: P J S Shipp **Man Dir**: D Shurden
Dir: P Harrison
Fleet: 54 - 28 single-deck bus, 18 coach, 1 midibus, 7 minibus.
Chassis: 35 Dennis. 4 Iveco. 1 LDV. 4 Mercedes. 4 Optare 6 Volvo.
Bodies: 2 Alexander. 4 Beulas. 1 Northern Counties. 4 Optare. 29 Plaxton. 1 Reeve Burgess. 10 UVG. 2 Wadham Stringer. 1 other.
Ops incl: local bus services, school contracts, excursions & tours, private hire, continental tours.
Livery: White/Blue/Yellow.
Ticket system: Wayfarer III

*WOODSTONES COACHES LTD

ARTHUR DRIVE, HOO FARM INDUSTRIAL ESTATE, WORCESTER ROAD, KIDDERMINSTER DY11 7RA
Tel: 01562 823073
Fax: 01562 827277
Man Dir: Ivan Meredith **Dir**: Richard Meredith
Fleet: 6 coach
Chassis: 6 Volvo.
Bodies: 6 Plaxton.
Ops incl: local bus services, school contracts, excursions & tours, private hire, continental tours.
Livery: White/Orange/Yellow/Red

YARRANTON BROS LTD

EARDISTON GARAGE,
TENBURY WELLS WR15 8JL.
Tel: 01584 881229.
Dirs: A. L. Yarranton (**Gen Man**), M. L. Yarranton, D. A. Yarranton.
Fleet: 12 - 10 coach, 1 minibus, 1 minicoach.
Chassis: 3 Bedford. 3 Dennis. 3 Mercedes. 2 Volvo. 1 Toyota.
Bodies: 2 Berkhof. 2 Caetano. 1 Jonckheere. 2 Mercedes. 4 Plaxton. 1 Duple.
Ops incl: local bus services, school contracts, excursions & tours, private hire, continental tours.
Livery: Green/White/Orange.

Do you want to keep your LITTLE RED BOOK up-to-date?
From *Buses* magazine carries updates every month.
See page 256 for Subscription details

Scottish Operators

ABERDEEN, CITY OF

*BLUEBIRD BUSES LTD

BUS STATION, GUILD STREET, ABERDEEN AB11 6GR
Tel: 01224 591381
Fax: 01224 584202
Recovery: 01224 591381
E-mail: eastscotland@stagecoachbus.com
Web site: www.stagecoachbus.com
Fleetname: Stagecoach Bluebird
Man Dir: Charlie Mullen **Dep Man Dir**: Robert Andrew **Ops Dir**: Robert Hall **Eng Dir**: Michael Reid **Ops Man**: Gus Beveridge **Com Man**: Jim Gardner **Depot Eng**: Ian Ferguson **Mktg Man**: Lisa Henry
Fleet: 369 - 65 double-deck bus, 141 single-deck bus, 17 coach, 61 midibus, 85 minibus.
Chassis: 42 Dennis. 52 Leyland. 38 MAN. 60 Mercedes. 25 Optare. 7 Scania. 155 Volvo.
Bodies: 268 Alexander. 5 Jonckheere. 11 Leyland. 10 Neoplan. 25 Optare. 43 Plaxton. 7 Wright.
Ops incl: local bus services, school contracts, excursions & tours, private hire, express.
Livery: Stagecoach/Megabus
Ticket System: Wayfarer TGX

FIRST

395 KING STREET, ABERDEEN AB24 5RP
Tel: 01224 650100
Web site: www.firstgroup.com
Man Dir: G Mair
Fleet: 185 - 34 double-deck bus, 107 single-deck bus, 12 coach, 20 articulated bus, 4 open top bus, 2 vintage, 6 minicoach.
Ops incl: local bus services, school contracts, excursions & tours, private hire, express, continental tours.
Livery: Coaches: Silver or White, Buses: Group Magenta Blue/Grey.

*FOUNTAIN EXECUTIVE

HILL OF GOVAL, DYCE, ABERDEEN AB21 7NX
Tel: 01224 729191
Fax: 01224 729898
E-mail: fountainexe@hotmail.com
Web site: www.fountainexecutive.co.uk
Prop: Michael Ewen
Fleet: 9 - 4 coach, 3 midicoach, 2 minicoach.
Chassis: 5 Mercedes. 4 Scania.
Ops incl: private hire, continental tours.
Livery: Gold

*GRAMPIAN COACHES

FIRST ABERDEEN LTD, 395 KING STREET, ABERDEEN AB24 5RP
Tel: 01224 650151
Fax: 01224 650123
E-mail: tom.gordon@firstgroup.com
Web site: www.grampian-coaches.co.uk
Man Dir: George Mair **Sec**: Alan Paterson
Coaching Man: Tom Gordon
Fleet: 28 - 3 single-deck bus, 17 coach, 2 midicoach, 6 minibus.
Chassis: 1 Bluebird. 2 BMC. 1 Dennis. 6 Mercedes.1 Optare. 6 Scania. 11 Volvo.
Bodies: 6 Alexander. 2 BMC. 1 Duple. 6 Irizar. 5 Jonckheere. 1 Optare. 4 Plaxton. 2 Van Hool.
Ops incl: school contracts, excursions & tours, private hire, continental tours.
Livery: First ("Barbie")
Ticket System: Setright

MAIRS COACHES

395 KING STREET, ABERDEEN AB24 5RP.
Tel: 01224 650150.
Fax: 01224 650123.
Man Dir: G. Mair. **Eng Sup**: R. Elrick.
Comm Dir: J. Mackie
Fleet: 26 - 2 double-deck bus, 14 coach, 10 midicoach.
Chassis: 1 DAF. 1 Dennis. 3 Leyland. 8 Mercedes. 3 Renault. 1 Scania. 7 Volvo.
Bodies: 2 Alexander. 2 Duple. 8 Mercedes. 1 Irizar. 6 Plaxton. 2 Van Hool. 3 Dodge.
Ops incl: school contracts, excursions & tours, private hire, express, continental tours.
Livery: Silver/Grey or Maroon/Gold.
Ticket System: Wayfarer/Setright.
Part of FirstGroup.

WHYTES COACH TOURS

SCOTSTOWN ROAD, NEWMACHAR, ABERDEEN AB21 7PP
Tel: 01651 862211
Fax: 01651 862918
E-mail: sales@whytescoachtours.co.uk
Web Site: www.whytescoachtours.co.uk
Ptnrs: Linda A Urquhart, W. J. Whyte, Ian A W Urquhart, Susan Whyte, Steven Whyte.
Fleet: 22 - 14 coach, 4 midicoach, 1 minibus, 3 minicoach.
Chassis: Bova. DAF. Ford Transit. Mercedes. Volvo.
Bodies: Autobus. Beulas. Bova. Caetano. Mellor. Mercedes-Benz. Plaxton. other.
Ops incl: local bus services, school contracts, excursions & tours, private hire, continental tours.
Livery: Two-tone Green.

ABERDEENSHIRE

AMBER TRAVEL

CROSSFIELDS FARMHOUSE, TURRIFF AB53 7QY.
Tel: 01888 563474.
Fax: 01888 563474.
Props: D. Cheyne, S. Cheyne.
Fleet: 5 - 4 coach, 1 midibus.
Chassis: 1 Bedford. 1 Mercedes. 3 Volvo.
Ops incl: school contracts, private hire.
Livery: White/Red/Amber

*CHEYNES COACHES

ALLANDALE, DAVIOT, INVERURIE AB51 0EJ
Tel: 01467 671400
Fax: 01467 671479
E-mail: lesley@cheynescoaches.co.uk
Web site: www.cheynescoaches.co.uk
Ptnrs: W A Cheyne, R Cheyne, L A Cheyne, M F Cheyne.
Fleet: 11 - 3 single-deck bus, 4 coach, 1 midibus, 1 minibus, 2 minicoach.
Chassis: 1 Ford Transit. 3 Leyland. 3 Mercedes. 4 Volvo.
Bodies: 2 Optare. 1 Plaxton. 4 Van Hool.
Ops incl: school contracts, excursions & tours, private hire.
Livery: Silver/Pink/Purple

HAYS COACHES

HALLHILL, COBAIRDY, HUNTLY AB54 7YB
Tel: 01466 740283.
Fax: 01466 740283
Web site: www.hays.co.uk
Ptnr/Man: Stuart Hay
Fleet: 15 - 9 coach, 2 midicoach, 4 minibus.
Chassis: 1 Bedford. 1 Ford. 2 Ford Transit. 4 Iveco. 1 Leyland. 2 Mercedes. 3 Volvo.
Bodies: 4 Beulas. 1 Duple. 1 Marshall. 1 Mellor. 2 Mercedes. 3 Plaxton. 1 Van Hool. 2 Mazda.
Ops incl: local bus services, school contracts, excursions & tours, private hire, continental tours.
Livery: Grey/Blue/Red

J W COACHES LTD

DYKEHEAD GARAGE, BLACKHALL, BANCHORY AB31 6PS.
Tel/fax: 01330 823300.
Chmn/Man Dir: J. S. Westaby.
Dir: J. I. Westaby.
Ops Man: A. Anderson.
Fleet: 15 - 5 coach, 6 midibus, 1 midicoach, 3 minibus.
Chassis: 1 Bedford. 6 Freight Rover. 1 Iveco. 4 Leyland. 1 MAN. 2 Mercedes.
Bodies: 5 Carlyle. 3 Duple. 2 Plaxton. 2 Reeve Burgess. 1 Devon. 2 Dormobile.
Ops incl: local bus services, school contracts, excursions & tours, private hire.
Livery: Blue/Turquoise/White.
Ticket System: Setright.

*KINEIL COACHES LTD

ANDERSON PLACE, WEST SHORE INDUSTRIAL ESTATE, FRASERBURGH AB43 9LG
Tel: 01346 510200
Fax: 01346 514774
Man Dir: Ian Neilson
Fleet: 24 - 2 single-deck bus, 14 coach, 1 midibus, 3 midicoach, 4 minicoach.
Chassis: 1 DAF. 2 Leyland. 13 Volvo.
Bodies: 2 Alexander. 1 Jonckheere. 3 Plaxton. 13 Van Hool. 5 other.

Ops incl: local bus services, school contracts, excursions & tours, private hire, continental tours.
Livery: Blue/White/Red
Ticket system: Wayfarer 2

*ALEX MILNE COACHES

THE GARAGE, 4 MAIN STREET, NEW BYTH AB53 5XD
Tel: 01888 544340
Fleet: 16 - 3 coach, 6 minibus, 7 minicoach.
Chassis: 6 Ford Transit. 7 Mercedes. 3 Volvo.
Ops incl: local bus services, school contracts, private hire

M W NICOLL'S COACH HIRE

THE BUSINESS PARK, ABERDEEN ROAD, LAURENCEKIRK AB30 1EY
Tel: 01561 377262.
Fax: 01561 378822.
E-mail: malcolm.nicoll@lineone.net
Man Dir: M. W. Nicoll. Dir: I. J. Nicoll.
Service Man: A. Gordon.
Gen Man: H. Thomson.
Fleet: 24 - 2 single-deck bus, 6 coach, 3 midibus, 6 midicoach, 2 minibus, 5 minicoach.
Chassis: 1 Bova, 4 Ford Transit, 1 Leyland, 9 Mercedes, 1 Optare, Setra, 2 Toyota, 6 Volvo.
Bodies: 1 Bova, 2 Caetano, 1 Duple, 10 Mercedes, 1 Solo, 6 Van Hool, 4 others.
Ops incl: local bus services, private hire.
Livery: White.
Ticket System: Almex.

REIDS OF RHYNIE

22 MAIN STREET, RHYNIE, BY HUNTLY AB54 4HB
Tel/Fax: 01464 861212
Recovery: 07831 173681
Owner: Colin Reid.
Fleet: 14 - 4 coach, 2 midibus, 1 midicoach, 7 minibus.
Chassis: 4 Ford Transit. 4 LDV. 3 Mercedes. 4 Volvo.
Bodies: include: 3 Caetano. 2 Mercedes. 1 Van Hool.
Ops incl: local bus services, school contracts, private hire.
Livery: White/Blue/Water Green
Ticket system: Wayfarer 3

*SHEARER OF HUNTLY LTD

OLD TOLL ROAD, HUNTLY AB54 6JA.
Tel: 01466 792410
Fax: 01466 793926
Dlrs: James W Shearer, Irene E Shearer.
Fleet: INCL: 2 coach
Chassis: 2 Dennis. 5 Ford Transit. 4 LDV.
Bodies: incl: 2 Wadham Stringer
Ops incl: school contracts, private hire.
Livery: White

*SIMPSON'S COACHES

21 UNION STREET, ROSEHEARTY, FRASERBURGH AB43 7JQ
Tel: 01346 571610
Fax: 01346 571070
E-mail: info@simpsonscoaches.co.uk
Web site: www.simpsonscoaches.co.uk
Prop: Ron Simpson.
Fleet: 6 coach.
Chassis: 1 Iveco. 5 Volvo.
Bodies: 1 Beulas. 2 Berkhof. 3 Caetano.
Ops incl: excursions & tours, private hire, continental tours.
Livery: Silver/Blue.

ANGUS

JAMES MEFFAN LTD

PARKEND, KIRRIEMUIR DD8 4PD.
Tel: 01575 572130.
Chmn: F. A. Carter. Co Sec: C. Mullen.
Dir/Gen Man: N. Meffan.
Fleet: 20 - 4 coach, 1 midibus, 3 midicoach, 10 minibus, 2 minicoach.
Chassis: 1 Ford Transit. 2 Freight Rover. 4 Leyland. 13 Mercedes.
Bodies: 4 Alexander. 1 Carlyle. 2 Duple. 6 Mercedes. 1 Plaxton. 1 Reeve Burgess. 1 PMT. 1 Scott. 1 Crystal. 1 Mellor. 1 Dormobile.
Ops incl: local bus services, school contracts, private hire.
Livery: Custard and Cream.
Ticket System: Wayfarer Saver.
Part of Traction Group.

*RIDDLER'S COACHES LIMITED

CAIRNIE LOAN, ARBROATH DD11 4DS
Tel: 01241 873464
Fax: 01241 873504
Dirs: Charles W Riddler, Gwenda M Riddler.
Fleet: 7 coach.
Chassis: 7 Volvo.
Ops incl: excursions & tours, private hire.

*SIDLAW EXECUTIVE TRAVEL (SCOTLAND) LTD

LISHEEN, THE BRAE, AUCHTERHOUSE DD3 0RE
Tel: 01382 320280
Fax: 01382 320482
E-mail: travel@sidlaw.co.uk
Web site: www.sidlaw.co.uk
Dir: Bob Costello Fleet Eng: Jamie Costello
Fleet: 14 - 2 coach, 4 minicoach, 4 midicoach, 4 minibus.
Chassis: 1 MAN. 13 Mercedes.
Ops incl: school contracts, excursions & tours, private hire.

ARGYLL & BUTE

BOWMAN'S COACHES (MULL) LTD

SCALLACASTLE, CRAIGNURE, ISLE OF MULL PA65 6BA.
Tel: 01680 812313.
Prop: A. Bowman, S. Bowman, I. Bowman, I. Bowman. Gen Man: A. Bowman.
Fleet: 12 coach.
Chassis: Bedford. Dennis. Ford. Leyland.
Bodies: Duple. Jonckheere. Plaxton.
Ops incl: local bus services, excursions & tours, private hire.
Livery: Cream/Red.
Ticket System: Setright, Almex.

CRAIG OF CAMPBELTOWN LTD

BENMHOR, CAMPBELTOWN PA28 6DN
Tel: 01586 552319.
Fax: 01586 552344
E-mail: d.halliday@westcoastmotors.co.uk
Web site: www.westcoastmotors.co.uk
Fleetname: West Coast Motors
Chmn/Man Dir: W G Craig Dir: C R Craig
Co Sec: J M Craig Tran Man: D M Halliday
Fleet Eng: D Martin
Fleet: 71 - 6 double-deck bus, 28 single-deck bus, 30 coach, 2 midibus, 3 midicoach, 1 minibus.
Chassis: 1 Bedford. 26 DAF. 17 Dennis. 1 Freight Rover. 5 Leyland. 1 MAN. 5 Mercedes. 5 Optare. 9 Volvo.
Bodies: 15 Alexander. 1 Ikarus. 1 Jonckheere. 1 Mellor. 1 Onyx. 5 Optare. 4 Park Royal. 13 Plaxton. 27 Van Hool. 2 Wright.
Ops incl: local bus services, school contracts, excursions & tours, private hire, express.
Livery: Multi-coloured
Ticket System: Wayfarer.

GARELOCHHEAD COACHES

WOODLEA GARAGE, MAIN ROAD, GARELOCHHEAD PA65 6BA
Tel: 01436 810200.
Fax: 01436 810050.
Prop: Stuart McQueen

HENDERSON HIRING

KINTYRE PLACE, TARBERT PA29 6UL.
Tel: 01880 820220
Fax: 01880 820900.
Prop: D & Mrs E. Henderson.
Fleet: 12 coach.
Chassis: Volvo.
Bodies: Van Hool.
Ops incl: excursions & tours.

A/c	Air conditioning
♿	Vehicles suitable for disabled
🍴	Coach(es) with galley facilities
WC	Coach(es) with toilet facilities
▼	Seat belt-fitted vehicles
R	Recovery service available (not 24 hr)
R24	24hr recovery service
✓	Replacement vehicle available
T	Toilet-drop facilities available
🚌	Vintage vehicle(s) available
🚐	Open top vehicle(s)

Scottish Operators

HIGHLAND HERITAGE COACH TOURS
CENTRAL ADMINISTRATION OFFICE, DALMALLY PA33 1AY
Tel: 01838 200453
E-mail: info@highlandheritage.co.uk
Web site: www.highlandheritage.co.uk
Man Dir: Ian Cleaver
Fleet: 15 coach.
Chassis: 15 Volvo.
Bodies: 15 Van Hool.
Ops incl: excursions & tours
Livery: Gold

*HIGHLAND ROVER COACHES
TAYNUILT PA35 1HT
Tel/Fax: 01866 822612
E-mail: angus.douglas@freeuk.com
Prop: Angus Douglas.
Fleet: 3 - 1 coach, 2 minibus.
Chassis: 1 Ford. 2 Mercedes.
Bodies: 2 Mercedes. 1 other
Ops incl: local bus services, school contracts, private hire
Ticket system: Setright.

*McCOLLS OF ARGYLL LTD

MCCOLLS HOTEL, WEST BAY, DUNOON PA23 7HN
Tel: 01369 702764
Fax: 01369 702764
Dir: David Wilkinson
Fleet: 8 coach
Chassis: 8 Iveco
Bodies: 8 Beulas
Ops incl: excursions & tours

OBAN & DISTRICT BUSES LTD
GLENGALLAN ROAD, OBAN PA34 4HH
Tel: 01631 570500
Fax: 01631 570311
E-mail: enquiries@obanbuses.co.uk
Web site: www.obanbuses.co.uk
Fleetname: Oban & District.
Man Dir: Colin Craig **Dir**: W. G. Craig
Depot Controllers: David Hannah, Donnie McDougal **Workshop Supervisor**: Iain McDonald
Fleet: 23 - 16 single-deck bus, 2 coach, 2 midicoach, 2 minibus, 1 midibus.
Chassis: 4 DAF. 3 Dennis. 2 LDV. 10 Leyland. 2 Mercedes. 1 Optare. 1 Volvo.
Bodies: 4 Alexander. 1 Optare. 5 Plaxton. 4 Wright. 1 Onyx. 2 KL Conversion.
Ops incl: local bus services, school contracts, private hire, express.
Livery: Red/Blue/Honeysuckle
Ticket System: Wayfarer 3
Subsidiary of West Coast Motors

L. F STEWART & SON LTD
DALAYICH, BY TAYNUILT PA35 1HN.
Tel: 01866 833342.
Fax: 01866 833237.
Dirs: R. Maceachen, M. A. Stewart.
Fleet: 4 - 2 coach, 2 minibus.
Chassis: 2 Mercedes. 2 Volvo.
Bodies: 1 Plaxton. 2 Reeve Burgess. 1 Berkhof.
Ops incl: local bus services, school contracts, private hire.
Livery: Red/White/Yellow.

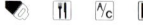

*AUSTIN TRAVEL
STATION ROAD, EARLSTON TD4 6BZ
Tel: 01896 849360
Fax: 01896 849623
E-mail: travelaustin@aol.com, info@scotlandtours.co.uk
Props: Douglas Austin, Barry Austin.
Fleet: 6 - 4 coach, 2 midicoach.
Chassis: 1 Bova. 2 Mercedes. 3 Volvo.
Bodies: 1 Bova. 2 Esker. 3 Plaxton.
Ops incl: excursions & tours, private hire, continental tours.
Livery: Pearlescent white

JAMES FRENCH & SON
THE GARAGE, COLDINGHAM, EYEMOUTH TD14 5NS.
Tel/Fax: 01890 771283.
Fleet: 12 coach.
Chassis: Volvo.
Bodies: Van Hool.
Ops incl: excursions & tours.

*MUNRO'S OF JEDBURGH LTD
OAKVALE GARAGE, BONGATE, JEDBURGH TD8 6DU
Tel: 01835 862253
Fax: 01835 864297
Recovery: 01835 864866
E-mail: ewan@munrosofjedburgh.co.uk
Web site: www.munrosofjedburgh.co.uk
Co Sec: Ewan Farish **Ops Dir**: Donald Cameron **Eng Dir**: Bruce Campbell
Fleet: 42 - 16 double-deck bus, 8 coach, 13 midibus, 2 midicoach, 3 minibus.
Chassis: 10 DAF. 3 Dennis. 3 LDV. 7 MAN. 9 Mercedes. 7 Optare. 1 Van Hool.
Bodies: 2 East Lancs. 1 Ikarus. 7 Marshall/MCV. 8 Optare. 6 Plaxton. 2 Transbus. 8 Van Hool. 5 Made-to-Measure. 3 Jaycas.
Ops incl: local bus services, school contracts, private hire.
Livery: White/Red stripes
Ticket System: Wayfarer TGX

PERRYMAN BUSES
WOODBINE GARAGE, BURNMOUTH TD14 5SL.
Tel: 01890 781533.
Fax: 01890 750481.
Web site: www.perrymansbuses.com
Man Dir: R. Perryman.
Fleet: 35 coach
Chassis: incl: 4 Volvo
Bodies: incl: 1 Wright
Ops incl: local bus services, private hire

TELFORDS COACHES LTD
TWEEDEN BRAE, NEWCASTLETON TD9 0TL
Tel/Fax: 01387 375677
Recovery: 07711 280475
E-mail: alistair@telfordscoaches.com
Web site: www.telfordscoaches.com
Fleetname: Telford's Coaches
Dir: Alistair S Telford **Ch Eng**: William Johnstone **Co Sec**: Shelagh Nixon
Fleet: 13 - 7 coach, 6 midicoach.
Chassis: 1 Ford. 6 Mercedes. 1 Scania. 5 Volvo.
Bodies: 4 Mercedes-Benz. 8 Plaxton. 1 Van Hool.
Ops incl: local bus services, school contracts, excursions & tours, private hire, continental tours.
Livery: Blue with white vinyls

M. LINE INTERNATIONAL COACHES
THE COACH HOUSE, RIVERBANK, ALLOA FK10 1NT.
Tel: 01259 212802.
Fax: 01259 213372.
E-mail: info@m-line.co.uk.
Web Site: www.m-line.co.uk.
Ops Man: T. Matchett.
Dir/Fleet Eng: C. W. Christie.
Fleet: 16 - 7 double-deck bus, 5 coach, 4 double-deck coach.
Chassis: 2 Bova. 2 Iveco. 4 Neoplan. 2 Volvo.
Bodies: 6 Alexander. 2 Bova. 4 Neoplan.
Ops incl: local bus services, school contracts, excursions & tours, private hire, continental tours.
Livery: Metallic Rainbow.
Ticket System: Almex.

*MACKIE'S COACHES
32 GLASSHOUSE LOAN, ALLOA FK10 1PE.
Tel: 01259 216180
Fax: 01259 217508
E-mail: enquiries@mackiescoaches.com
Web site: www.mackiescoaches.com
Fleet: 18 - single-deck bus, coach
Chassis: 3 Bova. 15 Volvo.
Bodies: 3 Bova. 2 Caetano. 1 Duple. 2 Jonckheere. 5 Van Hool. 5 Wright.
Ops incl: local bus services, school contracts, excursions & tours, private hire, continental tours.
Livery: White/Brown/Beige.
Ticket System: Wayfarer.

*WOODS COACHES
2 GOLF VIEW, TILLICOULTRY FK13 6DH
Tel: 01259 751753
Fax: 01259 751824
Fax: 07836 662919
E-mail: jwcoaches@btinternet.com
Web site: www.woodscoaches.net
Owner: James Woods **Ops Man**: John Woods.
Fleet: 10 - coach, midicoach, minicoach
Chassis: 2 Bova, 8 Mercedes.
Bodies: 2 Bova. 2 Esker. 6 Mercedes.
Ops incl: school contracts, excursions & tours, private hire
Livery: Silver

DUMFRIES & GALLOWAY

ANDERSON'S COACHES

BLUE BELL HILL, SKIPPERS, LANGHOLM DG13 0LH.
Tel: 01387 380553.
Fax: 01387 380553.
Ptnrs: I. R. Anderson, K. Irving.
Ch Eng: C. Anderson.
Fleet: 6 - 2 single-deck bus, 2 minibus, 2 minicoach.
Chassis: 1 AEC. 3 Ford Transit. 1 Freight Rover. 1 Leyland.
Bodies: 2 Plaxton. 1 Robin Hood. 1 PMT. 1 N/S Transit.
Ops incl: local bus services, school contracts, private hire.
Livery: Red/Orange/Yellow stripe.
Ticket System: Almex.

R. K. ARMSTRONG COACHES wc /c R24

THE PARK, BRIDGE-OF-DEE, CASTLE DOUGLAS DG7 1TR.
Tel: 01556 503391
Fax: 01556 504656
Recovery: 01556 503391
E-mail: rkarmstrong8@aol.com
Web site: www.armstrongcoaches.com
Prop: R. K. Armstrong.
Fleet: 14 - 1 single-deck bus, 5 coach, 4 midibus, 2 midicoach, 1 minibus, 1 minicoach.
Chassis: 5 mercedes. 2 Optare. 1 Scania. 1 Toyota. 2 Volvo.
Bodies: 1 Jonckheere. 1 Leyland. 5 Mercedes. 2 Optare. 1 Plaxton. 2 Reeve Burgess. 1 Van Hool.
Ops incl: local bus services, school contracts, excursions and tours, private hire, continental tours.

*WILLIAM BROWNRIGG

THE GARAGE, THORNHILL DG3 5LZ.
Tel/Fax: 01848 330203
Fleet: 9 - 4 coach, 5 minibus
Chassis: Bova. Leyland. Mercedes. Scania. Volvo.
Bodies: Bova. Duple. Mercedes. Plaxton. Reeve Burgess.
Ops incl: local bus services, school contracts, excursions and tours, private hire
Livery: Orange/White

*JAMES GIBSON & SON

16 CHURCH STREET, MOFFAT DG10 9HD
Tel: 01683 220200
Fax: 01683 220758
E-mail: enquiries@gibsonscoaches.co.uk
Web site: www.gibsonscoaches.co.uk
Fleet: 9
Chassis: 5 Setra. 4 Volvo.
Bodies: 1 Duple. 5 Setra. 3 Van Hool.
Ops incl: excursions & tours, private hire, continental tours.

Livery: Red/Maroon/Orange

JAMES KING COACHES

36 MAIN STREET, KIRKCOWAN, NEWTON STEWART DG8 0HG
Tel: 01671 830284
Fax: 01671 830499
E-mail: enquiries@kingscoachhire.com
Fleet: 25 - 3 single-deck bus, 11 coach, 4 midibus, 7 midicoach.
Chassis: 9 Mercedes. 3 Optare. 13 Volvo.
Bodies: 2 East Lancs. 2 Jonckheere. 3 Optare. 6 Plaxton. 9 Van Hool. 3 other.
Ops incl: local bus services, school contracts, excursions & tours, private hire.

*KIWI LUXURY TRAVEL

80 QUEEN STREET, NEWTON STEWART DG8 6JL
Tel: 01671 404294
Fax: 01671 403310
E-mail: kiwitravel@btconnect.com
Web site: www.kiwitravelltd.co.uk
Dirs: Ian Allison, Janet Allison
Fleet: 4 - 3 coach, 1 minicoach
Chassis: incl: 3 Volvo
Bodies: incl: 1 Caetano.
Ops incl: local bus services, school contracts, excursions & tours, private hire.

MacEWAN'S COACH SERVICES

JOHNFIELD, AMISFIELD, DUMFRIES DG1 3LS
Tel: 01387 256533
Fax: 01387 711123
Prop: John MacEwan **Ch Eng:** Peter Maxwell
Fleet: 65 - 5 double-deck, 22 single-deck bus, 9 coach, 1 double-deck coach, 12 midibus, 4 midicoach, 12 minibus
Chassis: 1 AEC. 2 Bedford. 1 Bristol. 1 DAF. 3 Dennis. 3 Ford Transit. 1 Iveco. 4 LDV. 2 Leyland. 5 MAN. 18 Mercedes. 3 Optare. 5 Scania. 2 Transbus. 9 Volvo.
Bodies: 10 Alexander. 2 Autobus. 2 Duple. 1 ECW. 1 East Lancs. 1 Irizar. 1 Jonckheere. 4 LDV. 4 Marshall/MCV. 5 MCW. 3 Optare. 17 Plaxton. 3 Crystal. 2 Drinkwater. 2 Transbus. 1 Van Hool. 3 Wright. 1 DAB. 2 Montano.
Ops incl: local bus services, school contracts
Livery: White/Red/Blue
Ticket system: ERG Transit 400

MCCULLOCH AND SON

MAIN ROAD, STONEYKIRK, STRANRAER DG9 9DH.
Tel/Fax: 01776 830236.
E-mail: mcculloch.coaches@virgin.net
Fleetname: McCulloch Coaches
Ptnrs: D F McCulloch, E A McCulloch
Fleet: 8 - incl: 1 single-deck bus, 3 coach, 1 midibus, 1 midicoach, 1 minicoach.
Chassis: 1 Bedford. 4 Mercedes. 2 Optare. 3 Volvo.
Bodies: 1 Caetano. 1 Duple.

2 Optare. 4 Plaxton.
Ops incl: local bus services, excursions & tours, school contracts, private hire
Livery: White/Blue lettering
Ticket System: Ticket books

*STAGECOACH WEST SCOTLAND

LEWIS STREET, STRANRAER
Web site: www.stagecoachbus.com
Man Dir: Tom Wileman **Eng Dir:** Sam Greer

*STAGECOACH WEST SCOTLAND

EASTFIELD ROAD, DUMFRIES
Tel: 01387 253496
Web site: www.stagecoachbus.com
Man Dir: Tom Wileman **Eng Dir:** Sam Greer

DUNDEE CITY

FISHERS TOURS

16 WEST PORT, DUNDEE DD1 5EP
Tel/Fax: 01382 455177
E-mail: fisherstours@btconnect.com
Web site: www.fisherstours.co.uk
Ptnrs: James Cosgrove, Catherine Cosgrove **Tran Man:** David Kidd
Fleet: 16 - 3 single-deck bus (70seat), 11 coach, 1 midicoach, 1 midibus, 2 minibus.
Chassis: 3 Iveco. 7 Leyland. 4 Mercedes. 2 Volvo.
Bodies: 1 Beulas. 2 ECW. 1 Marshall. 3 Mercedes. 1 Optare. 6 Plaxton. 2 Van Hool.
Ops incl: school contracts, excursions & tours, private hire, continental tours.
Livery: White/Blue/Turquoise/Yellow.

*SIDLAW EXECUTIVE TRAVEL (SCOTLAND) LTD

LISHEEN, THE BRAE, AUCHTERHOUSE DD3 0RE
Tel: 01382 320280
Fax: 01382 320482
E-mail: travel@sidlaw.co.uk
Web site: www.sidlaw.co.uk
Dir: Bob Costello **Fleet Eng:** Jamie Costello
Fleet: 14 - 2 coach, 4 minicoach, 4 midicoach, 4 minicoach.
Chassis: 1 MAN. 13 Mercedes.
Ops incl: school contracts, excursions & tours, private hire.

STAGECOACH EAST SCOTLAND

SEAGATE BUS STATION, DUNDEE DD1 2HR.
Tel: 01382 228345.
Fax: 01382 202267

- /c Air conditioning
- Vehicles suitable for disabled
- Coach(es) with galley facilities
- wc Coach(es) with toilet facilities
- Seat belt-fitted vehicles
- R Recovery service available (not 24 hr)
- R24 24hr recovery service
- Replacement vehicle available
- T Toilet-drop facilities available
- Vintage vehicle(s) available
- Open top vehicle(s)

Man Dir: Doug Fleming **Eng Dir**: Sandy Brydon **Mktg Man**: Lisa Henry
Fleet: 156 - 47 double-deck bus, 54 single-deck bus, 9 coach, 4 midibus, 42 minibus.
Chassis: 4 Daimler. 17 Dennis. 2 Dodge. 1 LDV. 55 Leyland. 35 MCW. 17 Mercedes. 4 Optare. 4 Renault. 17 Volvo.
Bodies: 68 Alexander. 4 Duple. 2 ECW. 18 East Lancs. 19 MCW. 8 Northern Counties. 4 Optare. 8 Plaxton. 11 Reeve Burgess. 5 Wright. 9 Other.
Ops incl: local bus services, school contracts, excursions & tours, private hire.
Livery: Orange/Blue/White.
Ticket System: Wayfarer.
Part of Stagecoach Group.

*TRAVEL DUNDEE
44-48 EAST DOCK STREET, DUNDEE DD1 3JS
Tel: 01382 201121
Fax: 01382 201997
E-mail: mailbox@traveldundee.co.uk
Web site: www.traveldundee.co.uk
Man Dir: James Lee **Traff Man**: William Murphy **Ch Eng**: Frank Sheach **Business Man**: Elsie Turbyne
Fleet: 127 - 18 double-deck, 88 single-deck, 19 coach, 2 double-deck coach
Chassis: 7 Dennis. 2 Leyland. 7 Mercedes. 12 Optare. 6 Scania. 93 Volvo.
Bodies: 3 East Lancs. 2 Leyland. 3 Mercedes. 12 Optare. 17 Plaxton. 90 Wright
Ops incl: local bus services, school contracts, excursions & tours, private hire.
Livery: Travel Dundee/Travel Greyhound

EAST AYRSHIRE

LIDDELL'S COACHES
1 MAUCHLINE ROAD, AUCHINLECK KA18 2BJ.
Tel: 01290 424300/420717.
Fax: 01290 425637.
Prop: J. Liddell. **Ch Eng**: J. Quinn. **Co Sec**: Ms J. Samson. **Ops Man**: Ms M. Milroy.
Fleet: 24 - 8 double-deck bus, 10 coach, 4 midicoach, 2 minibus.
Chassis: 1 Bova. 3 DAF. 2 Dodge. 2 Freight Rover. 10 Leyland. 6 Volvo.
Bodies: 8 Alexander. 1 Bova. 1 Caetano. 3 Duple. 1 ECW. 1 East Lancs. 2 Jonckheere. 4 Plaxton. 2 Reeve Burgess. 1 Wright.
Ops incl: local bus services, school contracts, excursions & tours, private hire, express.
Livery: White with Brown/Orange/Lemon stripes.
Ticket System: Setright.

*ROWE & TUDHOPE
WEST HILLHEAD, FARM ROAD, KILMARNOCK KA3 1PH
Tel: 01563 525631
Fax: 01563 571489
E-mail: geo.rowe@fsmail.net
Web site: www.roweandtudhope.com
Dir: George Rowe
Fleet: 22 - 1 double-deck bus, 3 single-deck bus, 12 coach, 2 midibus, 2 midicoach, 2 minicoach.
Chassis: 6 Dennis. 2 Ford Transit. 3 Leyland. 4 Mercedes. 2 Scania. 5 Volvo.

Bodies: 10 Alexander. 1 Irizar. 3 Jonckheere. 6 Plaxton. 2 other.
Ops incl: local bus services, school contracts, exursions & tours, private hire.
Livery: White/Blue flag
Ticket system: Wayfarer

EAST LOTHIAN

EVE CARS & COACHES
SPOTT ROAD, DUNBAR EH42 1RR.
Tel: 01368 865500.
Fax: 01368 865400.
Web site: www.eveinfo.co.uk
Ptnrs: Gary Scougall, Vona Scougall.

EAST RENFREWSHIRE

*HENRY CRAWFORD COACHES LTD
SHILFORD MILL, NEILSTON, GLASGOW G78 3BA
Tel: 01505 850456
Fax: 01505 850479
E-mail: henrycrawford@talk21.com
Web site: www.henrycrawfordcoaches.co.uk
Ops Man: James Crawford(**Dir**) **Ch Eng**: John Crawford(**Dir**) **Co Sec**: Isobel Crawford(**Dir**)
Fleet: 26 - 21 coach, 5 minicoach.
Chassis: 1 Bova. 2 Leyland. 5 Mercedes. 18 Volvo.
Bodies: 1 Bova. 2 Duple. 1 Indcar. 1 Optare. 3 Plaxton. 16 Van Hool. 2 other.
Ops incl: private hire, school contracts.
Livery: White/Red

SOUTHERN COACHES (NM) LTD
LOCHLIBO ROAD, BARRHEAD G78 1LF.
Tel: 0141-881 1147.
Fax: 0141 881 1148.
E-mail: reservations@southern-coaches.co.uk.
Web site: southern-coaches.co.uk
Dirs: R. Wallace, D. Wallace, Mary Wallace.
Fleet: 19 - 17 coach, 2 minicoach.
Chassis: 2 DAF. 2 Toyota. 15 Volvo.
Bodies: 2 Caetano. 1 Jonckheere. 8 Plaxton. 8 Van Hool. 1 Ikarus.
Ops incl: school contracts, excursions & tours, private hire, express.
Livery: Cream/Blue/Orange.

EDINBURGH, CITY OF

AAA COACHES
UNIT 7, RAW CAMPS INDUSTRIAL ESTATE, KIRKNEWTON EH27 8DF
Tel: 01506 883000
Fax: 01506 884000
E-mail: aaacoaches@hotmail.com
Web site: www.aaacoaches.co.uk
Man Dir: Sharon Renton

Fleet: 15 - 9 single-deck bus, 3 midibus, 3 minibus.
Chassis: 1 Dennis. 3 Ford. 2 Ford Transit. 1 LDV. 3 Mercedes. 2 Scania. 7 Volvo.
Bodies: 5 Jonckheere. 1 Leyland. 3 Mercedes. 2 Plaxton. 2 Sunsundegui. 2 Van Hool.
Ops incl: school contracts, excursions & tours, private hire
Livery: White with Highland scene.

*BROWNS OF EDINBURGH
DROVERS ROAD, EAST MAINS INDUSTRIAL ESTATE, BROXBURN EH52 5ND
Tel: 01506 857201
Fax: 01506 859096
E-mail: enquiries@brownscoaches.co.uk.
Web site: www.brownscoaches.co.uk.
Fleet: 15 - 12 single-deck coach, 3 minicoach
Chassis: 3 Mercedes. 12 Volvo.
Bodies: 7 Berkhof. 5 Van Hool. 3 other.
Ops incl: excursions & tours, private hire, continental tours.
Livery: White with blue writing.

*EDINBURGH BUS TOURS
ANNANDALE STREET, EDINBURGH EH7 4AZ
Tel: 0131 220 0770
Fax: 0131 225 7857
E-mail: info@edinburghtour.com
Web site: www.edinburghtour.com
Man Dir: Neil Renilson **Fin Dir**: N Strachan
Ops Dir: W W Campbell **Eng Dir**: W Devlin
Mktg Dir: I Coupar
Fleet: 24 open-top bus
Chassis: 4 Dennis. 20 Leyland.
Bodies: 17 Alexander. 4 Plaxton. 3 Roe.
Ops incl: local bus services, excursions & tours

FAIRWAY TRAVEL
6 BRIARBANK TERRACE, EDINBURGH EH11 1ST.
Tel: 0131 467 6717.
Fax: 0131 467 6717.
E-mail: davy@fairwaytravel.freeserve
Web site: www.fairwaytravel.co.uk
Prop: D. Innes.
Fleet: 4 - 1 coach, 2 midicoach, 1 minibus.
Chassis: 1 DAF. 1 Setra. 2 Toyota.
Bodies: 2 Caetano. 1 Leyland. 1 Setra.
Ops incl: school contracts, excursions & tours, private hire, continental tours.
Livery: Blue and Red on White.

*FIRST IN EDINBURGH LTD
CARMUIRS HOUSE, 300 STIRLING ROAD, LARBERT FK5 3NJ
Tel: 01324 602200
Fax: 01324 611287
Web site: www.firstgroup.com
Man Dir: Brian Juffs **Ops Dir**: Juliette Turner **Eng Dir**: Andrew Green **Fin Dir**: David Stewart
Fleet: 439 - 153 double-deck bus, 202 single-deck bus, 5 coach, 78 midibus, 1 minibus.
Chassis: 1 BMC. 78 Dennis. 21 Leyland. 2 MCW. 32 Mercedes. 188 Scania. 117 Volvo.

Bodies: 103 Alexander. 1 BMC. 24 East Lancs. 15 Northern Counties. 23 Optare. 80 Plaxton. 4 Transbus. 189 Wright.
Ops incl: local bus services
Livery: Pink/Purple/White

*LIBERTON TRAVEL
♥ wc 🍴 A/c

17-29 ENGINE ROAD, LOANHEAD EH20 9RF
Tel: 0131 440 4400
Fax: 0131 448 0008
E-mail: sales@libertontravel.co.uk
Dirs: Iain Smith, Alan Boyd
Fleet: 10 - 7 coach, 2 minibus, 1 minicoach.
Chassis: 1 Dennis. 1 Ford Transit. 1 Freight Rover. 1 Mercedes. 6 Volvo.
Bodies: 1 Caetano. 1 Marcopolo. 4 Plaxton.
Ops incl: school contracts, excursions & tours, private hire.
Livery: White

*LOTHIAN BUSES PLC ♿

ANNANDALE STREET, EDINBURGH EH7 4AZ
Tel: 0131 554 4494
Fax: 0131 554 3942
E-mail: mail@lothianbuses.co.uk
Web site: www.lothianbuses.co.uk
Ch Exec: Neil Renilson **Man Dir**: Ian Craig **Fin Dir**: N Strachan **Ops Dir**: W W Campbell **Eng Dir**: W Devlin **Mktg Dir**: I Coupar **Employee Dir**: J Dixon **Chmn**: P Smith **Non Exec Dirs**: W Gallagher, I Kitson, A Ross, J Saren, A Guest, B Cox
Fleet: 624 - 499 double-deck bus, 125 single-deck bus.
Chassis: 283 Dennis. 115 Leyland. 226 Volvo.
Bodies: 254 Alexander. 285 Plaxton. 85 Wright.
Ops incl: local bus services.
Livery: Maroon/Red/White/Gold
Ticket system: Wayfarer 3

*MAC TOURS LTD

ANNANDALE STREET, EDINBURGH EH7 4AZ
Tel: 0131 220 0770
Fax: 0131 225 7857
E-mail: info@mactours.co.uk
Web site: www.edinburghtour.com
Ch Exec: N Renilson **Fin Dir**: N Strachan **Ops Dir**: W W Campbell **Eng Dir**: W Devlin **Mktg Dir**: I Coupar
Fleet: 40 - 3 double-deck bus, 1 single-deck bus, 28 open-top bus, 7 midibus, 1 minibus.
Chassis: 20 AEC. 7 Dennis. 12 Leyland. 1 Mercedes.
Bodies: 17 Alexander. 20 Park Royal. 3 other.
Ops incl: excursions & tours.
Livery: Red/Cream, Blue/Yellow

*STANLEY MACKAY COACHES

BUTLERFIELD INDUSTRIAL ESTATE, BONNYRIGG EH19 3JQ
Tel: 01875 822862
Fax: 01875 822762
E-mail: mackay.coaches@virgin.net

Prop: Douglas Mackay.
Fleet: 5 coach.
Chassis/Bodies: 4 Setra. 1 Volvo.
Ops incl: private hire

SCOTIA TRAVEL
♥ wc 🍴 ✦ A/c T

ROSEBINE GARAGE, 29A MAIN STREET, COALTOWN, GLENROTHES KY7 6HU
Tel: 0131 553 1455/01592 773900
Fax: 01592 775588
Recovery: 01592 773900
E-mail: enquiries@scotiatravel.co.uk
Web site: www.scotiatravel.co.uk
Prop: Alex Henderson
Fleet: 4 - 2 coach. 2 minibus.
Chassis: 1 Bova. 1 DAF. 2 Mercedes.
Bodies: 1 Bova. 1 Reeve Burgess. 1 Van Hool.
Ops incl: private hire, excursions & tours, continental tours.
Livery: Blue/Gold/White.

*EDINBURGH COACH LINES LTD
♥ wc A/c R T

81 SALAMANDER STREET, LEITH, EDINBURGH EH6 7JZ
Tel: 0131 554 5413
Fax: 0131 553 3721
E-mail: enquiries@edinburghcoachlines.com.
Web site: www.edinburghcoachlines.com.
Dirs: Patric & Thomas Kavanagh **Gen Man**: Peter Fyvie **Traff Man**: John Blair
Bookings Cnsltnt: Jacqueline Bauld
Fleet: 25 - 20 coach, 4 midicoach, 1 minibus.
Chassis: 1 BMC. 1 MAN. 8 Mercedes. 14 Scania. 1 Volvo.
Bodies: 1 BMC. 1 Caetano. 1 Indcar. 8 Irizar. 4 Setra. 7 Van Hool.
Ops incl: excursions & tours, private hire, continental tours, school contracts.

FALKIRK

FIRST SCOTLAND EAST ♿
wc 🚌 🍴 ♥ R24 ✦ T

CARMUIRS HOUSE, 300 STIRLING ROAD, LARBERT FK1 5HP.
Tel: 01324 627175
Fax: 01324 611287.
Man Dir: B Juffs
Fleet: 481 - 176 double-deck bus, 247 single-deck bus, 22 coach, 36 midibus, 54 minibus.
Chassis: 91 Dennis. 91 Leyland. 12 Leyland-DAB. 37 MCW. 45 Mercedes. 23 Optare. 87 Scania. 95 Volvo.
Bodies: Alexander. East Lancs. MCW. Optare. Plaxton. Roe. Wright.
Ops incl: local bus services, school contracts, excursions & tours, private hire, express.
Livery: Cream/Blue or Cream/Green. New vehicles in First Group

White/Blue/Magenta.
Ticket System: Wayfarer 3.

P. WOODS MINICOACHES

20 CALDER PLACE, HALLGLEN FK1 2QQ.
Tel: 01324 613085.
Fax: 01324 717976.

FIFE

*FIFE SCOTTISH OMNIBUSES LTD
♿ wc ♥ T

GUTHRIE HOUSE, GLENFIELD INDUSTRIAL ESTATE, COWDENBEATH KY4 9HT
Tel: 01383 511911
Fax: 01383 516450
Recovery: 01383 511911
E-mail: eastscotland@stagecoachbus.com
Web site: www.stagecoachbus.com
Fleetname: Stagecoach in Fife
Man Dir: Tom Wileman **Dep Man Dir**: Robert Andrew **Ops Dir**: Doug Fleming
Eng Dir: Sandy Brydon
Fleet: 330 - 132 double-deck bus, 114 single-deck bus, 10 coach, 44 midibus, 34 minibus.
Chassis: 45 Dennis. 14 Leyland. 37 MAN. 19 Mercedes. 15 Optare. 10 Scania. 190 Volvo.
Bodies: 177 Alexander. 2 Jonckheere. 88 Northern Counties. 15 Optare. 48 Plaxton.
Ops incl: local bus services, school contracts, excursions & tours, private hire, express.
Livery: Stagecoach
Ticket System: ERG

KINGDOM COACHES

DEN WALK, METHIL KY8 3JH.
Tel: 01333 26109
Fleet: 3 coach.
Chassis: 2 DAF. 1 Ford.
Bodies: 2 Plaxton. 1 Van Hool.
Ops incl: private hire.
Livery: Yellow/White.

*MOFFAT & WILLIAMSON LTD
♿ wc ♥ 🍴 A/c R ✦

OLD RAILWAY YARD, ST FORT, NEWPORT-ON-TAY DD6 8RG
Tel: 01382 541159
Fax: 01382 541169
E-mail: enquiries@moffat-williamson.co.uk
Web site: www.moffat-williamson.co.uk
Gen Man: John Williamson **Ops Man**: Iain Williamson **Depot Man**: John Rodger
Fleet: 59 - 1 double-deck bus, 9 single-deck bus, 42 coach, 2 midibus, 3 midicoach, 2 minicoach.

A/c	Air conditioning
♿	Vehicles suitable for disabled
🍴	Coach(es) with galley facilities
wc	Coach(es) with toilet facilities
♥	Seat belt-fitted vehicles
R	Recovery service available (not 24 hr)
R24	24hr recovery service
✦	Replacement vehicle available
T	Toilet-drop facilities available
🚐	Vintage vehicle(s) available
🚌	Open top vehicle(s)

Scottish Operators

Chassis: 1 DAF. 18 Dennis. 1 LDV.
1 Leyland. 4 MAN. 6 Mercedes. 5 Optare.
23 Volvo.
Ops incl: local bus services, school contracts, private hire, express.
Livery: Brown/Cream/Orange
Ticket System: Almex

*RENNIES OF DUNFERMLINE LTD

WELLWOOD, DUNFERMLINE KY12 0PY
Tel: 01383 620600
Fax: 01383 620624
E-mail: gordon@rennies.co.uk
Web site: www.rennies.co.uk
Chmn: John Rennie Gen Man: Gordon Menzies Tran Man: Iain Robertson
Ch Eng: George Clark
Fleet: 52 - 20 double-deck bus, 25 coach, 3 midicoach, 4 minibus.
Chassis: 3 BMC. 10 Dennis. 1 Iveco. 1 LDV. 20 Leyland. 5 Mercedes. 12 Volvo
Bodies: 1 Beulas. 3 BMC. 4 Caetano. 7 Jonckheere. 1 Mellor. 4 Mercedes. 4 Plaxton. 1 Sunsundegui. 4 Van Hool. 6 Wadham Stringer. 17 other.
Ops incl: local bus services, school contracts, excursions & tours, private hire, continental tours.
Livery: Blue/White.
Ticket system: Almex

ST ANDREWS EXECUTIVE TRAVEL

UNIT 2, TOM STEWART LANE, ST ANDREWS KY16 8YB
Tel: 01334 470080
Fax: 01334 470081
E-mail: orders@saxtravel.co.uk
Web Site: www.saxtravel.co.uk
Dir: Gordon Donaldson.
Fleet: 7 - 1 coach, 2 minicoach, 4 midicoach.
Chassis: 6 Mercedes. 1 Toyota.
Ops incl: school contracts, excursions & tours, private hire.
Livery: Green/White.

GLASGOW, CITY OF

*ALLANDER COACHES LTD

19 CLOBERFIELD INDUSTRIAL ESTATE, MILNGAVIE G62 7LN
Tel: 0141 956 5678
Fax: 0141 956 6669
E-mail: enquiries@allandercoaches.co.uk
Web site: www.allandercoaches.co.uk
Man Dir: J F Wilson Dir: Mrs E E Wilson Ch Eng: G S Wilson Co Sec: Miss M Brown Ops Man: G F Wilson
Fleet: 22 - 2 double-deck bus, single-deck bus, 14 coach, 1 minibus, 2 minicoach.
Chassis: 8 Bova. 3 Dennis. 1 Mercedes. 1 Toyota. 9 Volvo.
Bodies: 1 Alexander. 1 Berkhof. 8 Bova. 5 Jonckheere. 1 Optare. 2 Plaxton. 1 Transbus. 3 Wadham Stringer.
Ops incl: local bus services, excursions & tours, private hire, school contracts.
Livery: Black/Gold/Orange.
Ticket system: Setright

*CITY SIGHTSEEING GLASGOW LTD

153 QUEEN STREET, GLASGOW G1 3BJ
Tel: 0141 204 0444
Fax: 0141 248 6582
E-mail: info@scotguide.com
Web site: www.scotguide.com
Dirs: A Pringle, Mrs C Pringle.
Fleet: 12 open-top bus.
Chassis: 3 Leyland. 9 MCW.
Ops incl: excursions & tours.
Livery: Red
Ticket system: Almex Microfare

DOIGS OF GLASGOW LTD

TRANSPORT HOUSE, SUMMER STREET, GLASGOW G40 3TB
Tel: 0141 554 5555
Fax: 0141 551 9000
E-mail: andy@doigs.com
Web site: www.doigs.com
Chmn/Man Dir: Andrew Forsyth Co Sec: Iain Forsyth Ops Man: Gerald Conner
Fleet: 15 - 1 double-deck bus, 1 single-deck bus, 1 articulated bus, 8 coach, 1 midicoach, 3 minicoach.
Chassis: 1 DAF. 1 Dennis. 1 LDV. 3 Mercedes. 8 Scania. 1 Volvo.
Bodies: 1 Caetano. 1 East Lancs. 7 Irizar. 1 Marcopolo. 2 Mercedes. 1 Optare. 1 Sunsundegui. 1 Wright.
Ops incl: school contracts, excursions & tours, private hire, continental tours.

FIRST GLASGOW

197 VICTORIA ROAD, GLASGOW G42 7AD.
Tel: 0141 423 6600
Fax: 0141 636 3228
Web Site: www.firstgroup.com.
Man Dir: Mark Savelli
Fleet: 992 - 396 double-deck bus, 496 single-deck bus, 100 minibus.
Chassis: 126 Dennis. 103 Leyland. 36 MCW. 85 Mercedes. 15 Optare. 130 Scania. 497 Volvo.
Bodies: Alexander. East Lancs. MCW. Optare. Plaxton. Wright.
Ops incl: local bus services.

NEIL MACKELLAIG

11 DUNSYRE PLACE, GLASGOW G23 5EB.
Tel: 0141 946 1895.
Prop: N. Mackellaig.
Fleet: 1 minicoach.
Chassis: Toyota. Body: Caetano.
Ops incl: school contracts, private hire.

*JOHN MORROW COACHES

18 ALBION INDUSTRIAL ESTATE, HALLEY STREET, GLASGOW G13 4DL
Tel: 0141 951 8888
Fax: 0141 952 6445
Prop: John Morrow.
Fleet: 15 - 14 single-deck bus, 1 midicoach.
Bodies: 1 Leyland. 9 Mercedes. 2 Optare. 1 Toyota. 2 Volvo
Chassis: 1 Caetano. 1 Leyland. 9 Mercedes. 2 Optare. 1 Plaxton. 1 Van Hool

Ops incl: local bus services, private hire, school contracts, excursions & tours
Livery: Brown/Cream
Ticket system: Wayfarer 3

SCOTTISH CITYLINK COACHES LTD

BUCHANAN BUS STATION, KILLERMONT STREET, GLASGOW G2 3NP
Tel: 0141 352 4454
E-mail: info@citylink.co.uk
Web site: www.citylink.co.uk
Man Dir: Neil Wood
Ops incl: private hire, express.
Livery: Blue/yellow
Ticket system: Wayfarer

SELVEY'S COACHES

HILLCREST HOUSE, 33 HOWIESHILL ROAD, CAMBUSLANG G72 8PW.
Tel: 0141 641 1080.
Fax: 0141 641 2065.
Owner: A. G. Selvey.
Fleet: 8 - 5 coach, 2 midicoach, 1 minicoach.
Chassis: 3 Bedford. 2 Leyland. 1 Mercedes. 2 Volvo.
Bodies: 1 Duple. 1 Jonckheere. 1 Mercedes. 3 Plaxton.
Ops incl: excursions & tours, private hire, school contracts.
Livery: Maroon/Red/Yellow.

*STAGECOACH WEST SCOTLAND

UNITS A,B,C, BLOCHAIRN ROAD, GLASGOW G21 2D7
Tel: 0141 552 5653
Web site: www.stagecoachbus.com
Man Dir: Tom Wileman Eng Dir: Sam Greer

HIGHLAND

BEAULY COACH HIRE

THE ROOKERY, WESTER BALBLAIR, BEAULY IV4 7BQ
Tel: 01463 782498
Fax: 01463 783298
E-mail: mhairicormack@aol.com
Prop: Gordon Cormack
Fleet: 4 - 2 midicoach, 2 minicoach
Chassis: Mercedes
Ops incl: school contracts, private hire

*BLUEBIRD BUSES LTD

6 BURNETT ROAD, LONGMAN INDUSTRIAL ESATE, INVERNESS IV1 1TF
Tel: 01463 239292
Fax: 01463 712338
Recovery: 01463 239292
E-mail: eastscotland@stagecoachbus.com
Web site: www.stagecoachbus.com
Fleetname: Stagecoach Inverness
Man Dir: Tom Wileman Dep Man Dir:

Robert Andrew **Ops Dir**: Robert Hall **Eng Dir**: Michael Reid **Ops Man**: Scott Pearson **Depot Eng**: Russell Henderson
Fleet: 63 - 7 double-deck bus, 12 single-deck bus, 9 coach, 27 midibus, 8 minibus.
Chassis: 27 Dennis. 1 Leyland. 4 MAN. 6 Mercedes. 2 Optare. 24 Volvo.
Bodies: 34 Alexander. 7 Jonckheere. 6 Northern Counties. 2 Optare. 14 Plaxton.
Ops incl: local bus services, school contracts, excursions & tours, private hire, express.
Livery: Stagecoach/Citylink/Megabus
Ticket System: Wayfarer TGX

*D&E COACHES

39 HENDERSON DRIVE, INVERNESS IV1 1TR
Tel: 01463 222444
Fax: 01463 226700
Recovery: 07770 222612
E-mail: decoaches@aol.com
Web site: www.decoaches.co.uk
Props: D Mathieson, E Mathieson
Fleet: 16 - 5 coach, 1 midibus, 5 midicoach, 5 minicoach.
Chassis: 3 LDV. 6 Mercedes. 1 Optare. 1 VW. 5 Volvo.
Bodies: 2 Alexander. 2 Berkhof. 2 Mercedes. 1 Optare. 2 Plaxton. 2 Reeve Burgess. 3 Van Hool. 2 other.
Ops incl: local bus services, school contracts, private hire.
Livery: Black/Red

DUNCAN MACLENNAN
HILL-SIDE, SHIELDAIG, STRATHCARRON IV54 8XN
Tel/Fax: 01520 755239
Prop: Duncan MacLennan
Fleet: 2 - 1 midicoach, 1 minibus.
Chassis/bodies: 1 Ford. 1 Mercedes.
Ops incl: local bus services, school contracts.

RAPSONS COACHES LTD
1 SEAFIELD ROAD, INVERNESS IV1 1TN
Tel: 01463 710555
Fax: 01463 711488
E-mail: info@rapsons.co.uk
Web site: www.rapsons.co.uk
Chairman: Sandy Rapson **Man Dir**: John Lornig **Ops Dir**: Neil MacDonald **Eng Dir**: Russell Henderson **Comm Services Dir**: Alistair Goodall.
Fleet: 250 - incl: 26 double-deck bus, 37 single-deck bus, 118 coach, 2 open-top bus, 50 minibus.
Ops incl: local bus services, school contracts, excursions & tours, private hire, express.
Livery: Blue
Ticket System: Wayfarer 3

SHIEL BUSES
BLAIN GARAGE, ACHARACLE PH36 4JY.
Tel/Fax: 01967 431272.
E-mail: shiel.buses@virgin.net

Dir: Donnie MacGillivray.
Fleet: 10 - 4 single-deck coach, 6 midibus.
Chassis: 1 Ford Transit. 4 Mercedes. 4 Volvo.
Bodies: 2 Mercedes. 2 Plaxton. 2 Van Hool. 2 Onyx.
Ops incl: local bus services, school contracts, private hire.
Livery: Red/White
Ticket system: Amex

SPA COACHES
R24
KINETTAS, STRATHPEFFER IV14 9BH.
Tel: 01997 421311.
Fax: 01997 421983.
Web site: www.spacoaches.com
Prop: N. MacArthur.
Fleet: 28 - 6 double-deck bus, 13 coach, 5 midibus, 2 minibus.
Chassis: 1 DAF. 2 Ford Transit. 5 Mercedes. 14 Volvo.
Bodies: 1 Duple. 7 Alexander. 2 Caetano. 3 Jonckheere. 5 Plaxton. 6 Van Hool. 4 other.
Ops incl: local bus services, school contracts, excursions & tours, private hire, continental tours.
Livery: Orange/White.
Ticket System: Punch Tickets.

GRAHAM URQUHART TRAVEL LTD
28 MIDMILLS ROAD, INVERNESS IV2 3NY
Tel: 01463 222292
Fax: 01463 238880
E-mail: graham@urquharttravel.fsnet.co.uk
Web site: www.grahamurquharttravel.co.uk
Dir: John P Urquhart
Fleet: 7 - 3 coach, 3 midicoach, 1 minicoach.
Chassis: 1 Ford. 1 Iveco. 1 Mercedes. 3 Scania.
Bodies: 1 Berkhof. 3 Irizar. 1 Van Hool. 2 Esker.
Ops incl: excursions & tours, private hire, continental tours.

WHITE HEATHER TOURS

ALGARVE, BADABRIE, BANAVIE PH33 7LX
Tel/Fax: 01397 772255
E-mail: enquiries@whitehethertravel.co.uk
Web site: www.whitehethertravel.com
Prop: Adam A MacIntyre
Fleet: 3 midicoach.
Chassis/bodies: 2 Caetano. 1 Mercedes.
Ops incl: school contracts, excursions & tours, private hire.
Livery: White/Gold/Green/Red

INVERCLYDE

*GILLEN'S COACHES LTD
UNIT 3, KINGSTON BUSINESS PARK, PORT GLASGOW PA14 5DP
Tel/Fax: 01475 744618
Recovery: 07785 873299
Dir: Michael Gillen
Fleet: 14 - single-deck bus, midicoach, minibus, minicoach
Ops incl: local bus services, excursions & tours, private hire.
Livery: White
Ticket system: Wayfarer

GLEN COACHES LTD

6 MACDOUGALL STREET, GREENOCK PA15 2TG.
Tel: 01475 783399.
Fax: 01475 888446.
Owners: W. Wilson, Ms C. Wilson.
Fleet: 10 - 6 coach, 2 midibus, 1 midicoach, 1 minibus.
Chassis: 1 Iveco. 2 Mercedes. 6 Volvo.
Bodies: 1 Beulas. 1 Jonckheere. 2 Plaxton. 5 Van Hool.
Ops incl: local bus services, school contracts, excursions & tours, private hire.
Livery: Blue/White.

MIDLOTHIAN

ALLAN'S GROUP
NEWTONLOAN GARAGE, GOREBRIDGE EH23 4LZ
Tel: 01875 820377.
Fax: 01875 822468
Recovery: 01875 820377
E-mail: allanscoaches@aol.co.uk
Web Site: www.allans-group.com
Dir: D W Allan **Ch Eng**: Neil Mitchell **Office Man**: Mrs D Allan
Fleet: 14 - 9 single-deck bus, 5 midicoach.
Chassis: 5 Mercedes. 9 Scania.
Bodies: 5 Sitcar. 9 Van Hool.
Ops incl: school contracts, private hire.
Livery: Blue/Silver.

WILLIAM HUNTER

OAKFIELD GARAGE, LOANHEAD EH20 9AE
Tel: 0131 440 0704
Fax: 0131 448 2184
E-mail: sales@hunterscoaches.co.uk
Props: G I Hunter, W R Hunter.
Fleet: 14 - 12 coach, 2 minibus.
Chassis: 3 Toyota. 11 Volvo.
Bodies: 3 Caetano. 11 Van Hool.
Ops incl: school contracts, private hire.
Livery: Brown/Cream

A/c	Air conditioning
	Vehicles suitable for disabled
	Coach(es) with galley facilities
WC	Coach(es) with toilet facilities
	Seat belt-fitted vehicles
R	Recovery service available (not 24 hr)
R24	24hr recovery service
	Replacement vehicle available
T	Toilet-drop facilities available
	Vintage vehicle(s) available
	Open top vehicle(s)

FIRST SCOTLAND EAST

14-16 ESKBANK ROAD, DALKEITH EH22 1HH.
Tel: 0131 663 1945.
Fax: 0131 660 3989.
Man Dir: Brian Juffs
Fleet: 481 - 176 double-deck bus, 247 single-deck bus, 22 coach, 36 minibus.
Chassis: 91 Dennis. 91 Leyland.12 Leyland-DAB. 37 MCW. 45 Mercedes. 23 Optare. 87 Scania. 95 Volvo.
Bodies: Alexander. East Lancs. MCW. Optare. Plaxton. Roe. Wright.
Ops incl: local bus services, school contracts, excursions & tours, private hire.
Livery: Cream/Yellow and Green, Light Grey/Dark Blue and Magenta.
Ticket System: Wayfarer 3.
See also Edinburgh, Falkirk.

*LIBERTON TRAVEL
See Edinburgh, City of

*STANLEY MACKAY COACHES
See Edinburgh, City of

*McKENDRY TRAVEL
RAMSAY COLLIERY, ENGINE ROAD, LOANHEAD EH20 9NP
Tel: 0131 440 1013
Fax: 0131 448 2160
E-mail: douglas.mckendry@virgin.net
Web site: www.mckendrycoaches.co.uk
Dir: Ann McKendry **Tran Man**: Stuart McCaw
Fleet: 15 - 1 double-deck bus, 12 coach, 2 minibus.
Chassis: 1 Dennis. 1 Ford Transit. 1 Freight Rover. 1 Leyland National. 4 Scania. 5 Volvo.
Bodies: 1 Caetano. 2 Jonckheere. 2 Plaxton. 5 Van Hool.
Ops incl: excursions & tours, private hire, school contracts.
Livery: White/Blue/Purple/Red vinyls

MORAY

*CENTRAL COACHES

CHURCH ROAD, KEITH AB55 5BN
Tel: 01542 882113
Fax: 01542 886945
E-mail: enquiries@centralcoaches.co.uk
Web site: www.centralcoaches.co.uk
Ptnrs: William W Smith, Veronica A Smith, William A Smith
Fleet: 10 - 7 coach, 3 minbus.
Chassis: 1 Bova. 3 DAF. 1 Ford Transit. 2 Mercedes. 3 Volvo.
Bodies: 1 Bova. 1 Caetano. 1 Jonckheere. 1 Mellor. 1 Mercedes. 3 Plaxton. 1 Van Hool. 1 other.
Ops incl: local bus services, school contracts, private hire.
Livery: White/Red

KINEIL COACHES
See Aberdeenshire

*MAYNES COACHES LTD

4 MARCH ROAD WEST, BUCKIE AB56 4BU
Tel: 01542 831219
Fax: 01542 833572
E-mail: maynescoaches@talk21.com
Web site: www.maynes.co.uk
Man Dir: Gordon Mayne **Dirs**: Sandra Mayne, David Mayne (**Tran Man**), Kevin Mayne **Eng**: Mike Lapka **Co Sec**: Jennifer Cowie
Fleet: 30 - 1 single-deck bus, 21 coach, 7 midicoach, 1 minicoach.
Chassis: 3 Bova. 1 Dennis. 1 Leyland. 3 MAN. 7 Mercedes. 13 Volvo.
Bodies: 4 Beluga. 2 Caetano. 3 Marcopolo. 1 Northern Counties. 4 Plaxton. 1 Reeve Burgess. 12 Van Hool.
Ops incl: local bus services, school contracts, excursions & tours, private hire, continental tours.
Livery: Blue/White/Gold

NORTH AYRSHIRE

*CLYDE COAST COACHES LTD
55 MONTGOMERIE STREET, ARDROSSAN KA22 8HR
Tel: 01294 605454
Fax: 01294 605460
E-mail: enquiries@clydecoast.com
Web site: www.clydecoast.com
Dirs: Kenneth G McGregor, David H Frazer.
Fleet: 20 - 8 double-deck bus, 10 coach, 2 midibus.
Chassis: 1 Ford Transit. 8 Leyland. 1 VW. 10 Volvo.
Bodies: 3 Alexander. 5 ECW. 2 Sunsundegui. 8 Van Hool. 2 other.
Ops incl: excursions & tours, private hire, school contracts.
Livery: Silver Blue metallic

T & E DOCHERTY

40 BANK STREET, IRVINE KA12 0LP
Tel/Recovery: 01294 278440
Fax: 01294 272510
E-mail: info@coach-hires.co.uk
Web site: www.coach-hires.co.uk
Owner: Hugh Tait **Gen Man**: Tom Hamilton
Fleet: 31 - 2 double-deck bus, 6 single-deck bus, 11 coach, 4 minicoach, 8 midibus.
Chassis: 7 Bova. 1 Dodge. 2 LDV. 2 Leyland. 10 Mercedes. 2 Optare. 8 Volvo.
Bodies: 2 Alexander. 1 Autobus. 7 Bova. 1 Caetano. 1 East Lancs. 2 LDV. 2 Optare. 6 Plaxton. 1 Reeve Burgess. 2 Van Hool. 6 Wright. 1 Sitcar.
Ops incl: school contracts, excursions & tours, private hire, express, continental tours.
Livery: Buses: Blue/Cream. Coaches: Cream/Beige
Ticket System: Wayfarer 3.

MARBILL TRAVEL

HIGH MAINS GARAGE, MAINS ROAD, BEITH KA15 2AP
Tel: 01505 503367
Fax: 01505 504736
E-mail: marbill@btclick.com
Web site: www.marbillcoaches.com
Man Dir: Margaret Whiteman **Eng Dir**: David Barr **Ops Dir**: Connie Barr
Fleet: 66 - 26 double-deck bus, 20 single-deck bus, 18 coach, 2 minicoach.
Chassis: 2 Bova. 34 Leyland. 2 Mercedes. 28 Volvo
Bodies: 26 Alexander. 2 Bova. 25 Plaxton. 12 Van Hool. 1 Beluga.
Ops incl: school contracts, excursions & tours, private hire.

MILLPORT MOTORS LTD
16 BUTE TERRACE, MILLPORT KA28 0BA.
Tel: 01475 530555.
Fleet: 4 single-deck bus.
Chassis: 3 Leyland. 1 Volvo.
Ops incl: local bus services, private hire.
Livery: Blue/Cream.
Ticket System: Almex.

*SHUTTLE BUSES LTD

CALEDONIA HOUSE, LONGFORD AVENUE, KILWINNING KA13 6EX
Tel: 01294 550757
Fax: 01294 558822
E-mail: dgranger@btconnect.com
Web site: www.shuttlebuses.co.uk
Man Dir: David Granger
Fleet: 25 - 1 single-deck bus, 3 coach, 13 midibus, 2 midicoach, 4 minibus, 2 minicoach.
Chassis: 1 AEC. 4 Dennis. 3 Ford Transit. 2 Leyland. 7 Mercedes. 7 Optare. 1 Scania.
Bodies: 3 Alexander. 1 Autobus. 2 Mercedes. 7 Optare. 5 Plaxton. 1 Reeve Burgess. 6 other.
Ops incl: local bus services, school contracts, private hire.
Livery: Yellow/White.
Ticket System: Almex

T PATERSON & BROWN LTD

51 HOLMHEAD, KILBIRNIE KA25 6BS.
Tel: 01505 683344.
Fax: 01505 684508
Recovery: 07787 530162
E-mail: patersonscoaches@tiscali.co.uk
Web site: www.patersonscoaches.com
Man Dir: Samuel Paterson **Ch Eng**: David Paterson **Co Sec**: Robert Brown.
Fleet: 7 coach.
Chassis: 4 Bova. 3 Volvo.
Bodies: 4 Bova. 1 Caetano. 1 Plaxton. 1 Van Hool.
Ops incl: excursions & tours, private hire, continental tours, school contracts.

*STAGECOACH WEST SCOTLAND

HEAD OFFICE, SANDGATE, AYR KA7 1DD
Tel: 01292 613700
Fax: 01292 613501
Web site: www.stagecoachbus.com

Man Dir: Tom Wileman **Eng Dir**: Sam Greer

NORTH LANARKSHIRE

A&C LUXURY COACHES
4 HILLHEAD AVENUE, MOTHERWELL ML1 4AQ
Tel: 01698 252652
Fax: 01698 259898
E-mail: enquiries@acluxurycoaches.co.uk
Web site: www.acluxurycoaches.co.uk
Prop: Alex Grenfell
Fleet: 6 - 3 coach, 2 midicoach, 1 minicoach.
Chassis: 3 Mercedes. 1 Neoplan. 2 Volvo.
Bodies: 1 Neoplan. 1 Plaxton. 1 Van Hool
Ops incl: school contracts, private hire, excursions & tours.

CANAVAN'S COACHES
CEDAR LODGE, COACH ROAD, KILSYTH G65 0DB.
Tel: 01236 822414.
Prop: M., G., H., & J. Canavan.
Ops incl: local bus services.

DUNN'S COACHES
560 STIRLING ROAD, RIGGEND, AIRDRIE ML6 7SS.
Tel: 01236 722385.
Fax: 01236 722385.
Owner: William G. Dunn. **Eng**: Craig Dunn.
Fleet: 7 - 4 coach, 3 minibus.
Chassis: 1 DAF. 3 Volvo. 1 Leyland. 2 Mercedes.
Bodies: 1 Alexander. 1 Marshall. 4 Plaxton. 1 Van Hool.
Ops incl: local bus services, school contracts, excursions & tours, private hire, express.

ESSBEE COACHES (HIGHLANDS & ISLANDS)

7 HOLLANDHURST ROAD, GARTSHERRIE ML5 2EG
Tel: 01236 423621
Fax: 01236 433677
Man Dir: B. Smith. **Gen Man**: J. Kinnaird.
Ops Man: S. Stewart.
Fleet: 56 - 14 single-deck bus, 19 coach, 2 double-deck coach, 6 midicoach, 19 minibus.
Chassis: 2 DAF. 3 Ford Transit. 13 Leyland. 6 Leyland National. 21 Mercedes. 2 Neoplan. 10 Volvo.
Bodies: 7 Duple. 1 ECW. 1 Jonckheere. 6 Leyland National. 2 Neoplan. 15 Plaxton. 3 Autobus. 2 Crystals.
Ops incl: local bus services, school contracts, excursions & tours, private hire.
Livery: Red/Silver.
Ticket System: Wayfarer.

GOLDEN EAGLE COACHES
MUIRHALL GARAGE, 197 MAIN STREET, SALSBURGH BY SHOTTS ML7 4LS
Tel: 01698 870207
Fax: 01698 870217
E-mail: general@goldeneaglecoaches.freeserve.co.uk
Web site: www.golden-eagle-coaches.co.uk
Ptnrs: Peter Irvine, Robert Irvine, Isabel Irvine.
Fleet: 15 - 5 single-deck bus, 10 coach.
Chassis: 1 Bova. 1 DAF. 6 Leyland. 7 Volvo.
Bodies: 1 Bova. 5 Leyland. 8 Van Hool. 1 other
Ops incl: private hire, excursions & tours, school contracts, .
Livery: White/Maroon/Gold

*HUTCHISON'S COACHES (OVERTOWN) LTD
5 CASTLEHILL ROAD, OVERTOWN, WISHAW ML2 0QS
Tel: 01698 372132
Fax: 01698 376933
E-mail: stewartanderson@hutchisoncoaches.co.uk
Web site: www.hutchisoncoaches.co.uk
Prop: S Anderson
Fleet: 48 - 27 single-deck bus, 21 coach.
Chassis: 2 DAF. 6 MAN. 9 Optare. 8 Scania. 23 Volvo.
Bodies: 1 Alexander. 1 Berkhof. 2 Duple. 4 Irizar. 1 Northern Counties. 9 Optare. 4 Plaxton. 12 Van Hool. 12 Wright.
Ops incl: local bus services, excursions & tours, private hire, continental tours, express.
Livery: Blue/Cream; Silver/Blue/Red
Ticket System: Wayfarer.

IRVINE'S OF LAW
LAWMUIR ROAD, LAW ML8 5JB.
Tel: 01698 372452
Fax: 01698 376200
Prop: Peter Irvine **Man**: Gordon Graham
Ch Eng: Scott Fisher
Fleet: 40 - 14 double-deck bus, 13coach, 13 midibus.
Chassis: DAF. Dennis. Optare. Scania. Volvo.
Bodies: Van Hool
Ops incl: local bus services, excursions & tours, school contracts, private hire, express, continental tours.
Livery: Red/Cream.
Ticket System: Wayfarer.

LONG'S COACHES LTD
157 MAIN STREET, SALSBURGH BY SHOTTS ML7 4LR.
Tel: 01698 870768.
Fax: 01698 870826.
E-mail: info@longscoaches.co.uk
Web site: www.longscoaches.co.uk
Dir: Peter I. Long **Co Sec**: Susan Long.
Fleet: 14 - 13 coach, 1 midicoach.
Chassis: 2 Bova. 12 Volvo.
Bodies: 2 Bova. 12 Van Hool.
Ops incl: excursions & tours, private hire, express, continental tours, school contracts.
Livery: Silver/Maroon.
Ticket System: Wayfarer.

MACPHAILS COACHES
409 HIGH STREET, NEWARTHILL, MOTHERWELL ML1 5SP
Tel: 01698 860249
Fax: 01698 861963
E-mail: macphailscoaches@hotmail.com
Web site: www.macphailscoaches.com
Dirs: Martin MacPhail, Henry MacPhail.
Fleet: 8 coach.
Chassis: 8 Volvo.
Bodies: 1 Plaxton. 7 Van Hool.
Ops incl: excursions & tours, private hire, continental tours.

MCKINDLESS EXPRESS
101 MAIN STREET, BOGSIDE, WISHAW ML2 9PP.
Tel: 01698 356991.
Prop: M. McKindless.
Ops Incl: local bus services, express, school contracts, private hire.
Livery: Cream/Green.

*MCT GROUP TRAVEL LTD
NETHAN STREET DEPOT, NETHAN STREET, MOTHERWELL ML1 3TF
Tel: 01698 253091
Fax: 01698 259208
Recovery: 01698 269301
E-mail: mctgrouptravel@hotmail.com
Web site: www.mctgrouptravel.com
Man Dir: Desmond Heenan **Exec Dir**: Oswald Heenan **Fleet Eng**: Alan Bruce.
Fleet: 14 - 4 coach, 6 midicoach, 4 minicoach.
Chassis: 5 Mercedes. 6 Toyota. 3 Volvo.
Bodies: 6 Caetano. 1 Esker. 3 Jonckheere. 4 Mercedes.
Ops incl: excursions & tours, private hire, continental tours.
Livery: Turquoise/Silver

MILLER'S COACHES
22 WOODSIDE DRIVE, CALDERBANK, AIRDRIE ML6 9TN.
Tel: 01236 763671.
Owner: W. Miller. **Tran Man**: T. Miller.
Fleet: 12 - 8 coach, 4 minicoach.
Chassis: 8 Leyland. 4 Mercedes.
Bodies: 2 Alexander. 1 Mellor. 8 Plaxton. 1 Reeve Burgess.
Ops incl: local bus services, school contracts, private hire.
Livery: Black/White/Grey.

A/c	Air conditioning
♿	Vehicles suitable for disabled
🍴	Coach(es) with galley facilities
wc	Coach(es) with toilet facilities
💺	Seat belt-fitted vehicles
R	Recovery service available (not 24 hr)
R24	24hr recovery service
🔧	Replacement vehicle available
T	Toilet-drop facilities available
	Vintage vehicle(s) available
	Open top vehicle(s)

Scottish Operators

STEPEND COACHES
92 WADDELL AVENUE, GLENMAVIS, AIRDRIE ML6 ONZ.
Tel: 01236 760500.
Prop: S. Chapman.
Ops incl: local bus services.

*TRAMONTANA
CHAPELKNOWE ROAD, CARFIN, MOTHERWELL ML1 5LE
Tel: 01698 861790
Fax: 01698 860778
E-mail: wdt90@tiscali.co.uk
Web site: www.tramontanacoach.co.uk
Prop: Douglas Telfer
Fleet: 6 coach
Chassis: 6 Volvo.
Bodies: 2 Caetano. 1 Irizar. 3 Plaxton.
Ops incl: private hire
Livery: White

ORKNEY

ORKNEY COACHES (FORMERLY PEACE'S COACHES)
SCOTTS ROAD, HATSTON INDUSTRIAL ESTATE, KIRKWALL KW15 1JY.
Tel: 01856 870555.
Fax: 01856 877501.
Man Dir: F. Rapson. **Ch Eng:** R. Henderson.
Ch Exec: A. H. Rapson. **Fin Dir:** J. Lornie.
Ops Dir: A. MacDonald.
Fleet: 44 - 28 coach, 6 midibus, 4 midicoach, 6 minibus.
Chassis: 26 Bedford. 2 Dennis. 4 Ford. 1 MCW. 7 Mercedes. 1 Renault. 2 Toyota. 1 Volvo.
Bodies: 7 Duple. 18 Plaxton. 1 Van Hool. 1 Berkhof. 2 Unicar. 14 Other.
Ops incl: local bus services, school contracts, excursions & tours, private hire.
Subsidiary of Rapsons Coaches.

PERTH & KINROSS

ABERFELDY MOTOR SERVICES
BURNSIDE GARAGE, ABERFELDY PH15 2DD
Tel: 01887 820433
Fax: 01887 829534
E-mail: john@aberfeldymotors.freeserve.co.uk
Web site: www.aberfeldycoaches.co.uk
Prop: John Stewart **Co Sec:** Lynda Stewart
Fleet Eng: David Matthew
Fleet: 11 - 8 coach, 1 midibus, 1 minibus, 1 minicoach.
Chassis: 1 Bova. 3 Mercedes. 7 Volvo.
Bodies: 1 Alexander. 1 Bova. 1 Plaxton. 6 Van Hool. 1 Onyx. 1 KVC.
Ops incl: excursions & tours, private hire, continental tours, school contracts.
Livery: Blue

*BLUEBIRD BUSES LTD
RUTHENFIELD ROAD, INVERALMOND, PERTH PH1 3EE
Tel: 01738 629339
Fax: 01738 643264
Recovery: 01738 629339
E-mail: eastscotland@stagecoachbus.com
Web site: www.stagecoachbus.com
Fleetname: Stagecoach in Perth
Man Dir: Tom Wileman **Dep Man Dir:** Robert Andrew **Ops Dir:** Robert Hall **Eng Dir:** Michael Reid **Ops Man:** Kenny Stewart **Depot Eng:** John Dick
Fleet: 77 - 16 double-deck bus, 25 single-deck bus, 6 coach, 10 midibus, 20 minibus.
Chassis: 10 Dennis. 16 Leyland. 16 MAN. 5 Mercedes. 15 Optare. 15 Volvo.
Bodies: 53 Alexander. 3 Jonckheere. 3 Neoplan. 15 Optare. 1 Plaxton. 2 Wright.
Ops incl: local bus services, school contracts, excursions & tours, private hire, express.
Livery: Stagecoach/Megabus
Ticket System: Wayfarer TGX

CABER COACHES LTD
CHAPEL STREET GARAGE, ABERFELDY PH15 2AS
Tel: 01887 870090
Fax: 01887 829352
E-mail: cabercoaches@btinternet.com
Man Dir: Kenneth Carey **Sec:** Alexandre Carey
Fleet: 5 - 1 single-deck bus, 1 coach, 1 midibus, 1 midicoach, 1 minibus, 1 minicoach.
Chassis: 1 LDV. 2 Leyland. 2 Mercedes. 1 Renault.
Bodies: 1 Alexander. 2 Mercedes. 2 Plaxton. 1 Reeve Burgess.
Ops incl: local bus services, school contracts, private hire, excursions & tours.
Livery: White
Ticket system: Almex

*DOCHERTY'S MIDLAND COACHES
PRIORY PARK, AUCHTERARDER PH3 1GB
Tel: 01764 662218
Fax: 01764 664228
Recovery: 01764 662218
E-mail: docherty.midland@virgin.net.
Web site: www.dochertysmidlandcoaches.co.uk
Props: Jim & Edith Docherty **Ops:** Colin Docherty **Eng:** William Docherty
Fleet: 21 - 2 single-deck bus, 10 coach, 1 midibus, 4 midicoach, 1 minicoach, 1 vintage.
Chassis: 1 Leyland. 6 Mercedes. 3 Scania. 9 Volvo.
Bodies: 1 Irizar. 1 Optare. 3 Plaxton. 1 UVG. 8 Van Hool. 2 Wright. 3 other.
Livery: White/Black/Grey
Ticket System: Almex

*EARNSIDE COACHES
GREENBANK ROAD, GLENFARG PH2 9NW
Tel: 01577 830360
Fax: 01577 830599
E-mail: info@earnside.com.
Web site: www.earnside.com
Dirs: David Rutherford, Fiona Rutherford, Gary Rutherford
Fleet: 9 - 1 double-deck bus, 7 coach, 1 midicoach.
Chassis: 1 DAF. 2 Leyland. 1 Renault. 1 Scania. 4 Volvo.
Bodies: 2 Berkhof. 1 Ikarus. 1 Irizar. 1 Leyland. 3 Plaxton. 1 other.
Ops incl: local bus services, school contracts, excursions & tours, private hire, continental tours.
Livery: Yellow/Maroon.

HIGHWAYMAN COACHES
STATION ROAD, ERROL PH2 7QB
Tel: 01821 642739
Fax: 01821 642683
E-mail: rng6@tesco.net.
Owner: Robin Gloag
Fleet: 2 double-deck bus, 8 coach, 1 double-deck bus, 2 midicoach.
Chassis: 3 Bova. 2 DAF. 2 Leyland. 4 MAN. 1 Mercedes. 1 Neoplan. 1 Toyota.
Bodies: 3 Bova. 1 Caetano. 2 Leyland. 1 Mercedes. 1 Neoplan. 1 Plaxton. 4 Van Hool.
Ops incl: school contracts, excursions & tours, private hire.
Livery: multicolour

MEGABUS
10 DUNKELD ROAD, PERTH PH1 5TW
Tel: 01738 522456
Web site: www.megabus.com
Fleet: 60 - incl: 25 double-deck coach
Chassis: incl: 25 MAN
Bodies: incl: 25 MAN.
Ops incl: express.
Livery: Stagecoach (White/Blue/Orange/Red)/Megabus

PEGASUS TRAVEL LTD
28 INVERALMOND ROAD, PERTH PH1 3TW
Tel/Fax: 01738 444070
E-mail: enquiries@pegasus-travel.co.uk, info@pegasus-travel.co.uk
Web site: www.pegasus-travel.co.uk
Man Dir: Duncan Graham **Co Sec:** Mairi Graham **Ops Man:** Trevor White **Ch Eng:** Guy Batchelor
Fleet: 9 - 6 single-deck bus, 3 midicoach.
Chassis: 1 DAF. 1 Iveco. 3 Mercedes. 4 Volvo.
Bodies: 1 Autobus. 8 Plaxton.
Ops incl: local bus services, excursions & tours, private hire, school contracts
Livery: White

SMITH & SONS COACHES
THE COACH DEPOT, WOODSIDE, COUPAR ANGUS PH13 9LW
Tel: 01828 627310
Fax: 01828 628518
E-mail: www.smithandsonscoaches.com
Prop: I. C. Smith. **Prop/Fleet Eng:** G. Smith.
Office Man: A. Osborne.
Prop/Traf Man: I. F. Smith.
Ops incl: local bus services, school

contracts, excursions & tours, private hire, continental tours.
Livery: White/Orange.
Ticket System: Setright.

*ELIZABETH YULE

STATION GARAGE, STATION ROAD, PITLOCHRY PH16 5AN
Tel: 01796 472290
Fax: 01796 474214
E-mail: info.elizabeth-yule@virgin.net
Web site:
www.perthshirecoaches.co.uk
Dirs: Elizabeth Yule, Alexandra M Bridges (Sandra)
Fleet: 9 - 5 coach, 3 midicoach, 1 minibus.
Chassis: 1 LDV. 3 Mercedes. 5 Volvo.
Ops incl: local bus services, school contracts, private hire.
Livery: White
Ticket System: Almex

RENFREWSHIRE

ALAN ARNOTT
16 TURNHILL CRESCENT, WEST FREELANDS, ERSKINE PA8 7AX
Fleetname: S & A Coaches, City Sprinter

ARRIVA SCOTLAND WEST
INCHINNAN, PAISLEY PA3
Web site: www.arrivabus.co.uk
Fleetnames: Arriva, SPT
Man Dir: Ian Craig **Ops Man:** Murray Rogers
Fleet: 170 - incl double-deck bus, single-deck bus, midibus
Chassis: incl: Dennis, Leyland. Optare. Scania. Volvo.
Bodies: incl: Alexander, Northern Counties, Plaxton. Wright.
Ops incl: local bus services
Livery: Stone/Aquamarine

JAMES BURNS
24 GLENDOWER WAY, FOX BAR, PAISLEY PA2 0TH.
Fleetname: Green Line Coaches.

IAN CHESTNUT
36D NORTH ROAD, JOHNSTONE PA5 8NF.
Fleetname: Reliable Bus.

*CLASSIQUE SUN SALOON LUXURY COACHES

8 UNDERWOOD ROAD, PAISLEY PA3 1TD
Tel: 0141 889 4050
Fax: 0141 848 7616
Web site:
www.classiquecoaches.co.uk
Prop: David N Dean
Fleet: 9 coach.

Chassis: 1 AEC. 4 Leyland. 1 Setra. 3 Volvo.
Bodies: 1 Duple. 4 Plaxton. 2 Harrington. 1 Ramseier+Jenzer. 1 Setra.
Ops incl: excursions & tours, private hire, continental tours.
Livery: Various.

VIOLET GRAHAM COACHES
93 IVANHOE ROAD, FOX BAR, PAISLEY PA2 0LF.
Tel: 01505 349758.
Fax: 01505 349758.
Owner: V. Rosike.
Fleet: 2 midicoach.
Chassis: 1 Ford Transit. 1 Freight Rover.
Ops incl: school contracts, private hire.

SHETLAND

R G JAMIESON & SON
MOARFIELD GARAGE, CULLIVOE, YELL ZE2 9DD
Tel: 01957 744214
Fax: 01957 744270
E-mail: rhjamieson@hotmail.com
Ptnr: Robert H Jamieson
Fleet: 5 - 2 coach, 2 minibus, 1 minicoach.
Chassis: 1 Dennis. 2 Ford Transit. 1 Marshall. 1 Mercedes.
Bodies: 1 Berkhof. 1 Plaxton. 3 other.
Ops incl: local bus services, school contracts, excursions & tours, private hire, continental tours.
Livery: White/Blue (three shades)

*JOHN LEASK & SON

ESPLANADE, LERWICK ZE1 0LL
Tel: 01595 693162
Fax: 01595 693171
E-mail: info@leaskstravel.co.uk
Web site: www.leaskstravel.co.uk
Ptnrs: Peter R Leask, Andrew J N Leask
Fleet: 19 - 7 single-deck bus, 7 coach, 1 midibus, 1 midicoach, 2 minibus, 2 minicoach.
Chassis: 12 DAF. 2 Dennis. 1 LDV. 3 Mercedes. 1 Optare.
Bodies: 1 Alexander. 5 Ikarus. 1 Optare. 4 Plaxton. 2 Van Hool. 3 Wright. 3 other.
Ops incl: local bus services, school contracts, excursions & tours, private hire.
Livery: Ivory/Blue.
Ticket system: ERG

SOUTH AYRSHIRE

*DODDS OF TROON LTD
4 EAST ROAD, AYR KA8 9BA
Tel: 01292 288100
Fax: 01292 287700
E-mail: info@doddsoftroon.com
Web site: www.doddsoftroon.com

Man Dir: James Dodds **Dirs:** Douglas Dodds, Norma Dodds
Fleet: 20 - 2 single-deck bus, 15 coach, 3 midicoach.
Chassis: 1 Dennis. 2 Leyland. 1 Scania. 3 Toyota. 13 Volvo.
Bodies: 2 Alexander. 3 Caetano. 1 Irizar. 6 Jonckheere. 3 Plaxton. 5 Van Hool.
Ops incl: school contracts, excursions & tours, private hire, express, continental tours.

IBT TRAVEL GROUP
CAIRN HOUSE, 15 SKYE ROAD, PRESTWICK KA9 2TA
Tel: 01292 477771
Fax: 01292 471770.
E-mail: briant@ibtravel.com
Partner: Ian Black
Fleet: 3 coaches
Chassis: Volvo
Bodies: Van Hool
Ops incl: continental tours, private hire
Livery: Blue/Gold flash

*KEENAN OF AYR COACH TRAVEL

DARWIN GARAGE, COALHALL BY AYR KA6 6ND
Tel: 01292 591252
Fax: 01292 590980
Dirs: Tony Keenan, Jamie Keenan
Fleet: 20 - 2 double-deck bus, 6 single-deck bus, 10 coach, 1 midibus, 1 midicoach.
Chassis: incl: 8 Leyland. 8 Volvo.
Bodies: 8 Alexander. 4 Duple. 2 Plaxton. 6 Van Hool.
Ops incl: school contracts, excursions & tours, private hire.
Livery: Red/Yellow/Orange/White

MILLIGANS COACH TRAVEL LIMITED
LOAN GARAGE, MAUCHLINE KA5 6AN
Tel: 01290 550365
Fax: 01290 553291
E-mail: milligans1@aol.com.
Web Site:
www.milliganscoachtravel.co.uk
Dir: William Milligan **Ops Man:** Morag Milligan
Fleet: 15 - 10 coach, 3 double-deck coach, 1 midicoach, 1 minibus.
Chassis: 2 DAF. 1 Mercedes. 3 Neoplan. 1 Scania. 8 Volvo.
Bodies: 1 Berkhof. 2 Bova. 1 Caetano. Duple. 1 Irizar. 1 Jonckheere. 1 Mercedes. 3 Neoplan. 2 Plaxton. 2 Van Hool. 1 other.
Ops incl: excursions & tours, private hire, school contracts.
Livery: Black/Red/Silver

 Seat belt-fitted vehicles
 Recovery service available (not 24 hr)
R24 24hr recovery service

✓ Replacement vehicle available
T Toilet-drop facilities available
Vintage vehicle(s) available
Open top vehicle(s)

Ac Air conditioning
Vehicles suitable for disabled
Coach(es) with galley facilities
wc Coach(es) with toilet facilities

*STAGECOACH WEST SCOTLAND

HEAD OFFICE, SANDGATE, AYR KA7 1DD
Tel: 01292 613700
Fax: 01292 613501
Web site: www.stagecoachbus.com
Man Dir: Tom Wileman **Eng Dir**: Sam Greer
Fleet: 431 - 100 double-deck bus, 100 single-deck bus, 42 coach, 16 articulated bus, 3 open-top bus, 105 midibus, 65 minibus.
Chassis: 1 AEC. 78 Dennis. 72 Leyland. 2 Leyland National. 2 MAN. 62 Mercedes. 3 Optare. 3 Scania. 204 Volvo.
Bodies: Alexander. Berkhof. Carlyle. Duple. ECW. East Lancs. Jonckheere. Leyland. Leyland National. Marshall. Mercedes. Northern Counties. Optare. Park Royal. Plaxton. Transbus. Wright.
Ops incl: local bus services, school contracts, private hire, express.
Livery: Stagecoach (White/Blue/Orange/Red)
Ticket System: Wayfarer

SOUTH LANARKSHIRE

ALFRA COACH HIRE

26 MACHAN ROAD, LARKHALL ML9 1HG.
Tel: 01698 887581.
Prop: F. Russell.
Fleet: 4 minibus.
Chassis: 2 Ford Transit. 1 Freight Rover. 1 Leyland.
Ops incl: private hire.
Livery: White.

BEATON COACHES LTD

46 JOHN STREET, BLANTYRE G72 0JG.
Tel: 01698 822514.
Fax: 01698 710590
Ops Man: J Beaton **Dirs**: R Beaton, J Beaton (jnr) **Co Sec**: Mrs E Beaton
Ch Eng: I Smith.
Chassis: 2 Bova. 2 DAF. 7 Leyland. 3 Mercedes. 5 Volvo.
Ops incl: school contracts, private hire.

R. & C. S. CRAIG

TOWNFOOT, ROBERTON, BY BIGGAR ML12 6RS.
Tel: 01899 850655.
Dirs: R. Craig, C. S. Craig.
Traf Man/Ch Eng: J. Harvie.
Gen Man: R. Craig.
Fleet: 3 - 2 minibus, 1 minicoach.
Chassis: Freight Rover.
Ops incl: school contracts, private hire.
Livery: White.

MUIRS COACHES

1 POWELL STREET, DOUGLAS WATER ML11 9PP.
Tel: 01555 880551.
Fax: 01555 880771.
E-mail: coaches@muirstravel.co.uk
Web site: www.muirstravel.co.uk
Gen Man: G. Muir.
Fleet: 6 - 1 single-deck bus, 1 coach, 1 midicoach, 3 minicoach.
Chassis: 1 Bova. 4 Mercedes. 1 Toyota.
Bodies: 1 Bova. 1 Caetano. 4 Mercedes. 1 Wadham Stringer.
Ops incl: local bus services, school contracts, excursions & tours, private hire, continental tours.

PARK'S OF HAMILTON LTD

14 BOTHWELL ROAD, HAMILTON ML3 0AY
Tel: 01698 281222
Fax: 01698 303731
Chmn: Douglas Park **Ch Eng**: Malcolm Fisher.
Co Sec/Dir: Gerry Donnachie. **Ops Man**: Michael Andrews. **Dir**: Hugh McAteer.
Fleet: 100 - incl: coach, double-deck coach.
Chassis: incl: Neoplan. 30 Volvo. Iveco.
Bodies: incl: 30 Jonckheere. Neoplan. Plaxton. Van Hool. Beulas.
Ops incl: local bus services, school contracts, excursions & tours, private hire, express, continental tours.
Livery: Black
Ticket System: Wayfarer

*SILVER CHOICE COACHES

1 MILTON ROAD, EAST KILBRIDE G74 5BU
Tel: 01355 249499
Fax: 01355 265111
Web site: www.silverchoicetravel.co.uk
E-mail: david@silverchoicetravel.co.uk
Dirs: D W Gardiner, S Gardiner **Ch Eng**: D Hurst
Fleet: 11 - 8 coach, 2 double-deck coach, 1 minicoach.
Chassis: 3 Bova. 1 Iveco.1 Mercedes. 2 Scania. 4 Volvo.
Bodies: 1 Beulas. 3 Bova. 2 Irizar. 1 Plaxton. 3 Van Hool. 1 other.
Ops incl: school contracts, private hire, express, continental tours.
Livery: Silver

WILLIAM STOKES & SONS LTD

22 CARSTAIRS ROAD, CARSTAIRS ML11 8QD
Tel/Fax: 01555 870344
E-mail: enquiries@stokescoaches.co.uk
Web site: www.stokescoaches.co.uk
Fleet: 22 - 13 single-deck bus, 7 coach, 2 midicoach
Chassis: 6 Dennis. 4 Leyland. 1 Mercedes. 9 Volvo. 2 other.
Bodies: 2 Alexander. 3 Berkhof. 1 Caetano. 1 Ikarus. 1 Marshall. 13 Plaxton. 2 Van Hool.
Ops incl: local bus services, school contracts, excursions & tours, private hire.
Livery: Red/Cream
Ticket System: Almex A90

STONEHOUSE COACHES

48 NEW STREET, STONEHOUSE ML9 3LT.
Tel: 01698 792145.
Prop: N. Collison.
Livery: White/Pink/Navy.

STUART'S OF CARLUKE

CASTLEHILL GARAGE, AIRDRIE ROAD, CARLUKE ML8 4UF
Tel: 01555 773533
Fax: 01555 752220
Dir: Stuart Shevill **Ops**: John Hane
Fleet: 49 - 10 double-deck bus, 20 single-deck bus, 15 coach, 2 minibus, 2 minicoach
Chassis: 15 Dennis. 1 Ford Transit. 10 Leyland. 3 Mercedes. 1 Optare. 15 Volvo.
Bodies: Alexander. Caetano. ECW. Jonckheere. Northern Counties. Optare. Plaxton. Reeve Burgess. Van Hool.
Ops incl: local bus services, school contracts, excursions and tours, private hire, express, continental tours.
Livery: Silver/Blue
Ticket system: Wayfarer

*WHITELAWS COACHES

LOCHPARK INDUSTRIAL ESTATE, STONEHOUSE ML9 3LR
Tel: 01698 792800
Fax: 01698 793309
E-mail: enquiries@whitelaws.co.uk
Web site: www.whitelaws.co.uk
Fleet: 37 - 23 single-deck bus, 11 coach, 2 midicoach, 1 minibus.
Chassis: incl: 1 Iveco. 3 Mercedes.
Bodies: incl: 1 Marshall/MCV. 1 Plaxton. 3 Sunsundegui. 2 Van Hool. 1 Volvo.
Ops incl: local bus services, school contracts, excursions & tours, private hire.
Livery: Silver with Red/White/Blue.
Ticket System: Wayfarer 3

STIRLING

*BILLY DAVIES EXECUTIVE COACHES

TRANSPORT HOUSE, PLEAN INDUSTRIAL ESTATE, PLEAN FK7 8BJ
Tel: 01786 816627
Fax: 01786 811433
Web site: www.daviescoaches.co.uk
E-mail: billy@daviescoaches.com
Prop: Billy Davies
Fleet: 10 - 5 double-deck bus, 3 coach, 1 minibus, 1 minicoach.
Chassis: LDV. MAN. MCW. Volvo
Bodies: Duple. MCW. Mercedes. Plaxton.
Ops incl: school contracts, private hire.
Livery: Red/Yellow/Black
Ticket system: Wayfarer

*FITZCHARLES COACHES LTD

87 NEWHOUSE ROAD, GRANGEMOUTH FK3 8NJ
Tel: 01324 482093
Fax: 01324 665411
E-mail: info@fitzcharles.co.uk
Web site: www.fitzcharles.co.uk
Man Dir: Ronnie Fitzcharles **Dir/Sec**: Olive King **Ops**: David Fitzcharles **Fleet Eng**: Stewart McArthur
Fleet: 16 - 15 coach, 1 midicoach.
Chassis: 3 DAF. 1 Mercedes. 12 Volvo.
Bodies: 2 Ayats. 4 Caetano. 8 Plaxton. 2 Sunsundegui.

Ops incl: excursions & tours, private hire, continental tours, school contracts, express.
Livery: Red/Cream.

WEST DUNBARTONSHIRE

D. P. BISHOP
14 LENNOX ROAD, MILTON, DUMBARTON G82 2TL.
Fleetname: DB Travel.

LOCHS AND GLENS HOLIDAYS
SCHOOL ROAD, GARTORCHARN G83 8RW
Tel: 01389 713 713
E-mail: enquiries@lochsandglens.com
Website: www.lochsandglens.com
Tran Man: Brian Nichols
Fleet: 15 coach
Chassis: 15 Volvo.
Bodies: 15 Jonckheere.
Ops incl: excursions & tours
Livery: White with blue letters

McCOLL'S COACHES LTD
BALLAGAN DEPOT, STIRLING ROAD, BALLOCH G83 8LY
Tel: 01389 754321
Fax: 01389 755354
E-mail: mccolls@btconnect.com
Web site: www.mccolls.org.uk
Man: William McColl Man Dirs: Thomas McColl, Janet McColl Co Sec: Ann McKinlay
Ops Man: Liam McColl Head mechanic: Eddie McKinley
Fleet: double-deck bus, single-deck bus, coach, minibus.
Chassis: DAF. Dennis. Ford. Ford Transit. Leyland. leyland National. MCW. Mercedes. Volvo. other.
Bodies: Leyland National. MCW. Mercedes. other.
Ops incl: local bus services, school contracts, excursions & tours, private hire.

WEST LOTHIAN

LES BROWN TRAVEL
9 HARDHILL ROAD, BATHGATE EH48 2BW
Tel: 01506 656129
Fax: 01506 656129
E-mail: les-brown@btconnect.com
Web Site: www.lesbrowntravel.com
Props: Les Brown, Colin Brown
Fleet: 8 - 2 midicoach, 6 minicoach.
Chassis: 5 Ford Transit. 3 Mercedes.
Ops incl: school contracts, excursions & tours, private hire.

BROWNINGS (WHITBURN) LTD
22 LONGRIDGE ROAD, WHITBURN EH47 0DE
Tel: 01501 740234
Fax: 01501 741265
E-mail: george@browningscoaches.fsnet.co.uk
Web site: www.browningscoaches.co.uk
Man Dir: G D Browning Co Sec: Mrs G Blyth
Fleet: 15 - 5 double-deck bus, 10 coach
Chassis: 5 Leyland. 10 Volvo.
Bodies: 2 Berkhof. 1 East Lancs. 1 Leyland. 2 Plaxton. 3 Roe. 6 Van Hool.
Ops incl: excursions & tours, private hire, school contracts.
Livery: Red/White/Blue.

GLENTANA COACHES LTD
GREENPARK, EDINBURGH ROAD, LINLITHGOW EH49 6AA.
Tel: 01506 670254.
Fax: 01506 846034.
E-mail: glentanacoaches@ic24.net
Web site: www.glentanacoaches.co.uk
Dir: William Ramage Co Sec: Alexander Calderwood
Fleet: 6 - 5 minibus, 1 midicoach.
Chassis: 6 Mercedes
Bodies: 5 Mercedes. 1 Optare.
Ops incl: private hire, incl. airport transfer.

E & M HORSBURGH
180 UPHALL STATION ROAD, PUMPHERSTON EH53 0PD
Tel: 01506 432251
Fax: 01506 438066
E-mail: horsburgh@btconnect.com
Web site: www.horsburghcoaches.com
Dirs: Eric Horsburgh, Mark Horsburgh
Fleet: 66 - 11 double-deck bus, 23 single-deck bus, 2 coach, 6 midibus, 4 minicoach, 22 minibus.
Chassis: 5 Dennis. 10 Ford Transit. 4 LDV. 14 Leyland. 18 Mercedes. 9 Optare.
Bodies: 4 LDV. 10 Ford. 14 Leyland. 8 Leyland National.14 Mercedes. 9 Optare. 9 Plaxton.
Ops incl: local bus services, school contracts, private hire.
Livery: Golden Yellow/White
Ticket System: Almex

HOUSTOUN TRAVEL
110 PUMPHERSTON ROAD, UPHALL STATION, LIVINGSTON EH54 5PJ
Tel: 01506 437773.
Fax: 01506 437206.
Prop: Ian Horsburgh.
Fleet: 9 - 1 minibus, 8 minicoach.
Fleet: 1 DAF. 5 Ford Transit. 1 Freight Rover. 2 Mercedes.
Bodies: 1 Carlyle. 1 Leyland. 1 Mercedes. 1 Plaxton. 5 other.
Ops incl: local bus services, school contracts, private hire.

*McKECHNIE OF BATHGATE LIMITED
2 EASTON ROAD, BATHGATE EH48 2QG
Tel: 01506 654337
Fax: 01506 654337
E-mail: pmkcoach@aol.com
Dir: Peter McKechnie Co Sec: Catherine McKechnie
Fleet: 8 - 4 coach, 2 midicoach, 2 minicoach
Chassis: 1 Leyland. 3 Volvo. 4 Mercedes
Ops incl: school contracts, private hire.

MARTIN'S COACH TRAVEL

1 SUMMERVILLE COURT, UPHALL STATION, LIVINGSTON EH54 5QG.
Tel: 01506 435968.
Fax: 01506 435968.
E-mail: martcoach@aol.com
Prop: Tony Martin
Fleet: 5 coach.
Chassis: 2 Bova. 1 MAN. 2 Volvo.
Bodies: 2 Bova. 3 Van Hool.
Ops incl: excursions & tours, private hire, school contracts.
Livery: White/Green/Orange/Blue

*PRENTICE WESTWOOD
WESTWOOD, WEST CALDER EH55 8PW
Tel: 01506 871231
Fax: 01506 871734
Recovery: 01506 871231
E-mail: sales@prenticewestwoodcoaches.co.uk
Web site: www.prenticewestwoodcoaches.co.uk
Dirs: Robbie Prentice, David Cowen
Ops Man: Jock Johnston
Chassis: 5 Bova. 1 DAF. 12 Leyland. 3 MCW. 3 Mercedes. 3 Neoplan. 1 Setra. 29 Volvo.
Bodies: 2 Berkhof. 5 Bova. 6 Caetano. 1 Duple. 9 ECW. 1 Ikarus. 5 Jonckheere. 3 MCW. 3 Neoplan. 1 Northern Counties. 6 Plaxton. 9 Van Hool. 2 Wadham Stringer. 3 other.
Ops incl: school contracts, private hire, continental tours.
Livery: White/Blue/Red.
Ticket System: Almex.

WESTERN ISLES

GALSON-STORNOWAY MOTOR SERVICES LTD
1 LOWER BARVAS, ISLE OF LEWIS HS2 0QZ
Tel: 01851 840269.
Fax: 01851 840445.
E-mail: info@galsonmotorsltd.co.uk
Web site: www.galsonmotorsltd.co.uk

❄c	Air conditioning	
♿	Vehicles suitable for disabled	
🍽	Coach(es) with galley facilities	
wc	Coach(es) with toilet facilities	
💺	Seat belt-fitted vehicles	
R	Recovery service available (not 24 hr)	
R24	24hr recovery service	
✓	Replacement vehicle available	
T	Toilet-drop facilities available	
	Vintage vehicle(s) available	
🚌	Open top vehicle(s)	

Dir: I. Morrison. **Ch Eng**: F. Smith.
Dir/Ops Man: I. Morrison.
Dir/Tran Man: C. Morrison.
Fleet: 14 - 9 coach, 1 midibus, 1 midicoach, 3 minibus.
Chassis: 3 Ford Transit. 6 Leyland. 2 Mercedes. 3 Volvo.
Bodies: 9 Plaxton. 1 Van Hool. 1 Autobus. 3 Ford Transit.
Ops incl: local bus services, school contracts, excursions & tours, private hire.
Livery: Yellow/Cream.
Ticket System: Wayfarer.

HARRIS COACHES

SCOTT ROAD, TARBERT, ISLE OF HARRIS HS3 3DL
Tel/Fax: 01859 502441
E-mail: harriscoaches@easynet.co.uk
Ptnr: Norman MacKay
Fleet: 5 - 3 coach, 1 midicoach, 1 minicoach.
Chassis: 2 Mercedes. 3 Volvo.
Bodies: 1 Mercedes. 4 Plaxton.
Ops incl: school contracts, excursions & tours, private hire.
Livery: Grey/Red.
Ticket System: Wayfarer.

HEBRIDEAN COACHES
R24

HOWMORE, SOUTH UIST HS8 5SH
Tel: 01870 620345
Fax: 01870 620301
Ptnrs: D. A. MacDonald, S. MacDonald
Fleet: 8 - 7 coach, 1 midicoach
Chassis: 2 Bedford. 2 Dennis. 2 Ford. 1 Leyland. 1 Mercedes.
Bodies: 1 Alexander. 5 Duple. 1 Plaxton. 1 Crystal Conversions.
Ops incl: local bus services, school contracts, private hire.
Livery: Cream/Green
Ticket System: Almex

KENNEDY COACHES
3 ORINSAY, LOCHS, ISLE OF LEWIS HS2 9RG
Tel: 01851 880375
Prop: Murdo M Kennedy

Fleet: 2 - 1 minibus, 1 midibus.
Chassis/Bodies: 1 Ford Transit. 1 Mercedes.
Ops incl: local bus services, private hire

LOCHS MOTOR TRANSPORT LTD
CAMERON TERRACE, LEURBOST, LOCHS, ISLE OF LEWIS HS2 9PE
Tel: 01851 860288.
Fax: 01851 705857.
Dirs: C. MacDonald, R. MacDonald, S. MacDonald, A. MacDonald.
Ch Eng: I. MacKinnon.
Fleet: 20 - 4 single-deck bus, 12 coach, 3 midibus, 1 midicoach.
Chassis: 12 Ford. 1 Freight Rover. 3 Leyland. 4 Mercedes.
Bodies: 5 Alexander. 1 Carlyle. 8 Duple. 2 Marshall. 2 M2M. 3 Plaxton.
Ops incl: local bus services, school contracts, private hire.
Livery: Blue/Cream.

ISLE of MAN

*DOUGLAS CORPORATION TRAMWAY
STRATHALLAN CRESCENT, DOUGLAS IM2 4NR
Tel: 01624 696420
E-mail: pcannon@douglas.gov.im
Fleet: 20 tramcars
Ops incl: tram services, private hire.

ISLE OF MAN TRANSPORT

TRANSPORT HEADQUARTERS, BANKS CIRCUS, DOUGLAS IM1 5PT
Tel: 01624 663366
Fax: 01624 663637
E-mail: info@busandrail.dtl.gov.im
Fleet: 109 - 75 double-deck bus, 10 single-deck bus, 24 tram.
Chassis: 33 DAF. 34 Dennis. 18 Leyland.
Bodies: 54 East Lancs. 8 Leyland. 10 Marshall. 10 Northern Counties. 3 Optare.
Ops incl: local bus/tram services, private hire
Livery: Red/Cream.
Ticket System: Wayfarer.

*PROTOURS ISLE OF MAN LTD

SUMMERHILL, DOUGLAS IM2 4PF
Tel: 01624 674301
Fax: 01624 675656
Email: info@protours.co.im
Chmn & Man Dir: Roy Lightfoot **Dirs**: D L Wilson, S F Cairns, F B Kinnear **Ops Man**: Dave Bennett **Holiday Man**: Colin Morgan
Ch Eng: Alan Lancaster
Fleet: 31 - 3 single-deck bus, 16 coach, 4 midicoach, 6 minibus, 2 minicoach.
Chassis: 8 Bedford. 1 Bova. 2 BMC. 6 DAF. 1 Ford Transit. 6 Iveco. 4 Leyland. 1 Scania. 1 Toyota. 2 LAG.
Bodies: 1 Berkhof. 1 Bova. 1 Caetano. 2 BMC. 1 Carlyle. 8 Duple. 5 Leicester. 7 Plaxton. 1 Reeve Burgess. 2 Van Hool. 1 Wadham Stringer. 1 other.
Ops incl: local bus services, excursions & tours, private hire, express, continental tours, school contracts.
Livery: White/Blue/Yellow

Welsh Operators

ANGLESEY

CARREGLEFN COACHES

CARREGLEFN GARAGE, AMLWCH LL68 0PR
Tel: 01407 710139
Fax: 01407 710217
Prop: Alun Lewis
Fleet: 10 - 1 single-deck bus, 8 coach, 1 minicoach.
Chassis: 2 Bedford. 1 Toyota. 7 Volvo.
Bodies: 4 Caetano. 1 Duple. 5 Plaxton.
Ops incl: local bus services, school contracts, excursions & tours, private hire.
Livery: Blue/Cream

ELLIS COACHES
CHURCH STREET, LLANGEFNI LL77 7EB
Tel: 01248 750304
Prop: F. B. Ellis.
Fleet: 14 - 5 double-deck bus, 1 single-deck bus, 8 coach.
Chassis: Bedford. Bristol. Daimler. Ford. Leyland. Volvo.
Bodies: Duple. Plaxton.
Livery: D/D -Yellow/Mushroom/Red, S/D - White/Mauve/Red.

W C GOODSIR
30 TRENWFA ROAD, LANDS END, HOLYHEAD LL65 1LE
Tel: 01407 764340
Livery: White/Black/Yellow/Orange.

GWYNFOR COACHES
ANEYLFA, 1 GREENFIELD AVENUE, LLANGEFNI LL77 7NU
Tel: 01248 722694
Prop: H. Hughes.

O R JONES & SONS LTD
 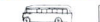
BUS & COACH DEPOT, LLANFAETHLU LL65 4NW
Tel: 01407 730204
Fax: 01407 730083
Prop: I. W. Jones (**Gen Man**), J. P. Jones.
Ch Eng: D. Williams. **Sec**: M. Cook.
Fleet: 27 - 4 double-deck bus, 10 single-deck bus, 7 coach, 3 midibus, 1 midicoach, 2 minibus.
Chassis: 3 Bedford. 4 Bova. 4 Bristol. 1 DAF. 2 Freight Rover. 10 Leyland National. 3 Mercedes. 2 Scania. 1 Toyota.
Bodies: 2 Alexander. 4 Bova. 1 Caetano. 1 Carlyle. 2 Duple. 1 East Lancs. 10 Leyland National. 3 Northern Counties. 3 Plaxton. 1 Reeve Burgess.
Ops incl: local bus services, school contracts, excursions & tours, private hire, express, continental tours.
Livery: Red/White/Green.

W E JONES & SON
THE GARAGE, LLANERCHYMEDD LL71 8EB
Tel: 01248 470228
Fax: 01248 852893
Prop: G E Jones
Fleet: 11 - 5 double-deck bus, 2 single-deck bus, 3 coach, 1 minibus.
Chassis: 1 Bedford. 1 Bristol. 1 DAF. 1 Daimler. 1 Dodge. 3 MCW. 1 Mercedes. 1 Volvo.
Bodies: 2 Alexander. 3 MCW. 1 Mercedes. 2 Northern Counties. 1 Plaxton.
Ops incl: school contracts, private hire.
Livery: Red/White

LEWIS-Y-LLAN
MADYN INDUSTRIAL ESTATE, AMLWCH LL68 9DL
Tel: 01407 832181
Fax: 01407 830112
Props: A. H. Lewis, R. M. Lewis.
Fleet: 10 - 2 double-deck bus, 4 coach, 4 midibus.
Chassis: 1 Bedford. 3 Leyland. 3 Mercedes. 2 Volvo. 1 Volkswagen.
Bodies: 1 Alexander. 1 East Lancs. 1 Jonckheere. 1 Leyland. 3 Optare. 3 Plaxton.
Livery: White/Blue.

BLAENAU GWENT

GARY'S COACHES OF TREDEGAR

42 COMMERCIAL STREET, TREDEGAR NP22 3DJ
Tel: 01495 726400
Fax: 01495 726500
Recovery: 01495 723264
E-mail: sales@garys-coaches.co.uk
Web site: www.garys-coaches.co.uk
Props: Mr & Mrs G A Lane **Ops Man**: D Williams **Ch Eng**: G Cresswell
Fleet: 14 - 12 coach, 1 midicoach, 1 midibus.
Chassis: 2 DAF. 1 Dennis. 1 Leyland. 2 Mercedes. 8 Volvo.
Bodies: 1 Duple. 4 Duple. 2 Mercedes. 5 Plaxton. 2 Van Hool.
Ops incl: excursions & tours, private hire, school contracts, continental tours.
Livery: White/Blue

HENLEYS BUS SERVICES LTD
HENLEYS COACH GARAGE, VICTOR ROAD, CWMTILLERY NP13 1HU
Tel: 01495 212288
Fax: 01495 320720
Dir: Martin Henley **Head Eng**: Michael Henley **Sec**: Daphne Henley
Fleet: 11 - 6 coach, 4 midibus, 1 minicoach.
Chassis: 4 Leyland. 4 Mercedes. 1 Setra. 2 Volvo.
Bodies: 1 Alexander. 1 Duple. 2 East Lancs. 1 Jonckheere. 1 Leicester. 5 Plaxton. 1 Setra.
Ops incl: local bus services, school contracts, excursions & tours, private hire.
Ticket system: Wayfarer

*STAGECOACH IN SOUTH WALES
See Torfaen

BRIDGEND

R & D BURROWS LTD

21 CEMETERY ROAD, OGMORE VALE CF32 7HR
Tel: 01656 840259
Fax: 01656 841866
E-mail: burrowscoaches@yahoo.co.uk
Web site: www.burrowscoaches.co.uk
Dirs: J G Jones, S A Jones, P J Jones
Fleet: 9 - 1 double-deck bus, 1 single-deck bus, 7 coach
Chassis: 1 DAF. 1 Ford. 3 Leyland. 1 Scania. 1 Setra. 2 Volvo.
Bodies: 1 Duple. 1 ECW. 3 Plaxton. 1 Setra. 2 Van Hool. 1 Wadham Stringer.
Ops incl: private hire, school contracts.

*G M COACHES LTD

MOUNTAIN VIEW GARAGE, TY-FRY ROAD, CEFN CRIBWR CF32 0BB
Tel: 01656 740262
Fax: 01656 746040
E-mail: carl@gmcoaches.com
Web site: www.gmcoaches.com
Man Dir: Carl Hookings **Dirs**: Katherine Hookings, Andrea Lockwood **Man**: Idris Hall
Fleet: 32 - 10 double-deck bus, 2 single-deck bus, 14 coach, 2 double-deck coach, 1 open-top bus, 1 midicoach, 1 minicoach, 1 minibus.
Chassis: incl: 3 DAF. 1 Dennis. 2 MAN. 1 Mercedes. 2 Neoplan.
Bodies: 3 Alexander. 4 Berkhof. 2 ECW.

- Air conditioning
- Vehicles suitable for disabled
- Coach(es) with galley facilities
- Coach(es) with toilet facilities
- Seat belt-fitted vehicles
- **R** Recovery service available (not 24 hr)
- **R24** 24hr recovery service
- Replacement vehicle available
- **T** Toilet-drop facilities available
- Vintage vehicle(s) available
- Open top vehicle(s)

3 East Lancs. 1 Ikarus. 2 Jonckheere.
1 Marshall/MCV. 1 Mercedes. 2 Neoplan.
1 Plaxton. 10 Van Hool.
Ops incl: local bus services, school contracts, excursions & tours, private hire, continental tours.

GWYN JONES & SON LTD

WHITE CROFT GARAGE,
BRYNCETHIN CF32 9YR
Tel: 01656 720300
Fax: 01656 725632
Recovery: 01656 720182
Chair: John Gwyn Jones **Dir**: Miriam J. Jones
Fleet: coach.
Chassis: Leyland. Mercedes. Scania. Volvo.
Bodies: Berkhof. Jonckheere. Mercedes. Plaxton. Van Hool.
Ops incl: excursions & tours, private hire, continental tours, school contracts.
Livery: White/Gold/Maroon

*PENCOED TRAVEL LTD

18 CAER BERLLAN, PENCOED
CF35 6RR
Tel: 01656 860200
Fax: 01656 864793
E-mail: pencoedtravel@aol.com
Web site: www.pencoedtravel.co.uk
Man Dir: Denise Cook **Ch Eng**: Neil Cook
Co Sec: Andrea Talbot **Ops**: David Momo
Fleet: 11 - 4 double-deck bus, 7 coach.
Chassis: 2 Bristol. 5 DAF. 2 Daimler.
1 Dennis. 1 Leyland.
Bodies: 1 Berkhof. 2 Leyland. 2 Northern Counties. 2 Plaxton. 4 Van Hool.
Ops incl: private hire, school contracts
Livery: White/Blue

PORTHCAWL OMNIBUS CO LTD

OLD STATION LANE, PORTHCAWL
CF36 5TL
Tel: 01656 783269
Fax: 01656 783959
Dirs: J. Williams (**Man Dir**), Mrs B. N. Williams. **Co Sec**: Mrs P. Phillips.
Man: J. Williams jnr. **Ops Man**: G. W. Morgan.
Fleet: 13 - 3 double-deck bus. 1 single-deck bus. 9 coach.
Chassis: 1 Bedford. 3 Daimler. 5 Leyland. 4 Volvo.
Bodies: 1 Duple. 1 Jonckheere. 2 MCW. 1 Northern Counties. 6 Plaxton. 2 Willowbrook.
Ops incl: private hire, school contracts.
Livery: Beige/Maroon or White/Maroon
Ticket System: Almex.

*STAGECOACH IN SOUTH WALES
See Torfaen

CAERPHILLY

CASTELL COACHES LTD

UNITS 3 & 4 EUROPEAN TERMINAL BUILDING, PANTGLAS INDUSTRIAL ESTATE, BEDWAS CF83 8DR
Tel: 029 2086 1863.
Fax: 029 2086 1864
Recovery: 07967 636659
E-mail: sales@castellcoaches.co.uk
Web site: www.castellcoaches.co.uk
Co Sec: Mrs S Kerslake (**Tel**: 07801 515119)
Dir: C Kerslake. **Ops Man**: B Kerslake (**Tel**: 07801 515117)
Fleet: 21 - 5 double-deck bus, 12 coach, 3 midicoach, 1 minibus.
Chassis: 2 Bova. 4 DAF. 6 Leyland. 4 Mercedes. 7 Volvo.
Bodies: 2 Bova. 1 Duple. 2 Jonckheere. 4 Leyland. 4 Mercedes. 6 Plaxton. 2 Van Hool.
Ops incl: excursions & tours, private hire, continental tours, school contracts.
Livery: White with multicolour

GLYN WILLIAMS TRAVEL

PENNAR CROSSING,
PONTLLANFRAITH NP12 2AW
Tel: 01495 229237
Fax: 01495 222880
Man Dir: G J Williams **Eng Dir**: T G Williams
Comm Man: I MacDonald
Fleet: 29 - 23 single-deck bus, 6 midibus.
Chassis: 23 Dennis. 6 BMC.
Bodies: 10 Caetano. 3 Marshall. 6 Plaxton. 4 UVG. 6 BMC.
Ops incl: local bus services.
Livery: Green/White.
Ticket System: Wayfarer TGX
Part of Stagecoach in Wales

HARRIS COACHES

BRYN GWYN STREET, FLEUR-DE-LIS NP2 1RZ
Tel: 01443 832290
Man Dir: John Harris
Fleetname: Shuttle
Ops incl: local bus services
Livery: Cream/Maroon/Red

*ISLWYN BOROUGH TRANSPORT LTD

PENMAEN ROAD DEPOT,
PONTLLANFRAITH NP12 2DY
Tel: 01495 235707
Fax: 01495 220871
E-mail: simsr@caerphilly.gov.uk
Web site: www.kingfishertravel.com
Chairmn: David Poole **Man Dir**: Roger Sims
Comm Dir: Paul Diaper **Traff Man**: Dow Jones
Fleet: 49 - 27 single-deck bus, 19 coach, 2 midicoach, 1 minibus.
Chassis: 3 Bova. 1 DAF. 3 Dennis. 1 Ford Transit. 6 Leyland. 16 MAN. 4 Mercedes. 15 Volvo.
Bodies: 1 Berkhof. 3 Bova. 1 Caetano. 11 East Lancs. 10 Jonckheere. 4 Marshall. 9 Optare. 4 Plaxton. 1 Reeve Burgess. 1 Setra. 2 Van Hool. 2 other.
Ops incl: local bus services, school contracts, excursions & tours, private hire, continental tours.
Livery: Blue/White
Ticket System: Wayfarer

*STAGECOACH IN SOUTH WALES
See Torfaen

CARDIFF

*CARDIFF BUS

SLOPER ROAD, LECKWITH,
CARDIFF CF11 8TB
Tel: 029 2078 7700
Fax: 029 2078 7742
E-mail: headoffice@cardiffbus.com
Web site: www.cardiffbus.com
Man Dir: David Brown **Eng Dir**: David Worsell **Fin Dir/Co Sec**: Cynthia Ogbonna
Fleet: 253 - 27 double-deck bus, 102 - single-deck bus, 105 midibus, 19 articulated single-deck bus.
Chassis: 180 Dennis. 6 Leyland. 21 Optare. 19 Scania. 27 Volvo.
Bodies: 15Alexander. 6 Leyland. 19 Northern Counties. 21 Optare. 161Plaxton. 19 Scania. 12 Transbus.
Ops incl: local bus services
Ticket System: Wayfarer

CROESO TOURS

13 WATERLOO ROAD, PENYLAN,
CARDIFF CF23 5AD
Tel: 029 2047 2313
E-mail: jmforster13@hotmail.com
Owner: John M. Forster
Fleet: 3 - 1 midicoach, 1 minibus, 1 minicoach
Chassis: 1 Iveco. 1 LDV. 1 Renault
Ops incl: private hire, school contracts.

GREYHOUND COACHES CO

COACH DEPOT, STATION TERRACE,
ELY BRIDGE, CARDIFF CF5 4AA
Tel: 029 2056 1467, 2055 2767
Ptnrs: T. James, Florence James.
Fleet: 14 - 13 coach, 1 minibus.
Chassis: 10 Bedford. 1 Ford Transit. 3 Volvo.
Ops incl: local bus services, excursions & tours, private hire.
Livery: White/Blue.

*STAGECOACH IN SOUTH WALES
See Torfaen

WALTONS COACHES

31 AVONDALE ROAD,
GRANGETOWN CF1 7DT.
Tel: 029 2039 9511.
Dirs: B. J. Walton, Mrs S. F. Walton, R. J. Walton, D. McCarthy.
Fleet: 6 - 4 coach, 2 midicoach.
Chassis: Bedford. Ford. Mercedes.
Ops incl: private hire, school contracts.
Livery: Blue/White/Red.

WATTS COACHES

OLD POST GARAGE, BONVILSTON CF5 6TT.
Tel/Fax: 01446 781277.
Prop: C. P. Watts. **Tran Man:** J. B. Watts.
Fleet: 23 - 3 double-deck bus, 16 coach, 4 midicoach.
Chassis: 2 Bristol. 2 DAF. 5 Ford. 4 Leyland. 2 MAN. 4 Mercedes. 4 Volvo.
Bodies: 3 Alexander. 3 Caetano. 5 Duple. 1 Optare. 8 Plaxton. 1 Reeve Burgess. 1 Made-to-Measure. 1 Robin Hood.
Ops incl: school contracts, private hire.
Livery: Cream/Red/Gold.

WHEADONS GROUP TRAVEL LTD

STATION TERRACE, ELY BRIDGE, CARDIFF CF5 4AA
Tel: 029 2057 5333
Fax: 029 2057 5384
E-mail: admin@wheadons-group.co.uk
Web site: www.wheadons-group.co.uk
Prop: Ernest K Wheadon **Ch Eng:** Steve Osling
Fleet: 34 - 20 coach, 10 midicoach, 4 minibus.
Chassis: Ford Transit. Leland. Mercedes. Toyota. Volvo.
Bodies: Autobus. Caetano. Mercedes. Toyota. Van Hool.
Ops incl: private hire, school contracts, excursions & tours, continental tours.

CARMARTHENSHIRE

*BYSIAU CWM TAF/TAF VALLEY COACHES

PENRHEOL, WHITLAND SA34 0NH
Tel: 01994 240908
Fax: 01994 241264
Dirs: Clive Edwards, Heather Edwards
Fleet: 14 - 10 coach, 2 midibus, 1 midicoach, minibus.
Chassis: Dennis. Iveco. LDV. Leyland. Mercedes. Optare. Volvo.
Bodies: Jonckheere. Mercedes. Optare. Plaxton. Reeve Burgess. Transbus. Van Hool
Ops incl: local bus services, excursions & tours, school contracts, private hire, continental tours.
Livery: White/Silver/Blue

CASTLE GARAGE LTD

BROAD STREET, LLANDOVERY SA20 0AA
Tel: 01550 720335
Man Dir: Derek Jones
Fleet: 12 - 4 midibus, 4 midicoach, 4 minibus.
Chassis: 2 Ford Transit. 2 Freight Rover.

8 Mercedes.
Bodies: Mellor. Mercedes. Optare. Plaxton. Reeve Burgess. Wadham Stringer.
Ops incl: local bus services, school contracts, private hire.

GARETH EVANS COACHES

80 GLYN ROAD, BRYNAMMAN SA18 1SS
Tel: 01269 823127
Fax: 01269 824533
Props: K. Davies, Mrs S. Davies.

FFOSHELIG COACHES

BLAENYCOED ROAD, CARMARTHEN SA33 6EG.
Tel: 01267 281211.
Fax: 01267 281232
Recovery: 07876 027926
E-mail: ffoshelig@aol.com
Owner: Rhodri Evans.
Fleet: 8 - 7 coach, 1 minibus.
Chassis: 1 Leyland. 1 Toyota. 6 Volvo.
Bodies: 1 Caetano. 1 Duple. 1 Jonckheere. 4 Plaxton. 1 Van Hool.
Ops incl: school contracts, excursions & tours, private hire.
Livery: Pale Cream/Brown

GWYN WILLIAMS & SONS LTD

DERLWYN GARAGE, LOWER TUMBLE SA15 5YT
Fleet: 27 - 3 double-deck bus, 8 single-deck bus, 17 coach, 7 minibus
Livery: Two tone Blue/Red.

JONES INTERNATIONAL

STATION ROAD, LLANDEILO SA19 6NG
Tel: 01558 822985
Fax: 01558 822984
Props: Meirion Jones, Myrddin Jones, Neil Jones **Office Man:** Carole Thompson
Ch Eng: Andrew Vale
Fleet: 7 - 2 single-deck bus, 5 coach.
Chassis: 3 DAF. 3 Leyland. 1 Volvo.
Bodies: 6 Van Hool. 1 Crossley.
Ops incl: excursions & tours, private hire, express, continental tours, school contracts.
Livery: Yellow/Blue

*JONES MOTORS (LOGIN) LTD

LOGIN, WHITLAND SA34 0UX
Tel: 01437 563277
Fax: 01437 563393
E-mail: info@joneslogin.co.uk
Web Site: www.joneslogin.co.uk
Man Dirs: E A Jones, A T Jones, E H Jones
Fleet: 17 - 14 coach, 1 midicoach, 2 minibus.
Chassis: 8 Dennis. 2 LDV. 11 Mercedes. 1 Scania. 5 Volvo.
Bodies: 1 East Lancs. 1 Irizar. 2 Leyland. 1 Mercedes. 12 Plaxton.

Ops incl: local bus services, school contracts, excursions & tours, private hire, continental tours.

LEWIS COACHES WHITLAND

THE GARAGE, WHITLAND SA34 0AA
Tel: 01944 240274
Dirs: E Lewis
Fleet: 11 - 8 coach, 1 midibus, 2 minicoach.
Chassis: 1 Bedford. 3 Dennis. 2 LDV. 3 Leyland. 2 Volvo.
Bodies: 1 Berkhof. 1 Duple. 2 Leyland. 1 Optare. 6 Plaxton.
Livery: White with Green/Mink stripes
Ops incl: local bus services, school contracts, private hire
Livery: White/Green with mink stripes
Ticket System: Wayfarer

*LEWIS-RHYDLEWIS

PENRHIW-PAL GARAGE, RHYDLEWIS, LLANDYSUL SA44 5QG
Tel: 01239 851386
Fax: 01239 858899
Ptnrs: Maldwyn Lewis, Meirion Lewis, Eirian James, Gwenda Savins, Rhianon Williams
Fleet: 18 - 14 coach, 1 minicoach, 3 minibus.
Chassis: 4 Bedford. 1 BMC. 3 Ford Transit. 5 Leyland. 1 Renault. 2 Setra. 3 Setra. 2 Volvo.
Bodies: 1 BMC. 1 Duple. 11 Plaxton. 2 Setra. 3 other.
Ops incl: school contracts, excursions & tours, private hire, continental tours.
Livery: Multicoloured/Cream/Red/Orange

MORRIS TRAVEL

ALLTYCNAP ROAD, JOHNSTOWN SA31 3QY
Tel: 01267 235090.
Fax: 01267 238183.
E-mail: sales@morristravel.co.uk
Web site: www.morristravel.co.uk
Man Dir/Chmn: T J Freeman **Ops Dir:** C J Freeman. **Dir/Co Sec:** C M Freeman
Ch Eng: A Jones. **Traf Man:** V Shambrook
Traff Controller: P Davies.
Fleet: 29 - 1 single-deck bus, 19 coach, 1 midibus, 6 minibus, 1 minicoach, 1 midicoach.
Chassis: 4 Bedford. 3 DAF. 1 Ford. 1 Freight Rover. 14 LDV. 2 Mercedes. 1 Optare. 4 Volvo.
Bodies: 1 Berkhof. 1 Duple. 14 Leyland. 1 Ford Transit. 2 Mercedes. 1 Optare. 9 Plaxton.
Ops incl: local bus services, school contracts, private hire.
Livery: Blue/Navy/White.
Ticket System: Wayfarer

A/c	Air conditioning
♿	Vehicles suitable for disabled
🍽	Coach(es) with galley facilities
WC	Coach(es) with toilet facilities
🎗	Seat belt-fitted vehicles
R	Recovery service available (not 24 hr)
R24	24hr recovery service
✓	Replacement vehicle available
T	Toilet-drop facilities available
🚌	Vintage vehicle(s) available
🚐	Open top vehicle(s)

Welsh Operators

THOMAS BROS
TOWY GARAGE, LLANGADOG
SA19 9LU.
Tel: 01550 777438
Fax: 01550 777807.
Prop: Gareth Thomas
Fleet: 19 - minibus, coach
Chassis/bodies: incl: 1 Mercedes/Optare Sorocco
Ops incl: local bus services, school contracts, excursions & tours, private hire.
Livery: Cream/Green.
Ticket System: Setright.

CEREDIGION

*BRODYR JAMES
GLANYRAFON, LLANGEITHO, TREGARON SY25 6TT
Tel: 01974 821255
Fax: 01974 251618
Dirs: D E James, T M G James
Fleet: 16 - 10 coach, 2 midibus, 2 midicoach, 2 minibus.
Chassis: 1 Bedford. 3 Dennis. 1 Ford Transit. 5 Mercedes. 1 Toyota. 5 Volvo.
Bodies: 2 Alexander. 1 Caetano. 1 Jonckheere. 1 Mellor. 1 Mercedes. 8 Plaxton. 2 Reeve Burgess.
Ops incl: local bus services, school contracts, private hire.
Livery: White/Red/Gold.
Ticket System: Almex

LEWIS'S COACHES
BRYNEITHIN, LLANRHYSTUD SY23 5DN.
Tel: 01974 202495.
Owner: M. M. Benjamin.
Fleet: 19 - 16 coach, 3 minibus.
Chassis: 4 Bedford. 4 DAF. 6 Dennis. 3 Ford Transit. 1 Volvo.
Bodies: 10 Duple. 2 Plaxton. 1 UVG. 3 Van Hool.
Ops incl: private hire, school contracts.
Livery: White.

MID WALES TRAVEL
BRYNHYFRYD GARAGE, PENRHYNCOCH, ABERYSTWYTH SY23 3EH
Tel: 01970 828288
Fax: 01970 828940
Dir: J Melvyn Evans **Ops Man**: Heddwyn Morgan
Fleet: coach, midibus, midicoach.
Chassis: 4 Dennis. 1 Leyland. 6 Mercedes. 6 Volvo
Bodies: 5 Alexander. 1 Autobus. 1 Jonckheere. 5 Plaxton. 4 UVG. 1 Wright.
Ops incl: local bus services, school contracts, private hire.
Livery: White/Blue

RED KITE COACHES
R24
UNIT 1, GLANDINAS, PENPARCIAU, ABERYSTWYTH SY23 1RR
Tel: 01970 627427
Fax: 01970 624412
E-mail: enquiries@redkitecoaches.co.uk
Web site: www.redkitecoaches.co.uk
Prop: P Bryan
Fleet: 4 - 2 single-deck bus, 1 double-deck coach, 1 midicoach.
Chassis: 1 DAF. 1 Leyland. 1 Scania. 1 Volvo.
Bodies: 2 Plaxton. 1 Wadham Stringer. 1 other
Ops incl: private hire, excursions & tours, express, continental tours.
Livery: White/Blue
Livery: Wayfarer

*RICHARDS BROS
MOYLGROVE GARAGE, PENTOOD INDUSTRIAL ESTATE, CARDIGAN SA43 3AG
Tel: 01239 613756
Fax: 01239 615193
E-mail: enquiries@richardsbros.co.uk
Web site: www.richardsbros.co.uk
Gen Man: W J M Richards **Ch Eng**: D N Richards **Traf Man**: R M Richards
Ops Man: S M Richards
Fleet: 67 - 23 single-deck bus, 22 coach, 4 midicoach, 4 minibus, 14 midibus.
Chassis: 8 Bedford. 23 DAF. 11 Dennis. 3 LDV. 1 MAN. 12 Mercedes. 2 Volvo.
Bodies: 5 Alexander. 1 Autobus. 1 Caetano. 3 Carlyle. 7 Duple. 2 Ikarus. 2 Marshall. 2 Northern Counties. 9 Optare. 15 Plaxton. 2 Reeve Burgess. 3 Transbus. 8 Van Hool. 3 Wright. 3 Cymric.
Ops incl: local bus services, school contracts, excursions & tours, private hire, continental tours.
Livery: Blue/White/Maroon
Ticket System: Wayfarer

ROBERTS COACHES
UNIT 4, GLANYRAFON INDUSTRIAL ESTATE, ABERYSTWYTH SY23 3JQ
Tel: 01970 611085
Fax: 01970 626855
Prop: G Roberts
Fleet: 5 coach.
Chassis: 2 DAF. 3 Leyland.
Bodies: Plaxton. Duple.
Ops incl: school contracts, private hire, tours & excursions.
Livery: White or Blue

CONWY

ALPINE TRAVEL
CENTRAL COACH GARAGE, BUILDER STREET WEST, LLANDUDNO LL30 1HH
Tel: 01492 879133
Fax: 01492 876055
E-mail: chris@alpine-travel.co.uk
Web site: www.alpine-travel.co.uk
Dirs: Bryan Owens, Patricia Owens, Christopher Owens, Christopher Bryan Owens.
Fleet: 90 - double-deck bus, single-deck bus, coach, minibus.
Chassis: Bedford. Bova. Bristol. DAF. Dennis. Ford. Leyland. Leyland National. MAN. Mercedes. Volvo.
Bodies: Alexander. Bova. Duple. ECW. East Lancs. Leyland National. Marshall. Noge. Northern Counties. Plaxton. Sunsundegui. Wadham Stringer. Willowbrook. Robin Hood.
Ops incl: local bus services, school contracts, excursions & tours, private hire, continental tours.
Livery: Green/Cream or White
Ticket System: Setright.

ARRIVA CYMRU LTD
IMPERIAL BUILDINGS, GLAN-Y-MOR ROAD, LLANDUDNO JUNCTION LL31 9RU
Tel: 01492 592111.
Fax: 01492 592968.
Man Dir: S. Green. **Eng Dir**: M. Evans.
Fin Dir: B. Pegg.
Fleet: 265 - 39 double-deck bus, 129 single-deck bus, 3 coach, 94 midibus.
Chassis: DAF. Dennis. Leyland. Mercedes. Scania. Volvo.
Bodies: Alexander. ECW. Northern Counties. Plaxton. Wright.
Ops incl: local bus services, school contracts, private hire, express.
Livery: Turquoise/Cotswold Stone
Ticket System: Wayfarer III.

GRWP ABERCONWY
MAESDU, LLANDUDNO LL30 1HF.
Tel: 01492 870870.
Fax: 01492 860821.
Fleetname: Great Orme Tours.
Dir: I. Trevette.
Tramway & Coach Man: Rosemary Sutton.
Fleet: 4 midicoach.
Chassis: 3 Bedford. 1 Guy.
Ops incl: local bus services, excursions & tours.
Livery: Blue/Cream.
Ticket System: Almex.

*LLEW JONES INTERNATIONAL
STATION YARD, LLANRWST LL26 0EH
Tel: 01492 640320
Fax: 01492 642040
E-mail: info@llewjones.com
Web site: www.llewjones.com
ManDir: Stephen Jones **Ops Man**: Kevin Williams **Fin Dir**: Eirlys Jones **Wkshp Man**: Erfyl Roberts
Fleet: 24 - 14 coach, 6 midibus, 4 midicoach.
Chassis: 6 DAF. 5 Dennis. 1 LDV. 1 MAN. 11 Mercedes. 1 Optare. 1 Setra. 1 Volvo.
Bodies: 3 Ayats. 1 Carlyle. 4 Duple. 1 Jonckheere. 2 Mercedes. 1 Noge. 1 Optare. 6 Plaxton. 1 Reeve Burgess. 2 UVG. 1 Van Hool. 2 Ovi.
Ops incl: local bus services, school contracts, excursions & tours, private hire, continental tours.
Livery: White/Silver/Magenta/Blue
Ticket system: Almex A90

ROBERTS MINI COACHES
RHANDIR GARAGE, RHANDIR LL22 8BW.
Tel: 01492 650449.
Prop: W. T. Roberts.

DENBIGHSHIRE

BRYN MELYN LTD
ABBEY ROAD, LLANGOLLEN
LL20 8SN
Tel: 01978 860701
Web site: www.bryn-melyn.co.uk
Ops Man: Chris Jones
Fleet: 14 - 3 double-deck bus, 3 single-deck bus, 3 midibus, 5 school bus.
Chassis: 5 BMC. 3 Dennis. 1 Leyland. 2 MAN. 3 Mercedes.
Bodies: 3 East lancs. 1 Leyland. 3 Marshall. 2 Optare.
Ops incl: local bus services, school contracts
Livery: Yellow/Blue/Red/White
Ticket system: Wayfarer 3

GHA COACHES
MILL GARAGE, BETWS GWERFIL GOCH, CORWEN LL21 9PU
Tel: 01978 753598
Fax: 01978 721441
E-mail: ghacoaches@aol.com
Web site: www.ghacoaches.co.uk
Prop: E. L. Davies, G. Davies, A. Davies.
Fleet: incl 10 coaches
Chassis: includes 10 Volvo
Bodies: includes 10 Plaxton
Livery: Grey/Red/Maroon.

M & H COACHES
8 TREWEN, DENBIGH LL16 3HF.
Tel: 01745 812057.
Prop: Mrs M. Owen.
Livery: Blue/White.

CLWYDIAN TOURS
LLANRHAEADR, DENBIGH LL16 4NT
Tel: 01745 890543
Fax: 01745 890546
Prop: R David Evans **Ch Eng**: M Terzo
Fleet: 14 - 12 single-deck coach, 2 midicoach.
Chassis: 2 Bedford. 4 Dennis. 2 Ford. 1 Iveco. 1 Leyland. 2 MAN. 1 Toyota. 1 Volvo.
Bodies: 2 Caetano. 4 Duple. 3 Marcopolo. 4 Plaxton. 1 Wright.
Ops incl: excursions & tours, school contracts, private hire
Livery: White with blue stripes
Ticket System: Almex, Wayfarer 3, Setright

VOEL COACHES LTD
PENISA FILLING STATION, FFORD TALARGOCH, DYSERTH LL18 6BP
Tel: 01745 570309.
Fax: 01745 570307
Web site: www.voelcoaches.com
Man Dir: W M Kerfoot-Davies **Com Man**: Michelle Kerfoot Higginson.
Fleet: 25 - 7 double-deck bus, 4 single-deck bus, 12 coach, 1 minibus, 1 midicoach.
Chassis: Dennis. Mercedes. Scania. Volvo

Bodies: Berkhof. Van Hool.
Ops incl: local bus services, school contracts, excursions & tours, private hire, continental tours.
Livery: Orange

FLINTSHIRE

EAGLES AND CRAWFORD

53 NEW STREET, MOLD CH7 1NY
Tel: 01352 700217/8
Fax: 01352 750211
E-mail: eaglesandcrawford@supanet.com
Ptnrs: J. F. J. K. & W. P. Eagles.
Fleet: 15 - 6 double-deck bus, 7 coach, 2 minibus.
Chassis: 6 Bristol. 2 Dennis. 1 Freight Rover. 4 Leyland. 1 Mercedes. 1 Toyota. 1 Van Hool.
Bodies: 1 Caetano. 1 Carlyle. 3 Duple. 6 ECW. 1 Mercedes. 1 Optare. 3 Plaxton. 1 Van Hool.
Ops incl: local bus services, excursions & tours, private hire, continental tours.
Livery: White/Blue/Orange.
Ticket System: Almex.

*FOUR GIRLS COACHES
THE OLD POST OFFICE YARD, CORWEN ROAD, PONTYBODKIN, MOLD CH7 4TG
Tel: 01352 770438
Fax: 01352 770253
Ptnrs: Mrs C J Thomas, Mrs M E Williams
Fleet: 9 - 7 coach, 1 minibus, 1 midicoach.
Chassis: 1 DAF. 1 Ford Transit. 6 Volvo.
Bodies: incl: 1 Caetano
Ops incl: school contracts, excursions & tours, private hire.
Livery: Turquoise/Red/Yellow

JONES MOTOR SERVICES

CHESTER ROAD, FLINT CH6 5DZ.
Tel: 01352 733292.
Fax: 01352 763353.
E-mail: tours@jonescoaches.co.uk
Ptnr: A. Jones.
Fleet: 10 - 9 coach, 1 midicoach.
Chassis: DAF, Iveco, Leyland.
Bodies: Caetano, Duple, Plaxton, Van Hool.
Ops incl: excursions & tours, private hire, express, continental tours, school contracts.
Livery: Blue.

OARE'S COACHES
TY DRAW, BRYNFORD, HOLYWELL CH8 8LP.
Tel: 01352 714868.
Fax: 01352 713339.
Prop: G. A. Oare.
Livery: White/Red/Silver.

P. & O. LLOYD
RHYDWEN GARAGE, BAGILLT CH6 6JJ.
Tel: 01352 710682.
Man Dir: David Lloyd.
Fleet: 36 - 17 double-deck bus, 4 single-deck bus. 6 coach, 7 minibus.
Chassis: incl: Optare. Leyland. Volvo.
Bodies: incl: MCW. East Lancs. MCW. Optare. Plaxton. Van Hool.
Ops incl: local bus services, private hire, school contracts.
Livery: Cream/Red or Cream/Maroon/Gold.
Ticket System: Almex.

PIED BULL COACHES
53 WOODLANDS CLOSE, MOLD CH7 1UU.
Tel/Fax: 01352 754237.
Prop: R. Williams.
Livery: Blue/White.

TOWNLYNX
CAETIA LLWYD, NORTHOP ROAD, HOLYWELL CH8 8AE.
Tel: 01352 710489.
Prop: S. A. Lee.
Livery: White/Yellow/Blue.

GWYNEDD

ARVONIA COACHES
THE SQUARE, LLANRUG LL55 4AA.
Tel: 01286 675175.
Fax: 01286 671126.
Prop: R. Morris.
Fleet: 9 - 6 coach, 2 midibus, 1 minibus.
Chassis: 1 Ford Transit. 1 MAN. 1 Mercedes. 1 Volvo. 3 EOS. 2 Van Hool.
Bodies: 2 Alexander. 1 Carlyle. 2 Van Hool. 3 EOS. 1 Noge.
Ops incl: local bus services, excursions & tours, continental tours.
Livery: White/Orange/Red.
Ticket System: Almex.

CAMBRIAN COAST COACH LINE
RIVERSIDE HOUSE, ABERGYNOLWYN LL36 9YR.
Tel/Fax: 01654 782235.
E-mail: ronbott@talyllyn.freeserve.co.uk.
Prop: Ronald C. Bott.
Fleet: 2 - 1 coach, 1 minicoach, plus 1 taxi.
Chassis: 1 Mercedes. 1 Toyota. 1 Seat.
Ops incl: excursions & tours, private hire.
Livery: Red/Blue.
Ticket System: Setright.

CERBYDAU BERWYN COACHES
BERWYN, TREFOR LL54 5LY
Tel: 01286 660315.
Fax: 01286 660110.

Prop: B. Japheth.
Livery: White/Yellow/Brown.

*CAELLOI MOTORS (T. H. JONES & SON)

UNIT 17, GLAN Y DON INDUSTRIAL ESTATE, PWLLHELI LL53 5YT
Tel: 01758 612719
Fax: 01758 612335
Fleet: 6 - 2 single-deck bus, 4 coach
Chassis: 1 DAF. 1 Marshall. 4 Volvo.
Bodies: 1 Berkhof. 1 Marshall. 3 Van Hool. 1 Wright.
Ops incl: local bus services, excursions & tours, private hire, continental tours
Livery: Multi
Ticket System: Almex

*CLYNNOG & TREFOR

TREFOR, CAERNARFON LL54 5HP
Tel: 01286 660208
Fax: 01286 660538
Dirs: D Jones, E Griffiths **Co Sec:** I Williams
Fleet: 40 - 1 single-deck bus, 13 coach, 14 double-deck coach, 12 minibus.
Chassis: 1 Bedford. 8 Bristol. 1 Dennis. 6 Leyland. 12 Mercedes. 12 Volvo.
Bodies: 8 Alexander. 2 Carlyle. 11 ECW. 3 Jonckheere. 1 Mercedes. 3 Northern Counties. 10 Plaxton. 2 Reeve Burgess.
Ops incl: local bus services, school contracts, private hire.
Livery: Red/Cream, White
Ticket system: Wayfarer

*EMMAS COACHES

BAKER STREET GARAGE, MARIAN ROAD, DOLGELLAU LL40 1EL
Tel: 01341 423934
Fax: 01341 423321
E-mail: info@emmascoaches.co.uk
Web site: www.emmascoaches.co.uk
Dir/Prop: Barry Thomas, **Sec:** Anita Thomas
Tran Man: Brett Thomas
Fleet: 11 - 1 single-deck bus, 5 coach, 1 double-deck coach, 1 midicoach, 2 minibus, 1 people carrier.
Chassis: 1 Bedford. 1 DAF. 1 Ford. 2 Leyland. 1 Leyland National. 2 Mercedes. 2 Scania. 1 Toyota.
Bodies: 1 Caetano. 2 Mercedes. 1 Optare. 23 Plaxton. 3 Van Hool. 1 other
Ops incl: local bus services, excursions & tours, continental tours.
Livery: Green

*EXPRESS MOTORS

THE GARAGE, LLYFNI ROAD, PENYGROES LL54 6ND
Tel: 01286 881108
Fax: 01286 882331
Web site: expressmotors.co.uk
Ptnrs: Eric Wyn Jones, Jean Ann Jones.
Managers: Ian Wyn Jones, Kevin Wyn Jones, Keith Jones.
Fleet: 36 - 2 double-deck bus, 8 single-deck bus, 8 coach, 2 double-deck coach, 1 open-top bus, 10 midibus, 2 midicoach, 2 minicoach, 1 vintage.

Chassis: 1 Bedford. 2 Bova. 2 Bristol. 4 DAF. 2 Dennis. 7 MAN. 10 Mercedes. 7 Optare.
Bodies: 3 Alexander. 2 Bova. 1 Duple. 2 ECW. 3 East Lancs. 1 Hispano. 1 Leyland. 3 Neoplan. 7 Optare. 3 Plaxton. 1 Transbus. 1 UVG. 3 Van Hool. 3 Wadham Stringer. 2 Wright.

GRIFFITHS COACHES

3 ELIM COTTAGES, SILOH, PORTDINORWIC LL56 4JR
Tel: 01248 670530
Fax: 01248 671111
Prop: Hefin Griffiths
Fleet: 11 - 5 double-deck bus, 1 single-deck bus, 5 coach.
Chassis: 5 Bristol. 1 Leyland. 5 Volvo.
Bodies: 1 Berkhof. 5 ECW. 3 Jonckheere. 1 Plaxton. 1 Van Hool.
Ops incl: private hire, school contracts.
Livery: Red/Grey/White

JOHN'S COACHES

NORTH WESTERN ROAD, GLAN-Y-PWLL, BLAENEAU FFESTINIOG LL41 3NN
Tel: 01766 831781
Mobile: 0777 167735
Fax: 01766 831781
Prop: J R Edwards
Fleet: 6
Chassis: 1 Berkhof. 3 DAF. 2 Mercedes.
Bodies: Berkhof. Mercedes. Plaxton.
Ops incl: local bus service, school contracts, private hire.
Livery: White/Red
Ticket System: Wayfarer

*KMP LLANBERIS LTD

Y ELYN INDUSTRIAL ESTATE, LLANBERIS LL55 4EL
Tel: 01286 870880
Fax: 01286 871191
E-mail: info@kmpbus.com
Web site: www.kmpbus.com
Man Dir: K A Williams **Co Sec:** E Williams
Eng Man: M A Williams **Ops Man:** D Hulme
Fleet: 28 - 4 double-deck bus, 15 single-deck bus, 4 coach, 1 open-top bus, 3 midibus.
Chassis: 9 Dennis. 1 Leyland. 4 MCW. 3 Mercedes. 1 Neoplan. 1 Optare. 9 Volvo.
Bodies: 3 Alexander. 1 Caetano. 2 East Lancs. 4 MCW. 3 Mellor. 1 Neoplan. 1 Optare. 5 Plaxton. 2 Reeve Burgess. 6 Wright.
Ops incl: local bus services, school contracts, private hire.
Livery: Blue/Black.
Ticket System: Wayfarer 3

NEFYN COACHES

WEST END GARAGE, ST DAVIDS ROAD, NEFYN LL53 6HE.
Tel: 01758 720904.
Fax: 01758 720331.
Props: B. G. Owen, M. A. Owen, A. G. Owen.
Fleet: 9 - 1 single-deck bus, 4 coach, 4 minicoach.
Chassis: 1 Freight Rover. 1 Leyland. 3 Mercedes. 3 Volvo. 1 Optare.
Bodies: Reeve Burgess, Plaxton.
Ops incl: local bus services, school contracts, excursions & tours, private hire.
Livery: Multi-colour.

SILVER STAR COACH HOLIDAYS LTD

13 CASTLE SQUARE, CAERNARFON LL55 2NF
Tel: 01286 672333
Fax: 01286 678118
Web site: www.silverstarholidays.com
Man Dir: Elfyn William Thomas **Co Sec:** Helen Jones **Ch Eng:** Barry Thomas
Ops Man: Eric Wyn Thomas
Fleet: 18 - 5 single-deck bus, 9 coach, 4 midibus. 1 vintage.
Chassis: 1 AEC. 1 Bedford. 3 Bristol. 3 Dennis. 1 Leyland. 8 Mercedes. 3 Neoplan. 1 Optare. 2 Setra. 2 Volvo.
Bodies: 1 Alexander. 3 ECW. 3 Neoplan. 1 Optare. 25 Plaxton. 2 Setra. 2 Van Hool. 1 Burlingham.
Ops incl: local bus services, school contracts, excursions & tours, private hire, continental tours.
Livery: Green coaches/Blue buses.
Ticket System: Wayfarer 3

MERTHYR TYDFIL

SIXTY SIXTY COACHES

THE COACH DEPOT, MERTHYR INDUSTRIAL PARK, PENTREBACH CF48 4DR
Tel: 01443 692060.
Fax: 01443 699061.
E-mail: enquiries@sixsixty.co.uk
Web site: www.sixtysixty.co.uk
Prop: G Handy, C T Handy.
Fleet: 18 - 3 single-deck bus, 9 coach, 2 double-deck coach, 3 midibus, 1 midicoach
Chassis: 6 DAF. 3 Dennis. 1 Leyland. 3 Mercedes. 2 Scania. 3 Volvo.
Bodies: 3 Alexander. 2 Caetano. 1 Duple. 3 Plaxton. 3 Reeve Burgess. 5 Van Hool. 1 LAG.
Ops incl: local bus services, school contracts, excursions & tours, private hire.
Livery: Silver
Ticket system: Wayfarer

*STAGECOACH IN SOUTH WALES

See Torfaen

MONMOUTHSHIRE

*REES MOTOR (TRAVEL)

LLANELLY HILL, ABERGAVENNY NP7 0PW
Tel: 01873 830210
Fax: 01873 832167
Recovery: 01873 830210
Prtnrs: Nigel A Rees, Neville A Rees, Margo E Rees
Fleet: 9 - 7 coach, 1 double-deck coach, 1 minicoach.
Chassis: 1 Bova. 3 DAF. 1 Dennis. 1 HestairDuple. 1 LDV. 2 Neoplan
Ops incl: local bus services, school

contracts, excursions & tours, private hire, continental tours.
Livery: Green/White

*STAGECOACH IN SOUTH WALES
See Torfaen

NEATH & PORT TALBOT

BLUEBIRD OF NEATH/ PONTARDAWE
9-10 LONDON ROAD, NEATH SA11 1HB.
Tel/Fax: 01639 643849.
Fleetname: Bluebird Coaches (Neath).
Prop: Ian S. Warren. **Ch Eng**: George Warren. **Sec**: Ms Melanie Evans.
Fleet: 21 - 2 double-deck bus, 18 coach, 1 midibus.
Chassis: 2 Bristol. 1 DAF. 1 Mercedes. 17 Volvo.
Bodies: 4 Jonckheere. 1 Mercedes. Leyland. 10 Plaxton. 6 Van Hool.
Ops incl: local bus services, excursions & tours, private hire, continental tours, school contracts.
Livery: White/Blue/Red.

MERLYN'S COACHES (SKEWEN) LTD
THE LODGE, 56 SIDING TERRACE, SKEWEN SA10 6RD.
Tel: 01792 813303.
Fax: 01792 813085.
Props: June John, Andrew Pearce.
Fleet: 14 - 1 single-deck bus, 10 coach, 1 midicoach, 1 minibus, 1 midibus.
Chassis: 4 Leyland. 1 MCW. 1 Renault. 6 Volvo.
Bodies: 1 Caetano. 1 Duple. 7 Plaxton. 4 Van Hool. 1 Cymric.
Ops incl: local bus services, school contracts, excursions & tours, private hire, continental tours.
Livery: White/multi coloured.
Ticket System: Wayfarer.

NELSON & SON (GLYNNEATH) LTD
74A HIGH STREET, GLYNNEATH SA11 5AW.
Tel: 01639 722252.
Fax: 01639 720308.
Fleetname: Nelson's Coaches.
Man Dir: J. L. R. Nelson.
Dir/Co Sec: Mrs J. Nelson.
Fleet: 11 - 10 coach, 1 midicoach.
Chassis: 4 DAF. 1 Ford. 4 Leyland. 1 Mercedes. 1 Volvo.
Bodies: 1 Duple. 1 Jonckheere. 5 Plaxton. 3 Van Hool. 1 Other.

Ops incl: school contracts, excursions & tours, private hire, continental tours.
Livery: White/Red/Orange.

*D J THOMAS COACHES
MILLAND ROAD INDUSTRIAL ESTATE, NEATH SA11 1NJ
Tel/Fax: 01639 635502
E-mail: mail@djthomascoaches.co.uk
Web site: www.djthomascoaches.co.uk
Dirs: Richard Thomas, Andrea Gibson
Fleet: 14 - 9 coach, 3 minicoach, 2 minibus.
Chassis: 1 Bristol. 4 Mercedes. 1 Renault. 9 Volvo.
Bodies: 9 Berkhof. 3 Plaxton. 3 Van Hool.
Ops incl: local bus services, excursions & tours, private hire, school contracts.

*TONNA LUXURY COACHES LTD
TENNIS VIEW GARAGE, HEOL-Y-GLO, TONNA SA11 3NJ
Tel: 01639 642727
Fax: 01639 646052
Dirs: K M Hopkins, A Hopkins
Fleet: 16 coach.
Chassis: 1 DAF. 1 Dennis. 3 Mercedes. 11 Volvo.
Bodies: incl: 1 Alexander. Plaxton. Van Hool.
Ops incl: school contracts, private hire.
Livery: White/Blue

NEWPORT

NEWPORT TRANSPORT LTD
160 CORPORATION ROAD, NEWPORT NP19 0WF
Tel: 01633 670563
Fax: 01633 242589
Web site: www.newporttransport.co.uk
E-mail: newporttransport@btconnect.com
Fleetname: Newport Bus
Chmn: J G Dally **Man Dir**: T G Roberts
Fleet: 80 - 6 double-deck bus, 51 single-deck bus, 7 coach, 1 open-top bus, 15 midibus.
Chassis: 17 Dennis. 4 Optare. 59 Scania.
Bodies: 42 Alexander. 7 Irizar. 4 Optare. 9 Wright. 18 Scania.
Ops incl: local bus services, school contracts, private hire.
Livery: Green/Cream.
Ticket System: Wayfarer TGX150

SHAMROCK COACHES
48 HIGH STREET, NEWPORT NP9 1GB
Tel: 01633 251917.
Fax: 01633 256822.
Web site: www.shamrock-travel.co.uk

Man: M. King. **Controller**: R. Cope.
Co Sec: A. Rowe. **Off Man**: C. Ward.
Fleet: 34 - 30 coach, 4 midicoach.
Chassis: 3 Bova. 18 Dennis. 2 MAN. 4 Mercedes. 4 Scania. 3 Volvo.
Bodies: 3 Bova. 8 Duple. 1 Jonckheere. 10 Plaxton.
Ops incl: local bus services, school contracts, excursions & tours, private hire, express, continental tours.
Livery: Yellow/Green.
Ticket System: Wayfarer 3.
See also Shamrock, Rhondda

*STAGECOACH IN SOUTH WALES
See Torfaen

WELSH DRAGON TRAVEL
21 BEAUFORT ROAD, NEWPORT NP19 7ND.
Tel: 01633 761397
E-mail: alan.smith5@ntworld.com
Prop: Alan Barrington Smith.
Fleet: 4 - 1 double-deck bus, 2 coach, 1 open-top bus.
Chassis: 1 Bedford. 1 Bristol. 2 Leyland.
Ops incl: local bus services, school contracts, private hire.
Livery: Red/Cream
Ticket System: Almex

PEMBROKESHIRE

W. H. COLLINS
CUFFERN GARAGE, ROCH, HAVERFORDWEST SA62 6HB.
Tel: 01437 710337.
Fleetname: Collins Coaches.
Prop: P. N. & M. Collins.
Fleet: 18 - 16 minibus, 2 minicoach.
Ops incl: school contracts, private hire.
Livery: Blue/Grey/White.

*EDWARDS BROS
THE GARAGE, BROAD HAVEN ROAD, TIERS CROSS, HAVERFORDWEST SA62 3BZ
Tel: 01437 890230
Fax: 01437 890337
E-mail: edwardsbros@tiscali.co.uk
Prop: Robert Edwards
Fleet: 20 - 8 coach, 4 midibus, 4 midicoach, 4 minibus.
Chassis: 1 Bova. 1 Dennis. 3 LDV. 9 Mercedes. 6 Volvo.
Bodies: 2 Autobus. 1 Bova. 4 Mercedes. 6 Plaxton. 1 Reeve Burgess. 3 Van Hool. 3 other.
Ops incl: local bus services, school contracts, excursions & tours, private hire.
Livery: Gold or White.
Ticket System: Wayfarer

Air conditioning	Replacement vehicle available
Vehicles suitable for disabled	Toilet-drop facilities available
Coach(es) with galley facilities	Vintage vehicle(s) available
Coach(es) with toilet facilities	Open top vehicle(s)
Seat belt-fitted vehicles	
Recovery service available (not 24 hr)	
24hr recovery service	

*MIDWAY MOTORS
R24
MIDWAY GARAGE, CRYMYCH
SA41 3QU
Tel: 01239 831267
Fax: 01239 831279
E-mail: reesmidway@hotmail.com
Ptnrs: Wyndham Rees, Elan Rees **Ch Eng**: Heulyn Phillips
Fleet: 15 - 3 single-deck bus, 8 coach, 2 midicoach, 2 minibus.
Chassis: 1 Bova. 4 Dennis. 2 Ford. 1 Ford Transit. 1 LDV. 1 Mercedes. 1 Optare. 4 Volvo.
Bodies: 1 Bova. 5 Caetano. 1 Mercedes. 1 Optare. 3 Plaxton. 1 Reeve Burgess. 1 Wadham Stringer.
Ops incl: local bus services, school contracts, excursions & tours, private hire, continental tours.
Livery: Silver/Blue

SILCOX COACHES
WATERLOO GARAGE, PEMBROKE DOCK SA72 4RR.
Tel: 01646 683143.
Fax: 01646 621787.
Man Dir: K. W. Silcox
Fleet: 74 - 42 single-deck bus, 19 coach, 14 midibus, 1 midicoach.
Chassis: 25 Dennis. 38 Leyland. 1 MAN. 10 Mercedes. 1 Optare. 1 Volvo.
Bodies: 2 Berkhof. 7 Caetano. 5 Duple. 1 East Lancs. 3 Marco Polo. 4 Marshall. 2 Mellor. 1 Optare. 40 Plaxton. 2 UVG. 1 Van Hool. 6 Wadham Stringer. 2 Wright.
Ops incl: local bus services, school contracts, excursions & tours, private hire, continental tours.
Livery: Red/Cream/Blue.

SUMMERDALE COACHES
SUMMERDALE GARAGE, LETTERSTON SA62 5UB.
Tel: 01348 840270.
Props: D. G. Davies, B. J. L. Davies, G. R. Jones.
Livery: Yellow/Blue

POWYS

A. & E. HIRE
PENYBRYN, LLANGYNIEW, WELSHPOOL SY21 0JS
Tel: 01938 810518
Dir: Arwyn P Davies
Fleet: 5 minibus
Chassis/bodies: 4 Ford. 1 Freight Rover.
Ops incl: school contracts, private hire

*ROY BROWNS COACHES
R24
15 HIGH STREET, BUILTH WELLS LD2 3DN
Tel: 01982 552597
Tel: 01982 552286
E-mail: neil@rbci.fsnet.co.uk
Web site:
www.roybrownscoaches.co.uk

Prop: N W Brown **Ops Man**: P H Davies
Fleet: 28 - 6 single-deck bus, 12 coach, 10 minibus.
Chassis: 4 Bedford. 5 DAF. 2 Dennis. 7 Leyland. 3 Optare. 1 Volvo
Bodies: 4 Caetano. 4 MCW. 10 Plaxton. 1 Wright. 1 other.
Ops incl: local bus services, school contracts, excursions & tours, private hire
Ticket System: Setright.

CELTIC TRAVEL
NEW STREET, LLANIDLOES SY18 6EH
Tel: 01686 412231/412232
E-mail: celtic@irc.ruralwales.org
Props: P. Jones, G. Jones.
Fleet: 20 - 17 coach, 3 minibus.
Chassis: 1 Bedford. 2 DAF. 3 Ford. 3 Leyland. 11 Volvo
Bodies: Bova, Duple, Ford, Plaxton, Van Hool.
Ops incl: school contracts, excursions & tours, private hire.
Livery: dark/light Grey with green lettering and Welsh Dragon emblem.

CENTRAL TRAVEL
OLD BULK YARD, STATION YARD, NEWTOWN SY16 1BA
Tel: 07710 432832
Tel/Fax: 01686 610224
Props: Richard W Bowen
Fleet: 4 - 1 coach, 1 midicoach, 1 minicoach, 1 minibus.
Chassis: 1 Ford Transit. 1 Mercedes. 1 Scania. 1 Volvo
Bodies: 1 Mercedes. 1 Plaxton. 1 Van Hool.
Ops incl: school contracts, private hire.

COACHING CONNECTION
14 GREAT OAK STREET, LLANIDLOES SY18 6BN
Tel: 01686 413714
Fax: 01686 411065
Props: David Corfield, Miss Betty Tonks
Fleet: 1 coach
Chassis/Body: Setra
Ops incl: excursions & tours.
Livery: Cream with orange/brown flashes.

*CROSS GATES COACHES
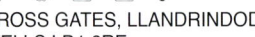
CROSS GATES, LLANDRINDOD WELLS LD1 6RE
Tel: 01597 852000
Fax: 01597 851748
E-mail: peter@llnk.co.uk
Dir/ Ops Man: Peter Knill **Dir/Co Sec**: Reg Knill **Ch Eng**: Chris Prynne
Fleet: 15 - 4 single-deck bus, 10 coach, 1 midibus
Chassis: 2 DAF. 2 Dennis. 2 Mercedes. 4 Optare. 5 Scania.
Bodies: 1 Carlyle. 1 Duple. 1 Irizar. 4 Optare. 4 Plaxton. 4 Van Hool.
Ops incl: local bus services, school contracts, private hire.
Livery: Blue/Graphite
Ticket system: Wayfarer

D G DAVIES
AFON MARTEG GARAGE, PANT-Y-DWR LD6 5NA
Tel: 05978 8232
Prop: D G Davies
Fleet: 2

Chassis: Ford.
Bodies: Duple, Plaxton
Ops incl: school contracts, private hire.
Livery: White with red/blue flashing

*R G GITTINS - COACHES
THE GARAGE, DOLANOG, WELSHPOOL SY21 0LQ
Tel/fax: 01938 810439
Prop: R G Gittins
Fleet: 3 - 1 coach, 1 midibus, 1 midicoach
Chassis: 1 Bova. 1 MAN. 1 Mercedes.
Bodies: 1 Bova. 1 Caetano. 1 Reeve Burgess.
Ops incl: school contracts, excursions & tours, private hire.

GWYN JONES (MEIFORD)
THE GARAGE, MEIFOD SY22 6DB
Tel: 01938 500249
E-mail: gwynmeifod@talk21.com
Ptnrs: Gwyn Jones, Jean Jones, Martin Jones
Fleet: 3 - 2 single-deck bus, 1 midicoach.
Chassis/Bodies: 1 DAF. 1 Caetano. 1 Mercedes.
Ops incl: school contracts, excursions & tours, private hire, continental tours.
Livery: Green/White

*HAPPY DAYS COACHES
See Shropshire

LAKELINE COACHES

EBRAN-DDU, FELINDRE, KNIGHTON LD7 1YN
Tel: 01547 7662
Dir: J E A Lakelin
Fleet: 4 - 3 coach, 1 minibus.
Chassis: 1 Bedford. 1 DAF. 1 Dennis. 1 Ford.
Bodies: 1 Duple. 1 LDV. 2 Plaxton.
Ops incl: school contracts, private hire
Livery: Pale Blue/Dark Blue

LLOYDS COACHES
R24
OLD CROSVILLE GARAGE, DOLL STREET, MACHYNLLETH SY20 8BH
Tel: 01654 702100
Fax: 01654 703900
Mobile: 07712 552953
E-mail: lloydscoaches@hotmail.com
Dirs: D W LLoyd
Fleet: 12 - 1 single-deck bus, 6 coach, 1 midicoach, 4 minibus
Chassis: 2 Leyland. 5 Mercedes. 5 Volvo.
Bodies: 3 Alexander. 1 Duple. 7 Plaxton. 1 other.
Ops incl: local bus services, school contracts, private hire.
Livery: Silver/Red/Yellow
Ticket system: Wayfarer

OWEN'S MOTORS LTD

TEMESIDE HOUSE, STATION ROAD, KNIGHTON LD7 1DT
Tel: 01547 528303
Fax: 01547 520512
Web site: www.owensmotors.co.uk

Ops Man: D. Owen. **Ch Eng**: T Owen.
Sec/Dir: J Owen
Fleet: 14 - 11 coach, 3 minibus.
Chassis: 3 Dennis. 1 Ford. 2 LDV. 7 Volvo.
Bodies: 2 Duple. 1 Ford Transit. 2 LDV. 8 Plaxton. 1 Van Hool.
Ops incl: local bus services, school contracts, excursions & tours, private hire, continental tours.
Livery: Blue/Grey

*STAGECOACH IN SOUTH WALES
See Torfaen

STOCKHAMS COACHES
TIMBERCRAFTS TRADING ESTATE, GILWERN ROAD, CRICKHOWELL NP8 1HW
Tel/Fax: 01873 810343
Prop: Nancy Stockham
Fleet: 8 - 4 coaches, 4 minibuses.
Chassis: 3 Volvo, 1 Leyland. 4 Ford Transit
Bodies: Ford, Plaxton, Van Hool
Ops incl: school contracts, private hire.
Livery: Green/White.

STRATOS TRAVEL
2 SHORTBRIDGE STREET, NEWTOWN SY16 2LW
Tel: 01686 629021
Fax: 01686 626092
E-mail: info@stratostravel.co.uk
Web site: www.stratostravel.co.uk
Prop: M Owen
Fleet: 5 - 1 single-deck bus, 3 coach, 1 midicoach.
Chassis: 1 Ayats. 1 Bova. 1 Dennis. 1 Iveco.1 Toyota.
Bodies: 1 Ayats. 1 Beulas. 1 Bova. 1 Caetano. 1 Plaxton.
Ops incl: local bus services, excursions & tours, private hire, continental tours.
Livery: Silver/Blue

TANAT VALLEY COACHES

THE GARAGE, LLANRHAEDR YM MOCHNANT SY10 0AD
Tel: 01691 780212
Fax: 01691 780634
Recovery: 01691 780212
E-mail: info@tanat.co.uk
Web site: www.tanat.co.uk
Dirs: R Michael Morris, Peter W Morris **Eng Man**: Alex Hughes **Co Sec**: Sara Morris
Ops Man: Nick Culliford
Fleet: 40 - 4 double-deck bus, 12 single-deck bus, 15 coach, 3 midibus, 1 midicoach, 5 minibus.
Chassis: 4 Bedford. 1 DAF. 8 Dennis. 2 LDV. 16 Leyland. 1 Marshall. 3 Mercedes. 1 Toyota. 4 Volvo.
Bodies: 6 Alexander. 1 Berkhof. 1 Bova. 2 Caetano. 7 Duple. 1 ECW. 5 East Lancs. 2 LDV. 2 Leyland. 1 Marcopolo. 1 Marshall/MCV. 6 Plaxton. 3 Reeve Burgess. 2 UVG.
Ops incl: local bus services, school

contracts, excursions & tours, private hire, express.
Livery: Beige/Cream/White
Ticket System: Almex A90

WILLIAMS COACHES
RICH WAY, THE WATTON, BRECON LD3 7EH.
Tel: 01874 622223
Fax: 01874 625218
E-mail: office@williams-coaches.co.uk
Web site: www.williams-coaches.co.uk
Chmn: J L Williams (Senr) **Dirs**: D M Williams (**Sec**), D E Williams, J L Williams (jnr),I T Parry (**Eng**), W Rees (**Ops Man**)
Fleet: 37 - 1 single-deck bus, 20 coach, 1 midibus, 2 midicoach, 13 minibus.
Chassis: 1 Bedford. 1 DAF. 8 Ford Transit. 1 Irisbus. 3 LDV. 1 MAN. 17 Mercedes. 4 Setra. 1 Scudo.
Ops incl: local bus services, school contracts, private hire, excursions & tours.
Livery: Orange/Cream
Ticket System: Setright

RHONDDA, CYNON, TAFF

*BEBB TRAVEL

THE COACH STATIOIN, LLANTWIT FARDRE CF38 2HB
Tel: 01443 215100
Fax: 01443 215134
E-mail: sales@bebbtravel.co.uk
Chmn: John O'Brien **Man Dir**: David Newman **Fleet Eng**: Dave Witte
Fleet: 44 - 26 single-deck bus, 18 coach.
Chassis: 26 Optare. 18 Volvo.
Bodies: 26 Optare. 18 Plaxton.
Ops incl: local bus services, school contracts, express
Livery: White/Blue/Red/Green
Ticket system: ERG

*EDWARDS COACHES
NEWTOWN INDUSTRIAL ESTATE, LLANTWIT FARDRE CF38 2EE
Tel: 01443 202048
Fax: 01443 217583
E-mail: admin@edwardscoaches.co.uk
Web site: www.edwardscoaches.co.uk
Owner: Mike Edwards **Dirs**: Shaun Edwards, Jason Edwards, Kelly Edwards, Jessica Edwards
Fleet: 84 - 28 double-deck bus, 47 coach, 5 midicoach, 4 minibus.
Chassis: 14 MCW. 14 Volkswagen.
Bodies: 13 Bova. 7 Irizar. 2 Jonckheere.

5 Marcopolo. 14 MCW. 1 Mellor. 5 Plaxton. 6 Setra.
Ops incl: school contracts, excursions & tours, private hire, continental tours.
Livery: White/Blue

GLOBE COACHES
BROOKLANDS, FFORCHNEOL ROW, GODREAMAN, ABERDARE CF44 6HD.
Tel: 01685 873622.
Fax: 01685 876526
E-mail: wayne@globecoaches.entadsl.com
Web site: www.globecoaches.co.uk
Prop: Wayne Jarvis
Fleet: 18 - 16 coach, 2 midicoach.
Chassis: 2 DAF. 1 Leyland. 1 MAN. 2 Mercedes. 12 Volvo.
Bodies: 2 Berkhof. 2 Caetano. 2 Duple. 6 Jonckheere. 4 Plaxton.
Ops incl: excursions & tours, private hire, school contracts, continental tours.
Livery: White/Blue.

*MAISEY
GELYNOG YARD, CASTELLAU ROAD, BEDDAU CF38 2RA
Tel/Fax: 01443 205462
E-mail: info@maiseybus.co.uk
Web site: www.maiseybus.co.uk
Ptnrs: Brian Evans, Graham Evans, Colin Evans.
Fleet: 10 - 2 minibus, 8 minicoach.
Chassis: 2 Ford Transit. 1 LDV. 7 Renault.
Ops incl: school contracts, private hire.
Livery: White/Red

*STAGECOACH IN SOUTH WALES
See Torfaen

*THOMAS OF RHONDDA

BUS DEPOT, PORTH CF39 0AG.
Tel: 01443 433714
Fleet: 56 - 20 double-deck bus, 6 single-deck bus, 22 coach, 3 double-deck coach, 3 midibus, 2 minibus.
Chassis: 7 Bova. 4 DAF. 4 Dennis. 26 Leyland. 3 MAN. 2 Scania. 10 Volvo.
Ops incl: local bus services, excursions & tours, school contracts, private hire, continental tours.
Livery: White
Ticket System: Almex

Air conditioning	Replacement vehicle available
Vehicles suitable for disabled	Toilet-drop facilities available
Coach(es) with galley facilities	Vintage vehicle(s) available
Coach(es) with toilet facilities	Open top vehicle(s)
Seat belt-fitted vehicles	
Recovery service available (not 24 hr)	
R24 24hr recovery service	

CITY & COUNTY OF SWANSEA

*D'COACHES (DIAMOND HOLIDAYS)

98/99 WOODFIELD STREET, MORRISTON SA6 8AS
Tel: 01792 795808
Fax: 01792 781173
E-mail: enquiry@diamondholidays.co.uk
Web site: www.diamondholidays.co.uk.
Man Dir: Chris Roberts. **Ops Dir**: Ryan Jones **Fin Dir**: David Rees
Fleet: 18 coach
Chassis: 18 DAF.
Bodies: 18 Bova.
Ops incl: excursions & tours, private hire, continental tours.
Livery: Cream/Gold/Green.

FIRST CYMRU BUSES LIMITED
HEOL GWYROSYDD, PENLAN SA5 7BN
Tel: 01792 582233
Fax: 01792 561356
Web Site: www.firstgroup.com
Man Dir: J W Davies **Fin Dir**: Mrs A Price **Ops Dir**: P F Collier **Eng Dir**: P J Davies
Fleet: 349 - 5 double-deck bus, 14 single-deck bus, 36 coach, 254 midibus, 39 minibus.
Chassis: 1 BMC. 1 DAF. 266 Dennis. 3 Iveco. 13 Leyland. 44 Mercedes. 3 Optare. 14 Volvo.
Bodies: 20 Alexander. 3 ECW. 3 Leyland. 21 Marshall. 1 Mellor. 268 Plaxton. 8 Reeve Burgess. 1 Wadham Stringer. 17 Wright. 6 BMC. 2 Robin Hood.
Ops incl: local bus services, school contracts, excursions & tours, private hire, express.
Livery: FirstGroup.
Ticket System: Wayfarer III.

*HAWKES COACHES LTD

BRIDGE ROAD, WAUNARLWYDD, SWANSEA SA5 4SP
Tel: 01792 873336
Fax: 01792 875172
E-mail: hawkescoaches@btconnect.com
Dirs: Brian Hawkes, Mrs Janet Hawkes
Fleet: 22 - 2 single-deck bus, 19 coach, 1 midibus.
Chassis: 1 DAF. 3 Dennis. 1 Optare. 17 Volvo.
Bodies: 2 Alexander. 4 Duple. 4 Jonckheere. 12 Plaxton.
Ops incl: local bus services, private hire, school contracts.
Ticket System: Wayfarer

*BRIAN ISAAC COACHES LTD

COACH HOLIDAY CENTRE, 99 WOODFIELD STREET, MORRISTON, SWANSEA SA6 8AS
Tel: 01792 701644
Fax: 01792 310233
E-mail: enquiries@brianisaac.co.uk
Web Site: www.brianisaac.co.uk
Man Dir: Brian H Isaac **Fin Dir**: David Rees
Ops Dir: Ryan Jones
Fleet: 10 coach
Chassis: 10 DAF.
Bodies: 10 Bova.
Ops incl: excursions & tours, private hire, continental tours.
Livery: Blue/Magenta/White

PULLMAN COACHES LTD
UNIT 41, PENCLAWDD INDUSTRIAL ESTATE, CROFTY SA4 3RT.
Tel: 01792 851430
E-mail: pullmancoaches@aol.com
Web site: www.pullmancoaches.co.uk
Dirs: C. W. Lewis, H. S. Rees.
Fleet: 34 - 8 single-deck bus, 25 coach, 1 minicoach.
Livery: Cream/White/Red/Fawn
(Part of Veolia Transport)

*STAGECOACH IN SOUTH WALES
See Torfaen

ARTHUR THOMAS COACHES
91 PONTARDULAIS ROAD, GORSEINON SA4 4FQ.
Props: A. A., J. T., B. E., G. A. Thomas.
Livery: Cream/Red/Blue.

TORFAEN

B'S TRAVEL

13 EAST VIEW, GRIFFITHSTOWN NP4 5DW.
Tel/Fax: 01495 756889.
E-mail: kay@bstravel.fsnet.co.uk
Ptnrs: James Benning, Kay Benning.
Fleet: 4 - 1 coach, 1 midicoach, 1 minibus, 1 minicoach.
Chassis: 1 LDV. 1 MAN. 2 Mercedes.
Bodies: 1 Autobus. 1 Jonckheere. 1 Gem. 1 LDV.
Ops incl: private hire, school contracts.
Livery: White

*JENSON TRAVEL

15 PONTNEWYNDD INDUSTRIAL ESTATE, PONTNEWYNDD, PONTYPOOL NP4 6YW
Tel/Fax: 01495 760539
E-mail: jenson01@btconnect.com
Tran Man: Nicola Jenkins **Owner**: Gwyn Jenkins **Ch Eng**: Peter Ryan
Fleet: 18 - 9 double-deck coach, 5 minibus, 4 midicoach
Chassis: 5 Dennis. 5 LDV. 1 MAN. 4 Mercedes. 3 Volvo.
Bodies: 1 Caetano. 2 Jonckheere.
4 Leyland. 1 Plaxton. 3 Reeve Burgess. 1 Van Hool.
Ops incl: school contracts, excursions & tours, private hire.
Livery: White/Blue/Navy

*STAGECOACH IN SOUTH WALES
1 ST DAVID'S ROAD, CWMBRAN NP44 1PD
Tel: 01633 838856
Fax: 01633 865299
Web site: www.stagecoachbus.com
Man Dir: John Gould **Comm Dir**: Richard Davies **Eng Dir**: David Howe
Fleet: 374 - 13 double-deck bus, 73 single-deck bus, 37 coach, 10 double-deck coach, 136 midibus, 105 minibus.
Chassis: 6 BMC. 136 Dennis. 12 Leyland. 77 Mercedes. 6 Neoplan. 33 Optare. 104 Volvo.
Bodies: 167 Alexander. 6 BMC. 6 Leyland. 7 Marshall/MCV. 6 Neoplan. 22 Northern Counties. 33 Optare. 115 Plaxton. 7 UVG. 5 other.
Ops incl: local bus services, school contracts, excursions & tours, private hire, express.
Livery: Stagecoach
Ticket System: Wayfarer III

VALE OF GLAMORGAN

EST BUS LTD
UNIT 26, TUMULUS WAY, LLANDOW TRADING ESTATE, LLANDOW CF71 7PB
Tel: 01446 793100
Dir: C Hookings
Ops incl: local bus services, school contracts
Livery: Maroon/Cream

HAYWARD TRAVEL (CARDIFF)
2 MURCH CRESCENT, DINAS POWYS CF64 4RF
Tel: 029 2051 5551
Fax: 029 2051 5113
E-mail: info@haywardtravel.co.uk
Web site: www.haywardtravel.co.uk
Ops incl: private hire

THOMAS OF BARRY
12 PARK CRESCENT, BARRY CF62 6HD
Tel/Recovery: 01446 722800
Fax: 01446 722766
E-mail: thomasofbarry@hotmail.com
Web site: www.thomasofbarry.com
Prop: A Jones **Ops Man**: K Jones
Fleet: 71 - 5 double-deck bus, 15 single-deck bus, 30 coach, 2 double-deck coach, 4 open-top bus, 5 midibus, 3 midicoach, 2 minibus, 5 minicoach.
Chassis: 20 Dennis. 2 Irisbus. 2 MAN. 20 Mercedes. 5 Optare. 20 Scania. 2 Volvo.
Bodies: 4 Beulas. 3 Caetano. 5 Duple. 12 Irizar. 6 Leyland. 5 MCW. 9 Mercedes. 15 Plaxton. 2 Sunsundegui. 3 UVG. 6 Van Hool.
Ops incl: local bus services, school

contracts, excursions & tours, private hire, express, continental tours.
Livery: White/Maroon.
Ticket System: Wayfarer 3
(Part of the Shamrock Group)

WREXHAM

ACTON COACHES
109 HERBERT JENNING AVENUE, ACTON PARK LL12 7YA
Tel/Fax: 01978 352470
Prop: D B Evans.
Fleet: 4 - 3 coach, 1 midibus
Chassis: 1 DAF. 2 Volvo. 1 Mercedes.
Bodies: 1 Plaxton. 1 Caetano. 1 Van Hool. 1 Optare.
Livery: Blue/White
Ops incl: school contracts, private hire

GEORGE EDWARDS & SON

BERWYN, BWLCHYWYN LL11 5UE.
Tel/Fax: 01978 757281
Props: G F & G Edwards.
Fleet: 7 - includes single-deck bus, coach
Chassis: 1 Bedford. 6 DAF
Bodies: 2 Duple. 1 Optare. 4 Van Hool
Ops incl: local bus services, school contracts, private hire.
Livery: Red/Ivory/Maroon

*HAPPY DAYS COACHES
See Shropshire

HAYDN'S TOURS & TRAVEL

BEVERLEY, FIELD HEAD, CHIRK LL14 5PU.
Tel/Fax: 01691 773267
E-mail: christopherwilliams@virgin.net
Ptnrs: M Williams, Chris Williams.
Fleet: 2 coach
Chassis: 1 DAF. 1 Volvo.
Bodies: 1 Duple. 1 Plaxton.
Ops incl: excursions & tours, private hire, school contracts.
Livery: Red/White/Yellow/Orange

JOHN'S TRAVEL WREXHAM

1 BRYN MAELOR, SOUTHSEA LL11 6RD.
Tel: 01978 753364
Prop: John F H Ithell
Fleet: 4 - 2 midibus, 2 minibus
Chassis: 4 Mercedes
Bodies: 1 Carlyle.2 Plaxton. 1 Reeve Burgess.
Ops incl: local bus services, private hire
Livery: White with red lettering
Ticket system: Wayfarer

D. JONES & SON
CLYDFAN, HALL STREET, RHOSLLANERCRUGOG LL14 2LG.
Tel: 01978 842540
Mobile: 07739 206623
Props: D. & G. Jones.
Fleet: 7 - 1 coach, 6 single-deck bus
Fleet: 1 DAF. 4 Dennis. 2 Mercedes.
Bodies: 3 Caetano. 1 Mercedes. 3Plaxton.
Ops incl: local bus services, school contracts, private hire.
Ops incl: local bus services, private hire
Livery: Blue/Cream.
Ticket system: Wayfarer

E JONES & SONS
MOUNTAIN VIEW, BANK STREET, PONCIAU LL14 1EN.
Tel: 01978 841613.
Props: J B & G Jones.
Fleet: 7
Livery: Blue/White/Orange.

*PAT'S COACHES LTD
GATEWEN ROAD, NEW BROUGHTON LL11 6YA
Tel: 01978 720171
Fax: 01978 758459
E-mail: enquiries@patscoaches.co.uk.fsnet.co.uk
Web site: www.patscoaches.co.uk
Ptnr: P C Davies, J M Davies, D K Davies
Chassis: 1 DAF. 1 LDV. 2 Mercedes. 2 Neoplan. 2 Scania. 8 Volvo.
Bodies: 1 Autobus. 4 Berkhof. 1 Jonckheere. 1 Marcopolo. 1 Marshall/MCV.
2 Mercedes. 2 Neoplan. 2 Plaxton. 1 Van Hool. 1 Wright. 1 other.

PRICES COACHES
THE HAVEN, BERSHAM ROAD, SOUTHSEA LL11 6TF
Tel/Fax: 01978 756834
Prop: Tecwyn Price
Fleet: 7 - 2 double-deck bus, 4 coach, 1 midibus
Chassis: 2 Leyland. 1 Mercedes. 1 Setra. 3 Volvo.
Bodies: 2 Leyland. 1 Kassbohrer. 1 Mercedes. 2 Plaxton. 1 Van Hool.
Ops incl: school contracts, private hire
Livery: Primrose/Green/Orange

*STRAFFORDS COACHES

UNITS 7/8, FIVE CROSSES INDUSTRIAL ESTATE, MINERA LL11 3RD.
Tel: 01978 756106
Fax: 01978 756106
Props: G A Strafford
Fleet: 12 - 1 double-deck bus, 5 coach, 3 midicoach.
Chassis: 1 Bova. 4 DAF. 1 Iveco. 1 Leyland. 4 Mercedes.
Bodies: 1 Bova. 1 Duple. 1 Iveco. 1 MAN. 4 Mercedes. 1 Plaxton. 2 Van Hool.
Ops incl: school contracts, private hire.
Livery: Cream/Brown/Orange

T WILLIAMS & SONS
CLARKE STREET BUS GARAGE, PONCIAU LL14 1RT
Tel: 01978 840062.
Prop: J S Williams.
Fleet: 4 coach.
Chassis: 2 Bedford, 1 DAF, 1 Volvo.
Bodies: Duple, Plaxton, Jonckheere.
Ops incl: private hire, school contracts, excursions & tours.
Livery: Blue/Cream.
Ticket System: Setright.

❄	Air conditioning
♿	Vehicles suitable for disabled
🍽	Coach(es) with galley facilities
WC	Coach(es) with toilet facilities
▼	Seat belt-fitted vehicles
R	Recovery service available (not 24 hr)
R24	24hr recovery service
🔧	Replacement vehicle available
T	Toilet-drop facilities available
	Vintage vehicle(s) available
🚌	Open top vehicle(s)

CHANNEL ISLANDS

ALDERNEY

RIDUNA BUSES
40C HIGH STREET, ALDERNEY
GY9 3TG
Tel: 01481 823760
Fax: 01481 823030
Prop: A. J. Curtis.
Fleet: 5 - 2 single-deck bus, 2 coach, 1 minibus.
Chassis: 3 Bedford. 1 Freight Rover.
Bodies: 2 Duple. 1 Pennine. 1 Heaver.
Ops incl: local bus services, excursions & tours, private hire.
Livery: Cream/Maroon

GUERNSEY

ISLAND COACHWAYS LTD
THE TRAMSHEDS, LES BANQUES, ST PETER PORT GY4 6SF
Tel: 01481 720210
Fax: 01481 710109
E-mail: sales@island-coachways.demon.co.uk
Web site: www.island-coachways.demon.co.uk
Man Dir: Mrs Hannah Beacom **Co Sec/Dir**: George Boucher **Works Man/Dir**: Ben Boucher **Traf Man**: John Drillot **Off Man**: Mrs Jenny Down **Customer Care Man**: Mrs Ann Belben
Fleet: 56 - 38 single-deck bus, 14 coach, 1 midicoach, 3 minibus
Chassis: 1 Cannon. 33 Dennis. 4 Iveco. 9 Leyland. 4 Optare. 4 Renault. 1 Toyota.
Bodies: 1 Caetano. 4 Camo. 33 East Lancs. 3 Elme. 3 Iveco. 2 Leicester. 4 Optare. 6 Wadham Stringer.
Ops incl: local bus services, school contracts, excursions & tours, private hire
Livery: Bus: Green/Yellow Coach: Cream/Gold
Ticket System: Almex, Smartfare

JERSEY

CONNEX JERSEY
2 CALEDONIA PLACE, WEIGHBRIDGE, ST HELIER JE2 3NG
Tel: 01534 877772
Gen Man: Phillipe Juhles
Fleetname: Connex
Fleet: 33 single-deck buses
Chassis: 33 Dennis
Bodies: 33 Caetano

TANTIVY BLUE COACH TOURS
70/72 LA COLOMBERIE, ST HELIER JE2 4QA
Tel: 01534 706706
Fax: 01534 706705
E-mail: info@jerseycoaches.com
Web site: www.jerseycoaches.com
Man Dir: Mike Cotilard **Ops Dir**: Paul Young
Fleet: 66 - 4 single-deck bus, 60 coach, 2 mdnicoach.
Chassis: 7 Bedford. 3 Cannon. 1 Iveco. 50 Leyland. 2 Optare.
Bodies: 2 Caetano. 6 Carlyle. 7 Duple. 3 Leicester. 2 Optare. 40 Wadham Stringer.
Ops incl: school contracts, excursions & tours, private hire.
Livery: Blue.

WAVERLEY COACHES LTD
UNIT 3, LA COLLETTE, ST HELIER JE2 3NX
Tel: 01534 758360
Fax: 01534 732627
Dir/Gen Man: S. E. Pedersen.
Ch Eng: Peter Evans.
Fleet: 18 - 12 coach, 2 midicoach, 4 minibus.
Chassis: 7 Bedford. 5 Leyland. 2 Mercedes. 1 Renault. 3 VW.
Bodies: 7 Duple. 5 Wadham Stringer. 4 other.
Ops incl: excursions & tours, private hire.
Livery: Yellow/White.

ISLES OF SCILLY

HERITAGE TOURS
SANTAMANA, 9 RAMS VALLEY, ST MARY'S TR21 0JX
Tel: 01720 422387
Props: G. Twynham, Mrs P. Twynham.
Fleet: 1 single-deck bus (1948 vehicle).
Chassis: Austin K2. **Body**: Barnard.
Ops incl: excursions & tours, private hire.
Livery: Blue/Cream.

NORTHERN IRELAND

A1 COACH TRAVEL
35 NORBURGH PARK, FOYLE SPRINGS, DERRY BT48 0RG
Tel/Fax: 028 7130 9323
Prop: J. Bradshaw.
Fleet: 2 midicoach.
Chassis: 1 Mercedes. 1 Renault.
Ops incl: private hire, continental tours, school contracts.

*CHAMBERS COACH HIRE LTD
11 CIRCULAR ROAD, MONEYMORE BT45 7PY
Tel: 028 8674 8152
Fax: 028 8674 8152
Web site: www.coachireland.com
Dirs: Des Chambers, Mary Chambers, Paul Chambers, Philip Harkness **Ops Man**: Mary McIver
Fleet: 48 - 16 coach, 2 double-deck coach, 4 midibus, 8 midicoach, 6 minicoach, 12 minibus.
Chassis: 2 Ford Transit. 1 Mercedes. 16 Scania.
Bodies: 2 Berkhof. 15 Irizar. 18 Mercedes. 12 Plaxton.
Ops incl: school contracts, excursions & tours, private hire

*CROSS COUNTRY COACHES LTD
63 BALLYLINTAGH ROAD, COLERAINE BT51 3SPP
Tel: 028 7086 8989
Fax: 028 7086 9191
E-mail: sales@crosscountrycoaches.com
Dirs: J R Telford, B Telford
Fleet: 6 - 5 coach, 1 midicoach.
Chassis: 1 Bedford. 1 DAF. 1 MAN. 1 Volvo.
Bodies: 1 Jonckheere. 4 Wadham Stringer. 1 OB.
Ops incl: excursions & tours, private hire, continental tours.
Livery: White/red/Yellow with green-blue logo

*DARRAGHS COACHES
22 LISHEEGHAN ROAD, BALLYMONEY BT53 7JY
Tel: 028 2954 0684
Fax: 028 2954 0785
E-mail: kdarragh@aol.com
Man: Robert Darragh

GILES TOURS
63 ABBEYDALE AVENUE, NEWTOWNARDS BT23 8RT
Tel/Fax: 028 9181 1099
E-mail: enquiries@gilestours.co.uk
Web site: www.gilestours.co.uk
Dirs: Neil Giles, Patricia Giles
Fleet: 4 - 3 coach, 1 midicoach.
Chassis: 1 Mercedes. 3 Van Hool.
Ops incl: excursions & tours, private hire, continental tours.

*LAKELAND TOURS
47 MAIN STREET, TEMPO BT94 3LU
Tel: 028 8954 1646
Fax: 028 8954 1424
Recovery: 07779 026597
E-mail: lakelandtours@btconnect.com
Web site: www.lakelandtours.co.uk
Prop: Ian McCutcheon
Fleet: 5 - 3 coach, 1 midicoach, 1 minicoach.
Chassis: 1 DAF. 1 Leyland. 2 MAN. 1 Mercedes.
Bodies: 1 Mercedes. 1 Noge. 1 Plaxton. 1 Setra. 1 Van Hool.
Ops incl: excursions & tours, private hire, school contracts.

*LOGANS EXECUTIVE TRAVEL
58 GALDANAGH ROAD, DUNLOY, BALLYMENA BT44 9DB
Tel: 028 2765 7203
Fax: 028 2765 7559
E-mail: coaches@loganstravel.com
Web site: www.loganstravel.com
Prop: Sean Logan
Fleet: 49 - coach, midicoach, minicoach, minibus.
Chassis: 6 Iveco. 5 LDV. 1 MAN. 12 Mercedes. 25 Volvo.
Ops incl: local bus services, school contracts, private hire, continental tours.

LONDONDERRY & LOUGH SWILLY BUS COMPANY LTD
STRAND ROAD, DERRY BT48 7PY
Tel: 00 353 74 22863
Fleet: 88 - single-deck bus, coach.
Ops incl: local bus services.

POOTS COACH HIRE LTD
118A PORTADOWN ROAD, TANDRAGEE BT62 2JX
Tel: 028 3884 1504
Fax: 028 3884 1724
Dirs: Jim T Poots, Samuel Poots
Fleet: 6 - 3 coach, 3 midicoach.
Chassis: 1 DAF. 3 Mercedes. 2 Leyland.
Bodies: 3 Plaxton. 3 Reeve Burgess
Ops incl: excursions & tours, private hire, express, school contracts.
Livery: White
Ticket system: Wayfarer

*O. ROONEY COACH HIRE LTD
4 DANA PLACE, HILLTOWN, NEWRY BT34 5UE
Tel: 028 4063 0825
Fax: 028 4063 8028
Recovery: 077721 510955
E-mail: oliver@orcoachireland.com
Web site: www.orcoachireland.com
Man Dir: Oliver Rooney **Ops Man**: Aaron Rooney
Fleet: 12 - 2 single-deck bus, 3 coach, 2 midibus, 5 minibus.
Chassis: 2 Dennis. 1 Leyland. 6 Mercedes. 1 Renault. 2 Volvo.
Bodies: 3 Alexander. 3 Plaxton. 6 Reeve Burgess.
Ops incl: local bus services, excursions & tours, school contracts, private hire.
Livery: White/Yellow

SLOAN TRAVEL
51 KILLOWEN OLD ROAD, ROSTREVOR, NEWRY BT34 3AE.
Tel: 028 4173 8459
Fax: 028 4173 9459
Dir/Ch Eng: B. M. Sloan. **Sec**: Ms M. Sloan.
Fleet: 7 - 6 coach, 1 minibus.
Chassis: 4 Bedford. 3 Ford.
Bodies: 2 Duple. 4 Plaxton.
Ops incl: local bus services, school contracts, excursions & tours, private hire, express, continental tours.
Livery: Mixed.

TRANSLINK
CENTRAL STATION, EAST BRIDGE STREET, BELFAST BT1 3PB
Tel: 028 9089 9400
E-mail: feedback@translink.co.uk
Web site: www.translink.co.uk
Fleetnames: Ulsterbus, Citybus
Chmn: Dr Joan Smyth **Ch Exec**: Keith Moffat **Dir of HR**: Alan Mercer **Dir of Ops**: Philip O'Neil **Fin Dir**: Stephen Armstrong **Mktg Exec**: Ciaran Rogan **Head of Projects**: David Laird **Infrastructure Exec**: Clive Bradberry
Fleet: 1,469 – 20 double-deck bus, 1,274 single-deck bus, 40 coach, 2 double-deck coach, 8 articulated bus, 4 open-top bus, 98 minibus, 23 minicoach.
Chassis: 1 Ayats. 84 Bristol. 10 DAF. 43 Dennis. 819 Leyland. 97 Mercedes. 23 Optare. 5 Renault. 43 Scania. 346 Volvo.
Bodies: 1,023 Alexander. 1 Ayats. 7 Caetano. 4 Duple. 3 ECW. 4 Irizar. 10 Mercedes. 23 Optare. 135 Plaxton. 2 Reeve Burgess. 6 Van Hool. 247 Wright. 6 Other makes.

	Air conditioning		Seat belt-fitted vehicles		Replacement vehicle available
	Vehicles suitable for disabled	R	Recovery service available (not 24 hr)	T	Toilet-drop facilities available
	Coach(es) with galley facilities				Vintage vehicle(s) available
	Coach(es) with toilet facilities	R24	24hr recovery service		Open top vehicle(s)

REPUBLIC OF IRELAND

AIRCOACH
DUBLIN
Web site: www.aircoach.ie
Chassis: incl Setra
Ops incl: express
Livery: Blue

*ALLIED COACHES
113 GRANGE WAY, BALDOYLE INDUSTRIAL ESTATE, BALDOYLE D13
Tel: 00 353 1 832 8300
Fax: 00 353 1 832 8299
E-mail: info@alliedcoaches.ie
Web site: www.alliedcoaches.ie
Man Dir: Jim Nolan **Man**: Seamus Nolan
Fleet: 7 - 3 coach, 2 minicoach, 2 minibus.
Chassis: incl: 1 DAF. 2 Mercedes.
Bodies: incl: 1 BMC. 2 Marcopolo
Ops incl: excursions & tours, private hire
Livery: Silver

ARAN TOURS LTD
14 LOWER ALBERT ROAD, SANDYCOVE, Co DUBLIN
Tel: 00 353 1 280 1899
Fax: 00 353 1 280 1799

BARRY'S COACHES LTD
THE GLEN, MAYFIELD, CORK CITY
Tel: 00 353 21 450 5390, 450 1669 (emergencies only)
Fax: 00 353 21 450 9628
Fleet: 15 - 12 coach, 2 minibus, 1 minicoach.
Chassis: 1 AEC. 3 Bedford. 6 Leyland. 2 Mercedes. 2 Volvo.
Bodies: 7 Duple. 1 Jonckheere. 2 Mercedes. 3 Plaxton. 2 Van Hool.
Livery: Blue/White

*BARTON TRANSPORT
STRAFFAN ROAD, MAYNOOTH, CO KILDARE.
Tel: 00 353 1 628 6026
Fax: 00 353 1 628 6722
E-mail: info@bartons-transport.ie
Web site: www.bartons-transport.ie
Man Dir: Patrick Barton **Man**: Fergal Barton
Fleet: 35 - 1 double-deck bus, 10 single-deck bus, 20 coach, 4 minicoach.
Chassis: 1 BMC. 28 DAF. 2 Irisbus. 4 Mercedes.
Bodies: 2 Ayats. 2 Beulas. 7 Berkhof. 1 BMC. 5 Ikarus. 8 Marcopolo. 4 Optare. 5 Plaxton. 1 Van Hool.
Ops incl: local bus services, private hire, excursions & tours, school contracts.
Livery: Cream

RONNIE BRUEN T/A BLUEBIRD COACHES
72 KILBARRON DRIVE, COOLOCK, DUBLIN 5.
Tel/Fax: 00 353 1 847 7896.
Dirs: Ronnie Bruen, Keith Bruen.
Fleet: 7 - 3 coach, 2 midicoach, 2 minibus.
Chassis: Ford Transit. Leyland. Mercedes. Volvo.
Bodies: Mercedes. Duple.
Ops incl: private hire, express, school contracts.
Livery: Cream/Red.

BUCKLEY'S TOURS
KILLARNEY, Co KERRY
Tel: 00 353 64 31945
E-mail: buckleys@iol.ie

BURKE BROS (COACHES) LTD
CLARETUAM, TUAM, Co GALWAY
Tel: 00 353 93 55416
Fax: 00 353 93 55356
Dirs: P .Burke, Ms M. Burke.
Ops Man: P. Steede.
Fleet: 12 - 10 coach, 2 midicoach.
Chassis: Mercedes-Benz, Toyota, Volvo.
Bodies: Caetano, Jonckheere, Plaxton.
Ops incl: local bus services, private hire, continental tours.
Livery: White with Blue/Orange stripes.

*BUS EIREANN/IRISH BUS
BROADSTONE, PHIBSBOROUGH, DUBLIN 7
Tel: 00 353 1 830 2222
Fax: 00 353 1 830 9377
E-mail: info@buseireann.ie
Web site: www.buseireann.ie
Chmn: Dr John Lynch **Ch Exec**: Tim Hayes
Co Sec: Martin Nolan **Ch Mech Eng**: Joe Neiland **Man HR**: Des Tallon **Man Sales&Mktg**: Barry Doyle
Fleet: 1,396 - 23 double-deck bus, 567 single-deck bus, 640 coach, 2 open-top bus, 87 midibus, 27 minibus.
Chassis: 201 DAF. 43 Dennis. 2 Ford. 155 GAC. 278 Leyland. 76 Mercedes. 20 Optare. 156 Scania. 415 Volvo.
Bodies: 86 Alexander. 176 Caetano. 24 East Lancs. 31 Hispano. 156 Irizar. 184 Leyland. 20 Mercedes. 1 Northern Counties. 20 Optare. 322 Plaxton. 20 Sunsundegui. 18 Van Hool. 106 Wright. 182 other.
Ops incl: local bus services, school contracts, excursions & tours, private hire, express.
Livery: White/Red.
Ticket System: Wayfarer.

BUTLERS BUSES
17 BROOKVALE, COBH, Co CORK
Tel/Fax: 00 353 21 811660
E-mail: butlersb@gofree.indigo.ie
Prop: Ian Butler

CAHALANE COACHES
UNIT 6, KILBARRY ENTERPRISE CENTRE, DUBLIN HILL, CORK
Tel: 00 353 21 430 4606
Fax: 00 353 21 430 1200
Fleet: includes 14, 24, 29 and 35-seat coaches

*CALLINAN COACHES LTD
KINISKA, GLAREGALWAY, Co GALWAY
Tel: 00 353 91 798324
Fax: 00 353 91 798962
Recovery: 00 353 8724 13691
E-mail: info@callinancoaches.ie
Web site: www.callinancoaches.ie
Fleet: 22 single-deck bus
Chassis: 22 Volvo.
Ops incl: excursions & tours, continental tours, private hire

CARROLL'S COACH HIRE
BALLYMAKENNY ROAD, DROGHEDA
Tel: 00 353 41 36074.
Props: G. Carroll, P. Caroll (**Man**).
Fleet: 8 coach.
Chassis: Bedford. **Bodies**: Duple.
Ops incl: local bus services, excursions & tours, private hire.
Livery: White.

CLASSIC COACHES
61 HEATHER ROAD, SANDYFORD INDUSTRIAL ESTATE, FOXROCK, DUBLIN 18
Tel: 00 353 1 295 2080.
Fax: 00 353 1 295 3982
Fleet: 1 coach

COLLIN'S COACHES
CARRICKAMOSS, Co MONAGHAN
Tel: 00 353 42 9661 631
Fax: 00 353 42 9663 462
E-mail: colcoach@iol.ie

CONWAY COACH AND CHAUFFEUR DRIVE
WILLOW GROVE, REDGATE, LIMERICK
Tel: 00 353 61 53366
Prop: R. Conway (Gen Man), Val Conway.
Prop/Ch Eng: Patrick Conway. **Prop/Sec**: Audrey Hurley. **Traf Man**: R. Hurley.
Fleet: 11 midicoach.
Livery: White/Red.

CORCORANS EXECUTIVE TOURS
10 COLLEGE STREET, KILLARNEY, CO KERRY
Tel: 00 353 64 36666
Fax: 00 353 64 35666
Fleet: coach, midicoach
Chassis: incl: Mercedes
Ops incl: private hire

COYLES COACHES
GWEEDORE, Co DONEGAL
Tel: 00 353 75 31208.
E-mail: coylescoaches@eircom.net

CREMIN COACHES
BANTRY, Co CORK

Tel/Fax: 00 353 2 766 906
E-mail: info@cremincoaches.com
Web site: www.cremincoaches.com
Fleet: incl: minicoach
Chassis: incl: Mercedes
Livery: White
Ops incl: private hire

CRONIN'S COACHES LTD

SHANNON BUILDINGS, MALLOW ROAD, CORK
Tel: 00 353 21 430 9090
Fax: 00 353 21 430 5508
Email: cork@croninscoaches.com.
Web Site: www.croninscoaches.com.
Dirs: D. & Joan Cronin. **Ch Eng**: Niall Cronin. **Gen Man**: Nora Cronin.
Fleet: 50 - 47 coach, 3 midicoach.
Chassis: DAF. Leyland. Volvo.
Bodies: Van Hool
Ops incl: private hire
Livery: White with red flash.

CROSSON MOTOR GROUP

UNIT 10/12 NEWTOWN INDUSTRIAL ESTATE, COOLOCK, DUBLIN 17
Tel: 00 353 1 848 5811
Fax: 00 353 1 848 5721
Fleetname: Crosson Coaches.
Chmn: S. Crosson. **Man Dir**: A. Kennedy.
Dirs: J. O'Reilly, B. Cullen, S. Crosson.
Fleet: 1 midicoach.
Chassis: Mercedes. **Body**: Euro Coach.
Ops incl: private hire, continental tours.
Livery: White

MARTIN CROWLEY

CLANCOOL BEG, BANDON, Co CORK
Tel/Fax: 00 353 23 42150
Fleet: incl: minicoach, midicoach
Ops incl: private hire

DERO'S COACH TOURS

22 MAIN STREET, KILLARNEY, Co KERRY
Tel: 00 353 64 31251
Fax: 00 353 64 34077
Email: deroscoachtours@eircom.net.
Web site: www.derostours.com
Prop: Ms E. O'Sullivan Quille. **Sales Dir**: Ms C. O'Sullivan, D O'Sullivan.
Fleet: 18 - 12 coach, 4 midicoach, 2 minicoach.
Chassis: 10 DAF. 6 Mercedes. 2 Volvo.
Livery: White with multi red/Silver/Red/Orange.
Relief drivers and guiding agency also.

JIMMY DONNELLY & SON

46 IRISH STREET, ENNISCORTHY, Co WEXFORD.
Tel: 00 353 54 33956
Fleet: 7 - 5 coach, 2 minibus

SEAN DONNELLY

MAIN STREET, GRANARD, Co LONGFORD
Tel: 00 353 43 86540
Fleetname: Pioneer Bus Service
Prop: Sean Donnelly.
Fleet: 20 – 3 single deck bus, 17 coach.
Chassis: Leyland, Leyland National, Scania.
Bodies: Leyland National, Plaxton, Van Hool.

DONOVAN'S COACH HIRE

HEADFORD, KILLARNEY, Co KERRY
Tel: 00 353 64 54041.
Fax: 00 353 64 54041
Props: Joe & Maureen Donovan.
Fleet: 8 - 5 coach, 2 midicoach, 1 minibus.
Chassis: 1 Ford Transit. 3 LDV. 2 Mercedes. 2 Volvo.
Bodies: 2 Jonckheere. 1 Duple. 2 Mercedes. 1 Plaxton.
Ops incl: school contracts, excursions & tours, private hire.

P. DOYLE LTD

ROUNDWOOD, Co WICKLOW
Tel: 00 353 1 281 8119
Fleetname: St Kevins Bus Service.
Prop/Traf Man: P. Doyle.
Gen Man/Ch Eng: J. Doyle.
Sec: John Doyle.
Fleet: 5 single-deck bus.
Chassis: 5 Leyland.
Bodies: 1 Plaxton. 4 others.
Livery: Blue/Cream.
Ticket System: Setright.

*TONY DOYLE COACHES LTD

BALLYORNEY, ENNISKERRY, Co WICKLOW
Tel: 00 353 1 286 7427
Fax: 00 353 1 286 7427
Email: info@tonydoyle.com
Web site: www.tonydoyle.com
Man Dir: Tony Doyle **Co Sec**: Margaret Doyle
Fleet: 12 - 8 coach, 3 midicoach, 1 minicoach.
Chassis: 1 DAF. 4 Iveco. 3 MAN. 1 Mercedes. 3 Scania.
Bodies: 3 Beulas. 3 Indcar. 3 Irizar. 1 Mercedes. 1 Noge. 1 Plaxton.

*THE DUALWAY GROUP

KEATINGS PARK, RATHCOOLE, Co DUBLIN
Tel: 00 353 1 458 0054
Fax: 00 353 1 458 0808
E-mail: info@dualwaycoaches.com
Web site: www.dualwaycoaches.com
Fleetnames: Dualway, City Sightseeing, Grayline
Man Dir: Anthony McConn **Gen Man**: David McConn **Fin Controller**: Trish McConn
Admin Man: Dawn Nolan

Fleet: 35 - 23 double-deck bus, 6 coach, 20 open-top bus, 6 midicoach
Chassis: 8 AEC. 1 Daimler. 14 Leyland. 7 Mercedes. 5 Volvo.
Bodies: 14 Alexander. 3 East Lancs. 1 Esker. 1 Jonckheere. 10 Leyland. 2 Marcopolo. 1 Northern Counties. 1 Optare. 2 Park Royal.
Ops incl: local bus services, excursions & tours, school contracts, private hire.

*DUBLIN BUS (BUS ATHA CLIATH)

59 UPPER O'CONNELL STREET, DUBLIN 1.
Tel: 00 353 1 872 0000
Fax: 00 353 1 873 1195
Email: info@dublinbus.ie
Web site: www.dublinbus.ie
Chmn: John Lynch **Ch Exec**: Joe Meagher **Dirs**: David Egan, Arnold O'Byrne, Tom Coffey, Peter Webster **Head of Finance**: Paul O'Neill **Ch Eng**: Shane Doyle
Business Dev Man: Paddy Doherty **Human Resources Man**: Gerry Maguire **Ops Man**: Mick Matthews
Fleet: 1,076 - 966 double-deck bus, 39 single-deck bus, 51 midibus, 20 articulated bus
Chassis: 25 DAF. 10 Dennis. 20 Leyland. 1021 Volvo.
Bodies: includes: Alexander. ECW. Wright.
Ops incl: local bus services.
Livery: Blue/Yellow with Dublin Blue/White/Darker Blue swoosh

DUBLIN MINI COACHES & CHAUFEUR HIRE

WASDALE HOUSE, 14 CAMAC PARK, OLD NAAS ROAD, DUBLIN 12
Tel: 00 353 861 780049
Fax: 00 353 1 6961001
Email: info.dmc@o2.ie
Web site: www.dublinminicoaches.com
Man Dir: Stephen Millar
Fleet: 8 - 2 midicoach, 6 minicoach.
Chassis/Bodies: 6 Mercedes.
Ops incl: excursions & tours, private hire, school contracts.
Livery: Green

*EIREBUS LTD

CORDUFF ROAD, BLANCHARDSTOWN, DUBLIN 15
Tel: 00 353 1 824 2626
Fax: 00 353 1 824 2627
E-mail: eirebus@iol.ie
Web site: www.eirebus.ie
Man Dir: Patrick Kavanagh **Dir**: Thomas Kavanagh **Tran Man**: Derek Graham
Gen Man: Paul Curtis
Fleet: 37 - 29 coach, 2 midicoach, 2 minicoach, 4 minibus.
Chassis: 2 MAN. 6 Mercedes. 24 Scania. 2 Toyota. 3 Volvo.
Bodies: 2 Indcar. 14 Irizar. 2 Jonckheere. 4 Plaxton. 11 Van Hool. 4 other.

Ac	Air conditioning	✓	Seat belt-fitted vehicles	✓	Replacement vehicle available
	Vehicles suitable for disabled	R	Recovery service available (not 24 hr)	T	Toilet-drop facilities available
	Coach(es) with galley facilities	R24	24hr recovery service		Vintage vehicle(s) available
WC	Coach(es) with toilet facilities				Open top vehicle(s)

ENFIELD COACHES LTD
RATHCORE, ENFIELD, Co MEATH
Tel: 00 353 1 824 2626
Fleet: 3 - 1 coach, 3 minibus

FAHERTY'S COACH HIRE
DRUMONEY, MOYCULLEN,
Co GALWAY
Tel: 00 353 91 85228
Fleet: 5 - 4 coach, 1 minicoach

FINEGAN COACH HIRE
29 MAIN STREET,
CARRICKMACROSS,
Co MONAGHAN
Tel: 00 353 42 61313
Fleet: 7 - 5 coach, 1 minicoach, 1 minibus

FINNEGAN - BRAY
OLD COURT INDUSTRIAL ESTATE,
BOGHALL ROAD, BRAY, Co
WICKLOW
Tel: 00 353 1 286 0061
Fax: 00 353 1 286 8121
E-mail: finnegan-bray@oceanfree.net
Dir: Eugene Finnegan
Fleet: 15 - 2 double-deck bus, 3 single-deck bus, 3 coach, 2 midicoach, 4 midibus, 1 minibus.
Chassis: 4 DAF. 1 Dennis. 6 Mercedes. 1 Optare. 3 Volvo.
Bodies: 1 Alexander. 2 Ikarus. 1 Leyland. 6 Mercedes. 1 Northern Counties. 1 Optare. 2 Plaxton. 1Van Hool.
Ops incl: local bus services, excursions & tours, school contracts, private hire.
Livery: Red

DECLAN FINNEGAN
THE COACH & CAB CAFE, 10 MAIN STREET, KENMARE, CO KERRY
Tel: 00 353 64 41491
Fax: 00 353 64 42636
Fleet: coach, minicoach
Ops incl: private hire.

TOM FOX
MONAGHAN ROAD, ROCKCORRY,
Co MONAGHAN
Tel: 00 353 42 42284
Fleet: 2 coach

MARTIN FUREY COACHES LTD
MILLTOWN, DRUMCLIFFE, Co SLIGO
Tel: 00 353 71 63092
Fleet: 5 - 3 coach, 2 minibus

GALVINS COACHES

MAIN STREET, DUNMANWAY,
Co CORK
Tel: 00 353 23 45125
Fax: 00 353 23 45407
Dir: R. E. Galvin
Chassis: Ford. Ford Transit. Leyland National. Scania. Volvo.
Bodies: Leyland National. Mercedes. Plaxton. Van Hool. Willowbrook. Duple.
Fleet: single-deck bus, coach, double-deck coach, midibus, midicoach.

GLYNNS COACH HIRE (ENNIS) LTD
KNOCKADERRY, TULLA ROAD,
ENNIS, Co CLARE
Tel: 00 353 65 682 8234
Fax: 00 353 65 684 0678
Recovery: 00 353 8625 97037
Email: info@glynnscoaches.com
Web site: www.glynnscoaches.com
Fleetname: Glynns of Ennis
Chmn: Jackie Cronin. **Sec**: Niamh Cronin.
Fleet: 14 - 5 coach, 4 midicoach, 2 minibus, 3 minicoach. 2 Irisbus.
Chassis: 2 Beulas. 1 DAF. 1 Iveco. 3 MAN. 5 Mercedes. 1 Setra. 3 Volvo.
Bodies: 1 Ikarus. 3 Indcar. 5 Mercedes. 1 Noge. 2 Plaxton. 1 Setra. 1 Euro.

JAMES GLYNN
GRAIGUE NA SPIDOGUE (POST GRAIGUECULLEN), NURNEY
Tel: 00 353 503 46616
Prop/Gen Man/Traf Man: J. Glynn
Prop/Ch Eng: A. Glynn **Prop/Sec**: Mrs J. Glynn.
Fleet: 4 - 3 single-deck bus, 1 coach.
Livery: Cream/Blue.

GRAYLINE TOURS
THE MALT HOUSE, GRAND CANAL QUAY, DUBLIN 2
Tel: 00 353 1 670 8822
Fax: 00 353 1 670 8731
E-mail: grayline@tlp.ie
Also at DUBLIN TOURIST CENTRE, SUFFOLK, DUBLIN 2
Tel: 00 353 1 605 7705

HALPENNY TRANSPORT
ASHVILLE, THE SQUARE,
BLACKROCK, DUNDALK
Tel: 00 353 42 21608
Fleetname: Halpenny Transport
Man Dir: John Halpenny
Fleet: 14 - includes 2 double-deck bus, 2 single-deck bus, 8 coach
Chassis: mainly Volvo.
Bodies: include 1 Sunsundegui
Ops incl: local bus services, private hire, continental tours
Livery: White with Red/Blue/Green

HEALY COACHES
CASTLEGAR, GALWAY
Tel: 00 353 91 770066
Fax: 00 353 91 753335
Web site: www.healybus.com
Email: healybus@iol.ie.
Prop: Michael Healy
Fleet: 13 - 2 single-deck bus, 8 coach, 1 open-top bus, 2 midicoach
Chassis: 6 Leyland. 1 MAN. 1 Mercedes. 4 Volvo.
Bodies: 2 Alexander. 1 Duple. 1 ECW. 2 Ikarus. 2 Leyland. 1 Mellor. 1 Noge. 2 Plaxton.

M. HOGAN
LIBERTY STREET, THURLES,
Co TIPPERARY
Tel: 00 353 50 421622
Fleetname: Shamrock Bus Service.
Prop/Gen Man: M. Hogan.
Ch Eng: T. Maher. **Sec**: J. Maher.

Fleet: 2 coach.
Livery: Cream/Orange.
Ticket System: Setright.

IRELAND COACHES
COOLQUAY, THE WARD, Co DUBLIN
Tel: 00 353 1 835 2714
Fax: 00 353 1 835 2715
E-mail: irelandcoaches@eircom.net
Fleet: 30 coaches, midicoaches, minicoaches

IRISH COACHES
R24
ULSTER BANK CHAMBERS,
2-4 LOWER O'CONNELL STREET,
DUBLIN
Tel: 00 353 1 878 8894/8898
Fax: 00 353 1 878 8916
E-mail: dch@irishcoaches.ie
Web site: www.irishcoaches.ie
Chmn: Patric Barton **Dir**: Dermot Cronin
Man Dir: D C Hughes
Fleet: 4 - 3 coach, 1 midicoach
Chassis: 4 DAF
Bodies: 1 Ayats. 1 Berkhof. 2 Marcopolo.
Livery: yellow

DONAL JOYCE MINIBUS HIRE
GENTIAN HILL HOUSE,
KNOCKNACARRA, Co GALWAY
Tel: 00 353 91 521427
Fax: 00 353 91 52 4284
Fleet: 8 -2 minicoaches,8 midibus
Ops incl: excursions & tours, private hire

*BERNARD KAVANAGH & SONS LTD
BRIDGE GARAGE, URLINGFORD,
Co KILKENNY
Tel: 00 353 56 31189
Fax: 00 353 56 31314
Email: info@bkavcoaches.com.
Web Site: www.bkavcoaches.com.
Fleet: 54 - 50 coach, 4 midicoach.
Chassis: incl: 3 Bova. 7 MAN. 2 Setra. 4 Volvo.
Bodies: 5 Beulas. 2 Indcar. 10 Irizar. 2 Jonckheere. 3 Plaxton. 2 Setra. 30 Van Hool.
Ops incl: excursions & tours, private hire, express, continental tours.
Livery: White/Multi

J J KAVANAGH & SONS
MAIN STREET, URLINGFORD, Co KILKENNY
Tel: 00 353 56 31106
Fax: 00 353 56 31106
E-mail: info@jjkavanagh.ie
Web site: www.jjkavanagh.ie
Joint Man Dir/Fin Cont: J. J. Kavanagh
Joint Man Dir/Ops Man: Paul Kavanagh
Maintenance Man: Edward Scully
Fleet: 38 - 1 double-deck bus, 36 coach, 1 open-top bus
Chassis: 6 MAN. 25 Setra. 45 Volvo.
Bodies: 15 Caetano. 2 Leyland. 4 Mercedes. 2 Northern Counties. 20 Plaxton. 25 Setra. 7 Van Hool. 1 Wright.

Ops incl: local bus services

M. KAVANAGH
LIMERICK ROAD, TIPPERARY
Tel: 00 353 62 51563
Fax: 00 353 62 51593
E-mail: mattkavanagh3@aol.net
Fleet: 19 - 12 coaches, 5 single-deck bus, 2 minibus.

PIERCE KAVANAGH COACHES
CHURCH VIEW, URLINGFORD, CO KILKENNY
Tel: 00 353 56 31213
Fax: 00 353 56 31599
E-mail: info@kavanaghscoaches.com
Web site: www.kavanaghscoaches.com
Dirs: Pierce Kavanagh, John Kavanagh **Ch Eng**: John Kenny
Co Sec: Jim Bannon
Fleet: 20 - 1 single-deck bus, 18 coach, 1 midicoach.
Chassis: 1 Bova. 1 DAF. 2 Ford. 5 Ford Transit. 4 Leyland. 5 MAN. 1 Mercedes. 3 Scania. 2 Volvo

KEENAN COMMERCIALS LTD
BELLURGAN, DUNDALK, Co LOUTH
Tel: 00 353 42 937 1405
Fax: 00 353 42 937 1893
Fleetname: Anchor Coaches
Man Dir: Seamus Keenan
Fleet: 17 - 8 single-deck bus, 7 coach, 2 minibus.

KENNEALLY'S BUS SERVICE LTD
BLENHEIM, WATERFORD
Tel: 00 353 51 872777
Fax: 00 353 51 872770
Joint Man Dirs: J J Kavanagh, Paul Kavanagh **Tran Man**: Tony Crean
Ops Man: Michael Ryan
Fleet: 27 - 6 double-deck bus, 3 single-deck bus, 18 coach
Chassis: 1 AEC. 2 Leyland. 5 MAN. 15 Setra. 30 Volvo.
Bodies: 4 Alexander. 5 Caetano. 4 Northern Counties. 15 Setra. 10 Van Hool. 1 Wright.
Ops incl: local bus services, excursions & tours, private hire, express, continental tours.
Livery: Green/Blue/Red on White
Subsidiary of J J Kavanagh, Urlingford

KENNEDY COACHES
ANNASCAUL, TRALEE, Co KERRY
Tel: 00 353 66 91 57106
Fax: 00 353 66 91 57427
Fleet: 5 - 3 double-deck bus, 3 minibus

K. M. KEOGH
39A WEXFORD ROAD, ARKLOW
Tel: 00 353 40 22560
Fleet: 4 coach

KERRY COACHES LTD
INISFALLEN, 15 MAIN STREET, KILLARNEY, Co KERRY
Tel: 00 353 64 31945
Fax: 00 353 64 31903
Email: buckleys@iol.ie
Web site: www.kerrycoaches.com
Ops Man: Alan O'Connor
Fleetnames: Buckley Tours, Kerry Tours
Man Dir: M Buckley
Fleet: 19 - 14 coach, 2 midicoach, 3 minibus
Chassis: incl: 2 Setra

DAVE LONG COACH TRAVEL
CURRAGH, SKIBBEREEN
Tel: 00 353 28 21138
Fleet: 1 coach

LESCLACHA LTD
28 AVONDALE, NEWMARKET-ON-FERGUS
Tel: 00 353 61 71233
Fleetname: Lovetts Coaches
Fleet: 9 - 1 single-deck bus, 6 coach, 1 midibus, 1 minibus.
Chassis: Leyland.

LUAS
LUAS DEPOT, RED COW ROUNDABOUT, CLONDALKIN, DUBLIN
Tel: 00 353 1 461 4910
Web site: www.luas.ie
Man, Strategic Planning/PR: Ger Hannon
Fleet: 40 tram
Chassis/bodies: Alstom Citadis
Ops: tram service

P. J. McCONNON
GREENLEE, CLONES ROAD, MONAGHAN
Tel: 00 353 47 82020
Fleet: 4 coaches
Chassis: Volvo
Bodies: Plaxton

JAMES McGEE (BUSES)
BALLINA MAIN ROAD, FALCARRAGH, LETTERKENNY
Tel: 00 353 74 35174
Fleet: 8 minibus.
Chassis: 1 Ford. 3 Toyota.
Ops incl: private hire.
Livery: White

JOHN McGINLEY COACH TRAVEL
MAGHEERCARTY, GORTAHEEK, Co DONEGAL
Tel: 00 353 7491 35201
Fax: 00 353 7491 35960

E-mail: info@jchhmcginley.com
Web site: www.jchhmcginley.com
Prop: James McGinley
Fleet: 16 - 8 coach, 8 minibus.
Chassis: Ford Transit. Mercedes. Volvo.
Bodies: Plaxton. Van Hool.
Ops incl: local bus services, excursions & tours, continental tours, school contracts, private hire, express, continental tours.

GERALD MANNING
CASTLE ROAD, CROOM, LIMERICK
Tel: 00 353 61 88311
E-mail: gmanning@indigo.ie
Fleet: 13 - 10 coach, 2 minibus, 1 midibus.

ALAN MARTIN COACHES
R24
1 KIRKFIELD COTTAGE, CLONSILLA, DUBLIN 15
Tel: 00 353 1 835 1560
Fax: 00 353 1 835 1816
Dirs: A. Martin, B. C. Martin. **Ch Eng**: M. Reilly. **Traf Man**: M. Clarke.
Fleet: 8 - 6 single-deck bus, 1 double-deck bus, 1 minibus.
Chassis: 6 Ford. 2 Leyland. 4 MAN. 2 Mercedes. 3 Scania. 2 Toyota. 5 Volvo.
Ops incl: local bus services, school contracts, excursions & tours, private hire, express.
Livery: White with two Blue stripes.

MARTIN'S COACHES (CAVAN) LTD
CORRATILLION, CORLOUGH, BELTURBET, Co CAVAN
Tel: 00 353 49 26222
Fax: 00 353 49 23116
E-mail: jimmartin@eircom.net
Dir: James G Martin
Fleet: 16 - 5 coach, 4 midicoach, 7 minibus.
Chassis: 5 DAF. 7 Ford Transit. 3 Mercedes. 1 Toyota.
Bodies: 4 Bova. 2 Caetano. 3 Mercedes.

MD COACH HIRE
25 TARA LAWN, THE DONAHIES, RAHENY, DUBLIN 13
Tel/Fax: 00 353 1 847 9591
Prop: Michael Dunne.

MICHAEL MEERE COACH HIRE
33 CHURCH DRIVE, CLARECASTLE, ENNIS, Co CLARE
Tel: 00 353 65 682 4833
Fax: 00 353 65 684 4544
E-mail: michaelmeere@clarelive.com

MIDLAND BUS CO LTD
LOUGHNASKIN, ATHLONE
Tel: 00 353 90 22427
Dir/Gen Man: N. Henry
Fleet: 14 coach
Chassis: Leyland, Volvo, Mercedes.
Ops incl: local bus services, excursions & tours.

A/c	Air conditioning	
	Vehicles suitable for disabled	
	Coach(es) with galley facilities	
WC	Coach(es) with toilet facilities	
	Seat belt-fitted vehicles	
R	Recovery service available (not 24 hr)	
R24	24hr recovery service	
	Replacement vehicle available	
T	Toilet-drop facilities available	
	Vintage vehicle(s) available	
	Open top vehicle(s)	

JOE MORONEY
HERMITAGE, ENNIS, Co CLARE.
Tel: 00 353 66 824146
Fax: 00 353 65 686 9480
E-mail: mcoachesennis@eire.com
Fleet: 7 - 1 double-deck coach, 1 coach

MORTON'S COACHES DUBLIN
TAYLORS LANE, BALLYBODEN, DUBLIN 16
Tel: 00 353 1 494 4927
Fax: 00 353 1 494 4694
E-mail: mortonscoaches@clubi.ie, info@circlelinebus.com
Fleet: Circle Line Bus Co
Prop: Paul Morton
Fleet: 13 - 1 double-deck bus, 3 single-deck bus, 6 coach, 3 double-deck coach
Chassis: 1 Ayats. 6 DAF. 6 Mercedes. 10 Volvo.
Bodies: 1 Ayats. 4 East Lancs. 2 Marcopolo. 1 Ovi. 1 Wright.
Ops incl: local bus services, school contracts, excursions & tours, private hire, continental tours.
Livery: White

THOMAS MURPHY & SONS
KILBRIDE HOUSE, KILBRIDE LANE, BRAY, Co WICKLOW
Tel: 00 353 1 286 2471
Fleet: 11 - 8 coach, 1 minibus, 2 minicoach.
Chassis: Volvo, Mercedes, Scania.

NAUGHTON COACH TOURS
SHANAGURRANE, SPIDDAL, Co GALWAY
Tel: 00 353 91 553188
Fax: 00 353 91 553302
E-mail: naugtour@iol.i.e
Web site: www.wombat.ie/pages/oneachtain-tours
Dir: Steve Naughton **Dir/Sec**: Maureen Naughton
Fleet: 8 - 5 coach, 1 double-deck bus, 2 midicoach.
Chassis: 1 Daimler. 1 MAN. 3 Mercedes. 1 Toyota. 2 Volvo
Bodies: 1 Caetano. 1 Jonckheere. 1 Leyland. 2 Plaxton.
Ops incl: excursions & tours, private hire

NESTORBUS LTD, GALWAY & DUBLIN
TURLOUGHMORE, ATHENRY, Co GALWAY
Tel: 00 353 91 797144, 00 353 1 832 0094
Fax: 00 353 91 797244
E-mail: busnestor@eircom.net
Web Site: www.busnestor.galway.net
Prop: P. Nestor
Fleet: 9 - 8 coach, 1 double-deck coach.
Chassis: 8 Mercedes. 1 Setra.
Ops incl: excursions & tours, private hire, express, continental tours.
Livery: Red/Cream

NOLAN COACHES
19 CLONSHAUGH LAWN, COOLOCK, DUBLIN 17
Tel: 00 353 1 847 3487
Mobile: 0862 592000
Prop: David Nolan
Fleet: 1 coach
Ops incl: school contracts, private hire.

O'CONNELL COACHES
PORTUMNA ROAD, BALLINASLOE
Tel: 00 353 905 43339
Prop: J. O'Connell
Fleet: 5 coach
Chassis: Ford. **Bodies**: Plaxton
Ops incl: private hire.

O'CONNOR AUTOTOURS LTD
ROSS ROAD, KILLARNEY
Tel: 00 353 64 31052
Fax: 00 353 64 31703
Dir/Gen Man: B. O'Connor.
Ch Eng: R. Downing. **Sec**: C. Enright.
Traf Man: D. Fenton
Fleet: 5 - 1 midibus, 4 minicoach.
Chassis: Leyland. Mercedes. Volvo.
Bodies: Reeve Burgess. Van Hool. Euro.
Ops incl: excursions & tours, private hire.
Livery: Maroon/Yellow.

TOM O'CONNOR
CLOGHANE, TRALEE, Co KERRY
Tel: 00 353 66 713 8140

FEDA O'DONNELL COACHES
RANAFAST, Co DONEGAL
Tel/Fax: 00 353 75 48114
Prop: Pat O'Flaherty.
Fleet: 13 - 9 coach, 2 minibus, 2 minicoach.
Ops incl: express

O'FLAHERTY TRANSPORT LTD
LISDOONVARNA, Co CLARE
Tel/Fax: 00 353 65 74117.
Fleet: 1 midicoach.
Prop: Pat O'Flaherty

LARRY O'HARA
13 SKIBBEREEN LAWN, WATERFORD CITY
Tel: 00 353 51 372232
Fax: 00 353 51 357566
E-mail: larryohara@eircom.net
Fleetname: O'Hara Autotours
Props: Larry O'Hara, Helen O'Hara
Fleet: 6 - 2 midicoach, 2 minibus, 2 minicoach.
Chassis/Bodies: 1 Ford Transit. Mercedes.

O'MALLEY COACHES
FOILDARRIG, NEWPORT, Co TIPPERARY
Tel: 00 353 61 378119
Fax: 00 353 61 378002
Owner: E. O'Malley
Fleet: 16 - 2 single-deck bus, 9 coach, 2 midibus, 2 midicoach, 1 minibus.
Ops incl: local bus services, school contracts, excursions & tours, private hire, express.

Livery: Blue/White.

*O'S COACHES
HOSPITAL, Co LIMERICK
Tel: 00 353 61 383 222
Fax: 00 353 61 383 222
E-mail: oscoaches@eircom.net
Prop: Sean F. O'Sullivan **Ch Eng**: Patrick Leahy.
Fleet: double-deck bus
Chassis: Leyland,Leyland National, Mercedes
Bodies: Leyland, Leyland National, Mercedes
Ops incl: school contracts
Livery: Blue/Cream

O'SULLIVANS COACHES
FARRAHY ROAD, KILDORRERY, MALLOW, Co CORK
Tel: 00 353 22 25185
Fax: 00 353 22 25731
Prop: C O'Sullivan
Fleet: 12 - 9 coach, 3 midicoach.
Chassis: 2 Bedford. 1 Ford Transit. 1 Leyland. 2 Mercedes. 4 Volvo.
Bodies: 1 Duple. 3 Plaxton. 3 Van Hool. 3 Van Conversions.

GEORGE PLANT
AREDNAGEEHA, BANTRY, Co CORK
Tel/Fax: 00 353 27 5064
Fleet: incl: minicoach, minibus
Ops incl: private hire, excursions & tours

JACKY POWER TOURS
2 LOWER ROCK STREET, TRALEE, Co KERRY
Tel: 00 353 66 713 6300
Fax: 00 353 66 712 9444
Fleet: 7 - 5 midicoach, 2 midibus.

JOHN ROSS
97 SLIAGH BREAGH, PEPPERSTOWN, ARDEE, Co LOUTH
Tel: 00 353 41 53158
Fleet: 8 - 3 coach, 2 midicoach, 2 minibus, 1 midibus

ROVER COACHES
LYNN ROAD, MULLINGAR, Co WESTMEATH
Tel: 00 353 44 40825
Fax: 00 353 44 42280
Recovery: 086 2571645
E-mail: pobrien@pobrien.ie
Man: Patrick O'Brien **Asst Man**: John Farrell
Eng: Edwin Craig
Fleet: 14 - 7 coach, 3 midibus, 2 minicoach, 2 minicoach.
Chassis: 1 DAF. 2 Ford Transit. 1 MAN. 1 Mercedes. 1 Renault. 5 Volvo.
Bodies: 1 Mercedes. 5 Plaxton. 1 Van Hool.

SEALANDAIR COACHING (IRELAND) LTD/PAB TOURS
51 MIDDLE ABBEY STREET, DUBLIN 1
Tel: 00 353 1 873 3411
Fax: 00 353 1 873 2639

E-mail: info@pabtours.com
Web site: www.pabtours.com
Fleetname: PAB Tours
Man Dir: Anthony Kelly
Fleet: 5 coach
Chassis: Leyland
Bodies: Duple

MATT SHANAHAN COACHES
ST MARTINS, LACKEN ROAD, KILBARRY, WATERFORD
Tel: 00 353 51 74192
Fleet: 2 - single-deck bus

ST KEVINS BUS SERVICE
See P Doyle, above

*SUIRWAY BUS & COACH SERVICES LTD

PASSAGE EAST, Co WATERFORD
Tel: 00 353 51 382209
Fax: 00 353 51 382676
E-mail: suirway@eircom.net
Web site: www.suirway.com
Fleetname: Suirway
Fleet: 15 - 4 single-deck bus, 11 coach.
Chassis: 4 Dennis. 1 Leyland. 10 Volvo.
Bodies: 7 Plaxton. 8 Van Hool.
Ops incl: local bus services, school contracts, excursions & tours, private hire.
Livery: White/Red

SWILLY BUS SERVICE
LETTERKENNY, Co DONEGAL
Tel: 00 353 74 22863
Ops incl: local bus service

TREACY COACHES
ERRIGAL, KILLALA ROAD, BALLINA, Co MAYO
Tel: 00 353 96 22563
Fax: 00 353 96 70968
E-mail: treacycoaches@eipcom.net
Dirs: A. Treacy (**Gen Man**). Sec: M. Treacy.
Fleet: 8 - 1 minibus, 7 coach.
Ops incl: excursions & tours, private hire, express.
Livery: White/Blue.

A/c	Air conditioning
♿	Vehicles suitable for disabled
🍴	Coach(es) with galley facilities
WC	Coach(es) with toilet facilities
♥	Seat belt-fitted vehicles
R	Recovery service available (not 24 hr)
R24	24hr recovery service
✓	Replacement vehicle available
T	Toilet-drop facilities available
	Vintage vehicle(s) available
	Open top vehicle(s)

Revised / Additional / Late Entries

Major Groups

THE GO-AHEAD GROUP PLC
3RD FLOOR, 41-51 GREY STREET, NEWCASTLE UPON TYNE NE1 6EE
Tel: 0191 232 3123
Fax: 0191 221 0315
E-mail: admin@go-ahead.com
Website: www.go-ahead.com
Ch Exec: Keith Ludeman **Fin Dir/Co Sec**: Ian Butcher **Non-Exec Chmn**: Sir Patrick Brown **Non-Exec Dirs**: Christopher Collins, Rupert Pennant-Rea
Fleet: 3371 - 1157 double-deck bus, 542 single-deck bus, 532 coach, 94 articulated bus, 1046 minibus/midibus.
Ops incl: local bus services, excursions & tours, express
Livery: local fleet identity
Ticket System: various
Subsidiary companies:
BUS: Birmingham Coach Company, Brighton & Hove Bus & Coach Company, Go North East, London General, London Central, Metrobus, , Oxford Bus Company, Solent Blue Line, Southern Vectis, Wilts & Dorset
RAIL: Southern Railway, South Eastern
PARKING: Meteor
AVIATION SUPPORT SERVICES: Aviance, Plane Handling

Hampshire

UNI-LINK
Tel: 023 8059 5974
Web site: www.uni-link.info
Fleet: 20 - 5 double-deck bus, 15 single-deck bus
Chassis: Dennis. Mercedes. Scania.
Bodies: Alexander. Caetano. East Lancs. Mercedes. Scania.
Ops incl: local bus services
Livery: White/Blue
Services operated for Uni-Link by Minerva Accord

West Yorkshire

*W T S MINICOACHES
49 PRIESTHORPE ROAD, FARSLEY, LEEDS LS28 5JR
Tel: 0113 257 6165
Web site: www.wyco.net/wts
Prop: R Favell
Fleet: 1 minibus.
Chassis: 1 LDV
Ops incl: school contracts, private hire, excursions & tours.
Livery: Green/White

London

LONDON SOVEREIGN
BUSWAYS HOUSE, WELLINGTON ROAD, TWICKENHAM TW2 5NX
Tel: 020 8400 6600
Web site: www.sovereignlondonbuses.co.uk
Man Dir: Nigel Stevens
Fleet: 100 - double-deck bus, single-deck bus.
Ops Incl: local bus services, private hire
Livery: TfL
Part of the Transdev Group

LONDON UNITED BUSWAYS LTD
BUSWAYS HOUSE, WELLINGTON ROAD, TWICKENHAM TW2 5NX
Tel: 020 8400 6600
Fax: 020 8977 0390
Web site: www.lonutd.co.uk
Fleetname: Transdev London United
Man Dir: Nigel Stevens
Fleet: double-deck bus, single-deck bus.
Chassis: 502 Dennis. 64 Scania. 190 Volvo.
Bodies: 235 Alexander. 119 East Lancs. 399 Plaxton.
Ops Incl: local bus services, private hire
Livery: TfL
Part of the Transdev Group

Do you want to keep your LITTLE RED BOOK up-to-date?
Buses magazine now carries updates every month.
See page 256 for Subscription details

SECTION 5
Indices

TRADE INDEX

Several of the traders listed in this index will have more than one entry; only the first is shown here in each case.

A

ABACUS TUBULAR PRODUCTS LTD	35
ABBOT BROWN & SONS LTD	18
AC IS	45
ACT	45
ACTIA UK Ltd	27
AD COACH SALES	12
ADGROUP	50
ADG TRANSPORT CONSULTANCY	50
ADVANCED VEHICLE BUILDERS	11
AFTERMARKET COACH SUPPLIES (UK) LTD	18
AIRCONCO	18
AIR DOOR SERVICES	25
AJP COMMERCIALS	13
AKM TECHSERVICES	50
ALBATROSS TRAVEL GROUP	60
ALBION AUTOMOTIVE LTD	26
ALEXANDER DENNIS LTD	8
ALLEN & DOUGLAS CORPORATE CLOTHING LTD	48
ALLIED VEHICLES	13
ALLISON TRANSMISSION	34
ALMEX INFORMATION SYSTEMS	45
ALSTOM TRANSPORT	9
ALTRO	32
AMA LTD	18
AP BORG & BECK / AP LOCKHEED - *see Automotive Products*	
ARDEE COACH TRIM LTD	41
ARRIVA BUS AND COACH	13
ARVIN MERITOR	21
ASHLEY BANKS LTD	22
ATKINS	53
ATLAS LIGHTING COMPONENTS	36
ATLANTIS INTERNATIONAL	49
ATOS ORIGIN	45
AUSTIN ANALYTICS	50
AUTOGLASS	49
AUTOLIFT LTD	36
AUTOMATE WHEEL COVERS	32
AUTOMOTIVE PRODUCTS GROUP LTD	21
AUTOMOTIVE TEXTILE INDUSTRIES LTD	32
AUTOPRO SOFTWARE UK	52
AUTOSAN	8
AUTOSOUND LTD	18
AVENTA	52
AVONDALE INTERNATIONAL LTD	13
AVS STEPS	20
AVT SYSTEMS	18
AYATS (GB) LTD	8

B

BALFOUR BEATTY RAIL PLANT LTD	39
BARNWELL SERVICES	38
BARRONS CHARTERED ACCOUNTANTS	50
B A S E	13
BBA FRICTION LTD	21
BELMONT INTERNATIONAL LTD	56
BEMROSEBOOTH LTD	45
BERNSTEIN ENGINEERING LTD	41
BESTCHART LTD	53
BEST IMPRESSIONS	51
BETA RESEARCH (ZEBRA)	19
M. BISSELL DISPLAY	45
BLACKPOOL COACH SERVICES	20
BLACKPOOL TRIM SHOPS LTD	37
BLUEBIRD VEHICLES LTD	11
BLYTHSWOOD MOTORS LTD	13
BMC UK	8
BOB VALE COACH SALES	13
BOMBARDIER TRANSPORTATION	9
BORLAND, WINDER-DIXON LLP	50
BOTEL LTD	60
BRADTECH LTD	26
BRECKNELL WILLIS	39
BRIAN NOONE	13
BRIDGE OF WEIR LEATHER CO LTD	49
BRIGADE ELECTRONICS	40
BRIGHT-TECH DEVELOPMENTS	25
BRISTOL BUS & COACH SALES	13
BRISTOL ELECTRIC RAILBUS	40
BRITANNIA ROLL/TICKETMEDIA	45
BRITAX PMG LTD	26
BRITISH BUS PUBLISHING	58
BRITISH BUS SALES	13
BRITTANY FERRIES	54
BROADWATER MOULDINGS LTD	45
DAVID BROWN VEHICLE TRANSMISSIONS LTD	34
BROXWOOD VEHICLE SPECIALISTS	18
BRT BEARINGS LTD	38
COLIN BUCHANAN & PARTNERS	50
BULWARK BUS & COACH ENGINEERING LTD	37
BURNT TREE VEHICLE SOLUTIONS	11
BUS & COACH BUYER	58
BUS AND COACH PROFESSIONAL	59
BUSES	58
BUS USER	59
BUS SHELTERS LTD	42
BUSS BIZZ	22
BUTTS OF BAWTRY	34
BUZZLINES LTD	51

C

SALVADOR CAETANO (UK) LTD	9
CALEDONIAN MACBRAYNE LTD	54
CALOTELS HOTELS	56
CAMIRA	48

CANN PRINT	45
CAPOCO DESIGN	50
CAREYBROOK LTD	53
CARLYLE BUS & COACH LTD	25
CARMANAH TECHNOLOGIES	42
CARRIER SUTRAK	18
CASH PROCESSING SOLUTIONS LTD	22
CENTAUR FUEL MANAGEMENT	33
CHAPMAN DRIVERS SEATING	41
CHASSIS DEVELOPMENTS	11
CI COACHLINES	60
CIE TOURS	56
CLAN TOOLS & PLANT LTD	40
CLAYTON HEATERS LTD	18
COACH-AID	22
COACH & BUS	54
COACH & BUS WEEK	59
COACH CARPETS	33
COACH DISPLAYS LTD	54
COACH DIRECT	50
COACHFINDER LIMITED	52
COBUS UK	20
COGENT PASSENGER SEATING LTD	41
COLDCARE	18
COLIN BUCHANAN & PARTNERS	50
COMPAK RAMPS	36
CONCEPT COACHCRAFT	11
CONDOR FERRIES	54
CONSERVE UK LTD	18
COURTSIDE CONVERSIONS	11
CRAIG TILSLEY & SON LTD	29
CREATIVE MANAGEMENT DEVELOPMENT	50
CRESCENT FACILITIES LTD	26
CREST COACH CONVERSIONS	18
CREWE ENGINES	29
CRONER CCH GROUP LTD	53
CROWN COACHBUILDERS LTD	11
CRYSTALKLEEN LTD	49
CSM LIGHTING	37
CUBIC TRANSPORTATION SYSTEMS LTD	31
CUMMINS UK	19
CUMMINS-ALLISON LTD	22
CVI	11
CYBERLYNE COMMUNICATIONS LTD	19

D

DAF COMPONENTS LTD	29
DATS	54
DAVID BROWN VEHICLE TRANSMISSIONS LTD	34
DAVID FISHWICK	13
R. L. DAVISON & CO LTD	56
DAWSONRENTALS	13
DAYCO — TRANSPORT & TRADE DISTRIBUTION LTD	29
DCA DESIGN INTERNATIONAL	53
DE LA RUE	45
DEANS POWERED DOORS	25
DECKER MEDIA LTD	50
DEFINER SAFETY TREADS	33
DFDS SEAWAYS	54

DIESEL POWER ENGINEERING	29
DINEX EXHAUSTS LTD	28
DIRECT PARTS LTD	21
DISTINCTIVE SYSTEMS LTD	52
T & E DOCHERTY	52
DRINKMASTER LTD	26
DRIVER HIRE	52
DRIVELINE	11
DRURY & DRURY	37
DUNLOP TYRES	48
DUOFLEX LTD	35

E

EAST LANCASHIRE COACHBUILDERS LTD	10
EASTGATE COACH TRIMMERS	20
EATON LTD	22
EBERSPACHER (UK) LTD	18
KEITH EDMONSON	45
ELITE SEATBELT SPECIALIST LTD	41
ELLIS TRANSPORT SERVICES	50
ELSAN LTD	47
EMINOX LTD	31
ENECO	19
ENSIGN BUS COMPANY LTD	13
ERENTEK	22
ERF MEADWAY	44
ERRINGTONS OF EVINGTON LTD	13
ESKER BUS & COACH SALES, IRELAND	10
ESKER BUS & COACH, UK	12
E T M SOFTWARE SERVICES	22
EURO COACH BUILDERS LTD	12
EUROTUNNEL	54
EVOBUS (UK) LTD	13
EXCEL CONVERSIONS	12
EXPO MANAGEMENT LTD	54
EXPRESS COACH REPAIRS LTD	19

F

FABER MAUNSELL LTD	53
R. W. FAULKS FCIT	53
FCAV & CO	19
FIGUREHEAD DATA SYSTEMS	51
FINANCIAL INSPECTION SERVICES LTD	53
FIREMASTER EXTINGUISHER LTD	32
FIRTH FURNISHINGS LTD	33
FIRST CHOICE NAMEPLATES	19
DAVID FISHWICK COACH SALES	13
FJORD LINE	54
FLEET AUCTION GROUP	13
FLEETMASTER BUS & COACH LTD	13
FLIGHTS COACH TRAVEL LTD	38
FORD	10
FRANK GUY LTD	12
FRASER EAGLE MANAGEMENT SERVICES	52
FTA VEHICLE INSPECTION SERVICE	28
FUMOTO ENGINEERING OF EUROPE LTD	30
FURROWS COMMERCIAL VEHICLES	13
FURTEX LTD see INTERFACE FABRICS	
FWT	51

G

GABRIEL & COMPANY LTD	35
GARDNER PARTS	34
GEMCO	43
GHE	20
GM COACHWORK	12
IAN GORDON COMMERCIALS	13
GOSKILLS	51
GRAMPIAN SOFTWARE	52
GRASSHOPPER INN	56
GREATDAYS TRAVEL GROUP, MANCHESTER	56
GREATDAYS TRAVEL GROUP, LONDON	56
TONY GREAVES GRAPHICS	51
LEONARD GREEN ASSOCIATES	53
JOHN GROVES TICKET SYSTEMS	22
FRANK GUY LTD	12

H

HANOVER DISPLAYS LTD	25
HANSAR FINANCE LTD	55
HANTS & DORSET TRIM LTD	37
HAPPICH V&I COMPONENTS LTD	32
THOMAS HARDIE - WIGAN	13
HART BROTHERS	22
HATCHER COMPONENTS LTD	49
HATTS COACHWORKS	21
P J HAYMAN	56
HAYWARD TRAVEL (CARDIFF)	52
HENRY BOOTH GROUP *(see* BEMROSE BOOTH*)*	
B HEPWORTH & CO	49
HILTECH DEVELOPMENTS LTD	28
J. HIPWELL & SON	49
HISPACOLD	18
HL SMITH TRANSMISSIONS	26
JOHN HOLDSWORTH & CO LTD	49
HOLLOWAY COMMERCIALS	13
B D HOLT	13
HWP (H W PICKRELL)	14

I

IAN ALLAN PRINTING LTD	58
IAN GORDON	13
IBPTS	45
IMAGE & PRINT GROUP	54
IMAGE FIRST CORPORATE CLOTHING LTD	48
IMEXPART LTD	22
IMPERIAL ENGINEERING	22
INDEPENDENT COACH TRAVEL	60
INDCAR	12
INDICATORS INTERNATIONAL LTD	25
INDUSTRIAL & COMMERCIAL WINDOW CO LTD	49
INIT	45
INOVAS LTD	19
INTELLITEC	27
INTERFACE FABRICS	41
INTERLUBE SYSTEMS LTD	33
INVERTEC	21
IRISBUS (UK) LTD	8
IRISH COMMERCIALS	13
IRISH FERRIES	54
IRIZAR	10
ISLE OF MAN STEAM PACKET COMPANY	54
IVECO	29
ANDY IZATT	50

J

J W GLASS LTD	49
JACOBS BABTIE GROUP LTD	53
JANES URBAN TRANSPORT SYSTEMS	59
JAYCAS	18
JBF SERVICES LTD	28
JDC	12
JES BUSCYCLE	21
JMW	33
JOHN GROVES TICKET SYSTEMS	22
JOHN BRADSHAW	10
JOHN HOLDSWORTH & CO LTD	49
JONCKHEERE	10
JOURNEYPLAN	39
JUBILEE AUTOMOTIVE GROUP	12

K

KAB SEATING LTD	41
KARIVE LTD	35
KEITH EDMONDSON	45
KELLETT (UK) LTD	22
KENT COACHWORKS	21
KERNOW ASSOCIATES	50
KING LONG	8
KNORR-BREMSE SYSTEMS	22
THOMAS KNOWLES - TRANSPORT CONSULTANT	53
KVC	10

L

LANTERN RECOVERY SPECIALISTS	51
THE LAWTON MOTOR BODY BUILDING CO LTD	18
LDV PLC	10
LEICESTER CARRIAGE BUILDERS	10
LEINSTER VEHICLE DISTRIBUTORS/LVD	14
LEISUREWEAR DIRECT	48
LEONARD GREEN ASSOCIATES	53
LEXCEL POWER SYSTEMS PLC	20
LEYLAND PRODUCT DEVELOPMENTS	11
LH GROUP (SERVICES) LTD	26
LHE FINANCE LTD	55
LONDON BUS EXPORT	14
LOOK CCTV	44
LOUGHSHORE AUTOS LTD	14
LRTA PUBLICATIONS	59
LUNAR SEATING LTD	41

M

M A C LTD	18
MACEMAIN + AMSTAD	12
MAJORLIFT HYDRAULIC EQUIPMENT LTD	34
MAJORLINE ENGINEERING LTD	14
MAN TRUCK & BUS UK LTD (MENTOR)	8
MARK TERRILL PSV BADGES	19
MARK TERRILL TICKET MACHINERY	22

MARKET ENGINEERING	60
MARTYN INDUSTRIALS LTD	21
MASS SPECIAL ENGINEERING LTD	14
MAUN INTERNATIONAL	53
MCE LTD	22
MCI EXHIBITIONS LTD	54
MCV BUS & COACH LTD	10
McKENNA BROTHERS LTD	25
MELLOR COACHCRAFT	12
MENTOR COACH & BUS LTD	14
MERCEDES-BENZ	8
MET UK LIMITED	25
METRONET REW LTD	42
MID WEST BUS & COACH SALES LTD	14
MIDLAND COUNTIES PUBLICATIONS	58
MINIBUS OPTIONS LTD	12
MINIMISE YOUR RISK	51
MINITRAM SYSTEMS LTD	9
MIRROR IMAGE MODELS	37
MISTRAL GROUP (UK) PLC	14
MOCAP LIMITED	38
MONOWASH (BRUSH REPLACEMENT SERVICE)	49
STEPHEN C MORRIS	51
MOSELEY (PCV) LTD	10
MOSELEY IN THE SOUTH LTD	14
MOTT MACDONALD	53
MTB EQUIPMENT LTD	41
MULTIPART PSV	20
MVA	51
MYSTERY TRAVELLERS	59

N

MIKE NASH	14
NATIONWIDE CLEANING & SUPPORT	49
NEALINE WINDSCREEN WIPER PRODUCTS	18
NEERMAN & PARTNERS	51
NEOPLAN (MENTOR)	8
NEXT BUS LTD	14
NOGE (MENTOR)	10
NORBURY BLINDS	21
NORFOLKLINE	54
W. NORTHS (PV) LTD	14
NORTON FOLGATE	55
NU-TRACK	11

O

OLYMPUS COACHCRAFT LTD	12
OMNI WHITTINGTON	56
OMNIBUS TRAINING LTD	54
OPTARE COACH SALES	12
OPTARE GROUP	8
ORVEC INTERNATIONAL	35
OWENS OF OSWESTRY BMC	14

P

P&O FERRIES	54
PACEL ELECTRONICS	27
PACET MANUFACTURING	18
PARTLINE LTD	24

PARRY PEOPLE MOVERS	9
PASSENGER LIFT SERVICES LTD	36
PAYPOINT	45
PERCY LANE PRODUCTS LTD	25
PENINSULA GROUP	52
PERKINS GROUP LTD	30
PETERS DOOR SYSTEMS LTD	25
PHOENIX SEATING	42
PIAGGIO	11
H W PICKRELL	14
PINDAR	57
PIONEER WESTON	31
PJ ASSOCIATES	53
PLAXTON LTD, *SCARBOROUGH*	8
PLAXTON COACH SALES CENTRE	14
PLUM CREATIONS	51
PNEUMAX LTD	26
POLYBUSH	43
POWER BATTERIES (GB) LTD	20
POWERTRAIN PRODUCTS LTD	26
PRE METRO OPERATIONS	40
PRESTOLITE	27
PROFESSIONAL TRANSPORT SERVICES	51
PSS - STEERING & HYDRAULICS DIVISION	43
PSV GLASS	42
PSV PRODUCTS	19
PVS MANUFACTURING LTD	12

Q

Q'STRAINT	41
QUEENSBRIDGE (PSV) LTD	28
QUEENSBURY SHELTERS	42

R

R & J HANDLEY UNIFORM	48
RAINBOW CORPORATEWEAR	48
RATCLIFF TAIL LIFTS LTD	36
RED FUNNEL	54
RENAULT UK LTD	11
RESCROFT LTD	42
RH BODYWORKS	21
RICON UK LTD	36
RIGTON INSURANCE SERVICES	56
ROADLEASE	55
ROADLINK INTERNATIONAL LTD	22
ROBERTSON TRANSPORT CONSULTING	54
ROEVILLE COMPUTER SYSTEMS	52
ROUTE ONE	59

S

SAFEGUARD	32
SAFETEX LTD	41
SALTIRE COMMUNICATIONS	51
SALVADOR CAETANO (UK) LTD	9
SAMMYS GARAGE	52
SC COACHBUILDERS	9
SCAN COIN	22
SCANDUS UK	42
SCANIA BUS & COACH (UK) LTD	14
SCANIA	8

Company	Page
SCHADES LTD	45
SEAFRANCE	54
SECURON (AMERSHAM) LTD	41
SERGEANT (P&P) LTD	22
SETRA	8
SHADES-TECHNICS	26
SHAWSON SUPPLY LTD	24
SIEMENS TRAFFIC CONTROLS	40
SIEMENS VDO	44
SILFLEX LTD	25
SKILLPLACE TRAINING	54
SMART CENTRAL COACH	49
SMITH BROS & WEBB	49
H L SMITH	26
SNOWCHAINS EUROPRODUCTS	48
SOMERS TOTALKARE	34
SOMERBUS	14
SOUTHDOWN PSV	14
SOUTHERN VECTIS PLC	59
SPECIALIST	54
SSL	39
STAFFORD BUS CENTRE	14
STAGE HOTEL — LEICESTER	56
STANFORD COACHWORKS	12
STENA LINE	54
STERTIL UK	37
STEPHEN C MORRIS	51
STEPHENSONS OF ESSEX	14
JOHN STEWART & CO	12
PHIL STOCKFORD GARAGE EQUIPMENT	34
STOKE TRUCK & BUS CENTRE	14
STUART MANUFACTURING CO LTD	45
SUPERFAST FERRIES	55
SUSTRACO	40
SUTRAK: See CARRIER SUTRAK	
SWANSEA CORK FERRIES	54

T

Company	Page
TACHOGRAPH BUREAUX LTD	45
TAGTRONICS LTD	52
TALISMAN	48
TARA SUPPORT SERVICES	52
TAS PARTNERSHIP	54
TAWE COACHBUILDERS	12
TAYLORS COACH SALES	14
TELMA RETARDER LTD	40
TERENCE BARKER TANKS	34
MARK TERRILL PSV BADGES	19
MARK TERRILL TICKET MACHINERY	22
THE THOMAS AUTOMATICS CO LTD	45
THOMAS HARDIE - WIGAN	13
THOMAS KNOWLES	53
TIFFANYS HOTEL	56
TIFLEX LTD	33
TIME TRAVEL (UK)	51
TONY GREAVES GRAPHICS	51
TOP GEARS DESTINATIONS	25
TOP LINE TRAVEL OF YORK LTD	52
TOWERGATE CHAPMAN STEVENS	56

Company	Page
TOYOTA	11
TRAMONTANA	15
TRAM POWER LTD	9
TRAMWAYS & URBAN TRANSIT	59
TRANMAN SOLUTIONS	53
TRANSIT	59
TRANSPORT DESIGN INTERNATIONAL	29
TRANSPORT STATIONERY SERVICES	58
TRANSPORT TICKET SERVICES	22
TRANSPORTATION MANAGEMENT SOLUTIONS	19
TRAVEL INFORMATION SYSTEMS	53
TRAVELPATH 3000	56
TREVOR WIGLEY & SON BUS LTD	15
TRIMPLEX	33
TRUCK ALIGN CO LTD	21
TRUEFORM ENGINEERING LTD	42
TUBE PRODUCTS LTD	42
TVAC	12

U

Company	Page
UK COACH & BUS	15
UNITEC PARTS & SERVICE LTD	19
UNITEC	18
UNITEC LONDON	18
UNITEC ROTHERHAM	18
UNITEC SCOTLAND	18
USED COACH SALES	15
UVMODULAR	12
UWE VERKEN AB	18

V

Company	Page
BOB VALE COACH SALES	13
VAN HOOL	8
VAPOR STONE	26
VARLEY & GULLIVER LTD	34
VARTA AUTOMOTIVE BATTERIES LTD	20
VAUXHALL	11
VBI TRISCAN	33
VCA	54
VDL BOVA	9
VDL BUS INTERNATIONAL	9
VDO KIENZLE UK LTD	28
VENTURA	15
VERIFEYE	44
VICTORIA COACH STATION	52
VISECT LTD (TACH:TRAK)	45
V L TEST SYSTEMS LTD	34
VOITH TURBO LTD	34
VOLKSWAGEN COMMERCIAL VEHICLES	11
VOLVO BUS LTD	9
VOLVO COACH CENTRE	15
VOLVO FINANCIAL SERVICES	55
VOLVO INSURANCE SERVICES	56
VOR TRANSMISSIONS LTD	34
VOSA	54
VULTRON INTERNATIONAL LTD	39

W

Company	Page
W. NORTHS (PV) LTD	14

WABCO AUTOMOTIVE UK LTD	22
WACTON COACH SALES & SERVICES	15
WALLMINSTER LTD	31
WALSH'S ENGINEERING	30
WARD INTERNATIONAL CONSULTING LTD	51
WAYFARER TRANSIT SYSTEMS LTD	45
WEALDEN PSV LTD	15
WEALDSTONE ENGINEERING	30
WEBASTO PRODUCT LTD	18
WEBB'S	54
WEDLAKE SAINT	56
WIDNEY UK LTD	40
ALAN WHITE COACH SALES	15
WHITELEY ELECTRONICS	42
WIGHTLINK ISLE OF WIGHT FERRIES	54
WIGLEY TREVOR	15
WILKER	12
WILLIS LTD	56
WILSURE INSURANCE BROKERS	56
WINDOW CLEAN SERVICES	49
WOODBRIDGE FOAM UK LTD	42
WRIGHTBUS LTD	9
WRIGHTSURE INSURANCE SERVICES	56
WS ATKINS *see* ATKINS	

Y

YORKSHIRE BUS & COACH SALES	15

Z

ZF POWERTRAIN	26

Do you want to keep your
LITTLE RED BOOK
up-to-date?
Buses magazine is now carrying updates
every month.
See opposite title page or page 256
for Subscription details

OPERATOR INDEX

1ST CHOICE SCORPIO TRAVEL, *SLOUGH*	87

A

AAA COACHES, *KIRKNEWTON*	202
A1 COACH TRAVEL, *LONDONDERRY*	225
A1 TRAVEL, *YEOVIL*	169
A1A LTD, *BIRKENHEAD*	151
A.2.B TRAVEL UK LTD, *PRENTON*	151
AtoB TRAVEL LTD, *LUTON*	86
A & C LUXURY COACHES, *MOTHERWELL*	207
A & E HIRE, *WELSHPOOL*	220
A & J COACHES OF WASHINGTON CO LTD, *WASHINGTON, TYNE & WEAR*	182
AA, KNIGHTS OF THE ROAD, *GREATER LONDON*	145
A B COACHES LTD, *PAIGNTON*	104
A M K, *LIPHOOK*	125
A. R. TRAVEL, *HEMEL HEMPSTEAD*	129
ABBEY COACHWAYS LTD, *CARLTON, Nr GOOLE*	157
ABBEY TRAVEL LTD, *HITCHIN*	129
G. ABBOTT & SONS, *LEEMING*	157
ABERFELDY MOTOR SERVICES,	208
ABUS, *BRISTOL*	89
ACE TRAVEL, *BISHOPS STORTFORD*	129
ACE TRAVEL, *BURNTWOOD*	175
ACKLAMS COACHES, *BEVERLEY*	114
ACRON TRAVEL, *HORSFORTH*	190
ACTON COACHES, *WREXHAM*	222
ADAMS TOURS, *BLOXWICH*	184
ADAMSON'S COACHES, *CRAMLINGTON*	162
ADLINGTON TAXIS AND MINICOACHES, *HORWICH*	122
ADRAINS OF BRINKWORTH	193
AINTREE COACHLINE, *BOOTLE*	151
AIRCOACH, *DUBLIN*	226
AIRLINKS — THE AIRPORT COACH CO LTD, *WEST DRAYTON*	145
AIRLYNX LTD, *SOUTHAMPTON*	125
ALAN ARNOTT, *ERSKINE*	209
ALANSWAY COACHES, *NEWTON ABBOTT*	104
ALDERMASTON COACHES, *ALDERMASTON*	86
ALEC HEAD, *LUTTON, PETERBOROUGH*	161
ALEX MILNE, *NEW BYTH BY TURRIFF*	199
ALEXCARS LTD, *CIRENCESTER*	120
ALFA COACHES LTD, *STOCKTON-ON-TEES*	110
ALFA TRAVEL, *CHORLEY*	137
ALFRA COACH HIRE, *LARKHALL*	210
A LINE COACHES, *GATESHEAD*	182
ALLAN'S GROUP, *GOREBRIDGE*	205
ALLANDER COACHES LTD, *MILNGAVIE*	204
ALLIED COACHES, BALDOYLE, *DUBLIN*	226
ALLIED COACHLINES LTD, *HAYES*	152
ALMAR TRAVEL, *CHESTER-le-STREET*	110
ALPHA COACH CO, *HULL*	114
ALPHA PERSONALISED TRAVEL LTD, *WATFORD*	129
ALPINE TRAVEL, *LLANDUDNO*	216
ALTERNATIVE TRAVEL, *SCARBOROUGH*	157
ALTONA COACH SERVICES & TRAVEL CONSULTANT, *GATESHEAD*	182
ALTONIAN COACHES, *ALTON*	125
AMBASSADOR COACHES, *SOUTHEND ON SEA*	116
AMBASSADOR TRAVEL (ANGLIA) LTD, *GREAT YARMOUTH*	154
AMBER TRAVEL, *TURRIFF*	198
AMK CHAUFFUER DRIVEN, *LIPHOOK*	125
GEOFF AMOS COACHES, *DAVENTRY*	161
AMPORT & DISTRICT COACHES LTD, *ANDOVER*	125
ANDERSON COACHES LTD, *SHEFFIELD*	172
ANDERSON TRAVEL LTD, *LONDON SE1*	145
ANDERSON'S COACHES, *CASTLEFORD*	190
ANDERSON'S COACHES, *LANGHOLM*	201
ANDREW JAMES QUALITY TRAVEL, *CHIPPENHAM*	195
ANDREW'S OF TIDESWELL LTD	101
ANDREWS COACHES, *FOXTON, CAMBRIDGE*	92
ANDYBUS AND COACH LTD, *MALMESBURY*	193
ANGEL MOTORS (EDMONTON) LTD, *TOTTENHAM*	145
ANGEL TRAVEL, *WARRINGTON*	94
ANGELA COACHES LTD, *BURSLEDON*	125
ANGLIAN COACHES LTD, *BECCLES*	177
ANITAS BRITISH & CONTINENTAL TOURS LTD, *STANSTED AIRPORT*	116
ANNTONY MINIBUSES, *SUTTON*	179
ANTHONYS TRAVEL, *RUNCORN*	94
APL TRAVEL, *CRUDWELL*	193
APPLEBYS COACHES, *LOUTH*	156
APT COACHES LTD, *RAYLEIGH*	116
ARAN TOURS, *SANDYCOVE, Co DUBLIN*	226
ARLEEN COACH HIRE & SERVICES LTD, *PEASEDOWN ST JOHN*	169
ARMCHAIR COACHES, *HOUNSLOW*	145
R. K. ARMSTRONG COACHES, *CASTLE DOUGLAS*	201
ARNOLD LIDDELL COACHES, *BRISTOL*	90
ARON COACHLINES LTD, *HAYES*	152
ARRIVA CYMRU LTD, *LLANDUDNO JUNCTION*	216
ARRIVA DERBY LTD	101
ARRIVA SURREY & WEST SUSSEX, *GUILDFORD*	179
ARRIVA LONDON	145
ARRIVA MIDLANDS, *LEICESTER*	141
ARRIVA MIDLANDS, CANNOCK	175
ARRIVA NORTH EAST LTD, *SUNDERLAND*	182
ARRIVA NORTH WEST & WALES, *AINTREE*	151
ARRIVA PASSENGER SERVICES	85
ARRIVA PLC	85
ARRIVA SCOTLAND WEST, *PAISLEY*	209
ARRIVA SOUTHERN COUNTIES, *MAIDSTONE*	133
ARRIVA THE SHIRES & ESSEX, *LUTON*	86
ARRIVA YORKSHIRE, *WAKEFIELD*	190
ARROWEBROOK COACHES, *CHESTER*	94
ARTHUR THOMAS COACHES, *GORSEINON*	222
ARUN COACHES/FAWLTY TOURS, *HORSHAM*	188
ARVONIA COACHES, *CAERNARFON*	217
ASHALL'S COACHES, *CLAYTON*	122

ASHFORD LUXURY COACHES, *FELTHAM*	153
ASHLEY TRAVEL LTD t/a GRANT & McALLIN, *SHEFFIELD*	172
G. ASHTON COACHES, *ST HELENS*	151
ASM COACHES, *WHITSTABLE*	133
ASMAL COACHES, *LEICESTER*	141
J. & F. ASPDEN (BLACKBURN) LTD	137
ASTONS COACHES, *WORCESTER*	196
ASTONS OF NEWPORT, *SHROPSHIRE*	167
H. ATKINSON & SONS (INGLEBY), *NORTHALLERTON*	157
AUSDEN CLARK LTD, *LEICESTER*	141
AUSTIN TRAVEL, *EARLSTON*	200
AUTOCAR BUS & COACH, *TONBRIDGE*	133
AUTODOUBLE LTD, *MILTON KEYNES*	90
AUTOPOINT COACHES, *HAILSHAM*	113
AVENSIS COACH TRAVEL, *ROMSEY*	125
AVON COACH & BUS COMPANY, *BIRKENHEAD*	151
AWAY DAYS, *SHANKLIN*	132
AWAYDAYS LTD T/A GEMINI TRAVEL, *IPSWICH*	178
AXE VALE COACHES, *AXBRIDGE*	169
AXE VALLEY MINI TRAVEL, *SEATON*	104
AYREVILLE COACHES, *PLYMOUTH*	104
AZTEC COACH TRAVEL, *BRISTOL*	89

B

B & H TOURS, *MIRFIELD*	190
B & J TRAVEL, *MIDDLESTOWN*	190
B B COACHES LTD, *HALESOWEN*	184
B'S TRAVEL, *PONTYPOOL*	222
BACK ROADS TOURING CO LTD, *LONDON W5*	145
BAGNALLS COACHES, *SWADLINCOTE*	101
BAILEY'S COACHES LTD, *WATNALL*	163
BAILISS TOURS, *BARTON-IN-THE-BEANS*	141
BAKERS COACHES, *BIDDULPH*	175
BAKERS COACHES, *YEOVIL*	169
BAKERS COMMERCIAL SERVICES, *ENSTONE*	166
BAKERS DOLPHIN COACH TRAVEL, *WESTON-SUPER-MARE*	169
BAKEWELL COACHES, *BAKEWELL*	101
IAN BALDRY, *FELIXSTOWE*	177
BALDRY'S COACHES, *YORK*	158
BANBURYSHIRE ETA LTD, *BANBURY*	166
BANSTEAD COACHES LTD, *BANSTEAD*	179
BARCROFT TOURS & EVENTS, *HASTINGS*	113
BARFORDIAN COACHES LTD, *BEDFORD*	86
BARNARD CASTLE COACHES, *RICHMOND*	158
BARNES COACHES LTD, *SWINDON*	194
BARNSLEY & DISTRICT TRACTION CO	172
BARRATT'S COACHES, *NANTWICH*	94
BARRY'S COACHES LTD, *CORK*	226
BARRY'S COACHES LTD, *WEYMOUTH*	108
BARTON TRANSPORT, *MAYNOOTH*	226
BASFORDS COACHES LTD, *TOWCESTER*	161
BATH BUS COMPANY	169
BATTERSBY SILVER GREY COACHES, *MORECAMBE*	137
BATTERSBY'S COACHES, *WALKDEN*	122
BEACON COACHES, *CHELMSLEY WOOD*	184
K. W. BEARD LTD, *CINDERFORD*	120
BEATONS COACHES LTD, *BLANTYRE*	210
BEAULY COACH HIRE, *WESTER BALBLAIR, BY BEAULY*	204
BEAVIS HOLIDAYS, *BUSSAGE*	120
BEBB TRAVEL, *LLANTWIT FARDRE*	221
BEECHES TRAVEL, *TWICKENHAM*	153
BEECROFT COACHES, *FEWSTON, NR HARROGATE*	158
BEELINE (R&R) COACHES LTD, *WARMINSTER*	194
BEESTONS COACHES LTD, *HADLEIGH*	177
BELLS LUXURY COACHES, *SALISBURY*	194
BEN GEORGE TRAVEL, *BROUGHTON*	156
BEN JOHNSON COACHES, *BRANDESBURTON*	115
BENNETT'S COACHES, *GLOUCESTER*	120
BENNETT'S TRAVEL, *WARRINGTON*	94
BENNETTS TRAVEL (CRANBERRY) LTD, *GATES HEATH*	175
BERKELEY COACH AND TRAVEL LTD, *PAULTON, BRISTOL*	89
BERRYS COACHES (TAUNTON) LTD	170
BESSWAY TRAVEL, *WEST HARROW*	153
BEST WAY TRAVEL, *SALTBURN*	110
BETTER MOTORING SERVICES, *STRATTON-ST MARGARET*	194
JAMES BEVAN LTD, *LYDNEY*	120
BEXLEY COACHLINES, *BEXLEY*	133
BIBBY'S OF INGLETON	158
BIG BUS COMPANY, *LONDON SW1W*	145
BILLIES COACHES LTD, *ROTHERHAM*	172
BIRCHWOOD TRAVEL, *WARRINGTON*	94
BIRMINGHAM COACH COMPANY LTD, THE, *WARLEY*	184
BIRMINGHAM INTERNATIONAL COACHES LTD, *TILE CROSS*	184
D. P. BISHOP, *DUMBARTON*	211
B J S TRAVEL, *GREAT WAKERING*	116
BLACKBURN BOROUGH TRANSPORT LTD	137
BLACKPOOL TRANSPORT LTD	137
BLAGDON LIONESS COACHES LTD, *BRISTOL*	170
BLAZEFIELD HOLDINGS	85
BLUE BUS & COACH SERVICES LTD, *BOLTON*	138
BLUE DIAMOND COACHES, *HARLOW*	116
BLUE IRIS COACHES, *NAILSEA*	89
BLUEBIRD BUS & COACH, *MIDDLETON*	122
BLUEBIRD BUSES, *ABERDEEN*	198
BLUEBIRD BUSES, *INVERNESS*	204
BLUEBIRD BUSES, *PERTH*	208
BLUEBIRD COACHES (WEYMOUTH) LTD	108
BLUEBIRD COACHES, *COOLOCK, DUBLIN*	226
BLUEBIRD OF NEATH/PONTARDAWE	219
BLUELINE COACHES, *MAGHULL*	151
BLUE TRIANGLE BUSES, *RAINHAM*	116
BLUEWAYS GUIDELINE COACHES LTD, *LONDON*	145
BLUNSDON'S COACH TRAVEL, *BLADON*	166
C. BODMAN & SONS, *DEVIZES*	194
A. S. BONE & SONS, *HOOK*	125
A & H BOOTH LTD, *HYDE*	122
BORDACOACH, *RAYLEIGH*	116
BOSTOCK'S COACHES LTD, *CONGLETON*	94

BOTTERILLS, *THORNTON DALE*	158
BOULTONS OF SHROPSHIRE, *CHURCH STRETTON*	167
BOURNEMOUTH TRANSPORT LTD	108
L F BOWEN LTD, *TAMWORTH*	175
BOWERS COACHES LTD, *CHAPEL-EN-LE-FRITH*	101
D K & N BOWMAN, *WREAY, CARLISLE*	99
BOWMAN'S COACHES (MULL) LTD, *CRAIGNURE*	199
BOWYER'S COACHES, *HEREFORD*	128
M. BOYDON & SONS, *WINKHILL*	175
BRADSHAWS TRAVEL, *KNOTT END ON SEA*	138
BRAZIERS MINI COACHES, *BUCKINGHAM*	90
BRENTONS OF BLACKHEATH, *LONDON SE3*	145
BRENTWOOD COACHES	116
BRIAN ISAAC COACHES LTD, *SWANSEA*	222
BRIGHTON & HOVE BUS & COACH CO LTD	113
BRIGHTONIAN COACHES, *BRIGHTON*	113
BRIJAN TOURS, *BISHOPS WALTHAM*	125
BRISTOL ELECTRIC RAILBUS	89
BRITANNIA COACHES, *DOVER*	133
BRITANNIA TRAVEL, *OTLEY*	190
BRITTAINS COACHES LTD, *NORTHAMPTON*	161
BRODYR JAMES, *TREGARON*	216
BROMYARD OMNIBUS COMPANY, *BROMYARD*	128
A T BROWN, *TELFORD*	167
EDDIE BROWN TOURS LTD, *YORK*	158
H E BROWN, *CONGLETON*	94
LES BROWN TRAVEL, *BATHGATE*	211
BROWNINGS (WHITBURN) LTD	211
S H BROWNRIGG LTD, *EGREMONT*	99
WILLIAM BROWNRIGG, *THORNHILL*	201
BROWNS COACHES LTD, *PONTEFRACT*	190
BROWNS COACHES, *ASHFORD*	133
BROWNS OF DURHAM, *DURHAM*	110
BROWNS OF EDINBURGH, *BROXBURN*	202
ROY BROWNS COACHES, *BUILTH WELLS*	220
RONNIE BRUEN, *COOLOCK, DUBLIN*	226
BRYANS OF ENFIELD	146
BRYLAINE TRAVEL, *BOSTON*	143
BRYN MELYN LTD, *LLANGOLLEN*	217
BUCKBY'S COACHES, *ROTHWELL*	161
BUCKLEYS, *DONCASTER*	172
BUCKLEY'S TOURS, *KILLARNEY*	226
BUDDENS COACHES LTD, *See AVENSIS*	
BUGLERS COACHES LTD, *BRISTOL*	89
R. BULLOCK & CO (TRANSPORT) LTD, *CHEADLE*	122
BURDETTS COACHES LTD, *MOSBOROUGH*	172
BURGHFIELD MINI COACHES LTD, *READING*	87
BURKE BROS (COACHES) LTD, *TUAM, Co GALWAY*	226
BURNHAM PARK COACHES, *PLYMOUTH*	105
BURNLEY & PENDLE	138
JAMES BURNS, *PAISLEY*	209
R & D BURROWS LTD, *OGMORE VALE, BRIDGEND*	213
BURTONS COACHES LTD, *HAVERHILL*	178
BURTONS COLCHESTER, *COLCHESTER*	116
BUS EIREANN/IRISH BUS, *DUBLIN*	226
TERRY BUSHELL TRAVEL, *BURTON-ON-TRENT*	175
BUSES4U, *TANDRIDGE*	179
BUTLER BROTHERS, *KIRKBY IN ASHFIELD*	163
BUTLERS BUSES, *COBH, Co CORK*	226
BUTTERS COACHES, *CHILDS ERCALL*	167
BU-VAL, *LITTLEBOROUGH*	122
BUZZLINES, *HYTHE*	133
BYNGS INTERNATIONAL COACHES, *PORTSMOUTH*	125
BYRAN COACHES LTD, *SHEFFIELD*	172
BYSIAU CWM TAF/TAF VALLEY COACHES, *WHITLAND*	215
LES BYWATER & SONS LTD, *ROCHDALE*	122

C

C & G COACH SERVICES, *CHATTERIS*	92
C & S COACHES, *HEATHFIELD*	113
C I COACHLINES, *CHELMSFORD*	116
C. L. COACHES, *LANCING*	188
C N ENTERPRISES, *ROMFORD*	116
CABER COACHES, *ABERFELDY*	208
CABIN COACHES, *HAYES*	153
CAELLOI MOTORS, *PWLLHELI*	218
CAHALANE COACHES, *CORK*	226
CALDEW COACHES, *CARLISLE*	99
CALL-A-COACH, *WALTON-ON-THAMES*	179
CALLINAN COACHES, *GLAREGALWAY*	226
CAMBRIAN COAST COACH LINE, *ABERGYNOLWYN*	217
CAMPBELL'S COACHES, *SOUTH SHIELDS*	182
CANAVAN'S COACHES, *KILSYTH*	207
DEN CANEY COACHES LTD, *BIRMINGHAM*	184
CANTABRICA COACHES, *WATFORD*	129
CARADOC COACHES, *CHURCH STRETTON*	167
CARADON RIVIERA TOURS, *LISKEARD*	97
CARAVELLE COACHES, *EDGWARE*	153
CARDIFF BUS, *CARDIFF*	214
CARMEL COACHES, *OKEHAMPTON*	105
J. W. CARNELL LTD, *SUTTON BRIDGE*	163
PETER CAROL PRESTIGE COACHING, *WHITCHURCH, BRISTOL*	89
CARR'S COACHES, *SILLOTH*	99
CARREGLEFN COACHES, *AMLWCH*	213
CAROUSEL BUSES, *HIGH WYCOMBE*	89
CARROLL'S COACH HIRE, *DROGHEDA*	224
CARS INTERNATIONAL A. C. T., *ASH*	179
CARSVILLE COACHES, *URMSTON*	122
CASTELL COACHES LTD, *BEDWAS*	214
CASTLE GARAGE LTD, *LLANDOVERY*	215
CASTLEWAYS LTD, *WINCHCOMBE*	120
CATTERALLS OF SOUTHAM, *SOUTHAM*	183
CAVALIER TRAVEL, *LONG SUTTON*	143
CAVALIER TRAVEL SERVICES, *BRENTFORD*	146
CEDAR COACHES, *BEDFORD*	86
CEDRIC COACHES, *WIVENHOE*	116
CELTIC TRAVEL, *LLANIDLOES*	220
CENTAUR TRAVEL MINICOACHES, *SIDCUP*	146
CENTRA, *ADDLESTONE*	179
CENTRAL COACHES, *KEITH*	206
CENTRAL GARAGE, *TODMORDEN*	191
CENTRAL MINI COACHES, *DOVER*	133
CENTRAL TRAVEL, *NEWTOWN*	220
CENTREBUS, *LUTON*	86
CENTURION TRAVEL, *MIDSOMER NORTON*	170

CERBYDAU BERWYN COACHES, *TREFOR, PWLLHELI*	217
CHADWELL HEATH COACHES, *ROMFORD*	116
CHALFONT COACHES OF HARROW LTD, *SOUTHALL*	153
CHALFONT LINE LTD, *WEST DRAYTON*	146
CHALKWELL COACH HIRE & TOURS, *SITTINGBOURNE*	133
CHAMBERS COACH HIRE LTD, *MONEYMORE*	225
CHAMBERS COACHES (STEVENAGE) LTD	129
H. C. CHAMBERS & SON LTD, *BURES*	178
CHANDLERS COACH TRAVEL, *WESTBURY*	194
CHAPEL END COACHES, *NUNEATON*	183
CHARIOTS OF CRAWLEY	188
CHARIOTS OF ESSEX LTD, *STANFORD-LE-HOPE*	116
CHARLTON-ON-OTMOOR SERVICES, *OXFORD*	166
CHARTER COACH LTD, *YORK*	158
CHASE BUS SERVICES, *BURNTWOOD*	185
CHAUFFEURS OF BIRMINGHAM, *EDGBASTON*	185
CHEAM COACHES, *CHEAM, SUTTON*	179
CHENERY, *DISS*	154
CHENEY COACHES LTD, *BANBURY*	166
CHERRYBRIAR, *LONDON E3*	146
CHESTERBUS, *CHESTER*	95
IAN CHESTNUT, *JOHNSTONE*	209
CHEYNE'S COACHES, *INVERURIE*	198
CHILTERN TRAVEL, *HENLOW*	86
CHIVERS COACHES LTD, *WALLINGTON*	180
CITYCIRCLE LTD, *HAYES*	146
CITY SIGHTSEEING GLASGOW LTD, *GLASGOW*	204
CLAPTON COACHES LTD, *RADSTOCK*	170
CLARIBEL COACHES, *TILE CROSS*	185
CLARKES OF LONDON, *LONDON SE26*	146
CLARKSON COACHWAYS, *BARROW IN FURNESS*	99
CLARKSONS HOLIDAYS, *SOUTH ELMSALL*	190
CLASSIC COACHES LTD, *ANNFIELD PLAIN*	110
CLASSIC COACHES, *DUBLIN*	226
CLASSIC COACHES, *LUTON*	86
CLASSIQUE SUN SALOON LUXURY COACHES, *PAISLEY*	209
CLEGG & BROOKING COACHES, *STOCKBRIDGE*	125
CLH TRAVEL, *PAIGNTON*	105
CLINTONA MINICOACHES, *BRENTWOOD*	117
CLOWES COACHES, *LONGNOR*	102
CLWYDIAN TOURS, *LLANRHAEADR*	217
CLYDE COAST COACHES LTD, *ARDROSSAN*	206
CLYNNOG & TREFOR MOTORS, *CAERNARFON*	218
COACH COMPANIONS LTD, *LEOMINSTER*	128
COACH HOUSE TRAVEL, *DORCHESTER*	108
COACHLINERS, *SOUTH SHIELDS*	182
COACH OPTIONS, *MIDDLETON*	122
COACH SERVICES LTD, *THETFORD*	155
COACHING CONNECTION, *LLANIDLOES*	220
COACHMASTER (BRYAN GARRATT), *LEICESTER*	141
COACHSTYLE LTD, *CHIPPENHAM*	194
COACHWAYS, *ROCHDALE*	122
COAST TO COAST PACKHORSE, *KIRKBY STEPHEN*	99
COASTAL & COUNTRY COACHES LTD, *WHITBY*	158
COASTAL COACHES, *NEWICK, LEWES*	113
COCHRANE'S, *PETERLEE*	110
COLISEUM COACHES LTD, *WEST END, SOUTHAMPTON*	125
COLLIN PHILLIPSON, *GOOLE*	115, 174
COLLIN'S COACHES, *CARRICKAMOSS, Co MONAGHAN*	226
COLLINS COACHES LTD, *LONDON W7*	146
COLLINS COACHES, *CAMBRIDGE*	92
COLLINS COACHES, *SELBY*	158
W. H. COLLINS, *ROCH*	219
COLRAY COACH HIRE, *BLACKPOOL*	138
COMPASS ROYSTON COACHES, *DURHAM*	110
COMPASS TRAVEL, *WORTHING*	188
CONFIDENCE BUS/COACH HIRE, *LEICESTER*	141
CONISTON COACHES LTD, *BROMLEY*	146
CONNEX BUS UK LTD, *St HELIER, JERSEY*	224
CONWAY COACH AND CHAUFFEUR DRIVE, *LIMERICK*	226
COOKS COACHES, *WELLINGTON, SOMERSET*	170
COOKS COACHES, *WESTCLIFF-ON-SEA*	117
COOMBS TRAVEL, *WESTON-SUPER-MARE*	170
HENRY COOPER, *ANNITSFORD*	182
COOPERS COACHES, *ROTHWELL*	161
COOPERS COACHES, *WOOLSTON*	125
COOPERS TOURS LTD, *KILLAMARSH*	172
COPELAND TOURS (STOKE-ON-TRENT) LTD, *MEIR*	175
DAVID CORBEL OF LONDON LTD, *EDGWARE*	146
CORCORANS EXECUTIVE TOURS, *KILLARNEY, Co KERRY*	226
CORPORATE COACHING, *LUTON*	86
COSY COACHES, *KILLAMARSH*	172
COTTRELL'S COACHES, *MITCHELDEAN*	121
COUNTRY HOPPER, *IBSTOCK*	141
COUNTRY LION (NORTHAMPTON) LTD	161
COUNTRYLINER COACH HIRE LTD, *GUILDFORD*	180
COUNTRYSIDE BUS SERVICES, *SCARBOROUGH*	158
COUNTY COACHES, *BRENTWOOD*	117
COUNTY MINI COACHES, *LEICESTER*	141
L. S. COURT LTD, *FILLONGLEY*	183
COURTESY TRAVEL, *SHREWSBURY*	184
COURTNEY COACHES, BERKSHIRE	87
COX'S OF BELPER	102
COYLES COACHES, *GWEEDORE, Co DONEGAL*	226
R. & C. S. CRAIG, *ROBERTON*	210
CRAIG OF CAMPBELTOWN, *CAMPBELTOWN*	199
CRAIGGS TRAVEL EUROPEAN, *AMBLE*	162
CRAKERS COACHES, *DEAL*	134
HENRY CRAWFORD COACHES LTD, *NEILSTON*	202
CRAWLEY LUXURY, *THREE BRIDGES*	188
CREMIN COACHES, *BANTRY, WEST CORK*	226
CRESSWELLS COACHES (GRESLEY) LTD, *SWADLINCOTE*	102
N N CRESSWELL, *EVESHAM*	196
CRISTAL HIRE COACHES OF SWANWICK	102
CROESO TOURS, *PENYLAN*	214
CRONIN'S COACHES LTD, *CORK*	227
CROPLEY, *FOSDYKE*	143
CROPPER COACHES, *TOTTINGTON*	122

Operator Index

CROSS COUNTRY COACHES, *COLERAINE*	225
CROSS COUNTRY COACHES, *SWINDON*	194
CROSS COUNTRY HIRE, *POOLE*	109
CROSS GATES COACHES, *LLANDRINDOD WELLS*	220
CROSSKEYS COACHES, *FOLKESTONE*	134
CROSSON MOTOR GROUP, *COOLOCK, DUBLIN*	227
MARTIN CROWLEY, *BANDON Co CORK*	227
CROWN COACHES, *BICKLEY*	146
CROWN COACHES, *LEIGH-ON-SEA*	117
CROYDON TRAMLINK	146
CRUISERS LTD, *REDHILL*	180
CRUSADE TRAVEL, *PENKRIDGE*	175
CRUSADER HOLIDAYS, *CLACTON-ON-SEA*	117
CRYSTALS COACHES LTD, *LONDON SW10*	146
CUCKMERE COMMUNITY BUS, *POLEGATE*	113
CUMBRIA COACHES, *CARLISLE*	99
CUMFI-LUX COACHES, *HILLINGDON*	153
CUMFY COACHES, *SOUTHPORT*	151
CUNNINGHAM CARRIAGE CO, *CORRINGHAM*	117

D

D & E COACHES, *INVERNESS*	205
D & G COACH & BUS LTD, *STOKE ON TRENT*	175
D & H TRAVEL, *KENDAL*	99
D A C COACHES, *GUNNISLAKE*	97
D H CARS OF DENSTONE LTD, *UTTOXETER*	175
D R M BUS & CONTRAC SERVICES, *BROMYARD*	128
D.R.M. MINIBUS & COACH TRAVEL, *CHASE TERRACE*	176
D. R. P. MINIBUS TRAVEL, *NEWPORT PAGNELL*	91
D-WAY TRAVEL, *BUNGAY*	178
DAGLISH COACHES, *FRIZINGTON*	99
DAIMLER, *HALL GREEN*	185
DAISHS TRAVEL, *TORQUAY*	105
DALESMAN, *GUISELEY*	190
DAM EXPRESS, *ARDWICK GREEN*	122
DAMORY COACHES, *BLANDFORD FORUM*	109
DANS MINI-BUSES, *LONDON E18*	146
DARLEY FORD TRAVEL, *LISKEARD*	97
DARRAGHS COACHES, *BALLYMONEY*	225
DARTLINE COACHES, *EXETER*	105
DAVID PALMER COACHES LTD, *NORMANTON*	192
BILLY DAVIES EXECUTIVE COACHES, *STIRLING*	210
D G DAVIES, *RHAYADER*	220
DAWLISH COACHES LTD	105
ALAN DAWNEY COACH HIRE, *SHEPPEY*	134
DAWSON'S MINICOACHES, *ALFRETON*	102
MIKE DE COURCEY TRAVEL LTD, *COVENTRY*	185
DELAINE BUSES LTD, *BOURNE*	143
DEN CANEY COACHES LTD, *BIRMINGHAM*	184
DERBY COMMUNITY TRANSPORT	102
DEREK HIRCOCKS COACHES, *UPWELL, Nr WISBECH*	92
DEROS COACH TOURS, *KILLARNEY*	227
DERWENT COACHES LTD, *STANLEY, CO DURHAM*	182
DERWENT TRAVEL, *AYLESBURY*	90
DEWHIRST COACHES, *BRADFORD*	190
DEWS COACHES, *SOMERSHAM*	92
D'COACHES (DIAMOND HOLIDAYS), *MORRISTON*	221

DIRECT COACH TOURS, *BIRMINGHAM*	185
DOBSON'S BUSES LTD, *NORTHWICH*	95
T. & E. DOCHERTY, *IRVINE*	206
DOCHERTY'S MIDLAND COACHES, *AUCHTERARDER*	208
DOCKLANDS MINIBUSES, *SILVERTOWN E16*	147
DODDS OF TROON LTD, *AYR*	209
J. DODSWORTH (COACHES) LTD, *BOROUGHBRIDGE*	158
DOIGS OF GLASGOW LTD	204
JIMMY DONNELLY & SON, *ENNISCORTHY, Co WEXFORD*	227
SEAN DONNELLY, *GRANARD, Co LONGFORD*	227
DONOVAN'S COACH HIRE, *KILLARNEY*	227
DONS COACHES DUNMOW LTD, *GREAT DUNMOW*	117
DORSET COUNTY COUNCIL	109
DOUGLAS CORPORATION TRAMWAY	212
DOWN'S MOTORS & OTTER COACHES, *OTTERY ST MARY*	105
P. DOYLE LTD, *ROUNDWOOD, Co WICKLOW*	227
TONY DOYLE COACHES, *ENNISKERRY, Co WICKLOW*	227
K&H DOYLE, *RIPLEY*	102
TIM DRAPER HOLIDAYS, *ALFRETON*	102
DRP TRAVEL, *MILTON KEYNES*	91
DRURY COACHES, *GOOLE*	114
DUALWAY COACHES, *RATHCOOLE, Co DUBLIN*	227
DUBLIN BUS	227
DUBLIN MINI COACHES, *DUBLIN*	227
DUDLEY'S COACHES LTD, *WORCESTER*	196
DUNCAN MACLENNAN, *STRATH-CARRON*	205
RAY DUNN COACH TRAVEL, *HEDGE END*	126
DUNN'S COACHES, *AIRDRIE*	207
DUNN-LINE, *NOTTINGHAM*	163
DURHAM CITY COACHES LTD	111

E

'E' COACHES OF ALFRETON	102
EAGLE COACHES, *BRISTOL*	89
EAGLE LINE TRAVEL, *CHELTENHAM*	121
EAGLE TRAVEL, *STAFFORD*	176
EAGLES & CRAWFORD, *MOLD*	217
EAGRE, *MORTON*	143
EALING COMMUNITY TRANSPORT, *LONDON W3*	147
EARNSIDE COACHES, *GLENFARG*	208
EASSONS COACHES LTD, *ITCHEN*	126
EAST TEIGNBRIDGE COMMUNITY TRANSPORT *DAWLISH*	105
EAST YORKSHIRE MOTOR SERVICES LTD, *HULL*	115
EASTBOURNE BUSES LTD	193
A. W. EASTON'S COACHES LTD, *STRATTON STRAWLESS*	155
EASTONWAYS LTD, *RAMSGATE*	134
EASTVILLE COACHES LTD, *BRISTOL*	89
EASTWARD COACHES, *IVYBRIDGE*	105
EAVESWAY TRAVEL LTD, *ASHTON-IN-MAKERFIELD*	138
EBLEY COACH SERVICES, *NAILSWORTH*	121
EDS MINIBUS & COACH HIRE, *EAST TILBURY*	117
EDINBURGH BUS TOURS, *EDINBURGH*	202
EDINBURGH COACH LINES, *EDINBURGH*	203

EDWARDS BROS, *TIERS CROSS*	219
EDWARDS CAR & COACH HIRE, *LONG EATON*	164
EDWARDS COACHES, *LLANTWIT FARDRE*	221
GEORGE EDWARDS & SON, *BWLCHYWYN*	223
L J EDWARDS COACH HIRE, *HAILSHAM*	113
EIREBUS LTD, *DUBLIN*	227
ELCOCK REISEN LTD, *MADELEY*	168
ELITE SERVICES LTD, *STOCKPORT*	122
ELIZABETH YULE, *PITLOCHRY*	209
ELLENDERS COACHES, *SHEFFIELD*	172
ELLIS COACHES, *LLANGEFNI*	213
P & J ELLIS LTD, *LONDON NW10*	147
ELLISON'S COACHES, *ASHTON KEYNES*	194
ELTHAM EXECUTIVE CHARTER, *LONDON SE9*	147
EMBLINGS COACHES, *GUYHIRN*	92
EMMERSON COACHES, *IMMINGHAM*	156
EMMAS COACHES, *DOLGELLAU*	218
EMPRESS COACHES LTD, *ST LEONARDS-ON-SEA*	113
EMPRESS MOTORS LTD, *LONDON E2*	147
EMSWORTH & DISTRICT, *SOUTHBOURNE*	126
ENDEAVOUR COACHES, *BIRMINGHAM*	185
ENFIELD COACHES, *ENFIELD, Co MEATH*	228
ENNIS COACHES, *MATLOCK*	102
ENSIGNBUS COMPANY, *PURFLEET*	117
ENTERPRISE TRAVEL, *DARLINGTON*	111
EPSOM COACHES GROUP, *EPSOM*	180
ERB SERVICES, *BYKER*	182
ESSBEE COACHES, *COATBRIDGE*	207
EST BUS LTD, *LLANDOW*	222
EUROLINK FOLKESTONE	134
EUROSUN COACHES, *CROMER*	155
EUROTAXIS, *BRISTOL*	89
EUROLINERS, *REDNAL, BIRMINGHAM*	185
GARETH EVANS COACHES, *BRYNAMMAN*	215
EVE CARS & COACHES, *DUNBAR*	202
EXCALIBUR COACHES, *LONDON SE15*	117
EXCALIBUR COACH TRAVEL, *SOUTHMINSTER*	147
EXCEL PASSENGER LOGISTICS LTD, *STANSTED AIRPORT*	117
EXCELSIOR COACHES LTD, *BOURNEMOUTH*	109
EXPERT COACH SERVICES LTD, *GRIMSBY*	156
EXPRESS MOTORS, *PENYGROES, CAERNARFON*	218
EXPRESSLINES LTD, *BEDFORD*	86
EXPRESSWAY COACHES, *ROTHERHAM*	172
F	
FAHERTY'S COACH HIRE, *MOYCULLEN, Co GALWAY*	228
FAIRWAY TRAVEL, *EDINBURGH*	202
FALCON TRAVEL, *SHEPPERTON*	153
FARELINE BUS & COACH SERVICES, *EYE*	178
FARESAVER BUSES, *CHIPPENHAM*	194
FARGO COACHLINES, *BRAINTREE*	117
FARLEIGH COACHES, *ROCHESTER*	134
FARNHAM COACHES, *FARNHAM*	180
FELIX BUS SERVICES LTD, *STANLEY, DERBYS*	102
FENN HOLIDAYS LTD, *MARCH*	92
FERNLEAF COACHES, *MORDEN*	180

FERRERS COACHES LTD, *SOUTH WOODHAM FERRERS*	118
FERRYMAN TRAVEL, *LEYBOURNE*	134
FFOSHELIG COACHES, *CARMARTHEN*	215
DAVID FIELD, *NEWENT*	121
FIFE SCOTTISH OMNIBUSES LTD, *COWDENBEATH*	203
FILER'S COACHES, *PENSFORD, Nr BRISTOL*	89
FILERS TRAVEL, *ILFRACOMBE*	105
FINEGAN COACH HIRE, *CARRICKMACROSS, Co MONAGHAN*	228
FINGLANDS COACHWAYS, *RUSHOLME*	122
DECLAN FINNEGAN, *KENMARE, Co KERRY*	228
EUGENE FINNEGAN (TRANSPORT), *BRAY, Co WICKLOW*	228
FIRST IN ABERDEEN	198
FIRST BERKSHIRE, *BRACKNELL*	87
FIRST BRADFORD	190
FIRST CHOICE TRAVEL, *PETERBOROUGH*	92
FIRST BRISTOL, *WESTON-SUPER-MARE*	89
FIRST CYMRU, *SWANSEA*	222
FIRST IN CHESTER & THE WIRRAL	95, 151
FIRST IN DEVON & CORNWALL	105
FIRST EASTERN COUNTIES, *NORWICH*	155
FIRST EDINBURGH	202
FIRST ESSEX BUSES, *CHELMSFORD*	118
FIRST, *GLASGOW*	204
FIRST HALIFAX, *HALIFAX*	191
FIRST HAMPSHIRE & DORSET LTD, *SOUTHAMPTON*	126
FIRST IN HUDDERSFIELD	191
FIRST IN LEEDS	191
FIRST LEICESTER	141
FIRST LONDON	147
FIRST IN MANCHESTER, *OLDHAM*	123
FIRST NORTHAMPTON	161
FIRST POTTERIES	176
FIRST IN SCOTLAND EAST	203, 206
FIRST SOMERSET & AVON, *WESTON-SUPER-MARE*	170
FIRST SOUTH YORKS, *ROTHERHAM*	172
FIRST IN WYVERN, *WORCESTER*	196
FIRST YORK	158
FIRSTGROUP PLC	85
FISHERS TOURS, *DUNDEE*	201
JOHN FISHWICK & SONS, *LEYLAND*	138
FITZCHARLES COACHES LTD, *GRANGEMOUTH*	210
FIVE STAR GROUP TRAVEL, *LIVERPOOL*	151
JOHN FLANAGAN COACH TRAVEL, *GRAPPENHALL, WARRINGTON*	95
FLIGHTS HALLMARK, *BIRMINGHAM*	185
FLYGHT TRAVEL, *COSHAM*	126
FOCUS COACHES, *PRESTON*	138
FORDS COACHES, *ALTHORNE*	118
FOREST COACHES, *LONDON E6*	147
FORESTDALE COACHES LTD, *CROYDON*	147
FORGET-ME-NOT (TRAVEL) LTD, *IPSWICH*	178
FORMBY COACHWAYS LTD, *FORMBY*	151
FOUNTAIN EXECUTIVE, *ABERDEEN*	198
FOUR GIRLS COACHES, *PONTYBODKIN*	217

FOWLERS TRAVEL, *HOLBEACH DROVE*	143
TOM FOX, *ROCKCORRY, Co MONAGHAN*	228
FRASER EAGLE LTD, *PADIHAM*	138
FREEBIRD, *BURY*	123
FREEBIRD, *TOTTINGTON*	138
FREESTONES COACHES, *BEETLEY*	155
JAMES FRENCH & SON, *EYEMOUTH*	200
FRODINGHAM COACHES, *DRIFFIELD*	115
MARTIN FUREY COACHES LTD, *DRUMCLIFFE, Co SLIGO*	228
L. FURNESS & SONS, *HIGH GREEN*	172

G

G & S TRAVEL, *RAMSGATE*	134
G. J. TRAVEL LTD, *OTTERSHAW*	180
G. M. COACHES, *CEFN CRIBWR*	213
G. P. D. TRAVEL, *HEYWOOD*	134
GAIN TRAVEL EXPERIENCE LTD, *BRADFORD*	191
GALES COACHES LTD, *HASLEMERE*	180
GALLEON TRAVEL LTD, *HUNSDON*	129
GALLOWAY EUROPEAN, *MENDLESHAM*	178
GALSON-STORNOWAY, *ISLE OF LEWIS*	211
GALVINS COACHES, *DUNMANWAY, Co CORK*	228
GANGE'S COACHES, *COWES*	132
GARDINERS TRAVEL, *SPENNYMOOR*	111
GARELOCHEAD COACHES	199
GARETH EVANS COACHES, *BRYNAMMAN*	215
GARNETT'S COACHES, *BISHOP AUCKLAND*	111
BRYAN GARRATT/COACHMASTER, *LEICESTER*	141
GARRETT COACHES LTD, *NEWTON ABBOT*	105
GARY'S COACHES OF TREDEGAR	213
STANLEY GATH COACHES LTD, *DEWSBURY*	191
GATWICK FLYER, *ROMFORD*	118
GEE-VEE TRAVEL, *BARNSLEY*	172
GEMINI TRAVEL, *IPSWICH*	178
GEMINI TRAVEL, *MARCHWOOD*	126
GENIAL TRAVEL, *STANWAY*	118
BEN GEORGE TRAVEL, *BRIGG*	156
GHA COACHES, *CORWEN*	217
JAMES GIBSON & SON, *MOFFAT*	201
GILES TOURS, *NEWTOWNARDS*	225
GILLEN COACHES, *PORT GLASGOW*	205
R G GITTINS, *WELSHPOOL*	220
G-LINE, *St ANNES ON SEA*	138
GLEN COACHES LTD, *GREENOCK*	205
GLENTANA COACHES LTD, *LINLITHGOW*	211
GLENVIC OF BRISTOL LTD	90
GLENWAY COACHES, *DEWSBURY*	191
GLIDER TRAVEL, *BROWNHILLS*	185
G-LINE MINICOACHES, *SWINDON*	194
GLOBE COACHES, *ABERDARE*	221
GLOVERS COACHES LTD, *ASHBOURNE*	102
GLYN WILLIAMS TRAVEL, *BLACKWOOD*	214
JAMES GLYNN, *NURNEY*	228
GLYNNS COACH HIRE (ENNIS) LTD	228
GO NORTH EAST, *GATESHEAD*	183
GO-AHEAD GROUP	85
J D GODSON, *CROSSGATES*	191
PETER GODWARD COACHES, *SOUTH WOODHAM FERRERS*	118
GOLD STANDARD, THE, *GREENFORD*	147, 153
GOLD STAR COACHES, *TORQUAY*	106
GOLD STAR TRAVEL, *BROMSGROVE*	196
GOLDEN BOY COACHES (JETSIE LTD), *HODDESDON*	129
GOLDEN EAGLE COACHES, *SALSBURGH*	207
GOLDEN GREEN LUXURY TOURS, LONGNOR, *BUXTON*	102
GOLDEN PIONEER TRAVEL, *HEREFORD*	128
GOLDENSTAND SOUTHERN LTD, *LONDON, NW10*	147
GOODE COACHES, *NORTHAMPTON*	161
GOODE'S COACHWAYS, *WEDNESBURY*	185
W. C. GOODSIR, *HOLYHEAD*	213
GOODWIN'S COACHES, *BRAINTREE*	118
W. GORDON & SONS, *ROTHERHAM*	172
GOSPEL'S COACHES, *HUCKNALL*	164
G. W. GOULDING, *KNOTTINGLEY*	191
GRA-CAR COACHES, *FEATHERSTONE*	191
GRAHAM URQUHART TRAVEL, *INVERNESS*	205
VIOLET GRAHAM COACHES, *PAISLEY*	209
GRAHAM'S COACHES, *BRISTOL*	90
GRAHAM'S, *KELVEDON*	118
GRAND HOTEL TOURS, *SANDOWN*	132
GRAMPIAN COACHES, *ABERDEEN*	198
GRAND PRIX COACHES, *BROUGH*	99
GRANGEWOOD TRAVEL, *POTTER HEIGHAM*	155
GRANT PALMER PASSENGER SERVICES, *DUNSTABLE*	86
GRAVES COACHES, *BROXBOURNE*	130
GRAY'S TRAVEL OF COVENTRY	185
GRAYLINE COACHES (HARTWOOL) LTD, *BICESTER*	166
GRAYLINE TOURS, *DUBLIN*	228
GRAYS LUXURY TRAVEL, *HOYLAND COMMON*	172
GRAYSCROFT BUS SERVICES LTD, *MABLETHORPE*	143
A. GREEN (COACHES) LTD, *WALTHAMSTOW*	147
GREEN BUS SERVICE (WARSTONE MOTORS), *GREAT WYRLEY*	177
GRETTON'S COACHES, *PETERBOROUGH*	92
GREY DE LUXE COACHES, *HULL*	115
GREYHOUND COACHES CO, *CARDIFF*	214
GREYS OF ELY	92
GRIERSONS COACHES, *STOCKTON-ON-TEES*	111
GRIFFITHS COACHES, *PORTDINORWIC*	218
JEFF GRIFFITHS COACHES, *ST ANNES*	138
GRIMSHAW COACHES, *BURNLEY*	138
GRINDLES COACHES LTD, *CINDERFORD*	121
GROUP TRAVEL, *BODMIN*	97
GROVE COACHES, *HERTFORD*	130
GRWP ABERCONWY, *LLANDUDNO*	216
GUSCOTT'S COACHES LTD, *BEAWORTHY*	106
GWYN JONES (MEIFORD), *MYFORD*	220
GWYN WILLIAMS & SONS LTD, *LOWER TUMBLE*	215
GWYNFOR COACHES, *LLANGEFNI*	213

H

HAGUES COACHES, *ROTHERHAM*	173

HAILSTONE TRAVEL, *LITTLE BURSTEAD*	118
PHIL HAINES COACHES, *BOSTON*	143
MIKE HALFORD, *BRIDPORT*	109
A. HALPENNY, BLACKROCK, *DUNDALK*	228
HALTON BOROUGH TRANSPORT LTD, *WIDNES*	95
O. J. HAMBLY & SONS LTD, *LOOE*	97
HAMILTON OF UXBRIDGE	151
R. HANDLEY & SONS LTD, *MIDDLEHAM*	156
HAPPY AL'S COACHES, *BIRKENHEAD*	151
HAPPY DAYS COACHES, *WHITCHURCH*	168
HAPPY DAYS COACHES, *STAFFORD*	176
HAPPY WANDERER TRAVEL, *BIRMINGHAM*	185
HARDINGS COACHES, *BETCHWORTH*	180
HARDINGS INTERNATIONAL, *REDDITCH*	186
HARDINGS TOURS LTD, *HUYTON*	151
HARDYS, *ILFRACOMBE*	106
HARGREAVES COACHES, *HEBDEN, Nr SKIPTON*	158
HARLEQUIN TRAVEL, *IPSWICH*	178
R. J. HARLEY, *MARLBOROUGH*	194
HARPUR'S COACHES, *DERBY*	102
HARRIS COACHES, *BLACKWOOD*	214
HARRIS COACHES, *GRAYS*	118
HARRIS COACHES, *TARBERT*	212
HARRIS EXECUTIVE TRAVEL, *BROMSGROVE*	196
HARRISON'S TRAVEL, *ALFRETON*	102
D & H HARROD (COACHES) LTD, *KING'S LYNN*	155
HARROGATE & DISTRICT TRAVEL LTD	159
HARWOOD COACHES, *WEYBRIDGE*	180
K. G. & R. HATTON, *ST HELENS*	151
HATTS COACHES, *CHIPPENHAM*	194
HAWKES COACHES LTD, *SWANSEA*	222
HAYS COACHES, *HUNTLY*	198
HAYDN'S TOURS & TRAVEL, *CHIRK*	223
HAYTON'S COACHES, *BURNAGE*	123
HAYWARD TRAVEL (CARDIFF)	222
HAYWARDS COACHES, *NEWBURY*	87
HAYWARDS COACHES, *BASINGSTOKE*	126
HEALINGS INTERNATIONAL COACHES, *OLDHAM*	123
HEALY COACHES, *GALWAY*	228
HEARD'S COACHES, *BIDEFORD*	106
HEARNS COACHES, *HARROW WEALD*	148
HEATON'S OF SHEFFIELD	173
HEBRIDEAN COACHES, *LOCHBOISDALE*	212
HEDINGHAM & DISTRICT OMNIBUSES LTD, *SIBLE HEDINGHAM*	118
HELLYERS OF FAREHAM	126
HEMMINGS COACHES, *HOLSWORTHY*	106
HENDERSON HIRING, *TARBERT*	199
HENLEYS BUS SERVICES, *ABERTILLERY*	213
HENRY CRAWFORD COACHES LTD, *NEILSTON*	202
HENSHAWS COACHES, *JACKSDALE*	164
HERBERTS TRAVEL, *SHEFFORD*	86
HERITAGE TOURS, *ST MARY'S, ISLES OF SCILLY*	224
HERRINGTON COACHES LTD, *FORDINGBRIDGE*	126
HEYFORDIAN TRAVEL LTD, *BICESTER*	166
HI-DECK EUROCRUISERS, *WESTBURY*	195
HIGHLAND HERITAGE, *DALLMALLY*	200
HIGHLAND ROVER COACHES, *TAYNUILT*	200
HIGHWAYMAN COACHES, *PERTH*	208
HILLS OF HERSHAM, *HERSHAM*	180
HILLS SERVICES, *TORRINGTON*	106
HILLARYS COACHES, *PRUDHOE*	162
DEREK HIRCOCKS COACHES, *UPWELL, Nr WISBECH*	92
JOHN HOBAN TRAVEL LTD, *WORKINGTON*	99
HODDER MOTOR SERVICES LTD, *CLITHEROE*	139
HODGE'S COACHES (SANDHURST) LTD, *SANDHURST*	88
HODGSONS COACHES, *BARNARD CASTLE*	111
HODSON COACHES LTD, *NAVENBY*	143
M. HOGAN, *THURLES, Co TIPPERARY*	228
HOGG EUROPEAN COACHES, *SHEFFIELD*	173
HOLLINSHEAD COACHES LTD, *BIDDULPH*	176
HOLLOWAY COACHES LTD, *SCUNTHORPE*	157
J. R. HOLLYHEAD INTERNATIONAL, *WILLENHALL*	186
G & J HOLMES, *CLAY CROSS*	103
HOLMES GROUP TRAVEL, *NEWPORT*	168
HOLMESWOOD COACHES LTD, *ORMSKIRK*	139
HOMEWARD BOUND TRAVEL, *WIMBORNE*	109
HOOKWAYS GREENSLADES, *EXETER*	106
HOOKWAYS JENNINGS, *BUDE*	97
HOOKWAYS PLEASUREWAYS, *OKEHAMPTON*	106
HOPLEYS BUS & COACH, *TRURO*	97
HOPWOOD COACHES, *ASKHAM BRYAN, YORK*	159
HORNSBY TRAVEL, *SCUNTHORPE*	157
HORROCKS, *LYDBURY NORTH*	168
E & M HORSBURGH, *PUMPHERSTON*	211
HORSEMAN COACHES LTD, *READING*	88
JOHN HOUGHTON, *LONDON W5*	148
HOUNSLOW COMMUNITY TRANSPORT	153
HOUNSLOW MINI COACHES, *FELTHAM*	148
HOUSTON'S OF LONDON, *LONDON N15*	148
HOUSTOUN TRAVEL, *LIVINGSTON*	211
HOWIE'S OF ROBERTTOWN, *LIVERSEDGE*	191
HOWLETTS COACHES, *WINSLOW*	91
JIM HUGHES COACHES, *SUNDERLAND*	183
VIC HUGHES & SON LTD, *FELTHAM*	153
HULLEYS OF BASLOW, *BAKEWELL*	103
HULME HALL COACHES LTD, *CHEADLE HULME*	95
HUMBLES COACHES, *SHILDON*	111
HUNTS TRAVEL, *ALFORD*	143
WILLIAM HUNTER, *LOANHEAD*	205
HUNTINGDON & DISTRICT	92
HUTCHISON'S COACHES (OVERTOWN) LTD, *WISHAW*	207
HUTTON COACH HIRE, *WESTON-SUPER-MARE*	170
J. F. HUXLEY, *MALPAS*	95
HYLTON & DAWSON, *GLENFIELD*	141
HYTHE & WATERSIDE COACHES, *HYTHE*	126

I

IAN BALDRY, *FELIXSTOWE*	177
IBT TRAVEL GROUP, *PRESTWICK*	209
ILLINGWORTH COACHES, *WAKEFIELD*	191
IMPACT OF LONDON, *GREENFORD*	148
IMPERIAL BUS CO LTD, *RAINHAM*	118
INDEPENDENT COACHWAYS LTD, *HORSFORTH*	191
INGLEBY'S LUXURY COACHES LTD, *YORK*	159

INTERNATIONAL COACH LINES LTD, THORNTON HEATH	148
IPSWICH BUSES LTD	178
IRELAND COACHES, Co DUBLIN	228
IRISH COACHES, DUBLIN	228
IRVINE'S OF LAW, LAW	207
IRVINGS COACH HIRE LTD, CARLISLE	100
BRIAN ISAAC COACHES LTD, SWANSEA	222
ISLAND COACH SERVICES, LAKE, IoW	132
ISLAND COACHWAYS, ST PETER PORT	224
ISLE COACHES, OWSTON FERRY	173
ISLE OF MAN TRANSPORT, DOUGLAS	212
ISLE OF WIGHT COUNCIL, NEWPORT	132
ISLEWORTH COACHES, HESTON	153
ISLWYN BOROUGH TRANSPORT LTD, BLACKWOOD	214
IVYBRIDGE & DISTRICT, IVYBRIDGE	106

J

J & C COACHES, NEWTON AYCLIFFE	111
J & D EURO TRAVEL, HARROW	153
J & Y COACHES, CLITHEROE	139
J B C MALVERNIAN TOURS, MALVERN	196
J C S COACHES, CORBY	161
J R J COACHES, CORBY	161
J R TRAVEL, YORK	159
J W COACHES LTD, BANCHORY	198
JACKSON'S COACHES, BLACKPOOL	139
ANDREW JAMES QUALITY TRAVEL, CHIPPENHAM	195
BRODYR JAMES, TREGARON	216
JAMES KING COACHES, NEWTON STEWART	201
JAMES MEFFAN LTD, KIRRIEMUIR	199
PAUL JAMES COACHES, COALVILLE	141
R. G. JAMIESON & SON, YELL	209
JANS COACHES, SOHAM, ELY	93
JAYLINE BAND SERVICES, HORDEN,	111
JAYCREST LTD, SITTINGBOURNE	134
JEFFS COACHES LTD, TOWCESTER	162
JEMS TRAVEL, STANNINGTON	173
JENSON TRAVEL, PONTYPOOL	222
JOHN MORROW COACHES, GLASGOW	204
JOHN'S COACHES, BLANEAU-FFESTINIOG	218
JOHN'S TRAVEL, WREXHAM	223
BEN JOHNSON, BRANDESBURTON	115
JOHNSON'S TOURS, HODTHORPE	164
JOHNSONS COACH & BUS TRAVEL, HENLEY-IN-ARDEN	186
D JONES & SON, RHOSLLANERCRUGOG	223
E JONES & SONS, PONCIAU	223
JONES EXECUTIVE COACHES LTD, WALKDEN	123
JONES INTERNATIONAL, LLANDEILO	215
JONES MOTOR SERVICES, FLINT	217
JONES MOTORS (LOGIN) LTD, WHITLAND	215
O. R. JONES & SONS LTD, LLANFAETHLU	213
P. W. JONES COACHES, HEREFORD	128
W E JONES & SON, LLANERCHYMEDD	213
JOSEPHS MINI COACHES, NEWCASTLE-UNDER-LYME	176
DONAL JOYCE MINIBUS HIRE, GALWAY	228

JUMBO MINI COACHES, NOTTINGHAM	164

K

K & B TRAVEL, CLIBURN	100
K & S COACHES, MANSFIELD	164
K. M. MOTORS LTD, BARNSLEY	173
KARDAN TRAVEL, COWES, IoW	132
BERNARD KAVANAGH & SONS LTD, URLINGFORD	228
J. J. KAVANAGH & SONS, URLINGFORD	228
M. KAVANAGH, TIPPERARY	229
PIERCE KAVANAGH COACHES, URLINGFORD	229
KEENAN OF AYR COACH TRAVEL, COALHALL	209
KEENAN COMMERCIALS, DUNDALK, CO LOUTH	229
KEIGHLEY & DISTRICT TRAVEL	192
KENNEALLY'S BUS SERVICE LTD, WATERFORD	229
KENNEDY COACHES, LOCHS	212
KENNEDY COACHES, TRALEE	229
KENT COACH TOURS LTD, ASHFORD	134
KENT COUNTY COUNCIL, AYLESFORD	134
KENZIES COACHES LTD, ROYSTON	130
K. M. KEOGH, ARKLOW	229
KERRY COACHES, KILLARNEY, Co KERRy	229
KESTREL COACHES, STOURPORT ON SEVERN	196
KETTLEWELL (RETFORD) LTD	164
R. KIME & CO LTD, FOLKINGHAM	144
KINCH BUS LTD, HEANOR	103
KINEIL COACHES, FRASERBURGH	198
JAMES KING COACHES, NEWTON STEWART	201
KINGDOM COACHES, LEVEN	203
KINGDOM'S TOURS LTD, TIVERTON	106
KINGFISHER MINICOACHES, READING	88
KINGS COACHES, STANWAY	118
THE KINGS FERRY, GILLINGHAM	134
KINGS LUXURY COACHES, MIDDLESBROUGH	159
KINGSNORTON COACHES, BIRMINGHAM	186
KINGSLEY COACHES, BIRTLEY	183
KINGSMAN INTERNATIONAL TRAVEL, FAVERSHAM	134
KINGSTON COACHES, SALISBURY	195
KINGSWINFORD COACHWAYS, BRIERLY HILL	186
KIRBYS COACHES, RAYLEIGH	118
KIRKBY LONSDALE COACH HIRE, CARNFORTH	139
KIWI LUXURY TRAVEL, NEWTON STEWART	201
KMP LLANBERIS LTD	218
KONECTBUS, DEREHAM	155
K-VALLEY MINI-COACHES, WOKING	180

L

LADYBIRD TRAVEL, WORKINGTON	100
LADYLINE, RAWMARSH	173
LAKELAND TOURS, TEMPO, Co FERMANAGH	225
LAKELINE COACHES, KNIGHTON	220
LAKES SUPERTOURS, WINDERMERE	100
LAKESIDE COACHES, ELLESMERE (SHROPSHIRE)	168
LAMBS COACHES, STOCKPORT	123
LAMBERT'S COACHES (BECCLES) LTD	178
LANCASHIRE UNITED, BLACKBURN	139
LANGSTON & TASKER, BUCKINGHAM	91
LEANDER COACH TRAVEL, SWADLINCOTE	103
JOHN LEASK & SON, LERWICK	209

LEE'S COACHES, *LANGLEY MOOR*	111
LENDOR, *MOSSLEY*	123
LEOLINE TRAVEL, *HAMPTON*	154
LEON MOTOR SERVICES LTD, *FINNINGLEY*	173
LEONS COACH TRAVEL, *STAFFORD*	176
LE-RAD COACHES & LIMOUSINES *WOODLEY Nr STOCKPORT*	95
LESCLACHA LTD, *NEWMARKET-ON-FERGUS*	229
LEVERS COACHES LTD, *SALISBURY*	195
LEWIS-RHYDLEWIS, *LLANDYSUL*	215
LEWIS TRAVEL UK, *LONDON SE1*	148
LEWIS'S COACHES, *LLANRHYSTUD*	216
LEWIS'S COACHES, *PAILTON*	184
LEWIS-Y-LLAN, *AMLWCH*	213
LIBERTON TRAVEL, *EDINBURGH*	203
ARNOLD LIDDELL COACHES, *BRISTOL*	90
LIDDELL'S COACHES, *AUCHINLECK*	202
LINK LINE COACHES LTD, *LONDON*	148
LINKFAST LTD T/A S&M COACHES, *BENFLEET*	118
LISKEARD & DISTRICT OMNIBUS CO LTD, *LAUNCESTON*	97
LITTLE BUS COMPANY, THE, *ELSTREE*	148
LITTLE JIM'S BUSES, *BERKHAMSTED*	130
LITTLE TRANSPORT LTD, *ILKESTON*	103
LIVERPOOL CITY COACHES	152
LLEW JONES INTERNATIONAL, *LLANWRST*	216
P&O LLOYD, *BAGILLT*	217
LLOYDS COACHES, *MACHYNLLETH*	220
LOCHS MOTOR TRANSPORT LTD, *LEWIS*	212
LOCHS & GLENS HOLIDAYS, *GARTOCHAN*	211
LODGE COACHES, *HIGH EASTER*	119
LOGANS EXECUTIVE TRAVEL, *DUNLOY*	225
LOGANS TOURS, *NORTHFLEET GREEN*	135
LONDON BUSES, *LONDON E8*	148
LONDON CENTRAL, *MITCHAM*	148
LONDON GENERAL, *MITCHAM*	148
LONDONDERRY & LOUGH SWILLY, *LONDONDERRY*	225
LONDON UNITED BUSWAYS LTD, *TWICKENHAM*	154
DAVE LONG COACH TRAVEL, *SKIBBEREEN*	229
LONG'S COACHES LTD, *SALSBURGH*	207
LONGMYND TRAVEL, *SHREWSBURY*	168
J. J. LONGSTAFF & SONS LTD, *DEWSBURY*	192
LONGSTAFF'S COACHES, *MORPETH*	162
LOTHIAN BUSES, *EDINBURGH*	203
LOVERINGS COACHES (see TAW & TORRIDGE)	107
LUAS, *DUBLIN*	229
LUCKETTS TRAVEL, *FAREHAM*	126
LUDLOWS OF HALESOWEN	186
LUGG VALLEY PRIMROSE TRAVEL, *LEOMINSTER*	128
LUXURY MINI COACH, *GREENFORD*	149, 154
A. LYLES & SON, *BATLEY*	192

M

M. LINE INTERNATIONAL COACHES, *ALLOA*	200
M & B COACHES & MINIBUSES, *TELFORD*	168
M & E COACHES, *HERSHAM*	180
M & H COACHES, *DENBIGH*	217
M & J TRAVEL, *CRAVEN ARMS*	168
M & M COACH LINES, *HARROW WEALD*	154
M & S COACHES, *LEOMINSTER*	128
M C H MINIBUSES, *UXBRIDGE*	154
M C T GROUP TRAVEL LTD, *MOTHERWELL*	207
M D COACH HIRE, *DUBLIN*	229
M P MINICOACHES, *TELFORD*	168
M T P CHARTER COACHES, *LONDON E11*	149
MAC TOURS LTD, *EDINBURGH*	203
MacEWAN'S COACH SERVICES, *AMISFIELD*	201
STANLEY MACKAY COACHES, *BONNYRIGG*	203
NEIL MacKELLAIG, *GLASGOW*	204
MACKIE'S COACHES OF ALLOA, *ALLOA*	200
DUNCAN MacLENAN, *STRATH-CARRON*	205
MacPHAILS COACHES, *MOTHERWELL*	201
MacPHERSON COACHES LTD, *SWADLINCOTE*	103
MAGPIE TRAVEL, HIGH *WYCOMBE*	91
MAIRS COACHES, *ABERDEEN*	198
MAISEY, *PONTYPRIDD*	221
MALCYS, *SHEFFIELD*	173
GERALD MANNING, CROOM, *LIMERICK*	229
MANOR TRAVEL, *BEEFORD*	115
MANSFIELD'S COACHES, *SWINDON*	195
MARBILL COACH SERVICES LTD, *BEITH*	206
MARCHANTS COACHES LTD, *CHELTENHAM*	121
MARCHWOOD MOTORWAYS LTD, *TOTTON*	126
MARPLE MINI COACHES	95
MARSHALLS COACHES, *LEIGHTON BUZZARD*	86, 149
MARSHALLS OF SUTTON-ON-TRENT, *NEWARK*	164
ALAN MARTIN COACHES, *DUBLIN*	229
WALTER MARTIN COACHES, *SHEFFIELD*	173
MARTIN'S OF TYSOE	184
MARTIN'S COACH TRAVEL, *LIVINGSTON*	211
MARTINS COACHES, *LONDON*	149
MARTINS COACHES, *CHAPELTOWN*	173
MARTINS COACHES, *KETTERING*	162
MARTINS SELF DRIVE, *REDFIELD*	90
MARTIN'S COACHES, *CAVAN*	229
MASS TRANSIT, *ANSTON*	173
MASTER TRAVEL, *WELWYN GARDEN CITY*	130
MATTHEWS COACHES, *KINGS LYNN*	155
MAUDES COACHES, *BARNARD CASTLE*	111
MAUN CRUSADER TOURS, *SUTTON-IN-ASHFIELD*	164
MAYDAY TRAVEL, *CROYDON*	180
MAYFIELD COACHES	173
MAYNE COACHES LTD, *WARRINGTON*	95
A MAYNE & SON, *CLAYTON, MANCHESTER*	123
MAYNES COACHES, *BUCKIE*	206
MAYPOLE COACHES, *MELLING*	152
ROY McCARTHY COACHES, *MACCLESFIELD*	95
McCOLLS OF ARGYLL, *DUNOON*	200
McCOLLS COACHES, *ALEXANDRIA*	211
P. J. McCONNON, *MONAGHAN*	229
McCULLOCH AND SON, *STRANRAER*	201
JAMES McGEE (BUSES), *LETTERKENNY*	229
JOHN McGINLEY COACHES, *LETTERKENNY, Co DONEGAL*	229
McKECHNIE OF BATHGATE LTD	211
McKENDRY TRAVEL, *LOANHEAD*	206
McKINDLESS EXPRESS, *WISHAW*	207

McLAUGHLIN'S TOURS, *PENWORTHAM*	139
McLEANS COACHES, *WITNEY*	166
MEADWAY PRIVATE HIRE, *BIRMINGHAM*	186
MICHAEL MEERE COACH HIRE, *ENNIS*	229
MEGABUS, *PERTH*	208
MEMORY LANE COACHES, *OLD BOLINGBROKE*	144
MEMORY LANE VINTAGE OMNIBUS SERVICES, *MAIDENHEAD*	84
MEREDITHS COACHES, *MALPAS*	96
MERLYN'S COACHES (SKEWEN) LTD	219
MERTON COMMUNITY TRANSPORT, *MITCHAM*	180
MERVYN'S COACHES, *MICHELDEVER*	127
MESSENGER COACHES, *ASPATRIA*	100
METRO COACHES, *STOCKTON-ON-TEES*	159
METROBUS LTD, *CRAWLEY*	189
METROLINE TRAVEL LTD, *HARROW*	154
METROLINK, *MANCHESTER*	123
MID DEVON COACHES, *CREDITON*	106
MIDLAND BUS CO LTD, *ATHLONE*	229
MIDLAND METRO, *WEDNESBURY*	187
MID WALES TRAVEL, *PENRHYNCOCH*	216
MIDWAY MOTORS, *CRYMYCH*	220
MIKES COACHES, *BASILDON*	119
MIL-KEN TRAVEL LTD, *LITTLEPORT*	93
MIL-KEN TRAVEL LTD, *NEWMARKET*	178
KEN MILLER TRAVEL, *SHENSTONE*	186
MILLER'S COACHES, *AIRDRIE*	207
MILLIGANS COACH TRAVEL, *MAUCHLINE*	209
MILLMAN COACHES, *GRIMSBY*	157
MILLMAN'S OF *WARRINGTON*	96
MILLPORT MOTORS LTD	206
ALEX MILNE, *NEW BYTH*	199
MINIBUS & COACH HIRE, *EARL STONHAM*	178
MINIBUS SERVICES, *WATFORD*	130
MINI-BUS SHUTTLE SERVICE, *LONDON SW1*	149
MINSTERLEY MOTORS, *SHREWSBURY*	168
MK METRO LTD, *MILTON KEYNES*	91
MOFFAT & WILLIAMSON LTD, *GAULDRY*	203
MOOR TO SEA, *NEWTON ABBOT*	106
MOORE'S COACHES LTD, *HOLMES CHAPEL*	96
MOORLAND BUSES, *WESTON COYNEY*	176
JOE MORONEY, *ENNIS*	220
MORRIS TRAVEL, *CARMARTHEN*	215
JOHN MORROW COACHES, *GLASGOW*	204
MORTON'S COACH, *DUBLIN*	230
MOSLEYS TOURS, *DEWSBURY*	173
MOTTS COACHES (AYLESBURY) LTD, *AYLESBURY*	91
MOUNTAIN GOAT LTD, *WINDERMERE*	100
MOUNTS BAY COACHES, *PENZANCE*	97
C. W. MOXON LTD, *OLDCOTES*	164
MUIRS COACHES, *DOUGLAS WATER*	210
MULLEYS MOTORWAYS LTD, *IXWORTH*	178
MUNRO'S OF JEDBURGH	200
THOMAS MURPHY & SONS, *BRAY, Co WICKLOW*	230
GAVIN MURRAY & ELLISONS COACHES, *ST HELENS*	152
MYKANN COACH HIRE, *SWADLINCOTE*	103
MYTTON TRAVEL, *MINSTERLEY*	168

N

NASHS COACHES LTD, *SMETHWICK*	186
NATIONAL EXPRESS GROUP PLC	85
NATIONAL EXPRESS LTD, *EDGBASTON*	186
NATIONAL HOLIDAYS, *HULL*	115
NAUGHTON COACH TOURS, *SPIDDAL*	230
N. C. B. MOTORS LTD, *WEM*	168
NEAL'S TRAVEL LTD, *ISLEHAM, ELY*	93
NEFYN COACHES, NEFYN, *PWLLHELI*	218
NEIL MACKELLAIG, *GLASGOW*	204
NELSON & SON (GLYNNEATH) LTD, *NEATH*	219
W. H. NELSON (COACHES) LTD, *WICKFORD*	119
NESBIT BROS LTD, *MELTON MOWBRAY*	141
NESTORBUS LTD, *GALWAY & DUBLIN*	230
NEVILLE'S TOURS, *SUTTON COLDFIELD*	186
NEW BHARAT COACHES LTD, *SOUTHALL*	149
NEW ENTERPRISE COACHES, *TONBRIDGE*	135
NEWBOURNE COACHES, *LEIGHTON BUZZARD*	149
NEWBURY COACHES, *LEDBURY*	128
NEWBURY & DISTRICT, *NEWBURY*	88
NEWBURY TRAVEL, *OLDBURY*	186
NEWPORT TRANSPORT LTD	219
M. W. NICOLL'S COACH HIRE, *LAUREiNCEKIRK*	199
NIDDRIE COACHES, *MIDDLEWICH*	96
NIELSEN TRAVEL SERVICES, *SHEFFIELD*	173
NIGEL JACKSON TRAVEL, *QUENIBOROUGH*	142
NITEFLITE BUS LEASING, *CLEVEDON*	170
NOLAN COACHES, *COOLOCK, DUBLIN*	230
NORFOLK GREEN, *KINGS LYNN*	155
NORTH BIRMINGHAM BUSWAYS LTD, *ERDINGTON*	187
NORTH SOMERSET COACHES, *NAILSEA*	99
NORTHERN BLUE, *BURNLEY*	139
NORTH WEST COACHES & LIMOS, *THORNTON CLEVELEYS*	139
NORTON MINI TRAVEL, *STOCKTON-ON-TEES*	112
NOTTINGHAM CITY TRANSPORT LTD	164
NOTTINGHAM EXPRESS TRANSIT	164
NOTTS & DERBY TRACTION CO LTD, *HEANOR*	103
NU-VENTURE COACHES LTD, *AYLESFORD*	135

O

OTS MINIBUS & COACH HIRE, *CONSTANTINE*	97
O'CONNELL COACHES, *BALLINASLOE*	230
O'CONNOR AUTOTOURS LTD, *KILLARNEY*	230
TOM O'CONNOR, *TRALEE*	230
FEDA O'DONNELL, *DONEGAL*	230
O'FLAHERTY TRANSPORT, *LISDOONVARNA*	230
LARRRY O'HARA, *WATERFORD*	230
O'MALLEY COACHES, *NEWPORT, Co TIPPERARY*	230
O'S COACHES, *HOSPITAL, Co LIMERICK*	230
O'SULLIVANS COACHES, *MALLOW, Co CORK*	230
OARE'S COACHES, *HOLYWELL*	217
OBAN & DISTRICT BUSES LTD	200
OCEAN COACHES, *PORTSLADE*	113
DAVID OGDEN COACHES, *ST HELENS*	152
OLYMPIA TRAVEL, *HINDLEY*	140
OLYMPIAN COACHES LTD, *HARLOW*	119
THE ORIGINAL LONDON TOUR, *WANDSWORTH*	149
ORKNEY COACHES, *KIRKWALL*	208

OWEN'S MOTORS LTD, *KNIGHTON*	220
OWENS COACHES, *OSWESTRY*	168
OXFORD BUS COMPANY	166
OXFORD INTERNATIONAL, *BASINGSTOKE*	166

P

P&M COACHES, *WICKFORD*	119
DAVID PALMER COACHES LTD, *NORMANTON*	192
PARAGON TRAVEL, *UTTOXETER*	176
PARAMOUNT MINI-COACHES, *PLYMOUTH*	106
PARK TOURS AND TRAVEL (MOUNTAIN GOAT), *WINDERMERE*	100
PARK'S OF HAMILTON	210
PARKERS COACHES, *SWADLINCOTE*	103
PARKSIDE TRAVEL, *BROXBOURNE*	130
PARRYS INTERNATIONAL TOURS LTD, *CHESLYN HAY*	176
PASSENGER TRANSPORT LOGISTICS LTD, *MILTON KEYNES*	91
PAT'S COACHES, *NEW BROUGHTON*	223
T PATERSON & BROWN LTD, *KILBIRNIE*	206
PATHFINDER MASONS, *WILLENHALL*	187
PATRON TRAVEL, *FLINTHAM*	164
PAUL'S TRAVEL, *HUDDERSFIELD*	192
PAVILION COACHES, *HOVE*	114
D. A. PAYNE COACH HIRE, *ST NEOTS*	93
PAYNES COACHES & CAR HIRE LTD, *BUCKINGHAM*	91
PC COACHES OF LINCOLN	144
PEARCES PRIVATE HIRE, *WALLINGFORD*	166
PEARSON COACHES, *HULL*	115
PEELINGS COACHES, *KING'S LYNN*	155
PEGASUS COACHWAYS LTD, *RETFORD*	165
PEGASUS TRAVEL, *PERTH*	208
PENCOED TRAVEL LTD, *BRIDGEND*	214
PENMERE MINIBUS SERVICES, *FALMOUTH*	97
PENINSULA DRIVERS, *IVYBRIDGE*	107
PEOPLE'S EXPRESS, *WEST BROMWICH*	187
PERRY'S COACHES, *MALTON*	159
PERRYMAN BUSES, *BURNMOUTH*	200
PETER CAROL PRESTIGE COACHING, *WHITCHURCH, BRISTOL*	89
PETERBOROUGH TRAVEL CONSULTANTS *PETERBOROUGH*	93
PETE'S TRAVEL - see PEOPLES EXPRESS	
PEWSEY VALE COACHES, *PEWSEY*	195
PHILLIPS COACHES, *SOUTH WOODHAM FERRERS*	119
COLLIN PHILLIPSON MINICOACHES, *OUSEFLEET*	115,174
PICKERING COACHES, *SOUTH GODSTONE*	181
PIED BULL COACHES, *MOLD*	217
JOHN PIKE COACHES, *ANDOVER*	127
PLANET TRAVEL, *EARITH*	93
GEORGE PLANT, *BANTRY, Co CORK*	230
PLANTS LUXURY TRAVEL, *CHEADLE, STAFFS*	176
PLASTOWS COACHES, *WHEATLEY*	166
DAVID PLATT COACHES & MINITRAVEL OF LEES, *OLDHAM*	123
PLYMOUTH CITYBUS LTD	107
POOTS COACH HIRE, *TANDRAGEE*	225
PORTHCAWL OMNIBUS CO LTD	214
JOHN POWELL TRAVEL, *HELLABY*	174
POWELLS COACHES, *CREDITON*	107
POWELLS COACHES, *SHERBORNE*	109
JACKY POWER TOURS, *TRALEE*	230
POYNTERS COACHES, *ASHFORD, KENT*	135
PRE METRO, *KINGS NORTON*	187
PREMIER TRAVEL, *BRISTOL*	90
PRENTICE WESTWOOD, *WEST CALDER*	211
PRESTON BUS LTD	140
PRICES COACHES, *SOUTHSEA, WALES*	223
PRIMROSE COACHES OF CORNWALL, *HAYLE*	98
PRINCESS COACHES, *WEST END, SOUTHAMPTON*	127
PRIORY MOTOR COACH CO LTD, *NORTH SHIELDS*	183
F PROCTER & SON LTD, *FENTON*	176
PROCTERS COACHES (NORTH YORKSHIRE), *LEEMING BAR*	159
PROSPECT COACHES (WEST) LTD, *STOURBRIDGE*	187
PROTOURS (ISLE OF MAN), *DOUGLAS*	212
PROVENCE PRIVATE HIRE, *ST ALBANS*	130
PULFREYS COACHES, *GRANTHAM*	144
PULLMAN COACHES LTD, *SWANSEA*	222
PULLMAN DINER , *KNOTTINGLEY*	192

Q

QUANTOCK MOTOR SERVICES, *TAUNTON*	170

R

R & B COACHES, *LUDLOW*	169
R. & R. COACHES LTD (BEELINE), *WARMINSTER*	194
R D H SERVICES, *PLUMPTON*	114
R. K. F. TRAVEL, *STROOD*	135
RADLEY COACH TRAVEL, *BRIGG*	157
RADMORES COACHES, *PLYMPTON*	107
RAINHAM COACH CO, THE, *GILLINGHAM*	135
RAMBLER COACHES, *HASTINGS*	114
RAMON TRAVEL, *BOSCOMBE*	109
RANGER TRAVEL, *SOUTH CROYDON*	181
RAPSONS GROUP, *INVERNESS*	205
RAYS COACHES, *PLYMOUTH*	107
RB TRAVEL, *PYTCHLEY*	162
READING & WOKINGHAM COACHES, *WOKINGHAM*	88
READING HERITAGE TRAVEL, *READING*	88
READING TRANSPORT LTD	88
REAYS COACHES LTD, *WIGTON*	100
RED ARROW COACHES LTD, *HUDDERSFIELD*	192
RED KITE COMMERCIAL SERVICES, *LEIGHTON BUZZARD*	87
RED ROSE TRAVEL LTD, *AYLESBURY*	91
REDROUTE BUSES, *NORTHFLEET*	135
REDBY BUS & COACH, *SUNDERLAND*	183
REDFERN COACHES (MANSFIELD) LTD	165
RED KITE COACHES, *ABERYSTWYTH*	216
REDLINE COACHES, *LEYLAND*	140
REDWING COACHES, *LONDON SE24*	149
REDWOODS TRAVEL, *CULLOMPTON*	107
REES MOTOR (TRAVEL), *LLANELLY HILL, ABERGAVENNY*	218
REEVES COACH HOLIDAYS, *CHORLEY*	140
REG'S COACHES LTD, *HERTFORD*	130

Operator Index

REGAL BUSWAYS, *CHELMSFORD*	119
REGENT COACHES, *WHITSTABLE*	135
REIDS OF RHYNIE, *RHYNIE, BY HUNTLY*	199
RELIANCE MOTOR SERVICES, *SUTTON-ON-FOREST*	159
RELIANT COACHES LTD, *HEATHER*	142
RENNIES OF DUNFERMLINE LTD	204
RENOWN COACHES, *BEXHILL*	114
REYNOLDS COACHES OF CAISTER, *GREAT YARMOUTH*	156
REYNOLDS DIPLOMAT COACHES, *WATFORD*	130
RICHARDS BROS, *CARDIGAN*	216
RICHARDSON COACHES, *HARTLEPOOL*	112
RICHARDSON TRAVEL LTD, *MIDHURST*	189
RICHMOND'S COACHES, *BARLEY*	130
RIDDLER'S COACHES, *ARBROATH*	199
RIDLERS, *DULVERTON*	170
RIDUNA BUSES, *ALDERNEY*	224
JOHN RIGBY TRANSPORT & TRAVEL, *BATLEY*	192
RIGBY'S, KIRKHAM'S, GRIMSHAW'S *ALTHAM*	139
RINGWOOD COACHES, *STAVELEY*	103
RIVERSIDE COACHES, *TELFORD*	169
ROADLINER PASSENGER TRANSPORT, *POOLE*	109
ROADLINER TRAVEL, *CREWE*	96
ROADMARK TRAVEL LTD, A*SHINGTON*	189
ROBERTS COACHES, *ABERYSTWYTH*	216
ROBERTS COACHES, *HUGGLESCOTE*	142
ROBERTS TOURS, *WINGATE*	112
ROBIN HOOD TRAVEL LTD, *LEEK*	176
ROBIN'S COACHES, *CHIPPENHAM*	195
ROBINSON KIMBOLTON, *KIMBOLTON*	93
ROBINSONS HOLIDAYS, *GREAT HARWOOD*	140
ROBINSONS COACHES, *APPLEBY*	100
ROBINSONS COACHES, *STUKLEY*	91
RODGER'S COACHES, *CORBY*	162
ROEVILLE TOURS LTD, *ADWICK-LE-STREET*	174
ROWLANDS GILL TAXIS & COACHES, *ROWLANDS GILL*	182
ROLLINSON SAFEWAY LTD, *LEEDS*	192
RONDO TRAVEL, *HARROGATE*	159
RONSWAY, *LEIGHTON BUZZARD*	130
O. ROONEY, *HILLTOWN*	225
ROPERS COACHES, *BRADFORD*	192
ROSELYN COACHES, *PAR*	98
JOHN ROSS, *ARDEE, Co LOUTH*	230
ROSS TRAVEL, *FEATHERSTONE*	192
ROSSENDALE TRANSPORT LTD, *RAWTENSTALL*	140
ROUNDABOUT BUSES, *SIDCUP*	135
ROVER COACHES, *MULLINGAR*	230
ROVER EUROPEAN TRAVEL, *HORSLEY, STROUD*	121
ROWE & TUDHOPE, *KILMARNOCK*	202
ROWELL COACHES, *LOW PRUDHOE*	162
ROY BROWNS COACHES, *BUILTH WELLS*	220
ROYLES TRAVEL, *SHEFFIELD*	174
ROY PHILLIPS, *SLEAFORD*	144
RUTHERFORDS TRAVEL, *EASTERGATE*	189

S

SAFEGUARD COACHES, *GUILDFORD*	181
SAFFORDS COACHES LTD, *SANDY*	87
SANDERS COACHES, *HOLT*	156
SANDGROUNDER, *SOUTHPORT*	140
SARGANTS BROS LTD, *KINGTON*	128
SCARBOROUGH & DISTRICT	159
SCARLET BAND, *WEST CORNFORTH*	112
SCHOFIELD TRAVEL LTD, *LOUGHBOROUGH*	142
SCOTIA TRAVEL, *GLENROTHES*	203
SCOTLAND & BATES, *APPLEDORE*	135
SCOTTISH CITYLINK COACHES LTD, *GLASGOW*	204
SEAVIEW SERVICES, *SANDOWN*	132
SEA VIEW COACHES (POOLE) LTD	109
SEAGER'S COACHES LTD, *CHIPPENHAM*	195
SEALANDAIR COACHING (IRELAND), *DUBLIN*	230
SEARLE'S AUTO SERVICES, *THORNHAUGH, Nr PETERBOROUGH*	93
SEATH COACHES, *EAST STUDDAL, Nr DOVER*	135
SELVEY'S COACHES, *CAMBUSLANG*	204
SELWYNS TRAVEL, *MANCHESTER AIRPORT*	96
H. SEMMENCE & CO LTD, *WYMONDHAM*	156
SERENE TRAVEL, *BEDLINGTON*	162
SEWARDS COACHES, *AXMINSTER*	107
SHAFTESBURY & DISTRICT MOTOR SERVICES	109
SHAMROCK COACHES, *NEWPORT*	219
MATT SHANAHAN COACHES, *WATERFORD*	231
HARRY SHAW, *COVENTRY*	187
SHAWS OF MAXEY, *PETERBOROUGH*	93
SHEARER OF HUNTLY LTD, *HUNTLEY*	199
WA SHEARINGS LTD, *EXHALL*	188
WA SHEARINGS LTD, *NORMANTON*	193
WA SHEARINGS LTD, *TORQUAY*	108
WA SHEARINGS LTD, *WARRINGTON*	96
WA SHEARINGS LTD, *WIGAN*	124
SHEN CARE VOLUNTARY TRANSPORT, *SELLY OAK*	187
SHERBURN VILLAGE COACHES	112
SHERWOOD TRAVEL, *IMMINGHAM*	157
SHIEL BUSES, *ACHARACLE*	205
SHIRE COACHES, *ST ALBANS*	131
SHIRE TRAVEL INTERNATIONAL, *HEDNESFORD*	176
SHOREY'S TRAVEL & TRANSPORT, *MAULDEN*	87
B. R. SHREEVE & SONS LTD, *LOWESTOFT*	179
SHROPSHIRE COUNTY COUNCIL, *SHREWSBURY*	169
SHUTTLE BUSES LTD, *KILWINNING*	206
SIDLAW EXECUTIVE TRAVEL, *AUCHTERHOUSE*	199, 201
SIESTA INTERNATIONAL, *MIDDLESBROUGH*	160
SILCOX COACHES, *PEMBROKE DOCK*	219
SILVER CHOICE TRAVEL LTD, *EAST KILBRIDE*	210
SILVER STAR COACH HOLIDAYS LTD, *CAERNARFON*	218
SILVERDALE LONDON LTD, *LONDON NW10*	149
SILVERDALE TOURS (NOTTINGHAM) LTD, *NOTTINGHAM*	165
SILVERLINE LANDFLIGHT, *SOLIHULL*	187
SIMS TRAVEL, *BOOT*	100
SIMMONDS COACHES LTD, *LETCHWORTH*	131
SIMONDS COACH & TRAVEL, *DISS*	156
SIMPSON'S COACHES, *ROSEHEARTY*	199

SIXTY SIXTY COACHES, *PENTREBACH*	218
D. W. SKELTON, *BRIDGWATER*	171
SKILLS MOTOR COACHES, *BULWELL*	165
SKINNERS OF OXTED	181
SKYLINERS LTD, *NUNEATON*	184
SLACKS TRAVEL, *MATLOCK*	103
H. & A. SLEEP, *BERE ALSTON*	107
SLEIGHTS COACHES, *SWINTON*	174
SLOAN TRAVEL, *ROSTREVOR*	225
SMITH & SONS COACHES, *COUPAR ANGUS*	208
JOHN SMITH & SONS, *THIRSK*	160
SMITH'S COACHES (BE & GW SMITH), *SHEPTON MALLET*	171
SMITH BUNTINGFORD	131
SMITHS COACHES (MARPLE) LTD	96, 120
SMITHS COACHES, *CORBY GLEN, Nr GRANTHAM*	144
SMITHS CONTINENTAL TRAVEL, *BRENZETT*	135
G. A. SMITHS COACHES LTD, *TRING*	131
SMITHS MOTORS (LEDBURY) LTD	128
SNOWDON COACHES, *EASINGTON*	112
SOLENT BLUE LINE, *SOUTHAMPTON*	127
SOLENT COACHES, *RINGWOOD*	127
SOLID ENTERTAINMENTS, *GRIMSBY*	157
SOMERBUS, *BRISTOL*	171
SOULS COACHES LTD, *OLNEY*	91
SOUTH COAST MOTOR SERVICES, *CROYDON*	181
SOUTH DORSET COACHES LTD, *SWANAGE*	109
SOUTH GLOUCESTERSHIRE BUS & COACH COMPANY, *PATCHWAY, BRISTOL*	90
SOUTH LANCS TRAVEL, *ATHERTON*	124
SOUTH MIMMS TRAVEL LTD	131
SOUTH WEST COACHES LTD, *WINCANTON*	171
SOUTHDOWN PSV, *COPTHORNE*	189
SOUTHERN COACHES (NM) LTD, *BARRHEAD*	202
SOUTHERN VECTIS, *NEWPORT, IoW*	132
SOUTHGATE & FINCHLEY COACHES LTD, *LONDON N11*	149
SOUTHNOR COACHES, *DARTFORD*	136
SOVEREIGN COACHES, *LYME REGIS*	110
SPA COACHES, *STRATHPEFFER*	205
SPENCERS COACHES, *NEWARK*	165
SPOT HIRE TRAVEL, *BEARSTED*	136
SPRATTS COACHES LTD, *WRENINGHAM*	156
SQUIRRELL'S COACHES, *HITCHAM*	179
ST ANDREWS EXECUTIVE TRAVEL	204
ST KEVINS BUS SERVICE (P. DOYLE), *ROUNDWOOD, Co WICKLOW*	227
STAGECOACH CAMBRIDGESHIRE, *CAMBRIDGE*	93
STAGECOACH EAST, *NORTHAMPTON*	162
STAGECOACH IN EAST KENT & HASTINGS	136
STAGECOACH IN HASTINGS, *ST LEONARDS ON SEA*	114
STAGECOACH EAST MIDLANDS, *CHESTERFIELD*	103
STAGECOACH EAST SCOTLAND, *DUNDEE*	201
STAGECOACH GROUP	85
STAGECOACH IN HAMPSHIRE, *BASINGSTOKE*	127
STAGECOACH HANTS & SURREY, *ALDERSHOT*	127
STAGECOACH IN HULL	115
STAGECOACH LONDON, *ILFORD*	149
STAGECOACH MANCHESTER, *ARDWICK*	124
STAGECOACH MERSEYSIDE, *LIVERPOOL*	152
STAGECOACH NORTH EAST, *SUNDERLAND*	183
STAGECOACH NORTH WEST, *CARLISLE*	100
STAGECOACH IN OXFORDSHIRE	167
STAGECOACH SOUTH, *CHICHESTER*	189
STAGECOACH IN SOUTH WALES, *CWMBRAN*	222
STAGECOACH SOUTH WEST, *EXETER*	107
STAGECOACH SHEFFIELD, *SHEFFIELD*	174
STAGECOACH SUPERTRAM, *SHEFFIELD*	174
STAGECOACH TRANSIT, *STOCKTON*	112
STAGECOACH IN WARWICKSHIRE, *RUGBY*	184
STAGECOACH WEST, *GLOUCESTER*	121
STAGECOACH WEST SCOTLAND, *AYR*	206, 210
STAGECOACH WEST SCOTLAND, *DUMFRIES*	201
STAGECOACH WEST SCOTLAND, *GLASGOW*	204
F. W. STAINTON & SON LTD, *KENDAL*	100
STALLION COACHES, *CHELMSFORD*	119
STAN'S COACHES, *MALDON*	119
STANLEY MACKAY COACHES OF EDINBURGH, *BONNYRIGG*	203
STANLEY TAXIS & MINICOACHES	112
STANSTED TRANSIT, *STANSTED*	119
STANWAYS COACHES, *KIDSGROVE*	177
STEELS LUXURY COACHES, *ADDINGHAM*	192
STEPEND COACHES, *GLENMAVIS*	208
STEPHENSONS OF *EASINGWOLD*	160
STEPHENSONS OF ESSEX LTD, *ROCHFORD*	119
STEVE'S OF AMBLESIDE LTD	100
L. F. STEWART & SON LTD, *DALAYICH, BY TAYNUILT*	200
STEVE STOCKDALE COACHES, *SELBY*	160
STODDARDS LTD, *CHEADLE, STAFFS*	177
STOCKHAMS COACHES, *CRICKHOWELL*	221
WILLIAM STOKES & SONS LTD, *CARSTAIRS*	210
STONEHOUSE COACHES	210
JIM STONES COACHES	96
STONES COACHES OF BATH	171
E STOTT & SONS, *MILNSBRIDGE*	192
STOTT'S TOURS (OLDHAM) LTD	124
STRAFFORD'S COACHES, *MINERA*	223
STRATOS TRAVEL LTD, *NEWTOWN, POWYS*	221
STREAMLINE, *MAIDSTONE*	136
STREETS COACHWAYS LTD, *BARNSTAPLE*	107
STRINGERS PONTEFRACT MOTORWAYS	192
STUARTS OF CARLUKE	210
SUIRWAY BUS & COACH SERVICES LTD *PASSAGE EAST, Co WATERFORD*	231
SULLIVAN BUSES, *POTTERS BAR*	131
SUMMERDALE COACHES, *LETTERSTON*	220
SUMMERFIELD COACHES LTD, *SOUTHAMPTON*	127
SUNBEAM COACHES LTD, *NORWICH*	156
SUNBURY COACHES, *SHEPPERTON*	154
SUNRAY TRAVEL, *EPSOM*	181
SUNSET COACHES, *PENZANCE*	98
SUPERTRAVEL MINICOACHES, *SPEKE*	152
SURELINE, *PORTLAND*	110
SURELINE COACHES, *WOKING*	181
SUSSEX COUNTRY COACH HIRE, *SHOREHAM*	189
SUSSEX PIONEER COACHES, *BRIGHTON*	114

SUTTON COMMUNITY TRANSPORT	181
SWALLOW COACH CO LTD, *RAINHAM, ESSEX*	119
SWANBROOK TRANSPORT LTD, *CHELTENHAM*	121
SWEYNE COACHES, *GOOLE*	115
SWIFTS HAPPY DAYS TRAVEL, *DONCASTER*	174
SWIFTSURE TRAVEL (BURTON UPON TRENT) LTD	177
SWILLY BUS, *LETTERKENNY, Co DONEGAL*	231
SWINDON VINTAGE OMNIBUS, *SWINDON*	195

T

T & S TRAVEL, *PONTEFRACT*	192
TF MINI COACHES, *BARKING*	120
T M TRAVEL, *STAVELEY*	104
T N C COACHES, *CASTLE BROMWICH*	187
F. T. TAGG COACHES, *SUTTON-IN-ASHFIELD*	165
TALLY HO! COACHES, *KINGSBRIDGE*	107
TANAT VALLEY COACHES, *LLANRHAEDR YM, OSWESTRY*	221
TANGNEY TOURS, *BOROUGH GREEN*	136
TANTIVY BLUE COACH TOURS, *ST HELIER, JERSEY*	224
TAPPINS COACHES, *DIDCOT*	167
TARGET TRAVEL GROUP LTD, *CRAMLINGTON*	163
TATES COACHES, *MARKYATE*	131
TAVISTOCK COMMUNITY TRANSPORT, *GREENLANDS*	98
TAW & TORRIDGE COACHES LTD	107
TAYLORS COACH TRAVEL, *YEOVIL*	171
TELFORD'S COACHES, *NEWCASTLETON*	200
TELLINGS GOLDEN MILLER COACHES LTD, *HEATHROW AIRPORT*	150
TERRY'S COACH HIRE, *COVENTRY*	187
TERRY'S COACHES, *HEMEL HEMPSTEAD*	131
TEST VALLEY TRAVEL, *WHITEPARISH*	195
TETLEYS MOTOR SERVICES, *LEEDS*	193
THAMESDOWN TRANSPORT LTD, *SWINDON*	195
ARTHUR THOMAS COACHES, *GORSEINON*	222
THOMAS BROS, *LLANGADOG*	216
D J THOMAS COACHES OF NEATH	219
EDWARD THOMAS & SON, *WEST EWELL*	181
THOMAS OF BARRY	222
THOMAS OF RHONDDA, *PORTH*	221
THOMAS PATERSON & BROWN LTD, *KILBIRNIE*	206
THOMPSON'S, *FRAMLINGHAM*	179
THOMSETT'S COACHES, *DEAL*	136
THORNES INDEPENDENT LTD, *HEMINGBROUGH*	160
F. E. THORPE & SONS LTD, *LONDON W10*	150
THREE STAR COACH HIRE	87
TILLEY'S COACHES, *BUDE*	98
TIMEBUS TRAVEL, *ST ALBANS*	150
TIM'S TRAVEL, *SHEERNESS*	136
TITTERINGTON COACHES LTD, *BLENCOW*	101
TOMORROWS TRANSPORT, *ENFIELD*	150
TONNA LUXURY COACHES LTD, *NEATH*	219
TOP LINE TRAVEL, *YORK*	160
TOP TRAVEL, *READING*	127
TOTNES & DARTMOUTH RING & RIDE, *TOTNES*	108
TOURIST COACHES LTD, *SALISBURY*	196
TOWER COACHES, *WIGTON*	101
TOWLERS COACHES, *WISBECH*	93
TOWN & COUNTRY COACHES, *NEWTON ABBOT*	108
TOWN & COUNTRY MOTOR SERVICES LTD, *HURWORTH MOOR, Nr DARLINGTON*	112
TOWNLYNX, *HOLYWELL*	217
TRACKS VEHICLE SERVICES, *ROMNEY MARSH*	136
TRAMONTANA, *MOTHERWELL*	208
TRANSDEV	85
TRANSIT EXPRESS TRAVEL, *LENTON*	165
TRANSLINC LTD, *LINCOLN*	144
TRANSLINK, *BELFAST*	225
THE TRANSPORT MUSEUM, *WYTHALL*	196
TRATHENS TRAVEL SERVICES, *PLYMOUTH*	108
TRAVEL DUNDEE	202
THE TRAVEL LINK, *GILLINGHAM*	136
TRAVEL LONDON, *LONDON SE5*	150
TRAVELMASTERS, *SHEERNESS*	136
TRAVELPATH 3000, *GRANTHAM*	144
TRAVEL RITE EAST KENT, *EYTHORNE*	136
TRAVEL WEST MIDLANDS, *BIRMINGHAM*	187
TRAVEL WRIGHT, *NEWARK-ON-TRENT*	165
TRAVELGREEN COACHES, *DONCASTER*	174
TRAVELINE, *MINEHEAD*	171
TRAVELLERS CHOICE, THE, *CARNFORTH*	140
TRAVELLERS CHOICE, THE, *DALTON IN FURNESS*	101
TRAVELSPEED - *see* NORTHERN BLUE	
TRAVELSURE, *SEAHOUSES*	163
TRAVEL-WRIGHT, *MOUNTSORREL*	142
TREACY COACHES, *BALLINA, Co MAYO*	231
TRELEY MOTORS, *PENZANCE*	98
TRENT BARTON, *HEANOR*	104
TRINGWOOD TRAVEL, *WALTON ON THAMES*	181
TRURONIAN LTD, *TRURO*	98
TRUSTLINE SERVICES LTD, *HERTFORD*	131
TUERS MOTORS LTD, *PENRITH*	101
TURNERS TOURS, *CHULMLEIGH*	108
TURNERS COACHWAYS (BRISTOL) LTD, *BRISTOL*	90
TW COACHES LTD, *SOUTH MOLTON*	108
TWIN VALLEY COACHES, *SOWERBY BRIDGE*	193
TYNE VALLEY COACHES LTD, *HEXHAM*	163
TYNEDALE GROUP TRAVEL, *HALTWISTLE*	163
R. S. TYRER, *CHORLEY*	140
TYRER TOURS LTD, *PADIHAM*	140

U

UNICORN COACHES LTD, *HATFIELD*	131
UNITY COACHES, *RETFORD*	165
UNO LTD, *HATFIELD*	131
GRAHAM URQUHART TRAVEL, *INVERNESS*	205

V

VALES COACHES (MANCHESTER) LTD	124
VENTURE TRANSPORT (HENDON) (1965) LTD, *HARROW*	154
VICEROY OF ESSEX LTD, *SAFFRON WALDEN*	120
VIKING COACHES, *HEYWOOD*	124
VIKING MINICOACHES, *BROADSTAIRS*	137
VIKING TOURS & TRAVEL, *SWADLINCOTE*	104
VILLAGER MINIBUS, *SHARNBROOK*	87

VINCE COACHES, *BURGHCLERE, Nr NEWBURY*	88
VISCOUNT CENTRAL COACHES, *BURNELY*	140
VISION TRAVEL INTERNATIONAL LTD, *WATERLOOVILLE*	127
VISTA COACHWAYS, *CLEEVE*	171
VOEL COACHES LTD, *DYSERTH*	217

W

W H MOTORS, *CRAWLEY*	189
W M TRAVEL, *WISBECH*	92
W T S MINICOACHES, *FARSLEY*	193
WAINFLEET MOTOR SERVICES LTD, *NUNEATON*	184
WAKEFIELD TUTORIAL SCHOOL, *MORLEY*	193
WALDEN TRAVEL LTD, *SAFFRON WALDEN*	120
WALLIS COACHWAYS, *BILSTHORPE, Nr NEWARK*	165
WALLIS LIMOUSINES, *BROMLEY*	137
WALTONS COACHES, *GRANGETOWN, CARDIFF*	214
WARRENS COACHES (KENT & SUSSEX) LTD, *TICEHURST*	114
WARRINGTON BOROUGH TRANSPORT LTD	96
WARRINGTON COACHES, *ILAM*	104
WARSTONE MOTORS LTD, *GREAT WYRLEY*	177
WATERSIDE TOURS - see HYTHE & WATERSIDE	
PAUL WATSON TRAVEL, *DARLINGTON*	112
WATTS COACHES, *BONVILSTON, Nr CARDIFF*	215
WAVERLEY COACHES LTD, *ST HELIER, JERSEY*	224
WEARDALE MOTOR SERVICES LTD, *STANHOPE*	112
WEAVAWAY TRAVEL, *NEWBURY*	88
WEBB'S *PETERBOROUGH*	94
WEBBER BUS, *BRIDGWATER*	171
WELLGLADE LTD	85
WELSH DRAGON TRAVEL, *NEWPORT, MONMOUTHSHIRE*	219
WELSH'S COACHES, *PONTEFRACT*	193
WEST END/RUTLAND TRAVEL, *MELTON MOWBRAY*	142
WEST MIDLANDS SPECIAL NEEDS TRANSPORT, *BIRMINGHAM*	188
WESTBUS COACH SERVICES LTD, *HOUNSLOW*	150
WESTERHAM COACHES, *OXTED*	181
WESTERN GREYHOUND, *NEWQUAY*	98
WESTRINGS COACHES, *EAST WITTERING*	189
WEST'S COACHES LTD, *WOODFORD GREEN*	120
WESTWAY COACH SERVICES, *LONDON SW20*	150
WHEADONS GROUP TRAVEL, *CARDIFF*	215
WHEAL BRITON COACHES, *TRURO*	98
WHIPPET COACHES LTD, *FENSTANTON*	94
WHITE BUS SERVICES, *WINDSOR*	88
WHITE HEATHER TOURS, *FORT WILLIAM*	205
WHITEGATE TRAVEL, *NORTHWICH*	96
WHITELAWS COACHES, *STONEHOUSE*	210
WHITTLE COACH & BUS, *KIDDERMINSTER*	197
WHYTES COACH TOURS, *NEWMACHAR*	198
WICKSONS TRAVEL, *BROWNHILLS*	188
WIDE HORIZON LUXURY TRAVEL, *HINCKLEY*	142
WIGHTROLLERS, *SANDOWN, ISLE OF WIGHT*	132
ALBERT WILDE COACHES, *HEAGE*	104
WILFREDA BEEHIVE, *ADWICK-LE-STREET*	174
WILKINSONS TRAVEL, *ROTHERHAM*	174
F R WILLETTS & CO, *PILLOWELL Nr LYDNEY*	121
T WILLIAMS & SONS, *WREXHAM*	223
WILLIAMS COACHES, *BRECON*	221
F. T. WILLIAMS TRAVEL, *CAMBORNE*	98
GLYN WILLIAMS TRAVEL, *BLACKWOOD*	214
GWYN WILLIAMS & SONS LTD, *LOWER TUMBLE*	215
T. WILLIAMS & SONS, *PONCIAU*	223
WILLIAMSONS OF *ROTHERHAM*	174
WILLS MINI COACHES, *KINGSBRIDGE*	108
WILSON'S COACHES, *ROSSINGTON*	174
WILTAX BUSES LTD, *ADDLESTONE*	182
WILTS & DORSET BUS COMPANY LTD, *POOLE*	110
WINDSOR-GRAY TRAVEL, *WOLVERHAMPTON*	188
WINDSORIAN COACHES LTD, *WINDSOR*	88
WINGS LUXURY TRAVEL LTD, *HAYES*	150
WINN BROS, *NORTHALLERTON*	160
PAUL S. WINSON COACHES LTD, *LOUGHBOROUGH*	142
WINTS COACHES, *BUTTERTON, Nr LEEK*	177
WISE COACHES LTD, *HAILSHAM*	114
WISTONIAN COACHES, *SELBY*	160
MAL WITTS EXECUTIVE TRAVEL, *GLOUCESTER*	121
WOLD TRAVEL, *DRIFFIELD*	115
WOOD BROTHERS TRAVEL LTD, *BUCKFASTLEIGH*	108
JOHN WOODHAMS VINTAGE TOURS, *RYDE IoW*	133
WOODS COACHES LTD, *LEICESTER*	142
WOODS COACHES, *TILLICOULTRY*	200
P. WOODS MINICOACHES, *HALLGLEN*	203
WOODS TRAVEL LTD, *BOGNOR REGIS*	189
WOODSTONES COACHES LTD, *KIDDERMINSTER*	197
WOODWARD'S COACHES LTD, *GLOSSOP*	104
WOOTTENS, *CHESHAM*	91
J.P.A. WORTH, *BUXTON*	177
WORTHEN TRAVEL, *LITTLE MINSTERLEY*	169
WORTHING COACHES	190
WORTHS MOTOR SERVICES LTD, *ENSTONE*	167
WRIGHT BROS (COACHES) LTD, *NENTHEAD*	101
LEN WRIGHT BAND SERVICES LTD, *WATFORD*	131
WRIGLEY'S COACHES, *IRLAM*	124

Y

YARDLEY TRAVEL LTD, *BIRMINGHAM*	188
YARRANTON BROS LTD, *TENBURY WELLS*	197
YELLOW BUSES, *BOURNEMOUTH*	108
YELLOW ROSE COACHES, *CARNFORTH*	140
YELLOWLINE TOURS LTD, *UPPER BEEDING*	190
YEOMANS CANYON TRAVEL LTD, *HEREFORD*	129
YESTERYEAR MOTOR SERVICES, *DISEWORTH, DERBY*	104
YORKS COACHES, *COGENHOE*	161
YORKSHIRE COASTLINER LTD, *MALTON*	160
YOUNGS OF ROMSLEY, *HALESOWEN*	188
YULE, *PITLOCHRY*	209

Z

ZAK'S BUS & COACH SERVICES, *GREAT BARR*	188

Take our 3 issue trial today*, and you will receive your first issue for FREE!

The UK's biggest selling PSV magazine

Delivering prompt and informed coverage every month, **BUSES** magazine has provided an essential overview of the UK's PSV industry for over fifty-five years.

Supported by quality editorial features and the latest news, **BUSES** magazine is essential reading for decision-makers within the bus industry.

The magazine is notable for its most unique feature, 'Fleet News', now an 18-page section detailing the latest additions to and departures from major and less major bus and coach fleets in the UK and Ireland.

Every month **BUSES** editorial features cover key areas of interest, including vehicle operation, technical developments, ticketing and publicity.

Subscribe today to receive **BUSES** on your desk every month, and keep abreast of the latest news and developments in the bus industry.

Great subscriber benefits!

A subscription to **BUSES** comes with **FREE MEMBERSHIP** to the Ian Allan Publishing Subs Club.

As a member of the **Ian Allan Publishing Subs Club**, you will receive a personalised Subscription Loyalty Card, plus a quarterly newsletter with great subscriber benefits, discounts, offers and competitions!

BUSES PRIORITY ORDER FORM   (Photocopies acceptable)

I would like to subscribe to *Buses*:   LRB07

☐ 3 issues trial subscription   £7.20
☐ 1 year full UK subscription   £43.20

Mr/Mrs/Miss/Ms: _____
Forename: _____
Surname: _____
Address: _____
_____
_____
Post Code: _____
Tel No.: _____
Email: _____

1 - Debit / Credit card

Please debit my:
☐ Mastercard   ☐ Visa   ☐ Switch / Maestro

☐☐☐☐☐☐☐☐ ☐☐☐☐☐☐☐☐

Exp date:_____ Start date: _____
Issue no: ____ Date: _____

Cardholders signature: _____

2 - Cheque

I enclose a cheque to the value of _____
(please make cheque payable to **Ian Allan Publishing Ltd** Eurocheques are not accepted)

3 - Invoice

☐ Please invoice me

Return to: Subscriptions Dept, Ian Allan Publishing Ltd, Riverdene Business Park, Molesey Road, Hersham, Surrey, KT12 4RG

* Offer valid until 31st January 2007.